Handbook of Counseling and Psychotherapy with Older Adults

Wiley Series on Adulthood and Aging
Michael Smyer, Editor

Psychopathology in Later Adulthood
by Susan K. Whitbourne

Handbook of Counseling and Psychotherapy with Older Adults
edited by Michael Duffy

Handbook of Geriatric Assessment
edited by Peter A. Lichtenberg

Handbook of Mid-Life Development
edited by Margie E. Lachman

Handbook of Counseling and Psychotherapy with Older Adults

Edited by
MICHAEL DUFFY, PhD, ABPP

JOHN WILEY & SONS, INC.

New York • Chichester • Weinheim • Brisbane • Singapore • Toronto

Library of Congress Cataloging-in-Publication Data:

Handbook of counseling and psychotherapy with older adults / edited by
  Michael Duffy.
        p.   cm.
  Includes bibliographical references and index.
  ISBN 0-471-25461-4 (cloth : alk. paper)
    1. Psychotherapy for the aged—Handbooks, manuals, etc.   2. Aged—
  Counseling of—Handbooks, manuals, etc.   I. Duffy, Michael, Ph.D.,
  ABPP.
  RC480.54.H36   1999
  618.97′68914—dc21   98–48310

Printed in the United States of America.

10 9 8 7 6 5 4 3 2 1

To Jo Ann
my wife and friend

To my children
Sarah, Clare, and Andrew
the lights of my life

To my parents Joseph and Lucy
who lived long and lovingly

To Ira Iscoe
mentor, teacher, and friend
who is more of a father than he realizes

Contributors

Editor

Michael Duffy, PhD, ABPP
Counseling Psychology Program
Department of Educational
    Psychology
Texas A&M University
College Station, Texas

Patricia M. Averill, PhD
University of Texas Medical School at
    Houston
Harris County Psychiatric Center
Houston, Texas

Stephen J. Bartels, MD, MS
Department of Psychiatry
Dartmouth Medical School
Director of Aging Services Research
New Hampshire-Dartmouth
    Psychiatric Research Center
Lebanon, New Hampshire

Iris R. Bell, MD, PhD
Tucson Veteran's Administration
    Medical Center
Director, Program in Geriatric
    Psychiatry
Tucson, Arizona

June Bredin, MD
Independent Practice of Medicine
Redmond, Washington

Jo Ann Brockway, PhD
Department of Rehabilitation
    Services
Providence Medical Center
Seattle, Washington

Claire M. Brody, PhD
Department of Psychology and
    Women's Studies
William Paterson University
Wayne, New Jersey

John E. Calamari, PhD
Director of Clinical Training and
    Director, Anxiety and Obsessive-
    Compulsive Treatment and
    Research Program
Finch University of Health Sciences
The Chicago Medical School
Department of Psychology
North Chicago, Illinois

Karen Lynn Cassiday, PhD
Anxiety and Agoraphobia Treatment
    Center
Northbrook, Illinois

Martha Li Chiu, PhD
Palo Alto VA Health Care System
Psychology Service
Palo Alto, California

David W. Coon, PhD
Associate Director,
Older Adult Center
VA Palo Alto Health Care System
Menlo Park, California

Elizabeth M. Cotton, MD
Independent Practice of Medicine
Bellevue, Washington

Royda G. Crose, PhD
Coordinator,
Center for Gerontology
Ball State University
Muncie, Indiana

Donna S. Davenport, PhD
Counseling Psychology Program
Department of Educational
    Psychology
Texas A&M University
College Station, Texas

Larry W. Dupree, PhD
University of South Florida/Louis de
    la Parte Florida Mental Health
    Institute
Department of Aging & Mental
    Health
Tampa, Florida

Beatrice Ellis, PhD
Department of Psychology
Clinical Psychology Supervisor
University of Washington
Seattle, Washington

Naomi Feil, MSW, ACSW
Validation Training Institute
Cleveland, Ohio

Deborah W. Frazer, PhD
Director of Behavioral Health
Genesis Elder Care
Kennett Square, Pennsylvania

Margaret Gatz, PhD
Department of Psychology
University of Southern California
Los Angeles, California

David L. Gutmann, PhD
Division of Psychology
Northwestern University Medical
    School
Chicago, Illinois

Suzanne B. Hanser, EdD
Department of Music Therapy
Berklee College of Music and
    Harvard Medical School
Boston, Massachusetts

J. Ray Hays, PhD, JD
University of Texas at Houston
    Medical School
Houston, Texas

E.A. Meyen Hertzsprung, BA
Department of Psychology
University of Calgary
Calgary, Alberta
Canada

Gregory A. Hinrichsen, PhD
Psychological Services and Geriatric
    Psychiatry Division
Hillside Hospital, North Shore-Long
    Island Jewish Health System
Glen Oaks, New York

Margaret Hellie Huyck, PhD
Institute of Psychology
Illinois Institute of Technology
Chicago, Illinois

Lee Hyer, PhD
University of Medicine & Dentistry
    of New Jersey
Edison, New Jersey

Jordan Jacobowitz, PhD
Chicago School of Professional
  Psychology
Chicago, Illinois

Audrey Kavka, MD
San Francisco Psychoanalytic
  Institute
San Francisco, California

Helen Q. Kivnick, PhD
School of Social Work
University of Minnesota
St. Paul, Minnesota

Candace Konnert, PhD
University of Calgary
Department of Psychology
Calgary, Alberta
Canada

M. Powell Lawton, PhD
Polisher Research Institute
Philadelphia Geriatric Center
Philadelphia, Pennsylvania

Kristin J. Levine, MS
New Hampshire-Dartmouth
  Psychiatric Research Center
Lebanon, New Hampshire

Damond Logsdon-Conradsen, PhD
Augusta Veterans Administration
  Medical Center
Augusta, Georgia

Victor Molinari, PhD
Houston Veterans Affairs Medical
  Center
Director, Geropsychology
Psychology Service
Houston, Texas

Pamilla Morales, PhD
Bolton Institute
Psychology Department
Bolton, Lancashire
England

Kim T. Mueser, PhD
Department of Psychiatry
Dartmouth Medical School
New Hampshire-Dartmouth
  Psychiatric Research Center
Lebanon, New Hampshire

Jane E. Myers, PhD
Department of Counseling and
  Educational Development
University of North Carolina at
  Greensboro
Greensboro, North Carolina

Nancy A. Newton, PhD
Chicago School of Professional
  Psychology
Chicago, Illinois

Sara Honn Qualls, PhD
Chair, Department of Psychology
  and Director, Center on Aging
University of Colorado—Colorado
  Springs
Colorado Springs, Colorado

Robert E. Reichlin, PhD
University of Texas Health Science
  Center at Houston and
  Independent Practice
Bellaire, Texas

Joseph Richman, PhD
Albert Einstein College of Medicine
Bronx, New York

Kenneth Rider, PhD
Pacific Graduate School of
  Psychology
Los Altos, California

Erlene Rosowsky, PhD
Harvard Medical School and
  Independent Practice of
  Psychology
Needham, Massachusetts

Joel Sadavoy, MD, FRCP
Head, Division of General Psychiatry
Mount Sinai Hospital
Toronto, Ontario
Canada

Karen Sanders, PhD
Department of Psychology
Clinical Psychology Supervisor
University of Washington
Seattle, Washington

Lawrence Schonfeld, PhD
Florida Mental Health Institute
Department of Aging and Mental
    Health
University of South Florida
Tampa, Florida

Gregory C. Smith, EdD
Department of Human Development
University of Maryland
College Park, Maryland

Michael A. Smyer, PhD
Dean, Graduate School of Arts and
    Sciences
Associate Vice President for Research
    and Professor of Psychology
Boston College
Chestnut Hill, Massachusetts

David G. Sprenkel, PhD
Cognitive Dynamic Therapy
    Associates
Director, Elder Health Program
Greenery Rehabilitation Center
Pittsburgh, Pennsylvania

Melinda A. Stanley, PhD
University of Texas Medical School at
    Houston
Houston, Texas

Dolores Gallagher-Thompson, PhD
Palo Alto VA Health Care System and
    Stanford University
Los Angeles, California

Larry Thompson, PhD
Palo Alto VA Health Care System and
    Stanford University
Los Angeles, California

Jules C. Weiss, EdD, ATR
Department of Counseling
    Psychology and Independent
    Practice
Texas A&M University—Texarkana
Texarkana, Texas

Maureen Wilson, MA
Department of Psychology
Boston College
Chestnut Hill, Massachusetts

Antonette M. Zeiss, PhD
VA Palo Alto Health Care System
Psychology Service
Palo Alto, California

Robert A. Zeiss, PhD
VA Palo Alto Health Care System
Psychology Service
Palo Alto, California

Contents

PART TWO:

TREATMENT APPROACHES FOR SELECTED PROBLEMS

PERSONALITY DISORDERS

ANXIETY AND MOOD DISORDERS

ADJUNCTIVE PSYCHOLOGICAL TREATMENTS FOR ORGANIC DISORDERS

BEHAVIOR DISORDERS

Preface

This is a book about psychotherapeutic interventions with older adults. In the infant field of clinical geropsychology, most of the emphasis and advances have been in the area of assessment and diagnosis; I believe this volume provides a much needed resource in treatment approaches for the increasing number of mental health professionals who provide counseling and psychotherapy to older clients.

This book is explicitly directed toward *practice.* While the contributors each draw from relevant conceptual and research material, the chapters focus on practice concepts and techniques. This volume provides both a state of the art in conceptual and clinical research and an account of best practice in specific psychotherapeutic strategy and techniques.

This is a book *for practitioners* written *by practitioners.* Given the practice orientation of the *Handbook,* it seemed important to enlist writers who have a direct experiential contact with the topic they discuss. This lends a *real* quality to the selection of conceptual and research material and to the presentation of particular interventions. Contributors are either practitioners, practitioner/trainers, science practitioners, or clinical researchers. They were encouraged to illustrate suggested interventions with a variety of case material. And while current research findings are emphasized, contributors were encouraged to draw on their own considerable direct experience and conceptual understanding.

This volume will be useful to a variety of interested persons. The level of conceptual and practice expertise of the chapter contributors will appeal both to experienced geropsychologists and geropsychiatrists as well as geropsychiatric nurses and social workers, and counselors who focus on mental health and aging. It will also serve as an important resource to experienced general therapists in these professions who wish to develop greater proficiency in working with older adults. This handbook will also serve well as a text for graduate and even advanced undergraduate courses or clinical practica.

The discussion of interventions is organized around two dimensions, *modalities* and *problems.* Thus, *Part One, Approaches to Psychotherapy with Older Adults,* focuses on a series of treatment modalities including the use of psychotherapy process, group and expressive approaches, family and intergenerational interventions, and social and community interventions. The inclusion of this latter group of interventions clearly signals that the connotation of counseling and psychotherapy interventions in this book extends beyond the medical model and illness model range to include health, prevention, and environmental interventions. *Part Two, Treatment Approaches for Selected Problems,* provides conceptual and best practice interventions for a series of specific problems clustered under personality disorders, anxiety and mood disorders, adjunctive psychological treatments for organic disorders and behavior disorders. The final chapter presents a review and discussion of current ethical issues in geropsychological interventions. The organization of this book diverges from the traditional theory-based approach of many texts on psychotherapy. This change follows a growing body of psychotherapy research that locates effectiveness, not in theoretical approach or specific technique, but in a series of transtheoretical *common factors.* These factors seemingly point to underlying efficacious processes that link and are consistent with a variety of theoretical approaches.

On a personal note, this book has been a labor of love. In my complicated and sometimes frenetic life as both an academic and a practitioner, I have always found doing therapy and the psychotherapeutic process to be the wellspring of my intellectual life. Far from being a technical task, doing psychotherapy seems to connect me with what is most important in life and has always been the richest source of my ideas. I have learned much from my clients. I have learned that when we are dealing with life's fundamental issues, age drops away and we find a connection with our older client that is enriching to us both. I have come to view therapy as a naturalistic process in which we can discover an intimacy with our clients that is frequently absent in the wider world. And when this intimacy is present, psychotherapy is not an exercise in work, but an engaging and energizing exercise in life. It is in this spirit that I offer this volume.

MICHAEL DUFFY

Acknowledgments

Editing a handbook on psychotherapy with 39 chapters gave some of my colleagues cause to wonder about my mental health! As a first-time editor, I certainly had my own apprehension about the scale and volume of the task. In fact, it has been an entirely positive experience! Armed initially with the precautionary, if pessimistic, expectation that much of the book plan would probably be modified and that it would take double the allotted time, I have been pleasantly surprised; the plan seems to have worked, the contributors have exceeded my expectations, and we completed the book at the scheduled time. But there is a rational explanation. As editor, I will claim credit for two achievements: I selected the very best contributors and found the best publisher.

I am very gratified to be associated with this group of contributing professionals. They were selected for their proven expertise and have lived up to the promise I hoped for. Perhaps their best testimony came from the production staff who found them unfailingly courteous and always (almost) on time. At that moment, my strong suspicion that I had chosen well was confirmed!

I would like to make special mention of the very sad loss of Richard Hussian to the community of geropsychologists. Richard died in North Carolina in December 1998. He was due to contribute a chapter on behavioral interventions with the severely cognitive impaired. Although unassuming by temperament, Richard Hussian contributed in a monumental way to the development of this much needed area in geropsychology and authored several books. I believe Richard was ahead of his time and will be greatly missed.

From the beginning, my association with John Wiley and Sons has been affirming to me personally as a professional and as an author. Jennifer Simon has been helpful, flexible, and constructive and has made the task of handbook editor a pleasure and a positive experience that I never anticipated. I have been especially grateful for the excellent working relationship with Nancy Marcus Land and her staff at Publications Development Company. I found the quality of text editing to be superb: it is delightful to find one's work enhanced through the concise elegance of a skillful editor.

Finally, I am especially grateful to Michael Smyer, Series Editor for Wiley, for his support and trust in me and in this project. I am also grateful to George Niederehe with the National Institute for Mental Health; here I must immediately give away some of the credit for choosing excellent authors, since both George and Michael provided many excellent suggestions. It would be difficult to identify two more knowledgeable and influential persons in the field of clinical geropsychology. I am grateful to them.

M.D.

APPROCHES TO PSYCHOTHERAPY WITH OLDER ADULTS

Issues in Psychotherapy Process with Older Adults

Group and Expressive Therapy Approaches

Family and Intergenerational Interventions

Social and Community Interventions

CHAPTER 1

Using Process Dimensions in Psychotherapy: The Case of the Older Adult

MICHAEL DUFFY

This chapter focuses on the understanding and use of process variables in psychotherapy with older adults. The chapter begins with a general discussion of the meaning of process dimensions in therapy and the reasons why this domain in psychotherapy has been, until recently, neglected. It includes a description of a new paradigm of psychotherapy research and practice based on process characteristics, a discussion of specific process themes in geriatric psychotherapy, and a discussion of the use of process as a therapeutic strategy.

PROCESS VERSUS CONTENT

Although the concept of process versus content is familiar, at least implicitly, to most practicing psychotherapists, this concept has not been adequately treated within traditional psychotherapy research that has tended to focus exclusively on content dimensions of the therapy process either in defining problems or in describing procedures and techniques. Process versus content in psychotherapy is essentially a focus on the *how* versus the *what* within psychotherapy. Within problem definition, for example, a content description of a personality problem would focus on the symptomatic profile (the *what*) whereas a process understanding would examine the dynamics (the *how*) that give rise to a particular personality problem. Process includes the unique set of interpersonal characteristics, coping style, and the myriad ways a person deals with his or her world and the people in it. A content definition of a psychological problem tends to describe what the problem *looks like* (e.g., depression), whereas a process portrayal of the disorder gives a sense of the *meaning* of the depression, such as psychological loss and grief. Thus process diagnosis involves a "moving picture" of the dynamic meaning of a problem whereas a content diagnosis gives a "still picture" of the problem. In my experience more than 80% of diagnostic understanding lies in process rather than in content descriptions. The understanding of the dynamic meaning of a psychological problem gives the therapist a road map for treatment strategy. A content symptomatic description of a disorder is helpful in problem identification, but gives little guidance for therapeutic strategy.

Process dimensions are also important in the area of therapeutic techniques. Contemporary research (Wampold et al., 1997) has begun to clarify that it is not the technique as such (content), but the manner of administration of the technique (process) that accounts for effectiveness in psychotherapy. We later discuss the mounting evidence for the superiority of therapist variables over technical variables in the efficacy of psychotherapy. This point is easy to appreciate if, for example, we imagine how RET techniques differ in the hands of Albert Ellis than in the hands of his followers, or how cognitive restructuring techniques are handled by Aaron Beck versus his followers, or the empty chair technique in the hands of Fritz Perls versus his disciples. Despite the natural force of these comparisons, therapist process variables have been under researched.

Research is now consistently supporting the role of process dimensions or *common factors*, in the efficacy of psychotherapy. In this article we will:

1. Review evidence for the significance of process variables both for research and clinical purposes.
2. Present a rationale for the neglect of process variables in the current philosophy of science that prevails in psychology.
3. Examine the characteristics of a process approach/paradigm to therapy.
4. Outline and illustrate selected process themes in working with older adults.
5. Discuss process itself as therapeutic strategy.

TRADITIONAL RESEARCH ON THEORIES AND TECHNIQUES OF PSYCHOTHERAPY

For the past several decades, psychotherapy research has focused on the efficacy of psychotherapeutic treatment using a clinical trials method comparing theoretically based (content) treatment approaches and techniques. More recently, two critical findings have emerged:

1. Despite earlier statements to the contrary, in general, psychotherapy is both efficacious and effective (Luborsky, Crits-Christoph, Mintz, & Auerbach, 1988). Note that the term "efficacy" typically is used to refer

to research on psychotherapy conducted in laboratory conditions, whereas the term effective is reserved to studies of actual psychotherapy in natural and minimally uncontrolled situations.

2. There are no consistent treatment differences to be demonstrated in psychotherapy research.

Luborsky et al. (1980) in a series of studies, has demonstrated that treatment differences are found between treatment methods and control or no treatment conditions and between placebo and no treatment controls; however, *no differences* can be systematically detected between psychotherapy treatment evolving from different theoretical positions. Wampold et al. (1997), in a recent meta-analytical study, made several improvements in both the logic and statistical analysis of meta-analytical strategy and has demonstrated that differences between psychotherapy approaches cannot be reliably detected in any *series* of research studies. Interestingly, he finds that placebo control conditions are about 50% as effective of bona fide treatment conditions. Wampold (1997) goes on to critique the current emphasis on validated treatments, which strangely seems to ignore the preponderance of research that fails to support treatment differences. He also asks why proponents of validated treatments would wish to homogenize therapies and therapists through the use of manuals, when we know that treatment differences are of little importance. Indeed, when differences *are* found in particular studies, little attention is paid to the *clinical significance* and *magnitude* of the differences or to the alternate hypothesis that in these cases of difference they may in fact be due to underlying common elements in the therapeutic process, for example, the therapeutic relationship itself. The use of a manual, in diminishing therapist differences, may also diminish therapist effect and therefore deny the most important treatment ingredient that has been demonstrated to date—the therapist variables.

Therapist and relationship variables are the primary examplar of process dimensions in psychotherapy. Relationship and interpersonal variables have been neglected in classical psychotherapy research as well as in the current content-related content and technical focus on validated treatments (Czogalik, 1995). Over the years, however, there has been a strand of research that, at least minimally, has investigated the role of therapist and interpersonal factors in the effectiveness of various aspects of psychotherapy. Sexton and Whiston (1994), reviewing research on the quality of the counseling relationship over time, have isolated a series of process dimensions that have variable effects on the effectiveness of outcomes of psychotherapy. In most of these cases, however, process variables are evaluated in their relationship to *outcome* measures. It is entirely appropriate, however, to use the *process itself* as a measure of efficacy and effectiveness. In the experimental or quasi-experimental/clinical trials research of psychotherapy that will be familiar to most contemporary psychologists, the several weeks of duration of treatment of the therapy under investigation is completely ignored as a source of data related to effectiveness in favor of a simple (often single) outcome measure that purports to be sensitive to changes in therapeutic process. Process data can often detect the *reasons* why outcome comparisons proved nonsignificant or, conversely, process data can often explain *why* and *where* the change in outcome took place within the therapeutic trajectory.

A limited amount of research is well-known within the interpersonal relationship domain [e.g., Rogers' (1957) work on the therapeutic conditions and, more recently, Bordin's work (1979) on the so-called therapeutic alliance]. Both of these research domains represent an emphasis on process research but are often overutilized and are limited in the range of explanation they give to effectiveness. In the case of Rogers' therapeutic conditions, for example, it has been found that while these conditions may indeed be necessary as a prelude to psychotherapeutic change, they may not in every case (although perhaps in most cases) be sufficient to produce change (Kolb, Beutler, Davis, Crago, & Shanfield, 1985). During the past few years, a range of less well-known studies focused on process dimensions of psychotherapy and different interpersonal, reciprocal aspects of the therapeutic relationships. In an earlier categorization of counseling relationship research, Gelso and Carter (1985) made the distinction between research into the *real* relationship, (for example, the work of Rogers on the facilitative conditions) and what they described as the *unreal* relationship, mainly the transferential aspects of the therapeutic relationship. Also with the real relationship, focus has been placed on the role of counselor *self-disclosure* with emphasis on a range of modifying variables that variously influence the effectiveness of disclosure (Watkins, Savickas, Brizzi, & Manus, 1990). Another critical area of research has been in counselor or therapist intentions (Hill, 1990). Certainly, within the world of empirical research, therapist intentions and intentionality are little studied. However, in our naturalistic, day-to-day experience, we routinely "scan" the behavioral and verbal world for the *intention* of the other person and adjust our response and behavior accordingly if implicitly. It seems unlikely that clients do not also behave and modify their behavior in accordance with their view of the intentionality of the therapist or, vice versa, therapists judge the intentionality of their clients as a routine matter.

Within the so called unreal relationship, the concept of transference, both in its effects and as an explicit therapeutic tool has been acknowledged by many theoretical positions from the classical psychoanalytic, through the psychodynamic, through behavioral concepts of generalization, and cognitive concepts of "working models." More recent formulations that extend across this theoretical range view transference as a nonpathological but natural phenomenon that exists in everyday life and to some extent in all circumstances. It is highly reasonable that a person judges and adjusts behavior to future conditions based on past experiences. Thus, in both psychodynamic and cognitive psychology there is a recognition of models (working models) in attachment literature (Ainsworth, 1989), that are used as templates in new situations. Therapists also are likely to use transferential behavior. In the traditional discussion of this topic, therapists are deemed to have *countertransferences* to their patients or clients; in fact, there is an equal possibility that the therapist will initially experience *transferential* re-action to a particular client who triggers associations with the therapists earlier life experiences.

Another useful process variable is the *working alliance* itself as developed by Greenson (1967) and later Bordin (1979). This concept has been used in a series of variations by process researchers and is well documented in current therapy research literature, although it is not always recognized as a process dimension of psychotherapy.

Finally, and perhaps most importantly, there is a small but much needed line of research dealing with the reciprocal nature of the relationship between therapist and client. The term *reciprocal,* as differentiated from the notion of *interaction,* is a dynamic concept that represents a circular and, perhaps *spiral* notion of continuing recursive influence within the relationship between any two human beings (including the relationship between therapist and client). This concept of reciprocity is different from the conventional or statistical notion of interaction, which tends to be linear and static. The notion of reciprocally inter-acting behavior connotes the idea of a *moving* picture versus a *still photo* de-scribed by linear and even statistically interactive behavior. One area of specific interest within reciprocal research is the notion of complementarity in the rela-tionship of client and therapist (Kiesler, 1987; Kiesler & Watkins, 1989). Com-plementarity, for example, is illustrated in the relative positioning of control within the relationship and also the negotiation of the central relationship is-sues of how friendly/ hostile to be within the relationship. Finally, topic initia-tion and determination (Tracey, 1986) has considerable power within the therapeutic relationship. Mutual understanding on this issue had significant relationship to effectiveness of the therapeutic relationship. This seems close to the often-asserted need for the client to *feel understood* in order to be willing to continue in therapy.

PSYCHOLOGY'S PHILOSOPHY OF SCIENCE: "WHAT YOU SEE IS WHAT YOU GET"

While psychology had its origins within the field of philosophy, it has become distinctly detached from and unaware of its own philosophical bases. Psycholo-gists are frequently quite innocently unaware of the particular philosophy of science that undergirds the scientific practice and research of contemporary psychology. This philosophical background may help clarify the current em-phasis in research methodology and the neglect of alternate research paradigms that may offer a much closer link with the day-to-day experiential practice of psychotherapy. Modern psychology and its research methods evolved from modernism and the philosophy of positivism or empiricism. In the post-Renais-sance and Enlightenment times, science and its methods were influenced by positivism and empiricism. This philosophical position, in reaction to fear of magic and religious superstitions of earlier times, placed total reliance on measurable external data, and de-emphasized the internal domains of experience as unmeasurable and therefore unverifiable. This scientific approach owes much to early British philosophy in the late 1700s, namely *Empiricism*, a tradition that developed into Positivism and Logical Positivism (Warnock, 1969). A scientific movement developed that limited scientific evidence to data that was measurable in observable and behavioral terms. This philosophical background, as a basis for the philosophy of science, has remained the dominant force within much European, British, and American psychology. Although, over the years, there have been significant alternative philosophies such as the introspectionism of early European psychology, psychoanalysis, existential positions in philosophy and science and the ideographic emphasis of some American psychologists such as Gordon Allport. The dominant philosophy of science that formed the basis for experimental and clinical psychology was dominated by a behaviorist philosophy and practice that was driven by empiricist view of the world. We needed empirical data to demonstrate truth. It therefore makes complete sense that psychotherapy research has focused on overt behavioral techniques that ostensibly derive from different theoretical positions and whose effectiveness and efficacy are demonstrated by behavioral outcome data. Thus, the fledging science of psychology, becoming detached from an understanding of its philosophical roots, set out to find respectability in the methodological world of the then modern, Newtonian physical sciences.

Psychology as a discipline, a profession, and a research area is still largely dominated by this empiricist philosophy. It is highly probable that the seemingly unbridgeable gulf between science and practice is maintained by the inflexibility of this empiricist philosophy. In actual daily practice, few psychotherapists who practice continuously find it adequate to explore therapeutic processes simply in terms of behavioral outcomes. Not only is this at odds with the actual experience of psychotherapy, but it also contradicts our day-to-day life experience. From morning to night, we examine communication with one another in terms not only of overt language but also we search for meaning, intention, and motivation. Our overt and covert behavioral response is heavily influenced by these internal (and not empirically verifiable) modes of behavior.

In the postmodern era, these alternate viewpoints are common not only in philosophy but also in the physical sciences. It is meaningful that, for example, the area of theoretical physics (surely a temple of empiricist philosophy) is an area where the traditional Newtonian empirical test of reality is most in question (Von Bertalanffy, 1975). Psychology lags behind not only science in general, but behind many of the social sciences in reviewing and extending its own, often misunderstood, philosophy of science. Psychology has been impoverished by its neglect of process dimensions in behavior, by its lack of attention to *fine grain* behavior and to the subvocal and nonverbal dimensions of communication. There are a number of ways in which process dimensions assist both in the understanding and changing of human behavior. Some of these ideas and strategies are based on the conceptual and research work of others but many are drawn from direct clinical experience in working with older adults.

TOWARD A NEW PARADIGM OF PSYCHOTHERAPY PRACTICE AND RESEARCH

This section briefly lists and describes a series of key differences that exist when psychotherapy is viewed from a process point of view:

1. *Phenomenological versus essential.* Process psychotherapy pays attention to the actual experienced world of the older client. The therapist sees the world through the client's eyes. This is perhaps the best basis for the concept we have denoted as *empathy* that leads to a client "feeling understood." There are several theorists who have emphasized this aspect of psychotherapy. These include Carl Rogers and his work on empathetic understanding, the phenomenological emphasis of an existentialist philosophy (such as Rollo May) and, more recently, an emphasis on social constructivist viewpoints within psychotherapy.

2. *Inductive versus deductive.* Process-oriented psychotherapy starts with observation rather than theory. This is not an atheoretical position but rather asserts that "theorizing " versus "theory" (note the process difference) is based on immediate observation of behavior versus hypothetico-deductive assumptions that drive the psychotherapy process. Most practicing psychotherapists, whatever their self-stated theoretical position, eventually become inductive in their practice; to do otherwise, seriously restricts the amount of observational data the therapist is able to gather.

3. *Ideographic versus nomothetic.* Most psychological research can be described as nomothetic, that is, the individual is described only as part of a class or group. This is part of the reason why much psychological research is of limited value to clinicians. From a process point of view, a clinical phenomenon (e.g., psychological effect of position and family) exists even if it does not assume a normative role of central tendency within a large group. Many important psychological dynamics have been neglected in research and ignored in development because they exist only in small numbers within the overall population.

4. *Reciprocal versus static dynamics.* Much of the psychological understanding of human behavior portrays a linear and static picture of human interaction; even the statistical concept of interaction falls within this linear description. In fact, human interaction is a "moving" phenomenon with many reciprocal dynamics. In what we often refer to as "just conversation," communication specialists (perhaps more expertly than psychologists) indicate the enormous complexity that is present in even the simplest human verbal exchange. This defines not just the simple back-and-forward interaction, but a constantly changing picture in which every communication is influenced by the reciprocal nature of the previous communication. A metaphor for this reciprocal dynamic may be expressed using the term of circular, but the concept of spiral is more apt in that it includes the forward movement of the circular reciprocal activity. The enormous complexity in human communication makes it evident that

it is insufficient to simply ignore the process dimension of ongoing psychotherapy in favor of outcome indicators. This is not to denigrate the importance of outcome variables, but simply to indicate that to miss process variables is to miss the most significant portion of the variance in understanding in psychotherapeutic change.

5. *Intentions versus behavior.* As has been indicated earlier, we naturalistically scrutinize each other and our clients for the *intentions* that drive the verbal and nonverbal behavior. Verbal communication is at many levels. How often after an organizational meeting do we gather for a covert discussion of the "real" meaning of a statement by an administrator or colleague?

6. *Verbal versus nonverbal and subvocal.* Intentions, motivations, and meanings are mediated both through direct verbal and nonverbal meanings. We also need to pay attention to the *subvocal* domain: that is, the meaning of the words within the words rather than simply the nonverbal domain. To use the same example, it is the varieties of *meaning within* the verbal narrative, which we analyze after a formal meeting.

7. *Micro versus macro level behavior.* Psychology, guided by a narrow empiricist philosophy has tended to emphasize macro level behavior and has neglected the "fine-grain" behavior to which we so often attend in daily life and especially (if implicitly) in the practice of psychotherapy. Again, communication theorists have made greater gains in understanding this fine-grain nonverbal, subvocal level of behavior. In our traditional behavioral analyses and behavior modification, it would be useful to ensure that the behavior of focus is in fine detail. For example, in encouraging and rehearsing social or dating behavior, frequently therapists will start at too large "denominations" of behavior: asking a person out for a date or an evening dinner may be too large an increment to change easily. Attention to micro, fine-grain levels of behavior would make the initial behavior goals much more reachable. This might include, for example, maintaining a glance, paying attention to movement and attitude as a basis for subtle behavior cues (e.g., smiling, maintaining eye contact, opening brief conversation).

A final point can be made about the influence of these process characteristics on research methods. It is common to suggest that research methods might be usefully more qualitative. However, this characteristic in many ways is the least essential of the non-empirical paradigm. Whether the behavior is counted or not counted is of minimal importance. A more critical issue is the *nature of the evidence* that is required to demonstrate change. So, for example, it may well be that research might be more descriptive of the process of psychotherapy as it occurs (quantitatively or qualitatively). Research might also in similar ways therefore pay attention to process as well as outcome (describe and measure what occurs *within* the psychotherapy session as well as what occurs at the end/outcome of the psychotherapy session). Research should pay attention to detailed *narrative analysis* where the moment-to-moment processes are related to each other and an inductive formulation can portray a theoretical understanding of what occurred in the therapy session. There are many available content analytical techniques, some of which are in computer scoring modalities. Finally, clinical research aided by the above techniques would do well to pay attention to ideographic phenomena and de-emphasize *nomothetic* trends (if I am the *only* person with a broken leg I can affirm most strenuously that I *do* have a broken leg even though others do not!). This cataloguing of ideographic experiencing is an important need within research or diagnostic areas. As contrasted with typical content-oriented empirical research, the clinical experience of psychotherapists is portrayed often derisively as "only antidotal." This process of collecting the informed observations of experienced therapists, perhaps more formalized, becomes a valuable alternate research method. It is noteworthy that in Great Britain a formal system of gathering clinical opinions of physicians on particular health problems has been formalized into a national database of process data by the British Medical Association. This approach can also include the valuable analytical data that is produced in the clinical supervision process where teams of clinicians view video recordings of a psychotherapy session and give their consensual observations of the meaning of the process. Such observations, from a process and phenomenological point of view, can easily be further formalized as a significant form of psychological research.

PROCESS THEMES IN GERIATRIC PSYCHOTHERAPY

A selection of process dimensions that are clinically significant in psychotherapy with older adults. These are presented to complement content or outcome variables, in a more complete understanding of the psychotherapy process as described earlier. I am indebted to the work of the late Bill L. Kell and colleagues (Kell & Burow, 1970; Kell & Meuller, 1966; Meuller & Kell, 1972) in a series of monumental if relatively unknown, works that provide a rich portrait of process dynamics.

AMBIGUITY AND UNCERTAINTY

In a world that prizes decisiveness, feelings of uncertainty and based on the ambiguity of human situations become difficult for both therapist and older clients. In many occasions, this ambiguity and resulting uncertainty is understood as a problem that needs to be solved rather than a *source of information* in the processes at hand. Very frequently, it is not that a client, or indeed the therapist, is *indecisive* but rather that they are *undecided*. In other words, the situation is complex and the ambiguity and associated uncertainty capture that complexity precisely. Understanding this is critical for the work of the therapists. Therapists who are intolerant of uncertainty and ambiguity will put pressure on older clients to resolve decisions such as moving to assisted housing rather than allowing the time to explore the situations and emotions involved. In many ways, psychotherapy is about decision making. We are often in the position of deciding: What to do about a significant relationship? What vocational direction best fits our talents and desires? Whether to retire or continue work? Whether to continue to see ourselves as a patient or as a healthy person? When these and similar decisions are life-involving, that is, involve a major change in our life trajectory, then it is understandable that they can be inherently ambiguous. It follows, therefore, that uncertainty or *undecidedness* is an appropriate expression of the complexity of this decision. Most major decisions involve pros and cons and balancing pro and con aspects of a decision is the dilemma of life decision making. Most of us have experienced the stress of deciding on an important life decision when there are significant advantages and disadvantages on both poles of the of decision. For example, when a person is deciding to enter or leave a significant relationship, such ambiguity exists. Therapists not infrequently place considerable pressure on abused spouses, for example, to leave the abusive partner without sufficient recognition for the intense internal ambivalence that is necessarily experienced in such cases. Failure to attend to this process dimension will usually lead to the client leaving the therapist who is applying so much pressure. In fact, the optimal therapeutic posture in such ambiguous decision-making situations is to permit the client to move "backwards and forwards" across the advantages and disadvantages of each pole of the decision without pressure to decide, or without the therapist being committed to or requiring a particular outcome. Under these conditions, which seem to slow down the process of therapy, the client is able to move forward more expeditiously in a manner that validates the complexity of their decision and allows them to be unencumbered by shame at being "indecisive" while focusing their complete energy on the decision itself.

UNDERSTANDING AND HANDLING IMPASSES

Case files frequently contain instances of terminations that were the potential beginning points of psychotherapy rather than legitimate end points. In some cases, client and therapist have "politely" agreed to terminate their relationship without either party feeling truly satisfied with the process or outcome of their work together. In other cases, the therapy termination is characterized by confusion, puzzlement, or some other form of interpersonal conflict, which is often ascribed to client dynamics or personality problems. The dynamic concept of impasse is the notion that when therapy breaks down, far from being a moment of unmitigated failure in the psychotherapeutic process, these moments are often the precise point that leads to the central therapeutic issues for this client. The moment of conflict, which seems intractable, is precisely pointing to the manner in which the client, or indeed the therapist, deals with this type of interpersonal process or challenge. The psychotherapeutic process, if successful, is a poignant example of a truly intimate relationship and it therefore is not unusual that, if successful, it will lead to a strain on the therapist-client relationship. Intimacy, while being enormously fruitful and satisfying, is inherently anxiety provoking. It is therefore not surprising that at moments of approaching intimacy, due to the skill rather than the failure of the therapist, the client will generate a conflict to forestall further intimacy. So, for example, the older adult in the nursing home will abruptly terminate the psychotherapeutic session, expressing angrily his wish that the therapist leave immediately, or that the therapist is "bothering" him. At moments like this, therapists often feel disempowered (an accurate perception) and therefore experiences a failure in his or her therapeutic skills. The experienced therapist will recognize these moments as being therapeutically of great significance and, while not pushing intrusively forward at that moment, will reflect on this seeming failure as an indication of therapeutic progress and as perhaps the most poignant and meaningful diagnostic clue in the therapy to that point. Initial symptomatic diagnoses of the observable problem will now be completed with a more dynamically meaningful diagnostic profile of the processes that make sense of the symptomatic picture. Another example of impasse in psychotherapy with older adults is when the therapist avoids the topic of the client's approaching death. In this situation, there may be a genteel and unspoken collusion in the avoidance of this topic as the client "protects" the therapist from anxiety. This may lead to an impasse in the therapeutic process that points to the therapist's dynamics rather than the client. Once again, this is a critical moment in therapy and effective supervision might restore the therapist to therapeutic potency, allow him to regain his composure and provide further assistance to the older client.

ELICITING BEHAVIOR

An important source of dynamic diagnostic information about the client is revealed in the behavior that is elicited in the psychotherapy process. Basically, the concept of *eliciting behavior* is that most human beings, short on self-esteem, rarely assume that they will get what they need by directly asking for it. That leads us to develop intricate and complicated strategies for getting our needs met without risking potential rejection involved in asking directly. Perhaps the supreme need is to feel loved, and most human beings find it difficult to ask directly for love and affection. This leads us to develop indirect strategies that provide affirmation of affection and regard. Most adults entering psychotherapy have come to confront the growing disadvantages of the life style of eliciting behavior that they have developed in earlier life. Those individuals, for example, who have been psychologically, physically, or sexually abused, will have developed some degree of hypervigilance in the area of trust. Actually, they have developed coping or survival skills to meet their needs in a world in which trust is doubtful, if not impossible. Later in life, however, this eliciting strategy which perhaps served them well in earlier more vulnerable times now becomes a major impediment in the formation of an intimate, mature relationship in which trust is a critical ingredient. The process of therapy then becomes, in part, an understanding of the intricate and unique eliciting behaviors of the client and the development and rehearsal and risk-taking of new, more direct and effective interpersonal behaviors. The major vehicle the therapist has in understanding these eliciting behaviors of the client is as they are played out in the therapeutic process. Namely, it is the client's distrust that the therapist experiences in relationship with the client, and the various strategies, sometimes destructive, that the older client uses to maintain the relationship, that will allow the therapist to come directly, and phenomenologically, to understand the client's world. Indeed, these eliciting behaviors might precisely be the source of the impasse discussed earlier. Therefore, it is critical for the therapist to use process awareness to uncover and ameliorate these eliciting behaviors.

Perhaps the most common understanding of eliciting behavior is under the rubric of *manipulation*. It is understandable and natural to feel manipulated when we come to realize that someone is indirectly trying to get what they need from us. Manipulation is an emotionally loaded word, often deriving affective intensity from the person who feels used and angry in such a relationship. It is not uncommon for therapists to feel manipulated and to devote much energy to uncovering and challenging the manipulation. However, this is a *reactive* stance toward manipulation and, understanding manipulation more empathetically, as an eliciting behavior, helps the therapist understand, work with, and find alternate and healthier methods of interpersonal communication.

Therapeutic "Failures"

Both the failure to detect impasses and therapist reactivity to eliciting behavior cause breakdowns in the therapeutic process that are frequently experienced by the therapist as a failure. Indeed, if the story ends here, then often the client or the therapist will leave the therapeutic process and both parties will feel dissatisfied. However, as indicated, these moments of nonrecognition and reactivity are symptomatic of the central therapeutic tasks that lay before the client. With appropriate self-awareness, often derived from effective clinical supervision, the therapist cannot only be restored in working with the client, but indeed, can be empowered to more completely understand the client dynamics that are now seen as the central theme of the therapeutic effort. In fact, the issue that can be described as a mistake, with good recovery, can intensify the quality of the therapeutic relationships. Anger and reactivity can quickly turn to empathetic understanding and therapy can move even more rapidly and effectively than if the therapeutic "mistake" had never occurred.

Transferential Dynamics

Although transference has been frequently viewed as a clinical and problematic phenomenon, it may be viewed, naturalistically, as a universal feature of human cognition and relationships. It is perfectly meaningful that human beings assume that the road ahead will not differ from the road already traveled. It is understandable, for example, that an older person who has experienced betrayal, and abandonment will assume that future relationships cannot be trusted. Or, when an older adult has learned an emotional style in relationships (e.g., anger is permissible, tender emotions are not, or the converse of this), then they will anticipate this same emotional style and system of constraints in future relationships. Although this phenomenon can assume a clinical and problematic level, in itself it remains a normal and naturalistic process. Even in the world of geriatric psychotherapy, tranferential phenomena have a particularly poignant meaning in the client-therapist relationship in which therapists are often considerably younger than clients. It is not unusual that an understandable transferential instinct will cause a therapist to "parentify" the relationship with older clients thus disempowering their own role and authority as therapists. Conversely, some therapists may "infantilize" the older client, reversing the age difference in a manner that increases their own comfort but again disempowers, in this case, the older person. These transferential movements tend to create a therapist-client relationship that is anemic and innocuous and will soon die of its own lethargy and ineffectiveness. In clinical supervision of geriatric psychotherapy, confronting these tranferential moments becomes critical in the continuance of effective therapy. It can help the younger therapist recognize that, despite chronological age, an older client approaches the therapeutic process in a needy and psychologically childlike manner. Many of the issues of older clients concern, not with dealing with late life, but rather with unfinished emotional issues from earlier life that are still psychologically active. It is critical that the therapist assume the authority to provide understanding and guidance for this older client as he or she deals with unfinished issues that may be chronologically from earlier life, but experientially, are very much in the psychological present.

DYADIC AND GROUP PROCESSES

It has been suggested that most problems are interpersonal in nature and, clinically, this seems to be the case. Even a "detached" behavioral problem like depression, when understood in its dynamic meaning as well as its symptoms, is frequently about loss, abandonment, deprivation, or grief, all of which involve interpersonal processes. It is important that therapists become sensitive to interpersonal and group processes that are available to them in the therapy process. Even though the therapist may be at the bedside of an individual older client, it is important to pay attention to dyadic relationships that occur in this person's world, either with a roommate in the nursing home or indeed, psychologically, with absent family members. The lack of physical proximity of significant friends and family members sometimes obscures the psychological importance of those relationships. While a older patient may have a seemingly indifferent reaction to an ever-present adult daughter, for example, they may be obsessed by an unfinished and guilt-filled relationship with an absent child who pays scant attention.

Being attentive to dyadic and group processes in the world of the client becomes critical in having a comprehensive diagnostic view of the client's world. One advantage to providing therapy services in nursing homes, for example, is that the therapist is more likely to perceive, understand, and confront the various dynamic interactive processes that occur. The therapist may come to understand, for example, that the difficulties that an older person is having in the nursing home are directly related to the eliciting interpersonal style. They may seek help from staff in an abrasive and confronting manner and bring reactions which at times could even be abusive or at least neglectful. Even if we are not able to physically observe interactive behaviors in the world of the client, it is critical to process these possibilities in our minds as we ask detailed, pertinent and detailed questions about the interpersonal world of the client. This detailed phenomenological questioning allows us to see the world through the eyes of the client and develop an empathic and sophisticated understanding of the dynamic interpersonal processes that have shaped this older client's feelings and behavior.

SUBVOCAL AND NONVERBAL PROCESSES IN DEMENTIA

Traditional psychotherapy has been so preoccupied with overt, macrolevel behavior and external language that it has often dealt inadequately with the more complex linguistic world of the dementia patient. Human beings, as well as psychotherapist, are so attuned to the apparent importance of language in maintaining relationships that we often assume that when language is ended this also signals the end of internal processing, emotional life, and the possibility of continued relationship. This almost intuitive position is curiously at odds with our actual human experience of intimate relationships. We understand that a precise signal of the intimacy of the relationship is that it is not language-dependent. In other words, we can judge the significance and depth of the relationship when we can be together physically without words. How strange it is that the therapist assumes that psychotherapy is not possible at the moment when conventional language becomes impossible. It is almost the case, metaphorically speaking, that when the person no longer is able to hold conversations using language then everyone, including professional staff, seem to become emotionally detached. A tragic example of this is when a person loses language because of a stroke and even close relatives abandon their emotional relationship with the person because of a loss of language communication. Being attuned to the nonverbal and subvocal processes in communication is critical in maintaining a therapeutic stance with patients suffering from dementia. It is in this way that we can stay psychologically connected with them and enter their emotional world while tolerating the deprivation of our understandable felt need for logical language. With dementia, language disappears but emotions remain vibrant and poignant; it is not by accident that depression is very frequently a comorbid problem with cognitive decline. If we understand depression as an interpersonal phenomena, then we can clearly understand its presence in cases where emotional intimacy has vanished along with logical language.

DEVELOPMENTAL PROCESSES

Much of human experience is developmental in nature in the sense that it is gradual, incremental, and follows an orderly and predictable path. Much of what is designated as developmental psychology in our field would indeed be better described as *developmental behavior.* There is little emphasis on internal psychological development within the field of developmental psychology. Work such as that of Erik Erikson begins to deal with these internal, psychological aspects of human development. Even in Erikson there is the tendency to limit development to a lifespan perspective, so that we look at the unfolding of human experience over the *years* and throughout the lifespan. However, from the therapist's perspective, the developmental principle and process occur within discrete human experiences, such as grieving, the process of separation and divorce, making a life decision, and the development process of training in psychotherapy itself. In each of these domains of human experience, there can be described a developmental trajectory. As the therapist understands and is increasingly in tune with this trajectory, he or she can help the client manage the process in a more empathic and precise manner. The therapist who is sensitive to developmental processes, for example, is attuned to the concept of *readiness* in the client's life and can avoid the inappropriate anxiety that leads to rushing stages that inherently take time. Having a sense of the developmental process in an experience the client is facing, allows the therapist to "look over the head of the client and down the road." This posture is highly effective in keeping the therapist in tune with the client and not missing moments of therapeutic potential, not rushing a client to make decisions they are not ready for, and generally, paradoxically, increasing the pace of the psychotherapeutic change. Older adults, for example, frequently go through a painful but orderly process of determining their living environments as they become more physically and psychologically debilitated. These choices are bound up with internal developmental processes and a person needs to progress to a moment of decision. For example, to have been in the position of caretaker, nurturer, and provider all of one's life, can make the transition to the more "passive" setting of assisted living or nursing home a significant psychological transition for an older adult. Recognizing this internal developmental process helps with therapeutic timing, support, and, ultimately, effectiveness.

PROCESS AS THERAPEUTIC STRATEGY

The term technique in psychotherapy is both multifaceted and ambiguous. In a typical text on techniques of psychotherapy the term *technique* means several different things. In many cases, such as in behavioral techniques, the word technique denotes a *procedure,* an actual physical sequence of steps as, for example, relaxation techniques or systematic desensitization. In another sense, technique can indicate verbal procedures including, for example, verbal reinforcement or, in a different context, reframing techniques, where the significance of an event is reconceptualized in the interests of affirming the client. Yet another sense of therapeutic technique or strategy might be described as *therapeutic posture.* Within psychotherapy, therapeutic posture is frequently a better descriptor for the various therapeutic strategies that we have described. These approaches are somewhat less behaviorally defined and more ambiguous than procedural behavioral techniques. Indeed, therapists may feel less ambiguity and more comfort in using behavioral, procedural techniques. In moments of ambivalence and uncertainty, a therapist might feel drawn to a specific and discrete activity such as diagnostic testing or relaxation techniques. However, such a decision may constitute a "flight" from the central therapeutic issue. The very ambiguity and uncertainty, as stated earlier, may give an entry point to the central therapeutic issue. If we consider therapy to be a naturalistic experience rather than a technical invention of psychology, we might use the natural developmental process as a paradigmatic model for the therapeutic or healing process. After all, as self-psychology would suggest, human beings grow into psychological health through the normal healthy interpersonal connections they have with significant persons in their life. The emerging self is supported and becomes intact through the mirroring and affirming processes of critical parental figures and other significant persons in the person's life. What seems to be important in life and perhaps also in therapy is the psychological "posture" assumed by critical and significant persons in our life. It is not the behavior, simply, of parents that influences our well being, but rather the perceived *quality* and *meaning* of that behavior that adds to human psychological health. Therefore, it is not surprising that one important domain of psychological technique and strategy is a sophisticated understanding of the nature and quality of the relationship and the necessary psychological posture of the therapist toward a client. This also makes sense of the sustained body of research that suggests that the critical ingredient in the efficacy of psychotherapy has little to do with theoretical or technical treatment differences and much more to do with what has been described as "common factors" or ingredients, namely, aspects of the therapist or relationship variables. From this point of view, training in psychotherapy becomes less a technical exploit than assuring a sophistication in the understanding and subsequent utilization of dynamic psychological processes. Thus, for example, it is the therapist's understanding of the older adult's need for control that allows the therapist to position him- or herself in a way that is maximumally therapeutically effective, as opposed to becoming entangled in reactive control struggles with the client. It is, likewise, an understanding of the older adult's need for "parental" support that encourages the therapist to assume their full authority (as opposed to authoritarian style) available to the client. These aspects of therapeutic posture are implicit rather than explicit in the moment-to-moment management of the therapeutic relationship. Such psychological posture is present *within* the various other procedural techniques that may be used to the benefit of the client, for example, in relaxation training, behavior rehearsal, and directives. As was mentioned earlier, it is perhaps the "feeling understood" that is the critical element in the therapeutic goal initiation and discussion that takes place between the therapist and client.

Many important moments of therapeutic posture may take place in what seems to be perfectly common, ordinary, everyday conversations with the client. However, it is feeling dissatisfied with "just talking" that often will lead the anxious therapist to "escape" into procedural business. In fact, as communication specialists have demonstrated perhaps better than psychologists, there is no such thing as "just talking" (Peyrot, 1995). Human conversation is an immensely complex phenomenon with many levels. In any given conversation, there are often many levels of meaning. While the topic of a conversation may be in a specific *content* area, we are frequently using the process of this conversation to *send signals* that reaffirm our therapeutic posture toward the client. This covert approach is particularly helpful when clients are at a self-protective stage that would not allow self-awareness or direct discussion of problem areas. With an extremely narcissistic older client, for example, (and narcissistic seems one of the most resilient personality problems to survive in late life!), it is unlikely that we will directly confront the narcissistic behavior. To do so would probably produce resistance to further discussion and block any further progress. In this case, therefore, the conversations and communication about selfish behavior will be indirect and focus on less overt aspects of the narcissistic behavior, such as testing out the interest that the older person might have in altruistic behavior toward close friends.

CONCLUSION

Process dimensions of psychotherapy are perhaps the most central and least emphasized aspect of therapeutic process. They receive attention, if implicitly, in all effective psychotherapy and can be utilized instrumentally to greatly increase the power of the therapeutic experience of older persons.

REFERENCES

Ainsworth, M.D.S. (1989). Attachment beyond intimacy. *American Psychologist, 44,* 709–716.

Bordin, E.S. (1979). The generalizability of the psychoanalytic concept of the working alliance. *Psychotherapy: Theory, Research and Practice, 16,* 252–260.

Czogalik, D. (1995). A Strategy of interaction process research in psychotherapy. In J. Siegeried (Ed.), *Therapeutic and everyday discourse as behavior change.* Norwood, NJ: ABLEX.

Gelso, C.J., & Carter, J.A. (1985). The relationship in counseling and psychotherapy: Components, consequences and theoretical antecedents. *Counseling Psychologist, 13,* 155–243.

Greenson, R.R. (1967). *Techniques and practice of psychoanalysis.* New York: International Universities Press.

Hill, C.E. (1990). Exploratory in session process research in individual psychotherapy: A review. *Journal of Consulting and Clinical Psychology, 58,* 288–294.

Kell, B.L., & Burow, J.M. (1970). *Developmental counseling and psychotherapy.* New York: Houghton Mifflin.

Kell, B.L., & Meuller, W.J. (1966). *Impact and change: A study of counseling relationships.* New York: Appleton-Century-Crafts.

Kiesler, D.J. (1987). *Checklist of psychotherapy transactions—revised (CLOPT-R) and checklist of interpersonal transactions—revised (CLOIT-R).* Richmond: Virginia Connonwealth University.

Kiesler, D.J., & Watkins, L.M. (1989). Interpersonal complimentarity and the therapeutic alliance: A study of relationship in psychotherapy. *Psychotherapy, 26,* 183–194.

Kolb, D.L., Beutler, L.E., Davis, C.S., Crago, M., & Shanfield, T. (1985). Patient and therapy process variables relating to drop-out and change in psychotherapy. *Psychotherapy, 22,* 702–710.

Luborsky, L., Crits-Christoph, P., Mintz, J., & Auerbach, A. (1988). *Who will benefit from psychotherapy? Predicting therapeutic outcomes.* New York: Basic Books.

Luborsky, L., Mintz, J., Auerbach, A., Crits-Christoph, P., Bachrach, H., Todd, T., Johnson, M., Cohen, M., & O' Brien, C.P. (1980). Predicting the outcome of psychotherapy: Findings of the Penn psychotherapy project. *Archives of General Psychiatry, 37,* 471–481.

Meuller, J.M., & Kell, B.L. (1972). *Coping with conflict: Supervising counselors and psychotherapists.* Englewood Cliffs, NJ: Prentice-Hall.

Peyrot, M. (1995). Therapeutic preliminaries: Conversational context and process in psychotherapy. *Qualitative Sociology, 18*(3), 311–329.

Rogers, C. (1957). The necessary and sufficient conditions of therapeutic personality change. *Journal of Consulting Psychotherapy, 21,* 95–103.

Sexton, T.L., & Whiston, S.C. (1994). The status of the counseling relationship: An empirical review, theoretical implication, and research questions. *Counseling Psychologist, 22*(1), 6–78.

Tracey, T.J. (1986). Control in counseling: Interpersonal versus interpersonal definitions. *Journal of Counseling and Development, 64,* 512–515.

Von Bertalanffy, L. (1975). *Perspective on general system theory: Scientific-philosophical studies.* New York: Braziller.

Wampold, B.E. (1997). Methodological problems in identifying efficacious psychotherapies. *Psychotherapy Research, 7*(1), 21–43.

Wampold, B.E., Mondin, G.W., Moody, M., Stitch, F., Benson, K., & Ann, H. (1997). A meta-analysis of outcome studies comparing bona fide psychotherapies: Empirically, "all must have prizes." *Psychological Bulletin, 122*(3), 203–215.

Warnock, G.J. (1969). *English philosophy since 1900.* London: Oxford University Press.

Watkins, C.E., Savickas, M., Brizzi, J., & Manus, M. (1990). Effects of counselor response behavior on clients' impressions during vocational counseling. *Journal of Counseling Psychology, 37,* 138–142.

CHAPTER 2

Transferential and Countertransferential Processes in Therapy with Older Adults

NANCY A. NEWTON AND JORDAN JACOBOWITZ

This chapter focuses on transference and countertransference in psychotherapy with the elderly. Transference has traditionally been defined as an unconscious process in which the client responds to the therapist in distorted ways reflective of the client's past relationships with significant caretakers during childhood. These reactions are not grounded in the reality of the therapist or of the relationship. Freud (1966) believed that by re-enacting themes and issues from very early childhood, transference provided entry into the client's neurosis. He maintained that a therapeutic relationship which facilitated the emergence, clarification, and interpretation of the transference was crucial to resolving neurotic conflicts. Unconscious reactions for the therapist also occurred, according to Freud. These included the therapist's reaction to the client (therapist transference) and to the client's transference (countertransference). Its unconscious nature inevitably meant that the therapist's transference and countertransference reactions influenced treatment in problematic ways.

Since Freud's original conceptualization, the terms *transference* and *countertransference* have been used more broadly to refer to all of the patient's and therapist's emotional reactions toward one another, whether based in reality or in neurotic needs (Kernberg, 1985). Once the sole domain of psychodynamic psychotherapy, other therapy models have begun to recognize and work with transference within their own perspective: modifying the impact of negative early relationships by providing corrective emotional experiences, cultivating positive transference to facilitate achievement of therapeutic goals, or relating to the client in a way that meets the psychological and developmental needs evident in the transference relationship.

Limiting the concepts of transference and countertransference to unconscious processes has also been abandoned. This conceptual reformulation has highlighted the complexity of the interpersonal dynamics and multiple layers of interpersonal meanings within the therapeutic relationship. It nevertheless has blurred the differential impacts of conscious and unconscious reactions on the therapeutic relationship. Menninger reportedly said that countertransference is dangerous only when it is forgotten about (quoted by Slakter, 1987). Unconscious reactions inevitably restrict the therapist's availability to the client. "They 'clutter up' the therapist's self-observing and self-responding so as to interfere or at least make difficult the task of focusing on the patient" (Muslin & Clarke, 1988, p. 298). Once conscious of them, the prior detrimental reactions may provide the basis for heightened understanding of and empathy for the client.

The assumption that these processes differ in significant ways between elderly clients and clients of other ages is inherent in focusing on transference and countertransference in psychotherapy. It also implies the existence of meaningful similarities in transference among clients within a given age range, even when this range can extend from 65 to 100. Similar assumptions can be made about countertransference: There are similarities in the factors that color a broad range of therapists' perceptions and responses to elderly clients and that these responses differ in significant ways from their countertransference reactions to clients of other ages.

Historically, the literature on transference and countertransference parallels the literature on psychodynamic psychotherapy with the elderly. The early literature primarily described supportive psychotherapy with physically frail, cognitively impaired, or emotionally depleted elders (Alexander, 1944; Grotjahn, 1955; Meerloo, 1953). Observations regarding countertransference focused on the detrimental impact of clinicians' discomfort with the elderly based on internalized cultural stereotypes (Butler & Lewis, 1977), the residual psychological impact of experiences with parental authority figures, the disability and frailty of older clients, or discomfort with a power position in relationship to people significantly their senior (Grotjahn, 1955; King, 1980). Discussions of transference illuminated the ways in which a lifetime of experiences, generational differences, and age differences between therapist and client influenced the elderly person's comfort in, as well as use of, a therapeutic relationship.

Within the past 15 years, case reports and research have addressed the use of psychodynamic psychotherapy, and even psychoanalysis, with more intact and highly functioning older adults (Cath, 1982; Myers, 1984; Nemiroff & Colarusso, 1985b). While a number of these case reports focus on clients in their 50s and 60s—age groups which one is reluctant to classify as "elderly" by today's standards—therapists also describe effective intensive psychotherapy with clients in their 80s and 90s (Riess, 1992; Settlage, 1996; Strauss, 1996). Increasingly, this literature brings clarity to the ways that age influences transference and countertransference and the subtle ways that age-related differences are played out. Several conclusions can be drawn from these reports:

1. Transference reactions can be as significant in older clients as in younger clients; some clinicians argue that they may be even more powerful. Within the context of psychodynamic psychotherapy, analysis of the transference is a meaningful and effective therapeutic technique for older clients.

2. Transference processes are as complex in older clients as they are in younger adults. Their manifestation can be rich and varied and, as with younger adults, can shift in both meaning and presentation as therapy progresses.
3. Even though countertransference reactions to the elderly are influenced by age-related issues and experiences, each therapist's reactions to a particular client are unique. Ongoing cultivation of self-awareness is crucial to managing these reactions.
4. Depending on the therapist's level of self-awareness, acknowledgment, and understanding of countertransference reactions, these reactions can provide either a powerful basis for understanding and empathy or a significant block to establishing a therapeutic relationship.

This chapter will present these conclusions in more detail and discuss their implications through case examples.

COUNTERTRANSFERENCE

Mrs. Jones presented at intake as a petite, attractive, well-dressed, wealthy woman. She was obviously intelligent, articulate, and in distress. She reported persistent and longstanding feelings of hopelessness, crying episodes, lack of self-confidence and periods of suicidal ideation. In the intake, her affect seemed depressed, but constricted. She identified the precipitant of her depression as marital problems. She described her husband as a successful businessman, and the couple as active in their church and other social obligations. However, she described him as constantly belittling and criticizing her in private, becoming enraged over even minor problems. Although when confronted he angrily denied her accusations, she believed that he had been involved in multiple extra-marital affairs, most recently a long-standing relationship with his secretary. On rare occasions, the marital fights escalated to the point that he hit her, although this behavior had not occurred for more than a year, after an incident in which she called the police. Mrs. Jones was clearly ashamed of the marital problems and reported that she never mentioned the fights to any of her friends. While unhappy and psychologically intimidated, she denied any concerns for her physical safety. The couple had no children and she had no close family relationships. Mrs. Jones reported that she had left her husband several times in the past, but always returned home after a few weeks. Previous therapy helped her realize that she feels better when she stands up to her husband, but this behavior escalates the marital problems; when she keeps her feelings to herself, her depression increases. Her husband consistently had refused marital therapy, although he did not actively oppose her involvement in therapy.

This client's presentation is not unusual for an outpatient clinic or private practice. A therapist, presented with such a client, is likely to consider interventions that focus on cultivating Mrs. Jones' confidence, self-esteem, and assertiveness, potentially with the objective of encouraging her to question ongoing involvement in the marriage, if it cannot be modified in ways that are healthier for her. The relevant issue for this chapter is whether the therapist's reactions to and attitudes toward Mrs. Jones change in any way because of her age. She is 84 and her husband is 73. A related issue is whether those reactions and actions should be influenced by the client's age.

Dewald (1964) identifies three types of countertransference: general reactions—hidden agendas that influence interactions with all clients; group-specific reactions—such as to the elderly, women, and so on; individual-client reactions—the specific response elicited by a particular client. Any or all of these countertransference types may influence psychotherapy with the elderly.

Dewald identifies a number of generalized expectations that can unconsciously influence a therapist's work with clients. The therapist's role may be used to gratify unconscious needs to feel omniscient, in control, or needed by others; to fulfill curiosity or voyeuristic needs; to satisfy unconscious masochistic needs through inadvertent encouragement of clients' excessive demands. These unconscious agendas and expectations can influence the therapist to lead the client in certain directions and to cultivate need-gratifying relationships with clients. While Dewald identifies these countertransference reactions as operative with clients of any age, they may take on particular meaning in psychotherapy with the elderly. The vulnerability and frailty of many older adults, or their lower status within the culture, may initially appeal to therapists with unmet needs to feel powerful or to rescue the vulnerable. Some therapists' insecurity may be alleviated by working with a less challenging and less personally threatening group of clients.

Working with elderly clients often challenges therapists' narcissistic investment in their therapeutic skills and competence. Treating older adults whose lifestyle choices are generally limited and whose remaining lifespan is relatively short requires therapists to identify different criteria for evaluating the meaningfulness of their work. Younger clients often have more opportunity in terms of both lifestyle and time to demonstrate therapy's beneficial effects; benefits of therapy for the older client may be more subtle and harder to discern. For example, even if therapy enables Mrs. Jones to be less depressed, feel better about herself, and question remaining in an abusive relationship, the choices and options she has for both lifestyle and establishment of more gratifying intimate relationships are necessarily more limited than if she had achieved these goals at age 40.

The second type of countertransference reaction Dewald identifies is toward groups of clients. These reactions often reflect internalized cultural stereotypes and norms. Age biases within the American culture are well-known (Sonderegger & Siegel, 1995), and the internalization of these stereotypes by physicians and mental health professionals well-documented (Butler, 1994; Grant, 1996). They inevitably contribute to an often unrecognized internalized image of aging and the aged—the basis for evaluating any particular older individual. Much of the literature on psychotherapy with the elderly focuses on the ways in which these stereotypes bias psychotherapy with the elderly (Butler & Lewis, 1977; Orbach, 1994).

Within the context of these broad cultural stereotypes, individual therapist expectations about aging are often largely determined by direct experiences with a very limited sample of older people—family members who did or did not age gracefully, an idealized mentor or role model. Particularly important are early life experiences with parents and grandparents. Pervasive age-segregation makes it highly unlikely that non-elderly therapists will relate to a wide variety of older people as friends, coworkers, or casual social acquaintances. For the clinician whose only ongoing experience of aging is with a particular segment of the elderly, often those with significant impairments, maintaining broad perspectives can be even more challenging.

Expectations based on a narrow, personal sample of elderly—whether an idealized image of the elderly person as wise and generative or the negative stereotype of the elderly as rigid, conservative, incapable of new learning, a financial burden to society—likely color the therapist's perceptions and expectations of clients such as Mrs. Jones. The therapist may be more likely to assume a protector role toward this appealing, frail woman, feeling overly responsible for her welfare and wanting to rescue her from her abusive husband. To the extent that this stance is based on countertransference rather than the reality of the marital dynamics, it can make it more difficult to identify Mrs. Jones' role in the marital difficulties and consequently, more difficult to identify and develop her strengths. An alternative reaction is that the therapist may be more likely to be frustrated with Mrs. Jones and dismissive of the possibility of change. After all, if she hasn't gotten herself together by now, what can the therapist realistically expect?

A case description by Semel (1993) illustrates the subtle ways in which ageism can emerge in countertransference reactions. When her 67-year-old client became demanding and relentlessly critical, Semel's ageism emerged as a way of justifying her own frustration:

> I was aware of a strong wish to discharge this patient. Ideas circulated through my mind about how I might not be the right therapist for this woman (a wish even I could recognize). I also began to become increasingly conscious of her age, something that had never concerned me before this point in the therapy. Suddenly it was as if Mrs. T. had become an old patient, perhaps too old to be successfully treated by analysis. Freud's admonitions about the elderly patient with rigid personality traits flitted through my mind. (p. 136)

Just as elderly clients often use age as a convincing form of resistance, the therapist's residual ageism can emerge selectively when confronted with a particularly frustrating client, even when the therapist has previously examined personal stereotypes and biases.

The impact of the therapist's personal issues about aging and agedness has long been identified as critical to countertransference with the elderly (Butler & Lewis, 1977; Stern, Smith, & Frank, 1953). Elderly clients can present vivid, and sometimes painful, images of the aging process and the inevitability of death; empathic connections awaken therapists to their own future. This reality provokes strong emotional reactions and the desire to deny or minimize those feelings is natural. However, persistence in that denial can lead the therapist to remain unknowingly detached and distant from the client (Lewis & Johansen,

1982). When therapist and client unconsciously collude, they may engage in a choreography of denial that protects both from directly acknowledging fears of separation, loss, and death (Strauss, 1996). It is only when the therapist communicates openness, in both subtle and obvious ways, that expression of these issues can come directly into the relationship.

In addition to issues about aging, specific situations that are more often seen when working with elderly clients (e.g., illness, dementia, disability, institutionalization, chronic illness, impending death) trigger their own countertransference reactions (Genevay & Katz, 1990; Horowitz, 1991). Some experiences, such as chemical dependency, suicide, and sexual problems, may trigger quite different therapist reactions when seen in older (vs. younger) adults (Genevay & Katz, 1990).

The nature of intergenerational dynamics have long been identified as the basis of significant differences in the countertransference processes elicited by elderly and younger adult clients (King, 1980). Therapists may respond to clients as a grandparent (Knight, 1986) or parent and often must manage older clients' response to them as a son or daughter (Hildebrand, 1982). Increasingly, clinicians are recognizing that intergenerational countertransference reactions are not static, but instead change with the therapist's age and developmental phase. While younger therapists may look to the older person as an idealized grandparent and identify themselves with a loved grandchild role, the countertransference reactions of these same therapists will likely change as they reach middle-age and are managing the current realities of changing roles in relationship to their own aging parents.

As a child, adolescent, and even young adult, the therapist's experience of relationships with parents was most likely that of the adult as authority and the self as vulnerable or needy. Clinicians have often noted, that unless worked through, these experiences can lead to unconscious acting out of lingering feelings of anger and aggression toward elderly clients or defensive maneuvers through idealization or an overly protective stance (Grotjahn, 1955). For many middle-aged therapists, however, these early and historical child-parent relationship dynamics have been superceded by current patterns. With midlife, therapists often face shifting power dynamics in their own relationships with aging parents—now they are assuming positions of authority while parents struggle with feelings of increased dependency and neediness. Parents who served as sources of support, validation, and guidance no longer fill those roles.

Even for therapists who through personal self-reflection and analysis have processed childhood-based feelings toward parents, the conflicts and emotions stirred up by these midlife power shifts can be immediate and powerful (Ellman, 1996). These dynamics can contribute to the complexity of the "reverse oedipal complex" identified by Grotjahn (1955). Countertransference reactions related to residual anger toward parents can emerge with renewed salience and force. On the other hand, defending against those feelings or needing to replace the need-gratifying functions formerly filled by their own parents can lead to idealizing the elderly client or needing the client to be strong and wise to fulfill the therapist's needs. Alternatively, assuming an overly protective stance toward the patient can alleviate therapists' guilt about failed caregiving toward their own parents.

The developmental perspective illuminates other important dimensions of countertransference. Late life is a unique developmental phase, with its own values, attitudes, and psychological tasks (Erikson, Erikson, & Kivnick, 1986; Gutmann, 1987; Nemiroff & Colarusso, 1990). The therapist who understands this phase through direct personal experience is rare, although several recent case reports discuss the unique aspect of the experiences of older therapists treating older adults (Riess, 1992; Settlage, 1996; Strauss, 1996). More commonly, therapists are significantly younger than their elderly clients. The consequence of viewing the life of the older person through the younger adult lens of values and attitudes can be subtle and pervasive. A revealing personal account by Martin Grotjahn (1985), a highly respected geriatric psychiatrist, on the ways in which his own values and attitudes shifted in unexpected ways in late life, illustrates how difficult it is to understand a developmental phase from an outsider perspective, even after a lifetime of study.

Malamud (1996) describes a case example illustrating how easy it is to impose younger adult values in making judgments about the elderly. Feeling shocked and horrified by the poor hygiene and living conditions of an elderly couple, he advocated for nursing home placement. It was only when directly questioned about their quality of life that he remembered other salient aspects of the interview—that the couple was happy, that the husband was talkative and appropriate, that there were no physical dangers apparent in their living situation.

As Malamud contends, often well-intentioned social service and mental health interventions can be out-of-sync with the actual preferences of the elderly client when they are defined and conceptualized from within the values of the younger adult. A very elderly widower exemplified this process. He was referred because a social worker had been unable to convince him to attend a nearby senior center for lunch. She was understandably concerned about his poor nutritional intake, social isolation, and depression. From her perspective, attending the center, where he would receive not only food but also companionship, seemed an ideal intervention. The social worker was frustrated by his resistance and concerned about the consequences of his failure to follow her suggestion. However, when given the opportunity, the client talked poignantly and convincingly about his disinterest in cultivating new friends. New social contacts would never replace the lifelong relationships he had known—friendships that had emerged from shared life experiences and developed through good times and bad. To him, new acquaintances felt superficial and useless. To consider such contacts as "friends" would be disloyal to the relationships he had lost.

While many case studies have shown that in and of itself age does not affect suitability for psychotherapy or even for analysis (Settlage, 1996; Simburg, 1985), factors such as duration of symptoms that do influence expectations of therapeutic process and success, often correlate with age. The convergence of these factors can further heighten and serve to justify age-based pessimism.

Even the therapist who has cultivated a balanced view of the process of aging and who recognizes the variety of aging experiences and adaptations, is likely to become more pessimistic when learning that Mrs. Jones' marital problems have persisted for over 40 years, despite previous lengthy episodes of therapy.

Another age-correlated factor that often influences therapist expectations is "hardiness"—intactness of physical health and cognitive functioning. Whatever their age, clients who are experiencing chronic, debilitating physical illness or whose intellectual functioning is compromised present unique challenges in psychotherapy. However, the fact that these conditions occur more frequently in the elderly and may occur very frequently in a particular subgroup of elderly can lead to overgeneralization. Much of the debate regarding the use of psychoanalytic and intensive psychodynamic psychotherapy with the elderly reflects this type of overgeneralization.

The third type of countertransference process identified by Dewald is the reaction triggered by a particular client's personality dynamics and presentation. Even if based in cultural stereotypes, intergenerational dynamics, or other age-related issues described above, each therapist's reaction to a particular client at a particular time is unique, reflecting the idiosyncratic nature of that specific moment of client-therapist interaction and the feelings (both conscious and unconscious) provoked in the therapist. Increasingly, case reports illustrate the ways in which individual client and therapist dynamics and client-therapist interactions result in countertransference reactions (Muslin & Clarke, 1988). Idiosyncratic aspects of the countertransference may relate to concurrent life experiences such as death of a spouse (Riess, 1992), to common developmental experiences between therapist and client (Ellman 1996; Strauss, 1996), or to the uniqueness of the client (i.e., genuinely wise and talented older adults who win the therapist's admiration) (Settlage, 1996).

On the most fundamental level, unrecognized countertransference impairs the therapist's ability to be open to the client's experience and empathize with the emotional impact of those experiences. Its influence can jeopardize the therapeutic process in subtle and pervasive ways. It can impede the therapist's judgment in evaluating and facilitating the client's realistic evaluation of expectations for psychological, behavioral, and lifestyle changes. Because available options and lifestyle choices are inevitably more limited for someone at 90 than at 40 or even 70, the therapist is often in the position of evaluating whether a client's experience of having fewer options is reality-based acceptance or psychologically-based resistance. The therapist's dilemma is to remain alert to the sometimes subtle interplay between agist stereotypes—the client's as well as his or her own—and the realities of late life experience.

Distinctions between the client's resistance and/or the therapist's countertransference versus realistic expectations are not always easily discerned. In their description of the analysis of a female client in her late 60s, Wylie and Wylie (1987) point out that often the client's seemingly age-related concerns were, when addressed therapeutically, reflective of neuroses and transference reactions. During the course of therapy, this particular client complained of diminished genital sexuality, somatic symptoms, and reduced opportunities for new relationships. When the analyst was able to move beyond his initial assumption that each of these issues was a reality-based, age-related concern, and treat it as resistance, its psychological basis became clear and the symptoms abated.

While Mrs. Jones is in overall excellent health, back problems incapacitate her for periods of time, and she is increasingly afraid of falling. Although she appears intelligent and articulate, Mrs. Jones reports that particularly since turning 80 (the age at which she identified "feeling old"), she's noticed significant changes in her memory. She has not been reassured by her physician's reports that she is not experiencing early stages of dementia. Awareness of her own increasing sense of physical frailty and potential further declines frightens Mrs. Jones. The overly idealistic therapist might minimize the reality of these factors and hold unrealistic expectations for Mrs. Jones. In contrast, the age-biased therapist might overestimate the importance of these factors and thus too quickly collude with her belief that her physical health prevents lifestyle changes.

Age-related countertransference reactions can so influence the therapist's reactions that the ability to see and relate to the client's uniqueness and individuality is jeopardized. Therapists often, without thinking, relate to elderly clients in ways that they would consider patronizing and overly solicitous when interacting with younger clients—helping clients with coats, touching and hugging, or talking in simplistic terms. Particularly when working with a more frail population, these behavior patterns can become automatic rather than based on sensitivity to a particular individual's needs. While intended to be nurturant, they can inadvertently reinforce the client's sense of self as frail and needy and enhance a pathological self-image.

Alternatively, these behaviors can damage the therapist's credibility. As Hiatt (1971) suggests, "The older patient has spent a lifetime sizing up other persons. Many can spot a 'phony' and it is useless to play games with them" (p. 597). A 90-year-old client once described an incident in which she had traveled alone to another city for a major medical work-up. After the examination, the physician said, "I'll ask your daughter to come in." Because of the client's age, he had assumed that her daughter had accompanied her on the trip, that she needed assistance and support in making medical decisions for herself, and that it was inappropriate to relate to her as a competent, independent, fully functioning adult. Not surprisingly, the client was insulted and angry.

Countertransference reactions also jeopardize therapists' ability to effectively manage clients' transference reactions. Two issues have received particular attention: discomfort with transferential dependency relationships and sexualized transference. Many writers have noted the difficulty younger clinicians experience in accepting sexuality in the elderly and the implications for psychotherapy: that sexual feelings do not get explored or sexual conflicts resolved (Nemiroff & Colarusso, 1985b). The therapist's discomfort can inadvertently confirm the older adult's own fears that sexual feelings are inappropriate (the "dirty" old man). However, sexualized transference reactions occur in older adults just as in younger adults; the therapist needs to respond in a way that validates and respects the client's sexuality and adult status as a sexual being (Crusey, 1985; Gitelson, 1965).

Unrecognized countertransference can impair the therapeutic relationship in many ways. It can lead therapists to gratify their own needs by inappropriately using clients; it can impede therapists' ability to perceive each client's uniqueness and individuality, it can interfere with a genuinely therapeutic response to the client's transference; or it can diminish the capacity for empathy. Conversely when brought to consciousness and analyzed, emotional reactions to clients that emerge during and after sessions can provide powerful insight into the clients' emotional and psychological worlds. Awareness of one's personal feelings, reactions, and struggles provide a meaningful basis for a mutual relationship with aging clients who are either actively engaged with their lives or who are coping with dying, disability, institutional placement, or dementia.

Working with one's own countertransference is inevitable in effective psychotherapy. Recognition that countertransference reactions are not static across patients or across one's career; belief that one's reactions, attitudes, and values influence therapy, often in unconscious ways; and awareness that many of the personal issues that emerge in working with the elderly are integral to the therapist's own lifelong journey underlie successful management of these reactions. Given the ingrained cultural antagonism toward the elderly, specific efforts are often necessary to counter agist stereotypes. Cultivating and maintaining connection with the diversity of aging experiences through personal journals (Berman, 1994), literature, films, and relationships with a broad range of older adults supports the therapist's efforts to counter stereotypes and balance narrow experiences with particular segments of the elderly population.

Willingness to recognize and sit with one's own fears and anxieties about aging and death, as they emerge and change throughout life, is crucial to effective psychotherapy with the elderly. Differences between young and old in needs, feelings, and perceptions are not as great as the young would like to believe. Whatever his or her age, the therapist is simply at a different place on an aging continuum. The therapist's self-awareness can cut through the client's avoidance of often unspoken, painful issues and provides common ground for mutual respect. Successful therapeutic relationships with elderly clients are based in fundamental human needs—for security, self-esteem, and human connection. The frailer the elderly client, the more likely the therapist is, for self-protective reasons, to deny commonalities and, ironically, the more crucial is their recognition for successful intervention.

TRANSFERENCE

Any therapeutic relationship develops out of the client's appraisal of the therapist as a real person as well as a transference object. The importance of the "real" relationship with the therapist, particularly for older people with few social supports has often been emphasized (Newton & Lazarus, 1986). The role of transference in psychotherapy with the elderly—its emergence, meaning, and therapeutic management—has historically received less attention.

However, this pattern is changing as more case studies of psychodynamic therapy and psychoanalysis with older clients emerge in the literature (Miller, 1987; Myers, 1984; Simburg, 1985; Wharton, 1996). These case studies illustrate that transference processes are as complex and fluid as they are in younger adults. Their manifestation is as rich and varied as in younger clients and can shift in both meaning and presentation as therapy progresses. Therapists who work with psychologically high-functioning older adults are finding that emergence and analysis of transference patterns can be as powerful in therapy with older adults as it is in psychotherapy with younger people.

Many gerontologists have argued that the types of transference relationships that develop with the elderly differ from younger clients (Berezin, 1972; Grotjahn, 1955; Nemiroff & Colarusso, 1990). Some of these differences relate to the long course of significant relationships that adults develop during their lifespans. In contrast to the younger adult whose relationships with parents or other childhood caregivers are likely to be the basis of transference, the older person has a much longer history of many significant relationships, particularly with spouse, partners, and children, that shape their expectations both of others and themselves in relationships. Hiatt (1971) and Nemiroff and Colarusso (1990) suggest three sources of transference reactions in adulthood:

1. Early childhood experience
2. Experience from all following developmental stages
3. Current stage-related developmental conflicts

Taking a lifelong developmental history can identify the contributing relationship influences from each period and thus whether transference dynamics are based on childhood or adult experiences (Nemiroff & Colarusso, 1990).

EARLY CHILDHOOD EXPERIENCE

Parental-based transference relationships in which clients relate to therapists as parental figures emerge throughout the lifespan, regardless of the chronological ages of either therapist or client. The timelessness of the unconscious and the powerfulness of early life experiences in the formation of personality structure underlies the persistence of the influence of early relationships on transference reactions throughout adulthood and into late life (Berezin, 1972). Often novice therapists are surprised by the extent to which elderly clients use therapy as a way of continuing to attempt resolution of early childhood issues, particularly when those experiences were psychologically traumatizing.

ADULT EXPERIENCES

By late life, there has been ample opportunity for many significant relationships which may modify internalized expectations of and needs within relationships. These experiences may contribute to the client's perception of the therapist as a son or daughter—often as the idealized contrast to real children; to assume a mentor or "wise elder" role toward the younger, more inexperienced therapist; or to look to the therapist as a trusted sounding-board or peer, who fulfills functions previously filled by a spouse, close friends, or business associates.

The extent to which adult experiences contribute to the transference of a particular client likely is a function of the client's developmental course. For some older adults, the relationship with their own parents continues to be most salient in shaping their perceptions of self and others. Other people who have continued to develop psychologically throughout adulthood have internalized significant relationships from that period, with related changes in possibilities for transference reactions.

CURRENT-STAGE RELATED DEVELOPMENTAL CONFLICTS

Lazarus and Sadavoy (1996) categorize the ways in which age-related conflicts contribute to the transference. For example, very frail elderly may be more likely to relate to the therapist as a powerful parental authority figure; socially-isolated widows may be more likely to relate to the therapist as a confidant, recently deceased spouse, or idealized child.

OTHER AGE-FACTORS INFLUENCING TRANSFERENCE

Berezin (1972) was the first clinician to note that the client's "secret inner age" affects the transference. While chronological age and physical appearance shape the therapist's perceptions of the client, often the client's self-concept is that of a much younger person. Aging is a gradual process, with different levels of impact on people. Many psychologically healthy, physically vital, active older people have an internalized self-concept that is much younger than their physical appearance suggests. The sense of continuity in one's own life is captured in Wilma Donahue's view of herself at 70:

> I have more measure of feeling about aging, when I see the people I was young with, at the university, and all of a sudden I see them in the version of old people. I may not have seen them for a long time, and then I see them after they've stepped over the threshold and are now looking old. I have never thought of them as older people and suddenly I see them as old and I gather a sense of their being different, and I have thought about this. To them, just like I am to myself, there is a consistent personality. I don't recognize that I was 20, 30, 40, 50, 60, and so forth. I just seem to be a consistent personality that's lived a whole life. I realize I look the same to them as they look to me. As far as my feeling is concerned, I don't have that sense. I have the sense of being a whole person with spirit and interests that are consistent with my life. (Weinberg, 1975, p. 2406)

At the other extreme, older people who have failed to integrate aging into their self-concept for defensive reasons often hold on to much younger images of themselves. In contrast to Dr. Donahue, their experience of their younger self is a static, fixed perception rather than reflecting a sense of ongoing continuity. Their relationships are pathologically based on the internalized age of a younger person. For example, the person with a life-long hysterical character disorder reflecting unresolved childhood issues may continue to dress and behave as the coquettish, flirtatious teenager, expecting the therapist to respond to her advances. Such transference reactions may, however, be particularly threatening to the younger therapist who is uncomfortable with the older person's sexuality and unprepared for those dynamics to be played out in therapy.

SELF-PSYCHOLOGY PERSPECTIVE ON TRANSFERENCE

The self-psychology model of transference and the functions it serves in maintenance of the self provides a particularly useful way of conceptualizing the diverse range of transference reactions in the elderly (Muslin & Clarke, 1988). The self may be defined as an experienced constancy formed in early childhood that constitutes a coherent, vital core of personality. Healthy adaptation involves maintenance of a coherent, stable, and continuous self-representation in the face of ongoing change in experiences and relationships throughout life. Some theorists (Lazarus, 1980; Muslin, 1992) argue that late-life changes and losses undermine psychological well-being to the extent that they disrupt a vital, cohesive sense of self. Even for older people whose investment in the self is healthy and whose self-image is realistic, expectable experiences of late life can disrupt sense of self-continuity and self-esteem. For less psychologically healthy individuals, aging can lead to loss of adult lifestyle and/or relationships that served to shore up defensive needs of character structure while providing few options for replacement activities or people (Jacobowitz & Newton, 1990).

Confronted with an assault to the sense of self, the older person attempts to find restitution. The therapist facilitates restitution by providing the specific functions essential to a cohesive sense of self that the client can no longer sustain on his or her own. These functions are mirroring, idealizing, and twinship (Wolf, 1988). In mirroring transference, the therapist's admiration and praise restores and affirms the client's depleted sense of self. In idealizing transference, the client's merger/connection with a strong self-object (the therapist) provides a sense of safety and security that evokes/sustains self-structure. In alter-ego or twinship transference, being understood by another who is perceived as like oneself is the fundamental need. In younger adults, the type of transference reflects the developmental level of the self-system; in older clients, the extent and nature of disruption of a cohesive self-structure due to aging events also likely influences the nature of the transference.

Just as late life presents unique challenges to maintenance of self-structure, some ways of preserving a healthy sense of self may also be specific to late life. For example, the capacity to maintain self-continuity through an ongoing strong connection with one's younger adult self becomes essential as late life changes diminish opportunities for current "mirroring" objects (Griffin & Grunes,

1990). Both internal capacities (i.e., accurate memories and exaggerated fantasies of past experiences and achievements) and external activities (i.e., transitional objects that remind one of past relationships and experiences) may serve important functions in sustaining self-continuity. The therapist also can serve a crucial role in this process by mirroring the client in ways previously provided by spouse, friends, or other supportive figures that the older person has lost. By interacting with clients based on who they were rather than how they perceive themselves now, their younger, more competent sense of self is supported. By seeing the clients both as they are now and how they were when younger allows the therapist to treat the demoralized older person as a genuinely competent, respected, and appealing person, thus girding up a failing sense of self. The therapist is also countering the older client's internalization of negative agist cultural stereotypes. On the other hand, a patronizing, overly caregiving stance that denies the older person's adult status, only serves to confirm the elderly person's fears that he or she is inadequate and incompetent.

A heightened sense of vulnerability and powerlessness may contribute in late life to emergence of an idealizing transference. Age-correlated cohort experiences can reinforce the idealizing transference. Many of the current elderly lived during a period in which physicians and other medical professionals were highly respected authorities who provided direction and assistance. The frail older person confronted with life-threatening assaults may perceive the therapist as a strong, powerful parental figure whose protection and power he or she courts (Goldfarb & Sheps, 1954). In such a relationship, the patient may attribute idealized, almost godlike powers to the therapist and seek to ally with this powerful figure. Based on their work with brain-damaged nursing home patients, Goldfarb and his colleagues (Aronson, 1958; Goldfarb, 1955, 1956) suggest that if the frail patient is helped to believe that he has some control and mastery over the perceived powerful parental figure, this transference relationship can serve to re-establish the client's self-esteem and sense of mastery over a world perceived as threatening and uncaring.

Idealizing transference also occurs in psychotherapy with more physically and cognitively intact clients, who use their relationship with the now special and powerful therapist to restore psychological equilibrium (Jacobowitz & Newton, this volume). In their study of psychodynamic brief psychotherapy with elderly clients, Lazarus, Groves, and Newton (1984), examined the transference reactions of 10 older adults to their younger adult therapists. Without exception, the elderly clients embued the therapist with power and authority, and then used the therapist to affirm and restore challenged aspects of self, even when at times this required idiosyncratic re-interpretation of what the therapist had done or said.

The twinship or alter-ego transference focuses on the client's self-validation through identification with a therapist who is perceived as similar. In discussing her work with a number of elderly clients, Strauss (1996), herself in her 80s, describes ways in which sharing similar age-related experiences served an important function in normalizing client's experiences and encouraging them toward further psychological development.

WORKING WITH TRANSFERENCE REACTIONS

While the nature of the transference may be affected by age, how it is managed seems to have little relationship to client age. The way in which the therapist works with the transference depends on the therapist's theoretical orientation and conceptualization of the treatment process, the client's psychological-mindedness and capacity for insight, nature of the transference, and treatment goals. To the extent that the transference relationship facilitates (or at least does not impede) meeting treatment goals, the therapist may pay little attention to transferential processes. In contrast, the therapist who works within a self-psychological perspective may focus on the client's transference as a way of identifying treatment needs, developmental processes, and therapeutic interventions that will restore sense of self. Recent case studies illustrate that within the context of insight-oriented psychodynamics psychotherapy and analysis, transference reactions emerge and can be analyzed as with younger clients (Myers, 1984, 1986; Settlage, 1992).

Mr. Smith provides an example of the use of the transference relationship to cultivate a therapeutic relationship with a reluctant client and, as therapy progresses, to restore a depleted sense of self.

CASE EXAMPLE

Mr. Smith, an 85-year-old childless, retired male, was referred for his first outpatient psychiatric treatment following the death of his wife after a lengthy illness. When initially seen, he was severely depressed, with marked sleep disturbance, loss of appetite (accompanied by a 40-pound weight loss over the preceding two years), frequent crying episodes, loss of interest in self-care and daily activities, social withdrawal, and active suicidal ideation. He was preoccupied with feelings of guilt about his wife's death despite the fact that he had been a devoted caregiver for many years. For him, life had ended and he was simply waiting to die.

The initial challenges confronting Mr. Smith's therapist were to engage him in treatment and minimize the risk of suicide. He had come to the interview reluctantly; he was highly ambivalent about establishing a new relationship with anyone. He was assessed as a serious suicide risk, but not in imminent danger due to his immediate focus on getting a headstone for his wife's grave. Despite his psychological depletion and fragility, glimpses of Mr. Smith's stubborn independence, willfulness, and intolerance of loss of control over his life were evident. He unwaveringly stated and strongly argued his belief that he was in charge of his own life, had the right to make his own decisions, and had only agreed to the session to satisfy the physician who had cared for him and his wife for many years. He also stated that he appreciated the therapist's concern even though it was clearly misplaced.

During that initial interview, the essential components to Mr. Smith's self-image were evident. He proudly revealed that he had left home at age 14, lying about his age to enlist in the army during World War I. For the next 27 years, he had spent his military career in some type of combat or semicombat situation, including China, the Spanish Civil War, and World War II. After reaching the rank of sergeant as a very young man, he had refused further promotions so that he could remain "where the action was." Mr. Smith's self-image was that of a tough, in-command leader who was also fair and even caring toward the younger men who served under him. The death of his wife had disrupted this image of himself as a strong care-provider. It had also reawakened the guilt related to a World War II incident in which a number of his men had died in a South Pacific battle. The fact that he had been severely injured himself and much decorated for his valor had never assuaged his guilt.

In the initial session, the therapist was anxious to engage Mr. Smith without further undermining his personal sense of control and independence. Despite her concerns for his safety, she chose to relate to him as an adult who was competent to make his own decisions. At the same time, she wanted to establish herself as an equal authority worthy of his respect, so as to increase the likelihood that she could overcome his ambivalence about psychotherapy and influence his decisions regarding suicide. Mr. Smith's military experiences had keenly socialized him to rank and hierarchy; his vision of the ideal sergeant gave him a strongly internalized image of the meaning of responsibility for one's subordinates. Through her demeanor and actions, the therapist worked to assume the type of authority in relationship to him that he had manifested toward his men—firm but fair—and to establish her right to feel responsible for his welfare as he had assumed that stance toward his men. Over time and numerous telephone contacts, this approach allowed Mr. Smith an acceptable rationale for entering therapy while still maintaining his pride and independence. Shortly into the treatment, Mr. Smith saluted the therapist as he left, stating that if she had been in the military, she would have been a major and thus his commanding officer.

As therapy continued over a three-year period, other transference reactions emerged. About a year into treatment, Mr. Smith began missing appointments. It was only when the therapist suggested to him that he might be uncomfortable with the closeness of their relationship that Mr. Smith revealed his sexual feelings for the therapist, his shame that he had become a "dirty old man" and his fear that he could not control those impulses, thus threatening the therapist with his relationship to her. Labeling these feelings for Mr. Smith and demonstrating that she was neither threatened nor put off by his impulses, the therapist alleviated his fears that his sexual and aggressive impulses were both shameful and unmanageable. She also worked to help him normalize his sexual feelings and feelings about the loss of intimacy in his life. After these issues were addressed, Mr. Smith was able, on his own initiative, to re-establish a social support system, first with a niece with whom he had not had contact for at least twenty years, and finally with several female neighbors. Mr. Smith introduced both his niece and closest neighbor to the therapist, thus creating a sense of community amongst his significant others. These relationships served as both a source of self-respect through his fatherly stance and a means for receiving nurturance and validation.

Balancing Mr. Smith's needs for independence and support remained an issue. Consistent with Griffin and Grunes (1990), the therapist continually reaffirmed Mr. Smith's connection with his own younger self, a function whose importance he validated by giving her a photograph of himself as a younger man. Reminiscences about his younger life intertwined with discussion of current experiences and processing feelings of grief and guilt to constitute the content of sessions. His right to maintain control over his own life and the frequency of contact with the therapist was respected.

This context provided a frame in which he could also acknowledge his fears and vulnerabilities. He increasingly sought the therapist's advice and counsel. As he began to develop confidence in her and to use her as a sounding board, he began to recount stories of strong but nurturant women who had been sources of strength for him in the past. For example, he often repeated a story of a nurse who stayed at his side while he was delirious and near death following a severe war injury. Thus, he identified figures from his past that provided models for the therapist's behavior and interactions with him.

The relationship between Mr. Smith and his therapist was grounded in a "real" connection that balanced the transference processes. For example, they were both fans of the local baseball team, and he often went home to watch a game after their session. A friendly dollar wager on the team's success became a routine session end.

CONCLUSION

Any psychotherapeutic process is fundamentally grounded in the personal connection between the client and therapist. It is inevitable that personal attitudes, needs, hopes, and expectations, and the ways in which these individual dynamics play out in their relationship, powerfully influence the benefits of psychotherapy for the client. The therapist's responsibility is to remain open and attentive to the client's transference based reactions as well as the therapist's own personal responses to the client. This chapter identified the obstacles that interfere with this often challenging task. Awareness of transference and countertransference processes provides a rich source of information about each individual as well as the interactions between therapist and client; it is often the basis of a healing relationship for the client and, sometimes in the process, a path of personal growth for the therapist.

REFERENCES

Alexander, F.G. (1944). The indications of psychoanalytic therapy. *Bulletin of the New York Academy of Medicine, 20,* 391–394.

Aronson, M.J. (1958). Psychotherapy in a home for the aged. *Archives of Neurology and Psychiatry, 79,* 671–674.

Berezin, M.A. (1972). Psychodynamic considerations of aging and the aged: An overview. *American Journal of Psychiatry, 128,* 1483–1491.

Berman, H.J. (1994). *Interpreting the aged self: Personal journals of later life.* New York: Springer.

Butler, R.N. (1994). Dispelling ageism: The cross-cutting intervention. In D. Shenk & W.A. Achenbaum (Eds.), *Changing perceptions of aging and the aged* (pp. 137–143). New York: Springer.

Butler, R.N., & Lewis, M.I. (1977). *Aging and mental health: Positive psychosocial approaches.* St. Louis: Mosby.

Cath, S.H. (1982). Psychoanalysis and psychoanalytic psychotherapy of the older patient. *Journal of Geriatric Psychiatry, 15,* 43–53.

Crusey, J.E. (1985). Short-term psychodynamic psychotherapy with a sixty-two-year-old man. In R.A. Nemiroff & C.A. Colarusso (Eds.), *The race against time* (pp. 147–166). New York: Plenum Press.

Dewald, P. (1964). *Psychotherapy: A dynamic approach.* New York: Basic Books.

Ellman, J.P. (1996). Analyst and patient at midlife. *Psychoanalytic Quarterly, 65,* 353–371.

Erikson, E.H., Erikson, J.M., & Kivnick, H.Q. (1986). *Vital involvement in old age: The experience of old age in our time.* New York: Norton.

Freud, S. (1966). Transference. In J. Strachey (Ed.), *Introductory lectures on psychoanalysis* (pp. 431–438). New York: Norton. (Original work published 1920)

Genevay, B., & Katz, R.S. (1990). *Countertransference and older clients.* Newbury Park, CA: Sage.

Gitelson, M. (1965). Transference reaction in a sixty-six year old woman. In M.A. Berezin & S.H. Cath (Eds.), *Geriatric psychiatry: Grief, loss and emotional disorders in the aging process* (pp. 160–186). New York: International Universities Press.

Goldfarb, A.I. (1955). Psychotherapy of aged persons: IV. One aspect of the psychodynamics of the therapeutic situation with aged patients. *Psychoanalytic Review, 42,* 180–187.

Goldfarb, A.I. (1956). Psychotherapy of the aged: The use and value of an adaptational frame of reference. *Psychoanalytic Review, 43,* 68–81.

Goldfarb, A.I., & Sheps, J. (1954). Psychotherapy of the aged. HI: Brief therapy of interrelated psychological and somatic disorders. *Psychosomatic Medicine, 16,* 200–219.

Grant, L. (1996). Effects of ageism on individual and health care providers' responses to healthy aging. *Health and Social Work, 21,* 9–15.

Griffin, B.P., & Grunes, J.M. (1990). A developmental approach to psychoanalytic psychotherapy with the aged. In R.A. Nemiroff & C.A. Colarruso (Eds.), *New dimensions in adult development* (pp. 267–283). New York: Basic Books.

Grotjahn, M. (1955). Analytic psychotherapy with the elderly. *Psychoanalytic Review, 42,* 419–527.

Grotjahn, M. (1985). Being sick and facing eighty: Observations of an aging therapist. In R.A. Nemiroff & C.A. Colarusso (Eds.), *The race against time: Psychotherapy and psychoanalysis in the second half of life* (pp. 147–166). New York: Plenum Press.

Gutmann, D. (1987). *Reclaimed powers: Toward a new psychology of men and women in later life.* New York: Basic Books.

Hiatt, H. (1971). Dynamic psychotherapy with the aging patient. *American Journal of Psychotherapy, 25,* 591–600.

Hildebrand, H.P. (1982). Psychotherapy with older patients. *British Journal of Medical Psychology, 55,* 19–28.

Horowitz, M. (1991). Transference and countertransference in the therapeutic relationship with the older adult. In R.J. Hartke (Ed.), *Psychological aspects of geriatric rehabilitation* (pp. 211–228). Gaithersburg, MD: Aspen Publishers.

Jacobowitz, J., & Newton, N. (1990). Time, context, and character: A life-span view of psychopathology during the second half of life. In R.A. Nemiroff & C.A. Colarruso (Eds.), *New dimensions in adult development* (pp. 306–330). New York: Basic Books.

Kernberg, O.F. (1985). *Borderline conditions and pathological narcissism* (Rev. ed.). New York: Aronson.

King, P. (1980). The life cycle as indicated by the nature of the transference in the psychoanalysis of the middle-aged and the elderly. *International Journal of Psycho-Analysis, 61,* 153–160.

Knight, B. (1986). *Psychotherapy with older adults.* Beverly Hills, CA: Sage.

Lazarus, L.W. (1980). Self psychology and psychotherapy with the elderly: Theory and practice. *Journal of Geriatric Psychiatry, 13,* 69–88.

Lazarus, L.W., Groves, L., & Newton, N. (1984). Brief psychotherapy with the elderly: A review and preliminary study of process and outcome. In L. Lazarus (Ed.), *Clinical approaches to psychotherapy with the elderly* (pp. 16–35). Washington, DC: American Psychiatric Press.

Lazarus, L.W., & Sadavoy, J. (1996). Individual psychotherapy. In J. Sadavoy, L.W. Lazarus, L.F. Jarvik, & G.T. Grossberg (Eds.), *Comprehensive review of geriatric psychiatry: II* (2nd ed., pp. 819–850). Washington: American Psychiatric Press.

Lewis, J.M., & Johansen, K.H. (1982). Resistances to psychotherapy with the elderly. *American Journal of Psychiatry, 36,* 497–504.

Malamud, W.I. (1996). Countertransference issues with elderly patients. *Journal of Geriatric Psychiatry, 29,* 33–41.

Meerloo, J.A.M. (1953). Contributions of psychoanalysis to the problems of the aged. In M. Heimann (Ed.), *Psychoanalysis and social work* (pp. 321–337). New York: International Universities Press.

Miller, E. (1987). The Oedipus complex and rejuvenation fantasies in the analysis of a seventy-year-old women. *Journal of Geriatic Psychiatry, 20,* 29–51.

Muslin, H.L. (1992). *The psychotherapy of the elderly self.* New York: Brunner/Mazel.

Muslin, H.L., & Clarke, S. (1988). The transference of the therapist of the elderly. *Journal of the American Academy of Psychoanalysis, 16,* 295–315.

Myers, W.A. (1984). *Dynamic therapy of the older patient.* New York: Aronson.

Myers, W.A. (1986). Transference and countertransference issues in treatments involving older patients and younger therapists. *Journal of Geriatric Psychiatry, 19,* 221–239.

Nemiroff, R.A., & Colarusso, C.A. (1985a). Issues and strategies for psychotherapy and psychoanalysis in the second half of life. In R.A. Nemiroff & C.A. Colarusso (Eds.), *The race against time: Psychotherapy and psychoanalysis in the second half of life.* New York: Plenum Press.

Nemiroff, R.A., & Colarusso, C.A. (1985b). *The race against time: Psychotherapy and psychoanalysis in the second half of life.* New York: Plenum Press.

Nemiroff, R.A., & Colarusso, C.A. (Eds.). (1990). *New dimensions in adult development* (pp. 306–330). New York: Basic Books.

Newton, N., & Lazarus, L. (1986). Treatment of the elderly neuropsychiatric patient: Psychodynamic psychotherapies: In G.J. Maletta & F.J. Pirozzolo (Eds.), *Advances in neurogerontology* (Vol. 4, pp. 86–112). New York: Praeger Press.

Orbach, A. (1994). Psychotherapy in the third age. *British Journal of Psychotherapy, 11,* 171–231.

Riess, B.F. (1992). Some thoughts and material on age-related psychoanalysis of the aged. *Psychoanalysis and Psychotherapy: The Journal of the Postgraduate Center for Mental Health, 10,* 17–32.

Semel, V. (1993). Countertransference and ageism: Therapist reactions to the older patient. In C.M. Brody & V.G. Semel (Eds.), *Strategies for therapy with the elderly: Living with hope and meaning* (pp. 131–138). New York: Springer.

Settlage, C.F. (1992). Psychoanalytic observations on adult development in life and in the therapeutic relationship. *Psychoanalysis and Contemporary Thought, 15,* 349–374.

Settlage, C.F. (1996). Transcending old age: Creativity, development and psychoanalysis in the life of a centenarian. *International Journal of Psychoanalysis, 77,* 549–564.

Simburg, E.J. (1985). Psychoanalysis of the older patient. *Journal of the American Psychoanalytic Association, 33,* 117–132.

Slakter, L. (1987). The question of countertransference. In L. Slakter (Ed.), *Countertransference.* New York: Aronson.

Sonderegger, T.B., & Siegel, R.J. (1995). Conflicts in care: Later years of the lifespan. In E.J. Rave & C.C. Larsen (Eds.), *Ethical decision making in therapy: Feminist perspectives* (pp. 223–246). New York: Guilford Press.

Stern, K., Smith, J.M., & Frank, M. (1953). Mechanisms of transference and countertransference in psychotherapeutic and social work with the aged. *Journal of Gerontology, 8,* 328–332.

Strauss, H.M. (1996). Working as an elder analyst. In B. Gerson (Ed.), *The therapist as a person: Life crisis, life choices, life experiences, and their effects on treatment* (pp. 277–294). Hillsdale, NJ: Analytic Press.

Weinberg, J. (1975). Geriatric psychiatry. In A.M. Freedman, H.L. Kaplan, & B.J. Sadock (Eds.), *Comprehensive textbook of psychiatry* (2nd ed.) (Vol. 2, pp. 2405–2420). Baltimore: Williams & Wilkins.

Wharton, B. (1996). In the last analysis: Archetypal themes in the analysis of an elderly patient with early disintegrative trauma. *Journal of Analytical Psychology, 41*, 19–36.

Wolf, E. (1988). *Treating the self: Elements of clinical self psychology*. New York: Guilford Press.

Wylie, H., & Wylie, M. (1987). The older analysis and countertransference issues in psychoanalysis. *International Journal of Psychoanalysis, 68*, 343–352.

CHAPTER 3

Adjusting to Role Loss and Leisure in Later Life

JANE E. MYERS

Aging typically has been viewed as a time of loss, with the major challenge of later life being the need for adjustment to loss (Atchley, 1988; Havighurst, 1972). Since the 1960s, studies of coping among older persons have focused on identifying factors that correlate with life satisfaction and have included conjectures about factors that mitigate for or against successful adjustment to the aging process (e.g., P. Coleman, 1992; Neugarten, Havighurst, & Tobin, 1968). Attention has begun to shift toward the identification of factors related to healthy aging (Beckingham & Watt, 1995; Bowling, 1993). A paradigm shift is occurring in medicine and social sciences away from an illness-oriented, disease model of functioning toward a model of health and wellness (Mill, 1997; Myers, 1992). The potential for wellness in later life is increasingly being recognized, and strategies for promoting healthy lifestyles for persons in their later years are being proposed (Ponzo, 1992; Walker, 1991). Healthy aging is both a possibility and a goal, and a phenomenon that requires a reconceptualization of our views of "normal" aging (Abeles, Gift, & Ory, 1994; Blue Cross Blue Shield, 1998; Kaplan & Strawbridge, 1994). In fact, research suggests that the majority of older persons are, in fact, satisfied with their lives and experience a robust level of life satisfaction (George & Clipp, 1991).

Two areas that are essential in understanding adjustment in later life, from the perspective of both the illness and wellness models of aging, are role loss and leisure. Role loss refers to changes in later life in one's social and personal roles as a consequence of loss as well as changes such as retirement. Leisure, including all of the nonwork uses of one's time, potentially increases during retirement, but adjustment to increased free time is not necessarily positive. A focus on healthy aging requires understanding these concepts and how older persons are affected by changes in roles and time commitments. In addition, counselors can benefit from models that promote assessment and provide paradigms for effective interventions.

In this chapter, role loss in later life is examined, and research relating to adjustment to role loss is reviewed. Similarly, leisure in later life is explored, with a focus on factors that affect leisure satisfaction. Two holistic models for understanding role loss and leisure in later life are presented: Super's (1980) Life Career Rainbow and Witmer, Sweeney, and Myers' (1997) Wheel of Wellness. Each model provides a basis for interventions with older individuals and groups. Case examples are presented and discussed to illustrate the use of these models as a basis for assessment and intervention with older persons.

ROLE LOSS IN LATER LIFE

Older persons experience a variety of losses. To the extent that each loss represents one or more roles, they experience significant role loss. Some of the major losses older persons experience include: sensory and physical losses, loss of a job at retirement, loss of family members and friends, loss of a family home, and loss of things that have personal value and meaning. All of these have been defined as "normal age-related losses" (Waters & Goodman, 1990, p. 136). The personal meaning or impact of each loss determines how well an older person copes with and adjusts to the ensuing changes in his or her life.

Common Later Life Losses and the Impact of Loss

Sensory and physical losses affect how older persons relate to the world around them. A perception that one can no longer handle physical stress is common. The loss of perceived physical attractiveness, vitality and stamina, and mobility affect self-esteem and perceptions of one's social desirability. Losses of physical capacities often result in withdrawal from activities and social participation and subsequent social isolation.

The loss of one's job at any time in life has emotional consequences. It appears that these consequences are the same regardless of the time at which one's job is lost, including retirement. In addition to the loss of income, older persons at retirement experience a loss of work-related social contacts, many of which are casual and informal (e.g., lunch with colleagues). The loss of a time structure for one's day creates what Havighurst called a "crisis in the meaningful use of time" (Havighurst, 1972). A significant loss of status also accompanies the loss of a work role in a society oriented toward productive use of time.

Family members and friends may die, move away, or simply be busy with their own lives and unavailable to an older person. Or, the older person may move away, with distance creating geographic barriers to continued close relationships. Divorce of adult children creates disruption in the life of an older person, and potentially creates distance in relationships with grandchildren. Pet loss similarly can be disruptive to the life of an older person.

Losing a family home when one retires, relocates to retirement housing, or moves to a nursing home often means considerable downsizing of one's lifestyle. A lifetime of accumulated objects needs to be culled through, with many objects of personal value of necessity being left behind to accommodate smaller living quarters. The personal meaning of one's home and the objects in it has a major impact on adjustment of the older individual.

ADJUSTING TO LOSS IN LATER LIFE

All losses require a process of grieving, which occurs over time, and the development of plans for the future. An essential ingredient in this process is what Schlossberg (1984; Schlossberg, Waters, & Goodman, 1995) termed "role change." Adjusting to loss requires that the older person grieve the loss of whatever roles were associated with a particular life change and develop a new sense of role involvement to compensate for that which has been lost. How well an older person adjusts depends on several psychological factors, notably the development of a sense of purpose in life, social support networks, and perceptions of personal control.

The emphasis on pathology rather than the ordinary experience of aging has resulted in a lack of emphasis on purpose in life for older persons (P. Thompson, 1993). As they experience personal loss, illness and disability, personal suffering, and impending death, the search for personal meaning becomes increasingly important (Wong, 1989). Purpose in life is significantly related to perceived health and sense of well-being for older persons (Sweeney, 1998; Witmer, 1997). The loss of a sense of purpose and meaning in later life is reflected in lower purpose in life scores for older persons than for those in midlife (Ryff & Heidrich, 1997).

Social support has been shown to be beneficial for healthy functioning regardless of age (Broman, 1993; Ishii-Kuntz, 1990; Ulione, 1996); however, low levels of social support are particularly damaging to both the physical and mental health of older individuals (Sherbourne, Meredith, & Ware, 1992). The quantity of social support is not the critical factor; rather, older persons' perceptions of support determine the effect on their sense of well-being (Adams & Bleiszner, 1995; M. Thompson & Heller, 1990). Employment in the retirement years is related to larger support networks (Mor-Barak, Scharlach, Birba, & Sokolov, 1992). Further, persons with high involvement in relationships are more likely to engage in preventive health behaviors (Broman, 1993), including proper nutrition, a key factor in healthy aging (Toner & Morris, 1992). Positive family and friendship relationships in later life are a source of self-esteem and instrumental assistance, and contribute to positive perceptions of role involvement (Arber & Ginn, 1994).

Kobasa (1979) proposed the concept of psychological hardiness as including three key dimensions: (1) a sense of control over one's experiences, (2) a feeling of commitment in various arenas of life, and (3) a perception of life events as challenging. Hardy individuals ". . . view stressful situations as meaningful and interesting (commitment), see stressors as malleable (control), and construe difficulties as challenges . . ." (Lightsey, 1996, p. 629). Having an internal locus of control has been correlated with lower levels of anxiety and depression, higher levels of self-esteem, and higher levels of life satisfaction (Cvetanovski & Jex, 1994). Further, perceptions of oneself as able to achieve and maintain control of one's environment and make decisions about one's life are strongly correlated with physical and mental health (Bowling, 1993), and a sense of well-being in later life (Housley, 1992).

Counselors face a significant challenge in helping older persons achieve a new or renewed sense of purpose in life, a strong social support network, and a feeling of control over their lives. Given the potential for increased amounts of discretionary time in later life, a potentially successful means of addressing these challenges is through a focus on leisure activities. This focus may promote empowerment of older persons at the individual as well as organizational and community levels (Myers, 1990; Schulz, Israel, Zimmerman, & Checkoway, 1995).

LEISURE IN LATER LIFE

Leisure has been defined as the discretionary use of time (Papalia, Camp, & Feldman, 1996), or "engaging in self-determined activities and experiences for mostly intrinsic satisfactions that are available due to having discretionary income and time" (Witmer, 1997, p. 91). It is generally accepted that free time increases during retirement, such that making effective use of one's free time is one of the most important challenges of later life (Riker & Myers, 1990). Leisure participation offers substantial opportunities for involvement and reinvolvement, and an alternate means to status for older persons who no longer have a work role (Pedlar, Dupuis, & Gilbert, 1996). Although older persons experience increased time for nonwork activities, they experience substantial psychological barriers to the enjoyment of leisure. In this section, these barriers are identified, types of leisure activities common in later life are discussed, and the importance of leisure satisfaction is explored.

BARRIERS TO ENJOYMENT OF LEISURE IN LATER LIFE

Today's older cohort were raised with a strong work ethic and taught to feel discomfort with "nonproductive" uses of time. They may feel guilty over being nonproductive, and they may lack a clear definition of value for leisure activities which is similar to the value placed on work. They may not have learned to enjoy leisure earlier in life, and they may simply lack hobbies or preferences for use of their free time. Leisure provides an important means of social contact. Factors that isolate older persons such as disability and mobility limitations, mental illness, depression, and loss of close friends and family may contribute to reduced socialization, and lack of participation in leisure activities (Patterson, 1996; Stanley & Freysinger, 1995).

LEISURE PREFERENCES OF OLDER PERSONS

McDaniels and Gysbers (1992) suggested that leisure activities may be one or a combination of five types: physical, social, intellectual, volunteer, and creative. Ninety-five percent of older persons watch television, 82% read daily newspapers, 66% listen to the radio, and 30% read one or more books in a six month period (Crandall, 1991). The U.S. Bureau of the Census (1990) reported that 32% of older persons exercise by walking, 11% enjoy fishing, 13% swimming, 10% bicycle riding, and 8% each camping and golfing. An estimated 0.5% participate in adult education. Additional activities identified through an earlier Harris poll included socializing with friends (47%), caring for older and younger family members (27%), gardening or raising plants (39%), and participating in clubs and organizations (17%) (Harris & Associates, 1975). More recently, Hersch (1990) found the most frequently mentioned leisure activities of older persons to be participation in formal groups, travel, participation in informal groups, reading, visiting relatives and friends, watching sports, participating in sports, theater, volunteer work, and library visits.

Volunteer work is frequently identified as desirable for older people as a means of helping them feel productive and useful (Ellis, 1993; Herzog & House, 1991). Volunteerism has been related to decreased boredom, an increased sense of purpose in life, and an enhanced sense of well-being (Crist, 1996). In addition, Crist noted that volunteerism helps mitigate the effects of depression due to role loss. Although most older persons do not engage in volunteer work (Crandall, 1991), for those who do, the intrinsic satisfaction gained from their activities contributes to wellness in later life.

LEISURE SATISFACTION IN LATER LIFE

Leisure activity increases feelings of emotional well-being among older persons (Hersch, 1990; Zimmer & Lin, 1996). Leisure has a positive effect on self-esteem, especially when role commitment is high (Reitzes, Mutran, & Verrill, 1995). This positive effect appears to be related to perceived sense of control, since older persons are able to choose how and when to use their leisure or free time (Iso-Ahola, Jackson, & Dunn, 1994). Iso-Ahola et al. refer to this as "perceived freedom" in leisure, or the freedom to choose one's activities. Perceived freedom is critical for leisure involvement as well as physical and emotional health and wellness (Ragheb, 1993).

In a study of the relationship between perceived wellness and leisure, Ragheb (1993) found that satisfaction with one's leisure is more important than participation in leisure activities. Further, the greater the extent of congruence between one's leisure activities and one's personality type, the greater one's sense of well-being (Melamed, Meir, & Samson, 1995). Leisure mitigates against stress (D. Coleman & Iso-Ahola, 1993), thus contributing to overall wellness and life satisfaction for older individuals.

The emerging concept of a leisure life style for older persons implies an intrinsic value for leisure apart from its replacement of the work function (Riker & Myers, 1990). The attribution of meaning in life through leisure, without the guilt older people may feel when they engage in nonproductive activities, can be an important means of defining new roles to replace those lost in the later years of life. The following holistic models are helpful in understanding the relationship between role loss, role replacement, and leisure in later life.

HOLISTIC MODELS FOR CONCEPTUALIZING ADJUSTMENT TO ROLE LOSS AND LEISURE IN LATER LIFE

Counselors can benefit from holistic models that present both the relationship between role loss and leisure in later life and a paradigm for understanding adjustment to these late life processes. Two such models appear in the literature. These are Super's (1980) Life-Career Rainbow and Witmer et al.'s (1997) Wheel of Wellness. Each model is briefly described in this section.

SUPER'S LIFE CAREER RAINBOW

Super (1954) proposed a developmental approach to career counseling that incorporated a series of five developmental stages: growth, exploration, establishment, maintenance, and decline. Following several decades of longitudinal research, Super (1980) proposed a modified theory to explain the development of one's life-career across the life span. The revised theory no longer limited stages and processes to vocational development and choice, but incorporates a more holistic perspective that includes leisure and other life roles.

Super's rainbow theory proposes six life roles that exist across the earlier five stages, extending before, through, and beyond each stage to include the entire life span. The six life roles of homemaker, worker, citizen, leisurite, student, and child are possible across the life span and may exist simultaneously. However, the salience of each role, and the investment of time, effort, and commitment to each role varies across the life span. The model presents role salience as variable, and further suggests that a reduction in one role, such as that of student, may be compensated by an increase in another role, such as leisurite.

Older persons who experience loss of roles in one area, according to this model can be helped to increase their role salience and role commitment in other areas to improve their life satisfaction and sense of well-being. By taking an active role in making these changes, older persons can be helped to experience a greater sense of personal control and freedom of choice. Drawing a picture of a rainbow with bands of varying widths representing each of their life roles can help them develop a metaphor for understanding and changing their role commitments.

WITMER, SWEENEY, AND MYERS' WHEEL OF WELLNESS

Sweeney and Witmer (1991) and Witmer and Sweeney (1992) noted that more than half of all deaths in the United States are caused by lifestyle and self-destructive and negative behaviors. In addition to death, negative lifestyle choices contribute to a lowered quality of life, often for extended years. At the same time, the federal government spends more than 75% of health care dollars to care for people with chronic diseases, such as heart disease, stroke, and cancer. Less than half of 1% is spent to prevent these same diseases from occurring (U.S. Department of Health and Human Services, 1990). Sweeney and Witmer presented a holistic model for wellness and prevention that incorporates research and theoretical concepts related to healthy functioning from a variety of disciplines, including anthropology, education, medicine, psychology, religion, and sociology. The model was revised based on empirical data collected by the authors, and is shown in Figure 3.1 (Witmer et al., 1997).

Wellness has been defined by many authors, most incorporating the "total person" as the target of intervention. It is a means of living that is oriented toward optimal health and well-being in which body, mind, and spirit are integrated in a purposeful manner by the individual with a goal of living life more fully within all spheres of functioning, including social, personal, and environmental (i.e., ecological). Witmer et al. (1997) propose that each component of the model is necessary for healthy functioning in a holistic manner, and that they are all interrelated. Change in any one area, for example, will affect and create changes in other areas as well. The wheel is a cross-section of healthy living. In actuality, the wheel "moves" through time and space across the life span. Change is a constant aspect of wellness, and change may be for better or worse.

As shown in Figure 3.1, there are five major life tasks which empirical data support as important characteristics of healthy persons. These life tasks are work, friendship, love, self-direction, and spirituality. These tasks interact dynamically with several life forces, including family, community, religion, education, government, media, and business/industry. The life forces and life tasks interact with and are affected by global events, both natural and human, positive as well as negative. In a healthy person, all life tasks are interconnected and interact for the well-being or detriment of the individual. The 12 tasks of self-direction function much like the spokes in a wheel, providing the strength required for the wheel to move freely and effectively. All of them are necessary for healthy functioning.

Applying the Wheel of Wellness to issues of role loss and leisure in later life and retirement allows counselors to select one or more of the components of wellness as a focus for interventions. Because it is a holistic model, attempts to

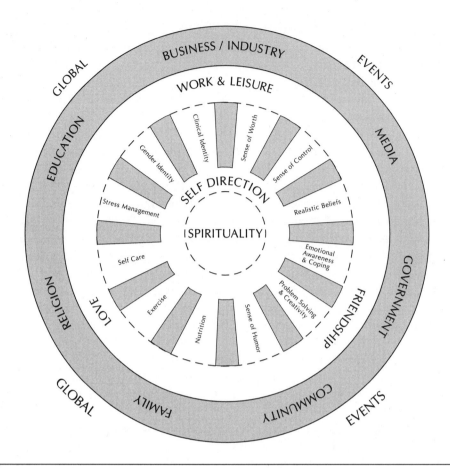

Figure 3.1 The wheel of wellness. (Copyright © 1992 by J.M. Witmer, T.J. Sweeney, and J.E. Meyers, Greensboro, NC. Reprinted with permission.)

promote change in any one or more areas may have a positive impact on leisure, roles, and total wellness.

ASSESSING ROLE LOSS AND LEISURE NEEDS

The two models presented in this chapter have implications for assessment of role loss and leisure needs as a basis for planning interventions with older persons. The elements in both models can be assessed through clinical interviews that focus on each aspect of the model using open-ended questions to determine older persons' role salience (Super's rainbow) and personal wellness (Wheel of Wellness). In addition, each model can be used as a paper-and-pencil assessment to provide a basis for further discussion and treatment planning.

Clients can be provided a copy of Super's rainbow and a set of colored pencils, along with instructions to draw bands of varying widths representing their investment in different life roles. With a second copy of the rainbow, clients can be encouraged to draw one rainbow showing their roles at an earlier time in life and one rainbow showing their roles now. In addition to functioning as a role/role loss assessment, this strategy provides opportunities for discussing adjustment to role loss and change, and reinforcing existing coping strategies for dealing with change. The width of the leisure band in the rainbow will provide a basis for understanding the older person's values attached to leisure and for stimulating discussion of leisure participation and leisure satisfaction.

The assessment of wellness in each area of the Wheel of Wellness can be done using the Wellness Evaluation of Lifestyle (WEL), a 123-item paper-and-pencil measure that provides a profile with 18 subscale scores for each component of the wheel as well as a score for total wellness (Myers, Witmer, Sweeney, & Hattie, 1998). The scores offer a baseline for counselors in examining personal wellness in later life and developing a plan to enhance wellness in one or more areas. Factors such as sense of worth and sense of control are important in adjusting to role loss, as discussed earlier. Leisure can be a focus for both assessment and intervention. The instrument has been normed with a variety of age groups, including older adults.

INTERVENTION STRATEGIES TO PROMOTE ADJUSTMENT TO ROLE LOSS AND LEISURE

A variety of intervention strategies may be proposed to assist older persons in adjusting to role loss and leisure in later life. These include individual and group interventions. Psychoeducational approaches, values clarification, support groups, and behavioral interventions may be effective. Any approaches used with clients of any age are appropriate for use with older persons. In this section, the focus is on using the two models presented earlier to help older clients cope with later life changes.

Many older persons do not understand counseling and have a perception based on earlier stereotypes that mental health care is appropriate for severe mental illness, not "normal" life transitions and events (Myers & Schwiebert, 1996). They tend to be reluctant to participate in counseling. On the other hand, psychoeducational programs tend to be less threatening and provide ample opportunity for structured interventions, referrals for counseling, and interventions in a group setting.

Group interventions can be easily structured according to either of the two models presented in this chapter. Paper-and-pencil assessments and rainbows or wellness profiles can be completed during sessions or given as homework assignments. It may be preferable to complete these in a counseling session, as older persons may have questions concerning the instructions or individual parts of the assignments which reflect their needs and concerns as a basis for counseling interventions.

Completed rainbows or profiles can be discussed individually or in small groups. A major advantage of groups with older persons is the opportunity for peer interaction and socialization. This can be especially important for older individuals who experience social isolation and loneliness. Case examples may help to illustrate these points.

In each of the following case examples, the client and his or her situation are described, with a focus on role loss, change, and adjustments in later life, and leisure activities. The two models presented earlier are used to conceptualize a treatment plan and outcomes of interventions are discussed.

CASE EXAMPLE 1

Description of Presenting Issues

Ed S., a 91-year-old, widowed, Caucasian male, was referred by his adult children and family physician for depression. His wife of 67 years had died a few months earlier, following a lengthy illness. For several years, Ed was the primary caretaker for his wife, who was largely homebound and severely disabled. He and his wife had lived independently in their own home in a retirement community located several hundred miles from their adult son and daughter. The adult son convinced his father to move to the area in which the son lived when long-term care was recommended for Ed's wife.

Ed and his wife moved near the son, with Ed taking an apartment and his wife being placed in a nursing home. Ed visited her daily and fed her all of her meals for six months, until she died. He remained living independently in his apartment, noting that all of the other residents were working and no one had time for "an old man." He became isolated, depressed, and soon was hospitalized with pneumonia. He stated that this was the lowest point in his entire life. When he was checked out of the hospital, his son took Ed to look at retirement communities, one of which he chose as his permanent living accommodations. The community had social support services as well as health care facilities. Ed remained depressed and isolated, such that the staff also requested a referral for mental health intervention.

Ed had a strong work history, having retired as a successful corporate manager at the age of 68. He returned to work shortly thereafter after obtaining a license as a real estate agent. He continued to work part-time in real estate until his mid-80s. He was an avid golfer who spent several days each week participating in golf with friends. He played tennis into his 80s as well. Prior to his wife's illness, the couple enjoyed traveling and social activities with friends.

In addition to his depression, Ed experienced a variety of health and sensory problems. He wore glasses and had had cataract surgery, wore hearing aids in both ears, and used a wheelchair due to severe arthritis. He took medication for high blood pressure as well.

Assessment

Using Super's rainbow and colored pencils, Ed was asked to draw his life-career rainbow as it would have looked 20 years earlier (when he was in his early 70s) and as it would look now. There was a clear difference in the drawings. His earlier drawing showed a balance of roles in the areas of work, leisure, citizen, and student. His current drawing showed almost no band width in leisure, he suggested that drawing anything related to work or being a student was irrelevant, as he had no work and could not be a student, and he drew only a thin line for citizen, noting that he was unable to be active in his community and could only vote if someone took him to the polls. When asked what he did with his time, the answer was "nothin.' There's nothin' I can do."

Ed also completed the WEL. His profile showed low scores in most areas, with sense of worth and sense of control being very low. His sense of meaning and purpose, as reflected in his score on the spirituality scale, was similarly low, as was his score on the leisure scale. His highest scores, which were all above average, were in the areas of self-care, nutrition, problem solving and creativity, sense of humor, and stress management.

Treatment Planning

Using the two rainbows as a basis for intervention, Ed's treatment plan included reviewing the two sets of rainbows, discussing the components of each one and the meaning each had for him, then discussing the differences between the two. Strategies for expanding the band width in areas that he depicted as having low role salience were a focus of intervention. In particular, since Ed had a lot of discretionary time, strategies for increasing his involvement in leisure activities were discussed at length. The setting of his retirement community offered ample opportunities for leisure activities that would bring Ed into contact with other older persons and help reduce his isolation. Behavioral strategies and contracts that encouraged his participation in group activities were also important.

When using an instrument such as the WEL for treatment planning, it is important to emphasize the client's areas of strengths and use these to help address areas of weakness. In Ed's case, his pattern of high scores reflected his need for intellectual stimulation, his problem-solving ability, and his ability to take care of himself in those areas where he felt he clearly had choices (i.e., choice of a balanced and healthy diet and choice to not drink, use illegal drugs, and manage his stress adequately). His sense of humor also was an asset, as he was able to laugh at himself and smiled readily when he could be convinced to join others for activities. His low scores in spirituality, sense of worth, and sense of control reflected his feelings of powerlessness over the circumstances of his life and his loss of a sense of purpose and meaning. His low score in leisure was a direct reflection of his sense of learned helplessness in responding to the circumstances of his life.

Based on his WEL scores, Ed's treatment plan included individual counseling as well as group and behavioral interventions. The focus of the individual sessions was on helping Ed process his grief over his wife's death and the loss of his physical strength and vitality. His coping resources and strengths and his sense of humor were used to help him gain new perspectives on the changes he had experienced in the past 10 years. He was encouraged to develop new leisure activities, starting with a daily game of cards with three other older men living in his facility. Ed's naturally extroverted nature soon became evident, and he quickly emerged as the designated, informal leader of the card players. This new role provided a sense of importance and esteem that had been missing in his life, and helped him experience a renewed sense of control as well as interest in his life. Choices made toward greater wellness are self-reinforcing, in that each such choice empowers the individual to make increasingly more choices that enhance personal wellness. This was the case with Ed, whose success with the card players led to increased social involvement with other older persons in the facility. He joined a regular afternoon discussion group, met friends with whom he ate each of his three meals each day, and became "the life of the party" at social gatherings in the retirement community. Ed engaged in several new roles, developed satisfying leisure pursuits, and developed a renewed sense of purpose in life, perceived control, and sense of well-being.

CASE EXAMPLE 2

Description of Presenting Issues

Susan and Bill were 74 and 75 years old, respectively, and had been married for 53 years. They were referred by their adult daughter with the admonition that "Dad thinks Mom needs to change, but Dad really is the one who needs to be different." Two weeks prior to the initial interview, Bill wrote a three-page letter to his adult daughter explaining that he "had had it" and "just wanted out" of the marriage. Susan had not seen the letter and could not understand what he had said and why he had written their daughter and not talked to her instead.

Bill retired at the age of 65 from a successful career as an outside salesperson. Since that time he has worked part time selling vitamins. Susan was a stay-at-home homemaker until Bill retired, at which time she began working for Mary Kay cosmetics. She was extremely successful in her work and rapidly advanced in the organization. As a couple, they taught Sunday school classes at their church, socialized with other couples 2 to 4 nights a week (dinner and cards), and attended social club events.

Bill found it difficult, if not impossible, to articulate his concerns, often saying either "I'm just not good at this" or "Oh, you know what I mean." Susan was hurt by his comments, but maintained that she loved him and could not understand why he was upset. He said she persisted in giving him directions when they were driving, which she said was correct but added that she had to do so as he always took the long way to get anywhere. He indicated that she was a wonderful wife and mother. She complained that he got excited about his yardwork and wore his muddy shoes into the house. In general, they verbalized a litany of small complaints about one another, but neither shared much initially in the way of significant issues.

Assessment

Susan and Bill were each asked to complete two life career rainbows, the first showing their role commitments prior to Bill's retirement, and the second showing their role commitments at the present time. Bill drew a very wide band for worker prior to his retirement, with no band width for homemaker, a small band for leisurite and citizen, and a wide band for student (he said he was always learning new things). His postretirement rainbow included a balance between worker, leisurite, student, and citizen, with a small band for homemaker. Neither Bill nor Susan drew a band representing "child." Susan drew her first rainbow with a very wide band for homemaker and small bands for each of the other areas. Her second rainbow included wide bands for leisurite and homemaker, and not quite as wide for worker. Although she worked only part time, her work was very important to her and had high role salience. She did not include bands for student or citizen.

Both clients completed the WEL. Their profiles showed very high scores on nutrition and self-care, and Bill also had a high score on exercise. His lowest scores were on locus of control, sense of worth, emotional awareness and management, work, and love. Susan's lowest scores were on sense of worth and exercise. Her highest scores were on friendship and work.

Treatment Planning

One area of concern that appeared in the rainbow drawings was Bill's addition since his retirement of a band for homemaker. Since he had traveled extensively during most of their marriage, Susan, who did not work, took care of the house. After his retirement, Bill began to intervene to "help" around the house. Susan felt that he was encroaching on her territory and resented his innuendos concerning areas where she could improve housekeeping. Bill was unaware of her resentment, stating only that he was just trying to help and she didn't understand his motives.

Bill noted that Susan had lots of friends, and made sure they had an active social calendar. At the same time, he noted a lack of intimacy in their relationship. Susan did not understand his feelings in this regard, and his difficulty expressing them made it even harder for her. When questioned about work, an area in which Bill scored low on the WEL and Susan scored high, it became evident that she had begun a successful career after his retirement during a time when he was drinking excessively. By the time he quit drinking, she was well established in a successful business and had no desire to quit. Bill did not enjoy "aggressive" women, which he seemed to define as any woman working outside the home. His attempts to help her improve her housekeeping were aimed at getting her to invest more time in the home and cheerfully relinquish her outside employment.

The treatment plan for this couple included homework assignments to make time to be together without the constant presence of another couple. Having "dates" where they held hands was a first step at getting them to communicate with one another on both an emotional and physical level. Taking time each day to express appreciation to one another for the other's good qualities was another assignment. Bill was challenged to redefine his sense of worth based on who he was now rather than who he was prior to his retirement. He was encouraged to reframe his sense of self in terms of his current work as a vitamin salesperson, his tremendous success at golf (he golfed his age, as Susan said), his work at the church, and his educational pursuits. As he began to do so, he began to lose interest in helping out around the house, which was fine with Susan. Without his "help," she was willing to invest more time in the home while still maintaining her business. Bill began to appreciate Susan's business success as yet another aspect of her intelligence and flexibility and was helped to see that just because she had a job did not mean she was, as he said, "in your face."

At the time of termination, the couple reported that they had spent the weekend together at the beach, had slept in the same bed close to one another, and were enjoying their time together. They were both working toward having a happier marriage, while continuing to enjoy time with their children, grandchildren, friends, and church affiliates.

CONCLUSION

Helping older persons adapt to role loss and change in later life, and enjoy their increased amount of time for leisure, requires a multifaceted approach. Holistic models can be helpful in conceptualizing late life changes as opportunities for development and growth. Comparing roles in later life to those in earlier years, and assessing dimensions of wellness, can provide a firm basis for treatment planning to help both older individuals and couples achieve greater life satisfaction in their later years.

REFERENCES

Abeles, R.P., Gift, H.C., & Ory, M.G. (Eds.). (1994). *Aging and quality of life*. New York: Springer.

Adams, R.G., & Bleiszner, R. (1995). Aging well with friends and family. *American Behavioral Scientist, 39*, 209–224.

Arber, S., & Ginn, J. (1994). Women and aging. *Reviews in Social Gerontology, 4,* 349–358.

Atchley, R.C. (1988). *Social forces and aging*. Pacific Palesades, CA: Wadsworth.

Beckingham, A.C., & Watt, S. (1995). Daring to grow old: Lessons in healthy aging and empowerment: Learning to live at all ages [Special issue]. *Educational Gerontology, 21,* 479–495.

Blue Cross/Blue Shield. (1998). *Ageless heroes*. Bismack, ND: Author

Bowling, A. (1993). The concepts of successful and positive aging. *Family Practice, 10,* 449–453.

Broman, C.L. (1993). Social relationships and health-related behavior. *Journal of Behavioral Medicine, 16,* 335–350.

Coleman, D.J., & Iso-Ahola, S.E. (1993). Leisure and health: The role of social support and self-determination. *Journal of Leisure Research, 25,* 111–128.

Coleman, P.G. (1992). Personal adjustment in later life: Successful aging. *Reviews in Clinical Gerontology, 2,* 67–78.

Crandall, R.C. (1991). *Gerontology: A behavioral science approach* (2nd ed.). New York: McGraw-Hill.

Crist, H.M. (1996). Efficacy of volunteerism for role-loss depression. *Psychological Reports, 79,* 736–738.

Cvetanovski, J., & Jex, S.M. (1994). Locus of control of unemployed people and its relationship to psychological and physical well being. *Work and Stress, 8,* 60–67.

Ellis, J.R. (1993). Volunteerism as an enhancement to career development. *Journal of Employment Counseling, 30,* 127–132.

George, L., & Clipp, E.C. (1991). Subjective components of aging well. *Generations, 15,* 57–60.

Harris & Associates. (1975). *The myth and reality of aging in America*. Washington, DC: Author.

Havighurst, R. (1972). *Developmental tasks and education*. New York: MacKay.

Hersch, G. (1990). Leisure and aging. *Physical and Occupational Therapy in Geriatrics, 9,* 55–78.

Herzog, A.R., & House, J.S. (1991). Productive activities and aging well. *Generations, 15, 49–54.*

Housley, W.F. (1992). Psychoeducation for personal control: A key to psychological well-being in the elderly. *Educational Gerontology, 18, 785–794.*

Ishii-Kuntz, M. (1990). Social interaction and psychological well being: Comparison across stages of adulthood. *International Journal of Aging and Human Development, 30,* 15–36.

Iso-Ahola, S.E., Jackson, E., & Dunn, E. (1994). Starting, ceasing, and replacing leisure activities over the life-span. *Journal of Leisure Research, 26,* 227–249.

Kaplan, G.A., & Strawbridge, W.J. (1994). Behavioral and social factors in healthy aging. In R.P. Abeles, H.C. Gift, & M.G. Ory (Eds.), *Aging and quality of life* (pp. 57–78). New York: Springer.

Kobasa, S.C. (1979). Stressful life events, personality, and health: An inquiry into hardiness. *Journal of Personality and Social Psychology, 37,* 1–11.

Lightsey, O.R. (1996). What leads to wellness? The role of psychological resources in well-being. *Counseling Psychologist, 24*, 589–735.

McDaniels, C., & Gysbers, N. (1992). *Counseling for career development: Theories, resources, and practice.* San Francisco: Jossey-Bass.

Melamed, S., Meir, E.I., & Samson, A. (1995). The benefits of personality-leisure congruence: Evidence and implications. *Journal of Leisure Research, 27*, 25–40.

Mill, J.E. (1997). The Neuman systems model: Application in a Canadian HIV setting. *British Journal of Nursing, 6*, 163–166.

Mor-Barak, M.E., Scharlach, A.E., Birba, L., & Sokolov, J. (1992). Employment, social networks, and health in the retirement years. *International Journal of Aging and Human Development, 30*, 145–159.

Myers, J.E. (1990). *Empowerment for later life.* Greensboro, NC: ERIC/CASS.

Myers, J.E. (1992). Wellness, prevention, development: The cornerstone of the profession. *Journal of Counseling and Development, 71*, 136–139.

Myers, J.E., & Schwiebert, V.S. (1996). *Competencies for gerontological counseling.* Alexandria, VA: American Counseling Association.

Myers, J.E., Witmer, J.M., Sweeney, T.J., & Hattie, J. (1998). *Wellness evaluation of lifestyle.* Greensboro, NC: Authors. (Also available through MindGarden, Palo Alto, CA.)

Neugarten, B., Havighurst, R., & Tobin, S. (1968). Personality and patterns of aging. In B. Neugarten (Ed.), *Middle age and aging.* Chicago: University of Chicago Press.

Papalia, D.E., Camp, C.J., & Feldman, R.D. (1996). *Adult development and aging.* New York: McGraw-Hill.

Patterson, I. (1996). Participation in leisure activities following a stressful life event: The loss of a spouse. *International Journal of Aging and Human Development, 42*, 123–142.

Pedlar, A., Dupuis, S., & Gilbert, A. (1996). Resumption of role status through leisure in later life. *Leisure Sciences, 18*, 259–276.

Ponzo, Z. (1992). Promoting successful aging: Problems, opportunities, and counseling guidelines. *Journal of Counseling and Development, 71*, 210–213.

Ragheb, M.G. (1993). Leisure and perceived wellness: A field investigation. *Leisure Sciences, 15*, 13–23.

Reitzes, D.C., Mutran, E.J., & Verrill, L.A. (1995). Activities and self-esteem: Continuing the development of activity theory. *Research on Aging, 17*, 260–277.

Riker, H.C., & Myers, J.E. (1990). *Retirement counseling: A practical guide for action.* New York: Hemisphere.

Ryff, C.D., & Heidrich, S.M. (1997). Experience and well-being: Explorations on domains of life and how they matter. *International Journal of Behavioral Development, 20*, 193–206.

Schlossberg, N. (1984). *Counseling adults in transition.* New York: Springer.

Schlossberg, N., Waters, E., & Goodman, J. (1995). *Counseling adults in transition.* New York: Springer.

Schulz, A.J., Israel, B.A., Zimmerman, M.A., & Checkoway, B.N. (1995). Empowerment as a multi-level construct: Perceived control at the individual, organizational, and community levels. *Health Education Research, 10*, 309–327.

Sherbourne, C.D., Meredith, L.S., & Ware, J.E. (1992). Social support and stressful life events: Age differences in their effect on health-related quality of life among the chronically ill. *Quality of Life Research, 1*, 235–246.

Stanley, D., & Freysinger, V.J. (1995). The impact of age, health, and sex on the frequency of older adults' leisure activity participation: A longitudinal study. *Activities, Adaptation, and Aging, 19*, 31–42.

Sweeney, T.J. (1998). *Adlerian counseling: A practitioner's approach.* New York: Taylor-Francis.

Sweeney, T.J., & Witmer, J.M. (1991). Beyond social interest: Striving toward optimum health and wellness. *Individual Psychology, 47*(4), 527–540.

Super, D.F. (1954). Career patterns as a basis for vocational counseling. *Journal of Counseling Psychology, 1,* 12–19.

Super, D.F. (1980). *Career choice and development: Applying contemporary theories to practice* (2nd ed.). San Francisco: Jossey-Bass.

Thompson, M.G., & Heller, K. (1990). Facets of support related to well-being: Quantitative social isolation and perceived family support in a sample of elderly women. *Psychology and Aging, 5,* 535–544.

Thompson, P. (1993). "I don't feel old": The significance of the search for meaning in later life. *International Journal of Geriatric Psychiatry, 8,* 685–692.

Toner, H.M., & Morris, J.D. (1992). A social psychological perspective of dietary quality in later adulthood. *Journal of Nutrition for the Elderly, 11,* 35–53.

Ulione, M.S. (1996). Physical and emotional health in dual-earner families. *Family and Community Health, 19,* 14–20.

United States Bureau of the Census. (1990). *Statistical abstract of the United States.* Washington, DC: U.S. Government Printing Office.

United States Department of Health and Human Services. (1990). *Healthy people 2000: National health promotion and disease prevention objectives.* Washington, DC: U.S. Government Printing Office.

Walker, S.N. (1991). Wellness and aging. In E.M. Baines (Ed.), *Perspectives on gerontological nursing.* Newbury Park, CA: Sage.

Waters, E.B., & Goodman, J. (1990). *Empowering older adults: Practical strategies for counselors.* San Francisco: Jossey-Bass.

Witmer, J.M. (1997). *Reaching toward wellness: A holistic model for personal growth and counseling.* Athens, OH: Author.

Witmer, J.M., & Sweeney, T.J. (1992). A holistic model for wellness and prevention over the lifespan. *Journal of Counseling and Development, 71,* 140–148.

Witmer, J.M., Sweeney, T.J., & Myers, J.E. (1997). *The wheel of wellness.* Greensboro, NC: Authors.

Wong, P. T. (1989). Personal meaning and successful aging: Psychology of aging and gerontology [Special issue]. *Canadian Psychology, 30,* 516–525.

Zimmer, Z., & Lin, H.S. (1996). Leisure activity and well being among the elderly in Taiwan: Testing hypotheses in an Asian setting. *Journal of Cross Cultural Gerontology, 11,* 167–186.

CHAPTER 4

Addressing Late Life Developmental Issues for Women: Body Image, Sexuality, and Intimacy

Royda G. Crose

In our rapidly aging society, two demographic phenomena are important for clinicians to recognize. First, there is no common group of older people. With increased longevity, multiple groups now exist among several cohorts of people over 50 years of age that make up the aging population. The 50–65-year-olds, who are confronting family and work-related role changes, bring different issues to therapy than the 80–95-year-olds, who are struggling with issues of numerous losses, disability, and dependency. The elders who were adults during the depression have had different life histories from those older adults who were adolescents during and after World War II. In only a few more years, the oldest of the baby boomers will join the ranks of elders bringing even greater diversity to this unique phenomenon of the aging population. As a result, this multigenerational, ever expanding, long-lived group of people bring a multitude of life experiences, needs, interests, and considerations to treatment and service programs for older adults (Crose, Leventhal, Haug, & Burns, 1997).

A second phenomenon of our times is the feminization of the aging population. Since significantly fewer men than women survive into very old age, the elders in our society are primarily women. In fact, among the oldest old populations there are two to three women for every man. This has important late life development implications for both men and women. For women who have grown up in a society where men have the power and privilege and where relationships with men are often based on sex appeal, submissive sexuality, and

Note. The author would like to thank Paula Hartman-Stein, Ph.D., Center for Healthy Aging, Akron, Ohio, for the contribution of case examples and clinical consultation in the development of this chapter.

intimacy within the context of marriage, late life development (without men as a reference point) may be a new and unsettling experience.

For many older women, the end of life is a time of blossoming and continued growth as independent, autonomous individuals. For others, it is a time of confusion, insecurity, and uncertainty without men as leaders, partners, and companions. For a great many, it is a time of caregiving for older husbands and parents that restricts opportunities and drains economic resources. Also, even though women live longer than men, they often live with a reduced quality of life due to chronic disabling conditions such as osteoporosis, rheumatoid arthritis, or other autoimmune type disorders. So, for many women, an extended lifespan does not necessarily mean that they enjoy equally long healthspans.

These two phenomena—the rapidly growing diversity of the aging population and the feminization of aging—mean that most of the late life therapy issues center around women's needs not only for treatment of disease and disorder, but also for continued growth and development (Crose, 1993). Therefore, it is important that clinicians be well informed about women's development across the lifespan and the implications for women of growing up and growing old in a sexist and ageist society.

THEORIES OF DEVELOPMENT

Traditional theories of psychology have viewed human development as gender neutral, but have based normal developmental patterns on models of autonomy, self-reliance, and separation that are more typical of males than females. In the past 20 years, feminist psychologists have argued that such narrow views of development are discriminatory to those (especially women) who follow developmental patterns that focus on relationships, interdependence, and connection. Miller (1976), in her landmark book, *Toward a New Psychology of Women*, describes this alternative pattern as the "self-in-relation" model of development. A few years later, Gilligan (1982), in her book, *In a Different Voice*, explains that this relational pattern of development is neither more authentic nor more deviant than the traditional autonomous view of development. It is simply different and should be recognized as equally valid and healthy. This distinction between gender differences in development has helped to depathologize women's ways of *being* (identity and social development) (Jordan, Kaplan, Miller, Stiver, & Surrey, 1991) and of *knowing* (intellectual development) (Belenky, Clinchy, Goldberger, & Tarule, 1986). These theorists believe that a self-in-relation model of development is not innate to women but is learned as a way in which to nurture others and to survive as the nondominant group in a society where men have ruled.

In this model, women typically identify themselves as people within relationships to others rather than as autonomous individuals outside relationships. Cooperation, rather than competition, is the preferred method of relating and an empathic, subjective affiliation with another person is more common than an analytic, objective relationship. This pattern of development keeps women connected, but may result in overinvolved, dependent, enmeshed relationships, just as the autonomous, self-reliant pattern of men may result in isolation, separation, and disconnection from others. Some geropsychologists (see Gutmann, 1987) theorize that in late life development women become more autonomous and agentic after their children are grown, and, likewise, men become more affiliative and communal after they retire from their occupational roles. It is generally agreed by subsequent researchers that women grow to become more autonomous with age, but it is not yet established whether men actually change to become more relational with age or if those men who have always been more relational are the ones who tend to survive into old age (see Crose, 1997).

In the past 30 or more years, several theories of late life development have been offered by gerontologists. The theory of disengagement (Cumming & Henry, 1961) held that growing old successfully meant giving up social roles and attachments. At the same time, proponents of activity theory believed that disengagement was not healthy and that older people must stay actively engaged. More recently, those that study aging have concluded that people do not change significantly with age to become more disengaged or more active, rather that patterns of continuity (Atchley, 1989) from youth to later life demonstrate typical aging. According to theories of continuity, deviation from earlier behaviors represent discontinuities and possible disorder in old age. Although such stability of personality and behavior is viewed favorably by many, others have begun to recognize the possibility of "gerotranscendence" or the ability of some older people to transform and change as they transcend the slings and arrows of growing old (Tornstam, 1996).

Recognition and understanding of all these different patterns of development are important for addressing lifespan developmental issues for women. From a clinical perspective, I find that continuity over the life span is typical of most of my older clients and sudden or extreme variations from former behaviors usually point to pathology. However, I also have learned that old age can bring transformation and growth, which enables clients to transcend the problems inherent in the aging process. The self-in-relation model of development, helps me understand the history of my older women clients and to support them as they struggle with new independence and autonomy as they become widowed, divorced, or are suffering from the empty nest. Although numerous issues for women in late life could be considered from a continuity theory of aging and a self-in-relation developmental model, this chapter will address only three important and interrelated aspects of women's lives: body image, sexuality, and intimacy.

THREE INTERRELATED ASPECTS OF FEMALE DEVELOPMENT: BODY IMAGE, SEXUALITY, AND INTIMACY

With age, physical appearance, sexual desire and involvement, and intimacy in relationships change and are often related to self-esteem, depression, anxiety, and loneliness for older women in therapy. Body image, sexuality, and formation of intimate relationships for women in their younger years are areas of particular interest for clinicians and researchers, but little has been studied or written about these issues for women in late life. The few studies that compare younger and older women's experiences usually find that older women have less disorder and despair about these issues than younger women. Although there is a common belief that women get more depressed, lonely, and asexual as they age, those who have taken the time to seriously investigate these questions have found that, as a group, women's depression actually lessens with age (McGrath, Keita, Strickland, & Russo, 1990) and loneliness among college students has been found to be greater than for elders (Hanley-Dunn, Maxwell, & Santos, 1985). It may be that younger people (clinicians and researchers included) feel despair when they view physical decline, lack of companionship, and isolation of the elderly through their own countertransferent projections. Actually, most older people view themselves as better off in later life than when they were young and foolish, and older people who are living productive and satisfying lives rarely feel that they would want to be younger. Of course, many older women continue to struggle with the unrealistic expectations for a perfect body, heightened sexuality, and self-sacrificing intimate relationships that have been placed on them throughout life. Some of the problems that older women bring to therapy come from these cultural expectations.

As the nondominant group in society, women's power has been in the ability to attract and to gain favor from the dominant group, men. Since sexual attractiveness is a primary method of gaining attention from men, body image becomes a major focus for women at a young age and continues to be so until later life. The youthful body is held to be ideal and the aging female body is viewed with disdain and even disgust by the dominant culture. This leaves many aging women with a sense of devaluation and powerlessness as their youthful attractiveness wanes.

Because women are expected to be the passive gender, they learn to wait for men to be the initiators of sexual activities and have typically followed the man's lead in sexual relationships. For the older heterosexual woman, this leaves few options if the man in her life dies or loses interest in sex due to health or psychological problems. Since women outlive men by many years and most marry men who are older, they often live for long periods of time without socially acceptable sexual outlets.

Whereas men often are the initiators of sex, women become the caretakers of intimate relationships throughout life. Indeed the primary task of women is often to nurture others and to build relationships. In late life after the children are grown and the husband has died, a woman may be left with significant role loss as well as loneliness without the kind of intimate relationships she has known at earlier times in her life.

These issues may be of concern for many women, but they do not become major distressors if the woman is able to adapt, adjust, and transcend the changes in life that come with age. A woman who feels good about herself, who enjoys good health, and who has weathered the difficulties of life throughout her earlier years, will continue to have positive feelings about her body and will find new ways to relate sexually and intimately with others as her life situation changes. However, the older woman who relies heavily on others for validation, who is suffering poor health, or who has been diminished by traumatic life events at earlier stages, will have more trouble accepting and adjusting to the problems that old age can bring. Therefore, the older woman's history, personality, health, cultural values, and outlook will influence her feelings about her body, her desire for sexual expression, and her need for intimacy. The younger therapist must be careful not to transfer his or her own ageist, sexist views on older women clients and to be willing to explore these vital areas of healthful living with people of all ages, even those in their 80s, 90s, and 100s. Since the literature on body image, sexuality, and intimacy in the lives of older women is sparse, much of what follows is based on research with younger populations and on anecdotal descriptions from clinical practice.

BODY IMAGE IN LATER LIFE

One look at popular magazines at the grocery store checkout counter reveals how much body image is an issue for women in this culture. Every month, in myriad magazines, there are new diets guaranteed to take weight off and to make the reader more desirable. Eating disorders on college campuses are rampant and girls as young as 8 years old are concerned about being fat. With such distortions of what the ideal woman should look like, no one, young or old, will measure up, and certainly, as women age, they veer further and further away from this ideal. Research on young women shows that significant numbers of women, no matter what their weight, want to weigh less and look younger and thinner. While the few studies that include older women also find that these subjects want to weigh less, the difference between actual and desired weight is less among older women than among younger women (Lamb, Jackson, Cassiday, & Priest, 1993). Such cross-sectional findings suggest that either older women become more accepting of their body size with age or that older cohorts of women are more realistic about weight loss.

No matter what ups and downs a woman has experienced with her body image at earlier ages, menopause and age bring changes in weight, fat distribution, and health that affect body image for most women. With the cessation of menses, a woman may rejoice or grieve the loss of monthly cycles; but the thickening of her waistline, the widening of her hips, and the graying of her hair are changes that affect the way she views her own attractiveness and the way she is viewed by others. When these normal occurances are combined with the changes that illnesses can bring to women with rheumatoid arthritis, incontinence, osteoporosis, surgeries, and side effects from cancer treatments, then older women, concerned with attractiveness, have many more challenges than younger women in maintaining good body image.

For women who were concerned about looking good at younger ages, this concern continues into old age. Sally, age 60, who has lupus, rheumatoid arthritis, and osteoporosis, feels that getting up each morning and putting on makeup is vital to health and well-being. "I don't want a pity party," she states emphatically. "So, I try to look my best and fake people out about how bad I feel." Sally, an artist, has had two divorces and is now widowed from her third marriage. When she gets to feeling really low about her losses and her pain, she locks her doors and gets in the shower to "cry my eyes out when I feel sorry for myself about all the things I can't do any longer." She likes to feel attractive and go out on an occasional date even though she doesn't want to get involved with another man because "it wouldn't be fair to him." In therapy, Sally is considering what her relationships would be like if she let others see her as she really feels rather than the image she projects through her makeup, fashionable clothes, and facade.

On the other hand, women who have never been concerned with their looks are not likely to begin to do so in old age. Alice, a 69-year-old professor, has always been more interested in books than in looks. Her rumpled, disheveled appearance makes her look much older than she actually is and her skin is pallid and puffy from lack of care and a recent illness. Though she has been widowed for 25 years, she has never considered dating or getting involved with another man. She says that she was surprised that any man had ever found her attractive enough to marry in the first place and that is certainly of no interest to her now. Her husband was an older educator who was impressed with her intellect. Since his death, she has devoted her life to rearing their three children and advancing her own scholarly endeavors. After a recent bout with a metabolic imbalance due to poor nutrition and medication effects, her grown children are concerned that she is not taking good care of herself and is at risk of serious health problems. They have enlisted the help of friends to look in on her and have hired a housekeeper and cook to see that her home and nutritional needs are met. Alice reluctantly accepts these changes but feels that these helpers interfere with her independence and privacy.

The women described here are unique, and emotionally stable, and their body images have stayed rather consistent throughout life. Sally puts on a good front that belies her underlying pain and distress, while Alice's scattered, haphazard look and lifestyle fit her image of the intellectual. While it might be helpful or even healthier for Sally to let down her guard and let others know how she is feeling, looking good makes her feel better and is a significant factor in her health plan. Alice's need to tidy up and pay more attention to her nutrition and hygiene might be important to her health but would require new attention to things that she has never felt were important. Mental health interventions can be effective in helping both these women process the changes in their lives that health problems are forcing them to make and cause them to see that clinging to old patterns of grooming and body imaging may be impeding their relationships with friends and family members.

Dramatic changes in interest about looks and body image are often indicators of depression, dementia, or other mental disorders. Marjorie and Edna are two women with chronic depression who have lost interest in how they look. Marjorie, age 90, lies in bed in a fetal position most of the time. The pictures on her bedside show her as a younger woman who dressed in the latest fashions and hairstyles. Once she was a wealthy, popular socialite who was active in community theater. She had no children and was pampered by her older, executive husband for whom she had been a secretary before they married. In a narcissistic manner, she had used beauty to attract a wealthy husband and to gain status; but now, in the nursing home, she is at the mercy of caregivers who do not respond in the way that others did when she was younger. Her control at this point in her life appears to be in refusing to comply with her caregivers' wishes. She will not eat, bathe, or get dressed. Unlike Sally, Marjorie gains benefits from having others pity her because she gets more attention by looking and feeling bad. If she gets up, gets dressed, and puts on makeup, she is expected to eat in the dining room, to do more self-care, and to participate in groups with other residents. She does not get special attention from the nurses when she looks good, so she has sacrificed her looks to get the attention she craves. Just as she used her good looks to get what she wanted as a young woman, now she is using her looks as a frail, helpless, sickly old woman to get the sympathy of others. This creates a cycle that keeps this formerly attractive woman deeply depressed, lonely, and dissatisfied. She does not want any of her former friends to visit her because she looks so bad, but she does not want to look good because she will not get the attention she needs. Her caregivers feel resentful and manipulated by her, and her friends have all abandoned her after repeatedly being rejected. She has had several physicians, psychiatrists, psychologists, and nurses attempt treatment with psychotherapy, medications, behavioral management, and even electroshock therapy, all to no avail. So, she lays in a fetal position, longing for relief from her unexplained physical pain and her emotional despair.

Edna is also upset about the way she looks. She has been depressed for many years and has been prescribed numerous medications for a multitude of physical and emotional problems. At age 69, she is overweight, plain, and poor. She has had two heart surgeries and suffers from severe angina. Edna was married at age 14 to a widower who had children only a few years younger than she. When the girls grew to be teenagers, her husband fobade his young wife to dress up or to wear makeup because he was afraid that his daughters' boyfriends would be attracted to her. She has always longed to look pretty but was hampered by lack of money and a threatening husband. For years, the only treatment for depression that she had received was antidepressant medication prescribed by her family physician, which increased her appetite and caused her to gain weight. In later life, when she was finally referred for psychotherapy, she realized that she had never been allowed to feel good about her body and her beauty. Edna decided that it was not too late to change. A change in medication helped this depressed woman begin to lose weight. She started to wear makeup and more contemporary clothing. After a few months of feeling better about her body image, she was able to confront other issues in her life and to function without the depression that had impeded her quality of life for so many years.

Although most women don't relish looking older in a youth-oriented, sexist society, healthy women gain maturity and confidence that allow them to accept their bodies in ways that they did not at younger ages. In fact, some older women have stated that they like their bodies better as they age and even that they feel safer on the streets as older women because they no longer feel "like a mark" for men who look at women only as sex objects. Women who do not feel good about themselves or their relationships at younger ages will not mature and develop healthy attitudes about their bodies in old age and will despair over the loss of their youthful appearance. This might be expressed by using heavy makeup and inappropriately revealing clothing or by turning to cosmetic surgery to alter their aging appearance.

In the few studies of body image that have been conducted on older women, researchers have found that women over 50 seem more accepting of heavier bodies (Lamb et al., 1993) and are concerned more with body function than with body appearance (Hart, 1998). Loomis and Thomas (1991) compared older women living independently with those living in nursing homes and found that body attitudes are more related to health problems than to age or living situations. These findings are consistent with unpublished studies that I have been conducting with women living with chronic disabling conditions. I have interviewed women with rheumatoid arthritis, lupus, multiple sclerosis, and osteoporosis; they express concerns with the changes in their appearance as a result of steroid medications (which cause weight gain and bloated contouring of their bodies), of bone and joint distortions (which cause hands, feet, and other body parts to protrude and swell), and of reductions in height (which cause improper fit of clothes). Improvement of health conditions and a physical fitness regimen for women of any age can be very beneficial to body function and will enhance body image as well. This seems to be of particular importance to the body image of older women (see Riddick & Freitag, 1984).

OLDER WOMEN'S SEXUALITY

Sexuality is an integral part of life at all ages. Whether it is behaviorally expressed or not, sexuality may be a part of dreams, fantasies, or memories that influence quality of life in old age. A look at the literature on older women's sexuality demonstrates how wide-ranging the topic of sex and aging can be. Some studies focus on frequencies of sexual activities in late life and lead the reader to believe that aging means a decline in sexuality. Other studies (Crose & Drake, 1993) focus on sexual satisfaction and interest in sex and find that older people tend to report stability in these qualitative aspects of sex across their life span. Most studies of sex and aging appear to take a rather traditional view of sexuality in that they investigate heterosexual, partnered, consensual sexual activities in old age and fail to explore aspects of sexual orientation and nonpartnered sexual expression and behavior. Because approximately half of all women over 65 are not married, such partnered, heterosexual investigations of late life sexuality may be more relevant for men than for women.

Sexual concerns of women in therapy cover a wide range of issues including desire for relational sex without availability of sexual partners, exploration of same-sex relationships, recovery from sexual assault and abuse during earlier times in their lives, disclosure of regrets about past sexual indiscretions, and the search for alternatives to partnered sexual satisfaction. Because literature is available about traditional, heterosexual, consensual sexual activity for older adults (see Chapter 18), this chapter focuses on some areas of sexuality for older women that have not been previously addressed but which may be the sexual issues that midlife and older women bring to therapy.

THE NEED FOR SENSUAL/SEXUAL PLEASURE

Given the gender differences in longevity (Crose, 1997), there is little doubt that older women are left with few resources for traditional, heterosexual partnerships. There simply are not enough men to go around and those few men who have survived into old age tend to be in monogamous marriages. Some older women who are married complain that their husbands are no longer able to or have lost interest in having sexual relations (Fog, Koster, Larsen, Garde, & Lunde, 1994).

Women, at all ages, have great variability in their sexual interests, experiences, or needs and such variability only increases with age. Eighty-three-year-old Dorothy, who has been divorced for most of her life, says, "I never liked sex that much anyway, so it is a relief to not have to be bothered." Others are like 85-year-old Nancy, a widow for 30 years, who feels just the opposite and says, "I have a very active sex life, mostly with younger men who are much more interesting than the men my age. Plus I have a steady relationship with a man who lives in another state and we visit each other on occasion." Most older women find themselves somewhere in between these two extremes, still interested in expressing their sexuality but without the sexual outlets that they had when they were younger (Campbell & Huff, 1995).

In old age, sensuality becomes an even more important aspect of sexuality than it was at earlier ages for older men and women alike. Helping older clients expand their views of sexuality to include sensual pleasuring provides more options for sexual satisfaction. Skin hunger for loving touch is one area of sensuality that may be satisfied in old age even when traditional sexual intercourse is no longer an option. Touch from family, friends, grandchildren, and even from strangers is important, as one older woman client revealed when she stated, "The main reason I go to church anymore is to get all the hugs and to be touched by the people there." Back rubs and foot massages in hospitals and nursing homes provide more than just lubrication for old, dry skin, but such care is increasingly difficult to obtain from overworked and undertrained staff. As a result, massage therapy for elders is gaining some acceptance and may be an important element of a treatment plan for those who have the resources to pay for the services.

Discussing and prescribing such sensual pleasures as masturbation, massage, bubble baths, aromatherapy, sexual reading, and erotic movies may be all that is needed to give older women clients permission to be sexual as a single woman (see Dodson, 1987). Masturbation for older women may not only be an excellent means of sexual expression but may actually improve overall health.

Clinicians who do not discuss these options with older women may be denying them options for greater life satisfaction and, in fact, may be missing important interventions for treatment of depression and anxiety, as exemplified by the two following cases.

After moving to a small apartment in an assisted living facility, 93-year-old Mary reported irritability and increased levels of anxiety. Such emotional stressors might typically be attributed to adjustment to a new environment; however, Mary's therapist noticed that she seemed especially unhappy that a particular table did not accompany her to her new residence. In exploring the meaning of her attachment to this table, Mary disclosed that she had used the table to rub against in a masturbatory practice for years and she missed this old "friend."

Lee, a 78-year-old, frail, depressed widow was suffering from insomnia. She missed her husband in bed beside her. In discussing her long relationship to her husband, she remembered that she used to masturbate as a young wife when her husband was out of town. Her therapist suggested that she might explore the possibility of using this strategy for sleep now. Lee was surprised to learn that she could still reach orgasm through masturbation and after this release she could fall asleep easily. This practice was satisfying to her and enabled her to discontinue the sleeping medication that her doctor had prescribed. By being open to the possibilities of masturbation for these rather frail, older women, their therapists were able to help them maintain sexual outlets that were beneficial to their health and well-being.

REMEMBERING THE PAST

Achievement of "ego integrity" (Erikson, 1963) is the late life developmental task that enables the older person to avoid despair about past failures, regrets, indiscretions, and missed opportunities. Life review (Disch, 1988) is a therapeutic method that helps older clients achieve this late life developmental task. A sexual history is an important part of life review and should not be left out of this process for older women in therapy. Though many older women may seem fragile and frail, they have survived into old age as women in a sexist society that is ripe with sexual assault and exploitation, resulting in many older women with histories of rape, incest, molestation, prostitution, abortion, or other sexually related traumas.

In the early part of the century when very young teen-age girls married, they often were escaping an abusive situation at home or were marrying an older, more financially secure man who could provide food and shelter. Edna, previously described, who, at age 14, married the widower with several small children, was not in love with her much older mate. Her husband needed a woman to take care of his children, and she needed a protector from a sexually abusive father. The price she paid was lifelong depression. Finally, at age 69, she was referred for therapy after becoming suicidal when her husband became ill and it appeared that he might die before her 93-year-old father. During life review in therapy, she began to deal with the sexual abuse from her childhood for the first time.

Marjorie, who was also described earlier, complained of a burning, excruciating pain in her stomach, but the doctors could find no cause for her symptoms. After one year of psychotherapy for depression, she finally disclosed that she felt shame and regret about an affair she had in her late 30s. She had fallen in love with a man her own age and felt she had betrayed her older, wealthy husband. When she became pregnant, she had to reveal her affair and her husband arranged an illegal abortion. Her lover moved away and Marjorie was left with chronic depression and somatization disorder. She believed that this affair was a sin and was fearful of facing God in the afterlife, so she lay in a fetal position, longing for death and clinging to life in great despair.

Laura, a 93-year-old former school guidance counselor, was referred for depression after her husband died. She was very psychologically minded and was enthusiastic about getting help. However, she became quite disoriented after a series of falls and her life review process began to continually focus on her many boyfriends from her much younger days. She kept going back to memories of one of her male high school students and wanted to talk about this relationship over and over. She remembered a consensual romance with this younger student and, though she never revealed whether or not it had consummated in sex, she now felt that she had been wrong in going against the norms of society and could not forgive herself. In her confused state, it was difficult to know the truth of this early life relationship; but whatever it was, it had strong sexual meaning and influence at the end of her life.

Such life experiences are not uncommon, but older women are reluctant to disclose sexually related histories as they feel shame or they have been discounted by others for clinging to traumas long past. Depressions and somatization disorders have been well established in younger women who have suffered sexual abuse and/or trauma (Bendixen, Muus, & Schei, 1994; Friedrich & Schafer, 1995; Golding, 1994, 1996a, 1996b; Golding, Cooper, & George, 1997; Kinzl, Traweger, & Biebl, 1995; Leserman & Drossman, 1995; Radomsky, 1995). To my knowledge, researchers have not yet looked at the relationship of hypochondriasis with histories of sexual assault or abuse in older women. However, such a connection has been evident with several older women clients in my practice. Such unresolved early traumas are often buried deep in memory but may continue to influence behavior and mental health, especially as a woman becomes fragile and frail in old age. A clinician who is aware and open to the possibility can facilitate the emergence of these issues during the course of therapy by simply inquiring about sexual history, attitudes, and relevant relationships.

SEXUAL ORIENTATION

There is perhaps no one who is more invisible in our society than the older lesbian. Since many older women are widowed and tend to be desexualized by the larger population, it is common for older women to live, travel, and socialize with other women without notice or stigma. At younger ages, two women or groups of women who showed little interest in male companionship might be suspected of being homosexual, but for midlife and older females these same sex social relationships are usually accepted without question. This acceptance of female companionship may allow older lesbians greater freedom in a homophobic society. Therapists who assume that all older women clients are heterosexual may miss important information about their older lesbian clients who are reluctant to reveal their sexual orientation (see McDougall, 1993; Shenk & Fullmer, 1996).

Sixty-year-old Meg's grief over her friend moving to another state immobilized her. She could not function in her teaching job nor could she concentrate to take care of her routine household tasks and responsibilities. Finally, she sought therapy to address the issues of such complicated grief reaction that no one really understood. It was only in therapy that she felt comfortable to reveal the lesbian relationship she had with this old friend. They had kept their relationship closeted for many years, and everyone assumed that they were just friendly companions who helped each other out. Now, Claudia had breast cancer and needed treatment and the support of her family. Her elderly mother and her grown children lived in another state and had insisted that she come there. Claudia decided to go, leaving Meg devastated. Therapy was the only safe place to turn for help with her feelings of grief, abandonment, and anger at this life trauma.

This kind of sexual invisibility and same-sex companionship in old age also allows those women who have formerly been in heterosexual relationships to experiment with changing their sexual orientation. Dancing, touching, and other intimacies become more and more common in a world of women. Given the unavailability of male partners and the history of exploitation and dysfunction that often occurs in heterosexual relationships, some older women decide to seek out same-sex companions for love and romance as well as for social support (Kellett, 1993). Although little has been written about this phenomenon, midlife and older women may come into therapy during such life transitions.

Forty-nine-year-old Alice sought therapy after she fell in love with a women she met over the Internet. Though she married as a teenager and now had two teenage daughters, she had always wondered about sex with women. With the wonders of the computer age, she was able to explore same-sex relationships anonymously. In a lesbian chatroom, she met Marie. They had much in common, and in time, they met and began a sexual relationship that was more satisfying than any she had known before with men. When she came into therapy, her life, as she had previously known it, was falling apart. Her church, family, friends, and coworkers had all condemned and abandoned her. Although she felt distraught, depressed and, at times, suicidal about all the upheaval in her life, she also felt that she had discovered her true sexual identity and wanted to explore the possibilities for herself as a lesbian.

This situation may seem unusual and though Alice is only in midlife, she represents a trend that I see among friends, colleagues, and midlife to older women clients who are not satisfied to live their lives in older ages without sexual partners. Like Alice, these women often need help from therapists in negotiating such controversial life changes with family and friends. They also need help in exploring their self-in-relation late life identity development.

SEXUAL RIGHTS AND PROTECTIONS

Many older women live with chronic illnesses that may interfere with sexuality. Effects of medication, incontinence, pain from arthritis, fragility of bones with osteoporosis, suppression of sexual desire with depression, and fatigue from caregiving responsibilities often put sex as a low priority or even as a health risk in late life. When an older woman becomes frail and dependent, freedom of sexual expression becomes compromised. Due to home care or institutionalization, she may no longer have the privacy to express her sexuality in ways that she desires. The sexual demands of domineering husbands or demented male residents in a nursing home may require protection from sexual assault or harassment in late life.

Alma was brought to the hospital with a broken hip after her husband had insisted on having sexual relations with her although her doctor had warned them about the risks of fractures due to her osteoporosis. She had always submitted to his sexual desires and believed that was the role of being a good wife. In her weakened condition, she did not have the motivation or energy to resist his sexual advances, though she understood the doctor's warning. Now, after this hospitalization, she had to be placed in long-term care where she would be protected from her husband's sexual demands.

On the other hand, women residents in long-term care sometimes need protection from demented male residents who make inappropriate sexual advances or try to get in bed with them during the nights. Staff often see these occurrences as harmless and unthreatening and may need education to understand the stress that living under such harassing conditions cause the older women residents.

Caregivers of older husbands or fathers also report sexual aggression from men suffering from dementing conditions. Greta suffered bruises and depression after her husband pushed her down in his desire to have sex. Before he developed Alzheimer's disease, they had enjoyed a mutually satisfying sexual partnership; but she sought therapy after he became so aggressive in his sexual demands that she was afraid for her safety. She felt that she was no longer able to care for him at home but was embarrassed to tell her grown children about this problem because she had never discussed such sexual intimacies with them before.

Conversely, long-term care staff and family members also need help in understanding the sexual needs, desires, and expressions of disabled, older women. It is not unusual for younger people to be disgusted by or to trivialize sexual expression in older people. Love and romance are energizing at any age, and older people who find such consensual relationships may need help from therapists to gain the respect and privacy needed to pursue such healthy experiences. A knowledgeable and understanding therapist can provide sex education (see White & Catania, 1982) for caregivers, adult children, and nursing home staff to assist older women in gaining the privacy needed for sexual expression, whether it be heterosexual, same-sex, or self-sexual experiences.

Transferences and Countertransferences

Therapists may fail to recognize the sexual components and issues in the treatment needs of older women because of their own countertransferences in working with clients old enough to be their mothers and grandmothers (see Genevay & Katz, 1990; Kellett, 1993). Romantic and sexual relationships between older men and younger women are culturally and socially acknowledged and even accepted, so the female therapist may not be so surprised at the sexual overtones in her relationships to older male clients. However, a younger male therapist can be taken off guard when an older woman client asserts herself sexually toward him.

Jeff, a doctoral student, developed a strong therapeutic alliance with Edna (the 69-year-old woman described earlier), but he ignored the sexual nature of her interactions with him. Because she was old enough to be his grandmother, it did not occur to him that she might be experiencing sexual feelings toward him. He did not notice her flirtatious remarks in the same way that he would with younger clients; and when she finally pulled up her blouse to show him her scars from heart surgeries, he was uncomfortable but could not believe this behavior was sexual. His supervisor asked him to explore the possibility that Edna was feeling sexual toward him and helped him address these issues with his client. By recognizing these transferences and his own countertransferences, Jeff was able to use Edna's sexual feelings to uncover the life review material regarding her older husband's jealousy of younger men and the unresolved sexual abuse by her father. This was a turning point in her therapy for depression.

Laura, the 93-year-old nursing home resident described earlier, has an active interest in the sex life of a male nurse who cares for her. Being a very dignified former schoolteacher, she probably would never make sexual advances to him, but she loves to know all about his current girlfriends. As she becomes more disoriented, she fantasizes that he is making love to his fianceé in a room above hers. She complains to her therapist that this keeps her awake at night but she seems to get great satisfaction in such voyeuristic delusions.

Older women have few males in their lives, especially nonrelatives. They value caring male health professionals and often respond to them with flirtatious or sexual overtones that are not so apparent in their relationships with female caregivers. Men who can accept and use these relationships supportively and therapeutically can be very effective in treating and enriching the lives of older, frail, or disabled women.

WOMEN'S INTIMATE RELATIONSHIPS IN LATE LIFE

The developmental path for most women in later life includes great changes in intimate relationships. As younger women, romantic, sexual relationships with one person took center stage as they built families and support systems. In old age, heterosexual women typically outlive the men with whom they were married and rely on their friends and families for intimacy. Because approximately one half of women over the age of 65 live alone, many believe that loneliness and desire for intimate companionship are common therapy issues for older women. Many older women do feel lonely, especially after the death of a spouse or close friend, but their therapy issues often center more around dynamic, changing relationships than on being alone in their later years. These relationships may be with adult children, grandchildren, and old friends, as well as new relationships in congregate environments (like senior centers, churches, apartment houses, retirement centers, and nursing homes). In my dissertation research (Crose, 1988), I learned that older women who are able to form satisfying new relationships were not lonely and tended to have greater life satisfaction than those who only relied on their older, long-term friends and family for companionship. These socially connected women also reported more affectionate relationships with their parents as young children. The people who despaired from loneliness in later life were more likely to have felt abandoned and lonely in earlier life.

The major intimacy issues in therapy with older women include loss of a spouse, stress in caregiving and care-receiving roles, living in congregate groups with new people, and grieving and replacing friendships as old friends become disabled and die. From a perspective of the self-in-relation model of development, the "self" in these intimate relationships must be redefined with the losses and changing living conditions that come with old age.

TRANSITIONS INTO WIDOWHOOD

Women typically report having more confidants than men (Connidis & Davies, 1990; Kendig, Coles, Pittelkow, & Wilson, 1988). Men tend to rely only on one woman, usually their wives, for intimacy and women tend to rely on several women, usually close friends, sisters, mothers, or daughters, in addition to their husbands. This gives women the advantage of having a supportive system for intimacy after the loss of their partners. Although women grieve the loss of their spouses, many develop new identities as single women whose capacities for intimacy grow and blossom in later life.

Studies of friendship connections of older women show a distinct difference between those who are married and those who are single, divorced, or widowed (Perkinson & Rockemann, 1996). After retirement, married women tend to stay focused on the social preferences of their husbands. If he wants to stay at home and watch television, she goes along with that. If he wants to be active in community events, she becomes active in such interests as well. Single women, on the other hand, are free to choose friends, interests, and activities according to their own preferences. After the death of a husband, the transition from identifying as a couple to identifying as a free agent in life is a major turning point in life for the surviving spouse. They will no longer be welcomed as part of the coupled world but may not have developed the skills to navigate in the world of single women. Apart from guiding her through the grief process, the therapist can assist a new widow during this time of transition to envision her many choices for intimacy during the remainder of her life.

For some, widowhood will be a time of increased involvement with family, whether it be with adult children, grandchildren, or siblings. When possible, women will reconnect and strengthen bonds with old friends and many will seek out new environments and relationships to experience increased growth and connection. While some women express a desire for remarriage and often find great satisfaction in becoming part of a couple again, most older women do not seek or find intimacy in a new heterosexual relationship. In old age, friendship and family are the sources for intimacy for most women.

FAMILY RELATIONSHIPS

Changing from the role of caregiver to care receiver presents crucial shifts in intimate relationships for women. Many times, women are referred for depression resulting from a major loss or health problem. For women, whose major role in life has been as caregiver to others, depression in late life may stem as much or more from role loss or role reversal than it does from the death of a loved one or the illness itself. Women who have been caregivers for most of their lives, first for children, then for ill parents or spouses, must find a new identity for themselves when they lose significant caregiving roles. Women, who become ill and are forced to receive care from those they usually care for, suffer from role reversal and identity adjustment. Therapy during these life changes should take these role and identity changes into account and honor their impact on the lives of older women. Ignoring such developmental processes can have serious consequences.

Mary, a 56-year-old caregiver for her mother, felt burdened and depressed. Her physician referred her to a psychologist for treatment. The therapist labeled Mary as "codependent" and insisted that Mary needed to place her mother in a nursing home and begin taking care of her own needs. Mary felt trapped between what her therapist believed and what she felt was the "right thing to do" for her mother. Placing her mother in a nursing home would make her feel guilty and irresponsible, but continuing to take care of her mother left her feeling overburdened and depressed. She quit therapy because the therapist only made her feel worse. Had this therapist understood the self-in-relation model of development, he would have been sensitive to the intimate, caring relationship that Mary had with her mother. Rather than labeling and pushing her toward severing her caregiving role, he would have guided her to explore the changing role with her mother and would have helped her find suitable options that honored the mother/daughter relationship as well as provided some relief for the caregiver.

Multigenerational families are relying on the older generations for caregiving of children more than ever before in history. With most mothers working outside the home and as conditions such as drug abuse, AIDS, alcoholism, and military service are rendering mothers and fathers incapable of caring for their children, grandmothers are becoming vital to family caregiving. These changing relationships in families can be a blessing for older women who want to continue caregiving roles with children, but they can also be a burden and major life stressor for those grandmothers who are not well or who want to move into new roles in late life. In either event, a therapist may help in sorting out these changing caregiving relationships for older women.

FRIENDSHIP

Friendships in later life are an important source of intimacy and life satisfaction for most older women. In her book, *Friendships through the Life Course,* Matthews (1986) identified three friendship styles of older adults: (1) the "independents," who involve themselves in friendly relations throughout life but who never achieve intimacy to the level that they can recall names of their past friends, (2) the "discerning," who form a small number of very close, important, intimate relationships during their lifetimes but are slow to get close to friendly acquaintances, and (3) the "acquisitive," who adapt to changing circumstances by easily making new close friends throughout life and expect potential friends will always be available. In my research (Crose, 1988), I found similar friendship patterns and concluded that those people who were both discerning and acquisitive had the greatest sense of well-being and were least lonely in their late life.

Close, intimate friendships are important to mental health at all ages. However, in late life when lifelong friends are also growing old, becoming ill, and dying, the ability to make new friends is crucial. With losses of close friends, older women may lose vital elements of their support systems, and therapists should encourage them to maintain social contacts and make new friends. Sometimes this means developing new skills or relearning social skills that have not been needed for a long time. Living in close proximity to others in retirement villages, assisted living facilities, or nursing homes brings increased social contact but may present challenges for developing intimate relationships. Getting along with difficult people and finding new friends in these congregate living environments are life skills that older women need to develop. I have described an intervention model for nursing home residents that takes into account their needs for resolving conflicts with staff and other residents, increases meaningful social interactions, and empowers them with feelings of self-worth (Crose, 1990a).

Maggie Kuhn, the founder of the Gray Panthers, recommended that old people reach out and make friends with younger people, so that they stay engaged with younger generations and also so that they prevent more losses, which are inevitable with older friends. Many of my older clients are struggling with establishing new relationships with young physicians, ministers, and lawyers, as they have outlived their older professional support systems. The relationship they establish with a younger therapist is equally important and must be nurtured and respected for the unique quality it brings to the lives of older women.

THERAPY CONSIDERATIONS

In this chapter, I have pointed to the complexities of body image, sexuality, and intimacy in the lives of older women. Space limitations have not allowed the many case examples and therapeutic interventions that might illustrate helpful therapy processes with older women, but the references and other chapters in this book provide guidance for therapeutic interventions. My hope is that I have triggered some new thoughts and considerations for therapists who are treating older women. I highly recommend an understanding of the self-in-relation model of development (Jordan et al., 1991) and of the continuity theory of aging (Atchley 1989). In my own work, I use life review combined with Gestalt techniques (Crose, 1990b) with individuals, family consultations (Crose, 1994), and friendship groups to assist women with late life developmental issues. The goal for all of us, older clients and therapists, should be to not only live longer but to live well and continue to grow throughout life.

REFERENCES

Atchley, R.C. (1989). A continuity theory of normal aging. *Gerontologist, 29*, 183–190.

Belenky, M.F., Clinchy, B.M., Goldberger, N.R., & Tarule, J.M. (1986). *Women's ways of knowing: The development of self, voice and mind.* New York: Basic Books.

Bendixen, M., Muus, K.M., & Schei, B. (1994). The impact of child sexual abuse: A study of a random sample of Norwegian students. *Child Abuse & Neglect, 18*(10), 837–847.

Campbell, J.M., & Huff, M.S. (1995). Sexuality in the older women. *Gerontology & Geriatrics Education, 16*(1), 71–81.

Connidis, I.A., & Davies, L. (1990). Confidants and companions in later life: The place of family and friends. *Journal of Gerontology: Social Sciences, 45*, S141–S149.

Crose, R. (1988). *The effects of parental bonding and perceptions of friendship on loneliness in institutionalized elderly.* Unpublished doctoral dissertation, Texas A&M University, College Station.

Crose, R. (1990a). Establishing and maintaining intimate relationships among nursing home residents. *Journal of Mental Health Counseling, 12*(1), 102–106.

Crose, R. (1990b). Reviewing the past in the here and now: Using gestalt therapy techniques with life review. *Journal of Mental Health Counseling, 12*(3), 279–287.

Crose, R. (1993). What's special about counseling older women? *Canadian Journal of Counseling, 25,* 617–623.

Crose, R. (1994). Family bonding and attachment patterns in late life. *Family Therapy, 21*(3), 217–221.

Crose, R. (1997). *Why women live longer than men . . . and what men can learn from them.* San Francisco: Jossey-Bass.

Crose, R., & Drake, L.K. (1993). Older women's sexuality. *Clinical Gerontologist, 12*(4), 51–56.

Crose, R., Leventhal, E.A., Haug, M.R., & Burns, E.A. (1997). The challenges of aging. In S.J. Gallant, G.P. Keita, & R. Royad-Schaler (Eds.), *Health care for women: Psychological, social, and behavioral influences.* Washington, DC: American Psychological Association.

Cumming, E., & Henry, W. (1961). *Growing old.* New York: Basic Books.

Disch, R. (Ed.). (1988). *Twenty-five years of the life review: Theoretical and practical considerations.* New York: Haworth Press.

Dodson, B. (1987). *Sex for one: The joy of selfloving.* New York: Crown.

Erikson, E.H. (1963). *Childhood and society.* New York: Macmillan.

Fog, E., Koster, A., Larsen, G.K., Garde, K., & Lunde, I. (1994). Female sexuality in various Danish general population age-cohorts. *Nordisk Sexologi, 12,* 111–117.

Friedrich, W.N., & Schafer, L.C. (1995). Somatic symptoms in sexually abused children. *Journal of Pediatric Psychology, 20*(5), 661–670.

Genevay, B., & Katz, R.S. (1990). *Countertransference and older clients.* Newbury Park, CA: Sage.

Gilligan, C. (1982). *In a different voice: Psychological theory and women's development.* Cambridge, MA: Harvard University Press.

Golding, J.M. (1994). Sexual assault history and physical health in randomly selected Los Angeles women. *Health Psychology, 13*(2), 130–138.

Golding, J.M. (1996a). Sexual assault history and limitations in physical functioning in two general population samples. *Research in Nursing & Health, 19,* 33–44.

Golding, J.M. (1996b). Sexual assault history and women's reproductive and sexual health. *Psychology of Women's Quarterly, 20,* 101–121.

Golding, J.M., Cooper, M.L., & George, L.K. (1997). Sexual assault history and health perceptions: Seven general population studies. *Health Psychology, 16*(5), 417–425.

Gutmann, D.L. (1987). *Reclaimed powers: Toward a new psychology of men and women in later life.* New York: Basic Books.

Hanley-Dunn, P., Maxwell, S.E., & Santos, J.F. (1985). Interpretation of interpersonal interactions: The influence of loneliness. *Personality and Social Psychology Bulletin, 11,* 445–456.

Hart, S. (1998). *The relationships among body image, sexuality, and emotional distress in older women with cancer.* Paper presented at the 23rd conference of the Association for Women in Psychology, Baltimore.

Jordan, J.V., Kaplan, A.G., Miller, J.B., Stiver, I.P., & Surrey, J.L. (1991). *Women's growth in connection: Writings from the Stone Center.* New York: Guilford Press.

Kellett, J.M. (1993). Sexuality in later life. *Reviews in Clinical Gerontology, 3,* 309–314.

Kendig, H.L., Coles, R., Pittelkow, Y., & Wilson, S. (1988). Confidants and family structure in old age. *Journal of Gerontology: Social Sciences, 43,* S31–S40.

Kinzl, J.F., Traweger, C., & Biebl, W. (1995). Family background and sexual abuse associated with somatization. *Psychotherapy and Psychosomatics, 64*(2), 82–87.

Lamb, C.S., Jackson, L.A., Cassiday, P.B., & Priest, D.J. (1993). Body figure preferences of men and women: A comparison of two generations. *Sex Roles, 28*(5/6), 345–358.

Leserman, J., & Drossman, D.A. (1995). Sexual and physical abuse history and medical practice. *General Hospital Psychiatry, 17*(2), 71–74.

Loomis, R.A., & Thomas, C.D. (1991). Elderly women in nursing home and independent residence: Health, body attitudes, self-esteem and life satisfaction. *Canadian Journal on Aging, 10*(3), 224–231.

Matthews, S.H. (1986). *Friendships through the life course: Oral biographies in old age.* Beverly Hills, CA: Sage.

McDougall, G.J. (1993). Therapeutic issues with gay and lesbian elders. *Clinical Gerontologist, 14*(1), 45–57.

McGrath, E., Keita, G.P., Strickland, B.R., & Russo, N.F. (1990). *Women and depression: Risk factors and treatment issues.* Washington, DC: American Psychological Association.

Miller, J.B. (1976). *Toward a new psychology of women.* Boston: Beacon Press.

Perkinson, M.A., & Rockemann, D.D. (1996). Older women living in a continuing care retirement community: Marital status and friendship formation. In K.A. Roberto (Ed.), *Relationships between women in later life.* Binghamton, NY: Harrington Park Press.

Radomsky, N.A. (1995). *Lost voices: Women, chronic pain and abuse.* Binghamton, NY: Harrington Park Press.

Riddick, C.C., & Freitag, R.S. (1984). The impact of an aerobic fitness program on the body image of older women. *Activities, Adaptation & Aging, 6*(1), 59–70.

Shenk, D., & Fullmer, E. (1996). Significant relationships women: Cultural and personal constructions of lesbianism. *Journal of Women and Aging, 8*(3/4), 75–89.

Tornstam, L. (1996). Gerotranscendence: A theory about maturing into old age. *Journal of Aging and Identity, 1*(1), 37–50.

White, C.B., & Catania, J.A. (1982). Psychoeducational intervention for sexuality with aged, family members of the aged and people who work with the aged. *International Journal of Aging and Human Development, 15*(2), 121–138.

CHAPTER 5

Developmental Issues in Psychotherapy with Older Men

MARGARET HELLIE HUYCK AND DAVID L. GUTMANN

THE MALE SEASONS OF EROS

A vast literature documents the eros of men—the ways in which men strive for intense sensual gratification, or turn against their appetites and dangerous excitements. There is substantial documentation about erotic development during the first half of life, and the special challenges posed by the need to regulate and direct strong desires into forms that are personally and socially acceptable. Many young men equate sexual desire with masculinity; feeling desire helps them feel masculine, and having their sexuality appreciated and fulfilled affirms a sense of masculinity. Therapists are used to dealing with younger men's sexual needs and their attendant conflicts. Our challenge is to understand the eros of older men well enough to recognize the signposts of sexual health and pathology in later life. Research and practice suggests that older men shift their erotic gears toward sexual appetites which rely less on hormonal surges, and more on the receptive pleasures of the mouth, the skin, the eyes, and secure, nurturing relationships (Gutmann, 1987/1994). Thus, more diffuse modes of erotic pleasure gradually replace the organ- and object-focused genital mode of the earlier years.

Thus, Gutmann (1999) asserts that, when we think of men generically and genetically, as members of the human species rather than as adherents of a particular culture or as members of a particular community, we can observe that the life cycle of the human male has four major divisions. He starts life, in the psychological as well as the physical sense as the child of his mother, and if things go as they should, he soon graduates to the status of "father's son." From there,

The "Parkville" research was funded by a grant from the National Institute of Mental Health Center on Aging, 1982–1986, M.H. Huyck, Principal Investigator.

he ascends to his own paternity as the father of sons and daughters. And finally, toward the end of life, he relapses back to the psychological status that predominated at the beginning of life—he becomes once again a "mother's son."

Early Development

The little boy who has been weaned in the physical sense but who remains bonded to the mother in the psychological sense directs all his erotic longings toward her and toward the parts of his own body that the mother tends and appreciates. The boy is needy for both physical and emotional nutriment during this time, and both seem to have their major source in the mother. Erotic gratification is diffuse, with intense pleasures gained from pleasures passively received: being fed, being caressed, gazing at the beloved mother, and being gazed at by her. Envy is directed at the other siblings, of either sex, particularly those who appear to be the mother's favorites. To the degree that the father receives evident donations of the mother's love, he too is envied—first, as a kind of larger sibling, the one who shares the mother's bed. Later, as the rivalry takes a more specifically sexual and oedipal form, the father will be resented, on narcissistic grounds, as a *successful* rival, and envied for the powers that gained him the victory. The stage of oedipal envy phases out when the boy, realizing that he cannot co-opt the father's powers by defeating him in open competition, decides to join him through identification and emulation. Accepting that he cannot steal the father's powers, the son accepts the principle of delay, becomes the father's apprentice, and begins, through protracted learning, to inherit the father's coveted powers. Now, as the father's son, he enters the latency period.

Adolescence and Young Adulthood

The son's dangerous oedipal dilemma is solved through a shift in allegiances. The son gives up the dangerous, envy-ridden status of mother's son and achieves a partial separation from her in the new, less dangerous, and "politically" advantaged status of father's son. The boy's rebirth as father's son, or as son of the collective father, is celebrated in many cultures with "rites de passage." The ritualized ordeal has always involved a test of the young candidate for manhood—a trial that is laid on by the communal fathers, who observe the youth closely for signs of weakness. If he cries, he still needs his mother and is not ready to learn the ways of men.[1]

   Bruno Bettelheim (1954) has documented the ways in which the ritual serves also to cool the boy's residual envy of women and their strange powers. As he

---

[1] Whiting and Child (1953) found that the severity of the ordeal varied, across cultures, with the length of the breast-feeding period. The ritual clearly marks a passage away from the mother, and since late weaning generates a strong maternal bond, a stringent ordeal is required to break it.

pointed out, the rites of passage allow the son to surrender his rivalrous envy with the powerful mother. During the time of young manhood and adulthood, his envy as well as his regard will be centered on his male peers, particularly those who surpass him in the manly pursuits earning praise and advancement from the fathers (see also Kimmel, 1996).

Men separate decisively from their mothers, bond to their fathers, and attempt the first tests of manhood at about the time when their bodies make the transition from the prepubertal to the pubertal condition. At that point in their bodies' history, when their physiology moves toward procreation, their psyche prepares for manhood and parenthood. Most men give up sexual bimodality, concede feminine qualities to the mate, and establish an unambiguous masculinity. Although the cultural definitions of what constitutes appropriate or desirable masculinity vary somewhat across cultures and historical periods (Kimmel, 1996), one of the core standards is that adult men should not rely too much on women, except for sexual pleasure. "Manly men" are expected to appreciate the special qualities of women—but not to emulate them or to yield to their control. The anxiety felt by many men when confronted by an angry, or even challenging, wife shows up in laboratory studies of marital interactions as physical symptoms such as increased blood pressure and various defensive strategies (Gottman, 1994). Gutmann (1987/1994) has argued, since 1974, that stereotypic masculinity arises and makes most sense in terms of the standard demands on men, as fathers, to provide physical security for their families and for the larger community. The male investment in the ways of the fathers, in the paternal orientation and to the suppression of feminine qualities begins with the onset of procreativity and phases out as the emergency period of active parenthood comes to a close.

MIDDLE AND LATER MANHOOD

As children mature, as the sense of parental emergency ebbs, men recover the feminine aspects of self as well as the maternal identifications that had been put on hold, lived out vicariously through the wife during the period of active paternity. In effect, the male engagement in unalloyed masculinity lasts about as long as the female window of fertility; as that window closes, men take over or reclaim the feminine qualities that the women begin to relinquish. In any event, in this postparental transformation, men return to the status of mother's son that they abandoned during their preparental and actively paternal years. Following this restoration of the status quo ante, maternal persons, both real and fantasied, again loom large in the mental life of the older man.

Across cultures, older men become preoccupied with women as powerful rather than seductive. They become aware, perhaps dimly, of their own disinterest in combat, their desire for peace and harmony, even their yearning to yield to a more powerful, nurturing other. They discover in women the aggressive strength that is diminishing in themselves. To some extent, their discovery may be rooted in reality: by midlife, many women do become more self-confident and assertive, more willing to disturb the status quo to push for their own agenda, and even angry or hostile toward men they feel have "held them down." On the other hand, many men perceive harmful female aggression when it does not really exist—when women are being self-assertive, rather than determinedly destructive. In actuality, the women are asserting themselves, without rancor, to redress imbalances of power sustained during the child-rearing period. Jung first described the basic pattern on the basis of clinical evidence (1933). Gutmann cited the evidence in cross-cultural texts (1987/1994), and from careful clinical studies of men and women suffering with late-onset psychiatric disorders (Gutmann, Grunes, & Griffin, 1982; Gutmann, 1999).

We have drawn on an intensive community study of approximately 150 geographically and maritally stable families—midlife couples and their young adult children, to describe gender styles (Huyck, 1994, 1996, 1999), marriage relationships (Huyck & Gutmann, 1992), and psychological functioning (Gutmann & Huyck, 1994; Huyck, 1991a, 1991b). These "Parkville" families do not reflect the full diversity of men and women in middle and later life, but what we have learned about normal development in Parkville is consistent with themes that emerge from the cross-cultural and clinical evidence. Because the extensive data from the Parkville respondents encompass self-report measures, lengthy interviews, and projective tests, we will draw on it for illustrations in our discussion of masculine developmental issues.

Although our emphasis here is on the patterns of change observed across time and across cultures, sociohistorical changes also affect the manner in which any underlying psychological patterns of change find expression. For example, the developmental changes in women, toward greater autonomy and more self-assertion, normally triggered by the phasing out of the parental emergency, have been augmented both by the recent social push for women to become more assertive in all realms, and by greater opportunities to do so. As one midlife Parkville woman said, when explaining why she now came back with a sharp retort when her husband was irritable with her, "Well, now the kids are finally out of the house and I don't have to keep it peaceful any more for them. Once the kids left, I got a little job, and learned that my opinions are valued. And I've been listening to the women's movement all these years and have decided they have a point—I should be more assertive" (Huyck & Gutmann, 1992).

Men feel the change in their wives—and their response is shaped by the meaning that it has for them. In the Parkville study, many of the men were having trouble with the changes in their wives.

Interdependent Men
A distinct minority of the men described their wives as increasingly autonomous and self-directing, and themselves as having accepted these changes as beneficial for them both. They also recalled being troubled when the changes first emerged, and struggling to recognize that greater equality of power and influence was fair and reasonable—and that no harm would come to them with the shift. They described their current marital relationship as egalitarian, with each partner reliant on the other. In their childhood memories of the parents, both

mother and father were described as strong, though in their own distinctive ways, and caring. A strong woman could, thus, also be a caring partner; she was not stealing the husband's masculinity by becoming self-directive. These men are more likely to retain their own independent involvement in either paid work or serious hobbies, not to escape closer links with the wife but because these activities represent compelling interests in their own right. Although these men sensed their wives midlife turn toward greater self-confidence and assertiveness, they were able to accommodate to the changes with minimal difficulty, and even to feel pride in the spouse's energy and accomplishments.

Syntonic-Dependent Men

Some middle-aged men seem to persist in, or revise, the stance of the wife's dependent son. Most are frank about their dependence: "She's always made most of the decisions; I'd be helpless without her." Gutmann and his colleagues have described such men as showing syntonic dependency (Gutmann, Grunes, & Griffin, 1982). Both in clinical accounts and in the Parkville studies, syntonic-dependent men describe a childhood where they experienced a blissful union with an indulgent mother and a remote or absent father. They never accomplished the usual transition of the young man, from being the mother's child in the home to being the father's child in some version of the outer world. As they see it, ultimate resource is not to be found in themselves, but belongs to the strong maternal persons on whom they continue to rely. Pushed by their desire to replicate the past relationship with a cherished mother, they usually select nurturing young women as mates. Nevertheless, during the period of parental emergency, they take pleasure in shared parenting and are willing to serve as the primary breadwinner. However, once the children are launched, they feel entitled to receive the extra measures of attention formerly directed at the young. The fate of such men in later life depends heavily on how their wives develop.

Some wives continue to accept syntonic-dependent men as cherished, if needy, loved ones; they operate as strong matriarchs in the family system. Their husbands typically express great satisfaction with the marriage; only themes in TAT stories and anxiety indicators on the psychosomatic distress measure suggest their underlying concerns with possible abandonment.

Dystonic-Dependent Men

Some men become hypersensitive to any hint that their wives are becoming less docile and dependent—on the assumption it means a return to being a fearful, compliant son of a domineering mother. The fear reflects, in part, the recognition of their own passivity and disinclination to engage in combat. Because of their developmental history, however, they distrust anything they regard as male passivity, fearing they will be emasculated by any woman who asserts her right to direct any part of his life. In their impressionable, formative years, these men had suffered weak and/or psychologically absent fathers and powerful, sometimes destructively aggressive mothers. They denied their own sense of oedipal complicity in the father's weakness or absence by blaming the overpowering mother. She (and not themselves) had gutted the father; *she* had driven him from the home.

In reaction, swearing that they would never suffer their father's shameful fate, these men typically married kindly, biddable, even adoring women—the perceived opposites of their intimidating mothers. Often they preserved their tenuous sense of masculinity by taking risks and demonstrating they were not like their cowardly fathers. In later years they, quite normally, mellow out, and no longer seek to be at the forefront of the battle. In addition, their wives have usually matured and become less docile and accommodating. Men who have serious problems with admitting anything soft or passive in themselves, for whom dependency is very toxic, may respond with shock.

The majority of midlife and older men are married. Married men are generally advantaged in health and longevity, although well-being may be threatened by marital discord. Discord is more likely to arise in the middle, child-launching years than in the later years (Huyck, 1996). Increasingly, women initiate a reconsideration of the relationship, either by changing themselves and implicitly requiring changes in their partners, or by directly negotiating changes in the relationship. To gain a better understanding of how midlife wives experience their husbands, it is useful to look more closely at the Parkville women. The focus of this chapter is not primarily on helping older women improve their marital relationships, but that the perspectives of wives are crucial in helping men.

WIVES' EXPERIENCES OF THEIR HUSBANDS

Our self-report measure of Marital Satisfaction entailed asking each woman to indicate how she felt about her marriage as a whole. The scale consists of six positive adjectives (loved, relaxed, stimulated, contented, grateful, confident) and six negative adjectives (bored, tense, frustrated, bothered or upset, neglected, unhappy). This is a measure of what a woman is willing to admit to others, and herself, about a relationship of long duration. Not surprisingly, most of the scores were positive. A more complex story emerged when we looked at the open-ended interview data. Usually responses to the first few questions about the marriage were quite rosy, reflecting on the early times of attraction and the ways in which the marital relationship was valuable to them. But by the second page of the protocol, the more covert doubts and yearnings emerged. The rosy and the difficult pictures of the marriage, and of the self in the marriage are both accurate, but we need to look at the complex reality that they depict.

On the basis of the interview data, we rated each woman's perception of control in the relationship; this measure we called the "Marital Politics" index (Huyck & Gutmann, 1992). Five styles of perceived control were identified: husband dominant; wife yielding but acknowledging covert resentment; wife asserting herself but ambivalent about it; wife unambivalently asserting herself in restructuring the marriage; and unchallenged matriarchy. In addition, the ways in which the wife described the marriage relationship were rated, as Marital Style. Five styles were identified: authoritative husband, nurturing husband, dyadic unity, vulnerable husband, and disappointed wife.

MORE SATISFIED WIVES

Some of the women who were most happy with their marriages said they deferred to their husband, giving priority to his wishes even when these were unstated. As one remarked, "My mother always used to say, 'If your husband wants to do something, you should grab your hat and go' and she was right. Many things I've come to do because he does. . . . Though he doesn't try to make me into what he wants. I do it because I want to." Some women remain deeply grateful to their husband for rescuing them from a bad fate. As one woman said, "I was always physically attracted to him. He always was and has been very gentle with me. This was extremely important to me because my parents had a very stormy violent marriage." The most satisfied women emphasize a sense of unity in the relationship. Many feel nurtured by their husband. Other women who felt especially good about their marriages said that they were in charge; they described themselves as matriarchs, using their strength to nurture in what they regarded as a caring and responsible way. Husbands were pictured in terms very similar to those used to describe their adult children.

A common and impressive theme in the marital accounts of the more satisfied women is their comfort with one partner being the "leader." The leader can be either the husband or the wife, but both partners are at ease with the arrangement: they do not struggle for control. (This finding contradicts much current exhortation about the desirability of egalitarian marriages.) The 22% of the wives who are granting authority to their husbands are likely to be younger (under 54 in this sample), still have children living at home, and the husbands are more likely to be managers or professionals. They are living the "traditional" marriage, and many of the women feel very benefited by this "patriarchal" arrangement. The matriarchical option, representing 11% of the sample, features older women who seem to have moved into matriarchy as the husband became ill.

DISAPPOINTED WIVES

Given the high scores for this sample on the Marital Satisfaction Scale, we were surprised to find that 42% of the women expressed significant disappointment in the relationship. Not surprisingly, these same women scored lower than average on the marriage satisfaction scale.

Why were they disappointed? No single cause. Disappointment implies that expectations, dreams, hopes, fantasies have been dashed or eroded by reality. One is not finally disappointed until one begins to realize that the dream can never come true. Sometimes the disappointment sets in early.

In a study of good marriages, Wallerstein (Wallerstein & Blakeslee, 1995) describes "rescue marriages" that serve as a haven from a troubled past. Wallerstein included only couples who agreed that the marriage was good, so in her case it is possible to build from the experience of being rescued to a durable, sustaining marital bond. While the Parkville sample also included some rescue marriages, we found that too often the rescue drama turns sour: the marriage turns into a repetition, for the wife, of the bad situation that she had escaped from, in the family of orientation. Thus, the rescued wife comes to realize that the man she married is much more like her rejecting or abusive father than she had been willing to recognize. Some masochistic women—those who desire punishment as well as rescue, automatically discredit their husband's favors, and turn him into their "bad father." But for the most part, even when the marriage went sour, the Parkville women did not choose divorce; as they said repeatedly, a combination of religious conviction, concern about the impact on their children, a belief that things could be worked out, and fear of the alternatives kept them in the marriage.

Other disappointments have a more developmental basis. Thus far, the Parkville couples have all stuck it out and are in the process of helping their children move into adulthood. They have the possibility of renegotiating their lives—how they spend time, money, attention. Most of the women and men talk about some visions for this phase of their lives, which includes some holiday period before they have to deal with serious illness. Actually though, about 40% of the husbands do have moderate to serious health problems; three women became widowed in the course of the study (and are not included in this particular report). Having to face health problems was one disappointment for women.

Many women have visions of self-expansion for this phase—after years of tending to the needs of children, they want to leave home and visit Ireland, or learn to play golf, or visit relatives in Tennessee. They want someone else to prepare dinner and clean up. Some want to enjoy sex with no one else in the house and no worries about pregnancy. They want to feel more like a partner, able to disagree without frightening the children. They want to have an ally in dealing with the complex problems presented by their adult children, frail parents, and extended families.

Next to illness, the strongest theme among the disappointed women is the passivity and vulnerability of their husbands. They speak often of husbands who won't leave home to explore the wider world, of husbands who retreat from golf when the wife begins to play, of husbands who become sullen or peevish if the same dinner is not on the table at the same time, of fathers who refuse to set limits on a slovenly grown son cluttering up the house. The disappointed women do not always express their resentments openly; about one-third say they do not share such feelings with their husband, about one-third complain at least some of the time but are either guilty or uncertain about the consequences, and another one-third are openly assertive about changing the relationship and criticizing behaviors they do not like.

When women begin to complain more openly, many men retreat, or alternately attack and retreat. Once these older men experience some impotence, related either to medication side effects, alcohol, or anger, many avoid further sexual encounters.

The disappointed wives feel frustrated in their hopes for this postparental period, which was expected to be a golden age of marriage. Disappointed wives had lower self-esteem and somewhat more evidence of depression, anxiety, and anger. Though chronic disappointment is difficult to take, the Parkville women describe strategies to make things better, to get closer to the kind of love they want at this stage in life. What can we learn from them?

Some women *reframe.* Thus, one subject described how important sexuality had become to her, and how disappointed she is that her husband's medication for hypertension affects his sexual response. She went on to explain that she had come to realize that the sexual relationship had simply shifted into another, "natural" phase where emotional contentment was more salient than sexual arousal and release.

Another characteristic of these women was *willingness to risk change.* For some women, sex was the arena. One said, "Sex is very important. I've gotten more adventuresome—I've left some of my Catholic girl background behind. The children are gone." For others, it was assuming more financial responsibility: "My husband wants to start his own business, so I'm trying to make a lot of money to provide that financial security."

Many women talked about *rebalancing self and other priorities.* As one said, "I try to do what he likes and yet not shy away from doing things I enjoy. He likes it when I take the initiative." Another worked out a specific compromise: "He bought a boat and I hate it, so the kids go with him. I love the time to read. We also like and dislike a lot of the same things." A more difficult issue is *resisting changes that are personally uncomfortable,* as in the case of the woman who reported, "He'd like me to be more motherly to him but I refuse. . . . His mother took care of him and he is unaware of so much that gets done in a home. I've told him, 'I'm your partner, not your mother.' Part of the attraction is that I'm a challenge to him but sometimes he'd like to be taken care of. . . . In the past, the biggest stress was this theme: He thought I gave too much attention to the children and not to him. I would say to him, 'They need me more now. You are grown up and it will pass.' What really resolved it is that the kids grew up."

Some women *vent their frustrations.* As one said, "When you're older, one minute you're sharp-tongued, the next minute you're on speaking terms. It's part of marriage; no big deal anymore. When you're younger it takes longer. Now you accept that you have to blow off."

Some *become resigned to nonchange.* While some women accept this reality, others recognize it but remain irritated. As one said, "I wish he'd be more interested in the house. He'd never notice if the place would fall down. We talk about it all the time but I have adjusted to it. It was really hard, but I accepted the fact that he was never going to do these things—took me about 15 years. I'd badger him about it and he'd just laugh at me."

And, finally—some more easily than others—some women *turn to others* for some version of understanding, affirmation, and love. None of the women in the Parkville research talked about sexual affairs during this phase (and infidelity was not explicitly inquired about). However, many find companionship, affirmation, and pleasure in the company of other women. Often the sought-out women are biological sisters, which seems to alleviate any guilt they sustain about moving outside the nuclear family circle for intimacy. Women also sought comfort in church circles. Some of the most disappointed women were what we came to call "widows in waiting"—they have given up on reconstructing the marriage, have mourned the lost relationship that will never be, and are building the networks of support to nurture them through the next phase. They may still be providing medical or household care for their husbands, but their heart is not in it.

Overall, disappointed wives are less psychologically invested in the marriage, as assessed in a self-report scale asking to what extent they thought about the marriage, arranged their schedule to spend more time with their partner, and so on. Perhaps because they were psychologically distancing from the relationship, they were also less invested in their husband's health (which certainly might impact his well-being, even survival), and somewhat more concerned about their own health. They were more invested in leisure, but less satisfied with their leisure activities than were the women who felt better about their marriages.

The Parkville women can help us understand some of the complexities of marital love in the later years. However, these women are still relatively young, and we need equivalent accounts from older cohorts. Our sense is that the Parkville women (and men) are telling us about the transition from a focus on parenting to another set of options. We hear many women struggling to make the apparent reality come closer to their vision of how this phase should refresh their lives. Data from those couples who are further along in this process suggest that some manage to renegotiate the relationship, most settle for companionship around a shared past, and some remain disappointed and increasingly eager for release. These are the patterns for today's postparental women; whether they will continue to shape the lives of tomorrow's senior class is an empirical question.

The Parkville women (like many others) can be extremely creative and persistent in trying different strategies to either modify a partner's behavior, alter their own perceptions and values, or change their own behavior. Women are more likely to come to therapists for help. Therapists need to recognize "his" and "her" marriage, while trying to detoxify any adverse side effects of later life developmental change. If they succeed, older men and women can indeed reclaim the powers suppressed earlier in the service of parenting.

THERAPEUTIC STRATEGIES

Broadly speaking, two kinds of men, the *dystonic-dependent* and the *syntonic-dependent* are put at risk by their own catastrophic reactions to the psychological contents released—in themselves and/or in their wives—by the developments of the postparental era. In both groups, men react to a potential expansion of self in themselves and in the spouse as though it were a profound threat—a diminishment.

The first at-risk type consists of men who are shocked by the emergence of their own strenuously denied sexual bimodality—their "feminine" side—and by the emergence of a hitherto closeted aggressive, unsentimental, and "masculine" side of the wife. These tend to be men who experienced their own mothers as destructive, particularly toward men: castrating toward their husbands, and potentially dangerous even toward their sons. In reaction, they tend to marry hyperfeminine women, nurturing and biddable, who do not fit the latent destructive mother transference. As long as the wife remains in this nonthreatening "Stepford" mode, these men are stabilized, able to tolerate the intimacy with a woman; but when the postparental wife comes out of the closet in a more self-asserting mode, the aggression that she now shares with the husband's internalized mother creates a subjective link, an *identity* between them, such that the wife now fits the husband's maternal transference. The archaic image of the destructive mother is in effect mapped onto the newly assertive wife, who then becomes unduly threatening to her newly feminized—hence newly vulnerable—husband. In his own eyes, the wife is transforming into the castrating mother, while he himself becomes the castrated father.

If they have the financial resources to cover divorce expenses, these men are apt to trade in the old, newly formidable wife, for a younger model who can be a still-dependent, still adoring "Daddy's girl." Through such trophy wives, they can restore the subjective status quo ante while staving off psychiatric symptoms. Men who possess these same lethal predispositions, but who lack the divorce option, are at risk to develop significant psychopathology, even including psychosis.

Despite blatant pathology, however, these complex, usually vital men can be successfully treated by intensive psychotherapy—though the nature of the treatment will vary depending on the sex of the therapist. By and large, male therapists will do well to position themselves in the transference as the "male ally" of these bedeviled men, thereby helping them deal with the shame of their feminization. Reminiscence is particularly useful with these clients, as they have usually—in their search for proofs of manhood—generated a dramatic history. Witnessing this narrative, and sponsoring its articulation, the therapist confirms the client's legend by dealing with him as though he is, now in the present, a worthy inheritor of his own history. Thus, the effective male ally is not only supportive in the warm and fuzzy sense; he supports the client's masculine identity by roughhousing with him, by confronting him, and by treating him as a worthy contender. Through the therapist, the client recontacts the legend that had been lost—or that had become persecutory—and makes it part of his present self-awareness.

Coming to trust the therapist as a reliable holder of his masculinity, the client can begin to explore the contramasculine aspects of self that later life development is pushing to the fore and that drive his symptoms. Often, these make their first appearance in the form of a homosexual transference toward the male therapist—a development that should be handled with the same combination of bluntness and sensitivity that the client has come to expect. When the homoerotic manifestation is properly interpreted, as an active, phallicized defense against what are ultimately very passive, oral wishes, the client can begin to explore, accept, and finally use—even appreciate— the contrasexual, sentient aspects of self. As the client comes to terms with his own *anima,* he incidentally accepts the *animus*—the masculine aspects of his wife. Once freed from the sense that he has become his own weak father, and freed from the sense that his wife is responsible for his castration, the interrupted development, toward the normal changes of later life, can then go forward—not only in the husband, but in both partners.

Where the male therapist helps these clients confront their own frightening inner life and their own emasculated father, the female therapist helps them deal with the frightening mother, now reappearing in the wife. The female therapist is likely—much like the wife—to take on the visage of the castrating mother (though at the outset, this transference will probably be masked by erotic fantasies, designed to blunt the therapist's fantasized powers). Working within the malign transference, the female therapist can demonstrate to her threatened client that a strong woman does not steal her strength, vampirelike, from a vulnerable man, and that her powers can be used in the service of healing rather than destruction. The therapist detaches herself, in the client's eyes, from the castrating mother transference, and in so doing lays the groundwork for undemonizing the client's wife. Though she has become a strong woman, the wife is no longer confounded, via the transference, with the client's "Witch-Mother." Again, normal post-parental development can go forward; and the wife can continue, without risking the marriage, to reclaim her powers.

Unlike the dystonic-dependent men, the syntonic-dependent men are not particularly threatened by postparental changes in themselves toward greater oral dependency; but they are hypersensitive to even minimal changes toward a tougher, less nurturing stance in their wives. In the quantitative sense, the actual changes may be minimal in the eyes of an outside observer, but may be very distressing to the vulnerable husband. The wife's announcement that she was going out with her sister one evening a week and that he could prepare his own dinner, or that she and a cousin were going to Italy—by themselves, if he refused to come—can be enough to trigger pathogenic trauma in these needy men. In addition, some newly liberated wives convey contempt for their husband's aggravated dependency, thereby rousing latent, potentially pathogenic feelings of shame.[2] Wives who are dismayed by their husband's desires for merger may try to protect themselves by pushing him to be more autonomous: they train him, usually unsuccessfully, in the household arts.

In the face of such disappointment and shame, some men shift to psychosomatic illness to justify receiving the care they crave. In other cases, men may

---

[2] Long-term studies of marriage (Gottman, 1994) indicate that spousal contempt is one of the most stressful and damaging sentiments in a relationship.

use their psychosomatic disorders to signal their wives that tender concern is now both welcome and justified: "If you don't want to take care of me, at least take care of my needy heart, liver, stomach . . ." They no longer need feel shame, because it is now their *soma* which requires care, and they are not responsible for the ills of their flesh. If this somatic message does not provoke TLC, significant depression can result.

The conflicts of these men are not intrapsychic, but external, with ungiving providers; accordingly, they are not promising candidates for insight-oriented psychotherapy. Given their reliance on psychosomatic resolutions, they tend to be referred by internists who see them as "crocks," or who recognize that covert psychological needs are driving the patient's intractable physical symptoms. They may also come in for outpatient aftercare, following hospitalization for a depressive episode. These long-term patients tend to develop passive-aggressive transferences where again, as with their wives, they put forward their physical symptoms instead of their emotions and then complain that their *soma* is not being properly cared for. These patients have to get worse, in the symptomatic sense, before they can get better. The therapist has to suggest, by an accepting, concerned manner, that the patient will not be shamed or rebuffed if he dispenses with the somatic defense, and brings his depressed, hungry feelings into the treatment. Meeting his feelings head on, the patient also encounters his underlying depression, but this is the price paid for eventual ego control over his inner life. Once aware of his volatile feelings, and made aware through the therapy of their source, the patient can begin to modulate them and take distance from them. In the case of his wife, for example, he can begin to recognize that his catastrophic reaction to her toughening is that of a helpless, abandoned child; they do not fit his condition as a seasoned adult, and they do not fit his wife, who can expand herself without shrinking or deserting him. She has not been driven away by the fear that he will suck her dry; nor will she return to nurse his body's pain.

The pathogenic experience of later life is that of being left alone with the "bad object": the castrating, engulfing, or abandoning mother, the weak father, the helpless, needy, draining baby. Later life psychotherapy can provide the patient with a strong ally, in the person of the therapist, against the bad objects, and with the adult tools to recognize them for what they are: the fevered creations of the inner eye. In this way, the child's bitter legacy to the adult is detoxified, and no longer blocks future development.

REFERENCES

Bettelheim, B. (1954). *Symbolic wounds*. Glencoe, IL: Free Press.

Gottman, J. with N. Silver. (1994). *Why marriages succeed or fail*. New York: Simon & Schuster.

Gutmann, D.L. (1994). *Reclaimed powers: Toward a new psychology of men and women in later life* (Rev. ed.). Evanston, IL: Northwestern University Press.

Gutmann, D.L. (1998). Male envy across the life-span (pp. 269–278). In Nancy Burke (Ed.), *Gender & Envy.* New York: Routledge.

Gutmann, D.L., Grunes, J., & Griffin, B. (1982). Developmental contributions to the late-onset disorders. In P. Baltes & O. Brim (Eds.), *Life-span development and behavior* (Vol. 4, pp. 244–263). New York: Academic Press.

Gutmann, D.L., & Huyck, M.H. (1994). Development and pathology in postparental men: A community study. In E. Thompson, Jr. (Ed.), *Older men's lives* (pp. 65–84). Thousand Oaks, CA: Sage.

Huyck, M.H. (1991a). Gender-linked self-attributions and mental health during the middle years. *Journal of Aging Studies, 5*(1), 111–123.

Huyck, M.H. (1991b). Predicates of personal control among midlife and older men and women in middle America. *International Journal of Aging & Human Development, 32*(4), 261–275.

Huyck, M.H. (1994). The relevance of psychodynamic theories for understanding gender among older women. In B. Turner & L. Troll (Eds.), *Women growing older: Theoretical directions in the psychology of aging* (pp. 202–238). Newbury Park, CA: Sage.

Huyck, M.H. (1995). Marriage and marital-like relationships. In R. Blieszner & V. Bedford (Eds.), *Handbook on aging and the family.* Westport, CT: Greenwood Press. (Reissued in paperback edition, 1996)

Huyck, M.H. (1996). Continuities and discontinuities in gender roles and gender identity. In V. Bengtson (Ed.), *Continuities and discontinuities in the adult life course and aging: Contributions in honor of Bernice Neugarten.* New York: Springer.

Huyck, M.H. (1999). Gender roles and gender identity in midlife. In S.L. Willis & J.D. Reid (Eds.), *Life in the middle* (pp. 209–233). New York: Academic Press.

Huyck, M.H., & Gutmann, D.L. (1992). Thirtysomething years of marriage: Understanding husbands and wives in enduring relationships. *Family Perspective, 26*(2), 249–265.

Jung, C. (1933). *Modern man in search of a soul.* New York: Harcourt, Brace.

Kimmel, M. (1996). *Manhood in America: A cultural history.* New York: Free Press.

Wallerstein, J., & Blakeslee, S. (1995). *The good marriage: How and why love lasts.* New York: Houghton Mifflin.

Whiting, J., & Child, I. (1953). *Child training and personality: A cross-cultural study.* New Haven, CT: Yale University Press.

CHAPTER 6

Existential Issues of Hope and Meaning in Late Life Therapy

CLAIRE M. BRODY

There are all kinds of hazards and changes associated with old age, but the one I think may be the worst of all is hardly noticed. It is what happens when an old person is confronted with a simulacrum of a youthful self, a mocking shadow, an echo of lost possibilities—and loses all moral independence.

—Doris Lessing
Walking in the Shade: 1949 to 1962

RELEVANT EXISTENTIAL CONCEPTS FOR TREATMENT STRATEGIES

One of the prevailing stereotypes that needs to be confronted is that "older adult" is always equated with dependence and needing to be protected, Older people are one of the last groups with whom the concept of empowerment has become associated (Meyers, 1995). Yet most older adults are like everyone else: capable of self-determination and autonomy. Having choices and maintaining control over decisions lends importance and meaning to these later years.

Also relevant is that psychotherapists traditionally regarded clients as objects, to be understood but also manipulated and changed. From an existential, humanistic point of view, the client is seen as the "primary subject in the therapeutic encounter" (Bugental & Sterling, 1995, p. 230), with the therapist as helper/consultant/companion in the effort to make the client's life less stressed. Chemical or behavioral interventions have been routinely used but these do not acknowledge the potential in each person for redirecting the pain to achieve relief.

Victor Frankl (1988) said that life holds a meaning for everyone; even the tragic and negative aspects of life can be turned into an achievement by the attitude one is helped to adopt toward the predicament. What truly matters in therapy is the personal encounter between therapist and client. It is the responsibility of the therapist to help the client cope with the "existential vacuum" to show that life really does have meaning. The lack of meaning in the client's life may be manifested as boredom or apathy—an existential frustration—but this can be the challenge, and engaging the client to find meaning becomes the task.

Alice is a woman who was helped to take some charge of her life by redirecting her activities.

CASE EXAMPLE

At 86, she suffers from moderately severe arthritis and a lifelong personality disorder. She had recently been placed in the long-term residence by her daughter. She was unpredictably agreeable or hostile with staff and toward the therapist, as well. This served to distract from her basic neediness and panic at the loss of control over her life. The therapist tried to both focus the past and look toward future activities which might lighten Alice's life in the new setting. At the same time, the therapist stated directly that she would not be put off by hostile encounters, but would stay to help the client maintain control. Alice responded to positive reinforcements. Once she learned to acknowledge that arthritis pain made her cranky, she made the choice to participate in exercise therapy with a recreational aide. Over a period of six months, Alice's behavior became more predictable, which made her life at the home less stressful.

Another existential concept to be considered in treatment is how people "re-experience the psycho-social tensions of a lifetime" (Erikson, Erikson, & Kivnick, 1986). When one has confidence in one's own willful self-determination and independence, then one can achieve autonomy and a feeling of being able to balance these tensions. Rollo May first described an existential approach to conceptualizing life's anxieties and problems (May, Angel, & Ellenberger, 1958), and noted psychotherapists' tendency to become preoccupied with technique when they were anxious or had doubts about what they were doing. If the therapist accepts the existential view of humans as always in a state of "becoming," of being in a state of crisis without despairing, then a therapist can work with any cohort, including the elderly in a participatory, helpful way. May refuted the therapist manifesto that "the less we are involved in a given situation the more clearly we can describe the truth." At the same time, he advocated clarifying what one's particular emotions and involvement in a given situation are, to avoid disruption of the therapeutic process. In working with older adults, it is certainly essential, he says, to get a "feeling" of, and to become "involved" with the client. If we resent the relationship or are hostile, then we "keep the other person out" and would thereby be unable to help that person realize his or her potential for being or becoming what he or she truly is.

In the therapeutic situation, it becomes imperative that the therapist stay involved. For example, anxiety can strike at the core of a client's self-esteem and sense of value. Severe anxiety can be a state of, and way of relating to one-self and others, destroying "being." Anxiety always involves inner conflict and often occurs at a point where a sense of potentiality and the possibility of ful-filling one's existence is emerging. When one denies these potentialities, the state that results can be interpreted as 'locking up" the possibility of experi-ence or being.

CASE EXAMPLE

Michael is a 75-year-old man who had a responsible job in an academic setting until re-cently. He suffers from seizures due to an old head injury, and although he has been hos-pitalized many times after grand mal episodes, he continues to deny that he has them at all. He refuses to acknowledge that his placement in a long-term care setting is appropri-ate and may be permanent. While the seizures are controlled with medication, they still recur occasionally and without warning. He prefers to claim he is being seen by the ther-apist because he is "crazy." Actually, he was referred because of problems he was having with staff: he would not bathe, and filled his clothing drawers with old newspapers that he wouldn't allow to be thrown away. In the first few therapy sessions, although he obviously enjoyed the opportunity to talk about current events or something he read in the paper, he assiduously avoided any allusion to his personal life. He also would find some reason to become enraged at the therapist just before tile time was up and would angrily ask her to leave immediately. The therapist remained "involved," noting that Michael's anxiety was palpable; his self-esteem and sense of "being" had been shattered in the course of losing his independence and autonomy. He was truly engaged in "locking up" the possibility of continuing to fulfill his existence. Over many months of talking with the therapist, prog-ress was made in that he had less need to resist the staff and less fear of losing total con-trol over his future. He was also more consistently cordial to the therapist. Michael's capacity to be more trustful was manifested when he allowed himself to become engaged in reminiscing.

One of the techniques that seemed to inspire Michael to let go of his anxiety, get closer to "being," was for the therapist to self-disclose. Michael, who had worked in an academic setting, was curious about the therapist in her teaching role. For example, the therapist would tell him about conferences she attended in another part of the country, about travel experiences and Michael, in turn, might recall having been there and then cautiously add some data about a fam-ily member. Thus, a modicum of trust was initiated, and the therapy proceeded.

For me, the existential explanation of behavior observed in many residents of long term care facilities makes the most sense. In May's early collaborative book, *Existence* (May et al., 1958), he summarizes Harry Stack Sullivan's and Frieda Fromm Reichmann's description of the mental state of the person who has lost his world. May discusses the problems of isolation and alienation where the "re-lation to the world has become broken." The person often exhibits schizoid be-havior like being detached, unrelated, lacking in affect.

CASE EXAMPLE

Martha, an 89-year-old former graphic artist is still capable of creative expression. However, she has gradually withdrawn into a morose state of introspection, complicated by beginning dementia She responds to questions, if at all, with either one-word answers or by saying, "I can't . . . I can't talk to you today. Go away." She rarely smiles. She also has become increasingly focused on details of her existence, asking the therapist to move her clock or her pocketbook a few inches. She worries about whether something she can't find has been stolen. After months of weekly visits she does not allow herself to become verbally engaged.

A key element of this detached, depressed, and anxious behavior is a distorted attitude toward the future. May (1958) says that severe anxiety or depression "blots out the sense of time; annihilates the future." It is this inability to "have" a future that leads to anxiety and depression, according to May. He says, "A man can understand himself only if he can project himself forward" (into the future). Thus, the anxiety-creating issues of the present cannot be avoided by the "determinism of the past" (pp. 68–69). With Martha, the therapist was accepting of her obsessive behavior, and very patient in expecting change. If she said, "I can't talk to you today . . . go away," the therapist said, "Oh, let's spend a little time together anyway . . ." and went with her to her room. The therapist also helped her arrange her shoes and clothing in the closet when she was bothered by the "disorder." The therapist brought her a calendar and helped Martha connect events and time. When encouraged, she was able to draw a picture of a remembered place or person, and to label it. As her competencies decreased and her depression was enhanced, she allowed the therapist to spend more time with her.

The capacity to transcend the immediate situation and to see beyond it, is often lacking in nursing home residents because the vast range of possibilities for their future is now eroding. The loss of ability is often the distinguishing mark, May says, of psychological disorder. It is a challenge to both client and therapist to continue in the face of diminishing capacities and potential. Simply being "present" and not looking to the future may be the answer in some cases. Awakening a dream or hope in an institutionalized, declining client can bring her face to face with painful reality, thereby creating anxiety. The therapist must not only awaken a dream, but one that has a connection to the client's current capacities or realistic potential.

Moss (1989) says that when psychotherapy can "awaken a lost dream or a lost hope," it can serve as a powerful vehicle for overcoming negativism and apathy. He refers to the positive role that anxiety can have as a medium for growth and change. Golomb (1995) says that the existential question today is not whether to be or not to be, but how one can become what one truly is. The goal is to help people achieve some measure of *authenticity*, but there is no single, exclusively valid path to authenticity and Golomb emphasizes that "attaining authenticity is by no means a solitary pursuit . . . cannot be achieved outside a social context . . . but (only) in a community" (p. 201). The therapist helps provide—and may be the only—"community."

In talking about an existential, humanistic approach to therapy that is adaptable to work with the elderly, Bugental and Kleiner (1993) suggest particular attention to the client's patterns of response to typical life questions: "Who and what are you?" "What brings you satisfaction?" "What is hurtful and disappointing?" "What sources of power can you draw on to aid you in your life?" (p. 106). It is in looking at a client's "subjectivity" that their world can be understood and worked with. If current behavior or thought patterns are painful or failing, then the client needs to be helped to change them through "continuously accessing their experience of being." That is the task of an existential approach. The therapist is not simply a "reflector" but an alive person, concerned with understanding and experiencing the being of the client in the sense that Rogers (1955) meant. Just as with a younger cohort, the relationship between the therapist and the client must be seen as a real one. Papouchis and Passman (1993) also view this relationship as the most significant agent in therapy.

Papouchis and Passman urge therapists to keep an open mind about the aging person's capacities and to have a case-specific dynamic treatment plan emphasizing the client's unique capacities in his environment. Assessment activities in the initial stages of existential psychotherapy with older adults, according to Lantz and Gomia (1995), help to reveal and identify meaning potentials in their lives that the therapist can then "respect, appreciate, admire, confirm, honor, and enjoy" (Lantz, 1993). These activities also provide an opportunity for the clients to determine whether they want to trust the therapist. Lantz makes the important observation that when the existential therapist makes a commitment of availability to the older client, it is implicit that although the therapist hopes for improvement and change, the therapist will not reject the older client who does not live up to the therapist's or the client's hope for change. Angie is an example of a client with whom one might not ordinarily choose to work because her condition and assessment both indicated a poor prognosis.

CASE EXAMPLE

Over the year that she was seen regularly in the assisted living residence, Angie, 82, had slipped from a state of early dementia to more moderate symptomatology. She was also depressed. Of Middle Eastern cultural background, she used to discuss cooking, her experience of working as a single parent, bringing up two small children by herself when her husband died, and her old neighborhood and friends in a large urban environment. She now must be reminded of the therapist's name each week, and the stories *she* has told, when repeated back by the therapist, are unfamiliar to her. Occasionally, she remembers former events and people in her life. Angie was also subject to unpredictable outbursts of anger—expressed verbally and physically with staff and other residents. These were often accompanied by curse words in her native language, but she denied these outbursts afterward. The therapist reminded Angie that she would return even if Angie said angry things to her. The staff was encouraged to distract her when she was irrationally angry, and to reward her more acceptable behavior, as with a cup of tea. After about two years, Angie's physical condition became more frail. Her angry outbursts decreased. When her antidepressant medication was adjusted, she showed fewer mood swings and was less abusive with staff and residents. The therapist accepted her declining mental status, hugged her, and smiled when Angie kissed her on both cheeks when she arrived and departed. The therapist did not abandon her.

Voerwoerdt (1987) says that as a client gets older, she may despair; hope dwindles, and she can become embittered. Those who have always been on good behavior may feel entitled to rewards, and in their absence may reach out for them with a vengeance, getting back at the (imagined) authority who has kept them from gratification. Angie's angry and aggressive behavior with staff and residents could be explained by Voerwoerdt's theory.

In existential therapy with older adults, "primary reflection treatment activities," are directed toward solving problems. "Secondary reflection" is the way to discover more abstract connections, unity, wholeness, and meaning (Lantz, 1993). The purpose of what Lantz refers to as "secondary reflection treatment" is to facilitate the client "noticing" and "honoring" meanings from their past that can still be accessible, even though they may be clouded or repressed due to stress or physical problems, or just the fears that go with becoming worse; when the meaning potentials become less or when feeling hopeless. In working with Angie, it was hard to associate her changes in mood or accessibility with anything particular, except that both her mental status and physical condition continued to worsen. The aim in the middle stage of seeing her was to keep hope in the forefront, hopelessness at bay.

It was pointed out recently by Tallmer (1993) that professionals in the field of gerontology mirror the societal philosophy and attitudes about the elderly that do not hold them in high esteem. Stereotypes and ageism prevail, not only in the population at large but in the training of professionals who expect to work with them. Nevertheless, mental health practitioners are increasingly becoming versed in issues that impinge on the well-being of the elderly: their problems, understanding the physical aspects of aging and mental functioning, and their psychosexual problems. Most important is the evolving realization that meaningful psychotherapy can be accomplished with older adults wherever they are found: in nursing homes, in senior residences or community centers, as well as in private practice settings. And these treatment efforts are most effective when they reflect the hope and meaningfulness which can pervade the later years, even in the face of loneliness, illness, depression, or when end-of-life issues predominate.

A FEMINIST EXISTENTIAL APPROACH TO THERAPY WITH ELDERLY WOMEN

Fodor (1993) differentiates feminist therapy from existential therapy with the elderly. Feminist therapy emphasizes change as related to empowerment, which helps the client focus how she is *currently* structuring experience, and it encourages her to find new ways of thinking. One aspect of existential therapy, for me, includes empowerment. To be empowered, the client takes the responsibility for her own choices and the change process. Even when the client has difficulty accomplishing goals and berates herself for this, the therapist's role is to encourage her to continue the process. Fodor, too, emphasizes modeling and self-disclosure by the therapist as aiding in empowering the client, especially if each was shaped by the same culture. In doing this, significant conflict areas can be understood, including dealing with anger, self-assertion, and body image.

Through recent times, women have had conflict when they became more independent and autonomous, defying the cultural roles for which they were prepared. A woman's view of motherhood is often central to the adjustment she makes. Whether in their original families, in their midlife years, or when they finally find themselves alone or in nursing homes, the optimism—or lack of it—they bring to their later years is related to the models provided by their mothers (Brody, 1993a, p. 30). It is in the crucible of the mother/daughter relationship that myths about roles get fired.

Caplan (1989) talks of the, "perfect mother" myth as largely responsible for the barriers that often grow up between mothers and daughters. If both need to fulfill traditional feminine stereotypes (e.g., a mother needs to shape her daughter for marriage), it can feed the conflict if the daughter—trying to break out of this stereotypical mold—goes to work and fulfills her mother's fear that she will be a "bad mother." Some daughters, for whatever reason, may decide *not* to have children at all, or to have children without marrying, choosing to have an atypical societal life style. They must be strong enough to contend with defied expectations to survive. As Chodorow (1989) has pointed out, if mothers are seen as totally responsible for the outcomes of their children's lives, then myths are formed that relate to either blame or idealization of mothers; two sides of the same belief in the all-powerful mother. However, if childrearing is shared by *both* parents in a new feminist interpretation, then a child's potential anger against less-than-perfect caretakers is divided equally. In the 1990s, a woman could expect to be 45 when her last child left home, and widowed at age 65, while her life expectancy was 83. Then she will have many years to deal with significant issues regarding her worth and her expectations outside the context of family life (see Brody, 1993a, p. 39ff. for reference to these statistics).

Women of previous generations who are elderly now also expect to spend more time caring for their aging parents, and to require help from *their* daughters. Women are thus at higher risk for being admitted to nursing homes; having been shaped to be caretakers, there are fewer possibilities of someone being available to help *them*. It is this loss of autonomy when old and infirm, along with the feelings of helplessness that had been a societal norm for women until the current generation, which contribute to the feelings of hopelessness and depression in elderly women. Home care for the elderly is often a feminist issue. When considering the mothers one treats in residential settings, and their daughters, the cultural changes that have taken place in the twentieth century must be looked at first.

A FEMINIST APPROACH TO TREATING DEPRESSION: WOMEN
EMPOWERING WOMEN

For women who grew up between 1910 and 1950, confronting interpersonal relationships can be a key therapy issue. Women's significance, their values and self-esteem, was more often tied up with their marital, helping, and caretaking roles. Thus, loss of these roles could have a devastating effect. A feminist therapist who is willing to self-disclose her own values, who models autonomy and purposefulness, who does not emphasize pathology or victimization can begin to counter depression.

Melva Steen (1996) reports on interviews with women recovering from depression. Although they report an existential alienation or pain in crises of adulthood, they were able to view their depression in a positive framework. They could even see the depression as a beneficial experience, a kind of coping mechanism for dealing with the stresses of their life, in particular the stressors related to lowered self-esteem. Steen states that when she shared the results of the study with the women interviewed, it enabled them to "become more personally empowered and promote social change by looking at new ways of knowing and being for women" (p. 91). This approach, leading to achieving one's potential and empowerment, is illustrated by the case of Roslyn.

CASE EXAMPLE

Roslyn, 62, with a very responsible job in a prestigious company, was left with extensive debts when her husband died. The relationship had deteriorated before he died and some of the debts were ones of which she was not aware. An attractive older woman who prided herself in her outward appearance, the blows to her self-esteem were considerable. She was seriously depressed. After working individually and in a group with women, her initial despair and depression were replaced with rage. The women in the group were especially helpful in helping her to focus her assets: her good appearance, her worthwhile job performance, her "good mother" role with her children. Her rage was now transformed into a sense of empowerment, that enabled her to sell the house and draw up a plan to repay the debts.

Nobler (1992), writing about the benefits of group therapy for older women, also remarks on the older women's disturbances around role loss and lack of marketable skills, as well as fear of loneliness and social isolation when there is divorce or death of a spouse. In a group using an existential framework, the women are encouraged to take the ultimate responsibility for *themselves* and to face the future realistically, although it may require major changes in strategies of living. Nobler points out that a female therapist who is at a comparable stage of *her* life, cannot only tune in to these women's problems, but can determine issues for the group to deal with based on her own stage of life development. She might do this consciously or unconsciously, but she will ultimately evoke changes in feelings about the aging process and body image that have created conflict. The group can be directed to explore new possibilities for productivity and personal development, along with introspective sharing around these issues. If the therapist can, in fact, model a more assertive, less passive role and can exhibit personal satisfaction with her work and home responsibilities, then she can help the group's older women to override despair.

McLeod and Ryan (1993) report on a British group of older women working on problems of anxiety, panic attacks, isolation, depression, and unresolved bereavement reactions. The authors report that the group developed existential awareness, group cohesiveness, installation of hope, and catharsis over a period of time. Such a group also reflected the psychological issues faced by women at this life stage and the (positive) attitude of the group leader. Typically, they report, women coming to this group felt their life had no purpose without children to bring up or paid employment. In addition, in their earlier life experiences they had less opportunity to assert their needs or express feelings. These authors restate what has been said previously by existential therapists: what is helpful in treatment with older women is not psychodynamic insight into past events or behavior strategies for anxiety management, but something more like the process of integration and review of life choices described by Erikson (1963) and Fry (1986). They especially point to the value of using Yalom's (1975) "existential factors" for focusing group members' current experience, since this is constantly changing while individual members of the group are making choices and facing their responsibilities with each other.

CASE EXAMPLE

Lillian, age 60, returned to therapy 10 years after an earlier brief stint of looking at her life. She came ostensibly because of a crisis in her relationship with two grown daughters and to continue her review of her earlier problems with them when they were on the verge of adulthood. While the therapist acknowledged the psychodynamic basis for the earlier problems, Lillian was encouraged to keep the focus on current issues. Maintaining her autonomy in her relationship with her husband was one issue. He had bullied her most of their marriage. She is depressed—as she has been for a long time—but perhaps she is now at a point where she can entertain options of assertiveness, personal fulfillment, and the possibility of more gratifying relationships with her grown children than when she was younger.

When the therapist recommended that Lillian join a women's group at this stage of resolving leftover life issues, it was with the anticipation of four or five mirrors reflecting back Lillian's potential. A group, even more than individual therapy could capitalize on her inherent assertiveness and ability to get what she wanted from both her spouse and her daughters, as well as help her focus her current crisis.

As seniors, women's power in society is changing as new social roles are evolved. Women who reach middle and old age after the year 2000 will have lived different lives than their mothers and grandmothers. They may, indeed, feel more empowered than *their* mothers and be able to confront their old age with more self-determination and autonomy.

EXISTENTIAL ISSUES IN WORKING WITH THE COGNITIVELY IMPAIRED

With Michael, who was described earlier, cognitive impairment leaves him feeling powerless, especially when he is in denial of his impairment altogether. The therapist's role is to clarify for the client his own power of will and decision, without directing him one way or another. When the therapist can truly refrain from directing him, can listen without judgment to his raging but can also enlist him in the exploration of some of those "deterministic forces" in his life and remind him that he is still in control of many activities that make his life more fulfilling, she is serving him well. In Michael's case, the therapist's aim was to help him acknowledge that despite his serious neurological disorder he was not "crazy" and could be respected. Rollo May (1969) said that no matter how much the client is a victim of forces of which he is unaware, he is "opening himself in some particular way to the data" by simply exploring these deterministic forces in his life and thus, no matter how seemingly insignificant, he is engaged in some choice (p. 201).

Frieda, the following case illustration, is another example that elderly clients' cognitive capacities to understand and respond may decline, but they still need to feel in control over events and interactions in their lives. If one works with a client for several years while this decline is taking place, the cognitive changes may be slow and subtle but will ultimately become very apparent. Jane Meyers (1995) says that such individuals need to feel they can still influence the people who affect them, and she also notes that they are especially vulnerable to perceived and actual losses of power. A decreased sense of power can result in lowered self-esteem.

CASE EXAMPLE

Frieda, 85, brought her small piano with her to the assisted living residence, where it was placed in the living room. When she first came there, she would spontaneously sit down from time to time to play a popular song—to the delight of the staff and other residents. Over a period of about a year, however, she did this less and less as her Alzheimer's disease progressed from early to middle stage. Now when staff asked her to play, she declined, saying simply, "I don't remember what to play . . . ," and looked defeated. The staff encouraged her to do another creative activity, like finger painting, and when she walked past the piano she said, "I used to play, but now I like to paint." The sense of efficacy thus produced enabled her to cope, and she was not depressed.

In helping her shift her creative expression from music to art, the staff enabled Frieda to keep some control over her diminishing capacities and to maintain her self-esteem. Woods (1996) has said that hopelessness is involved in linking depression to giving up (as in suicide attempts). When the cognitively impaired client *cannot* anticipate a positive outcome for their declining abilities, and a negative outcome seems inevitable, then new options are needed. And Erikson et al. (1986) have pointed to "activity" as an antidote for meaninglessness and depression. A small group experience, where meaningfulness of the activity is stressed, is often more helpful than an individual therapy experience for a cognitively impaired client in a long-term care residence. Even wide variations in skill levels and attention span can be incorporated into the activities provided: identifying smells, word association, drawing human figures, and matching games can be tried (see Brody, 1993b, pp. 51–55 for a description of these activities).

In therapeutic situations with the cognitively impaired an important existential element is optimism. Therapists who believe clients can have some level of control over their impairments, reflect this optimism. Meaningful activities also offer cues for diagnostic differentiation of the participants, so that maximum performance levels can be elicited by the therapist. Saul (1988) and Brody (1993b) both describe group therapy opportunities for confused, disoriented, and cognitively impaired clients. Saul tells the participants what the purpose of the group is: to provide a chance for social experience and to discuss matters of mutual concern, and that the therapist will help the participant "think." When family caregivers joined the clients in Saul's groups, this often led to innovative new strategies of caregiving and support. He reports changes in existential experiences, in the realms of thinking, recalling, and using judgment.

Brody (1993b) describes small (four person) activity-oriented groups for moderately impaired nursing home residents. These groups were intended to reinforce overlearned activities and to enhance the clients' feelings of control, and to allow them to express emotions that were often hidden. Brody reports that in one small group where drawings of a whole human figure were the tasks, one elderly woman drew a naked male figure with a large, explicit penis. This, in turn, elicited a heated response from the other group members on her daringness, but also a sharing of sexual fantasies. Sexual desires and fantasies are neglected areas of study in the elderly, but are clearly related to the quality of life and meaningfulness, at any age.

Reifler and Teri (1986) said that diagnoses are usually done carelessly or not at all in nursing homes. This goes along with the more nihilistic view of the elderly, in general. "Why bother making a diagnosis you can't do much about?" Treatment strategies are possible for all phases of Alzheimer's and other cognitive impairments. An existential approach requires a therapist with an outlook of hopefulness applying these strategies.

EXISTENTIAL THERAPEUTIC APPROACHES TO END-OF-LIFE ISSUES

Death and dying are still the subjects hardest for most therapists to deal with in their work with the elderly. Professional training for mental health workers and medical doctors is still insufficient in this area. Beckmann and Olesen (1987) say, "The closeness of death brings me into emotional contact with what the (self) that must die and what the life I am now anxious about, actually contains and means to me" (p. 37). The death and dying experience that is so full of fear and anxiety for the clients, is also difficult for the therapist. What the therapist must somehow convey to the clients is that the anxiety that they flee from—and often have before, in their lifetime—is also a basic condition for an "authentic life"; while the fact of death cannot be changed, the relationship—of the person to his or her life—can be shaped, so that the *quality* of life remaining can be more meaningful. These authors state, "It is paradoxical that (it is) death and fear of death which *could* bring a person into existence . . . only when he accepts that death is an ever-present truth in a meaningful life, will (his life) gain real value. . . ." (p. 40).

The impact of the death of an older parent for a family survivor is sometimes diminished by its predictability. Since our society's values are no longer linked to those of the nuclear family, death, too, can elicit ambivalent feelings in survivors. Working with elders near the end of their lives often involves therapists in a subtle preparation for their own death. Kastenbaum (1987) interprets the frequent devaluation of the death of an older person as less important than, say, that of a younger one, as a final expression of ageism. This devaluation happens more readily for elders whose lives have had less impact on those around them. The death of a person who has had a long and productive life *can* be an occasion for celebration of a life well-lived, with meaning. Yalom (1980) has told us that every human being's life requires meaning, whereas "to live without meaning, goals, values or ideals . . . provokes considerable stress" (p. 422). Individuals facing death are also able to live with fullness and zest if they have a sense of purpose. He suggests that a client who asks, "What is the meaning of life?" is different from the one who asks "What is the meaning of *my* life?" A therapist can help clients personalize this latter goal, enabling them to live more fully and to face death with less despair. One way this can be done is through life review, focusing on the productive, gratifying moments there have been in most people's lives.

Another tactic is to suggest to the client that to be useful to *others* can be a powerful source of meaning. Yalom talks of the ways this can be accomplished: creating something new can be an antidote to meaninglessness; "to live fully, to retain one's sense of astonishment at the miracle of life, to plunge oneself into the natural rhythms of life, to search for pleasure in the deepest sense possible . . ." (p. 437).

CASE EXAMPLE

Marie, age 88, had been a schoolteacher and was interested in whatever intellectually stimulating activities were available when she first arrived at the long-term care residence. Her physical condition and mental status deteriorated during her first year there. She began to wander, try to leave the residence, saying "I have to get to the library." Then one day she fell and broke her hip. After a brief hospitalization, she returned to the residence but she was now limited to a walker or wheelchair and had minimal mobility. She also communicated verbally less and less. She was clearly depressed and her physical condition deteriorated further. However, at this point her affect changed, She became more aware of the other residents, was less self-absorbed than before. She would watch and listen intently as someone told a funny story or another resident painted a picture. In a curious way, she even seemed to enjoy her days more, although immobilized and physically declining. It was as if each moment of life had become more precious; death did not appear to preoccupy her.

Marie's new attention to others' lives seemed to provide her with the sense of connectedness, belonging, and meaning that had been lacking. Her depression lifted after her accident when she became involved in what other residents were doing and feeling.

Describing the later stage of life as one of "generativity," would put purposefulness in the context of self-transcendence—caring for (and about) others. Marie seemed to exemplify this when she became more ill and frail. This is in sharp contrast to the meaninglessness that Yalom (1980) describes as an "existential vacuum" characterized more by boredom, apathy, and emptiness. He also says that anxiety about death or fear of loneliness often masquerades as meaninglessness, and may project one into a search for identification with a cause, a longing to be part of a larger group. Yalom says that a good therapist is one who can listen carefully and more sensitively to these subtle meanings in clients' lives. Where the clients have previously only been able to focus on themselves, now they can find and focus on the "meaning-seeking" and "meaning-providing" activities of their lives; and sometimes this happens when the therapist can help them focus on the lives of those around them, as we saw in Marie.

Older people are especially vulnerable to depression when physical health declines or close relationships are sundered by death. These events can also be significant sources of stress. Hopelessness is closely linked to loneliness. To be without hope for the future is to believe that life cannot improve. The losses can appear irreversible and problems unsolvable (Walton, Schultz, Beck, & Walls, 1991). However, to accept one's own mortality, to transcend pain or discomfort is also to transcend loneliness, to seek out new relationships or pleasures. Spiritual well-being also affects loneliness, so that existential well-being often encompasses a set of beliefs that life *is* purposeful, meaningful, and positive. If survivors are offered the opportunity to experience grief and to find meaning in the loss over time, then they, too, can view the future more positively.

Reminiscence groups are another therapeutic medium for participants to find meaning in their later years. Viney (1995) reported research with reminiscence groups in nursing homes. It shows that people in such groups have lower mortality and greater happiness (compared with measurements at an earlier time). The therapist listened to the stories (reminiscences) for content implying answers to self-defeating attitudes. The stories without hope made life for those who told them more difficult, she reported. There is so much in the lives of elders that can lead to hopelessness, and stories that reflected this, were self-limiting. The opposite, positive effect came from stories that acknowledged control, competence, or other abilities that allowed them to cope.

Bolen (1996) discusses the dehumanization that occurs when illness forces someone to relinquish control to caregivers; choice after choice is stripped away as energy and competencies decrease. If this moment is transcended in a positive way, however, it can favorably change the lives of both those affected and those around them. The therapist can encourage and empower the person afflicted by the way she "frames" the situation to the client. Frank is an example of this empowerment.

CASE EXAMPLE

Frank, 82, had been a successful lawyer up to the time of his illness. He was respected by his colleagues and a wide coterie of close friends and family. His wife had died when he was about 70, but he continued his professional work and associations. He filled the vacuum with a new interest, sculpting, for which he found he had an aptitude. When he fell ill with a life-threatening disease, his "choices" would become circumscribed by the treatment options open to him, and he weighed them carefully. He allowed the therapist to help him "frame" his options, and to continue to find meaningfulness in the limited activities he was reduced to by his illness. He was able to transcend the changes in his life that were forced on him by illness, to look positively toward the future, and to accept the modicum of hope offered. He said he did not fear death.

An interesting point made by Bolen is that she is less able to help a client transcend in a positive way the changes brought about by major illness if that person has been "marginalized" by society up to this point—someone for whom a sense of choice has not been there before, as for socioeconomic reasons. This observation by Bolen would lend itself to further research. A socioeconomic or cultural distinction is not often acknowledged by therapists, although the way one offers services—the modality, the setting—is often different for any age cohort depending on racial or social caste.

A Jungian or existential framework in therapy with older, sick clients can be more meaningful than traditional modes. Tales of remarkable remissions brought about by unconventional methodologies are often discounted as "anecdotal." Bolen's recent reports reflect that of Bernie Siegel (1986), who worked with cancer patients. Bolen says that medicine often ignores the "complicity and subjectivity of getting sick and getting well; the fact that belief (hope) can play a part in getting well." She notes the additional factor of emotional support and the power of the therapist's (doctor's) own positive attitude toward the client.

This positive attitude on the part of mental health workers in settings where the elderly are coping with end-of-life issues seems especially apt to consider. The aides who assist stroke victims or late-stage Alzheimer's clients or cancer patients, whether in hospitals or long-term care settings, are among the most important members of a team, and can bring light to a long, dark passageway. Bolen (1996) says, "fear of loss and fear of abandonment are what keep us from being fully ourselves with others" (p. 116). In working with ancillary staff, as well as nurses and family caregivers for elderly clients who are dying, this attitude of hope and meaning can be transmitted best by a therapist who can risk authentic feelings and intimacy.

REFERENCES

Beckmann, J., & Olesen, H. (1987). The anxiety of the unknown: Dying in a psycho-existential perspective. In A. Gilmore & S. Gilmore (Eds.), *A safer death: Multidisciplinary aspects of terminal care* (pp. 31–40). New York: Plenum Press.

Bolen, J.S. (1996). *Close to the bone: Life-threatening illness and the search for meaning.* New York: Scribner.

Brody, C.M. (1993a). Mothers and daughters: Caretaking and adjustment issues. In C.M. Brody & V.G. Semel (Eds.), *Strategies for therapy with the elderly: Living with hope and meaning* (pp. 30–43). New York: Springer.

Brody, C.M. (1993b). Working with residents of a nursing home who have Alzheimer's disease. In C.M. Brody & V.G. Semel (Eds.), *Strategies for therapy with the elderly: Living with hope and meaning* (pp. 44–56). New York: Springer.

Bugental, J.F.T., & Kleiner, R.I. (1993). Existential psychotherapies. In G. Stricker & J.R. Gold (Eds.), *Comprehensive handbook of psychotherapy integration* (pp. 101–112). New York: Plenum Press.

Bugental, J.F.T., & Sterling, M.M. (1995). New perspectives in existential-humanistic psychotherapy. In A.S. Gurman & S.B. Messer (Eds.), *Essential psychotherapies: Theory and practice* (pp. 226–260). New York: Guilford Press.

Caplan, P. (1989). *Don't blame mother: Mending mother-daughter relations.* New York: Harper & Row.

Chodorow, N. (1989). *Feminism and psychoanalytic theory.* New Haven, CT: Yale University Press.

Erikson, E.H. (1963). *Childhood and society.* New York: Norton.

Erikson, E.H., Erikson, T.M., & Kivnick, H.Q. (1986). *Vital involvement in old age.* New York: Norton.

Fodor, I.G. (1993). A feminist framework for integrative psychotherapy. In G. Stricker & R. Gold (Eds.), *Comprehensive handbook of psychotherapy integration* (pp. 217–235). New York: Plenum Press.

Frankl, V.E. (1988). *The will to meaning: Foundations and application of logotherapy.* New York: New American Library.

Fry, P. (1986). *Depression, stress, and adaptation in the elderly.* Rockville, MD: Aspen.

Golomb, J. (1995). *In search of authenticity: Kierkegaard to Camus.* New York: Routledge & Kegan Paul.

Kastenbaum, R.M. (1987). When a long life ends: The search for meaning. *Generations, 11*(3), 9–13.

Lantz, J. (1993). *Existential family therapy.* Northvale, NJ: Aronson.

Lantz, J., & Gomia, L. (1995). Activities and stages in existential therapy with older adults. *Clinical Gerontologist, 16*(1), 31–40.

May, R. (1969). *Love and will.* New York: Norton.

May, R. (1958). Contributions of existential psychotherapy. In R. May, E. Angel, & H.F. Ellenberger (Eds.), *Existence: A new dimension in psychiatry and psychology* (pp. 37–91). New York: Basic Books.

May, R., Angel, E., & Ellenberger, H.F. (1958). *Existence: A new dimension in psychiatry and psychology.* New York: Basic Books.

McLeod, J., & Ryan, A. (1993). Therapeutic factors experienced by members of an outpatient group for older women. *Group, 16*(3), 146–155.

Meyers, J. (1995). The psychological basis for empowerment. In D. Thursz, C. Nusberg, & J. Prather (Eds.), *Empowering older people: An international approach* (pp. 111–119). Westport, CT: Auburn House.

Moss, D. (1989). Psychotherapy and human experience. In R.S. Valle & S. Halling (Eds.), *Existential phenomenological perspectives in psychology: Exploring the breadth of human experience* (pp. 193–213). New York: Plenum Press.

Nobler, H. (1992). It's never too late to change: A group psychotherapy experience for older women. *Group, 16*(3), 146–155.

Papouchis, N., & Passman, V. (1993). An integrative approach to the psychotherapy of the elderly. In G. Stricker & J.R. Gold (Eds.), *Handbook of psychotherapy integration* (pp. 437–451). New York: Plenum Press.

Reifler, B.V., & Teri, L. (1986). Rehabilitation and Alzheimer's disease. In S.J. Brody & R.E. Ruff (Eds.), *Aging and rehabilitation: Advances in the state of the art* (pp. 107–121). New York: Springer.

Rogers, C. (1955). Persons or science? A philosophical question. *American Psychologist, 10,* 267–278.

Saul, S.R. (1988). Group therapy with confused and disoriented elderly people. In B.W. Maclennan, S. Saul, & M.B. Weiner (Eds.), *Group psychotherapies for the elderly* (pp. 197–208). Madison, CT: International University Press.

Siegel, B. (1986), *Love, medicine, and miracles.* New York: Harper & Row.

Steen, M. (1996). Essential structure and meaning of recovery from clinical depression for middle-adult women: A phenomenological study. *Issues in Mental Health Nursing, 17,* 73–92.

Tallmer, M. (1993). Foreword. In C.M. Brody & V.G. Semel (Eds.), *Strategies for therapy with the elderly: Living with hope and meaning* (pp. xiii–xvi). New York: Springer.

Viney, L.L. (1995). Reminiscence in psychotherapy with the elderly: Telling and retelling their stories. In B.K. Haight & I.D. Webster (Eds.), *The art and science of reminiscing: Theories, research methods and applications* (pp. 243–254). Philadelphia: Taylor & Francis.

Voerwoerdt, A. (1987). Psychodynamics of paranoid phenomena in the elderly. In J. Sadavoy & M. Leszcz (Eds.), *Treating the elderly with psychotherapy: The scope for change in later life* (pp. 67–93). Madison, CT: International University Press.

Walton, C.G., Schultz, C.M., Beck, C.M., & Walls, R.C. (1991). Psychological correlates of loneliness in the older adult. *Archives of Psychiatric Nursing, 5*(3), 165–170.

Woods, R.T. (1996). *Handbook of the clinical psychology of ageing.* Chichester, England: Wiley.

Yalom, I. (1975). *The theory and practice of group psychotherapy.* New York: Basic Books.

Yalom, I. (1980). *Existential psychotherapy.* New York: Basic Books.

CHAPTER 7

It Takes Two: Therapeutic Alliance with Older Clients

HELEN Q. KIVNICK AND AUDREY KAVKA

Psychotherapy may be defined as the treatment of mental and emotional disorders through verbal and nonverbal communication between a therapist/counselor and a patient/client, conducted to bring about changes in the client's thoughts, feelings, and behaviors (Goldfarb, 1950). On the surface, this enterprise requires that a client (often seeking relief from distress), participate in a relationship with a therapist (a professional with certified skills in ameliorating emotional and mental disorders). This relationship most often involves regular meetings, dominated by communication that reflects thoughts, feelings, and actions on the part of the client, and, depending on therapeutic orientation, thoughts, instructions, and feelings on the part of the therapist. However, for psychotherapy to be therapeutic, several additional ingredients are necessary. First, the client must engage in a measure of internal processing or "work" (thinking; free-associating; experiencing affect; understanding) that ultimately results in the changed thoughts, feelings, and behaviors identified as goals at the outset. But what defines this internal work as therapy (as opposed to spontaneous growth or normative development) is that it is catalyzed by something in the client-therapist relationship. And that "something" is what we refer to as the therapeutic alliance, which we regard as a *sine qua non* of effective psychotherapy.

BACKGROUND: THERAPEUTIC ALLIANCE

Defined as the "active and purposeful collaboration between patient and therapist" (Gaston, Thompson, Gallagher, Cournover, & Gagnon, 1998, p. 190), the alliance represents a common thread among disparate therapeutic schools of thought. It has been described as the "active ingredient" of psychodynamic psychotherapy (Frieswyk et al., 1986; Greenson, 1965) and of behavior and cognitive therapy (Bordin, 1979; Gelso & Carter, 1985; Rush, 1985; Wilson & Evans, 1977). It has been examined across therapeutic modalities (e.g., Gaston, Marmar, Thompson, & Gallagher, 1988; Gaston et al., 1998); across disorders [e.g., depression (Marmar, Gaston, Gallagher, & Thompson, 1989); assorted neuroses (Hatcher & Barends, 1996); personality disorders (Barber, Morse, Krakauer, Chittams, & Crits-Christoph, 1997); alcoholism (Amodeo, 1990); opiate addiction (Belding, Iguchi, Morral, & McLellan, 1997); psychosis (Beauford, McNiel, & Binder, 1997)]; and across therapeutic settings [e.g., pseudotherapy (Robiner & Storandt, 1983); outpatient psychotherapy (Marmar, Gaston, et al., 1989; Marmar, Weiss, & Gaston, 1989); psychiatric hospitalization (Beauford et al., 1997); community care (Priebe & Gruyters, 1993)].

As discussed by practicing psychotherapists and psychotherapy researchers alike, establishing a therapeutic alliance is the first major task of therapy, and maintaining it remains an underlying task throughout the course of treatment. The alliance is formed during the initial processes of assessment and treatment planning (Finkel & Anderle, 1990; Goldstein, 1990). When client and therapist feel that progress has been made in the first session, they may well be reacting to the experience of a rudimentary alliance. When a first session ends less hopefully, the experienced absence of a burgeoning alliance may be responsible.

One major thrust of research on the therapeutic alliance concerns its relationship to psychotherapy outcome. What kind of outcome is predicted by what kind of alliance? What kinds of disorders predict what kinds of alliance? How does the alliance differ—in terms of its strength, its valence, its trajectory, and its relation to outcome—across therapeutic modalities? Across specific therapeutic techniques? Across diagnostic categories? Other questions address the ways the therapeutic alliance relates to client age, to therapist age, and to the relative ages between them. Although research provides preliminary answers to many of these questions, studies to date have been so specific to client population and therapeutic modality that generalized answers indicating practice strategies are premature.

Empirical investigation of the research questions posed here requires valid, reliable, quantifiable measures of the overall construct of therapeutic alliance, and of its component subconstructs. The development of such measures is far from complete. The patient's appraisal of the alliance in psychotherapy is shown to have the strongest association with psychotherapy outcome (e.g., in contrast to the therapist's appraisal) regardless of whether outcome is assessed by patient, therapist, or observer (Horvath & Symonds, 1991). It is therefore not surprising that most alliance theorists and psychometricians have focused their attention on measuring this perception (Hatcher & Barends, 1996). Three tools have been relatively widely used. The Penn Helping Alliance Questionnaire (Alexander & Luborsky, 1986) comprises two component subscales: (1) Helping Alliance (measuring the extent to which the patient perceives the therapist as providing, or being able to provide, needed help); and (2) Collaboration (measuring the extent to which the patient perceives therapy as a collaborative effort). The Working Alliance Inventory (Horvath & Greenberg, 1989) attempts to tap the following three components of the working alliance in psychotherapy, based on Bordin's (1979) research on working alliance: (1) Goals (patient's perception of agreement between self and psychotherapist about the goals of his or her treatment); (2) Tasks (patient's perception of agreement between self and psychotherapist about the specific tasks through which the goals of treatment are to be achieved); and (3) Bonds [patient's rating of the bond between him- or herself and the therapist (e.g., "I feel comfortable with [Therapist's Name]")].

The last measure, the California Psychotherapeutic Alliance Scales (Gaston, 1991; Marmar, Gaston, et al., 1989; Marmar, Horowitz, Weiss, & Marziali, 1986), attempts to address both client and therapist contributions to the alliance with the four subscales: (1) Patient Working Capacity (the extent to which therapist comments or interpretations raise new situations and connections for the patient); (2) Patient Commitment (extent to which the patient feels that therapy is worthwhile, despite momentary setbacks or frustrations); (3) Working Strategy Consensus (patient's perception of agreement between him- or herself and the therapist around treatment goals and tasks); and (4) Therapist Understanding and Involvement (patient's experience of the therapist as demonstrating accurate understanding vs. pressuring him or her to make changes prematurely). Some research suggests that a single, general factor essentially measuring the strength of the overall alliance represents the therapeutic alliance more accurately than do the component subscales and the specific constructs they represent (Salvio, Beutler, Wood, & Engle, 1992; Tracey & Kokotovic, 1989). Recent work by Hatcher and Barends confirms this suggestion (1996).

Hatcher and Barends (1996) also conducted an exploratory factor analysis of the three preceding measures, ultimately identifying six components of the patient's view of the therapeutic alliance: (1) Confident Collaboration (extent to which the patient is confident and committed to a process that feels promising and helpful); (2) Goals and Tasks (patient-therapist agreement on therapeutic tasks and goals); (3) Bond (extent to which the patient feels liked, accepted, and respected by the therapist; perceived mutual liking and respect); (4) Idealized Relationship (extent to which patient is able/unable to disagree with or express hostility toward the therapist; (5) Dedicated Patient (patient's downplaying feelings of frustration with therapy); and (6) Help Received (extent to which patient perceives progress in therapy and is hopeful of a good outcome). They found that the vital core of the therapeutic alliance is conveyed by the Confident Collaboration factor, as related to the patient's estimate of personal improvement. An alliance rated highly in these terms is seen as positive, valuable, and purposeful, with a forward-looking quality that propels the therapy ahead.

Researchers disagree about the way the working alliance contributes to psychotherapy. According to one view, the alliance is an "active ingredient" of psychotherapy. This view holds that therapeutic change results both from the patient's engagement with treatment tasks (complete assigned tasks; discuss the process), *and also* from the affective bond that takes shape as the therapeutic alliance (Frieswyk et al., 1986; Rogers, 1957). A certain amount of change takes place as a result of the existence of the therapeutic alliance, itself, regardless of patient fulfillment of therapeutic tasks. According to a second view, the alliance is necessary to therapeutic success, but is not, alone, responsible for therapeutic progress (Gaston et al., 1998). All change requires client engagement both in treatment tasks and also in the alliance's real relationship. A third view describes the working alliance as nothing more than a component of the transference, necessary to therapeutic success only insofar as the transference is considered necessary (Brenner, 1979).

Psychotherapy literature includes references to the "working alliance," "helping alliance," "working relationship," "real relationship," "patient-therapist rapport" in addition to "therapeutic alliance." Although the terms denote subtly different constructs within specific therapeutic approaches, we have chosen, in this chapter, to use them interchangeably, to refer to the patient-therapist collaboration through which both patient and therapist maximize their involvement in therapy. The therapeutic alliance is created and maintained by client and therapist, together. It requires the effective, ongoing participation of both; it can be corrupted or undermined by either. With respect to psychotherapy with elders, therapist bias against older clients' capacity for insight or change can seriously interfere with the initial formation of the alliance. On the client's part, the very problems that led her or him to seek treatment can prevent initial engagement in the alliance.

BACKGROUND: PSYCHOSOCIAL DEVELOPMENTAL PROCESS

We consider the working alliance in psychotherapy with older adults in the overall context of psychodynamic psychotherapy with older adults. Sigmund Freud and other early psychoanalytic thinkers were erroneously convinced that emotional depletion rendered older adults incapable of engaging in or benefiting from any form of psychotherapy that required intense affect, and that cognitive decline interfered insurmountably with elders' involvement in any insight-oriented treatment. Perhaps more important, early views of psychodynamic development held that important psychosexual development takes place in childhood, and that individual personality structure, defenses, and coping mechanisms are solidified before the end of life's second decade. For decades, Freud's early assertion, "Near or above the fifties the elasticity of the mental process, on which the treatment depends, is as a rule lacking . . . Older people are no longer educable" (1905/1953, p. 264), met with little opposition.

Traditional psychoanalytic theory is developmental in maintaining that personal growth begins with a human organism that is inherently satisfaction-seeking. Development arises from the repetitive, and progressive process of adaptation to the inevitable frustrations of this satisfaction seeking. The basic language of psychoanalytic theory—psychosexual stages, conflict, tension, regression, ego maturation—conveys its fundamental commitment to understanding, in complex ways, the simultaneity of challenge and opportunity in each stage of life. Intrinsic to the theory is the belief that the mind develops in dynamic response to emotional challenge; growth arises in response to inevitable, painful frustrations, and disappointments.

Freud's assertions of old-age rigidity notwithstanding, the inherently developmental nature of psychoanalytic theory supports the practice of psychotherapy with older adults, and offers three major principles as a basis for such practice: (1) the lifelong tension of the human as an organism seeking homeostasis and stable continuity while constantly adapting to change, and integrating that change into their stable sense of self; (2) the simultaneous, opposing pressures toward regression and toward progression at every stage of life; and (3) insight about the dynamic, always changing interplay of external life experiences with internal mental life and character structures. Two additional theoretical cornerstones complete the foundation of psychoanalytic psychotherapy: recognition of both conscious and unconscious determinants of behavior, thought, and feeling; and appreciation of the influence of the past in the present.

Building on psychoanalytic developmental theory, Erik Erikson (1950/1963) explicitly articulated a process of lifelong psychosocial development, proceeding through eight stages that begin at birth and do not end until death. Erikson emphasized the tension between emotional challenge and emotional growth at each stage of life from infancy to the end of life, positing that if extreme, this tension can precipitate temporary regression, and that if inadequately resolved it can lead to fixation. The most recent formulations of Erikson's life-cycle developmental theory (Erikson, Erikson, & Kivnick, 1986; Kivnick, 1993; Kivnick & Jernstedt, 1996) highlight three principles: (1) Process in Time, (2) Dynamic Balance of Opposites, and (3) Vital Involvement. The first two principles emphasize life-cycle development and tension (see Figure 7.1). According to the third theme, the eight psychosocial themes serve as a conceptual scaffolding around which people construct their lives, from beginning to end.

PROCESS IN TIME

Overall epigenetic psychosocial development (the lifelong process of balancing psychosocial themes) is thought to be a product both of biology and of the environment. Like cognition and physical stature, psychosocial capacities develop according to a genetic program, under the influence of a great number of environmental factors. Each theme comes to ascendancy at one stage or another (e.g., toddlers focus enormous amounts of energy on Autonomy and Shame/Doubt). But all themes are operational at every stage in the life cycle, and psychosocial development takes place in all 64 boxes of the life-cycle chart shown in Figure 7.1. Themes that will be focal in adulthood are previewed or anticipated in early life, when they are dealt with in age-appropriate, rudimentary form—as a toddler learning to walk struggles with Industry and Inferiority. Themes that are focal in childhood are revisited and reviewed in subsequent stages. Even those themes which are adequately balanced when ascendant must perpetually be reworked in age-appropriate terms, as elders must rework issues of Autonomy and Shame/Doubt when physical deterioration and disease constrict mobility.

Older Adulthood 57	58	59	60	61	62	63	64 Integrity & Despair WISDOM
Middle Adulthood 49	50	51	52	53	54	55 Generativity & Self-Absorption CARE	56
Young Adulthood 41	42	43	44	45	46 Intimacy & Isolation LOVE	47	48
Adolescence 33	34	35	36	37 Identity & Confusion FIDELITY	38	39	40
School Age 25	26	27	28 Industry & Inferiority COMPETENCE	29	30	31	32
Play Age 17	18	19 Initiative & Guilt PURPOSE	20	21	22	23	24
Toddlerhood 9	10 Autonomy & Shame/Doubt WILL	11	12	13	14	15	16
Infancy 1 Basic Trust & Basic Mistrust HOPE	2	3	4	5	6	7	8

Figure 7.1 Psychological stages of life. (Adapted from *Vital Involvement in Old Age*, by E.H. Erikson, J.M. Erikson, and H.Q. Kivnick, 1986, New York: W.W. Norton. Copyright © 1986 by W.W. Norton & Co. Used with permission.)

DYNAMIC BALANCE OF OPPOSITES

For each psychosocial theme, healthy development involves the individual in balancing personal strengths with weaknesses—skills with awkwardnesses, capacities with deficits. Dystonic tendencies are brought into dynamic balance with syntonic, each catalyzing the other and relying on the other for its own meaning.

VITAL INVOLVEMENT

At each stage throughout the life cycle, themes are balanced or "worked on," as they are enacted through involvement in everyday feelings, activities, dreams, relationships, and more. Each theme—each pair of opposing tendencies—is enacted through characteristic behaviors and attitudes. Reciprocally, life's activities, experiences, feelings, and attitudes are all understood as somehow involved with balancing one theme or more. This vital involvement gives psychosocial process—a synthesis of the psychological and internal with the social and external—its full meaning.

DYNAMIC PSYCHOTHERAPY AND THE THERAPEUTIC ALLIANCE WITH OLDER PEOPLE

In the absence of definitive research clarifying the precise role the working alliance plays in psychotherapy, we conceptualize the alliance in an iterative relationship with other elements of therapeutic practice. An alliance forms, as part of initial therapeutic encounters. This alliance influences patient and therapist involvement in the treatment, which, in turn, determines the course of treatment. Progress and stagnation, satisfaction and frustration in therapy influence the ongoing development of the alliance. With every session, the current nature of the alliance influences the involvement—verbal, affective, cognitive, behavioral—both patient and therapist demonstrate in treatment. The alliance provides the medium in which therapy develops. Therapeutic progress and stalling are both influenced by the alliance relationship and, in turn, contribute nourishment or bile to the alliance. Because of this close relationship between the helping alliance and therapy itself, we interpret the many therapeutic modifications recommended for work with elders as applicable to developing and enhancing the therapeutic alliance.

Eriksonian theory identifies an ongoing, normative developmental effort to reinterpret past history in terms of present needs, and to meet present demands on the basis of past experience. Reflecting a similar pattern, dynamic psychotherapy integrates past with present and considers both external and internal factors that contribute to a patient's state of being. Aging, itself, does not lead patients to seek psychotherapy; age itself is not necessarily unduly stressful. Certain conditions associated or combined with aging may be stressful, but it is each individual's internal structure for coping with and adapting to the stress at hand that determines his or her need for therapeutic help. In working with an elder, the therapist must take into account features of the normal aging process as a backdrop for physical changes and impairments of this particular individual, and dynamic psychosocial principles as a backdrop for this individual's psychodynamics (or theoretical principles underlying a different psychotherapeutic orientation)—both weaknesses and strengths. The therapist is challenged to understand how much emphasis to place on this individual's being old, and how much to place on his or her being a patient. Therapeutic work with elder clients requires an understanding of both psychotherapy and aging, as well as knowledge of how to use each understanding in the service of the other. A robust therapeutic alliance requires comparable simultaneous understandings.

Knight (1996) has identified three categories of characteristics in terms of which elders normatively differ from middle- and young adults, and according to which specifics of therapeutic practice should be modified: (1) maturational, (2) cohort, and (3) social context. We must emphasize at the outset that any individual elder may demonstrate some, none, or all of these characteristics, in degrees ranging from mild to profound. Determination of each elder's ability to engage in dynamic (as opposed to purely supportive) therapy, and of the requisite technical accommodations, must rest on the therapist's accurate assessment of each client's unique combination of strengths and weaknesses.

Maturational characteristics of aging include a slowing of cognitive processing, and deteriorations in hearing and vision—both of which can interfere with smooth communication between older and younger adults. Age-related diminution of working memory decreases the number of things an elder can actively keep in mind and work on at one time. Impairment of fluid intelligence may limit the elder's capacity to think through the implications of abstract interpretations. Newton, Brauer, Gutmann, and Grunes (1986) discuss a later-life focus on self that may be associated with an elder's decreased stores of psychological energy, orientation toward his or her inner world and affective experience, and reminiscence and life review. Whereas these normative characteristics of aging are most often presented as obstacles to elders' participation in dynamic psychotherapy and involvement in a robust therapeutic alliance, some of these same characteristics may actually enhance elders' ability to engage productively in such therapeutic work. Indeed, some characteristics of aging are properly discussed in terms of necessary therapeutic modifications. For example, therapists are urged to *compensate* for a client's hearing impairment by speaking slowly and facing her or him at all times, and to offset limited working memory by communicating in short sentences, conveying one idea at a time. In the other direction, however, we urge therapists to take advantage of elders' characteristic focus on the self and the interior life as a unique, age-related readiness for the introspection, life review, and reminiscence that are essential to the work of dynamic treatment.

Knight describes *cohort-related* issues as including connotations of words (e.g., "dementia" seems consistently to connote psychosis where "senility" connotes cognitive disruptions and disorientations), life expectations (e.g., individuals who married early in the twentieth century do not have the same expectation for marital happiness and intimacy held by those born in later cohorts), and specific values (e.g., although elders—like "youngers"—will spontaneously criticize family members and relationships, elders will most often answer direct questions about change by denying that they would like anything to be different). Elders' having lived through historical eras that predate the personal experience of younger therapists require the therapist to develop an understanding for the relevant history. All such cohort-related issues create the possibility of fundamental patient-therapist misunderstandings, interfering with establishing and maintaining a therapeutic alliance. With respect to cohort-related issues, the therapist must recognize the likelihood of his/her ignorance or misunderstanding, and must convey to the patient a sincere respect for assistance in remedying this ignorance. Clients value being asked questions when the therapist does not appreciate a historical issue, and they feel both more clearly understood and more closely allied when they, personally, have explained such an issue. This process has much in common with the "ordinary" therapeutic process of exploring what a specific concept, word, or aphorism means to particular client. Regardless of specific focus, this kind of exchange provides an opportunity for expert information to flow from client to therapist, and for both individuals to share this reversed teaching and learning experience.

Older clients may inhabit two different gerontological *social contexts*. One encompasses the age-segregated community of senior citizens, involving residence, recreation, and daily maintenance activity. The second involves the macrosystemic social policies, practices, and attitudes that govern the lives of elders. Elder clients are likely to be retired and living on fixed incomes; for many, health care decisions are dictated by Medicare regulations rather than by best practice. Older men are most likely to be married; older women are most likely to be alone. To understand an individual elder client and his or her dynamic adaptation, the therapist must understand the obstacles and constraints society imposes on elders as a whole. Concretely, the therapist must also understand the social context well enough to intervene effectively if necessary. As indicated by the following clinical example, active therapist participation in the client's network can greatly strengthen the therapeutic alliance.

Establishing a robust therapeutic alliance and conducting effective dynamic psychotherapy with elder clients require the skillful integration of standard therapeutic practice with creative interpersonal adaptation to the specific demands posed by normative characteristics of aging. This dual set of requirements may arouse unconscious resistance in the clinician, either to the boundary uncertainty triggered by self-initiated modifications of standard therapeutic technique, or to mastering a clearly essential additional body of information. This resistance may deter therapists from engaging with older clients, supporting the gerontophobic stereotypes and biases that still pervade the professional psychotherapy community (Duffy, 1992; Kavka, 1995; Molinari, 1996). These biases include therapeutic nihilism regarding the possibility of change, devalued professional status associated with aged clientele, the therapist's own aging concerns (personal transferences and countertransferences; unconscious fears of disability and dependence), and eagerness to avoid considering mortality. In addition to interfering with case-by-case therapeutic work, these biases mitigate, systemically, against including geropsychology in therapy training. Thus, most therapists continue to receive little, if any, training in geriatric practice, and they participate, inadvertently, in reinforcing negative biases. These negative therapist feelings jeopardize a therapeutic alliance from the very beginning.

CASE EXAMPLE

A woman in her early 70s was referred for psychotherapy by her rheumatologist. She had a chronic systemic disease that was progressively disabling. The overt basis for the referral was concern about depression. Less overt was the exhaustion on the part of the doctor and his office staff, in response to the patient's frequent calls and complaints. It was evident after several consultation visits that the patient was quite narcissistic and had suffered two major narcissistic injuries. First, her husband had divorced her and remarried. More recently, her previously beautiful face and body, and her vivacious personality had been transformed by age and illness. She was now obese and overly made up. She moved slowly and painfully, elegant high heels replaced with bulky athletic shoes, and she no longer had the energy for go-getting. Nonetheless, the vivaciousness of her personality rang through spirited accounts of her frenetic younger life, providing a clear picture of who she had been before she became who she was—or was most clearly identified—now. The therapist could appreciate the patient's life challenges, respect her strengths, and understand the dynamics underlying her current feelings and behaviors. The patient could appreciate the therapist's empathy and understanding. She was lonely and depressed. More powerfully, she projected a hunger for a relationship in which she felt very special.

This therapeutic understanding of her character (how it had been assaulted by her particular illness and losses) and her immediate relationship needs suggested a treatment strategy that included action in the patient's life in the community, as well as reflection in psychotherapy. Rather than beg her three children for sporadic and ambivalently supplied help, patient and therapist agreed that she could be of great help to someone by offering them the opportunity to live with her, in exchange for providing her some assistance at home. She found someone on her own and developed a satisfying relationship in which she received needed caretaking while enjoying the sense of being a grand benefactor.

The therapist recommended this regal approach to the referring physician and his staff when he phoned, concerned that he needed to place her in the hospital and feared that would worsen her depression. The therapist advised that because of her loneliness and shame at her neediness, the patient might actually benefit from the attentions she would automatically receive in the hospital. He was dubious, but later described entering her hospital room. The patient was holding court, with all the hospital personnel in attendance. (Coincidentally, this understanding of the patient helped relieve *the doctor's* wounded narcissism as well. Initially he had enjoyed this very special woman picking him out to be her very special doctor, but her illness was refractory to all treatment. He felt he was failing, and her constant calls and complaints pained him narcissistically. The therapist actively encouraged him to feel that he was doing a heroic job with a patient who was unusually challenging both medically and psychologically.)

Psychotherapy could not undo the narcissistic wounds that age and illness were wreaking upon this patient, but understanding her intense need to feel appealing and special helped the therapist begin, realistically, to bolster her self-esteem in a way that also restored some sense of continuous identity. Patient and therapist talked with good humor about her clothes closet. Once it had been filled with party dresses and elegant high heels; now it contained soft slippers, athletic shoes, and housecoats. This mutual conversation about past and present helped revive her sense of herself as an elegant, socially engaged woman. "Can you imagine?" she challenged the therapist. "A woman like me with shoes like this in her closet!"

ESTABLISHING AND MAINTAINING THE THERAPEUTIC ALLIANCE

Clinicians and researchers agree that dynamic psychotherapy with older adults rests on the same developmental principles and ageless issues of unresolved conflict, maladaptive behavior patterns, and efforts at positive change that support dynamic therapy with clients of all ages. Experts also confirm the necessity for modifying certain therapeutic practices, to accommodate the maturational, cohort-based, and society-based issues previously discussed (Brink, 1986; Duffy, 1992; Knight, 1996; Lazarus & Sadavoy, 1988; Molinari, 1996; Newton et al., 1986; Nordhus, Nielsen, & Kvale, 1998; Spar, 1988; Weinstein & Khanna, 1986; Wheeler & Bienenfeld, 1990). As noted earlier, these modifications and therapeutic guidelines constitute creative interpersonal adaptations to each elder client's unique configuration of weaknesses and strengths. As such, they are central to establishing and maintaining the interpersonal relationship that is the therapeutic alliance.

The therapeutic alliance provides a relationship context in which the elder client experiences growth and change that may then be expressed in outside relationships and circumstances. Actual growth and change take place on an unconscious level, as part of the ongoing developmental work of balancing and rebalancing psychosocial themes. In psychotherapy, this internal, dynamic process is catalyzed by the therapist's verbalizations (comments; questions; observations; interpretations). In the context of the real relationship we refer to as a therapeutic alliance, therapist verbalizations stimulate the elder's conscious psychological effort, which ultimately translates into unconscious psychosocial work; in the absence of an alliance relationship, therapist interventions do not necessarily lead to client progress.

From the outset of each treatment, the alliance relationship is facilitated by reciprocal patient-therapist experiences, related to the eight psychosocial themes that have been described as underlying all of life's thoughts, feelings, and behaviors (Erikson et al., 1986; Kivnick, 1993). As illustrated by Erikson et al., the primary psychosocial task of old age—balancing a sense of integrity with an opposing sense of despair—includes age-appropriate reworking and renewing of balances around the seven other psychosocial themes (refer to the top row of Figure 7.1). In dynamic psychotherapy, therapist and client make use of the working alliance as a context for the patient's accomplishing this reworking and rebalancing. Early in treatment, the therapist must communicate with the part of the client that is ready to form and maintain an alliance relationship. This real relationship engages many—if not all—of the psychosocial themes, while it encourages the client to do necessary reworking and reintegrating around these eight themes.

Reciprocally, this relationship engages the therapist's own balances around the themes. Indeed, those therapist variables that are often cited as mitigating against elders receiving effective mental health services (Duffy, 1992; Molinari, 1996) may be seen as the therapist's own problematic thematic balances. For example, a therapist's fears of disability and dependency, avoidance of confronting mortality, ignorance about biopsychosocial norms of later life, belief in negative stereotypes about aging, and susceptibility to the professional devaluation associated with seeing low-status clients—all of which interfere with practicing effective psychotherapy with older clients—are clearly related to the therapist's personal concerns around her or his own Autonomy and Shame/Doubt, Integrity and Despair, Industry and Inferiority, and

Identity and Confusion. Establishing and maintaining a working alliance requires, minimally, that the therapist not let personal thematic imbalances interfere with meeting appropriate client needs.

TRUST AND MISTRUST

> From its earliest ascendancy at the beginning of the life cycle, the theme of Trust
> & Mistrust concerns the individual's reliance on a predictable, responsive environment, in balance with discriminating caution and skepticism about the realistic unpredictabilities and malignancies of that same environment. Individual
> heritage, demographics, and basic life circumstances constitute a stable foundation—that is shaken and must be re-established with each major circumstantial
> change. Rules and customs provide additional security. Routines, cultural practices, and religious behaviors and strictures all contribute to the sense of knowable reliability that informs daily conduct and that colors individual response to
> the actions of others. (Kivnick & Jernstedt, 1996, p. 142)

Perhaps the most fundamental element in a working alliance is a realistic feeling of hope shared by patient and therapist, that progress is possible. Elder clients come for psychotherapy as a last resort, despairing over a past that cannot be changed, a present that seems unendurable, and a future that seems to hold no possibility of improvement. Accustomed coping patterns and thematic balances are either quantitatively insufficient or qualitatively inappropriate to managing the accumulating pains of old age's exigencies, along with a lifetime of unconscious conflicts and anxieties. Changing societal customs, practices, and values threaten long-established senses of predictability and "knowable reality."

From the outset, the therapist for an older adult must provide a trustworthy perception and reliable reflection of the elder's reality. The therapist must acknowledge the real losses, limitations, and pains that impinge on the elder's everyday life, in physical, social, and emotional terms. The therapist must grasp the magnitude of these very real problems and, nonetheless, offer hope that is equally real. Over the course of treatment, this realistic shared hope supports both client and therapist in overcoming inevitable obstacles.

The psychotherapy relationship is characterized by a unique structure, in which participant roles, demands, and expectations are clear and predictable. Emphasizing these sources of stability enhances an elder's ability to experience reality-based trust, in balance with the mistrust elicited by changing social systems and values. Clarity of patient role behaviors and responsibilities contributes to the elder's sense of predictability about personal demands and expectations. Clarity of therapist role behaviors and responsibilities makes it safe for the elder to experience hope, related to a set of behaviors that may safely be expected to be caring and competent, while respectful of personal boundaries and individual needs. For the therapist, trust in underlying principles of theory and practice must be firm enough to permit the technical modifications that are widely accepted as essential to psychotherapy with older adults.

Autonomy and Shame/Doubt

> . . . Throughout life, the theme of Autonomy & Shame/Doubt concerns the body. It concerns capacities and limits. It concerns injuries, illnesses, and health. It concerns ability and helplessness, power and victimization. And it concerns boundaries—physical and emotional—and their capacity to contain the essential goodness or badness of what is within. . . . Associated with every element of this theme is the notion of control, of determination. Who controls me? What and whom do I control? With whose suggestions and instructions will I comply? Whom and what will I oppose? With whom will I cooperate? How much assistance can I accept, and from whom, without somehow denying my fundamental control over my self and my destiny—without denying my essential self? (Kivnick & Jernstedt, 1996, p. 144)

As older adults are referred into psychotherapy by primary physicians, elder therapy clients are likely to suffer from a complexity of physical weaknesses, limitations, and diseases that challenge lifelong capacities and overall self-reliance. Particularly in a culture that prizes independence and self-control far more than cooperation and responsible group membership, old age's deteriorations—whether normative or disease-related—threaten the balance between controlling and being controlled that lies at the core of a lifelong sense of self. Re-equilibrating this balance is part of the therapeutic alliance.

Issues of autonomy are immediately triggered by the elder's recognizing his or her need for help, and then by acting to seek that help. To effectively utilize available help, the elder will have to steer a course between feeling overcome by helplessness (boundaries fail to contain internal helpless feelings), and overwhelmed by the helper (boundaries fail to withstand perceived external takeover). The difficulties of steering this course while developing the therapeutic alliance will almost certainly parallel the difficulties he or she is experiencing outside the office. In facilitating the early establishment of an alliance, the therapist must convey an ability to provide assistance, along with a healthy respect for the client's capacity to use that help as he or she sees fit. As part of the process of rebalancing autonomy with shame/doubt, the client works to utilize personal strengths to compensate for disabilities, to maximize meaningful independence on the basis of necessary supports and assistance. Within the working alliance, the therapist and client must agree on the importance of identifying the client's strengths and acknowledging their ongoing centrality to the independent sense of self.

More often than any other quality, researchers and clinicians cite the importance of empathy in forming and strengthening the therapeutic alliance. The therapist must be empathically attuned to the patient's degree of readiness to receive understanding, concern, and attention. The patient must be ready to receive the therapist's empathy, and to do so without feeling pressured to express unfelt agreement, to make premature changes, or to take dystonic courses of action. In an illustrative exchange, a middle-aged therapist watched an arthritic patient settle herself, painfully, into a chair after climbing a long flight of stairs to the second-floor therapy office. "Do you realize what an accomplishment it is for you to make it up those stairs?" the therapist asked, acknowledging that she recognized and respected the patient's physical triumph. The patient smiled briefly and replied, "Do you realize how important you are to me?" Ready to hear the therapist's expressed empathy for her physical accomplishment, the patient felt free to verbalize her deep commitment to the overall therapeutic alliance. For the therapist, personal tensions between dependency and helplessness, on one hand, and independence on and power, on the other, must be well balanced to sustain an alliance that can promote client autonomy. Similarly, to promote the client's self-determined progress, the therapist must be able to offer help without imposing control.

INITIATIVE AND GUILT

Within this theme, the individual shifts focus from exercising capacities simply to demonstrate control, to using capacities for the purpose of accomplishing goals. Expansive tendencies toward curiosity, creativity, and ingenuity must be balanced by the anticipatory guilt that becomes the capacity for self-restraint.

> Over the life cycle, the individual learns to act on some good ideas and not on others, to express some products of an active, whimsical imagination, and to refrain from expressing others. . . . This is the lifelong theme most closely associated with playfulness, recreation, and enjoyment. It supports humor and exuberance. It is associated with the arts, with aesthetics, with a sense of beauty. Initiative sustains the enterprise that prompts elder and child, alike, to abandon the inertia of rest in favor of purposeful . . . activity. When inadequately balanced with self-restraint, initiative can impel ill-considered—and often later-regretted—courses of action. In the opposite direction, imbalance can result in a failure to follow through, and can lead to entanglement in an immobilizing web of painful anticipations, recriminations, and hesitations. (Kivnick & Jernstedt, 1996, p. 146)

In the treatment context, an elder patient's seeking help and following through on a referral both require a measure of initiative to counteract the inertia of rest and to overcome the hesitations associated with self-restraint. Similarly, returning for regularly scheduled appointments requires ongoing initiative on the part of the elder patient that must be supported in the alliance. From the very beginning, the therapist must convey an active willingness to help, so that clients leave the first session already engaged in a therapeutic alliance and feeling that they have received something valuable. Often this initial support will take the form of demonstrating to elders that psychotherapy offers an opportunity to think creatively and constructively about themselves.

We emphasize that the elder patient uses the therapeutic relationship to make creative changes—in outer life behaviors and structures, as well as in inner dynamic processes and patterns. These creative changes rest on the patient's ability to work out an age-appropriate balance between urges toward creativity and exploration, on one hand, and those toward restraint and hesitancy, on the other. To promote essential expressions of patient enterprise and ingenuity, the therapist must demonstrate a kind of parallel ingenuity, in flexibly adapting elements of therapeutic technique to establishing and sustaining an alliance with older patients.

To compensate for elder clients' sensory and cognitive impairments, the therapist may need to be unusually active in obtaining early information, and in working through both client and family resistances to treatment. The therapist may need to speak slowly, loudly, and in short, concrete sentences with frequent repetitions. He or she may need to use sound amplifying devices and to position him- or herself far closer to the client than would otherwise be customary (Lazarus & Sadavoy, 1988). Spar (1988) identifies four technical modifications for therapists to consider using to strengthen the alliance with older clients: (1) Adopt an explicitly optimistic stance; (2) engage the client actively, as opposed to listening more passively; (3) participate in symbolic and real giving; and (4) express concern for the client (e.g., facial expression; arm squeeze). In these concrete ways, the therapist demonstrates the use of initiative in adapting to painful client limitations and losses.

The pace of therapist/client interaction must be regulated to give the client ample time to respond; the initial visit may require more than an hour. Subsequent visits may need to be scheduled more frequently than with younger clients, or supplemented by telephone check-ins, both to facilitate the early establishment of a working alliance, and also to enable the therapist to monitor client response to treatment. Termination, too, may need to be implemented flexibly, with ongoing sessions scheduled periodically, as necessary, to enable each client to maintain progress and continue to utilize the therapeutic alliance in the service of psychosocial health (Brink, 1986; Nordhus et al., 1998; Spar, 1988). Knight (1996) and Wheeler and Bienenfeld (1990) note that home visits may be appropriate for elder clients and can, in the context of clear structure and boundaries, strengthen a working alliance and maximize an elder's progress in therapy.

In addition to flexibility around therapeutic technique, the therapist can work most effectively with older adults by demonstrating flexibility in therapeutic modality. Molinari (1996) encourages therapists to be familiar with the three major therapeutic approaches (psychodynamic; cognitive-behavioral; operant-behavioral), in order to introduce interventions from all approaches as they become appropriate for a given elder client. (In the previous case example, the psychodynamic therapist made an operant-behavioral intervention in raising the possibility of the client's finding a boarder.) In a similar vein, Nordhus et al. (1998) suggest that therapists be prepared to shift between exploratory, supportive, and didactic interventions—within the space of a single session, if necessary. These practice modifications require therapists to develop a less formal and more flexible style than that into which they have been professionally socialized. And it requires that they demonstrate considerable initiative in balance with self-restraint, in determining when to modify which principles of technique and modality with which client.

INDUSTRY AND INFERIORITY

> This psychosocial theme challenges the individual to balance a tendency toward hard work and accomplishment with opposing feelings of inadequacy and ineptitude . . . Underlying the pull toward mastery and the push away from inadequacy is an ever-growing competence, characterized both by demonstrable skills and knowledge, and also by an invisible, experienced sense of fundamental ability. Perhaps even more important than specific competencies are the internal capacity[ies] to work hard and . . . continue to learn. . . . (Kivnick & Jernstedt, 1996, p. 148)

Older clients bring to therapy a lifetime of skills, survival strategies, and hard work. These may not be adequate to deal effectively with current vicissitudes of old age, but they *have* enabled these individuals to make it through several decades of life. Essential to establishing an early working alliance, the therapist must often help clients recognize and identify their strengths and, in so doing, convey realistic respect for them. Such attention to identified competencies not only helps catalyze client industriousness. It also helps clients renew a lifelong sense of the self as whole within boundaries (related to Autonomy & Shame/Doubt), and of overall self-respect (associated with Identity & Confusion). The therapist often needs to assume an active stance in addressing concrete client concerns, but while doing so he or she must also convey a clear expectation for the clients' active participation in the problem-solving required both in treatment and, by extension, in life outside the office (Newton et al., 1986).

To do good work in psychotherapy, elder clients must experience their own realistic competence at living life; their own ability to work hard, learn, and grow; and their respect for the therapist's competence at guiding the process. All these are reinforced in the context of a robust therapeutic alliance, as illustrated by the following elder client's response to the way his younger therapist had heard a particular story. "I feel so smart talking to you. I'm just telling you what I think. But when you say it back to me I think, 'That old man really knows what he's talking about.'"

For many older clients, the learning that is part of psychotherapy must begin with learning *about* psychotherapy. Despite the presence of psychotherapy throughout mainstream popular culture, contemporary elders may well not have learned about therapy and "clienthood" in their everyday lives; they may require education about the complementary roles of client and therapist and about the overall parameters of treatment before being able to engage in the alliance or in any other treatment component. The therapist is responsible for clarifying such basic understandings as (1) elders can use psychotherapy to help learn new ways to solve problems with living; (2) talking about problems to a trained listener can be helpful; (3) putting feelings into words can be helpful; (4) elders don't have to be crazy to experience these benefits; (5) therapist and client work together to set and accomplish goals; (6) outpatient psychotherapy usually involves meeting regularly to work on problems, and often takes more than a few visits to experience major progress; (7) therapy is subject to confidentiality; (8) fees are assessed and collected on an established basis (Knight, 1996).

Maintaining a therapeutic alliance with older clients requires that the therapist, too, engage in learning. Therapists who lack specific gerontological training must learn basic information about biological, psychological, and social processes of aging. They must also learn to demonstrate the practice of flexibilities discussed earlier. Perhaps most important, however, to maintain a productive working alliance, therapists must be open to learning directly from their elder clients. Some of this learning concerns the kinds of specific cohort-related facts that emerge when a patient clarifies early life choices. (For example, through at least the 1920s, the University of California permitted male undergraduates to marry, whereas female undergraduates who married were automatically terminated; marriage for an 18-year-old woman had far broader life ramifications in 1925 than it carries today.) Some of this learning concerns cultural specifics and individual family traditions. (For as long as she could remember an elder Latina had made tamales at Christmastime, and had given them as gifts—one dozen per person—to each of her siblings, children, grandchildren, and great-grandchildren. Although the meaning of this practice has remained constant over the years, the magnitude of the enterprise greatly increased when she moved away from her home community in southern Texas and no longer had ingredients readily accessible.) Some therapist learning concerns information specific to client professions over time. (The demands and expectations of owning a successful family farm have changed considerably over the course of this century—through which today's agricultural patriarch has lived.)

In addition to being willing to learn from elder clients, therapists must learn to utilize—and also to display—their client-learned knowledge in the service of client progress. The strength of the therapeutic alliance can be significantly enhanced when elder clients experience teaching and learning as flowing in both directions. This perceived mutuality reinforces for clients the value of the very industriousness on which they will have to rely in making the changes required in treatment.

Paralleling the elder client's need to learn new skills and perspectives in therapy, the therapist must also be open to learning new skills and perspectives in the process of working with older adults. Conducting psychotherapy in unaccustomed settings (e.g., in the client's home or hospital room) and according to new technical and methodological parameters (e.g., sitting close to elder clients; offering behavioral directives along with dynamic interpretations) can allow therapists to develop new insights about the essential nature of the therapeutic process, new strategies for working with elder clients, and new perspectives on their own lives and relationships. As with all countertransference material, this learning must be examined by the therapist and used explicitly in the service of client progress in treatment. A therapist's ability to learn from clients has much in common with the ability to be inspired by clients, as explored by Kahn & Harkavy-Friedman (1997). Research has not clarified how much of this client-induced inspiration is a product of client characteristics (e.g., charisma), therapist characteristics (e.g., openness to inspiration in the therapy setting), or an interaction of the two. However, the fact that clinicians *do* report being inspired by clients confirms the presence of mutuality and reciprocity in the patient-therapist alliance relationship.

IDENTITY AND CONFUSION

> In later life the individual is challenged to make sense of the self that has lived through many decades of past, that lives in a moment experienced as present, and that will continue to live into a future that looms ever more finite. "What is it that lets me feel most like myself?" is a question that becomes increasingly meaningful and, for the fortunate, increasingly easy to answer. Family, ethnicity, and status continue to influence the sense of self from outside, along with personality traits, preferences and dislikes, appearance, and physical attributes from within. Inevitably, the elder must struggle with the role of limitations and disabilities in essential identity. (Kivnick & Jernstedt, 1996, p. 150)

Within the therapeutic alliance, the patient works to construct a "consistent enough" identity based on personal perception and experience, as reflected by the observations and interpretations of the therapist. Confronted with undeniable losses and limitations at the internal, personal, interpersonal, and societal levels, the elder struggles to reconcile "who I've always been" with "who I am now." A crucial task of the alliance is to facilitate this reconciliation, reassuring the elder from the outset that seeking psychotherapy is *not* the same thing as being crazy, that having problems is not the same thing as being a "mental case." Through reminiscence, the patient works at reestablishing self-continuity; through reviewing life's strengths and achievements he or she works at renewing self-respect. Patient and therapist, together, forge an alliance in which they perceive the patient in various stages of his or her past, and in the present. Acknowledging painful losses in the context of the alliance, they validate enduring strengths, identify new opportunities, and develop a shared understanding that integrates these multiple identities.

CASE EXAMPLE

Dr. X kept a consultation appointment scheduled by his wife. A distinguished-looking but ailing man in his 70s, he mentioned no medical disorders and could identify no problems except his wife's increasing faultfinding. He identified himself as a successful orthopedic surgeon, and suggested that his wife talk with the therapist instead of himself. Mrs. X subsequently described her husband as having been a successful orthopedic surgeon until, several years ago, he developed severe heart disease; since heart surgery he has been unable to recover sufficient stamina to resume even office practice. His various medications leave him fatigued, less mentally alert than his previous norm, and unable to meet his professional obligations. He has never formally retired or claimed his entitled disability insurance. When his wife urges him to contact his insurance agent, he accuses her of undermining his recovery. When his former partners try to discuss his changed status, he accuses them of jealously trying to oust him from the practice. He is always angry and blaming it on others. She loves him very much, but he is making her life miserable.

Dr. X reluctantly returned to the therapist, who encouraged him to tell his story in his own time. Initially, he spoke of his successful years as a physician, father, and member of the community. Then he told more. Dr. X had been the middle child of three boys, and he grew up with a constant, unrelenting envy of his two brothers. Only after making a great effort did he get the same respect from his father that his older brother received without trying; nothing he did could elicit the same affection his parents lavished on the baby brother. He felt neglected and hungry for attention and admiration.

As an adult he worked very hard, earning respect and appreciation from his patients, colleagues, community members, and family—eventually including his parents. These were the happiest years of his life. He fell totally unprepared for a retirement without daily pressures toward achievement and distinction. Indeed, he had neither planned nor chosen to retire. Now that he was not working, he envied everything about everyone else. He could not experience his office's continuing success in his absence as a tribute to his own achievements in earning a reputation, and in choosing and mentoring excellent partners. He did not feel pride in his partners; he did not even feel pride in his children. He could not stop himself from comparing himself to these younger adults in the present, and he felt diminished by the comparisons. He complained of their being too busy to give him respect or pay him attention. He described them as selfish. Rather than feeling fortunate that his wife was devoted, healthy, and able to care for him, he resented her energy and enthusiasm as constant reminders of how he, himself, did not feel.

As he recalled how he had felt like nothing in his parents' eyes until he achieved worldly success, he was able to acknowledge how hard he was fighting off feeling like nothing again, fighting to prevent this painful identity from the distant past from displacing the positive identity he had labored—in the more recent past—to construct. Focusing his anger and disappointment on his temporally distant parents and away from himself and the people who had loved him more recently, he came to be able to imagine that these people—his wife, his children, his partners, his patients—did value him even now. With the therapist, he identified internal resources that were still available to him. He had a good mind and loved to learn, but he could only concentrate for short periods of time and he could not predict when he would be alert and when he would feel too sleepy to work at all. He permitted his son to teach him to use the computer, finding the activity to be both physical and intellectual. He could work whenever he wanted and for whatever length of time suited him. He accomplished something he had never accomplished before. He let his son be the teacher, and he enjoyed being the student.

INTIMACY AND ISOLATION

By participating in relationships of closeness and in experiences of being alone, the individual fashions a capacity to engage with others whom he/she can love and be loved by, with true mutuality. . . . Throughout life, the individual participates in many different kinds of close, loving relationships, all of which, together, contribute to an overall capacity for love. In renewing earlier-life balances between intimacy and isolation, elders find themselves both revisiting earlier issues and also confronting the new demands that accompany new circumstances. . . . [Elders] find themselves forging new intimacies across generational lines, within and across family boundaries, and based on qualities and criteria that acquire new meaning as former criteria become irrelevant. (Kivnick & Jernstedt, 1996, p. 152)

By definition, the therapeutic alliance is a relationship. Also by definition, then, a strong therapeutic alliance involves client and therapist in the mutuality that characterizes any strong relationship. Forged for the purpose of facilitating the client's growth, the alliance is a collaboration in which both partners work together, facing a mutually understood reality to achieve their shared purpose.

Crucial to any therapeutic alliance, the therapist must function as an empathic, nonjudgmental listener. Clinicians agree that establishing and maintaining an alliance with an older client requires the therapist to project more empathy, more support, and more symbolic giving than analytic neutrality conventionally permits (Brink, 1986; Knight, 1996; Molinari, 1996; Newton et al., 1986; Nordhus et al., 1998). The alliance with older clients requires more mutuality than with younger clients, and the therapist may well have less time to establish its foundations. Particularly when the therapist is considerably younger than the client, he or she is challenged to (1) understand the client's life, history, and feelings; (2) effectively convey this understanding to the client; and (3) reveal enough about him- or herself that the client perceives their common life experiences and begins to engage in a real relationship. This relationship becomes the "shared world" (Molinari, 1996, p. 199) of the therapeutic alliance.

Where the stance of a psychodynamic therapist is, with younger patients, that of a semidetached listener or interpreter, this stance shifts, with older patients, to that of a participant observer. No longer is the therapist primarily a screen for the patient's projections and transferences or a mirror for the patient's thoughts. With older adults, the therapist must be a full, participating partner in a relationship that is demonstrably mutual. The patient must feel understood and accepted, and the therapist must demonstrate and communicate real understanding and acceptance. The patient must feel respect for the therapist's competence in response to competence demonstrated and confidence conveyed. And the patient must receive clear confirmation of being respected, in return. Such confirmation requires that the therapist both feel real respect for the patient and express that respect clearly enough—in words; in voice tone; in gesture; in action—that the patient is absolutely secure in the alliance.

GENERATIVITY AND SELF-ABSORPTION

Throughout life, the generative providing of selfless, loving care must be balanced with the capacity to take necessary care of the self. In order to provide consistent nurturance for those for whom one is responsible, the individual must see to it that he/she, too, receives essential care. . . . In later life, elders continue to seek a balance between caring for others and securing necessary care for themselves. . . . Elders continue to provide the next generations with all possible supports while, at the same time, counting on receiving essential services in return. At this stage, however, indirect expressions of generativity assume increasing importance. Elders take particular pleasure in identifying with members of the next generations, in seeing family ties remain strong, and in celebrating the myths and traditions according to which the family continues to grow and thrive. (Kivnick & Jernstedt, 1996, p. 155)

The act of coming for psychotherapy expresses an elder's need for help. Engaging in an alliance expresses his or her feeling of trust that this therapist will also provide care. But caring in a therapeutic alliance involves additional dimensions. The elder must be able to accept care and be nurtured by it. He or she must be able to reciprocate care and concern. And, as with the outside care that is increasingly necessary from friends, family, and formal providers, the elder's way of receiving care must, itself, be caring enough to provide gratitude that is meaningful and supportive to the ones who care. For older clients, psychotherapy offers a caring relationship that stands apart from accustomed parenthood or childhood relationships. Indeed, elders often come for therapy because—in one way or another—they are unable to secure the caring they feel they need from expected family sources. Although we do not suggest that the therapist provide the actual services clients require in daily life, we argue that the therapist must convey to the client a real sense of being cared about, and of having care to give, in return.

Within the therapeutic alliance, perhaps the most important dimension of care concerns the elder's reworking his or her earlier-life balance around generativity and self-absorption. Dr. X, in the previous example, did not experience unconditional parental care and nurturance when he was a relatively helpless child. He structured his own adulthood around effort and achievement, through which he could exert control, provide care for others, and depend on little, if anything, in return. When disease destroyed his adult capacities to care through hard work and control, his early imbalance around generativity left him unable to receive care from those closest to him, and equally unable to be caring to himself. The opposite of care and concern, he expressed anger and hurtful disapproval toward himself and others. As a result of care appropriately expressed in the therapeutic alliance, Dr. X was able to rework this theme enough to allow his son to take the upper hand in a teaching-and-learning relationship, and to allow himself to enjoy working as his stamina permitted.

Therapist generativity, in the working alliance, involves the sensitive giving and receiving of care and concern. It requires such appropriate symbolic gestures as, indicated in a quote cited earlier, the therapist's appreciation of a client's effort at overcoming physical obstacles to reaching the therapy session. And, suggested in the same quote, it requires the therapist's appropriate acceptance of the client's appreciation in response. With elder clients, therapist generativity also includes appropriate involvement with the client's outside relationships and circumstances. The therapist may need to become directly involved with family caregivers, to help the client secure services from professional providers, or to help the client develop creative strategies for giving and receiving necessary care in the community. This direct involvement has much in common with case management, through which the client receives services that are—more euphemistically than accurately—conventionally referred to as care. Just as the working alliance requires therapist flexibility with respect to issues of technique, identity, and relationship, so it requires therapist flexibility with respect to caring and being cared for.

INTEGRITY AND DESPAIR

> In its final stage the life cycle turns back to its beginnings, as the individual weaves a lifetime of strengths and weaknesses, joys and sorrows, gains and losses, dreams and disappointments into a unique fabric of experience. This is the integration that must guide the elder through the life time that remains— whether it be marked in months or in decades. The process of integration involves far more than simple life review and uniform acceptance of the past. It requires a real, and often painful, coming to terms with choices made and not made, actions taken and not taken, hopes fulfilled and not fulfilled. This kind of honest stock-taking, taken with the perspective of time, is essential to clarifying the lessons learned from a lifetime of experience. It is these lessons that give rise to the wisdom that makes it all worthwhile. (Kivnick & Jernstedt, 1996, p. 158)

Paradoxically, elder psychotherapy clients are both more fully focused on dealing with current concerns than younger clients may be, and are also developmentally readier to process the personal past. We noted early in this chapter that working with elders requires the therapist to understand each client in terms of two distinct conceptual frameworks: (1) maturational, cohort, and social issues related to aging; and (2) theoretical structure of a therapeutic orientation, and also in terms of how these distinct frameworks can support one another. An elder's realistically foreshortened future creates a pressure to make every moment of therapy count toward solving problems; there is little time for engaging in what might appear to be aimless exploring and drifting. On the other hand, this same sense of finitude creates an unconscious pressure to solve long-standing dynamic problems, rather than resisting or avoiding them. Together with the normative developmental push to reconcile the experiences of a whole lifetime, these apparently opposing pressures leave many elders uniquely ready to use the therapeutic alliance to access and process distant origins of dynamic conflicts in the service of dealing effectively with issues in the present.

In psychotherapy, elders seek practical solutions to immediate problems, rather than overall personality reconstruction. However, as illustrated by our two lengthy case examples, productive life review in the context of a strong therapeutic alliance facilitates the creation of these immediate, practical solutions based on overall psychodynamic understanding. By using the elder's past to understand and strengthen his or her present, the therapist is both meeting the client's goals for psychotherapy, and also facilitating the essential psychosocial developmental work of old age. With younger clients, recalling the past may, indeed, involve great attention to past failures—particularly the pains and failures of childhood. With elder clients, however, the recalled past explicitly includes joys along with pains, successes along with failures, strengths along with weaknesses. And the past, itself, includes the experiences of recent, as well as distant, decades. It is the normative task of old age to integrate life's whole range of experience as the basis for progressing into the future. A robust therapeutic alliance assists the older client in conducting this essential life synthesis while working out integral, practical solutions to immediately pressing problems that may be both behavioral and affective in nature.

As emphasized throughout this chapter, the essential therapeutic alliance with older adults rests on the therapist's sincere and meaningfully expressed respect for their having overcome the obstacles that are present in every long life, and for their struggling, now, to place personal life and work in critical review. This appreciation supports the elder's reconsolidation of a continuous identity, as noted earlier. Germane to the current discussion, this appreciation supports the review and reintegration that are central both to progress in psychotherapy, and also to the elder's psychosocial development in life as a whole. As illustrated in the following comment, attending to a robust therapeutic alliance allows the therapist to give the elder no smaller a gift than life, itself: "When I tell you about things, I get to live them all over again. It's almost like you're giving me my own life back again."

REFERENCES

Alexander, L.B., & Luborsky, L. (1986). The Penn helping alliance scales. In L.S. Greenberg & W.M. Pinsoff (Eds.), *The psychotherapeutic process: A research handbook* (pp. 325–366). New York: Guilford Press.

Amodeo, M. (1990). Treating the late life alcoholic: Guidelines for working through denial integrating individual, family, and group approaches. *Journal of Geriatric Psychiatry, 23*(2), 91–105.

Barber, J.P., Morse, J.O., Krakauer, I.D., Chittams, J., & Crits-Christoph, K. (1997). Change in obsessive-compulsive and avoidant personality disorders following time-limited supportive-expressive therapy. *Psychotherapy, 34*(2), 133–143.

Beauford, J.E., McNiel, D.E., & Binder, R.L. (1997). Utility of the initial therapeutic alliance in evaluating psychiatric patients' risk of violence. *American Journal of psychiatry, 154*(9), 1272–1276.

Behrends, R., & Blatt, S. (1985). Internalization, psychological development through life cycle. *Psychoanalytic Study of the Child, 40,* 11–40.

Belding, M.A., Iguchi, M.Y., Morral, A.R., & McLellan, A.T. (1997). Assessing the helping alliance and its impact in the treatment of opiate dependence. *Drug & Alcohol Dependence, 48*(1), 51–59.

Bordin, E.S. (1979). The generalizability of the psychoanalytic concept of the working alliance. *Psychotherapy Theory, Research and Practice, 16,* 252–260.

Brenner, C. (1979). Working alliance, therapeutic alliance, and transference. *Journal of the American Psychoanalytic Association, 27*(S), 137–158.

Brink, T.L. (1986). Editor's introduction to psychodynamic therapy with the aged: A review. In T.L. Brink (Ed.), *Clinical gerontology: A guide to assessment and intervention* (pp. 205–206). New York: Haworth Press.

Duffy, M. (1992). Challenges in geriatric psychotherapy. *Individual Psychology, 48*(4), 432–440.

Erikson, E.H. (1950/1963). *Childhood and society.* New York: Norton.

Erikson, E.H., Erikson, J.M., & Kivnick, H.Q. (1986). *Vital involvement in old age.* New York: Norton.

Finkel, S.I., & Anderle, T.E. (1990). Treatment planning. In D. Bienenfeld (Ed.), *Verwoerdt's clinical geropsychiatry* (3rd ed., pp. 197–203). Baltimore: Williams & Wilkins.

Freud, S. (1905/1953). *On psychotherapy: Standard edition* (Vol. 7, pp. 255–268). Toronto: Hogarth Press.

Frieswyk, S.H., Allen, J.G., Colson, D.B., Coyne, L., Gabbard, G.O., Horowitz, L., & Newsom, G. (1986). Therapeutic alliance: Its place as a process and outcome varia dynamic psychotherapy research. *Journal of Consulting and Clinical Psychology, 54*, 32–38.

Gaston, L. (1991). Reliability and criterion-related validity of the California psychotherapy alliance scales—patient version. *Psychological Assessment: A Journal of Consulting and Clinical Psychology, 3*, 68–74.

Gaston, L., Marmar, C.R., Thompson, L.W., & Gallagher, D. (1988). Relation of pretreatment characteristics to the therapeutic alliance in diverse psychotherapies. *Journal of Consulting & Clinical Psychology, 56*(4), 483–489.

Gaston, L., Thompson, L., Gallagher, D., Cournover, L.G., & Gagnon, R. (1998, Summer). Alliance, technique, and their interactions in predme of behavioral, cognitive, and brief dynamic therapy. *Psychotherapy Research, 8*(2), 190–209.

Gelso, C.J., & Carter, J.A. (1985). The relationship in counseling and psychotherapy: Components, consequences, and theoretical antecedents. *Counseling Psychologist, 13*, 155–243.

Goldstein, M.Z. (1990). Evaluation of the elderly patient. In D. Bienenfeld (Ed.), *Verwoerdt's clinical geropsychiatry* (3rd ed., pp. 47–58). Baltimore: Williams & Wilkins.

Goldfarb, A.I. (1950). Psychotherapy of aged persons: IV. One aspect of the psychodynamics of the therapeutic situation with aged patients. *Psychoanalytic Review, 42*, 180–187.

Greenson, R.R. (1965). The working alliance and the transference neurosis. *Psychoanalytic Quarterly, 34*, 155–181.

Greenson, R.R. (1967). *The technique and practice of psychoanalysis* (Vol. 1). New York: International Universities Press.

Hatcher, R.L., & Barends, A.W. (1996). Patients' view of the alliance in psychotherapy: Exploratory factor analysis of three alliance measures. *Journal of Consulting & Clinical Psychology, 64*(6), 1326–1336.

Horvath, A.O., & Greenberg, L.S. (1989). Development and validation of the working alliance inventory. *Journal of Counseling Psychology, 64*, 561–573.

Horvath, A.O., & Symonds, B.D. (1991). Relations between working alliance and outcome in psychotherapy: A meta-analysis. *Journal of Counseling Psychology, 38*, 139–149.

Kahn, W.L., & Harkavy-Friedman, J.M. (1997, Summer). Change in the therapist: The role of patient-induced inspiration. *American Journal of Psychotherapy, 52*(3), 403–414.

Kavka, A. (1995). *How psychoanalysis looks at getting older.* Unpublished paper presented at the San Francisco Psychoanalytic Institute.

Kivnick, H.Q. (1993). Everyday mental health: A guide to assessing life strengths. *Generations, 17*(1), 13–20.

Kivnick, H.Q., & Jernstedt, H.L. (1996). Mama still sparkles: An elder role model in long-term care. *Marriage and Family Review, 24*(1, 2), 123–164.

Knight, B.G. (1996). *Psychotherapy with older adults* (2nd ed.). Thousand Oaks, CA: Sage.

Lazarus, L.W., & Sadavoy, J. (1988). Psychotherapy with the elderly. In L.W. Lazarus (Ed.), *Essentials of geriatric psychiatry: A guide for health professionals* (pp. 147–172). New York: Springer.

Marmar, C.R., Gaston, L., Gallagher, D., & Thompson, L.W. (1989). Alliance and outcome in late-life depression. *Journal of Nervous and Mental Disease, 177*(8), 464–472.

Marmar, C.R., Weiss, D.S., & Gaston, L. (1989). Toward the validation of the California therapeutic alliance rating system. *Psychological Assessment, 1*(1) 46–52.

Marmar, C.S., Horowitz, M.J., Weiss, D.S., & Marziali, E. (1986). The development of the therapeutic alliance rating system. In L.S. Greenberg & W.M. Pinsoff (Eds.), *The psychotherapeutic process: A research handbook* (pp. 367–390). New York: Guilford Press.

Molinari, V. (1996). Current approaches to therapy with elderly clients. In *The Hatherleigh guide to psychotherapy* (pp. 193–213). New York: Haworth Press.

Newton, N.A., Brauer, D., Gutmann, D.L., & Grunes, J. (1986). Psychodynamic therapy with the aged: A review. In T.L. Brink (Ed.), *Clinical gerontology: A guide to assessment and intervention* (pp. 205–230). New York: Haworth Press.

Nordhus, I.H., Nielsen, G.H., & Kvale, G. (1998). Psychotherapy with older adults. In I.H. Nordhus & G.R. VandenBos, R. (Eds.), *Clinical geropsychology* (pp. 289–311). Washington, DC: American Psychological Association.

Priebe, S., & Gruyters, T. (1993). The role of the helping alliance in psychiatric community care: A prospective study. *Journal of Nervous and Mental Disease, 181*(9), 552–557.

Robiner, W.N., & Storandt, M. (1983). Client perceptions of the therapeutic relationships as a fuion of client and counselor age. *Journal of Counseling Psychology, 30*(1), 96–99.

Rogers, C.R. (1957). Necessary and sufficient conditions of therapeutic personality change. *Journal of Consulting Psychology, 21*, 95–103.

Rush, A.J. (1985). The therapeutic alliance in short-term directive psychotherapies. In American Psychiatric Association (Ed.), *Psychiatry update* (Vol. 4). Washington, DC: American Psychiatric Association.

Salvio, M.A., Beutler, L.E., Wood, J.M., & Engle, D. (1992). The strength of the therapeutic alliance in three treatments for depression. *Psychotherapy Research, 2*(1), 31–36.

Spar, J.E. (1988). Principles of diagnosis and treatment in geriatric psychiatry. In L.W. Lazarus (Ed.), *Essentials of geriatric psychiatry: A guide for health professionals* (pp. 102–112). New York: Springer.

Tracey, T.J., & Kokotovic, A. M. (1989). Factor structure of the working alliance inventory. *Psychological Assessment: A Journal of Consulting and Clinical Psychology, 1*, 207–210.

Weinstein, W.S., & Khanna, P. (1986). *Depression in the elderly: Conceptual issues and psychotherapeutic intervention.* New York: Philosophical Library.

Wheeler, B.G., & Bienenfeld, D. (1990). Principles of individual psychotherapy. In D. Bienenfeld (Ed.), *Verwoerdt's clinical geropsychiatry* (3rd ed., pp. 204–222). Baltimore: Williams & Wilkins.

Wilson, G.T., & Evans, I.M. (1977). The therent relationship in behavior therapy. In A. Gurman & A. Razin (Eds.), *Effective psychotherapy: A handbook of research.* New York: Pergamon Press.

CHAPTER 8

The Impact of Cultural Differences in Psychotherapy with Older Clients: Sensitive Issues and Strategies

PAMILLA MORALES

CULTURE AND ETHNICITY OF THE CULTURALLY DIVERSE ADULT

The impact of ethnicity and traditional culture has major implications for the culturally diverse elder adult. Culture is what has been learned from experiences in the environment, interactions with others, and the interpretations and influence of those experiences. Members of a cultural group tend to reinforce certain attitudes and behaviors in one another, and those become identifiable, constant features. Culture can be described as the totality of learned, socially transmitted behavior of a group that emerges from its members' interpersonal interactions. It is important that the helping professions and the helping process be sensitive to the cultural background and experiences of identifiable groups of people. Professionals who are sensitive to cultural dynamics and culture environments will be able to understand and respond better to the development of clients in counseling.

Kinship systems are an important aspect of culture for the culturally diverse elder adult. These systems are natural, collective, social relationship patterns that define group life. The system governs their relationships and status within their culture. Kinship systems include institutions such as marriage, parenthood, patriarchal and matriarchal lineage, family unit, nuclear family, extended family, and the ethnic community.

The social definitions of the distinctiveness of an ethnic group varies with time and is generally different between individuals. The same historical backgrounds, the same demographic processes and the same social structure can result in different interpretations and conceptions among individuals.

The culturally diverse elder adult in the United States has been impacted by a system of socialized institutional racism. Their culture, attitudes, and interactions with majority society have been limited by fear, prejudice, and racism. Their social identity is therefore in part created in reaction to external pressures and extreme forms of racism.

Most culturally diverse elder adults have been victimized by policies that denied them access to basic public institutions. For example, African Americans, were forced to attend separate schools that were deemed at the time as being educationally equal to white schools and were later proved to be inadequate and inferior. Native Americans were often separated from family members at young ages, sent to reservation boarding schools, and not allowed to practice their native language, religious traditions, or traditional mode of dress. For these individuals, the denial of their culture has far-reaching consequences not only for them but for their children and future generations. Hispanics were not allowed to attend public schools unless they could pass for white. If they were allowed to attend public schools, they were not allowed to speak their native language and many children were sent home until they could speak English well enough to attend public school. As a result they were often uneducated and learned to devalue the educational experience. Educational institutions were also utilized as a way of discovering whether individuals were legal residents, creating additional mistrust and fear of public institutions. Asians were also disallowed from attending public educational institutions, but unlike the Hispanics, many Asians had been educated in their countries of origin and in turn educated their children within the home environment and whenever possible sent them back to their home countries for further education, an option that the other groups did not have. This practice strengthened ties between Asian Americans and their originating country and allowed the development of closed, isolated self-governing communities.

CHARACTERISTICS OF THE CULTURALLY DIFFERENT OLDER ADULT—FAMILIAL AND COMMUNITY RELATIONSHIPS

Culturally diverse elder adults are somewhat different from the younger members as a result of the institutional polices of racism and discrimination. In recent years, the improvement in race relations and the reduction of institutional racial discrimination has created a dichotomy of experience between elder adults and their younger members. As a result of being isolated and segregated into minority communities for protection and support, elder adults rely more on their minority communities, their cultural traditions and kinship systems than their younger counterparts and are suspicious and often fearful of the majority culture. They have a tendency to be more entrenched in folk beliefs, religious affiliations and cultural traditions and norms. These elder adults retain a great deal of their culture and maintain close ties with family and community. Therefore, many continue to speak their traditional languages, to the exclusivity of a second language, and often see themselves as the keeper of cultural traditions and feel compelled to practice them openly to preserve their culture and pass on these traditions to future generations.

Within all four minority groups, the kinship system acts as their support and provides them with roles as they become elders within their communities. Elders in all four groups become more respected within their communities and cultural groups as they age. They become guiding influences within the family units and govern family interactions, family traditions, and cultural celebrations. They become the teachers of culture and provide the younger generations with oral history of their past and their cultural traditions.

For culturally diverse elder adults, familial and community ties are the most important facets in their lives. They resist outside influences and pressure and prefer to solve all individual issues with the family whenever possible. When situations present themselves that the family is unable to overcome, they seek out community support, but rarely will go outside the minority culture to seek help within social institutions. This is especially true with mental illness and any other psychological issues. In general, families in all four cultures believe that family solidarity is best in regard to the treatment of emotional disorders and that the individual should remain within the family. There is great reluctance to expose a family member to any services outside the family or minority community as such exposure usually results in the person being separated from their family with the end result of the family losing control. When working with individuals from these four cultural groups, it is important to keep this in mind as family solidarity is not simply a cultural commitment, but a psychological one as well.

As a result of past discriminatory social institutional practices, many culturally diverse elder adults do not have an institutional support system in place for assisting them in their elder years. For example, many were never registered for Social Security and retirement benefits. Additionally, due to the minority traditions of extended families elder adults invested the entirety of their income in the care and education of their children in lieu of their own personal retirement accounts. Instead they relied on their children to take care of them and provide for them in their elder years. Cultural norms and traditions also dictate this policy as well as the belief that elders should remain within the family for care and treatment, until their deaths. Families resist placing their elders in institutions such as nursing home facilities and prefer to care for them within the family environment regardless of the amount of care, time, and physical impairments.

CHARACTERISTICS OF ELDER NATIVE AMERICANS

Native people, American Indians, Indians; are all names applied to the people whose ancestors lived in the Americas previous to the European settlement. There are approximately 263 distinct nations, tribes, bands, clans, or communities of native people with approximately 38 percent living on reservation land

(Schaefer, 1979). About 50 to 75 different tribal languages continue to be spoken (Schaefer, 1979). The reservation system has produced a mixture of positive and negative influences. On the negative side it has isolated Native Americans from mainstream culture and economic opportunities. On the positive side they have reestablished native culture, pride, and traditions in reaction to the government's past policy of integrating and assimilating native children and have kept tribes relatively intact.

Within Native American culture, land is a central cultural concept, specifically their tribal lands. Tribal land usually refers to land occupied by an individual's tribe prior to resettlement; reservation land was land provided by the government and may or may not have any relation to tribal land. Reservation land was used solely for the resettlement of Native Americans. Most religious ceremonies, culture, and custom revolve around tribal lands. For the elder Native American, land is more meaningful than for their younger members as they vividly remember their parents, friends, and communities dying for the right to exist on sacred native lands. Therefore, land is a symbol for them of their very fight for existence and autonomy. On many reservations, the elders continue to fight for land that was taken from them and they have instilled in the younger generations the importance of their tribal lands along with the need to continue fighting for native land that was taken from them.

Another major component that affected the lives of many elder Native Americans was the requirement for all Native American children to attend boarding schools. All Native American children were forced into boarding schools created by the government and various religious groups whose main goals were to replace the practice of Native American language, dress, beliefs, and religions with the practice of the white civilization and assimilation into the majority culture. Often these schools were located hundreds of miles from their families and communities. Many children in these schools were only allowed to see their parents once a year and contact was severely restricted.

Elder adults specifically males, are generally respected and often help to govern the tribe. Many become members of the tribal council and dictate policy to younger members. They view themselves as being the gatekeepers of the tribe, their traditions and their belief systems. Religion for native people is an integral part of the culture and praying is a part of daily life. On many tribal lands, the only ones who continue to speak the native languages are the elders.

Within the Native American culture, the elder adults are the keepers of tradition and they are relied on to maintain and keep oral histories. Native American people place emphasis on traditional forms of communication such as storytelling. The elders are considered the "tellers" while younger members are designated as the "listeners." Emphasis is placed on the ability to communicate feelings and emotions through nonverbal forms of communication.

The elder adult is provided for within the culture and it is expected that their children and the Native American communities will maintain them until their deaths. There is a strong sense of tribalism and if children have left the reservation or are unable to care for their elder adult, the responsibility falls on the tribe. For the Native American, the family, the extended family, and the tribe are primary, with self being secondary. The strong sense of tribal bonding creates an atmosphere that all elders are "grandmothers" and "grandfathers" regardless of blood ties.

Native Americans place more emphasis on the administration of the family by the father and older relatives than on any other type of authority. Therefore the elder adult in the Native American community has a great deal of status and respect. There is mutual respect between wife and husband, between parents and children, between family members and relatives, and between family members and the tribe. All members are given a voice within the community regardless of how young or old. Strong family relationships are emphasized, but a sense of independence among family members is rewarded, particularly among children and adolescents. Native Americans set few rules for their children and instead prefer for them to learn from their peers and their own mistakes and will chastise children by laughing at their mistakes or misfortunes. The elders also provide examples of appropriate or inappropriate behaviors for children by telling them traditional stories.

As a result of a strong sense of tribalism, everything is shared among Native Americans, including the solution to problems, material goods, and time. Native Americans treat time as a natural event and do not believe it should control their natural way of living. Native Americans generally reject the traditional sense of individualism leading to competition among family members and the tribe. Elder Native Americans take pride in sharing their resources and time with family members and their tribe. They are respected for their longevity and wisdom and are bound by tradition and culture.

CHARACTERISTICS OF ELDER HISPANICS

Hispanics are members of a single cultural group in the sense that they share a fairly common history, beginning with the Spanish conquest of the Americas. Hispanics share a common language, and have similar values and customs. Despite these similarities Hispanic culture is not homogeneous; it makes more sense to conceptualize Hispanic culture as an aggregate of parallel but distinct subcultures, each emanating from a different geographic area (Parrillo, 1966).

Hispanic, as distinct from Spanish, history begins in the early sixteenth century with the arrival of the Spaniards in the new world. By the middle of the sixteenth century, the original immigrants from Spain, native Indians, and variations of mixed Spaniards and Indians founded permanent settlements. In some areas, slaves from Africa were imported for labor, and yet another genetic and cultural strain was introduced. This complex process of Indo-Hispanic marriage, exploration, colonization, and cultural fusion created what is today's Hispanic people and culture (Parrillo, 1966).

The Spanish language is an important unifying factor in Hispanic culture. Of the Hispanics surveyed 68.9% identified Spanish as the "mother tongue" with English a remote second-place choice; 48.7% of Hispanics speak only Spanish in the home; the remaining 32% speaking variations of both Spanish and English and only 20% state that English is their only language (Schaefer, 1979). Most elder Hispanic adults speak Spanish exclusively and, if they do speak English, prefer to conduct most conversations in Spanish. Many elders take great pride in their native language and often will chastise younger members for not addressing them in Spanish as they see this behavior as disrespectful. The Spanish language is an emotional language and many elder adults feel that they can only convey their feelings and emotions appropriately through the Spanish language.

The Hispanic family is considered to be one of the most important culture-specific values of Hispanics (Sabogal, Marin, Otero-Sabogal, Marin, & Perez-Stable, 1987). Familism is described as a strong identification and attachment of individuals with their families and strong feelings of loyalty, reciprocity, and solidarity (Sabogal et al., 1987). The family remains the single most important reference group for most individuals throughout life, providing emotional security and a sense of belonging to its members (Padilla, Ruiz, & Alvarez, 1975). To a significant extent, individual Hispanics may view themselves much of the time as agents or representatives of their family (A. Padilla & Ruiz, 1976).

Within the Hispanic family there are two conceptual distinctions (A. Padilla & Ruiz, 1976): the nuclear family, consisting of husband, wife and children; and the extended family, which encompasses grandparents, uncles, aunts, and cousins. Because of the patrilineal factor, relatives on the father's side of the family may be considered more important than those on the mother's side. Both family concepts blend to create the intimate Hispanic family circle often forming a common council in crisis or time of decision, even if the decision directly affects only one member of the nuclear family. Several generations are likely to live within the same dwelling. This type of living arrangement is generally not created out of economic necessity, rather out of a sense of community and familism (Miranda, 1985).

In addition to the nuclear and extended family, unrelated friends are often symbolically incorporated into the family by the custom of godparentage. Familial friends along with uncles and aunts are chosen as godparents of children, who then participate in the raising of children and are often parent substitutes. Each child may have a different set of godparents. Godparents take part in family gatherings, familial decisions, and provide monetary support for children (Miranda, 1985). The practice of godparentage exists within other cultures; however, the difference within the Hispanic culture is the level of participation in intimate familial decisions (Miranda, 1985).

The interpersonal relations among parents and children who constitute the nuclear family are usually dictated by defined patterns of deference. The pattern that predominates is "the elder order the younger, and the men order the women (Murillo, 1976, p. 21)." This pattern establishes two central themes around which the interpersonal relations within the family are usually organized. The first is respect and obedience to elders and the second is male dominance. The husband and father is the autocratic head of the household. Few decisions can be made without his approval or knowledge. All other family members are expected to respect him and to accede to his will or direction.

Should he misuse his authority, however, he will lose respect within the community (Murillo, 1976).

The wife and mother role is to serve the needs of her husband, support his actions and decisions, and take care of the home and children. She represents the nurturent aspect of the family's life. Her life tends to revolve around her family and a few close friends. Usually, a close continuing relationship between mother and children perpetuates throughout her life (Murillo, 1976). Children receive training in responsibility and are often assigned tasks or responsibilities according to their age and ability, which they are expected to assume. This may take the form of caring for younger brothers or sisters, doing errands, taking care of grandparents, taking a job to help finance the family's needs, or some similar activities. This develops interdependence and a feeling of importance as a family member. Much of the individual's self-esteem is related to how he or she perceives him- or herself and how others perceive them in carrying out assigned family responsibilities (Murillo, 1976).

The importance of the family to a Hispanic and the close interpersonal ties that exist among family members, including those of the extended family, are not often appreciated in the Anglo society. Among Anglos a breaking away from familial dominance in adolescence is commonly looked on as being a state of growing maturity and independence and a necessary step toward adulthood. Within the Hispanic family, this same independence is viewed as a rejection of the family and the culture. Often adult Hispanic children marry and continue to live within the parental home even with the addition of children. To the Hispanic, family needs and demands have highest priority (Murillo, 1976).

The most important organization in the Hispanic community is the church, specifically the Roman Catholic Church. Only 5% of Hispanic people do not belong to the Roman Catholic Church (Schaefer, 1979). The Catholic Church has functioned as an aid in maintaining the importance of family within the Hispanic community and publicly chastises members who breach the customs. The church acts as the "rule keeper"; it participates in births, marriages, and funerals and is inextricably interwoven into the socialization of Hispanics (Parrillo, 1988).

Characteristics of Elder Asians

People described as Asians represent many different races, countries/areas of origin, religions, and traditional customs and cultures. Asians overall tend to be more urbanized than other minority cultures, and usually foreign rather than native born with closer ties to their countries of origin and birth. As a result of early socialization within Asian families, they have been taught to be relatively inhibited and tend to be less socially aggressive than white Americans. Traditional families emphasize the old countries' culture, including language, ceremonies, religion, arts, and the morals and ethics of proper social and interpersonal behavior.

The first group to immigrate into the United States were the Chinese whose work ethic was very desirable, but as a people and culture were very much unwanted. The anti-Chinese attitude led to the passage of the exclusion act in 1892. This act suspended specifically all Chinese immigration and other Asian immigration for nearly 50 years with no allowances made for spouses and/or children to join their fathers/husbands. This act also made Asians born in foreign countries ineligible for American citizenship.

Many Asians who immigrated to the United States intended to bring their families later and then found out that this was impossible. Most of the western states at the time also prohibited interracial marriages and in fact a federal law was passed that stated that any American woman who married an Asian man lost her citizenship. Compounding the problem for the Chinese was the traditional viewpoint that discouraged marrying out of their native village or province and certainly prohibited marriage outside the country or race. Between 1930 and 1946, the sex ratio of Chinese in the United States was approximately 80% male to 20% female (Schaefer, 1979). Because there were few American-born Chinese before 1930, the Chinese were essentially a community of men.

Asians typically have a history of organizational membership that is carried over from their country of origin. The Chinese have a history of clans that are extended governing units bound together by common ancestry. The clans are declining in their influence but the clans of the past provided mutual assistance, provided loans, settled disputes among their members, and provided cultural norms and traditions (Schaefer, 1979). Chinatowns are the result of past and present immigration and represent not only Chinese culture but their institutions as well. Chinatowns also define the culture, traditions, and family interactions. They are not without their social ills, and have problems with high suicide rates, run-down housing, rising crime rates, poor working conditions, and population density. The barrier that Chinese Americans created around their communities, which protected them in the past, has a tendency to deny them needed social services.

Within the traditional Asian families, parental authority, especially the father's, is seen as absolute. Loyalty to the family is important as it is the basis of the group's unity, cohesion, and control. Conservatism and self-control especially of emotions are taught as a emphasis on showing maturity. Asian parents use very little physical or corporal punishment; instead, they will ridicule or tease their children into conformity. Parents have positions of authority and privilege along with responsibility and obligation to the children. The expression of deference toward those in a superior position guides proper conduct in moments of social ambiguity that might arouse emotional feelings of embarrassment or confusion. Asians are basically patrilineal, emphasizing and placing importance on descent or kinship through the male line. The most important relationship in most Asian families is that of the father and son, specifically the firstborn son. All other relationships in the family system are extensions of or subordinated to this relationship. There is only one father, but parents always desire many sons. The mutual dependency between father and son is continuous and includes deceased male kin from the past, present, and future. The son owes his father services, obedience, and respect and the father is expected to assist the son in his education, to arrange his marriage, and when he dies to give his son his possessions. The kinship obligation between mother and son is derived by virtue of her marriage to the father, thus the son owes her the same obligations that he owes the father.

Romantic love, as defined in the Western world, is not expressed in traditional Asian families. Often the father arranges the marriages for all his children and these marriages are based on strengthening the family rather than love. Divorce is generally disapproved of and is considered to bring shame on the family, regardless of the abuse or situation.

Elder Asians are often grateful for what they have been granted by the United States government in exchange for their labor and typically seek very little from social institutions. They rely solely on Asian communities and their families for support on all levels. Typically, Asians do not seek individual wealth or individual status, rather they focus on collectivism and all resources are pooled within the family system and then divided according to need by the male head of the household. There is no single Asian faith, rather a conglomeration of many. The people of South Asia (Indian, Pakistani) are typically Hindu and Muslims, the people of Southeast Asia (Burma, Cambodia, Laos, Vietnam, Thailand, Malaysia, Indonesia, and the Philippines are a mixture of Christian and Buddhist. China, Japan, and Korea have a mixture of Confucianism, Buddhism, Shintoism, and Christianity.

CHARACTERISTICS OF ELDER AFRICAN AMERICANS

Most Africans who arrived in the United States from 1619 until the end of the slave trade in 1808 were unwilling immigrants. Between 1899 and 1922, 135,000 West Indian Blacks were admitted (Schaefer, 1979). Differences in culture prevented any unifying racial bond from forming between Black immigrants and native-born Blacks. During the age of exploration, Black crew members served under Columbus and sixteenth-century Spanish explorers such as Balboa and Cortez. They came as indentured servants, worked off their debts and then lived in the New World as free men. The labor demands of the southern colonies soon resulted in the enslavement of millions of other Africans and their forced migration to the United States. Slavery replaced indentured servitude in the South. Blacks were forcibly taken from their African homelands and sold into a lifetime of slavery in a land they did not choose and in which they had no opportunity to advance themselves.

To ease transition into a new country, many other ethnic groups re-created in miniature the society they left behind, but the Africans were not allowed to do so. They were forced to give up their culture, language, and country of origin. Southern state laws made the education of Black slaves a criminal offense.

Two hundred years of master-slave relations did much more than just prevent their assimilation; they shaped values and attitudes that continue today. The institution of slavery created an inferior status for Blacks and led to a great deal of prejudice and discrimination.

Myths about Black racial inferiority emerged as a rationalization of slavery. Although an extremely small percentage of White Southerners actually owned slaves, they were the most influential, and other Southern Whites were strong supporters of the system. Blacks were treated as if they were biologically inferior; as a result, the Blacks became socially inferior, first because of slavery and then as a result of discrimination in jobs, housing, and education. Suppression and restriction of educational endeavors as commonly practiced by slave owners was so effective that approximately 1% or 2% of the slaves were literate (Schaefer, 1979). Slaves were allowed to become Christians and a higher level of literacy grew out of Bible-reading, creating a powerful institution for African Americans.

Slavery has had major long-term consequences on the Black family (Schaefer, 1979). Many slaves owners separated males and females and did not allow marriages between them for two reasons, (1) if a slave were sold, it provoked dissension in the remaining slave and (2) it kept slaves from escaping. Additionally after 1910, a period of mass migration of Black men in search of employment in northern cities created an even higher incidence of broken or matriarchal homes (Brigham & Weissbach, 1972).

The Black person was not accorded any significant constitutional safeguards until after the Civil War. Following emancipation, thousands of unskilled and undereducated Blacks wandered the country in search of a new existence. Many Northern cities absorbed the freed slaves, but by 1900 the Black communities were crowded and efforts to help often turned to anger and antagonism. The discriminatory system known as Jim Crow (i.e., separate facilities and institutions) became firmly established in the South by 1900. The term Jim Crow refers to an offensive Black stereotype in a nineteenth century song-and-dance act. The United States separate-but-equal policy only further strengthened the double standards for Whites and Blacks. World War II began to erode this policy and helped to discredit racism. The 1954 Supreme Court decision in *Brown v. Board of Education* declared that segregated school facilities were inherently unequal and unconstitutional (Brigham & Weissbach, 1972).

African American elders have strong religious beliefs that are rooted in American Protestantism. The African American churches have merged long-lost tribal traditions of African religion with Christianity. Some of the cultural components of African religion emphasized a belief system that enabled the people to cope with extreme environmental conditions. These beliefs were pragmatic, magical and mysterious, secular, and family oriented.

Elder African Americans have a more vivid memory of prejudice and discrimination and sadly have accepted a restricted role in society and continue to have a great fear of White authority. As a result, elder Blacks are more firmly entrenched in Black communities and often during familial and or personal crisis will rely on the help of Black religious leaders such as the pastor of their local church.

African Americans and Anglos appear to have developed a moderately integrated position within the general society; however, the unresolved nature of the relationship still generates major societal issues and African Americans react angrily to unfair treatment or perceived injustices. The riots in Miami in 1989 and in Los Angeles in 1992 are examples of this pattern. African Americans also continue to experience attacks by the Ku Klux Klan and White supremacy groups.

ACCULTURATIVE STYLES AND COUNSELOR EFFECTIVENESS WITH OLDER ADULTS

The concept of acculturation is a factor to be considered within the culture and identity of the elder adult. Acculturation is defined as a process that occurs when an individual of an ethnic minority relinquishes traditional values, customs, beliefs, and behaviors of the minority culture and adopts those of the majority culture (Sodowsky, Lai, & Plake, 1991). This concept is important in counseling because certain evidence demonstrates that the effectiveness of counseling can be affected by the client's level or degree of acculturation into the dominant society (Cuellar, Harris, & Jasso, 1980). For example, a Hispanic individual whose primary childhood language was Spanish, chooses to speak only English, both in the home and in the outside environment, reflecting a high process of acculturation and the individual's relinquishment of the minority culture in favor of the dominant culture.

Acculturation is therefore an important aspect to determine before proceeding with counseling (Cuellar et al., 1980). Research has shown that acculturation has been found to be associated with a person's mental health status (Golding, Burnam, Timbers, Escobar, & Karno, 1985; Griffith, 1983; Szapocznik & Kurtines, 1980); levels of social support available (Griffith & Villavicencio, 1985); deviancy (Berry & Annis, 1974); alcoholism and drug use (Graves, 1967; Padilla et al., 1977); and political and social attitudes (Alva, 1985; Kranau, Green, & Valencia-Weber, 1982). An individual's acculturation level affects the counseling and the counseling relationship and needs attention when working with culturally diverse elder adults who may be less acculturated than their younger members and generally retain a greater percentage of culture, language, and customs. Acculturation is a fundamental variable in the interpretation of the clinical interview and psychological test data. Acculturation of a minority individual can be measured on two dimensions: the degree of assimilation to the majority culture and the degree of retention of the minority culture (Berry, 1980; LeVine & Padilla, 1980; Mendoza & Martinez, 1981; Sanchez & Atkinson, 1983). Either dimension can be used, and many types of acculturation measures are available. Counselors should know the specific minority culture and utilize the measures that have been designed for that cultural group.

CLINICAL PRACTICE OF CULTURALLY DIVERSE ELDER ADULTS

Counselors working with the culturally diverse elder adult must take into consideration acculturation factors, language, historical features of racism and discrimination for each distinct group and cultural norms and traditions. Another central issue is the counselor's ability to differentiate between psychiatric disorders and/or mental health issues and cultural norms. In the past, mental health literature has reported a higher level of mental illness and mental disorders among ethnic groups than among Whites. More recent literature has suggested three possible reasons for this: (1) a lack of uniformity in the definition of mental problems among culturally different groups, (2) lack of epidemiological studies and (3) biases in reporting mental problems within culturally diverse groups (Paniagua, 1994).

Because English is not the first language for many culturally diverse elder adults, miscommunications between the counselor and the client can easily occur. Culturally diverse elder adults may have difficulty expressing themselves in English, struggle to find appropriate words, and become more emotionally withdrawn as a result of expending energy in the attempt to communicate their thoughts and feelings. Many individuals must first think in their native language, translate the words into English for themselves and then finally respond to the counselor.

Many culturally diverse elder adults practice and follow religious/folk beliefs that maybe unfamiliar to the counselor. Beliefs in spirits, hexes, and other unseen events are culturally accepted among some members of the four multicultural groups and are especially prevalent among elder adults. If those beliefs are not recognized as normal within the individuals' culture during the formulation of a clinical diagnosis, the client may be erroneously diagnosed with a psychiatric disorder. In addition, if the counselor does not treat these folk beliefs with respect, the elder adult may disregard the counselor's expertise creating resistance within the counseling relationship.

For counselors to work competently with culturally different elder adults, they must understand biological, psychological, and social issues that impact this group in our society. They must be aware of the assumptions and precepts of theories relevant to their practice and how these may apply differently to culturally diverse groups. These theories and models may proscribe or limit the therapies that will be beneficial for culturally diverse elder adults. Counselors must continue to explore and learn issues related to culturally diverse elder adults and discriminatory practices. They need to be knowledgeable and aware of verbal and nonverbal process variables and how these may affect minorities in counseling.

COUNSELING THE ELDER NATIVE AMERICAN

Although Native Americans have been described as an ethnic group, the counselor should recognize that the many tribes are diverse in their cultural values, religions, and traditions. To work effectively with elder Native Americans, counselors must spend a great deal of time learning about the specific tribe they will be working with and making themselves known to the Indian community. Rarely are counselors or any type of mental health service providers accepted into the community without first consulting the tribal council and receiving permission. The tribal council acts as a screening agent to its community and, as a result of the U.S. government's long history of past abuse, is highly suspicious of non-Native Americans wanting to provide health and social services.

When working with Native American elders, it is best to keep rules at a minimum and those rules that are necessary must be flexible as Native Americans rarely respond well to formally structured environments. If you are conducting family therapy, it is important that counselors not look at the elders as being the "head" of the family. Although elders occupy places of respect and governship, they do not make decisions individually. Generally, decision making is conducted with the entire family/tribe, and each member from the oldest to the youngest has input, with each person's input being evaluated and measured.

The counselor must also accept the client's consultation of tribal leaders, the elderly family members, and the medicine man or woman when problems or issues emerge. A Native American may bring such individuals into the counseling environment without consulting with the counselor. They play a major role in the elder's life and he or she respects their advice. The use of traditional healers is becoming more common and many Native American elders expect this to be integrated into their sessions.

Native American elders are generally also tribal leaders. This position is highly respected within the tribe and the elder will expect the same level of deference from the counselor. If this respect is not forthcoming, the elder Native American will reject the counselor and become very resistant within the counseling environment. Elder Native Americans will generally seek help from within the tribe prior to going outside the Native American community. The counselor usually represents a last effort in solving an overwhelming problem and needs to be aware that a crisis situation probably has brought the individual into counseling.

Native Americans place a great deal of emphasis on listening and are trained from birth to place a great emphasis on nonverbal forms of communication. Counselors should be prepared to expect long periods of silence during counseling sessions. Native American elders are generally slow in their speaking patterns, utilize few words, and sometimes prefer to tell their problems embedded in stories. Elders also will communicate their emotions on a subtle level through cues with their bodies, eyes, and tone of voice. Direct and prolonged eye contact is generally seen as a challenge and is a sign of lack of respect among elders.

Counselors should avoid taking too many notes in the sessions as this will create an atmosphere of suspicion. The focus on note taking may make the individual uncomfortable as this information can be released to other social organizations and create harm. In the counseling relationship, it is also important to avoid asking questions that are unrelated to the core clinical problem as this creates mistrust about the real purpose of the sessions.

Counselors should clarify those issues using a nondirective approach and then use a directive problem-solving approach for concrete and feasible solutions. The counselor needs to be flexible in making appointments as Native American elders do not plan their lives around a specific time frame. Counseling sessions may vary in time as the elder will decide when he or she has finished talking.

Native American elders disclose slowly and may need to attend many sessions before they begin to feel comfortable sharing any type or amount of information. Initial sessions may consist of the Native American elder first telling the counselor historical stories to determine whether the counselor will be a respectful listener. The establishment of the counseling relationship will often be time consuming and prolonged; however, once the counselor has gained the elder's trust, it will be complete and open.

During the first session with the elder Native American client, the counselor should discreetly pay attention to the screening for alcoholism and watch for signs of depression as these are common issues in this community. The onset of illness and limited mobility is often followed by depression, feelings of inadequacy, and low self-esteem.

Behavioral approaches have been recommended with American Indian clients rather than psychodynamic models as these approaches emphasize the cause of behavior as determined primarily by external events. Psychodynamic theories and models do not take into consideration the reservation environment and the extreme racism and discrimination that Native American elders have faced.

COUNSELING THE ELDER HISPANIC

Hispanics turn to family members during times of stress and economic difficulties and often consult with other members in the family before they decide to seek outside help. The next most common solution is to consult with a priest. Approximately 95% of all Hispanic people are Catholics and often look for answers within the environment of the church and their priests. This is especially true for elder Hispanics who view religion as an important part of their lives and believe that prayer will cure a physical or mental health problem. Only after exploring these options do they seek help from a counselor.

In general, Hispanics are family oriented and often incorporate nonfamily members in helping professions such as a physician into their familial circle. Hispanic people have a need to know about the individual(s) providing services before they will commit to a helping relationship. It is not unusual for the

Hispanic individual/family to request personal information about the counselor prior to addressing client's concerns. Elder Hispanic individuals will be very curious as to the counselor's relationship with his or her family, both nuclear and extended as they often judge a person by their familial commitments. Elder Hispanics may seek out a counselor who is married with children or an older individual as they believe that age brings wisdom and a younger person is often not mature enough to provide these services. Hispanics also often bring gifts, this is their way of expressing gratitude for the services provided by the therapist and they can become very offended if these gifts are turned away.

Nevertheless counselors should maintain a courteous and formal relationship with the elder Hispanic until clearly invited to treat the client in a more informal manner. Although Hispanics tend to incorporate nonfamily members into their familial circle, they also want the person to be a professional and have high credentials. To this end, counselors should use titles and the surnames as opposed to the first name as this is a sign of respect, both of status and age.

Elder Hispanics often believe that a divine providence governs the world and that the individual cannot control or prevent adversity. Fatalism can imply a sense of vulnerability and lack of control in the presence of adverse events, as well as the feeling that such events are "waiting" to affect the life of the individual (Casas & Vasquez, 1996). Fatalism may also be interpreted in terms of an adaptive response to uncontrollable life situations. The counselor must be aware that the issue of fatalism cannot be dismissed or explained away as these are major belief systems often rooted in religion and need to be incorporated into therapy.

Hispanics lump many different systems under a general description of a nervous condition. This may imply anything from severe depression to occasional migraines. The counselor must make a special effort to determine whether pathology, a physical condition, or a cultural explanation is present and obtain a detailed description of the actual symptoms.

A major component in the counseling of elder Hispanics is acculturation and language. Many elder Hispanics are less acculturated, more entrenched in folk beliefs and culture, and feel more comfortable in their native language of Spanish. It is not unusual to find elder Hispanics who do not speak English either at all or well enough to converse with a counselor. Therefore, those counselors who are working with this population need to either be fluent enough in Spanish to converse with these clients or obtain a professional interpreter. It is highly suggested that counselors not use family members as interpreters as the elder Hispanic may want to discuss or disclose information with the counselor that he or she may be hesitant to share with the family. Using a casual acquaintance such as a secretary can be problematic as these individuals are not bound by confidentiality and often have ties with the community and may share confidential information.

Many elder Hispanics may have folk beliefs or spiritual interpretations of mental disorders. It is important that counselors explore and understand these interpretations and learn how to utilize them in the counseling process. These beliefs are part of the elder Hispanic's culture and have specific meaning for the individual. Often elder Hispanics will consult with a folk healer either prior to counseling or in addition to the counselor.

Elder Hispanics see the counselor as an expert and will expect specific suggestions for helping them solve their issue/problem. They often do not understand the differences between counselors, psychologists, psychiatrists, and physicians and may request medication to help with their problem or discuss medical complaints that may be troubling them along with the psychosocial components. Hispanic individuals tend to focus on monitoring their health and often place a great deal of emphasis on medications and medical interventions. It is important to discuss these differences with clients along with their expectancy for a prescription of medication and the fact that medication may or may not offer a solution to their issue.

Elder Hispanics are polite to individuals they see as being authority figures and will not correct a counselor who has misunderstood them, as they see this as being disrespectful of authority. The counselor needs to routinely restate the information given and ask if it is correct and the meaning that the elder wants to convey. By asking for clarification, the counselor allows for the elder to be involved in the therapeutic process and essentially gives the elder permission to clarify issues without embarrassing the counselor.

Behavioral approaches and cognitive behavioral therapies have been suggested as modalities that are effective with elder Hispanics as they focus on problems and solutions, are less insight oriented, and focus on helping the individual restructure. Therapies that are not recommended in this population include insight-oriented modalities, psychodynamic approaches, and rational emotive therapy (RET).

COUNSELING THE ELDER ASIAN

Asians do not encourage members of their group to reveal their problems to people outside the group. All problems must be shared only among family members, just as all credits and successes received by an individual must also be shared by the entire family. Shame and guilt are mechanisms used by Asian families to enforce norms in the family (Kitano & Maki, 1996). Therefore Asians rarely seek out counseling unless forced by an outside authority (i.e., the police) or the situation has reached crisis proportions and the family and community can no longer cope.

An Asian person who attempts to contact an outside support agency without family permission may lose confidence and support from the family. This can exacerbate an already strong sense of shame and guilt leading in turn to additional anxiety and depression. Elder Asians will not contact a counselor on their own initiative. When an elder Asian does come in for counseling, there will be a great deal of hesitancy and resistance. Because the very act of coming for help to someone outside the Asian community brings a sense of failure and shame, counselors need to be sensitive to these issues and feelings.

Elder Asians have a high belief in self-control that extends into all facets of their lives including emotions and behavior. They believe that an individual must show stoicism, patience, and an uncomplaining attitude in the face of adversity and to display tolerance under the most extreme painful conditions. When an individual breaks from these norms, they become an embarrassment to the family. Like the Hispanics, elder Asians also believe in fatalism and that events are predetermined with individuals being powerless and having little control over their own lives.

As a result of a past history of abuse and racism, elder Asians fear exposing any difficulties outside their families and community. When asked questions by non-Asians they will often look quiet and act passive to avoid offending others and sometimes will avoid eye contact and will answer all questions affirmatively to be polite when they do not understand the counselor's questions. Typically, elder Asians will be deferential in the presence of the counselor because they perceive the counselor to be the authority. Among Asians, silence is a sign of respect and direct eye contact during direct verbal communication is considered to be disrespectful.

When an elder Asian comes to counseling it is usually a crisis situation. The families have often refused to seek professional help for many years until the problem has become so chronic and severe that the family is unable to continue handling the situation. When they seek professional help, they expect the counselor to tell them what is wrong and how to resolve the problem immediately. The counselor needs to emphasize concrete and tangible goals and give the impression that a tentative solution is possible. It is best to avoid comments suggesting that the solution will take a long time. Again, counselors need to keep in mind that the elder Asian will see the therapist as an authority figure and will have certain expectations of expertise. Counselors must define the services they can provide, describe prior experiences and education, and use a professional title while maintaining a formalized relationship in which they address the elder by title and surname.

Elder Asians' mental or emotional problems have probably brought shame and guilt to the family; therefore, it is important to understand that an open discussion will be difficult. In the first session, the therapist must show both verbally and nonverbally that he or she will wait until the client is ready to discuss mental problems in public (Paniagua, 1994). Elder Asians also have a tendency to express psychological disorders in somatic terms such as headaches, back pain, weight loss, and fatigue. Again, this is because psychological disorders bring a sense of shame, humiliation, and guilt as it is felt that the individual is responsible for the lack of mental self-control. Psychological disorders can also stigmatize the entire Asian family within the Asian community and therefore physical complaints are more acceptable.

The counselor needs to acknowledge all somatic complaints and determine whether these should be referred for a medical consultation. Once physical complaints have been ruled out, the counselor should help the elder Asian to move from somatic complaints to mental health problems. The first meeting should always be considered a potential crisis and the counselor should be prepared to provide the family with specific guidelines for immediate treatment and outline a plan of action. It is important to avoid suggestions regarding inpatient treatment as many Asians consider hospitalization as the last resort and the family must be consulted and provide approval.

Behavioral approaches provide more concrete and directive solutions and do not emphasize the exploration of internal conflicts that can lead to an increase in the shame felt by the Asians. Therapy with elder Asians should be problem focused, goal oriented, and symptom relieving on a short-term basis.

COUNSELING ELDER AFRICAN AMERICANS

Elder African Americans often hesitate to enter a counseling relationship in part because racism and discrimination have left them suspicious of social institutions. Instead, they prefer to seek help from extended family members, the community, and the church. For many elder African Americans, the church is one of the most significant influences in their lives. Therefore it is important that the counselor assess the level of religious involvement.

For many elder African Americans, familism is also an important variable in the counseling relationship. The family systems of African Americans often include friends in addition to blood relations. There is a great deal of role flexibility in African American families, and it is not unusual for the mother to play the role of the father and function as the head of the family. This role may extended beyond a single generation with the elder female African American providing the father role for grandchildren, great-grandchildren, nieces, and nephews. As a result, elder African Americans often become involved in counseling both on behalf of troubled junior family members or because they are no longer able to cope with these same members. Although it is necessary in these situations to place attention on the problematic junior family member, it is important not to overlook the perhaps unspoken needs of the elder African American.

Elder African Americans often have many folk beliefs that counselors should be aware of and, when appropriate, incorporate into counseling as these can be important belief systems. Many elder African Americans believe that mental problems can be the result of occult or spiritual factors and that folk medicine can effectively treat their medical and mental problems. There are three basic types of healer/spiritual figure in African American communities: the elder female folk healer who deals with common ailments and provides advice and gives folk medication; the spiritualist/voodoo priest, and the African American Protestant pastor.

Most elder African American clients prefer to discuss the core or most essential problem he or she feels should be considered first, additional problems may be handled in later sessions. The elder will expect the counselor to suggest a focused, brief intervention to deal with the problem quickly. An important issue is to avoid linking the mental health problem with child rearing or with past parental behavior as African Americans see this type of direction as blaming and ridiculing individuals deserve respect and who did their best under the extreme circumstances of racism and discrimination.

Counselors working with elder African Americans should initially acknowledge that racial differences exist and encourage clients to talk about their feelings concerning this issue. After this discussion, the topic should not be dealt with in subsequent sessions unless raised by the client. Racial issues should not be discussed during brief or emergency interventions involving crisis.

Initial sessions with elder African Americans should emphasize the collection of preliminary clinical data more than the therapeutic process. The counselor should have a clear understanding of the client's environment, familial relationships, religious affiliation, and support systems. It is also important to reinforce the concept of empowerment and relate it to the client's experience with therapeutic changes. Counselors should communicate acceptance and respect for the elder African American client in terms that are intelligible and meaningful in his or her cultural frame of reference.

Recommended therapeutic modalities of therapy with elder African American clients are problem-solving and social skills training. The central goal of problem-solving training is to teach the elder to deal quickly with the solution of one or more problems in a series of problems. This strategy may be perceived by the client as a way of taking power or control over his or her own behavior or over other family members. Insight-oriented therapies are also not recommended when working with this population.

PSYCHOLOGICAL ASSESSMENT WITH THE CULTURALLY DIVERSE ELDER ADULT

Inaccurate psychological assessment and diagnosis of mental disorders is a major issue when working with culturally diverse elder adults. These inaccuracies can have three consequences: overdiagnosis, underdiagnosis, and misdiagnosis (Lonner & Ibrahim, 1996). Biases in testing are generally found to be a major factor in inaccuracies with psychological assessment. Attempts have been made to eliminate or control biases in the assessment and diagnosis of multicultural groups, including the translation of tests into the language of the group being tested and the development of culturally appropriate norms (Paniagua, 1994). However, biases continue to exist and to be problematic in the assessment of the elder adult.

Dana (1993) suggests that counselors should first conduct an assessment of acculturation to determine the level of integration. After this important determination, the therapists should provide a culture-specific service delivery style utilizing the client's native language and selecting assessment measures appropriate for the cultural orientation and client preferences. Finally, the therapist should use a culture-specific strategy when informing the client about findings derived from the assessment process.

Psychological assessments are important in that instruments are used to provide a common language in the assessment and diagnosis of psychiatric disorders. To facilitate reimbursement and meet institutional requirements, many such instruments may be required in the clinical practice of counselors involved in the assessment and treatment of mental problems. Therefore, counselors should use these instruments when working with culturally diverse elder adults, but understand the need for modifications and individual plans of assessment. Many elder adults have not completed any type of formal education and may not be able to read or write either in English or their native languages. Counselors should also understand the compounding factor of age and cultural diversity when testing clients. For example, tests designed for Native Americans may be appropriate for most members of this group, but inappropriate for Native Americans over the age of 60 years. It is not uncommon for assessment instruments to be normed solely on younger populations of culturally diverse individuals.

CONCLUSION

Counselors should be aware that the lack of knowledge and recognition of cultural influences could reduce their effectiveness in counseling culturally diverse elder adults. Counselors need to understand the appropriate culture as well as the aging process and how these two variables interact within the culturally diverse elder's life. This understanding is often necessary to effectively overcome culturally diverse elders' resistance to a counseling process that is in conflict with their values and culture. The experiences of many culturally diverse elder adults have left them suspicious of social institutions and it will be necessary for the counselor to allay their fears.

Counselors often fail to consider the culturally diverse elder adult's unique frame of reference and psychosocial history before deciding whether to work with him or her. For all four groups, establishing a working relationship is often time consuming and requires flexibility on the part of the counselor. These clients are often the most challenging and rewarding for the counselor, who must integrate culture, folk beliefs, acculturation, and language to a greater degree than when working with their younger counterparts.

To make informed choices about entering, continuing, or terminating therapy, culturally diverse elders and their families must receive the necessary information in a context they can easily understand. Elder adults are generally unfamiliar with the counseling process and should be told explicitly about the procedures and goals of counseling. Clients should not only be informed of the treatment plan but also be alerted to possible alternative intervention methods. Counselors should also be aware of the organizational factors that can create barriers for the elder to attend counseling sessions (types of services to the racial/ethic community, accessibility via public transportation, intake procedures, professional background of staff, foreign language capability of staff, and race/ethnicity of staff and planning boards).

Additionally, counselors should be aware and sensitive to their own cultural heritage, be aware of how their biases may be perceived by their culturally diverse elder clients. Counselors wanting to work within these populations should expose themselves to the different cultural groups, enroll in experiential courses, and be supervised by individuals with prior experience in working with the culturally diverse elder adult.

Finally, counselors must explore different ways of reaching this group. It may be that counselors need to take an outreach role approach that requires them to spend less time in their offices and more time in their clients' communities. As stated earlier, all four minority groups often mistrust social institutions because of both past and perceived present racism and prejudice. Counselors may have to make the initial contact with culturally diverse elders in their communities and establish themselves as helpers within the community. By making him- or herself available in the client's environment, the counselor is in a better position to respond to the client's needs. This exposure may also help the counselor understand the cultural experience of the elder and enhance the counselor-client relationship. Counselors who become actively involved in the social programs and the activities in their minority clients find this visibility within the community greatly enhances their ability to provide effective counseling.

REFERENCES

Alva, S.A. (1985). Political acculturation of Mexican American adolescents. *Hispanic Journal of Behavioral Sciences, 7*, 345–364.

Berry, J.W. (1980). Acculturation as varieties of adaptation. In A.M. Padilla (Ed.), *Acculturation theory, model and some new findings.* (pp. 9–25). Boulder, CO: Westview Press.

Berry, J.W., & Annis, R.C. (1974). Acculturative stress; the role of ecology, culture, and differentiation. *Journal of Cross-Cultural Psychology, 5*, 382–406.

Brigham, J.C., & Weissbach T.A. (1972). *Racial attitudes in America: Analyses and findings of social psychology.* New York: Harper & Row.

Casas, J.M., & Vasquez, M.J.T. (1996). Counseling the hispanic: A guiding framework for a diverse population. In P.B. Pedersen, J.G. Draguns, W.J. Lonner, & J.E. Trimble (Eds.), *Counseling across cultures* (pp. 146–177). London: Sage.

Cuellar, I., Harris, I.C., & Jasso, R. (1980). An acculturation scale for Mexican Americans normal and clinical populations. *Hispanic Journal of Behavioral Sciences, 2*, 199–217.

Dana, R.H. (1993, November 5). Can *"corrections" for culture using moderator variables contribute to cultural competence in assessment?* Paper presented at the annual convention of the Texas Psychological Association, Austin, TX.

Golding, J.M., Burnam, M.A., Timbers, D.M., Escobar, J.I., & Karno, M. (1985). Acculturation and distress: Social psychological mediators. *Hispanic Journal of Behavioral Sciences, 7*, 339–344.

Graves, D.T. (1967). Acculturation, access, and alcohol in a tri-ethnic community. *American Anthropologist, 69*, 306–321.

Griffith, J., & Villavicencio, S. (1985). Relationships among acculturation, sociodemographic characteristics and social supports in Mexican American adults. *Hispanic Journal of Behavioral Sciences, 7*, 75–92.

Kitano, H.H.L., & Maki, M.T. (1996). Continuity, change and diversity: Counseling Asian Americans. In P.B. Pedersen, J.G. Draguns, W.J. Lonner, & J.E. Trimble (Eds.), *Counseling across cultures* (pp. 124–146). London: Sage.

Kranau, E.J., Green, V., & Valencia-Weber, G. (1982). Acculturation and the Hispanic woman: Attitudes toward women, sex-role attribution, sex-role behavior, and demographics. *Hispanic Journal of Behavioral Sciences, 4,* 21–40.

LeVine, E., & Padilla A. (1980). *Crossing cultures in therapy: Pluralistic counseling for the Hispanic.* Belmont, CA: Wadsworth.

Lonner, W.J., & Ibrahim, F.A. (1996). Appraisal and assessment in cross-cultural counseling. In P.B. Pedersen, J.G. Draguns, W.J. Lonner, & J.E. Trimble (Eds.), *Counseling across cultures* (pp. 293–323). London: Sage.

Mendoza, R.H., & Martinez, J.L. (1981). The measurement of acculturation. In A. Baron, Jr. (Ed.), *Explorations in Chicano psychology* (pp. 71–82). New York: Praeger.

Miranda, M., & Kitano, H.H. (1976) Barriers to mental health services: a Japanese-American and Mexican-American dilemma. In C.A. Hernandez, M.J. Haug, & N.N. Wagner (Eds.), *Chicanos: Social and Psychological Perspectives* (2nd ed., pp. 242–252). Saint Louis, MO: Mosby.

Murillo, N., (1976). The Mexican American family. In C.A. Hernandez, M.J. Haug, & N.N. Wagner (Eds.), *Chicanos: Social and Psychological Perspectives* (2nd ed., pp. 15–25). Saint Louis, MO: Mosby.

Padilla, A.M., & Ruiz, R.A. (1976). Prejudice and discrimination. In C.A. Hernandez, M.J. Haug, & N.N. Wagner (Eds.), *Chicanos: Social and psychological perspectives* (2nd ed., pp. 110–124). Saint Louis, MO: Mosby.

Padilla, E.R. (1976). The relationship between psychology and Chicanos: Failures and possibilities. In C.A. Hernandez, M.J. Haug, & N.N. Wagner (Eds.), *Chicanos: Social and psychological perspectives* (2nd ed., pp. 282–290). Saint Louis, MO: Mosby.

Paniagua, F.A. (1994). *Assessing and treating culturally diverse clients: A practical guide.* London: Sage.

Parrillo, V.N. (1966). *Strangers to these shores, race and ethnic relations in the United States.* Boston: Houghton Mifflin.

Sabogal, F., Marin, G., Otero-Sabogal, R., Marin, B.V., & Perez-Stable, E.J. (1987). Hispanic familism and acculturation: What changes and what doesn't. *Hispanic Journal of Behavioral Sciences, 9*(4), 397–412.

Sanchez, A.R. (1981). *Chicano student's use of counseling services: Cultural and institutional factors.* Unpublished master's thesis, California State University.

Schaefer, R.T. (1979). *Racial and ethnic groups.* Boston: Little, Brown.

Sodowsky, G.R., Lai, E.W.M., & Plake, B.S. (1991). Moderating effects of sociocultural variables on acculturation attitudes of Hispanics and Asian Americans. *Journal of Counseling and Development, 70,* 194–204.

Szapocznik, J., & Kurtines, W. (1980). Acculturation, biculturalism and adjustment among Cuban Americans. In A.M. Padilla (Ed.), *Acculturation theory, model and some new findings* (pp. 139–159). Boulder, CO: Westview Press.

CHAPTER 9

Using Reminiscence and Life Review as Natural Therapeutic Strategies in Group Therapy

VICTOR MOLINARI

In his seminal article, Butler (1963) defined life review as a universal process triggered by the realization of approaching death and characterized by the progressive return to consciousness of past experiences, particularly unresolved conflicts. Rather than viewing the reminiscence of older adults as a sign of failing memory or boredom, Butler saw it as a natural adaptive response to the challenges of late life. This concept has spawned numerous articles attesting to life review's utility as a conceptual framework for understanding the developmental crises associated with aging, and as a clinical tool for constructively channeling the reminiscence process.

This chapter first situates life review within the general literature on reminiscence. I then discuss life review's initial Eriksonian and Jungian theoretical underpinnings and the varied and overlapping perspectives evolving from current dominant clinical theoretical orientations. This is followed by a presentation of neglected advances in psychodynamic thought that nestles the concept in a broader and more viable theoretical framework. I then reflect on the varied forms that reminiscence interventions have taken and which of these can be construed as therapy; posit life review to be the prime mode of reminiscence therapy; and outline those aspects of life review therapy as a clinical technique that have been supported across varied settings by the empirical and qualitative literature. Guided by these considerations, I then propose a model life review therapy program. Finally, I present recommendations for further research in this area.

I would like to acknowledge Mr. Jeffrey Webster's thoughtful review of an earlier version of this chapter.

REMINISCENCE LITERATURE

Research on reminiscence has challenged some of Butler's major assumptions concerning the life review process. Certainly his ideas that life review occurs mostly among old people, and that all older persons engage in life review have not been validated. Romaniuk and Romaniuk (1983) found no differences between older and younger adults in frequency of reminiscence (although both groups reminisced more than middle-aged groups). In a study of centenarians, Merriam, Martin, Adkins, and Poon (1995) discovered that just under half of the centenarians had never reviewed their lives. She also found that centenarians did not reminisce nor review their lives more than the 60- or 80-year-olds, thus calling into question Butler's idea that approaching death sparks the life review.

However, in an exploratory analysis of the content and structure of life review deVries, Blando, and Walker (1995) discovered that older adults do review a greater number of events than younger adults. They also report that negative events are processed in a more complex manner than positive events, which suggests that personal transformation at any age is triggered by tension or conflict. Webster (1993) developed the Reminiscence Functions Scale (RFS) to assess the functions of reminiscence across the life span. The RFS was found to consist of seven factors: boredom reduction, death preparation, identity/problem-solving, conversation, intimacy maintenance, bitterness revival, and teach/inform. Research with this instrument across different age groups suggests that reminiscence is a process that begins early and continues throughout life. Nevertheless, although reminiscence frequency in general may remain relatively stable throughout the life span, specific reminiscence functions change with age. In particular, older adults utilize the identity/problem-solving function of reminiscence relatively less than the young or middle aged, but exercise the intimacy maintenance and death preparation functions more than the other age groups. These results are consistent with the findings of Taft and Nehrke (1990) who discovered no relationship between general reminiscence and ego integrity, but detected a significant relationship between life review dimensions and ego integrity, and age and ego integrity. Watt and Wong (1991) used qualitative analyses to develop a taxonomy of reminiscence that includes six types: integrative, instrumental, transmissive, narrative, escapist, and obsessive. They consider the most adaptive types of reminiscence to be integrative and instrumental, and obsessive reminiscence to be the least adaptive.

This brief review of the reminiscence literature leads to some general conclusions. Life review is not synonymous with reminiscence. It is a special form of reminiscence with an evaluative component—it is not the simple remembering of past events, but an active grappling with the past for the sake of settling unresolved tensions. This type of evaluative reminiscence is probably more frequently engaged in by older adults, although all older adults do not necessarily review their lives. The life review process is both intrapersonal and interpersonal, and encompasses personal integrative and social transmissive functions. The outcome may be reduction in death anxiety (Fishman, 1992) and possible acquisition of wisdom (but see Staudinger, Smith, & Baltes, 1992) or failure and depressive recrimination. The research of Webster (1993) and Watt and Wong (1991) have refined previous reminiscence taxonomies (Coleman, 1974; LoGerfo, 1980–1981; Romaniuk & Romaniuk, 1981), which may pave the way for conceptual advances, make sense of conflicting empirical findings, and offer guidance to clinicians working with older adults in varied settings.

THEORETICAL FORMULATIONS

Although Butler was careful not to embrace any specific theoretical perspective other than a life span developmental one, life review was almost immediately linked with the well-known theories of Erikson and Jung. Erikson's (1959) idea of ego integrity has a natural association with the life review process, because his theory postulates that the last stage of life is concerned with the task of self-integration. It has been proposed that ego integrity is achieved via the soul-searching attendant upon the life review process, and that depression awaits the failed life reviewer. Although these ideas make intuitive sense, research results have been inconsistent (Cooke, 1991; Fishman, 1992; Taft & Nehrke, 1990) probably related to the well-known difficulty of operationalizing Eriksonian concepts. Jung (1933) has also written about the need to synthesize the disparate aspects of the self, and how older adults are particularly open to accept the disowned contrasexual (e.g., animus, anima) aspects of their personality. Although life review appears to be a possible mechanism for such personal transformation, Jung's ideas however heuristic, are difficult to subject to rigorous quantitative or qualitative analysis probably related to the strong spiritual/mystical strain in his thinking.

More recent psychological, philosophical and social theories have conceptualized the life review process from a variety of other distinct but overlapping viewpoints. Viney (1995) has used personal construct theory to inform her reminiscence work with older adults. From this constructivist perspective, she postulated that older adults lose many of the sources of confirmation for the positive stories that are necessary for good mental health. Life review may be a way that some older persons affirm their identity by integrating their experiences into an empowered view of themselves. Watt and Cappeliez (1995) conceptualize the use of reminiscence from a cognitive-behavioral viewpoint. They note that the instrumental and integrative aspects of reminiscence act as adaptive coping strategies to stave off depression by reaccessing prior effective problem-solving strategies and developing positive self-attributions.

Gutmann (1987) explored the evolutionary function of reminiscence for older adults, and documented the role of the elder as storyteller across a range of different societies and time periods. Throughout history, older people have been the repositors of cultural values that traditionally they have transmitted in oral form. There are thus compelling sociobiological reasons why older people reminisce and why life reviews are often conducted in public forums. Older persons get societal affirmation for their accumulated wisdom, and bestow this legacy to younger generations. In this regard, it is interesting to speculate that the age-related maintenance of verbal over performance intellectual abilities may be due to the societal need for the elder to be spokesperson for oral tradition (see also Mergler & Goldstein, 1983). Consistent with the preceding analysis, Coleman (1994) has argued that the social function of reminiscence has long been neglected. He emphasizes that reminiscence teaches important shared moral values and links the individual adventure with society's journey. A life review not only changes a psyche but transforms society as well. The discourse-analytic perspective of Buchanan and Middleton (1994) builds on these analyses and offers a radical slant on the changing historical views of reminiscence. These authors note that prior to Butler's (1963) formulation, reminiscence was viewed at best as of little constructive advantage or at worst as a sign of mental illness. The life review concept depathologized reminiscence by promoting it to be of personal value for the older person. However, it has only been with recent social and demographic changes that the aforementioned societal benefits of reminiscence have been publicized. In a sense, modifications in the definition of reminiscence have mirrored the changes in the political clout that older adults have achieved.

Recent developments in psychoanalytic thinking may help realize a broader conceptualization of the life review process. Self-psychological theory has concentrated on the construct of the self as the major organizing force of the person (Kohut, 1984). Although the self is built on the "reflected appraisals of others," the major emphasis in self psychology has been on the varied aspects of the self schema. From this perspective, the life review can be viewed as a vehicle to achieve self-cohesion in late life. Renewed interest in object relations (Winnicott, 1971) and interpersonal theories (Klerman & Weissman, 1993; Sullivan, 1953) has focused attention less on the individual and more on the connection between psychopathology and failed interpersonal relationships. It follows that examination of the nuances of current and past relationships is essential for successful personality change, and that the therapeutic relationship is a prime vehicle for healing to occur. Extrapolating from the attachment theory of Mahler (1967), Molinari and Reichlin (1984–1985) have proposed that the life review process is similar to the mourning experience undergone by those who have suffered losses. With life review, losses can be personal and intangible, and the therapeutic goal may be that of promoting strategies for grief work and reattachment. Overreliance on the self as an explanatory device has also been confronted by feminist critics of psychoanalytic thought who emphasize the self-in-relation-to-others as the prime unit for psychological analysis (Jordan, 1989). Self-actualization of individual interests takes a less prominent role in feminist therapeutic goal-setting, because of a heightened realization of the reciprocation between individual and societal needs. The therapeutic goal might be to assist the individual to get along with others and cultivate a mutual social support system to satisfy natural desires to nurture and be nurtured. The narrative movement in psychoanalytic thought (Schafer, 1992) has heightened our awareness of how patients enter therapy with maladaptive stories ill-fitting to their current life situation and related to atavistic templates tied to historical circumstance. A therapeutic goal would be to create new stories that are more consonant with present realities. Insight into literal truth is abandoned as a hopeless endeavor, and therapeutic progress is gauged by the congruence and functionality of a protean narrative truth.

LIFE REVIEW AS A CLINICAL ACTIVITY

Because reminiscence has so many functions for older adults, it is little wonder that there have been diverse clinical uses for this activity. Structured reminiscence occurs in community, medical, psychiatric inpatient, psychiatric outpatient, and in long-term institutional settings. It has been utilized to alleviate depression (Watt & Cappeliez, 1995), reduce stress in a medical setting (Rybarczyk, 1995), and enhance self-esteem in patients with early dementia (Woods & McKiernan, 1995). The clinical applications of reminiscence have taken myriad forms via oral and written storytelling, autobiography, gestalt exercises, poetry, music, drama, pilgrimages, reunions, and scrapbooks (Garland, 1994; Haight & Hendrix, 1995).

The heterogeneity of these methods implemented by a diverse array of volunteers and professionals including occupational therapists, recreational therapists, nurses, social workers, psychiatrists, and psychologists has sparked a debate about the term life review "therapy." Bender (1994) has argued that therapy occurs only when a self-defined patient seeks treatment from a specialist who assesses the problem and offers the most suitable intervention for which the patient consents. It follows that by this definition most reminiscence groupwork is not therapy, although it still can be helpful. deVries, Birren, and Deutchman (1995) also eschew the therapy label for their guided autobiography approach because it is not problem-centered and emotions are not delved into or solicited.

These definitions are unnecessarily restrictive when stringently adhered to. I view reminiscence activity along a therapeutic continuum based on the nature of the setting (community vs. clinical), the personal and physical characteristics of the reminiscer (cognitively impaired vs. verbal and introspective), the qualifications of the provider (layperson vs. professional), the psychological relevance of the content areas covered (best loved talk shows vs. experiences with death), format (loose vs. structured), and types of goals sought (education and/or diversion vs. symptom relief and/or self-actualization). A simple reminiscence exercise conducted by a volunteer asking nursing home residents to describe an experience with their favorite singer of the 1930s is almost certainly not therapy, but a psychologist facilitating the processing of new nursing home residents' feelings about previous relocations during a weekly orientation group may be.

I propose that the term therapy be reserved for those structured activities of a professionally trained therapist who attempts to access and process the evaluative reminiscences that typically occur in a personal life review. Life review intervention can thus be conceived as "the" therapeutic form of reminiscence.

LIFE REVIEW THERAPY

Researchers' failure to adequately delineate the life review by specifying the therapeutic conceptualization underlying the intervention, the population for whom it is applied, the specific method utilized, and the goals sought has probably led to the continued debate over its efficacy (Haight, 1991; Molinari & Reichlin, 1984–1985). However, from a review of the recent literature, there now appears to be an emerging consensus on certain facts that may help guide the clinician in selecting the appropriate type of life review therapy.

Although individuals in all age groups evaluate their lives, life review is particularly salient for older adults since aging may trigger a natural developmental crisis that can be resolved by gaining an overall perspective on one's life. In a sense, many (though not all) older adults appear to be primed for the life review. Life review therapy differs from spontaneous life review in that it represents a unique opportunity for therapeutic influence because it is more structured and guided toward positive outcome. Convergent taxonomies of reminiscence reflect at least three core functions of the life review: to integrate disparate aspects of the self, to assist with current problem-solving strategies, and to bequeath a legacy. Psychologists working within self-psychological and Jungian perspectives will probably emphasize the first goal and use techniques that promote self-integration. Assistance with ferreting out prior means of coping and how to implement them in the here and now may be the province of those with more cognitive-behavioral orientations. The social goal of leaving a legacy for others might be emphasized by adherents of the object relations school. Life review conducted in an individual context is more likely to focus on self-development, while a group format will draw more social elements. Proponents of all clinical theories agree that an overarching goal is to deconstruct an individual's perspective of his or her life history into a more positive and coherent narrative emphasizing strengths, successes, and lessons learned.

However, if an individual becomes so mired in depressive recriminations that the facilitator is unable to draw out more positive experiences, life review therapy should be suspended until the psychiatric symptomatology is treated via other modalities. As with all therapies, negative outcomes occur, particularly if the intervention is so brief that it stirs up but does not consolidate distressing emotions (Coleman, 1994), or the environment is not receptive to the individual's change in self-concept (Bender, 1994). Indeed, some institutions are so bleak and nonrewarding that they engender negative life reviews as residents strive to make sense of how they ended up in this situation. In such nontherapeutic environments, caution is advised in the determination of whether to implement life review therapy. In short-stay psychiatric units, it has been reported that older adults frequently undergo a "reminiscence crisis," which may need to subside before life review work can be initiated (Blankenship, Molinari, & Kunik, 1996).

Since the life review is such an intimate form of reminiscence, life review therapy is best conducted in an individual or small-group context. Individual life review therapy is much more similar to psychotherapy which focuses on self-consolidation, particularly since one's past is explored to some extent in most forms of psychotherapy (Knight, 1996). If a group format is chosen, it is important to bear in mind that the major curative factors of cohesion and group feedback (Yalom, 1985) remain operative, and hence the group should be relatively homogeneous in terms of cognitive ability and psychiatric stability. Indeed, as discussed in the following section, group life review has some decided advantages over other formats.

A MODEL GROUP LIFE
REVIEW PROGRAM

With the previous considerations in mind and the caveat that all therapy should be tailored to the unique needs of the clients served, I propose in this section a general life review therapy program with relevance to most of the populations and settings that the clinician deems appropriate for conducting the life review. In addition to the well-known benefits of group therapy as an efficient form of therapy in settings increasingly concerned with cost-cutting, the group format has the decided advantage over individual life review therapy of allowing participants to affirm each other's life histories and to bequeath a lasting legacy by publicly telling their stories. Because all older adults do not undergo a life review, it would be advisable to select only those who are most motivated for the task, who are verbal, who are psychologically introspective, and who are not in an acute crisis that could set a negative tone for the life review. The number of participants should range from six to ten. Too many members may preclude the opportunity for everyone to have a chance to relay their story each session, but too few members may trigger problems when illness or transportation difficulties (notable for this age group) cause predictable attrition from session to session.

To assure continuity, arrangements should be made for weekly meetings. A week allows members enough time to prepare for the next session, but not so much intervening time to disrupt the flow of recounted autobiographical events. Sessions should be 60 to 90 minutes in duration to allow each participant enough time to tell his or her story in some detail, without exhausting the capacity of the oldest members to pay attention. The atmosphere of the group should always be warm and supportive. Soft drinks or snack foods create a genial social atmosphere that promotes comfort and trust. A well-lit and relatively soundproofed area permits ease of reading and listening. As opposed to a traditional therapy group, a unique feature of life review groups is that out-of-the-group socializing is not discouraged. Indeed, a secondary benefit may be that it buttresses an individual's flagging social support system. Because cohesion is so important, closed groups are preferred, since a new member might upset the natural rhythm and rapport that develops among the original participants.

The life review group should be organized around a different topic for each meeting, and a syllabus handed out at the opening session. Such structure serves two main purposes. It assists older adults who may be unfamiliar with what is required of them in therapy. More importantly, the structure of the life review group provides the organization necessary to gain perspective on the seeming disparate experiences of their lives. To this end, the first session should always include an introduction about the distinction between reminiscence and life review, the specific value of life review, and the particular objectives of the life review group. Members should be encouraged to prepare for each week's theme—preferably by writing down their thoughts. Ten to twelve meetings should suffice to cover major life events and transitions. Topics can include early and most important figures in their lives; relationships with parents, siblings, or friends; school experiences; work histories; relationships with spouses or lovers; earliest memories; most significant events; accomplishments; turning points; unfulfilled desires; regrets; major transitions; experiences with death or dying; spirituality; and purpose in life. These can be supplemented with more specific subject matter relevant to the particular group or setting (e.g., joys and pangs of childbirth for women; service experiences for groups conducted in VA settings).

The major task of the group leader is to keep members on target with psychologically relevant talk of their past, and to bear witness to the recital of their life stories. The leader should be both directive and supportive. A significant difference between the life review group and some other types of insight groups is that content rather than process is made the focus of the sessions. Denial mechanisms should be gently confronted only if interfering with discussion of the designated topic area. Process comments are made by the facilitator only to improve the flow of the presentations (e.g., if another member constantly interrupts or speaks out of turn), and are not proffered as a therapeutic end in of themselves (e.g., to give feedback to members about how others react to them). However, although the group is structured around topic areas, too rigid adherence to a set theme may not allow for the spontaneity that reflects the natural ebb and flow of human interaction and enhances group bonding. My rule-of-thumb is that if group members are discussing valuable psychological material but in a non-topic-related area then I go with the flow. However, if the group goes astray with psychologically irrelevant talk (e.g., weather, television program), I redirect them to the assigned topic. Digression should not necessarily be interpreted as resistance because many older adults have limited experience with therapy groups and may initially need assistance with distinguishing those particular events that are most psychologically compelling for discussion.

If significant negative reactions occur in a member, the group facilitator will need to make a decision concerning whether the person should remain in the group or be referred for other more intensive psychotherapeutic work. This decision might be guided by a general principle that older participants should be primed for a life review, and that if they are found to be steadily avoiding this process or find it overwhelming then they were not suitable candidates for this type of therapy.

Time should be left at the end of the last session to summarize what has been accomplished in the group, tie up loose ends, and encourage a more affirming view of the past and a more positive self-concept. There should be recognition that the wisdom born of long experience can be put to good use in dealing with the aging process. I find it advantageous to let members know how much I have learned from them and how they have certainly left a legacy for me to pass on to others.

DIRECTIONS FOR FUTURE RESEARCH

As Webster and Haight (1995) note, experimentalists and clinicians should communicate better. Findings from the general reminiscence literature need to inform practice and vice versa, and theory needs to guide both research and clinical work. The probable reason for the equivocal and at times disappointing results yielded by life review research is the exuberance of clinicians in utilizing this approach willy-nilly without explicit rationale with any older population with whom they have contact. Researchers need to define their life review interventions and specifically describe samples, hypotheses, and procedures. As a good example, Birren and Deutchman (1991) delineate their guided autobiography format in sufficient theoretical and practical detail to yield easy replication. Although not technically a clinical intervention, their structured approach allows an easy interface between research and practice that can serve as a model for those interested in life review therapy. There are now well-validated research instruments to assist with program evaluation (Kovach, 1993; Webster, 1993), and taxonomies of reminiscence have been developed and continue to be refined. For example, Webster (1997) has now added an eighth factor to the RFS by separating the seemingly distinct identity and problem-solving factors. But it is important to note that these classification schemes reflect general categorization for empirical purposes and should not be used to pigeonhole individual reminiscences (Adams, 1994). We now need not only empirical studies, but also qualitative content analyses (M. Duffy, November 1997, personal communication) examining the overall gestalt of reminiscence (Kovach, 1993) and its unique meaning for individuals. We should interview older adults and ask them why they reminisce and what value they receive from participating in life review sessions. Surprisingly, personality, gender, age, culture, and early family dynamic variables have been given short shrift in the literature as factors that affect the life review process (Webster & Haight, 1995).

Research also needs to pay closer attention to the development of assessment instruments identifying those who are most likely to benefit or to be traumatized from particular forms of life review. The length of the life review intervention must be made clear, since single-session interventions are unlikely to be powerful enough to bring about detectable change. It may be unreasonable to assume that brief reminiscence interventions with cognitively impaired patients will have the lasting effects of an intensive structured life review group composed of cognitively intact older persons (although certainly staff or family caregivers may transiently provide better care when they are primed to view the person with dementia in a life-span context). Long-term follow-up is now necessary (Stones, Rattenburg, & Kozma, 1995). Are the benefits of evaluating the past in a group setting short-lived or do these benefits accrue during a period of consolidation after the group ends? We need to explore whether the life review intervention has specific benefits yoked to the underlying theory of the process. Does life review really consolidate an identity and assist with current problem-solving, or are the effects nonspecific to the rapport gained with the therapist and fellow participants? Do those in life review therapy possess more coherent perspectives on their past than nonparticipants or others engaged in different forms of therapy? Guild issues have now emerged. What are the best qualifications for a life review therapist? Can paraprofessionals be prepared to do this type of work? Or does training in geropsychology offer particular benefits?

CONCLUSION

The life review literature has now come of age. We need to avoid general debates over whether reminiscence in old age has good or bad consequences, and instead take the next step and determine which older adults in which settings benefit from which forms of life review therapy. Life review therapists need to gain perspective on their own clinical work by evaluating past research so that wisdom can guide current practice.

REFERENCES

Adams, J. (1994). A fair hearing: Life review in a hospital setting. In J. Bornat (Ed.), *Reminiscence reviewed: Perspectives, evaluations, achievements* (pp. 84–95). Bristol, PA: Open University Press.

Bender, M. (1994). An interesting confusion: What can we do with reminiscence groupwork? In J. Bornat (Ed.), *Reminiscence reviewed: Perspectives, evaluations, achievements* (pp. 32–45). Bristol, PA: Open University Press.

Birren, J., & Deutchman, D. (1991). *Guiding autobiography groups for older adults: Exploring the fabric of life.* Baltimore: Johns Hopkins University Press.

Blankenship, L., Molinari, V., & Kunik, M. (1996). The effect of a life review group on the reminiscence functions of geropsychiatric inpatients. *Clinical Gerontologist, 16*(4), 3–18.

Buchanan, K., & Middleton, D. (1994). Reminiscence reviewed: A discourse analytic perspective. In J. Bornat (Ed.), *Reminiscence reviewed: Perspectives, evaluations, achievements* (pp. 61–73). Bristol, PA: Open University Press.

Butler, R. (1963). The life review: An interpretation of reminiscence in the aged. *Psychiatry, 26,* 65–76.

Coleman, P.G. (1974). Measuring reminiscence characteristics from conversation as adaptive features of old age. *International Journal of Aging and Human Development, 5,* 281–294.

Coleman, P.G. (1994). Reminiscence within the study of ageing: The social significance of story. In J. Bornat (Ed.), *Reminiscence reviewed: Perspectives, evaluations, achievements* (pp. 8–20). Bristol, PA: Open University Press.

Cooke, E. (1991). The effects of reminiscence on psychological measures of ego integrity in nursing home residents. *Archives of Psychiatric Nursing, 5,* 292–298.

deVries, B., Birren, J., & Deutchman, D. (1995). Method and uses of the guided autobiography. In B. Haight & J.D. Webster (Eds.), *The art and science of reminiscing: Theory, research, methods and applications* (pp. 165–177). Washington, DC: Taylor & Francis.

deVries, B., Blando, J.A., & Walker, L.J. (1995). An exploratory analysis of the content and structure of the life review. In B. Haight & J.D. Webster (Eds.). *The art and science of reminiscing: Theory, research, methods and applications* (pp. 123–137). Washington, DC: Taylor & Francis.

Erikson, E. (1959). *Identity and the life cycle.* New York: International Universities Press.

Fishman, S. (1992). Relationships among an older adult's life review, ego integrity, and death anxiety. *International Psychogeriatrics, 4*(2), 267–277.

Garland, J. (1994). What splendor, it all coheres: Life review therapy with older people. In J. Bornat (Ed.), *Reminiscence reviewed: Perspectives, evaluations, achievements* (pp. 21–31). Bristol, PA: Open University Press.

Gutmann, D.L. (1987). *Reclaimed powers: Towards a new psychology of men and women in later life.* New York: Basic Books.

Haight, B. (1991). Reminiscing: the state of the art as a basis for practice. *International Journal of Aging and Human Development, 33*(1), 1–32.

Haight, B., & Hendrix, S. (1995). An integrated review of reminiscence. In B. Haight & J.D. Webster (Eds.), *The art and science of reminiscing: Theory, research, methods and applications* (pp. 3–21). Washington, DC: Taylor & Francis.

Jordan, J. (1989). Relational development: Therapeutic implications of empathy and shame. *Work in Progress, 39,* 1–13.

Jung, C.G. (1933). *Modern man in search of a soul.* New York: Harcourt Brace Jovanovich.

Klerman, G.L., & Weissman, M.M. (1993). *New applications of interpersonal therapy.* Washington DC: American Psychiatric Press.

Knight, B. (1996). *Psychotherapy with older adults.* Beverly Hills, CA: Sage.

Kohut, H. (1984). *How does analysis cure?* Chicago, IL: University of Chicago Press.

Kovach, C. (1993). Development and testing of the autobiographical memory coding tool. *Journal of Advanced Nursing, 18,* 669–674.

LoGerfo, M. (1980–1981). Three ways of reminiscence in theory and practice. *International Journal of Aging and Human Development, 12*(1), 39–48.

Mahler, M.S. (1967). On human symbiosis and the vicissitudes of individuation. *Journal of the American Psychoanalytic Association, 15,* 740–763.

Mergler, N.L., & Goldstein, M.D. (1983). Why are there old people: Senescence as biological and cultural preparedness for the transmission of information. *Human Development, 26,* 72–90.

Merriam, S.B., Martin, P., Adkins, G., & Poon, L. (1995). Centenarians: Their memories and future ambitions. *International Journal of Aging and Human Development, 41*(2), 117–132.

Molinari, V., & Reichlin, B. (1984–1985). Life review reminiscence in the elderly: A review of the literature. *International Journal of Aging and Human Development, 20,* 81–92.

Romaniuk, M., & Romaniuk, J.G. (1981). Looking back: An analysis of reminiscence functions and triggers. *Experimental Aging Research, 7,* 477–489.

Romaniuk, M., & Romaniuk, J.G. (1983). Life events and reminiscence: A comparison of the memories of young and old adults. *Imagination, Cognition, and Personality, 2,* 125–136.

Rybarczyk, B. (1995). Using reminiscence interviews for stress management in the medical setting. In B. Haight & J.D. Webster (Eds.), *The art and science of reminiscing: Theory, research, methods and applications* (pp. 205–217). Washington, DC: Taylor & Francis.

Schafer, R. (1992). *Retelling a life: Narration and dialogue in psychoanalysis.* New York: Basic Books.

Staudinger, U.M., Smith, J., & Baltes, P. (1992). Wisdom-related knowledge in a life review task: Age differences and the role of professional specialization. *Psychology and Aging, 7,* 271–281.

Stones, M.J., Rattenburg C., & Kozma, A. (1995). Group reminiscence: Evaluating short- and long-term effects. In B. Haight & J.D. Webster (Eds.), *The art and science of reminiscing: Theory, research, methods, and applications* (pp. 139–150). Washington, DC: Taylor & Francis.

Sullivan, H.S. (1953). *The interpersonal theory of psychiatry.* New York: Norton.

Taft, L.B., & Nehrke, M.F. (1990). Reminiscence, life review, and ego integrity in nursing home residents. *International Journal of Aging and Human Development, 30,* 189–196.

Viney, L. (1995). Reminiscence in psychotherapy with the elderly: Telling and retelling their stories. In B. Haight & J.D. Webster (Eds.), *The art and science of reminiscing: Theory, research, methods and applications* (pp. 243–264). Washington, DC: Taylor & Francis.

Watt, L.M., & Cappeliez, P. (1995). Reminiscence interventions for the treatment of depression in older adults. In B. Haight & J.D. Webster (Eds.), *The art and science of reminiscing: Theory, research, methods and applications* (pp. 221–232). Washington, DC: Taylor & Francis.

Watt, L., & Wong, P.A. (1991). A taxonomy of reminiscence and therapeutic implications. *Journal of Mental Health Counseling, 12,* 270–278.

Webster, J. (1993) Construction and validation of the reminiscence functions scale. *Journal of Gerontology, 48,* 256–262.

Webster, J. (1997). The reminiscence functions scale: A replication. *International Journal of Aging and Human Development, 44*(2), 137–148.

Webster, J., & Haight B. (1995). Memory lane milestones: Progress in reminiscence definition and classification. In B. Haight & J.D. Webster (Eds.), *The art and science of reminiscing: Theory, research, methods and applications* (pp. 273–286). Washington, DC: Taylor & Francis.

Winnicott, D. (1971). *Playing and reality.* New York: Basic Books.

Woods, B., & McKiernan, F. (1995). Evaluating the impact of reminiscence on older people with dementia. In B. Haight & J.D. Webster (Eds.), *The art and science of reminiscing: Theory, research, methods and applications* (pp. 233–242). Washington, DC: Taylor & Francis.

Yalom, I.D. (1985). *The theory and practice of group psychotherapy.* New York: Basic Books.

CHAPTER 10

Integrated Group Approaches with the Early Stage Alzheimer's Patient and Family

ROBERT E. REICHLIN

The use of psychotherapeutic and psychosocial techniques with patients carrying the diagnosis of an irreversible, progressive neurological disorder may seem somewhat unconventional at this stage of medical treatment. By far the greatest attention has been directed toward pharmacological interventions and caregiver burden. At every turn, it seems as if healthcare professionals and the public are tantalized by putative breakthroughs, such as acetylcholinesterase inhibitors, anti-oxidants, and herbal preparations, and sobered by how the caregiver role can be interminably stressful. All of us who work with this population hope for some potion that will slow the progression, stop it, or prevent the disease itself from occurring. As we wait, more patients come to our attention, many of whom are being diagnosed at an earlier age. Much remains to be done and much can be done.

This chapter describes the Early Stage Alzheimer's Program initiated in 1993 by the Alzheimer's Association-Greater Houston Chapter. After a brief literature review, the development of the program is described in detail. This includes a discussion of the eligibility and selection procedures for the patient group, the integration of a concurrent caregiver's group, and the inclusion of an open-ended aftercare program. Patient and caregiver discussion topics are also presented, The use of a projective drawing technique with both patients and caregivers is described and examples of their productions are presented. Finally, recommendations for the implementation of an early stage program are offered.

166

REVIEW OF THE LITERATURE

The literature on the use of group treatment with the early stage dementia patient is limited. Gilewski's (1986) critical review of studies of group therapy with cognitively impaired older adults indicated that diagnostic accuracy/reliability, sample selection, mixed treatment modalities, and lack of methodological rigor and outcome measures were common problems. However, important exceptions to this conclusion have appeared recently in the literature.

Dye and Erber (1981) assigned newly admitted nursing home residents with varying degrees of cognitive impairment and their families to resident-only and family counseling groups. Groups met twice a week for seven sessions and followed a structured format. Resident-only groups focused on adaptation to the nursing home, and the family counseling groups emphasized communication of feelings among family members. They found immediate post-test results for participants in the resident-only group: less trait anxiety, and more internal locus of control when compared to a control group of nonparticipating residents. Participants in the family counseling group did not differ from controls. Shoham and Neuschatz (1985) conducted ego-supportive group therapy sessions with six to eight nursing home residents with mild to moderately severe confusion. The group was ongoing, meeting twice a week. The group model was based on the following assumptions:

- Creation of an accepting emotional environment
- Frequent intervention by the group leaders to help facilitate group interaction
- Provision of opportunities to "reachieve a sense of self by expressing personal opinions" (p. 71)
- Emotional ventilation
- The experience of belonging to a group
- Reminiscence to facilitate a sense of coherence across the life span.

Clinical observation suggested that cognitively impaired patients could benefit from group work through the experience of successful social interactions and increased self-esteem.

In a third nursing home study, Fernie and Fernie (1990) examined group composition. They sought to clarify whether patients who are mentally alert, mildly confused, or severely confused should be in the same (homogeneous) or different (heterogeneous) groups. Patients were selected on the basis of diagnosis, prior group experience, ability to communicate verbally, adequate hearing and vision, and cooperativeness. Each week, groups met daily for three consecutive days with eight patients in a group. Different topics or themes were selected for each session. Results indicted that groups comprised of mildly and severely confused patients, or mildly confused and mentally alert members appeared effective, while the integration of mentally alert members with severely confused patients was contraindicated.

Studies of group treatments with community residing dementia patients have also appeared. McAfee, Ruth, Bell, & Martichuski (1989), in conjunction with the Metro Denver Chapter of the Alzheimer's Association initiated a support/strategy group with early-stage, community residing patients and their family members. Goals included discussion of strategies for the future, and an opportunity to address issues of importance to caregivers and Alzheimer's patients. Criteria for participation included a medical diagnosis of irreversible dementia, a commitment by patient and family member to attend all sessions, independence in personal care activities of daily living, and the ability to participate in a group setting. Seven families were included. The first phase of the program consisted of six weekly meetings with patients and their family members. Speakers were invited to address diagnostic and medical concerns, financial issues, and family conflict. A reminiscence task about family life prior to the disease was included. The second phase lasted eight sessions, and patients and caregivers met separately. Discussion in both groups centered around topics such as emotional support, ventilation, coping strategies, driving, bothersome behaviors, and role changes. Patients' awareness of the implications of the disease for themselves and their family increased. Furthermore, following their participation, family members expressed a sense of empowerment from having their family member included in discussions about matters that impacted the entire family.

In 1991, David reported on the use of group therapy with day center participants with moderate cognitive impairment. Intact social and interpersonal skills were required for participation, and selection was based on the observations of staff and individual interviews. An attempt was made to select patients with similar educational background and life experiences. The group of five patients met twice weekly, and particular themes were selected to help generate discussion. Meetings were videotaped and discussed by the group at the following session. In addition, monthly caregiver support groups were provided that often incorporated the patient group's videotapes. As a consequence, caregivers were able to witness their family member's positive behavior in a mutually supportive and caring environment. This enhanced caregiver morale and encouraged caregivers to maintain these strengths at home. David concluded that patients felt a sense of autonomy when participating in the group which, in turn, increased their self-esteem. The structured environment of the patient group improved functioning, and elicited feelings of belongingness and usefulness.

Snyder, Quayhagen, Shepherd, and Bower (1995) reported on the effects of a closed, time-limited, eight-week seminar with community residing patients who had a diagnosis of Alzheimer's disease or a related disorder. Criteria for inclusion included a complete medical/diagnostic workup, having the ability to converse, sit for 90 minutes without agitation, and read handouts. Patients demonstrating major psychiatric disabilities that would impair group participation were not included. As a general measure, a score of 20 or above on the Mini Mental State Exam (MMSE; Folstein, Folstein, & McHugh, 1975) was a useful screening tool in predicting successful participation. However, it was noted that some patients had the necessary conversational and social skills required for participation while at the same time having lower MMSE scores. Specific topics were reviewed in one hour weekly sessions with patients and caregivers. Patients and caregivers then met separately for 30 minutes for further discussion of topics. Examination of evaluative statements made by the patients in the closed group about the selected topics indicated that their positive comments concerning purposefulness, survival, gratification, and belongingness emerged out of their experience of the intervention process and/or group interaction. Negative patient comments reflected the turmoil of the disease process itself, including feelings such as helplessness, devaluation, and unpredictability.

Robin Yale's work (1989, 1991, 1995) has been particularly instructive, especially her published manual for the planning, implementation, and evaluation of groups with community residing patients diagnosed with early stage Alzheimer's disease. Emphasis in these groups is directed toward establishing rapport, fostering meaningful interpersonal interactions, facilitating grief work, and assisting patients to come to terms with their situation. Members are identified on the basis of a medical diagnosis of probable Alzheimer's disease, an awareness of deficit, evidence of mild cognitive impairment, adequate communicational skills, and appropriate social behavior. Selection occurs in a two-stage process consisting of telephone screening and an interview with the patient and caregiver. Patients must score 18 or above on the MMSE. Groups usually consist of six to eight participants, and are time-limited to eight weeks. Concurrent caregiver groups are offered if resources permit. Meetings are structured around the discussion of topics such as the diagnosis of Alzheimer's disease, social stigma associated with the diagnosis, changes in life style and abilities, driving, dependency, communication, family issues, and preparation for the future. Outcomes based upon interviews with patients and caregivers include caregiver reports of enhanced patient self-esteem, ongoing interest in attending the group, and feelings of being better understood and less isolated. Yale found that patients were more likely to discuss problems related to the disease following the group program than patient controls.

THE EARLY STAGE ALZHEIMER'S PROGRAM (ESP), ALZHEIMER'S ASSOCIATION — GREATER HOUSTON CHAPTER

In 1993, the executive director of the Greater Houston Chapter asked me to develop a program to serve individuals diagnosed with early stage dementia, primarily of the Alzheimer's type. Up to this time, Association services to patients had been primarily indirect. Family support groups, education, and respite aide training have been the mainstays of the Chapter, and to a larger extent of the National Association. At the Greater Houston Chapter, we had observed that early stage patients were underserved in the community because adult day programs typically were not oriented toward patients who were reasonably functional, despite some cognitive deficits. In our community, adult day programs have been structured to serve middle stage Alzheimer's patients and/or individuals with physical and cognitive disabilities. We were also concerned about patients facing the development of excess disabilities such as anxiety and depression, that could intensify the symptom picture and decrease functioning. With important exceptions (McAfee et al., 1989; Yale, 1989, 1991, 1995), few chapters at that time had initiated programs addressing these concerns.

To meet the needs of early stage patients and their families, the chapter elected to follow Yale's suggestions for a program of group treatment. We also decided to provide a concurrent caregiver group that would assist in educating and providing support to the patient's family/caregiver. It was our intention to expose caregivers to experts in a variety of areas, such as legal, financial, and behavioral management, as well as provide them with the opportunity to share experiences and problem solve with other caregivers. We viewed this caregiver support group as an introduction to the larger, well-established, family support program available throughout the 18 counties the association serves.

Since the onset of the program, we have conducted 16 groups. The program evolved from offering patients and their caregivers one 12-week group to offering two consecutively run time-limited groups (seven weeks each) and an open-ended aftercare group. The program is described as follows:

ELIGIBILITY AND SELECTION PROCEDURES

1. Early stage dementia patients are typically referred to the ESP program by physicians, social workers, and geriatric clinics throughout the community. Early stage does not necessarily mean recently diagnosed since many individuals who have been diagnosed recently may not have come to the attention of medical personnel until well into the disease process. Our protocol is designed to accept early stage patients only. On rare occasions, we have accepted non-Alzheimer's (and non-vascular) dementia patients who otherwise met our eligibility criteria. These have included patients diagnosed with Huntington's corea, normal pressure hydrocephalus, and Parkinson's disease.

2. A two-step screening process is initiated when a caregiver or patient calls the association. Brief screening for appropriateness is conducted by phone, and information about the program is provided. An appointment for formal interviewing is also made at that time.

3. Patients and caregivers are screened at the association offices by a licensed clinical psychologist, participating clinicians, and the association's social worker.

4. Patients are administered the Mini Mental State Exam (Folstein et al., 1975). Eligible patients have generally achieved scores ranging from 20 to 25. Patients who are anxious occasionally score somewhat lower. Regardless of the MMSE score, individuals are interviewed to determine their awareness of their dementia and deficits and their ability to communicate in a group. Hence, we observe the prospective participant's ability to

interact appropriately, respond with some depth in his or her conversation, and spontaneously converse with the interviewers. Communicative ability is viewed as the most important variable in selection. Staging using the Global Deterioration Scale (Reisberg, Ferris, deLeon, & Crook, 1982), indicates that patients are in the early confusional clinical phase, (GDS = 3), or the late confusional clinical phase (GDS = 4).

5. Caregivers are administered the TRIMS Behavioral Problem Checklist (Niederehe, 1988) and interviewed to determine the caregiver's burden of care and interest in the program. The checklist also allows for a comparison of problems caregivers have identified with the impaired prospective participant's self-report regarding his or her own functioning; thus a check of the patient's awareness or denial of deficit is available.

6. Immediately following these interviews, clinicians and caregivers meet separately to discuss the patient's eligibility and answer any questions.

7. Patient groups are limited to eight to ten participants. Typically, a patient group has two to four members who have been through the group process before. Their presence has a calming and helpful effect on members who are new to the program. Caregiver groups tend to be larger in size because we are flexible about who attends (e.g., spouses, other family members, professional caregivers).

STRUCTURE/LENGTH

1. Each patient may participate in two consecutive phases, each consisting of a seven-part program that meets weekly. Group sessions last approximately one hour. The seventh meeting is scheduled to last 1½ hours to allow for review and socializing between the groups.

2. Caregivers are provided a concurrent educational/support group of the same length and duration.

3. Upon completion of two seven-week programs (Phase I and II), patients and caregivers are invited to continue in an aftercare program we call "Transitions." Patients and caregivers again have their own separate group. These groups meet every other week for one year.

GROUP PROCESS: THE PATIENT GROUP

Over the years, we have developed a generic list of "orienting topics" that serves to provide some structure to the patient group process and allows for discussion of issues introduced by group members. Topics selected are based on concerns that patients traditionally have expressed in the program. Patients report these topics to be of great importance, and we have observed that their discussion fosters group cohesion while offsetting the patient's growing sense of inadequacy, loss of self-esteem, and feelings of being different and discounted. Opportunities for spontaneous peer support have been especially poignant and beneficial to the group. As patients become more accustomed to the group, we have observed frequent expressions of humor and reminiscence about meaningful life experiences. Attention to the patient's affective expression is particularly salient because early stage patients often do not have the opportunity or perhaps the ability to express their outrage and despair about the disease.

We have found that our participants require considerable support from the therapeutic team during these interactions. Maintaining the group's focus and assisting with word-finding difficulties and loss of train of thought are frequently necessary. Accordingly, we have tried interactive tasks that do not depend solely upon open discussion. For example, psychodrama, presentation of personal photographs, a "hang man's" type activity, group viewing of a video interview with an Alzheimer's patient, drawings, and picture selection for a reminiscence task have all been used. Most of these activities have not worked because they were generally too complex, required sustained attention, and an intact ability to abstract or to carry out cognitive activities involving sequential tasks. We have found the use of the drawing and picture selection tasks to be most useful, and we continue to utilize them in each group. Table 10.1 lists activities scheduled for the patient group

An important element in the ESP program has been to foster a sense of safety and cohesiveness so that patients may bond with each other, and concurrently, develop a natural support group among caregivers (see discussion on caregiver group that follows). The provision of two consecutive groups has proven to be effective in reaching this goal. As patients become accustomed to the group and comfortable with expressing their feelings and concerns about their growing dependencies, deficits, and losses, the therapeutic team is able to actively reinforce expressions such as examples of remaining strengths. We encourage group members to speak about their own difficulties as a way of fostering empathy among members and improving awareness and tolerance of deficit. After four to five meetings, members begin commenting about how they are less anxious, less embarrassed by their memory difficulties, and less concerned about stigma.

Table 10.1   Activities scheduled during phase I and phase II patient groups.

Week	Topic/Activity
1	Introduction of group members, brief biography, purpose of the group, goal setting, areas of interest
2	Coping skills; memory problems and aids; what it means to have this diagnosis; issues about self-esteem
3	Expression through art: the drawing task
4	Coping with stress
5	Reminiscence: a picture selection task
6	Changes in family and social relationships; coping with caregivers
7	Review, wrap up, and party with the caregivers

This observation suggests that patients can experience themselves as able to maintain their self-esteem in the face of the negative emotional experiences that are associated with the recognition of loss of control over one's thoughts and life. Additionally, the group provides members with an opportunity to present themselves as capable of functioning appropriately with other adults. This again reinforces remaining strengths and improves self-esteem. However, it also can create a disparity in the perceptions of the therapists and caregivers, since the latter are typically identifying and discussing problem areas rather than strengths. Disparities are discussed with the caregivers (see below).

GROUP PROCESS: THE CAREGIVER GROUP

The caregiver group is led by a licensed social worker or a post-doctoral psychology fellow, or advanced graduate social work student. Meetings are structured around topic areas that have been salient for many caregivers over the years, including communication skills, behavioral management techniques, opportunities for sharing and providing emotional support, problem solving, identification of community resources, financial matters, legal issues, and information about the disease process and medications. Typically, these sessions are emotionally intense. Caregivers are direct, candid, and forthright in the expression of their uncertainties, disappointments, anger, and profound sense of loss. After the third or fourth meeting with the patient group, I join the caregiver group to answer general questions (usually about behavior management of a particular patient). Using the drawings that both patients and caregivers have produced, I discuss each patient and facilitate discussion concerning feelings of loss and anticipatory grief. Caregivers are asked to fill out the Behavioral Problems Checklist again during their sixth meeting, and complete an evaluation of the program during their seventh meeting.

TRANSITIONS

The need for aftercare was evident from the inception of the program. Early stage families who had completed two group sessions continued to need a form of support unavailable in the community. Recently, one group of caregivers who had completed the first seven-week phase began to meet on their own in the interim between Phase I and Phase II group sessions. These meetings often included their respective patients and were social and supportive in nature. In turn, the chapter was prompted to offer an aftercare program designed to facilitate caregiver interaction and problem solving, and to continue fostering patient self-esteem and belonging. Following completion of Phase I and II, participants are now invited to join the ongoing transitions aftercare groups held every other week for one year. As the size of the Transitions program grows, it may become necessary to limit the size of both the patient and caregiver groups to approximately 10 to 12 people for each group. We have noted that as time has passed, patients have become less able to use and participate in their group. Caregivers who have gradually learned the skills attendant to their role have different issues than newcomers to the Transitions program. Accordingly, we now limit participation to one year in order to maintain size requirements and relative homogeneity in the groups. After one year, caregivers are referred to their neighborhood Alzheimer's family support groups, and patients may be placed in appropriate day programs.

THE PROJECTIVE DRAWING TASK

From its inception, the ESP incorporated a projective drawing task in the patient group (Reichlin, 1999). Asking patients to draw their experience of the disease and/or its effect upon them was intended to provide an opportunity to discuss losses that were highly specific to each individual. Also, drawings could be used as a very powerful teaching tool for students and paraprofessionals. For the caregiver, exploration of patient drawings is a dramatic way to enhance empathy for their patient, and express feelings of loss previously unexpressed. For developing healthcare professionals (e.g., residents and fellows in geriatric medicine, social workers, nurses, long-term care administration graduate students) these drawings have proven to be poignant reminders that early stage patients are people still capable of expressing their emotional experience. While neuropsychological impairments are sometimes evident in these drawings, their primary usefulness resides in their dramatic and stark portrayal of hope, deficit, uncertainty, loss, and anger.

To conduct the drawing task, patients are given paper and a choice of colored pencils and instructed to draw their experience of the disease. We have found that encouragement is often necessary because of performance fears, impaired executive dysfunction, or visual-constructional deficits. The interactive elements in the task, however, are critical moments of therapeutic intervention. As we assist the patient in completing the task, we elicit the emotional context of the drawing, clarify what is being represented pictorially, and foster a sense of competence in the expression of feelings. This, in turn, provides a rich opportunity for the group to identify commonalities in their experience, and brings them closer together. Additionally, the patients have a chance to see how the group leaders interact with each person, and therapeutic trust is enhanced. When a patient is unable to draw anything, the therapists are able to address how group members sometimes falter, and yet carry on. For example, when one patient wrote a sentence saying that he was unable to draw, we presented his comment as demonstrating good effort, insight (awareness of deficit), and courage.

Recently, I have asked the caregiver group to draw their experience of caring for a person with Alzheimer's disease. As with the patients' drawings, these drawings are stunning in their frank portrayals of loss, burden, and uncertainty.

The following drawings by patients and caregivers are illustrative of those we have obtained throughout the program.

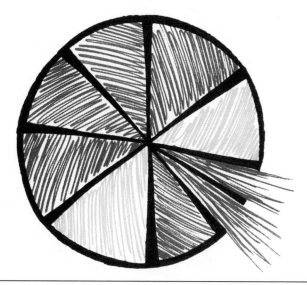

Caregiver (daughter). A pie chart with happy colors. Two pieces of the pie are coming out. I feel like I'm losing my parents. They are the 2 pieces. The rest of my life is in control.

Caregiver (husband). I'm in a black tunnel. No light at the end. No hope. No solutions. I don't feel like I have any good days. The red = 's anger and frustration, all around the tunnel. I'm no longer successful. I used to be successful because I could identify a problem and find a solution.

Caregiver (wife). Tears build up behind my eyes. Lost plans. We had plans for the future; all our friends are busy.

Patient. (Self expanatory).

Patient. Helpless.

Patient. I feel very controlled. My husband is nice but understanding is zero. He tells me everything to do. I feel like I'm in prison. I want to go somewhere but I cant.

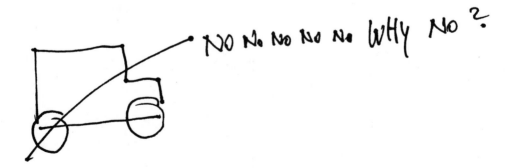

WHERE ARE IS MY CAR KEYS ?
" IS " WALLET

WHAT DO YOU MEAN?
THAT THEY ARE IN AS
SAFE PLACE

OH! ARE YOU SURE
AFTER MEETING WITH THE
ADVISOR (OR LEADER? OR DR)
I WILL GET THEM BACK ??

WHAT DO YOU MEAN?
MAYBE!!

Patient. My wife is not concerned with driving. I'm going along like this. She wants to be safe. I'm tired of hearing . . .

NO No No No No WHY NO?

Patient. An important part, the remainder of my life and I don't like it . . . I'll get used to it with time, reluctantly . . .

RECOMMENDATIONS
FOR THE IMPLEMENTATION OF
AN EARLY STAGE PROGRAM

SELECTION OF APPROPRIATE PARTICIPANTS

Both Fernie and Fernie (1990) and Yale (1995) have advocated for homogeneity of cognitive and communicational functioning in the selection of group members. Initially, however, we attempted to incorporate a broader mix of patients because of a mandate to offer services to as many patients and families as possible. Combining early and middle stage patients was found to be cumbersome, frustrating, and inefficient in view of the significant differences in ability to communicate adequately in a group setting. Also, inclusion of non-Alzheimer's (and non-vascular dementia) patients has not been effective, again because of differences in functional level. As described in the Eligibility and Selection section, subsequent refining of screening procedures emphasizing communication abilities, and a review of the items endorsed by caregivers on the Behavioral Problem Checklist has reduced the number of inappropriate patients, and enhanced homogeneity. This, in turn, has resulted in smoother group interactions, richer communications, and greater empathy among group members.

CO-THERAPY AND MULTIDISCIPLINARY TRAINING OPPORTUNITIES

Conducting groups with early stage patients is a complex affair requiring two therapists. Frequent active intervention by therapists is necessary to keep the conversation flowing, ensure that everyone who wants to has a chance to speak, and maintain focus on the topic or feelings being expressed. I have had the privilege to work with post-doctoral fellows in geropsychology and advanced social work students for the past 4 years, and have found their contributions essential and invaluable. Post-doctoral fellows or advanced social work students typically co-lead the patient group with me first, then lead the caregiver group, and then rejoin me for another patient group. Such a sequence provides a broad exposure to the problems of early stage families, and an opportunity to employ newly learned techniques and sensitivities. We are fortunate as well in having advanced and new social work students assisting with the Transitions group. These groups provide trainees with a unique clinical experience not found elsewhere in our community.

BLENDING THERAPEUTIC AND RESEARCH APPROACHES

The Early Stage Alzheimer's Program also offers a rich clinical setting for research. Recently, we began collaborating with the University of Texas at Houston, Center on Aging, to examine significant clinical themes in the patient group using audio recordings of group sessions. A variety of measures have been employed to investigate depression in dementia, awareness of deficit, health status, and caregiver burden. Patients and families are evaluated and selected for the ESP program prior to meeting with a researcher who subsequently enlists their participation in the research activity. Should any selected patient or family refuse to participate, the patient remains in the program, and research data are not collected for that group. Interestingly, patients have never complained about the presence of the researchers in their sessions, and patients and their families have been uniformly cooperative in the research.

ADVANTAGES OF WORKING WITH THE ALZHEIMER'S ASSOCIATION

Offering the ESP requires considerable secretarial and organizational support. We have found the Greater Houston chapter to be exceptional partners in our effort: they provide telephone screening, space for patient and caregiver sessions, secretarial assistance, and mailout to many organizations that announce the program as a regular service. The Program is now one of many services budgeted by the chapter. Most important, the Alzheimer's Association has considerable legitimacy in the community. Hosting these groups at the chapter's offices has lent great legitimacy to our program.

CONCLUSION

The most important conclusion we have drawn from our work with early stage patients is that these individuals continue to have a complex internal life, adult concerns about themselves and their families, and a growing sense that as their deficits emerge, the world is less interested in them as people. Professionals and students who have observed or participated in the program repeatedly note astonishment about how expressive the early stage patient can be. We should never been have surprised by this observation. We have always known that people can thrive in a warm, encouraging, and emotionally safe environment. Yet, in our appropriate efforts to attend to the early stage family, offset caregiver burden, and advocate for patient welfare, professionals tend to focus on functional deficit to the exclusion of understanding and interacting with *the early stage patient as an adult with a chronic illness* (Cotrell & Schultz, 1993; Gwyther, 1997; Sabat, 1994). As Cohen (1991) noted, while the Alzheimer's patient may be losing his or her cognitive abilities, "not all skills and abilities deteriorate at the same rate" (p. 8). Hence, a differentiated, more experience-near comprehension of the patient's subjectivity is essential to an understanding of how the disease is experienced. Such knowledge enables clinicians and families to more effectively communicate with the patient and intervene in the most effective and humane way possible. When we attend to a person in this manner, we are much more likely to interact with him or her as an individual who struggles to adapt and live with a progressive illness, rather than as someone who is, for all intents and purposes, already lost to us. Working with early stage families offers the clinician the opportunity to explore a still uncharted world, and provide services to an underserved population that is responsive to what well trained psychotherapists already know how to do.

REFERENCES

Cohen, D. (1991, May/June). The subjective experience of Alzheimer's disease: The anatomy of an illness as perceived by patients and families. *American Journal of Alzheimer's Care and Related Disorders and Research, 6*–11.

Cotrell, V., & Schultz, R. (1993). The perspective of the patient with Alzheimer's disease: A neglected dimension of dementia research. *Gerontologist, 33,* 205–211.

David, P. (1991, July/August). Effectiveness of group work with the cognitively impaired older adult. *American Journal of Alzheimer's Care and Related Disorders and Research,* 10–16.

Dye, C.J., & Erber, J.T. (1981). Two group procedures for the treatment of nursing home patients. *Gerontologist, 21,* 539–544.

Fernie, B., & Fernie, G. (1990). Organizing group programs for cognitively impaired elderly residents of nursing homes. *Clinical Gerontologist, 9,* 123–134.

Folstein, M.F., Folstein, S.E., & McHugh, P.R. (1975). "Mini-mental state": A practical method for grading the cognitive state of patients for the clinician. *Journal of Psychiatric Research, 12,* 189–198.

Gilewski, M.J. (1986). Group therapy with cognitively impaired older adults. *Clinical Gerontologist, 5*(3/4), 281–296.

Gwyther, L.P. (1997). The perspective of the person with Alzheimer's disease: Which outcomes matter in early to middle stages of dementia? *Alzheimer Disease and Associated Disorders, 11*(Suppl. 6), 18–24.

McAfee, M.E., Ruth, P.A., Bell, P., & Martichuski, D. (1989, November/December). Including persons with early stage Alzheimer's disease in support groups and strategy planning. *American Journal of Alzheimer's Care and Related Disorders and Research,* 18–22.

Niederehe, G. (1988). TRIMS behavioral problem checklist (BPC). *Psychopharmacology Bulletin,* 771–778.

Reichlin, R.E. (1999). *Exploring the experience of early stage Alzheimer's disease through a projective drawing task: Patients and caregivers.* In preparation.

Reisberg, B., Ferris, S., de Leon, M., & Crook, T. (1982). The Global Deterioration Scale for the assessment of primary degenerative dementia. *American Journal of Psychiatry, 139,* 1136–1139.

Sabat, S. (1994, May/June). Recognizing and working with remaining abilities: Toward improving the care of Alzheimer's disease sufferers. *American Journal of Alzheimer's Care and Related Disorders and Research,* 8–16.

Shoham, H., & Neuschatz, S. (1985). Group therapy with senile patients. *Social Work, 30,* 69–72.

Snyder, L., Quayhagen, M.P., Shepherd, S., & Bower, D. (1995). Supportive seminar groups: An intervention for early stage dementia patients. *Gerontologist, 35,* 691–695.

Yale, R. (1989). Support groups for newly diagnosed Alzheimer's clients. *Clinical Gerontologist, 8*(3), 86–89.

Yale, R. (1991). *A guide to facilitating support groups for newly diagnosed Alzheimer's patients.* Los Altos: Alzheimer's Association, Greater San Francisco Bay Area Chapter.

Yale, R. (1995). *Developing support groups for individuals with early-stage Alzheimer's disease.* Baltimore: Health Professions Press.

CHAPTER 11

The Role of Art Therapy in Aiding Older Adults with Life Transitions

JULES C. WEISS

A rt Therapy is a psychotherapeutic tool that can offer significant psychological, social, and physical health benefits for older adults. This chapter discusses the needs of older adults, the uses of art therapy, and how mental health professionals can use expressive art activities to aid older adults in coping with biopsychosocial challenges, developing psychosocial skills, and improving their quality of life.

THE BIOPSYCHOSOCIAL CHALLENGES FACING OLDER ADULTS

Older adults face multiple psychological, social, and physical health changes that involve numerous intrapsychic and interpersonal issues. Older adults strive to re-define their identity and sense of self-worth when developmentally they may feel lost, obsolete, and alienated. Changes in their physical health, environmental conditions, and sense of identity can trigger emotional crises fostering feelings of anxiety and depression along with phobias and fears. Older adults, in the midst of major life changes, reflect on the quality and significance of their lives, along with their values and beliefs. They re-examine experiences and achievements as they ponder critical existential questions related to the meaning of their life, the legacy of their past, and the direction of their future. Therapists can employ the expressive arts to amplify and clarify older adults' sense of identity and relationship with others providing further insight, direction, and meaning in their life.

Carl Jung (Campbell, 1971, p. 17) described the period from early to middle adulthood as a change from the extroversion of youth to the introversion of adulthood. Jung's view was that the first half of life was to develop identity, occupation, and family and the second half of life was to develop spirituality. Art experiences offer an expressive outlet that can guide individuals in re-evaluating their life and refocusing their view from an outer-world orientation to an inner-world perspective.

MENTAL AND PHYSICAL STIMULATION

Aging is often viewed in terms of a biological decremental model exhibiting a decline in all physiological systems. But physical exercise and mental stimulation have been shown to significantly enhance older adults physiological systems and psychological health by slowing the rate of decline, maintaining, or improving health (Madden, Allen, Blumenthal, & Emery, 1989). Mental exercises, like physical exercises, can enable adults to sustain and improve their mental capacities. Furthermore, mental exercise appears to be essential for the mind just as physical exercise is essential for the body (Restak, 1988). Therapeutically designed art activities can provide older adults with invigorating mental exercises offering visual, kinaestheic, and auditory stimulation along with an outlet to learn new skills, develop existing skills, and promote communication and interaction.

DEPRESSION, DEMENTIA, AND PSEUDO-DEMENTIA

Older adults who live in isolated or impoverished environments and experience a decrease in visual and motor activity often suffer from depressive symptoms of blunted affect, withdrawn behavior, and diminished cognitive awareness. Many individuals who appear to have dementia may actually be displaying signs of pseudo-dementia as a result of a lack of environmental, physical and cognitive stimulation, various stressors, and physiological imbalances. Creative art experiences can aid older adults in providing psychosocial, cognitive, and physical stimulation to offset a deprived environment. Physically, the process of creating art aids in eye-hand coordination and upper body mobility. Psychologically, it provides an intimate experience that reflects the individual's feelings and thoughts. Cognitively, the art experience provides opportunities for creative decision making, along with representational and problem-solving activities that expand the ability to conceptualize and create. Socially, the creative experience provides a shared activity and a meaningful dialogue that can expand the view of the world and of life.

ART THERAPY ADDRESSING THE OLDER ADULT'S EXPERIENCE

Expressive art experiences can help older adults reflect their personal journey and history, serving as a legacy for individuals and as an expression of the current state of affairs. Words, lines, colors, and shapes express how people view their world. Through art, older adults acknowledge their inner experience. By discussing their art with others, they shed their isolation and find a sense of universality in their life experiences. Within the expressive art process, they can re-evaluate their life, reframe erroneous notions, and gain a new perspective and sense of personal power. Similar to cognitive therapy, which looks at individuals' cognitions and self-talk, the therapeutic use of art enables individuals to portray and re-evaluate how they think and feel about themselves, their world, and their future. The art experience can give clarity to thoughts and feelings that may be difficult verbally to acknowledge but which are freely shared in the privacy of an art activity.

The creative expression of older adults activates the story of their lives. Older adults are not defined by their art, but they define themselves through creating art and sharing their story which lies behind the lines, colors, and images they create. As older adults verbalize and describe their expressive activity, they further clarify their past, present, and future outlook.

ART THERAPY OVERVIEW

The therapeutic use of art refers to the concept that the images created, the art-making process, and individuals' responses to the created products are reflections of their personality, interests, concerns, and conflicts. The marks we make, the colors, shapes, and graphic expressions we portray are articulations of our life experiences. Freud used free association to tap the power of unconscious images and dreams; in a similar manner, art therapists use art expression to tap unconscious images, feelings, and thoughts. Early analysts had patients draw and paint their dreams and then free associate to their pictures. Clients' unconscious conflicts expressed through drawings, were sometimes brought to awareness easier and more fully than through discussing dreams.

Art Therapy Pioneers

A major pioneer in the field of art therapy, Margaret Naumburg, was an art educator who saw art making as a cathartic process, sublimating aggressive drives. She viewed the client's artwork as symbolic speech. Using the symbolic potential of art work, she felt that psychological healing came through the communicative process. In the therapeutic dialogue, the client and therapist work together to understand the symbolic communication of the artwork. Through discussion of clients' artwork, they identify distorted perceptions and underlying conflicts and work toward reintegrating the perceptions and conflicts into a new perspective.

Edith Kramer, another pioneer in art therapy, guided clients to not only re-experience and resolve conflicts but to learn from the healing qualities of the art experience whereupon art becomes a "means of widening the range of human experience" (Kramer, 1958; Ulman, 1987). Kramer coined the phrase "art as therapy" focusing on the therapeutic "healing" qualities of the art-making process as the primary psychotherapeutic work.

Naumburg and Kramer are examples of two distinct and overlapping art therapy approaches. These approaches highlight how the art process can be used to acknowledge and reconcile conflicts (art psychotherapy—Naumberg) and to foster self-awareness and personal growth (art as therapy—Kramer) (Ulman, 1987).

PERSON, PRODUCT, AND PROCESS PARADIGM

Bob Ault (1986), an innovator in the art therapy field, developed an art therapy theoretical paradigm portraying three intertwined components: the person, the product, and the process. All art activities include components of the person, process, and product context.

The person component reflects the intrapsychic aspect of the creative activity, where individuals conceptualize and freely express ideas and feelings through art materials. The art piece mirrors the participants concerns, conflicts, and feelings. The process component refers to how individuals engage in creating and using art materials. It reflects how they work with various media, problem solve, and make decisions by themselves and in group activities. The process component includes interpersonal and intrapsychic issues. Intrapsychically, the art process highlights the relationship individuals have with their art piece, reflecting how clients feel about themselves as portrayed in the process of creating artwork. Interpersonal concerns may arise as we view how clients work with and relate to others.

In examining the process component of an art activity, the therapist may consider the following items:

- When clients are working with clay, do they hold the clay close to them and actively work with the materials in an intimate manner, or do they hold it at a distance, or as though it was fragile?
- Do they feel comfortable with the clay? Are they able to take command of the media or do they feel that the media is limiting their ability to express themselves?
- If there are problems in working with the media how do they cope with their difficulties? Are they able to develop new skills in working with the media and find new solutions to problems?
- When clients are working with others on a mural or collage what is their role and how do they interact? Do they freely express themselves or do they wait for others to first begin and then work in a more secondary or ancillary role?

To more fully understand the process component of the clients' activity, we reflect on how clients care for their artwork while creating it and how they present and discuss their artwork when it is finished.

The product component is the finished art piece which can range from an intricate sculpture to a simple drawing or craft. It is a nonverbal statement about individuals' lives. Clients may reflect on the significance of the product by themselves or with others. When discussing the finished product, clients may examine intrapsychic issues expressed in their art and reflect on others' insights to the art piece. A finished product brings a sense of accomplishment and pride to individuals which in turn helps to raise their self-esteem. The finished product exemplifies individuals' care of their art piece which can reflect their investment and care in other aspects of their life. It also demonstrates their level of artistic skill and sense of creativity.

ART ACTIVITIES: EXPRESSIVE ARTS, CRAFTS, AND SKILLED ART PRODUCTIONS

Art activities can be categorized within three groupings: expressive arts, craft activities, and skilled art productions. Within the person, process, and product paradigm, art activities can involve more person-focused expression, such as spontaneous expressive arts, or more product-focus, such as a craft activity of making a clay cup, or use both equally, such as designing and creating a model of a dream home.

A person-focused activity is central to spontaneous art or theme-related expressions. In contrast, a product-focused activity is structured to develop a finished piece and is central to craft-type activities. A skilled art production is an activity that reflects the advanced learning of new art skills. However, a craft activity could be elaborated and develop into an expressive activity or a very skilled art production; a skilled art activity can evolve into an expressive activity; and an expressive activity can progress into a skilled art production. The three types of art activities described are not exclusive but often overlap and can be transformed into others types of self-expression.

ART THERAPY INTERVENTION

In using art as a vehicle for psychotherapy, both the art process, the insight gained, and the sharing with others is used to help individuals find a more compatible relationship intrapsychically and interpersonally. Expressive art activities can help older adults in multifaceted ways. It can aid as an expressive outlet for older adults to share feelings and thoughts, help to gain insight into situations and clarify conflicts, offer a permanent record of experiences to reflect upon, provide a hobby and a chance to learn new skills, and give older adults an opportunity to develop new ways to view themselves and the world.

In counseling, therapists may find that clients' intellectualize and defend against their true feelings for fear of being vulnerable. But, in art therapy, the art media does not criticize, evaluate, or reject the individual. The art activity provides a nonthreatening modality that accepts the person as he or she is. The materials are waiting to be formed and molded by the individual.

In the art process, individuals have the opportunity to express themselves and reflect on their art expression. The art piece creates a conversation between the client's conscious and unconscious, inner self and persona, the client and therapist, and with other group members. Participants may find that the colors they use reveal their emotions, the shapes and lines they draw reflect their thoughts, and the art expression becomes their mirror, a direct reflection of their inner lives. The art product is also a medium clients can speak through, thereby making sensitive issues easier to discuss.

As older adults develop new skills in expressing their vision, they more closely examine their world and begin to re-evaluate how they have previously experienced the world. During the re-evaluation and contemplation process, older adults begin to gain a clearer sense of themselves and others. Their insights guide them in their emotional development and help them to experience a greater awareness of their inner-self. The expressive arts process helps older adults to validate their sense of identity and clarify their purpose in life.

The art product provides a concrete documentation of the older adults' legacy to contemplate, to share with others, and to hand down. It reflects the past, and enables individuals to view their current life and future possibilities with a greater sense of meaning and value.

MEDIA

In conducting art activities, one of the first decisions the older adult must make is which materials to use. The type of media chosen depends on the type and purpose of the art activity. When clients are given a very restricted or expansive selection of art materials, they may be uncomfortable with the activity. It is advisable to discuss with clients the variety of art mediums available, demonstrate how to use the art materials, and provide a healthy selection of art tools such as colored pencils, fine-tip magic markers, pastels, craypas, acrylics or oils, poster paints, collage material, finger paints, and clay. The art materials should be well organized for easy reach and use.

When clients have no instruction or practice before beginning an activity they can feel overwhelmed, frustrated, and inhibited due to their inexperience. Clients need to practice with various art mediums to learn the expressive qualities of the different materials and to find out which media they feel most comfortable with. Because creating art is a physical activity, before beginning clients should stretch using range of motion exercises to limber up their body.

Art mediums have a personality of their own. In deciding which media to use, it is important to look at the expressive qualities of each medium. Certain media are more pliable and easier to use, and each has a different expressive quality. The type of art medium used will effect the expression, color, line, shape, tone, and possibly placement of the image. Different art media elicit particular feelings, responses, and associations be it tactile, kinesthetic, visual as well as verbal, and have different potentials for expression (Rubin, 1984, p. 57).

Art mediums may be viewed on a continuum from highly confined pencil drawing to the very expressive use of finger paints. The following mediums are listed from the most restrictive media to most unrestrictive media: pencil drawing, craypas and pastels, clay work, collage, oil and acrylic painting, and finger paints. If individuals would like to use a very expressive medium, paints would be appropriate. If they feel overwhelmed by emotions and want to control the intensity of their feelings, they may want to use colored pencils. The qualities of certain media can have a therapeutic potential, such as using fingerpainting to free up a very tensely controlled individual who is afraid of making a mistake.

Being comfortable with the art media is very important, allowing clients to more easily express themselves and to enjoy the creative experience. For example, older adults may feel inhibited when using crayons because it may make them feel childish. Therapists may want to dignify the art activity by using more "adult type" art tools such as craypas or pastels.

GROUP ART ACTIVITIES

Group art activities enable older adults to share their experiences by working, helping, and learning with others. Discussion of clients' art work evokes memories, feelings, and thoughts in which participants become aware of having similar feelings and see the universality of life experiences. In the group experience, members become a witness to others' situations and through their support they develop closer alliances between members and a sense of companionship.

In group sessions, it is vital for members to have respect for each others' efforts and feelings, and to have a sense of ease about one's own artistic limitations. When members compare their artistic abilities to others, they instigate a sense of competition that can be detrimental. The process of expressing oneself in art is an exiting adventure and not an exhibitionistic talent show.

THE THERAPIST'S ROLE IN LEADING THERAPEUTIC ART ACTIVITIES

The setting should be a room with few distractions or onlookers and where participants can feel uninhibited. The room should be a pleasant environment where there is enough space to work, the tables and chairs are comfortable, and the art materials are accessible.

In conducting therapeutic art experiences, there are specific elements of the art activity that need to be discussed. At the beginning of the session, clients should be told how much time they have so they can pace themselves. The therapist also needs to discuss with clients whether they will be taking their art pieces home, leaving them to be worked on in the future, or if they will be put in their file for reflection at a later time. It is important that clients do not throw away or destroy their art work unless it is part of the therapeutic process. Destroying art work often reflects an inner struggle.

The therapist may want to begin the session by discussing clients' current issues and then have them explore their feelings and thoughts through an art media. The art activity and theme should develop from the clients' concerns and expressive needs. If clients have no particular topics for expression, the therapist can suggest spontaneous drawing/painting or a creative project. In deciding upon an art activity with clients, the therapist should be supportive and encouraging, not intrusive, aggressive, or intimidating. If the therapist has an activity in mind but the client wants to do something else, the therapist needs to be flexible and supportive, validating the client's needs and desires.

While the client is engaged in an art activity, the therapist also needs to plan what she or he himself will be doing. Some therapists draw when the client draws, while others watch and take notes. Parallel drawing or painting may ease the client's anxiety over having to "draw on command" or be the reluctant center of attention (Henley, 1986). The therapist should not be hypervigilant in watching over clients during the art-making process, which may make them nervous or uncomfortable. "Having the art therapist engaged in the art process creates a studio atmosphere where everyone has mobilized his or her creative energies and is taking stimulation and inspiration from others in the art room" (Henley, 1986).

The therapist is responsible for the group milieu and should be careful that the activity is not filled with excessive conversation. Clients may feel nervous about creating art and cope with their anxiety by talking throughout the activity. When clients talk excessively, the therapist should simply acknowledge their feelings and gently guide the clients' focus back to the art activity, asking them to talk as little as possible so that everyone can become fully invested in the creative experience. It is important to inform clients that they can discuss the activity when everyone finishes working. Excessive talking by the therapist or client during the art process reduces the value and power of the creative experience, making it into a social encounter.

After the art experience, it is recommended that clients discuss their experience and art work. Through discussion of their artwork older adults uncover feelings, thoughts, and new insights. But, there are times when clients do not want to speak about their art expression; this should be respected. Creating art in itself is therapeutic which brings a new awareness and sense of self to older adults.

When discussing clients' art work, therapists should view their role as a guest in someone's home who would like to be shown around. A useful comment to begin the discussion of a client's artwork is "Could you tell me about your art piece and your experience of creating it." Clients can then guide the therapist through their art production as they discuss the colors, images, symbols, people, and their associated meanings.

It is often helpful and less threatening if the therapist tries to understand the art piece from the client's point of view and then share his or her insights in a conditional manner. The therapist can assist clients to acknowledge their feelings and thoughts related to the art piece and experience, and help them to relate the significance of the art to their past experiences, present situation, and future plans. The focus of the interpretive process is to empathetically acknowledge the client's experience and to understand the significance of the client's expression.

When discussing the art piece, it is important to look at how the aesthetic elements of color, line, and form combine with the psychological elements of the story. In a phenomenological perspective, the client and therapist may want to view the art piece in varied ways (for example, from a distance) and discuss how changing the way we view the artwork changes the feelings it evokes. With the passage of time, when clients re-examine their artwork, they may gain a new perspective. At times, it is beneficial for clients to take an important image or theme from a previous art piece and re-create it in a new manner provoking new ideas, feelings, and perspectives.

INTERPRETING ART WORK

Therapists who exhibitionistically analyze artwork may alienate participants. When therapists overly interpret clients' artwork, reducing it to psychological lingo, they strip the soul and life out of the artwork. McNiff labels the misinterpretation of art by therapists as image abuse (McNiff, 1988). The power and life of the image often tells a deeper story than the therapist may recognize. When therapists interpret pictures in an autocratic manner, clients feel vulnerable and often lose trust in the therapist and the therapeutic relationship. When discussing artwork, the therapist should serve as a collaborator in the process as opposed to being the sole analyzer of the art work. Sensitive and insightful discussions of the art work, the clients' experience, and associated references can create a sense of intimacy, trust, and discovery between the client and therapist.

THERAPEUTIC ART ACTIVITIES

Art activities can enable older adults to share the story of their life and assist in their psychosocial development. Reflecting on their self-expression allows participants to witness their life in a new way by helping them share their feelings and thoughts. The activity enables individuals to integrate past experiences, find strength in the present, and can offer hope for the future.

Listed are several art activities that can be used therapeutically by licensed mental health professionals. Only a Registered Art Therapist can classify their work with clients as *art therapy*. Mental health professionals would label their work as the *therapeutic use of the arts*.

For all activities, a variety of art mediums and colors are recommended. For drawing activities, it is advised that participants work on sheets of paper sized

18 by 24 inches and have two or more of the following art tools: boxes of 24 color pastels, craypas, colored pencils, or colored fine-tip markers.

ACTIVITIES

Life Review

A *life review* is defined as a type of reminiscence which covers the whole life span (Butler, 1963). Dr. Butler claimed that the life review provides an individual with a means for the successful integration of experiences. Life reviews are commonly observed with the elderly due to the increasing awareness of the termination of life or aspects of one's life (retirement) which promotes a desire for resolution of intrapsychic conflicts, reconciliation with people, issues, and concerns and a longing to find or give meaning to one's experience.

To begin the life review activity, clients draw a line representing the path of their life from birth to the present. On the line they designate important milestones in their life with drawings and words. After completing the activity, clients discuss their life line and drawings.

A second life line can be done that includes their future. Clients draw a life line from birth to twenty years after their death. They should note the approximate year they expect to die and list on the life line their major accomplishments, experiences of the past, and their hopes for their future. In addition, they write how they will be remembered up to twenty years after they die and the effect their life will have on others. Participants include their hopes for what their family and friends will accomplish after their death.

The life review activity invites older adults to discuss their past, uncover positive experiences and inner strengths along with unresolved issues and conflicts, and plan for the future. It enables them to reminisce while staying focused on the present. Members may discuss how the past has shaped them and affected their attitudes, actions, and personal decisions and how they can shape the present and the future. The activity can help members come to terms with their past and present situation, along with acknowledging the legacy they will leave.

By combining an expressive arts life review process with cognitive therapy, older adults can recall and re-evaluate their life experiences, followed by re-examining and reframing dysfunctional thoughts and corresponding emotions. By itself, life review is a technique to increase awareness of an individual's life history. Cognitive therapy focuses on re-evaluating the meanings given to a client's perceptions of life. Together, both therapeutic approaches offer a way to view a client's life in a healthy self-affirming manner.

Clinical observations of a weekly cognitive group therapy program with older adults at a personal care facility (Weiss, 1995) found that participants would frequently engage in reminiscing (without prompts by the therapist) to inform members of their background and to provide added relevance to the content of the sessions. Participants used reminiscence to develop rapport with others and to establish their identity in the group. An expressive arts life review group therapy that incorporates cognitive therapy can increase the therapeutic efficacy of the group (Weiss, 1995).

Reality Orientation with Drawing and Writing

Reality therapy as developed by Taublee and Folsom (1966) has been a popular therapeutic treatment for disorientation. It aids confused individuals in becoming more aware of their life through verbally repeating fundamental facts about their life. The goal of reality therapy is to help confused individuals regain clarity about their lives and a connection to their world. But just the repetition of reality-based facts does not always foster an individual's understanding and clarity. Rather, it may be a rote activity that does not allow for a true synthesis of the individual's experience, emotions, and reality. Augmenting reality orientation with a drawing and writing activity (related to aspects of their lives) can help clients in acknowledging their past and present in a very concrete manner. The physical activity of drawing and writing can help individuals to recall and more fully express their experiences. Gaining an increased awareness of their lives can be very positive, but it can also raise issues of unresolved grief and loss which then need to be addressed.

The format of a reality orientation session using drawing and writing begins with participants filling out a reality orientation questionnaire stating who and where they are, describing their current activities, feelings, and thoughts. For clients who have difficulty writing, the therapist can help fill out the questionnaire. Next, a life theme is presented for a brief discussion, followed by a drawing/writing activity. Specific themes are used based on client issues and needs. Particular themes can help individuals recall specific aspects of their life and orientate them to the present. Some relevant themes are: where one lived and now currently lives; relationships; work experiences; hobbies; dreams; struggles of the past and the present. At the end of the activity, participants discuss their drawings and writings, their past experiences, and current feelings. The discussion enables participants to obtain feedback and re-evaluate their view of their lives. For optimal benefit, the group should be held for four to eight weeks with two sessions per week, using a closed group format to promote group cohesion and trust (Weiss, 1984).

Journal

Keeping a daily journal of writings and drawings allows clients to record their experiences and validate their daily life. Participants may want to create a journal book and decorate the cover or buy a large book with blank pages.

As we get older, we often do not have markers designating the daily successes and the personal losses in our life. Older adults may feel their life progresses from day to day without any record, validation, or recognition. By writing down their experiences accompanied by drawings and pictures, older adults can validate their daily life and later be able to reflect on how they portrayed their struggles and successes. It provides participants with the opportunity to re-evaluate their perspective of life. By describing their life experiences, older adults become more in touch with their feelings. The journal creates a legacy reflecting their ideas and experiences which can be shared with friends, family, and future generations.

Wishes—Three Things

There are things and feelings that we all wish to have or give to others that we believe would make us feel whole and complete. To begin the activity, fold a large sheet of paper in half and on one side of the paper have participants name and draw three objects or feelings that they would like to *receive* from three different people (one from each person) that they feel would make their lives complete. They can be things that they may never be able to have but could only dream of obtaining. The objects can be real or imaginary. They may be tangible such as a billion dollars or intangible such as wanting the love of a parent or a deceased relative.

Next, on the other side of the paper have participants write and draw three objects or feelings that they would like to *give* to three different people (one to each person) if they had the ability to give anything in the world. These things can be real or imaginary, tangible or intangible. Following the exercise, participants discuss what they would like from others and what they would like to give to others to make their lives complete.

The wish activity helps individuals look at their personal needs and unfinished business with significant others. Participants should discuss how they can realistically give to others and if possible how to accept from others what they would like to receive, while recognizing the limitations of their situation. Participants may need to discuss how to come to terms with their circumstances and unfulfilled dreams.

Family Drawing Done in Shading

Often when we try to draw an object or person we focus on how accurately we can portray the image. To enable participants to focus more on their feelings and less on their artistic skill, have clients draw their family members using only shading with various colors. No lines are to be used in the picture, only shades of colors to represent the clients' feelings about family members. An interesting theme for the picture is drawing shaded images of family members sitting around the dinner table, which can be a setting of highly evocative feelings. At the completion of the activity, participants discuss how they portrayed family members and their insights. From the activity, participants often obtain a heightened awareness of their emotional relationship with family members and the family dynamics.

Symbol of My Life

Have clients draw symbols that represent their inner strength and its outward expression. Using colors clients are to draw and embellish three symbols: one which reflects their inner self; another which reflects how they portray themselves to others (persona); and a third which expresses their interactions with the world. On a separate sheet of paper, clients are to draw the symbol of the inner self and their persona in relation to important experiences they have gone through. The art activity focuses on clients' inner strength and their self-image as it pertains to their struggles, successes, and relationships.

Life in the Jungle

Sometimes we feel that life is a struggle and it seems that we are living in a jungle. Have participants draw themselves, their friends, and family members as animals. What type of animals would they, their friends, and family members be? How would their life look if they lived in a jungle struggling with their current difficulties and successes? After the drawing activity, have members discuss why they chose particular animals to represent them and others, and how as an animal they would cope in the jungle.

The activity provides a metaphor for clients' lives by symbolizing their struggles. It is sometimes easier and less threatening for individuals to describe their life experiences through puppetry or an animal characterization because the activity enables clients to create a disguise in which to voice their feelings and concerns.

Making Your Own World

The activity focuses on a particular problem in participants' lives and helps them to look at their difficulties in a new light, bringing new insights. On a large sheet of paper, participants draw a large round circle. Inside the circle, clients are to draw a difficult situation they are facing. Have them include in the picture (in words and images) their strengths and weaknesses, coping abilities, and social supports. Next, draw lines going out of the circle with pictures and words describing what they need to take out of the situation to resolve their problem. Then draw lines going into the circle with pictures and words to describe what they need to add to their life to change their situation. At the end of the drawing activity, clients discuss their picture along with the new perspective they have gained from drawing the problem and the possible solutions.

Tree of Life

Trees are universal symbols which can be seen as reflections of growth, strength, and wholeness. Portraying a tree can be viewed as a symbol and reflection of our own life. Two therapeutic activities are listed which use the tree as a theme.

In the first activity, clients draw a tree that symbolizes their life. They include people and things in and under the tree as it reflects the clients' relationships, achievements, and difficulties. At the completion of the activity, participants share their pictures and the meaning behind them. The activity can be seen as an autobiographical statement and a metaphor about participants' lives.

The next activity, person picking an apple from a tree (PPAT), has been extensively researched by Gantt and Tabone (1998). The instructions are simply to draw a person picking an apple from a tree. For more information about the client's life, the therapist may suggest that participants include their home, family members, and/or friends in the picture. After the drawing is completed, there are several items in the picture which may be helpful and insightful to discuss. How do clients pick apples from the tree (for example, do they climb up on a strong or a weak ladder, do they just reach up, do they wait for the apples to drop); are there few or many apples in the tree (apples may symbolize opportunities or emotional wealth); is it a strong, weak, or dying tree (the tree may reflect their view of themselves); is it a nice day or is it cloudy (can reflect environmental conditions); are there other people helping to pick apples (other individuals can reflect dependency or a supportive network of friends and family)?

These tree activities are rich in symbolism and provide insight into clients' perceptions of their life.

Draw Your Future

Draw a picture of the future you desire. Include in the picture your family, friends, goals, hopes, and dreams. Then add to the picture the problems you may face when trying to achieve your desired future plans. Next to the problems, write out or draw possible solutions to those problems.

This activity can help individuals clarify their future goals and note the difficulties that may arise that they can prepare for. Problem solving their difficulties through a drawing activity can help participants find new solutions to existing problems. Drawing a problem and possible solutions accesses clients' intuition and imagination and can offer new insights and/or perspectives to their situation.

CONCLUSION

The expressive arts can be used therapeutically to aid older adults with developmental, psychological, social, and physical health issues and conflicts. Participants have an opportunity to find their inner voice to tell the story of their life, to share their legacy, and to create an avenue for meaningful communication.

Art activities can aid participants with new beginnings and endings and serve as rituals, creating objects that represent our passing through life. It can memorialize the moment and offer an opportunity to contemplatively look back. It serves to reflect the meaning and significance for many aspects of their lives that may have been silent. It may note the lives that have touched them and those that they have touched.

By sharing their art, clients recall years of memories, describing aspects of their life which others may have never known. Within each person there is a wealth of history, an accumulation of experiences, which is greater than the tribulations of the moment. Experiences, reflected in art, do not define individuals, but rather clarifies how they coped with their circumstances. When participants are aware of their full life experience, from birth to the present, they become more cognizant of the riches in their life, the trials they have gone through, the decisions they have made, and the fruits of their journey. The expressive arts can be a special gift to older adults; a gift of giving and receiving, of touching and being touched, a gift of sharing one's life.

REFERENCES

Ault, B. (1986). *Art therapy: The healing vision* (Video). Kansas: Menninger Foundation.

Butler, R.N. (1963). The life review: An interpretation of reminiscence in the aged. *Psychiatry Journal for the Study of Interpersonal Process, 26,* 65–67.

Campbell, J. (Ed.). (1971). *The portable Jung.* New York: Viking Press.

Diamond, M.C., Johnson, R.E., Protti, A.M., Ott, C., & Kajika, L. (1985). Plasticity in the 904-day-old male rat cerebral cortex. *Experimental Neurology, 87,* 309–317.

Gantt, L., & Tabone, C. (1998). *The formal elements art therapy scale: The rating manual.* Morgantown, WV: Gargoyle Press.

Henley, D. (1986). Approaching artistic sublimation in low-functioning individuals. *Art Therapy,* 67–73.

Kramer, E. (1958). *Art therapy in a children's community.* Springfield, IL: Thomas.

Kramer, E. (1971). *Art therapy with children.* New York: Schocken Books.

Madden, D.J., Allen, P.A., Blumenthal, J.A., & Emery, C.F. (1989). Improving aerobic capacity in health older adults does not necessarily lead to improved cognitive performance. *Psychology and Aging, 4*(3), 307–320.

McNiff, S. (1988). *Fundamentals of art therapy.* Springfield, IL: Thomas.

Restak, R. (1988). *The mind.* New York: Bantam Books.

Rubin, J.A. (1984). *Child art therapy* (2nd ed.). New York: Van Nostrand-Reinhold.

Taublee, L.E., & Folsom, J.C. (1966). Reality orientation for geriatric patients. *Hospitals and Community Psychiatry, 17.*

Ulman, E. (1987). Variations on a Freudian theme: Three art therapy theorists. In J. A. Rubin (Ed.), *Approaches to art therapy: Theory and technique* (pp. 277–298). New York: Brunner/Mazel.

Wadeson, H. (1987). *The dynamics of art psychotherapy.* New York: Wiley.

Weiss, J. C. (1984). *Expressive therapy with elders and the disabled: Touching the heart of life.* New York: Haworth Press.

Weiss, J. C. (1995). Cognitive therapy and life review therapy: Theoretical and therapeutic implications for mental health counselors. *Journal of Mental Health Counseling, 17*(2), 157–172.

CHAPTER 12

Using Music Therapy in Treating Psychological Problems of Older Adults

SUZANNE B. HANSER

Music therapy is not found in most textbooks of counseling and psychotherapy. Yet, as its clinical practice grows more widespread, empirical research is providing convincing evidence of its efficacy. For many older adults who do not respond to traditional forms of treatment, the impact of music therapy is particularly noteworthy. This chapter introduces the field of music therapy, reviews the literature with older adults, presents a sampling of successful strategies, outlines typical music therapy sessions, and offers case examples demonstrating effective interventions. The focus is on those diagnoses that have shown the most significant gains as a function of music therapy. The first section deals with cognitively impaired older adults who are in various stages of dementia, and highlights applications with individuals who have Alzheimer's disease and related disorders (ADRD). The next section of this chapter covers older adults who are diagnosed with psychiatric disorders, and details a music-facilitated stress reduction strategy for treating affective disorders. The last section covers the end of life and the work of music therapists in hospice settings and palliative care.

THE FIELD OF MUSIC THERAPY

Music was said "to soothe the savage beast" (Congreve, 1697) well before psychotherapy was known to humankind. In addition to biblical references to calming influences of music, the ancient healing practices of many cultures included music as a significant part of their rituals. Humane practitioners in asylums advocated using music, and early American physicians and authors claimed its medicinal value as an analgesic and a mood alterer (Heller, 1987).

Later, post-war shell-shock victims were found to respond to music when nothing else could reach them. The Musicians' Emergency Fund began to sponsor musicians in hospitals while a small group of specialists opened clinics to treat a variety of ailments using music as therapy.

In 1950, the National Association for Music Therapy established the field as an official discipline. Currently, the newly formed American Music Therapy Association, with its Standards of Practice and Code of Ethics, oversees 69 approved academic curricula in the United States and over 150 approved full-time clinical internships. It has approximately 5000 professional and student members who practice in schools, clinics, community agencies and hospitals as well as privately (NAMT, 1997). The Certification Board for Music Therapists conducts a national examination for applicants who have completed an approved degree program and six-month internship.

Currently, music therapists work with individuals and groups by assessing each client's needs, establishing goals and objectives consistent with the treatment team, and designing strategies that incorporate nonverbal, creative ways to reach specified psychotherapeutic aims (Hanser, 1988). They may use any genre of music along with improvisation, singing, moving or dancing to music, playing instruments (notably percussion with older adults), composing music, talking about and analyzing music, learning music, or listening to music. Combining these methods of musical interaction with counseling and psychotherapy techniques, music therapists have developed protocols such as Guided Imagery and Music (GIM) (Bonny, 1978, 1980), Clinical Music Therapy Improvisation (Lee, 1996), and Stress Reduction through Music Therapy (Hanser, 1996).

Music therapists specializing in gerontology work at all levels of care, from nursing homes to community-based senior programs and with individuals who are severely involved both physically and cognitively to those who are enhancing their quality of life by building musical abilities and talents. Several books detail music therapy procedures with older adults (Bright, 1981, 1988, 1991; Chavin, 1991; Clair, 1996b; Cordrey, 1995; Gfellar & Hanson, 1995; B. Smith, 1995). In addition, data have been gathered to guide practice, including the most comfortable loudness levels (Riegler, 1980b), vocal ranges (Salzberg, 1979), and repertoire (Moore, Staum, & Brotons, 1992). In choosing the type of music for a therapeutic intervention, that which is familiar and has been associated with positive memories may be most likely to enhance functioning. Music that was popular during the individual's youth or young adulthood may be indicated. However, individual preferences are the most significant predictor of responsiveness to music.

MUSIC THERAPY WITH COGNITIVELY IMPAIRED OLDER ADULTS

Individuals with extensive cognitive impairment tend to respond dramatically to music. Well into the course of a progressive, degenerative condition such as Alzheimer's disease, musical abilities, particularly the response to rhythm, often continue to flourish (Clair, Bernstein, & Johnson, 1995). There is considerable documentation of preserved performance abilities (Beatty et al., 1988; Crystal, Grober, & Masur, 1989). Using an analysis of P3 event-related potentials in the brains of individuals with Alzheimer's disease compared with healthy controls, Swartz, Hantz, Crummer, Walton, and Frisina (1989; Swartz, Walton, Crummer, Hantz, & Frisina, 1992) conclude that certain music perception and discrimination abilities may, likewise, be maintained. What might account for these and even more astounding anecdotal reports of caregivers who witness spontaneous outpouring of singing after months of silence?

Perhaps music, with its formal and referential elements, its potential to evoke both analytical and emotional responses, its passive and active sides, and its simplicity and complexity may be processed in so many ways that it can be experienced somehow by even the most impaired person. Music making is a continuous activity. As such, there is an ongoing flow of stimuli. Each note, each beat, each sound is a cue for the next. If the listener or participant misses one cue, there are many to come, maximizing the potential for an ongoing performance or reception of musical activity. This success may offer the person a rare sense of mastery or competence, contributing to the overall self-esteem of individuals who have lost so many abilities.

Another important mechanism is the ability of music to enhance emotion which is often heightened in the cognitively impaired individual. It is common to encounter crying, laughing, and other strong emotions as music evokes memories, images, associations, or connections to spirituality, childhood, and other personal meanings (Sacks & Tomaino, 1991). Music gives the person a unique opportunity to feel and experience a range of emotions in a protected and healthy manner.

Because people encounter music throughout their lives in many contexts and situations, musical responses are well-practiced. When an auditory stimulus is heard, they may respond without thought, as they would with any overlearned behavior. This automatic stimulus-response connection may hold for those who have difficulty processing the stimulus cognitively. In this way, music may evoke many complex behaviors: singing, dancing, tapping the toe, expressing feelings, reliving memories, or reacting emotionally to music that has held some meaning earlier in life.

Clearly, listening to music elicits many learned responses. But, with the assistance of a music therapist, new and different behaviors may be developed as well.

Music Therapy Research

Music therapists have reported an extensive array of positive effects for individuals with dementia, including maintaining or actually enhancing functional abilities and decreasing undesirable behaviors such as wandering and agitation. While early work in ADRD consists primarily of descriptive research and a few experimental studies (Gibbons, 1988; D. Smith, 1990), taken as a whole, this literature provides convincing evidence for music therapy. D. Smith's review cites behavioral interventions as the most effective in reducing inappropriate behavior in long-term care settings.

In a review of different therapies for Alzheimer's disease, Rabins (1996) reports modest gains for music therapy, tacrine, and other diverse approaches to dementia. He calls for the development of guidelines that would facilitate the comparative analysis of treatment protocols. Another problem in interpreting such literature is that health professionals' use of recorded music may be seen as comparable to music therapy strategies for specific problem behaviors. This biases any meta-analysis of the research while possibly misleading the reader about the efficacy of music therapy.

A review by Brotons, Koger, and Pickett-Cooper (1997) delineates the empirical research that has investigated specific music therapy strategies. The authors examined 69 references between 1986 and 1996, of which 42 were empirical studies and of these, 30 were clinically based studies. Out of a subset of 22 studies which were designed to test the outcome of music therapy trials, 21 yielded improvement, 11 of which demonstrated statistically significant results in comparison to control or comparison conditions.

The research has generated some interesting protocols for both developing new behaviors and decreasing inappropriate ones. Clinical studies report how music therapy enhances functioning. Encouraging results have been achieved on diverse behaviors, including face-name recognition (Carruth, 1997), cognition (G. Smith, 1986), socialization (Pollack & Namazi, 1992), reality orientation (Riegler, 1980a), and active participation (Christie, 1992; Clair & Bernstein, 1990a, 1990b; Kovach & Henschel, 1996; Smith-Marchese, 1994). Case studies report enhanced quality of life using a music therapy protocol (Lipe, 1991) and songwriting techniques (Silber & Hes, 1986). Other researchers have examined the effects of singing on such variables as alertness in patients with late stage dementia (Clair, 1996a), enhanced social interaction (Olderog-Millard & Smith, 1989), and increased recall of words when sung as opposed to spoken (Prickett & Moore, 1991). Taped music has been applied successfully to enhance responsiveness (Norberg, Melin, & Asplund, 1986; Sambandham & Schirm, 1995) and to change affect (Gaebler & Hemsley, 1991). Intergenerational music programs have resulted in reduced agitation and enhanced social interaction between older adults with dementia and young children (Newman & Ward, 1993; Ward, Los Kamp, & Newman, 1996).

While these studies examine a comprehensive music therapy treatment or single methods such as singing, songwriting, or music listening, other literature provides comparative evidence of different music therapy techniques. Recent findings (Hanson, Gfeller, Woodworth, Swanson, & Garand, 1996) suggest that more purposeful behavior is generated with movement experiences as opposed to singing and with activities which demand fewer responses compared with those of greater difficulty. In this study, activities that did not require expressive or receptive verbal skills, like moving to music, yielded the greatest compliance. Singing was performed most effectively when familiar songs were used and participants were not asked to sing every word. Similarly, activities where individuals chose a rhythm to play on percussion instruments resulted in more participation than when they were asked to duplicate a given rhythm. Brotons and Pickett-Cooper (1994) found that individuals with ADRD participate longer when playing instruments, dancing, moving, and playing games as opposed to composing or improvising. Clair and Bernstein (1993) observed higher rates of involvement with vibrotactile stimulation while playing drums compared with singing. The vibrotactile techniques consisted of the use of percussion instruments with large vibrating skins that created more volume and physical vibration for participants.

Much evidence has been amassed to support music therapy as a behavior management strategy for people with ADRD. Music therapy has been found to improve sleep (Lindenmuth, Patel, & Chang, 1992), decrease wandering (Fitzgerald-Cloutier, 1992; Groene, 1993), reduce agitation (Brotons & Pickett-Cooper, 1996; Clair & Bernstein, 1994; Gerdner & Swanson, 1993; Goddaer & Abraham, 1994; Tabloski, McKinnon-Howe, & Remington, 1995; Ward, Los Kamp, & Newman, 1996), decrease inappropriate verbalizations (Casby & Holm, 1994), and diminish aggressiveness during bathing (Thomas, Heitman, & Alexander, 1997).

MUSIC THERAPY STRATEGIES

This section presents a format for music therapy groups which may be applied in any of the stages of dementia. It also describes individual strategies for whom group music therapy is contraindicated.

Group Music Therapy

When a cognitively impaired person is referred to music therapy, the first task is to determine the types of musical experiences which will be most favorably received and most easily mastered. With this emphasis on success, the music therapist proceeds to assess musical interests and abilities. Musical background and taste is assessed first through interview. Informants such as caregivers and family members are questioned when the degree of dementia prevents the cognitively impaired person from reporting preferences. Then, the therapist plays musical excerpts from various periods and styles and observes the individual's response. Percussion instruments are introduced and the person is asked to imitate simple patterns as the therapist accompanies a song which seemed familiar or yielded some response during the observation period. A variety of songs may be sung and the individual will be asked to sing along.

More formal evaluation may take place, giving the therapist more clues to the music activities that most likely will be experienced with competence. An assessment tool such as the Residual Music Skills Test (RMST; York, 1994) offers a more comprehensive look at musical functioning. Depending on the goals and objectives of the music therapy program, the therapist may use other standardized psychological tests or mood scales to determine progress during the course of therapy.

The following is a sample format, introduced by the author (Hanser, 1987) as an adaptation of the "sonata form." Its labels are the features of a musical sonata form, namely, an introduction, exposition or theme, development, recapitulation, and coda or closing. It was developed to describe the parts of a music therapy session in which individuals with dementia and their family caregivers were invited to participate. This general outline was followed in weekly programs for cognitively impaired older adults and their family members. Level of functioning determined the length of sessions and the degree of complexity of the tasks and activities. Sessions lasted from 45 minutes to one hour and music experiences were based on group members' assessed abilities and preferences. The number of participants varied widely, ranging from 6 to 26 people. Obviously, small groups allow for more individualization and attention to individual needs. This outline offers some general parameters for musical experiences in the typical music therapy session. Other clinical applications of this format appear in Hanser and Clair (1995).

Part I Introduction

Participants are greeted with a song or chant that incorporates their names in a musical welcome. Group members are encouraged to sing along or chant the words as they greet each participant. Familiar melodies may form the basis for the greeting song. A popular example is singing "Hello, (first name)" to the tune of "Good Night, Ladies." The names are announced one by one as the therapist moves around the circle of participants.

When chants are employed, a rondo form (ABACA) is a useful structure for the greeting. A theme chant (A) is introduced e.g., "It's a beautiful day today. Let's hear what you have to say." Attention is turned to the first participant, who is called by name and greeted (B). The chant is repeated by the entire group (A). The next participant is greeted and given an opportunity to speak (C). The chant is spoken again (A) and the rondo continues around the circle until everyone is greeted and given a chance to say something.

While this introduction is designed primarily to set the stage for an orientation to group members, it also involves a great deal of repetitive material over a steady rhythm. This maximizes the chance that participants will be able to attend to the task and participate during at least part of the activity.

Part II Exposition

The theme of the session is introduced. Based upon the goals and objectives for the group, activities are designed to offer opportunities for successful expression of targeted responses. Examples include music-accompanied movement to enhance body awareness and coordination, singing to increase attention and focus, rhythmic improvisation to promote self-expression and nonverbal communication, dancing to improve socialization, music listening to change mood, performing on musical instruments to support self-esteem, composing songs to develop communication of ideas and feelings, and any creative approach to maximize functional abilities. Instruments such as xylophones and metallophones are tuned to various modes and scales, particularly the pentatonic, where no two notes are closer than a major second apart. This means that no matter what notes are played together, there is little sense of dissonance, maximizing the aesthetic qualities of the experience. This success orientation in the music therapy session is central to its effectiveness in achieving positive self regard and competence.

Part III Development

This activity takes the theme one step further or approaches the objective in another way. For instance, if the previous activity evoked memories and associations, this activity might focus on expressing that feeling using tuned instruments or percussion. If singing brought out active participation from group members, this activity might involve writing new words to a familiar song to communicate something about the group. If the group exercised to music, this part of the session might have the group listen to relaxing music and slow their movements.

Part IV Recapitulation

This repetition of previously experienced material provides another chance to engage in purposeful behavior or communication. Repeating a particularly successful or meaningful part of the session may reinforce the sense of mastery in the participants. Alternatively, if the group members are sufficiently aware cognitively, the group may discuss a favorite activity or present ideas for subsequent sessions.

Part V Coda

This acitivity provides closure and a clear cue that the session is ending. It is usually the same song or activity from session to session, reminding the group that it is time to end.

Individual Music Therapy

Individual referrals for music therapy are indicated when the person is not capable of participating in groups because of physical incapacity or antisocial behavior. In the case of physical incapacity, a brief individual session can help to change mood or orient a bedridden patient. Having undertaken the assessment process, the therapist will be prepared to use live or recorded music which is familiar and enjoyable to the individual.

Another purpose of individual therapy is to manage problem or catastrophic behavior. The stress reduction strategy described later in this chapter addresses agitation and anxiety in the person with dementia and may be applied on an individual or group basis. Techniques to handle bathing or difficult times of the day usually involve distraction from the task or anxiety-provoking stimulus by attracting attention with a familiar song or piece of music. In the case of Mr. L., a unique method was effective in preventing a catastrophic response in the dining hall.

CASE EXAMPLE

Mr. L. had been a resident in the nursing home for two years and became known to the nursing staff as one of the more difficult patients to manage. He was 69 years old, with a diagnosis of probable Alzheimer's disease, and in severe cognitive decline, Stage 6, according to the Global Deterioration Scale (GDS; Reisberg, Ferris, De Leon, & Crook, 1982). Several times a day, Mr. L. would become agitated and would exhibit sudden outbursts of screaming. The staff could find no observable cause for this behavior and had difficulty controlling him as well as the other patients whom he would upset in the process.

One day in the dining hall, Mr. L. was eating in his customary way, off the plate of another resident. As he did so, the resident started to yell and Mr. L. began to wail and raise his fists in the air, ready to strike. Observing the action, the music therapist quickly took a portable cassette player from her pocket and threw it on the table between them. The loud Souza March it played so startled both of them that the distraction silenced them immediately. Several residents started clapping in rhythm, and soon, Mr. L. was clapping along, oblivious of the near crisis and happy to be hearing the music.

The next day, the music therapist invited Mr. L. to attend the group session. Mr. L. enjoyed singing and participated in an improvisation on xylophones tuned to the pentatonic scale. He stayed on task to the activities for a solid hour and interacted appropriately with the other residents. After the session, the music therapist provided the staff with a cassette tape of the songs they had sung and a recorder for Mr. L. to use in the dayroom. After an hour without any outbursts or disruptions, the staff gave him the recorder and tapes, which he enjoyed without interruption.

The staff observed that they could prevent disruptive behavior by offering Mr. L. music while he remained calm or as soon as they suspected that another resident's behavior might bother him. He never had an outburst while listening to the tapes, and Mr. L.'s music collection grew as he participated in more music therapy groups.

MUSIC THERAPY WITH GEROPSYCHIATRIC PATIENTS

Numerous music therapists function as part of an interdisciplinary team on geropsychiatric units. Their nonverbal approach to relieving psychiatric symptomatology is often sought when other methods fail. Indeed, there is an increasing body of evidence that supports newer, nontraditional psychotherapeutic treatments. Shealy, Cady, and Cox (1995) report that as many as 85% of their 351 depressed clients were responsive to music, photostimulation, insight meditation, education and other treatments within two weeks, avoiding drug therapy.

Published music therapy methodologies address a variety of psychiatric problems, not limited to geropsychiatry. Some are based on well known philosophical approaches and others are unique to music therapy. Popular books include a multimodal music therapy strategy (Cassity & Cassity, 1993), two analytical models (Benenzon, 1981; Tyson, 1981), and a broad overview of treatment methods (Unkefer, 1990). An entire issue of the journal, *Music Therapy Perspectives*, was devoted to psychiatric music therapy (Goldberg, 1994). Shaw's *The Joy of Music in Maturity* (1993) addresses the needs of older adults in general through a presentation of creative music therapy techniques. Another book presents intergenerational programs (Shaw & Manthey, 1996).

MUSIC THERAPY RESEARCH

The music therapy literature presents a preponderance of descriptive research and philosophical papers. Much has been written on Guided Imagery and Music (GIM) and its positive effects in producing psychological insights (Blake & Bishop, 1994; Bonny, 1994; Clarkson & Geller, 1996). GIM is applied in therapist-client dyads or in groups. The technique involves:

1. A prelude—preliminary conversation to assess personal history and set goals
2. Induction—relaxation and focus as music is played
3. The music program—whereby a therapist guides clients through the experience of listening to music
4. Postlude—in which clients share their reactions or imagery and may review the session goals.

Songwriting is another important therapeutic tool for developing awareness, communicating feelings and enhancing group cohesion (Cordobes, 1997; Ficken, 1976). Musical improvisation has been utilized with psychiatric patients in an attempt to express emotions and interact with others (Bruscia, 1987; Nolan, 1994; Pavlicevic, Trevarthen, & Duncan, 1994). Patients with residual schizophrenia have benefited from singing and music listening by reducing their social isolation (Tang, Yao, & Zheng, 1994). Healthy older adults have found that communal drumming allows them to enhance their modes of expression and interaction (Reuer & Crowe, 1995).

In research by the author, symptoms of depression, distress, and anxiety were significantly reduced in older adults suffering from major or minor depression as compared with no contact control subjects (Hanser & Thompson, 1994). The protocol was a stress reduction through music listening program (Hanser, 1996) which is summarized here.

A MUSIC THERAPY STRESS REDUCTION STRATEGY

An advantage of this strategy is that it can be practiced by individuals who are physically and/or cognitively limited, in a clinical setting or at home. It can be done alone or in groups, and its methods may be adapted to accommodate individual needs. The method is based on cognitive behavioral approaches, using music to cue elevated mood, muscle relaxation, and pleasant imagery. The music therapist assists the clients to identify recorded music which they find relaxing and which may evoke positive associations, memories and visual images. Interview and behavioral observation provide the background material to aid in selecting appropriate music. Clients learn and practice eight techniques over a period of eight weeks, the first three for body relaxation, the next two for evoking positive imagery, and the last three for specific effects:

1. A musical workout—gentle exercise to preferred music
2. Music massage—facial massage to calming music
3. Building a bond with music—progressive muscle relaxation to specific music to accompany waves of tension and relaxation
4. Painting peaceful images—guided imagery which lets the music evoke a desirable place
5. Creative problem solving—special imagery to provide a relaxing environment for approaching problems or worries
6. Lullabye and good night—music to aid sleep
7. A musical boost—music to energize
8. Creativity through music—ideas for making music a regular part of the day

CASE EXAMPLE

Mrs. E. (74 years old, in good physical health, living alone) was diagnosed with late onset dysthymic disorder after her husband died. At that time, she began to isolate herself, did not eat well, and stopped paying attention to self-care. Bills accummulated and she experienced serious symptoms of anxiety.

Mrs. E. was referred for individual music therapy when the family expressed concern to her physician that she was not leaving the house and seemed unable to function independently. They considered nursing home placement, but preferred to explore psychotherapy options first. Unfortunately, Mrs. E. was resistant to making an appointment. Her family was relieved when she appeared more receptive to the idea of music therapy.

Her husband had loved music and owned an extensive record collection. When she first met with the music therapist, Mrs. E. talked easily about her memories of attending concerts with her husband and shared her feelings of loss. When asked to identify music which had positive associations, she immediately selected a recording of the opera, *Tristan and Isolde*, and the third symphony of Beethoven. Practicing the body relaxation exercises, Mrs. E. reported that listening to the music gave her "a way to be with" her husband again. She said that she began to feel a freedom that she had not experienced since the loss of Mr. E. She became aware of a loosening of tension throughout her body and a physical sense of release as she listened to the music. During the imagery exercises, her sense of relaxation deepened. When she practiced the Creative Problem-Solving imagery, she imagined herself getting her house in order as she walked from room to room in time with the music. Consequently, she turned on the same music and actually starting organizing and cleaning up the house.

Mrs. E. spent a few hours each day listening to different recordings while practicing the relaxation techniques and reported feeling alive again for the first time in a long while. Over time, she started getting out of the house to attend concerts. She gave attention to her appearance again, and greatly reduced her symptoms of depression and anxiety.

MUSIC THERAPY AT THE END OF LIFE

West (1994) likens the music therapist attending and supporting the death of an individual to a midwife who helps birth a new life. Music therapy provides one way for an individual near the end of life to find a sense of control when everything appears uncontrollable. By selecting music and music experiences that cause an obvious change in focus or mood, the person may feel empowered again. In another way, music may offer a means of expressing personal and transpersonal experience in a safe and indirect, nonverbal manner. Music is sometimes referred to as a symbolic language to communicate what cannot be said with words. This contributes to the ability of music to heighten awareness and offer a way to experience the moment fully and at times, joyfully.

As evidenced in the many books published about this work, there are cases where music therapy has evoked a peak experience in individuals who produce insights about the meaning of their lives (Lane, 1994; Martin, 1991; Munro, 1984). Because music can be enjoyed both passively through listening and actively through performance, singing or composition, it allows for many meaningful shared experiences with family, friends, and loved ones.

MUSIC THERAPY RESEARCH

Several music therapists have described their roles in palliative care settings (Burns, 1993; Gilbert, 1977; Mandel, 1993; Salmon, 1993; Yamamoto, 1993). A more recent explanation by Aldridge (1995) cites the connection between music and spirituality as central to music therapy. An overview of the state of the art in clinical practice, found in the proceedings of the International Conference: Music Therapy in Palliative Care (Lee, 1995), cites diverse processes which contribute to the impact of these techniques at the end of life.

Music therapy methodologies are similar to those used in psychiatry. Guided Imagery and Music has been effective for many who seek an avenue to express feelings and prepare for separation from loved ones (Wylie & Blom, 1986). Songwriting provides a legacy for significant others in the form of an original piece of music (Rykov, 1994). Music therapists report that writing songs offers an opportunity to give compliments to important people, articulate messages of positive feelings for others, and relive memories (O'Callaghan, 1996). The interactive musical dialogue which comes alive in clinical improvisation is another unique and significant feature of music therapy (Aldridge, 1989). In a moving account of the journey of a musician dying from AIDS, Lee (1996) details insights gathered through collaborative piano improvisation.

Other interesting effects of music therapy have been documented in the literature. Research by Curtis (1986) demonstrates some efficacy for music therapy procedures with terminally ill patients in managing pain. Remarkably, Boyle and Greer (1983) observed responsiveness in comatose patients when music was played contingent upon movement. These effects point out the tremendous potential for music as therapy.

MUSIC THERAPY STRATEGIES

In the case of the dying person, music therapy is an individualized process to meet unique needs. It calls upon all of the resources of the therapist to determine what choices the client should make, how active the music making or listening experience will be, and how much the person wishes to deal with issues of loss and death. The therapist must be extremely versatile musically to provide a favorite song or begin an improvisation to match the mood of the moment.

Music therapy is an intuitive process in this setting which works to support the person rather than attempting to achieve a particular goal. It involves an immensely creative interaction which is largely nonverbal and difficult to replicate. Families who participate in music therapy along with their loved one say that it is hard to verbalize what they gain from such an experience. This is truly the nature of music at the end of life. When it is effective, it can be transcendent in its impact.

CASE EXAMPLE

This is a song composed by Ken, his wife, Margaret, and daughter, Peggy. It is sung to Ken's favorite tune, "San Francisco":

> Hey there, Ken
> Here we go again
> Singing a song again
>   for you today.
>
> Hey there, Margaret
> She's a nice lady
> And she loves Peggy and Ken.
>
> Hey there, Peggy
> She's a nice daughter
> We love her,
>   she's number one!

Ken (71 years old) was hospitalized with pneumonia, when his physician declared that he was in the final stages of his terminal illness. He was extremely weak and could barely speak when his wife and daughter visited. The music therapist had noticed that during visits, no one said anything, and the family appeared quite morose. She asked if she could come in and sing some songs for Ken.

Margaret volunteered that "San Francisco" was a favorite of theirs. The therapist took out her guitar and as she sang, Ken opened his eyes and whispered some of the words. The women started singing and tears came to their eyes. They spoke about a trip to San Francisco and shared many pleasant memories. As they talked, Ken smiled and even laughed at one of the anecdotes.

When the therapist returned later, the three were reminiscing about Peggy's childhood and seemed rather animated. The therapist complimented the family on their musicality and suggested that they write a song about each other. She asked if they could find some appropriate words to fit the melody of "San Francisco." They came up with the lyrics printed here, with the verse about Margaret coming from Ken himself.

After Ken's death, Peggy copied the words to their song in calligraphy and created an artistic plaque for her mother. She said that their singing had helped her to reframe the experience of the last days with her father. She felt she had been able to give something to her father and mother just when she was feeling worthless in her inability to help or change the circumstances. Margaret said she was grateful for the opportunity to unite the family in such a creative way. She believed that her darkest moments in the hospital were brightened to an extent that she had not experienced in the many months of Ken's illness. She cherished the song and the memories that it elicited.

CONCLUSION

This chapter has summarized the recent research in music therapy with older adults, offer sample strategies and present clinical cases to illustrate applications. It was written to acquaint the reader with the field of music therapy and to present techniques which are based on research and clinical work with this population. If it has accomplished that effectively, it is hoped that the reader will view this approach to counseling and psychotherapy with openness and an interest in examining the potential for clinical music therapy interventions.

REFERENCES

Aldridge, D. (1989). A phenomenological comparison of the organization of music and the self. *Arts in Psychotherapy, 16,* 91–97.

Aldridge, D. (1995). Spirituality, hope and music therapy in palliative care. *Arts in Psychotherapy, 22,* 103–109.

Beatty, W., Zavadil, K., Bailly, R., Rixen, G., Zavadil, L., Farnham, N., & Fisher, I. (1988). Preserved musical skill in a severely demented patient. *International Journal of Clinical Neuropsychology, 10,* 158–164.

Benenzon, R.O. (1981). *Music therapy manual.* St. Louis, MO: MMB.

Blake, R.L., & Bishop, S.R. (1994). The Bonny method of guided imagery and music (GIM) in the treatment of post-traumatic stress disorder with adults in the psychiatric setting. *Journal of Music Therapy, 12,* 125–129.

Bonny, H. (1978). *Facilitating GIM sessions.* Salina, KS: Bonny Foundation.

Bonny, H. (1980). *GIM therapy: Past, present and future implications.* Salina, KS: Bonny Foundation.

Bonny, H. (1994). Twenty-one years later: A GIM update. *Music Therapy Perspectives, 12,* 70–74.

Boyle, M.E., & Greer, R.D. (1983). Operant procedures and the comatose patient. *Journal of Applied Behavior Analysis, 16,* 3–12.

Bright, R. (1981). *Practical planning in music therapy for the aged.* Melbourne, Australia: Alfred.

Bright, R. (1988). *Music therapy and the dementias: Improving the quality of life.* St. Louis, MO: MMB.

Bright, R. (1991). *Music in geriatric care: A second look.* Australia: Music Therapy Enterprises.

Brotons, M., Koger, S.M., & Pickett-Cooper, P. (1997). Music and the dementias: A review of literature. *Journal of Music Therapy, 34,* 204–245.

Brotons, M., & Pickett-Cooper, P. (1994). Preferences of Alzheimer's disease patients for music activities: Singing, instruments, dance/movement, games, and composition/improvisation. *Journal of Music Therapy, 31,* 220–233.

Brotons, M., & Pickett-Cooper, P. (1996). The effects of music therapy intervention on agitation behaviors of Alzheimer's disease patients. *Journal of Music Therapy, 33,* 2–18.

Bruscia, K. (1987). *Improvisational models of music therapy.* Springfield, IL: Thomas.

Burns, S. (1993). In hospice work, music is our great ally. *Pastoral Music, 17,* 11–13.

Carruth, E.K. (1997). The effects of singing and the spaced retrieval technique on improving face-name recognition in nursing home residents. *Journal of Music Therapy, 34,* 165–186.

Casby, J.A., & Holm, M.B. (1994). The effect of music on repetitive disruptive vocalizations of persons with dementia. *American Journal of Occupational Therapy, 48,* 883–889.

Cassity, M.D., & Cassity, J.E. (1993). *Multimodal psychiatric music therapy for adults, adolescents, and children: A clinical manual.* Weatherford, OK: C & C.

Chavin, M. (1991). *The lost chord: Reaching the person with dementia through the power of music.* Mount Airy, MD: Eldersong.

Christie, M.E. (1992). Music therapy applications in a skilled and intermediate care nursing home facility: A clinical study. *Activities, Adaptation and Aging, 16,* 69–87.

Clair, A.A. (1996a). The effect of singing on alert responses in persons with late stage dementia. *Journal of Music Therapy, 33,* 234–247.

Clair, A.A. (1996b). *Therapeutic uses of music with older adults.* Baltimore: Health Professions Press.

Clair, A.A., & Bernstein, B. (1990a). A comparison of singing, vibrotactile and nonvibrotactile instrumental playing responses in severely regressed persons with dementia of the Alzheimer's type. *Journal of Music Therapy, 27,* 119–125.

Clair, A.A., & Bernstein, B. (1990b). A preliminary study of music therapy programming for severely regressed persons with Alzheimer's type dementia. *Journal of Applied Gerontology, 9,* 299–311.

Clair, A.A., & Bernstein, B. (1993). The preference for vibrotactile versus auditory stimuli in severely regressed persons with dementia of the Alzheimer's type compared to those with dementia due to alcohol abuse. *Music Therapy Perspectives, 11,* 24–27.

Clair, A.A., & Bernstein, B. (1994). The effect of no music, stimulative background music and sedative background music on agitation behaviors in persons with severe dementia. *Activities, Adaptation and Aging, 19,* 61–70.

Clair, A.A., Bernstein, B., & Johnson, G. (1995). Rhythm playing characteristics in persons with severe dementia including those with probable Alzheimer's type. *Journal of Music Therapy, 32,* 113–131.

Clarkson, G., & Geller, J.D. (1996). The Bonny method from a psychoanalytical perspective: Insights from working with a psychoanalytic psychotherapist in a guided imagery and music series. *Arts in Psychotherapy, 23,* 311–319.

Cordrey, C. (1995). *Hidden treasures: Music and memory activities for people with Alzheimers.* Mt. Airy, MD: G & H.

Cordobes, T.K. (1997). Group songwriting as a method for developing group cohesion for HIV-seropositive adult patients with depression. *Journal of Music Therapy, 34,* 46–67.

Crystal, H.A., Grober, E., & Masur, D. (1989). Preservation of musical memory in Alzheimer's disease. *Journal of Neurology, Neurosurgery, and Psychiatry, 52,* 1415–1416.

Curtis, S.L. (1986). The effect of music on pain relief and relaxation of the terminally ill. *Journal of Music Therapy, 23,* 10–24.

Ficken, T. (1976). The use of songwriting in a psychiatric setting. *Journal of Music Therapy, 13,* 163–172.

Fitzgerald-Cloutier, M.L. (1992). The use of music therapy to decrease wandering: An alternative to restraints. *Music Therapy Perspectives, 11,* 32–36.

Gaebler, H., & Hemsley, D. (1991). The assessment and short-term manipulation of affect in the severely demented. *Behavioural Psychotherapy, 19,* 145–156.

Gerdner, L.A., & Swanson, E.A., (1993). Effects of individualized music on confused and agitated elderly patients. *Archives of Psychiatric Nursing, 7,* 284–291.

Gfeller, K., & Hanson, N. (Eds.). (1995). *Music therapy programming for individuals with Alzheimer's disease and related disorders.* DesMoines, Iowa: The University of Iowa College of Liberal Arts and College of Nursing.

Gibbons, A.C. (1988). A review of literature for music development/education and music therapy with the elderly. *Music Therapy Perspectives, 5,* 33–40.

Gilbert, J. (1977). Music therapy perspectives on death and dying. *Journal of Music Therapy, 14,* 165–171.

Goddaer, J., & Abraham, I. (1994). Effects of relaxing music on agitation during meals among nursing home residents with severe cognitive impairment. *Archives of Psychiatric Nursing, 8,* 150–158.

Goldberg, F.S. (Ed.). (1994). *Music therapy perspectives, 12.* Silver Spring, MD: National Association for Music Therapy.

Groene, R.W., II. (1993). Effectiveness of music therapy: 1:1 intervention with individuals having senile dementia of the Alzheimer's type. *Journal of Music Therapy, 30,* 138–157.

Hanser, S.B. (1987). *Music therapists handbook.* St. Louis, MO: Warren Green.

Hanser, S.B. (1988). Controversy in music listening/stress reduction research. *Arts in Psychotherapy, 15,* 211–217.

Hanser, S.B. (1996). Music therapy to reduce anxiety, agitation, and depression. *Nursing Home Medicine, 10,* 20–22.

Hanser, S.B., & Clair, A.A. (1995). Retrieving the losses of Alzheimer's disease for patients and caregivers with the aid of music. In T. Wigram, B. Saperston, & R. West (Eds.), *The art and science of music therapy: A handbook* (pp.342–360). Switzerland: Harwood Academic.

Hanser, S.B., & Thompson, L.W. (1994). Effects of a music therapy strategy on depressed older adults. *Journal of Gerontology, 49,* 265–269.

Hanson, N., Gfeller, K., Woodworth, G., Swanson, E., & Garand, L. (1996). A comparison of the effectiveness of differing types and difficulty of music activities in programming for older adults with Alzheimer's disease and related disorders. *Journal of Music Therapy, 33,* 93–123.

Heller, G. (1987). Ideas, initiatives, and implementations: Music therapy in America, 1789–1848. *Journal of Music Therapy, 24,* 35–46.

Kovach, C., & Henschel, H. (1996). Behavior and participation during therapeutic activities on special care units. *Activities, Adaptation and Aging, 20,* 35–45.

Lane, D. (1994). *Music as medicine.* Cleveland, OH: Zondervan.

Lee, C.A. (Ed.). (1995). *Lonely waters.* Oxford, England: Sobell.

Lee, C.A. (1996). *Music at the edge: The music therapy experiences of a musician with AIDS.* London: Routledge & Kegan Paul.

Lindenmuth, G.F., Patel, M., & Chang, P.K. (1992). Effects of music on sleep in healthy elderly and subjects with senile dementia of the Alzheimer type. *American Journal of Alzheimer's Disease and Related Disorders and Research, 2,* 13–20.

Lipe, A. (1991). Using music therapy to enhance the quality of life in a client with Alzheimer's dementia: A case study. *Music Therapy Perspectives, 9,* 102–105.

Mandel, S.E. (1993). The role of the music therapist on the hospice/palliative care team. *Journal of Palliative Care, 9,* 37–39.

Martin, J.A. (Ed.). (1991). *The next step forward: Music therapy with the terminally ill.* Bronx, NY: Calvary Hospital.

Moore, R.S., Staum, M.J., & Brotons, M. (1992). Music preferences of the elderly: Repertoire, vocal ranges, tempos, and accompaniments for singing. *Journal of Music Therapy, 29,* 236–252.

Munro, S. (1984). *Music therapy in palliative/hospice care.* St. Louis, MO: MMB.

National Association for Music Therapy. (1997). *NAMT member sourcebook.* Silver Spring, MD: Author.

Newman, S., & Ward, C. (1993). An observational study of intergenerational activities and behavior change in dementing elders at adult day care centers. *International Journal of Aging and Human Development, 36,* 321–333.

Nolan, P. (1994). The therapeutic response in improvisational music therapy: What goes on inside? *Music Therapy Perspectives, 12,* 84–91.

Norberg, A., Melin, E., & Asplund, K. (1986). Reactions to music, touch, and object presentation in the final stage of dementia: An exploratory study. *International Journal of Nursing Studies, 23,* 315–323.

O'Callaghan, C.C. (1996). Lyrical themes in songs written by palliative care patients. *Journal of Music Therapy, 33,* 74–92.

Olderog-Millard, K.A.O., & Smith, J.M. (1989). The influence of group singing therapy on the behavior of Alzheimer's disease patients. *Journal of Music Therapy, 26,* 58–70.

Pavlicevic, M., Trevarthen, C., & Duncan, J. (1994). Improvisational music therapy and the rehabilitation of persons suffering from chronic schizophrenia. *Journal of Music Therapy, 31,* 86–104.

Pollack, N.J., & Namazi, K.H. (1992). The effect of music participation on the social behavior of Alzheimer's disease patients. *Journal of Music Therapy, 29,* 54–67.

Prickett, C.A., & Moore, R.S. (1991). The use of music to aid memory of Alzheimer's patients. *Journal of Music Therapy, 28,* 101–110.

Rabins, P.V. (1996). Developing treatment guidelines for Alzheimer's disease and other dementias. *Journal of Clinical Psychiatry, 47,* 37–38.

Reisberg, B., Ferris, S.H., De Leon, M.J., & Crook, T. (1982). The global deterioration scale for assessment of primary degenerative dementia. *American Journal of Psychiatry, 139,* 1136–1139.

Reuer, B., & Crowe, B. (1995). *Best practice in music therapy: Utilizing group percussion strategies for promoting volunteerism in the well older adult.* St. Louis, MO: MMB.

Riegler, J. (1980a). Comparison of a reality orientation program for geriatric patients with and without music. *Journal of Music Therapy, 17,* 26–33.

Riegler, J. (1980b). Most comfortable loudness level of geriatric patients as a function of seashore loudness discrimination scores, detection threshold, age, sex, setting, and musical background. *Journal of Music Therapy, 17,* 214–222.

Rykov, M. (1994). *Last songs: AIDS and the music therapist.* St. Louis, MO: MMB.

Sacks, O., & Tomaino, C. (1991). Music and neurological disorder. *International Journal of Arts Medicine, 1,* 10–12.

Salmon, D. (1993). Music and emotion in palliative care. *Journal of Palliative Care, 9,* 48–52.

Salzberg, R.S. (1979). Vocal range of geriatric clients. *Journal of Music Therapy, 16,* 172–179.

Sambandham, M., & Schirm, V. (1995). Music as a nursing intervention for residents with Alzheimer's disease in long-term care. *Geriatric Nursing, 16,* 79–83.

Shaw, J. (1993). *The joy of music in maturity.* St. Louis, MO: MMB.

Shaw, J., & Manthey, C. (1996). *Musical bridges: Intergenerational music programs.* St. Louis, MO: MMB Music.

Shealy, C.N., Cady, R.K., & Cox, R.H. (1995). Pain, stress and depression: Psychoneuro-physiology and therapy. *Stress Medicine, 11,* 75–77.

Silber, F., & Hes, J. (1986). The use of songwriting with patients diagnosed with Alzheimer's disease. *Music Therapy Perspectives, 13,* 31–34.

Smith, B.B. (1995). *A song to set me free.* St. Louis, MO: MMB.

Smith, D.S. (1990). Therapeutic treatment effectiveness as documented in the gerontology literature: Implications for music therapy. *Music Therapy Perspectives, 8,* 36–40.

Smith, G. (1986). A comparison of the effects of three treatment interventions on cognitive functioning of Alzheimer patients. *Music Therapy, 6A,* 41–56.

Smith-Marchese, K. (1994). The effects of participatory music on the reality orientation and sociability of Alzheimer's residents in a long-term care setting. *Activities, Adaptation and Aging, 18,* 41–55.

Swartz, K.P., Hantz, E.C., Crummer, G.C., Walton, J.P., & Frisina, R.D. (1989). Does the melody linger on? Music cognition in Alzheimer's disease. *Seminar in Neurology, 9,* 152–158.

Swartz, K.P., Walton, J., Crummer, G., Hantz, E., & Frisina, R. (1992). P3 event-related potentials and performance of healthy older adults and AD subjects for music perception tasks. *Psychomusicology, 11,* 96–118.

Tabloski, P., McKinnon-Howe, L., & Remington, R. (1995). Effects of calming music on the level of agitation in cognitively impaired nursing home residents. *American Journal of Alzheimer's Care and Related Disorders and Research, 10,* 10–15.

Tang, W., Yao, X., & Zheng, Z. (1994). Rehabilitative effect of music therapy for residual schizophrenia: A one-month randomised controlled trial in Shanghai. *British Journal of Psychiatry, 165,* 38–44.

Thomas, D.W., Heitman, R.J., & Alexander, T. (1997). The effects of music on bathing cooperation for residents with dementia. *Journal of Music Therapy, 34,* 246–259.

Tyson, F. (1981). *Psychiatric music therapy.* New York: Weidnert & Sons.

Unkefer, E.F. (1990). *Music therapy in the treatment of adults with mental disorders: Theoretical bases and clinical interventions.* St. Louis, MO: MMB.

Ward, C.R., Los Kamp, L., & Newman, S. (1996). The effects of participation in an intergenerational program on the behavior of residents with dementia. *Activities, Adaptation and Aging, 20,* 61–76.

West, T.M. (1994). Psychological issues in hospice music therapy. *Music Therapy Perspectives, 12,* 117–124.

Wylie, M.E., & Blom, R. (1986). Guided imagery and music with hospice patients. *Music Therapy Perspectives, 3,* 25–28.

Yamamoto, K. (1993). Terminal care and music therapy. *Japanese Journal of Psychosomatic Medicine, 22,* 25–28.

York, E. (1994). The development of a quantitative music skills test for patients with Alzheimer's disease. *Journal of Music Therapy, 31,* 280–296.

CHAPTER 13

Therapeutic Issues and Strategies in Group Therapy with Older Men

David G. Sprenkel

The process of growing older is one of inexorable change, which challenges all who live to experience it. For some, growing older may be defined by greater opportunities and challenges. For others, the process is defined by increasing losses over time. Most who live beyond their sixth decade, however, do so without experiencing significant emotional difficulties (Reedy, 1982; Romaniak, McAuley, & Arling, 1983). Many elderly men do experience psychological difficulties that are due, at least in part, to either the direct or indirect effects of aging. This chapter focuses on these age-related changes and the use of group psychotherapy techniques in assisting those men who experience emotional or psychological difficulties associated with these changes.

When addressing psychotherapy with the elderly male, one must address those issues that have been linked to increased emotional sequelae for the older adult. By doing so, one risks ignoring the many strengths and positive attributes associated with the elderly. This may be a legitimate criticism of much of the literature on aging. However, for those professionals who work with elders and witness their courage and ability to adapt and cope, positive visions of aging are undeniable and cannot go unnoticed.

A second consideration needs to be made regarding the topic of this chapter. In discussing issues related to gender, it is easy to become diverted by comparisons between men and women. Although such comparisons have an important place in the literature, they seem to be of less use here. Thus, comparisons tend to focus on intragender differences and intergender comparisons are kept to a minimum.

Finally, many issues addressed in psychotherapy with elderly men are similar to issues faced in group psychotherapy with younger males. Likewise, group techniques with men share similarities across the ages. Others have provided excellent discussions of therapeutic issues with younger male populations

(Andronico, 1996; Kupers, 1993). There are issues, however, that, if not unique to the elderly male, certainly occur more frequently with an aged population. This chapter highlights several of the themes and therapeutic issues that occur more often when working with elderly males.

WHO IS THE ELDERLY MALE?

The process of aging is one of change. Such change is often presented by statistics documenting differences between younger and older populations. These statistical presentations can mask that aging is a developmental process and that one does not become "old" overnight. Rather, changes typically occur gradually over extended periods. The statistical representations merely reflect a moment in the process of change. Thus, the elderly male is often undergoing changes that are unnoticeable to others yet are likely noticed by the individual himself and, over time, can have a significant impact on his physical and emotional functioning. Three areas in which age-related changes seem to have potential for significant impact are physical health, social opportunities and support, and changes in job roles and economic status.

PHYSICAL HEALTH

One of the more obvious and dramatic areas of change experienced with increasing age is the physical development of the body. With increasing age, the male body undergoes numerous transformations. The skin becomes increasingly wrinkled and loses elasticity. Hair becomes whiter and continues to thin, with many men eventually becoming bald. Teeth weaken and are often removed and replaced by dentures. The body's gastrointestinal process changes. There is a reduction in digestive juices and decreased peristalsis leading to more frequent bouts with constipation. The bladder experiences a decreased capacity which, with an enlarging prostate, leads to more frequent urination. Sensory abilities such as vision and hearing suffer greater impairments and disease with advancing age.

Whereas professionals working with elderly men generally consider these changes "normative," they may or may not be seen as normal by the man himself. And, normative or not, many of these changes affect both the male's ability to function as well as his physical appearance. Although the decrease in physical functioning and its subsequent impact on emotional well-being is often addressed in the professional literature, the changes in physical appearance can also affect a man's self-image and esteem. This impact was evident in one male patient's response to gaining weight in a nursing home and being placed on a restricted diet. Although he was wheelchair-bound following a stroke and required assistance for most activities of daily living (ADLs), this patient had adapted to his living situation. When told he was overweight, however, he became very sensitive about his appearance and began to make critical comments about the appearance of many nursing home personnel. He had retained, or developed, a sense of self to which physical appearance was important. Apparent criticism of his appearance threatened his self-image even though he had seemingly more significant physical disability.

Physical changes associated with aging that are not normative include increased disease and illness rates. These changes differ from those previously described in that their onset tends to be less insidious, and the physical limitations they create can be more dramatic and occur over a brief period of time. An example of this is the onset of a cerebral vascular accident. The incidence of stroke increases with age after 65 years and contributes not only to increased mortality but also to increased disability (Zamula, 1986). The rates of cancer, especially cancer of the prostate and lung, increase for the elderly male. Although lung cancer is the leading cause of cancer death in older men, prostate cancer is the most frequently occurring cancer among elderly males (Satariono, 1997). Heart disease shows a significant increase in incidence for males with advancing age and is associated with increased disability (Boult, Kane, Louis, Boult, & McCaffrey, 1994; Verbrugge & Patrick, 1995). Sexual functioning is also often impaired to varying degrees with advancing age, often due to numerous chronic medical conditions and/or medication regimens (Panser et al., 1995).

Unlike physical changes associated with normal aging development, disease and disability are experienced by a minority of the overall population of elderly males. Such changes, however, are significant and pertinent for the mental health professional due to their increased frequency with advancing age and because of their association with emotional disturbances in late life.

SOCIAL FACTORS

A consequence of decreasing physical functioning and health with advancing age is an obvious increase in mortality. The average life span for males in the United States is 72.3 years (U.S. Bureau of the Census, 1995). Thus those males who live beyond their seventh and eighth decade will likely lose a number of male friends, coworkers, and family members. The age-related reduction in social network size is a consistent finding in the social gerontological literature, although the reasons for the reduction remain debatable (Harvey & Singleton, 1989; Lang & Carstensen, 1994; Lee & Markides, 1990). With advancing age, both males and females report a decrease in their number of friends, with males reporting fewer friends than females (Allan, 1989). Coupled with retirement and other factors, elderly males' social network undergoes increased loss with advancing age. Men's social contacts dwindle even further following the death of their spouse, a finding which has been attributed to the wife's role in maintaining the social network for the older couple (Johnson & Troll, 1994). In addition to increased isolation, a wife's death has also been associated with increased mortality for the elderly male (Jacobs & Ostfeld, 1977). Again, explanations emphasize the male's reliance on his wife for emotional and social support (Barer, 1994).

With increasing age, men are also more likely to live alone or in an institutional setting, with the age of male nursing home residents averaging approximately 84 years (Koff, 1997). With increased disability comes the need for greater assistance to care for oneself and, for many, their needs exceed their ability to live independently. Moving into an institutional setting can impact the well-being of the elderly, independent of their physical or social functioning. Individuals living in nursing home settings generally report decreased feelings of psychological well-being compared with peers of similar physical and social functioning who reside outside such facilities (Qassis & Hayden, 1990).

JOB ROLE AND FINANCIAL STATUS

Most elderly men were employed outside the home and were the primary source of income for their families. Thus, providing for their own and their families financial needs was a significant part of their self-concept. Retirement is a common experience for elderly males that is often expected or even mandated by society, and that often necessitates a change in self-concept. The loss of the job role, while not universally traumatic for males, does have significant mental health outcomes for approximately one-third of all retirees (Bosse, Spiro, & Kressin, 1996). In addition to the loss of the job role, a significant loss of income frequently accompanies retirement. Again, the importance of being able to provide financially for their families does not disappear even when other important struggles and obstacles are present. One patient, who had been retired for several years but suffered a serious stroke requiring nursing home care, filled his time in psychotherapy expressing concerns about the cost of his rehabilitation and the despair he felt in not being able to assist his wife in managing the expenses.

EMOTIONAL FUNCTIONING AND THE OLDER MALE

The age-related changes previously noted are each associated with the emotional health and well-being of the elderly male. This is particularly true for changes in physical health. Medical illness and disability have consistently been found to be significant predictors of depression in geriatric populations (Hays et al., 1998; Lyness et al., 1996), with illness seemingly impacting mood through the limitations it places on one's overall level of activity (Schulz & Williamson, 1993; Williamson & Schulz, 1992). In fact, some have found that depression among the elderly is "almost completely attributable to the joint effects of chronic medical conditions and functional disability" (Roberts, Kaplan, Shema, & Strawbridge, 1997, p. 1386). However, others have found social and economic variables to be related to the emotional functioning of the elderly in addition to one's physical health and level of disability (Callahan et al., 1994; Hays et al., 1998; Roberts et al., 1997).

These same variables are also correlated with late-life suicide rates for males. Males over the age of 65 have a higher rate of completed suicides than any other group (McIntosh, Pearson, & Lebowitz, 1997). Factors associated with suicide in older males include depression related to physical illness (Conwell, Rotenberg, & Caine, 1990), economic factors (McIntosh, Santos, Hubbard, & Overholser, 1994), losses related to retirement (Osgood & McIntosh, 1986), and social factors such as widowed status and social isolation (McIntosh et al., 1994).

While impaired health, increased disability, loss of job and income, and social isolation are not unique to the elderly population, their incidence increases with advancing age, and they appear to have a particular relevance for professionals working with older males. Again, for most men, changes in these areas are generally manageable and do not result in significant emotional turmoil. For those who experience a heavier burden because of changes in these areas, or for those who do not have the resources available to manage and cope with the changes, significant psychological distress is often the result. In some cases, this distress can be life threatening.

Factors that determine who experiences significant emotional distress associated with age-related changes include internal variables, such as coping skills and personality, as well as external variables, such as the size of one's social network. In addition, there may be qualities in the change process that make it easier or more difficult for the individual to accommodate. The impact of age-related changes on emotional health may vary due to the extent it impacts on one's life, the pace of its onset, and the meaning ascribed to it by the individual. That is, if the change affects many aspects of living, if it occurs quickly and unexpectedly, and if it affects significant aspects of the self, its impact on psychological health is likely to be greater.

The onset of a stroke is an excellent example of a sudden change that can have significant impact on many areas (e.g., ambulation, speech, cognition) and that often challenges central aspects of the self. Many patients, who exhibit significant anxiety symptoms during the first few weeks following a stroke, talk in therapy of its sudden onset and their feelings of being overwhelmed by the deficits incurred over a brief period of time. A stroke provides little opportunity for the individual to prepare for its subsequent impairments. If the stroke impairs a number of functional areas, the individual is at greater risk of increased dependency and social isolation, which often contributes to feelings of depression and loneliness. However, changes that occur more gradually can also interfere with an individual's emotional well-being (regardless of its speed of onset or its range of effect) if it is of significant meaning and importance to the individual. For example, elderly male patients often speak about feelings of loss and inadequacy if they experience changes in their abilities to function sexually. Such changes can occur slowly over time and without significant changes in other areas of living, with the subsequent feelings of loss shared by men who are sexually active as well as by those who are not. For these men, sexual ability is of particular importance to their sense of who they are, and its loss is often emotionally painful.

SUCCESSFUL AGING

There is a growing body of literature that examines factors related to successful aging, that is, people's ability to adapt and cope with the aging process and its concomitant effects (Baltes & Baltes, 1990; Coleman, 1996). Most of these theories describe an inherent, adaptive process within the aging individual that accounts for the fact that the majority of elderly do not experience significant loss of life satisfaction or decreases in self-esteem. The theories differ in delineating the exact nature of this process but tend to emphasize the individual's acceptance of what has changed and cannot be remedied, the focusing of energy and time on remaining strengths and capabilities, and the adapting of self-concept, daily routines, and coping strategies to accommodate the age- or disease-related changes (Baltes & Baltes, 1990; Coleman, 1996).

Such adaptive processes are supported by empirical evidence showing their relation to the maintenance of life satisfaction and well-being (Baltes & Baltes, 1990). If these processes are inherent, for those elderly men who do experience significant emotional or psychological distress, the processes must be in some way inadequate. That is, the age-related changes must prove too great for the inherent adaptive process to accommodate their subsequent impact. The impact of the changes may prove too great because of the nature of their onset, the range of effect on functional areas, and/or the meaning ascribed to the changes. For those whose adaptive process proves inadequate, the result is psychological distress. Group psychotherapy can assist those elderly males who experience decreased self-esteem and subsequent emotional disturbance.

GROUP PSYCHOTHERAPY

The changes experienced by aging men include changes in their objective life (e.g., physical functioning) and in their subjective, experiential life (e.g., sense of self). Psychotherapy can assist patients in modifying some of the changes in the objective realm, through techniques such as relaxation training, providing information regarding resources available to them, and other psychoeducational procedures. Group psychotherapy also holds great potential in addressing the more subjective, self-related changes associated with aging.

TREATMENT GOALS

Treatment goals associated with group psychotherapy vary depending on, among other things, the nature of the group (e.g., support group vs. depression-focused group), the theoretical orientation of the group leader, and patient characteristics. Certain treatment goals, however, are consistent with the literature on successful aging and seem to be applicable to most psychotherapy groups with elderly males:

- Identifying the impact that age-related changes are having on the male's self-concept and self-esteem.
- Identifying areas of loss (physical, social, etc. . . .) and assisting the patient in learning to accept nonreversible losses.
- Recognizing the reactions to the identified losses and differentiating those that appear to be realistic and contributing to healthy adaptation from those that may be contributing to poor adaptation and feelings of depression and anxiety.
- Empowering the male to revise those responses which appear to be contributing to poor adaptation.
- Assisting the male in modifying his future goals and expectations in a realistic manner that will lead to more adaptive behavior and improved emotional health.

THERAPEUTIC FACTORS

In achieving these goals with the elderly male, group psychotherapy has several qualities that appear to be of particular significance. These qualities are derived from Yalom's (1975) therapeutic factors for group psychotherapy. All of Yalom's therapeutic factors are relevant for groups with elderly males, but the three discussed here are especially powerful in treatment of emotional disturbances in the elderly male.

1. *Universality.* Given the changes noted in the social functioning discussed earlier, growing old can be an isolating and lonely experience for many men. Many elderly men in psychotherapy believe that the changes they are experiencing are unique to them. These beliefs often contribute to feelings of embarrassment, shame, and incompetence, which can lead to increased isolation, lowered self-esteem, and greater emotional distress. Groups in which other men discuss their reactions, thoughts, and feelings about growing older challenge the males' feelings of uniqueness and decrease their isolation and feelings of shame. The group also provides the elderly male with opportunities for making social comparisons that may be more appropriate than comparisons with younger, healthier groups. Baltes and Baltes (1990) cite the process of appropriate social comparison as one reason for the general resiliency of the self in later life. For many men who experience emotional distress in late life, failure to modify their expectations about themselves and their capabilities is a contributing factor to lowered self-esteem. Groups in which members have similar physical and social functioning assist men in making more realistic comparisons and in modifying their expectations for themselves accordingly.

2. *Altruism.* One loss associated with advancing age for many men is a decreased sense of purpose and decreased feelings of being useful. With decreased physical functioning comes greater dependence on others and, for many, fewer opportunities to provide assistance to their family and friends. Many men report similar feelings following retirement, and feelings of

decreased utility are especially prevalent for men who reside in institutional settings (e.g., nursing homes). Inclusion in a group not only provides the elderly patient with opportunities to provide assistance to others but also places a certain responsibility on him to do so. Group members are expected to listen and provide feedback to other members who are there for assistance. The opportunity to feel helpful and needed by others can have tremendous therapeutic meaning for elderly men.

3. *Development of socializing techniques.* Many elderly men are reliant on their wives for developing and/or maintaining their social network. They frequently report, especially early in group sessions, discomfort with talking in front of others, whether it be about their personal lives or some other topic. Group psychotherapy offers them, again, opportunities and responsibilities to socialize with others. Many men report increased comfort in talking with others, initiating conversation, and acting assertively in social settings after their experiences within a group setting. New social skills are taught through vicarious social learning and through direct techniques aimed at certain social skills (e.g., role-playing assertiveness skills).

ISSUES AND TECHNIQUES

Many of the issues that arise in groups with elderly men are similar to issues that develop in groups with women or younger men. Likewise, many of the techniques and procedures used in these groups will be similar and reflect little variation because of the age or gender of the participants. Certain issues, however, arise with greater frequency in groups with older men and seem to be age and/or gender-related.

Initiation of Treatment

Others have noted the particular difficulty that men have experiencing the vulnerability associated with discussing their internal emotional lives with others (Krugman & Osherson, 1993; Kupers, 1993). This difficulty may be attributed, in part, to their socialization as males in society. For many elderly men, the fear of talking with others about their emotions and inner experiences, coupled with the shame of needing assistance from others, leads them to deny a need for help and/or avoid seeking help from mental health professionals. Patients who are referred for psychotherapy from their primary care physician often report for their initial meeting without a clear understanding of why they were referred or how psychotherapy can be of assistance to them. Educating the patient can be of help in addressing some of their misconceptions about the mental health profession and about the type of people who can benefit from the services. For some men, this may be a time when they will be adapting to the very idea that they are in psychotherapy. One male patient spent the first few sessions in individual psychotherapy talking of his past experiences with psychologists and psychiatrists while he was in the military. Although his encounters with these professions were not necessarily negative, he maintained his belief that one must be "crazy" to see a mental health professional. By addressing these beliefs early in therapy, he was able to see that many of the stereotypes about psychotherapy, and about those who are in therapy, were false and he came to feel less shame about his need for mental health services.

Many men will resist group psychotherapy initially because of their feelings of shame and embarrassment, and will opt for individual psychotherapy. As a man becomes comfortable addressing his difficulties in individual psychotherapy, he may be more open to the idea of participating in a therapy group. Some men, however, report greater comfort in a group setting in which the focus is not entirely on them but is diffused among several patients, and these men will be more open to groups as their initial treatment choice. Each treatment option has its own strengths and limitations and having the flexibility to offer both is a benefit for any therapist.

"Doing Better"

McPhee (1996) notes that in group work with men, he often reminds the participants that they are in therapy not only to feel better but to do better as well. In group psychotherapy with elderly men, especially for men who are new to the process of psychotherapy, focusing on behaviors and actions may be a less threatening introduction to therapy than initially talking of emotions. Most men in therapy can identify at least one concrete, behavioral task or goal that they would like to change in some way and that is somehow related to the reason they are seeking therapy. Introducing the male patient to psychotherapy by discussing specific behaviors and objective situations allows time for him to become comfortable in the group setting without having also to confront the often significant vulnerability associated with emotions or feelings. As the patient becomes more comfortable with the group, he will be more willing to risk his feelings of vulnerability and introduce topics that cause him greater discomfort. For example, one nursing home patient talked in group of his displeasure in the manner he was being treated by a male nursing aide. He had been quiet about this, not reporting his displeasure, and was not happy with how he was handling the situation. Rather than focusing on his emotional reactions to the situation, the group engaged in active problem-solving and was able to provide several options the patient could employ to address the situation. Over time, however, other patients reported similar experiences that led to discussions of their feelings of dependency, vulnerability, and decreased control. The topic of feelings and emotions was not introduced by the group's leader. Rather, it came naturally from the shared experiences of the members and the discussion of their reactions to these experiences.

Self as Competent and in Control

Issues of competence and control are strongly related to men's sense of self (Krugman & Osherson, 1993). With advancing age, the male's sense of his competence in a variety of domains and the amount of control he wields over his life are frequent issues in group. Many men need to modify their definition of what it means to be competent and in control. Their beliefs and self-expectations from previous ages are often unrealistic and may contribute to lowered self-esteem. The very nature of group psychotherapy can be therapeutic by providing a peer group that may be more appropriate for the individual as a comparison group. And as the issues of competency and control occur with such frequency in so many areas, there are numerous opportunities to discuss not only specific behavioral strategies to accommodate the changes in capabilities, but also the feelings of loss and shame that often accompany the acknowledgment of these changes.

Decreased feelings of competence can result from normal, age-related changes as well as changes due to disease or illness. Normal changes in sexual functioning (e.g., increased time to obtain erection) are often experienced by men as a sign of decreased competence. This belief can lead to feelings of embarrassment and shame and to avoidance of sexual intercourse. Individual psychotherapy can provide information about the nature of age-related changes in sexual functioning in an attempt to normalize the individual's experiences and assist him in exploring behavioral options other than avoidance to handle the changes. Group psychotherapy, however, provides lived experiences in the form of other members, which can be much more persuasive in normalizing the changes. Members may share their experiences with these changes as well their previous attempts at accommodating the changes and solutions. These accommodations can be adopted by others.

Issues of control often accompany changes in physical functioning with advancing age and can have particular relevance for those living in institutional settings. The process of accommodating these changes is similar to the process of accommodating changes in one's sense of competency. Many men must accept loss that is not remediable and adopt new standards of what it means to be in control. Men living in nursing homes often talk in groups of the cost of institutional living and the strain their placement is having on their families. The strain they discuss is not only in terms of finances but also in relation to the time and hassle associated with the paperwork, phone calls, and other numerous tasks associated with long-term care. Many men feel they can provide little assistance to their families in this area. This is particularly distressing to those men who felt one of their biggest roles in the family was to provide for them financially. These men feel that not only can they not assist in this area but that they are now a financial burden to their family. In essence, they feel they have little control over the situation. Group psychotherapy can assist these men in acknowledging that they do not have the type of control or influence they once had but that they may be able to provide for their family in a different manner. Men have been able to remove some of the burden from their families by taking a more active role in talking with the nursing home officials or assisting in making phone calls to funding sources. These men have been able to modify their belief of what it means to be in control. In addition, they have been able to accept new roles and behaviors that allow them to exert some control and a continued sense of competence and usefulness.

Expression of Affect

Many men are not comfortable in expressing affect, especially the verbal expression of emotion. The fear of talking about feelings and the concomitant feelings of vulnerability are often reasons behind some men's avoidance of psychotherapy. However, with time and increased cohesion within the group, men increase their comfort with topics related to emotion and are more willing to tolerate hearing about and discussing feelings. In groups with both men and women members, the women may be more comfortable initiating discussion of feelings and are often the ones to introduce topics referring to emotional experiences. Once the topic is introduced, men often feel more comfortable and are more willing to discuss their own emotional reactions to topics presented in the group. Elderly men, however, often have difficulty expressing their thoughts and feelings about other group members who are present. They often are uncomfortable giving or receiving feedback, especially positive, emotionally-ladened feedback. The group leader will often need to give permission to the members to give such feedback by modeling this skill in the group. The giving of direct feedback, however, can remain a difficult skill to develop for many group members.

Watching Out for Stereotypes

Everyone in the group, members and leaders, holds beliefs about aging and the elderly. The group leader needs to be sensitive to beliefs held by members that may be stereotypical of the elderly and limiting the group members in some way. It is not uncommon for some members in the group to cite their age as their explanation for not changing some behavior or expectation. "What do you expect? I'm eighty-four years old" can be said by group members in response to attempts to get them to examine their behavior and explore possible changes. Although group members tend to be vigilant in identifying ageist beliefs in other members, and in challenging these beliefs, the group leader needs to remain aware of the difference between the acceptance of genuine loss and the use of age as an excuse to resist change.

Group leaders also need to be aware of their own biases and stereotypes related to the elderly. It is not uncommon to feel a desire to take a more paternalistic role with patients who have significant limitations, even if these limitations are unrelated to their ability to act on their own. The therapist may be more willing to act on the elderly patient's behalf and serve as an advocate outside the group because the patient is elderly rather than because there is any true need. By doing so, the therapist unwittingly may be reinforcing dependency beliefs held by group members and limiting opportunities for empowering the patient to act on his own behalf. The therapist's desire to take a more active role outside the group may be stronger for patients who experience increased disability and dependency (e.g., nursing home patients). However, it is especially important to be sensitive to areas of unneeded dependency within these groups because of their valid need for assistance in so many other areas. Their reduced control increases the significance of those areas in which they retain influence and independence. One frustrating experience for many men residing in nursing homes is the difficulty they have in acting as a true partner in their health care. Family members, nursing home staff, and their physician often attempt to make decisions for them and to exclude them in discussion of important aspects of their care (e.g., treatment options). The mental health professional working with the elderly may also feel a desire to take a more active role in the care of the patient, who may be willing to forfeit their input to others who "know better." The psychotherapy group, however, is a wonderful setting to explore the patient's reliance on others and, if appropriate encourage him to take a greater role in his own health care.

Allowing for Storytelling

The use of reminiscence, whether it is a structured component of the group or occurs spontaneously within the group setting, is an important aspect of group therapy with the elderly male. By talking about their past, group members are able to review their past strengths and capabilities, past struggles and coping responses, and to identify aspects of themselves that they have retained despite growing older. Reminiscing allows for the identification of positive attributes of the individual that goes beyond its immediate therapeutic impact. It also allows the man to communicate to others in the group a fuller understanding of who he is and was and how he views himself. Group members, as well as group leaders, come to see the patient not as an elderly man but as a man who has had a lifetime of feelings, experiences, struggles, and accomplishments.

Suicide

Elderly patients may be less likely to communicate their thoughts or plans for suicide than are younger populations (Osgood & McIntosh, 1986). For this reason and because elderly males have the highest rates of completed suicide, it is important for the group leader to introduce the topic of suicide. This topic should be introduced early in therapy and members should be encouraged to discuss suicide at any time during the course of treatment. Many times, the leader does not have to introduce the topic. Rather, a member often talks about having had suicidal thoughts at some point. One patient talked about his thoughts for suicide during the initial group therapy session following his stroke. He talked about the despair he felt immediately following his hospitalization and how the depression only deepened during his initial weeks in rehabilitation. He told the group that if he had had the means to kill himself while in rehabilitation he would be dead today. This led to other members admitting to having had thoughts of suicide and to their struggles with the subsequent fear of these thoughts. By talking about suicide early in therapy and normalizing thoughts of suicide among group members, the men felt more comfortable introducing the topic in later sessions and likely decreased the risk of members attempting suicide in the future.

CONCLUSION

For most elderly males, aging is a challenging process but does not result in significant emotional disturbances or distress. For those men who do experience emotional difficulties associated with aging, group psychotherapy offers unique opportunities for assistance. By talking about their struggles with others experiencing similar difficulties, listening to others share their stories, and being of assistance to others, group therapy can facilitate the acceptance of loss, the focusing of energy on retained skills and abilities, and the development of new and more adaptive goals and expectations for their futures.

REFERENCES

Allan, G.A. (1989). *Friendship: Developing a sociological perspective*. Boulder, CO: Westview Press.

Andronico, M.P. (1996). *Men in groups: Insights, interventions, and psychoeducational work*. Washington, DC: American Psychological Association.

Baltes, P.B., & Baltes, M.M. (1990). Psychological perspectives on successful aging: The model of selective optimization with compensation. In P.B. Baltes, & M.M. Baltes (Eds.), *Successful aging: Perspectives from the behavioral sciences* (pp. 1–34). New York: Cambridge University Press.

Barer, B. (1994). Men and women aging differently. *International Journal of Aging and Development, 48*, 29–39.

Bosse, R., Spiro, III, A., & Kressin, N.R. (1996). The psychology of retirement. In R.T. Woods (Ed.), *Handbook of the clinical psychology of aging* (pp. 141–157). New York: Wiley.

Boult, H.C., Kane, R.L., Louis, T.A., Boult, L., & McCaffrey, D. (1994). Chronic conditions that lead to functional limitations in the elderly. *Journal of Gerontology: Medical Sciences, 49*, M28–M36.

Callahan, C.M., Hendrie, H.C., Dittus, R.S., Brater, D.C., Hui, S.L., & Tierney, W.M. (1994). Depression in late life: The use of clinical characteristics to focus screening efforts. *Journals of Gerontology: Medical Sciences, 49*, M9–M14.

Coleman, P.G. (1996). Identity management in later life. In R.T. Woods (Ed.), *Handbook of the clinical psychology of aging* (pp. 93–113). New York: Wiley.

Conwell, Y., Rotenberg, M., & Caine, E.D. (1990). Completed suicide at age 50 and over. *Journal of the American Geriatrics Society, 38*, 640–644.

Harvey, A.S., & Singleton, J.F. (1989). Canadian activity patterns across the life span: A time budget perspective. *Canadian Journal on Aging, 8*, 268–285.

Hays, J.C., Landerman, L.R., George, L.K., Flint, E.P., Koenig, H.G., Land, K.C., & Blazer, D.G. (1998). Social correlates of the dimensions of depression in the elderly. *Journal of Gerontology: Psychological Sciences, 53B*, P31–P39.

Jacobs, S., & Ostfeld, A. (1977). An epidemiological review of the mortality of bereavement. *Psychosomatic Medicine, 39*, 344–357.

Johnson, C.L., & Troll, L.E. (1994). Constraints and facilitators to friendships in late late life. *Gerontologist, 34*, 79–87.

Koff, T.H. (1997). The institutionalization of elderly men. In J.I. Kosberg & L.W. Kaye (Eds.), *Elderly men: Special problems and professional challenges* (pp. 279–293). New York: Springer.

Krugman, S., & Osherson, S. (1993). Men in group therapy. In A. Alonso & H.I. Swiller (Eds.), *Group therapy in clinical practice* (pp. 393–420). Washington, DC: American Psychiatric Press.

Kupers, T.A. (1993). *Revisioning men's lives; gender, intimacy, and power*. New York: Guilford Press.

Lang, F.R., & Carstensen, L.L. (1994). Close emotional relationships in late life: Further support for proactive aging in the social domain. *Psychology and Aging, 9,* 315–324.

Lee, D.J., & Markides, K.S. (1990). Activity and mortality among aged persons over an eight-year period. *Journals of Gerontology: Social Sciences, 45,* S39–S42.

Lyness, J.M., Bruce, M.L., Koenig, H.G., Parmelee, P.A., Schulz, R., Lawton, M.P., & Reynolds, III, C.E. (1996). Depression and medical illness in late life: Report of a symposium. *Journal of the American Geriatrics Society, 44,* 198–203.

McIntosh, J.L., Pearson, J.L., & Lebowitz, B.D. (1997). Mental disorders of elderly men. In J.I. Kosberg & L.W. Kage (Eds.), *Elderly men: Special problems and professional challenges* (pp. 193–215). New York: Springer.

McIntosh, J.L., Santos, J.F., Hubbard, R.W., & Overholser, J.C. (1994). *Elder suicide: Research, theory, and treatment.* Washington, DC: American Psychological Association.

McPhee, D.M. (1996). Techniques in group psychotherapy with men. In M.P. Andronico (Ed.), *Men in groups: Insights, interventions, and psychoeducational work* (pp. 21–34). Washington, DC: American Psychological Association.

Osgood, N.J., & McIntosh, J.L. (1986). *Suicide and the elderly: An annotated bibliography and review.* Westport, CT: Greenwood Press.

Panser, L.A., Rhodes, T., Girman, C.J., Guess, H.A., Chute, C.G., Oesterling, J.E., Lieber, M.M., & Jacobsen, S.J. (1995). Sexual function of men ages 40–79 years: The Olmsted County study of urinary symptoms and health status among men. *Journal of the American Geriatrics Society, 43,* 1107–1111.

Qassis, S., & Hayden, D.C. (1990). Effects of environment on psychological well-being of elderly persons. *Psychological Reports, 66,* 147–150.

Reedy, M.N. (1982). Personality and aging. In D.S. Woodruff & J.E. Birren (Eds.), *Aging: Scientific perspectives and social issues* (2nd ed., pp. 112–136). Monterey, CA: Brooks/Cole.

Roberts, R.E., Kaplan, G.A., Shema, S.J., & Strawbridge, W.J. (1997). Does growing older increase the risk for depression? *American Journal of Psychiatry, 154,* 1384–1390.

Romaniak, J., McAuley, W.J., & Arling, G. (1983). An examination of the prevalence of mental disorders among the elderly in the community. *Journal of Abnormal Psychology, 92,* 458–467.

Satariono, W.A. (1997). The physical health of older men: The significance of the social and physical environment. In J.I. Kosberg & L.W. Kaye (Eds.), *Elderly men: Special problems and professional challenges* (pp. 159–174). New York: Springer.

Schulz, R., & Williamson, G.M. (1993). Psychosocial and behavioral dimensions of physical frailty. *Journals of Gerontology, 48,* 39–43.

U.S. Bureau of the Census. (1995). *Statistical abstract of the United States, 1994.* Washington, DC: U.S. Government Printing Office.

Verbrugge, C.M., & Patrick, D.L. (1995). Seven chronic conditions: Their impact on U.S. adults' activity levels and use of medical services. *American Journal of Public Health, 85,* 173–182.

Williamson, G.M., & Schulz, R. (1992). Physical illness and symptoms of depression among elderly outpatients. *Psychology of Aging, 7,* 343–351.

Yalom, I.D. (1975). *The theory and practice of group psychotherapy.* New York: Basic Books.

Zamula, E. (1986). Stoke: Fighting back against America's number three killer (*The Consumer* HHS Publication No. 86-1131). Washington, DC: U.S. Government Printing Office.

CHAPTER 14

Realizing Power in Intergenerational Family Hierarchies: Family Reorganization When Older Adults Decline

SARA HONN QUALLS

Becky Jones called me at the urging of her daughter, Andrea, who was concerned that Becky's mother, Grammy, was not progressing properly after surgery. Something seemed to be wrong, but Becky could not figure out what it was. Grammy had "not been herself" since the surgery. She was frightened about everything, demanding that family members stay with her round the clock. She refused to come to their homes or hire assistance. Her typical independence was missing; she had become as vulnerable as a child while being as demanding as ever. Andrea was worried enough about her Mother's exhaustion to insist that she seek help. Becky was serving Grammy several hours every day and trying to run a business on the side. The business was suffering, and Becky's husband was anxious to see some kind of long-term plan put into place. Clearly, Becky could not sustain this for long without burning out, yet Grammy was insistent that only Becky or Andrea could provide adequate comfort and care.

The challenges facing Becky, Andrea, and Grammy are well known to anyone working in geriatric health care. The complexity of the case is evident when viewed within a biopsychosocial model that advocates for clear articulation of the psychological and social issues as well as biological concerns. This chapter focuses on the impact of health decline in older adults on the psychological and social aspects of family relationships. In the first section, I describe the developmental history of families that serves as a backdrop for the challenging transitions of later life. Next, I discuss the transitions required of families when an older adult becomes more dependent. Finally, I present strategies a therapist can use to facilitate those transitions.

TRANSITIONS IN INDEPENDENCE AND AUTONOMY THROUGHOUT THE FAMILY LIFE CYCLE

The transition toward increased dependence in later life family members is one among many similar transitions throughout the family life cycle. The negotiation of power and authority first occurs early in the development of a primary relationship such as marriage. From the time an initial structure is established by a couple, these dimensions must be re-negotiated many times throughout the family life cycle.

INDEPENDENCE AND AUTONOMY IN CHILD AND ADOLESCENT DEVELOPMENT

The birth and rearing of children produces many transitions in the structure of independence and autonomy within the family because the increasing capacity of children to care for themselves requires parents to alter their approaches to fostering independence while protecting the well-being of the child. The total dependence of a newborn child is followed by ever-increasing independence and autonomy that requires adjustment in all family members. Parents accommodate their parenting strategies to the capacities of the child to make decisions for self. Even siblings' behaviors toward each other are affected by the child's capacity to function autonomously. For example, the role of a 15-year-old sister babysitter with her brothers will vary depending on their self-care capacities. In other words, families must alter the balance of relationships to accommodate changes in members' autonomy many times during the child-rearing years.

The key periods in which parents and children experience rapid changes in the levels of autonomy in children are associated with labels that reflect the level of difficulty experienced by all. For example, the *terrible twos* and the *adolescence nightmare* are two periods that are infamous for the stress in the parent-child relationship. At about age two, children's emerging physical, cognitive, and emotional capacities lead them to experience the pleasure of their own will. They want to do nearly everything themselves, and reap considerable frustration as they hit the limits of their capacities. The parent's role in protecting them and guiding them to behave in ways that are tolerable to those around them inevitably place the parent at odds with the will-enamored child. Temper tamtrums, emotional storms, and frustration on everyone's part are normative. Similarly, adolescence is defined by emerging capacities to reason, socialize independently, and establish adult goals and aspirations. Parents' roles switch between guidance for the purpose of protection and assistance, and observation of the adolescent's struggle to negotiate their needs in the external world. Adolescents often reject parents' assistance, and at times even the parents' values and lifestyles, in an effort to ensure that they are indeed functioning independently. These are but two of the periods in childrearing when emerging capacities enhance autonomy and require adjustment in family relationships.

Families vary in their style and skill of adjusting to emerging independence in their children. Several models of family style in relationships exist. For purposes of illustration, consider the Olson Circumplex Model of Marital and Family System (Olson et al., 1983) Olson and colleagues focus on two primary dimensions: cohesion (ranging from disengaged to enmeshed) and adaptability (chaotic to rigid). Related to the issue of how families change to meet the changing autonomy of members, these authors report two interesting patterns. First, families who use more extreme approaches to cohesion or adaptability show a much higher rate of clinical involvement (e.g., mental disorders or behavior problems with children) (Olson & Lavee, 1989). Second, they find that families shift in style across stages of the family life cycle, presumably to adapt to the unique demands of that period (Olson & Lavee, 1989). For example, during the early stages of the family life cycle (pre-children and young children phases), family cohesion styles are more commonly connected than separated. Later, when the children are teens or are out of the house, separated styles of cohesion are more common than connected styles. Adaptability styles also show change across the lifespan with the most frequent use of structured styles in place during childrearing and the greatest use of flexible styles in pre-children, adolescent children, and post-children phases. In other words, families naturally adjust their style to manage the roles necessary to support the autonomy capacity of the members. When rearing dependent children, families form highly connected and structured ways of managing family life. When the children are launching and after children have left home, family styles tend to be more separated-flexible.

GROWING INTO AUTONOMY: THE TRANSITION TO ADULTHOOD

Although it is a process that takes time and is fraught with ambiguous moments, the transition to adulthood ultimately establishes the child's role in society as an adult. Legally, there are several benchmarks for the transition: access to a driver's license at the state's defined legal age (e.g., 16); access to voting rights (and sometimes, alcohol) at 18; access to trust funds and other legal privileges at 21; and termination of access to parents' insurance or tax status (usually in the early 20s).

The benchmarks of the transition to adulthood within the family is far more ambiguous and subtle. The transition to being defined as an adult is muddied by confusions as to which rights and responsibilities are now available within the family. For example, the privilege and responsibility of serving as host or hostess for family gatherings or making joint decisions about family vacations may not be afforded until quite late in midlife. Furthermore, adults often rely on their parents for financial, housing, social, and psychological assistance well into middle adulthood, suggesting a form of dependence. Other role transitions that are common in early adulthood (e.g., becoming a parent, moving away from the hometown to take a job) establish new roles within the family that demand recognition of legal and psychological autonomy. Early adulthood is typically focused on establishing a life structure (Levinson, 1978; Williamson, 1982, 1991) through creating social structures such as marriage and parenting, and by establishing work or career that structures time, social class, and occupational identity.

Viewed from the family development perspective, the phase in family life when young adults move out of the nuclear family sphere into the larger world is referred to as *launching*. Family members launch the young adults into the external world where they must define their own space, roles, and challenges. The timing of launching varies across families (e.g., "you're on your own at 18" versus fully funding the young adult throughout college and professional education) as do the family dynamics. For example, enmeshed families, the extreme form of Olson's connected style of cohesion, often find the launching task especially challenging because it calls upon family members to differentiate life styles, values, thoughts, and feelings from one another. By definition, launching requires the family to send the adult into the external world to establish his or her own self and place. Of course, this task is the antithesis of enmeshed style of functioning. Enmeshed families do not find it safe for young adults to fully leave (e.g., they live with the parents well into adulthood or next door to them) or to establish full independence (e.g., financially or emotionally). Within the extreme opposite cohesion style, disengaged families risk providing no support to the launching young adult at a time when the outside world is potentially dangerous due to its complexity and lack of support structures for naïve or unprepared members of adulthood.

PARENTS AS PEERS: STAKING THE CLAIM FOR PERSONAL AUTHORITY

Williamson (1982, 1991) argues that it is not until the mid- to late-30s that one is positioned to establish true mutual autonomy with other adult generations within the family. The claim of full personal authority within the family system requires adults of all generations to recognize not only their equality of their legal status as independent adults, but their psychological equality. The power that has seemed inherent in the generational hierarchy to date is renegotiated to acknowledge the full mutual psychological and social autonomy of both (or all) generations. Williamson postulates that this degree of mutual autonomy cannot be established until adults fully establish a personal life style structure (the task of early adulthood) and they are willing to confront their parents as peers. In some families, it is never established because the family values the hierarchy (as is often true in traditional cultures), or cannot tolerate the anxiety of renegotiating power and recognizing the limits of the older generation.

The last stage of the family life cycle is when adults recognize the growing dependence of their parents on others. The points that are key for considering the challenges of late life families are that:

1. Families come to later life with considerable experience negotiating transitions in autonomy in members.
2. The style the family uses to manage basic family functions of cohesion and change (adaptability) will change as the members' capacity for autonomy change.
3. The style the family uses to manage those basic family functions may well predict their success at key transition points.

SOMETHING'S WRONG, BUT I'M NOT SURE WHAT IT IS: THE DAWNING OF AWARENESS OF DEPENDENCY

The Jones family described earlier is entering a new phase of adult family relationships. The signal of the change is that the second and third generation are noticing changes in Grammy that concern them. Becky and Andrea are no longer focused on establishing or even maintaining their personal authority. Their focus has now shifted to watching for changes in the oldest generation that threaten independence and autonomy. They are engaged in a transition that is as predictable as the earlier family development transitions during which the emergence of children's autonomy drives changes in family structures. Figure 14.1 outlines the sequence, showing that the shifts in later life reverse the order that was experienced during child rearing although the stages of the transition are similar.

OBSERVING AND MONITORING: ANTICIPATION OF RESPONSIBILITY

Like many members of the midlife generation in families, Becky Jones has been monitoring her mother's behavior for a while. Most midlife adults begin this process without being consciously aware that their role has changed. Siblings

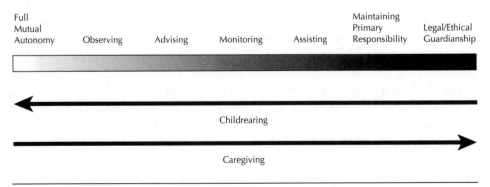

Figure 14.1   Family involvement with members.

will check in with each other about their mutual impressions of a parent's functioning. The older generation is queried about health concerns and medication use in a way that simply never occurred when the children were 20 and parents were 45. Parents will be encouraged to fly rather than drive cross country to visit family members, a change intended to protect the parents from harm. All of these changes in behavior reflect an increase in the observation and monitoring of one family member by another. In many cases, the observation and monitoring is mutual. For example, aging parents may check for evidence of excessive work stress on the face of a daughter, or may inquire about the impact of changes on Wall Street on their son's retirement account. Certainly, monitoring and observing is a common occurrence in families that is not limited to a focus on the aged members of the family. What is unique in many families is that the midlife adults begin to monitor in consistent ways that reflect a growing awareness of the declining physical, and possibly cognitive, capacities of their aging parents. Behavior which was once casual becomes a routine, purposive part of visits. Over 30 years ago, Blenkner (1965) described this transition as the move toward "filial maturity."

With increasing health difficulties and disabilities, the parent may offer the opportunity for increasing intrusions into what was once private information about bodily functioning, legal affairs, or finances. At this point the family moves down the continuum depicted in Figure 14.1 to begin offering assistance. Unfortunately, we have learned very little about how families move along this continuum. What cues do they use to decide to become more involved in monitoring or assistance? With whom do they discuss this decision? What happens if they move along the continuum too quickly? Or if other family members disagree about what kind of involvement is appropriate? Although it is clear that caregiving is a career (Aneshensel, Pearlin, Mullan, Zarit, & Whitlatch, 1995) that involves transitions in the degree and type of involvement, we know relatively little about how families move through the career. What is apparent is that families are often unsure about how much assistance is needed.

Denial or Ignorance: "Nothing Major, It's Just That . . ."

As family members take on the mantel of filial maturity, they are often confused by what they are observing. When the initial telephone call is finally made to a formal care provider, the opening line is often a disclaimer of the importance of what they have observed. I have commonly had the experience of hearing from an adult child, "It's nothing major—just normal aging, but I'm a little concerned. She doesn't have memory trouble like in Alzheimer's, but she's just not like herself anymore. She doesn't manage her finances very well, and sometimes she gets lost when she's driving." This adult child knows something is wrong, but cannot bring himself to recognize the degree of loss (basic self-care), the nature of the loss (memory and problem solving), or the possible causes (brain disease). Whether due to a psychological defense such as denial, or simple ignorance of normal versus diseased aging processes, this family member is struggling with the ambiguity involved in declining competence that is compromising autonomy.

Boss and colleagues (Boss & Greenberg, 1984) have written extensively about the challenge families experience when the status of one member within the family is ambiguous. Her initial research focused on the difficulties of families with one member who was missing in action during war. Families struggled with how to consider the missing person: was he inside or outside of the family? Were his needs and preferences to be maintained despite the growing unlikelihood that he would return to function within the boundaries of the family? In recent years Boss, Caron, and Horbal (1989) drew a parallel to the boundary ambiguity experienced by families of cognitively impaired elders. Is the person inside or outside the family decision making circle? How should family members respond to inappropriate behavior, unrealistic or unsafe preferences, and questionable judgment? Like Becky Jones, adult children often state their confusion about how to handle their parent's resistance to accepting assistance in the home that is critical to the safety of the parent, or to consider moving into a housing arrangement that affords more monitoring and assistance.

FAMILY REVERBERATIONS: "IF SHE'S DECLINING, IT MEANS THAT I'M . . ."

One consequence of acknowledging the degree of decline in an elderly parent is that the adult child(ren) must face the inevitable changes in their own role. The future holds an inevitable imbalance of personal power within the relationship as the balance of autonomy declines. Adult children and grandchildren often experience anxiety about taking the reins of power with their parents for many reasons. Long-term patterns of communication will be altered as children take on an authoritative role with their parents.

REALIZING POWER: FACILITATING MULTIGENERATIONAL RESPONSIBILITY

The role of the clinician during the last stage of the family life cycle focuses on facilitating the realization of power, authority, and responsibility for the care of one whose autonomy is compromised. The family's style of managing problems will determine how much intervention is needed. I follow the principle of minimal intervention, presuming that the family will be able to manage the transition on their own until they demonstrate otherwise. Thus, I begin with simple interventions such as labeling and education, and proceed to more intrusive interventions only as the family demonstrates that they cannot adapt to meet the needs of all members. In this section, I describe four types of intervention. These are presented in a sequence from least to most intrusive.

LABELING AND EDUCATING

Given the important role of ignorance or denial of the cause or nature of the older family member's increasing dependency, a critical and highly valuable intervention is labeling the problem and educating the family about it. For many families, this is the sole intervention that is needed. Once they know what they are dealing with, they have the resources to renegotiate roles, including issues of power and authority. They begin to label and address the problems, to anticipate what is coming down the road, and to prepare the entire family, including the older person, to make the necessary transitions. They celebrate the life lived autonomously, grieve its demise, and plan for the future needs of the declining person.

Other families, however, have difficulty accepting the validity of the information and struggle to hold onto the facts. Some family members are quite well defended against the fact of an elderly family member's dependency and adamantly refuse to acknowledge the information given them. They form alternative attributions, change (or simply fire) care providers, and proceed as if the information was never given to them. These families become serious problems for the formal helpers in their world (e.g., physicians, nursing home staff, hospital discharge planners) because they are willing to place the declining older person at risk or add unnecessary stress for the formal providers in order to maintain their denial.

CASE EXAMPLE

Becky Jones described her difficulty in making sense of her mother's behavior. Grammy had always been "difficult." Now that she was having trouble functioning completely independently, she was even more frustrated. Becky presumed that this frustration decreased her competence further due to anxiety.

Neuropsychological testing helped Becky understand that her mother was experiencing a vascular dementia that created specific, predictable difficulties for her. Grammy's lack of insight was probably due to a combination of her lifelong personality difficulty and the effects of the dementia. For the first time in her life, Becky really needed to take control of Grammy's affairs to protect her, rather than simply try to placate and avoid conflict.

Families that ignore or deny the information available to them require strong multidisciplinary, multiagency work. Hearing the same message from all providers can help the family break through the denial. If denial persists, I tend to take one of two approaches. First, I try to identify one professional provider whose relationship with even one family member might offer the chance to get accurate information into the system. The family as a whole may maintain its denial, but at least one person in the family may be open to holding the information for the family until such time as the denial no longer can be sustained. This person may provide a safety net for the older person's well-being by monitoring more closely the imminent danger. The alternative is to communicate well and provide support within the professional provider network so no provider expends useless energy or risks the legal or professional integrity of their organization to protect the family from themselves. There are, of course, cases where the older person's deterioration is sufficient to place him or her at risk of danger to self or others, and the professional must step in against the will of all family members to ensure safety for the older person (e.g., by hospitalizing).

FACILITATING COMMITMENT TO TAKE THE REINS

Assuming the family, or at least a significant person in the family, has accepted an accurate label and information about the health deterioration that threatens the older person's autonomy, the next step is for family members to step forward to take responsibility for providing needed assistance. This step refers to the family assuming *filial maturity* as described above.

Several factors can make this challenging. Family members whose lives are overwhelmingly busy may resist accepting one more demanding role. They may prefer to use a formal care delivery system to remove them from the psychological or time commitment to provide care directly.

A history of a conflicted relationship almost always complicates the transition to dependency because the potential caregiver experiences immediate and significant ambivalence about taking the reins. Sometimes the ambivalence is not immediately obvious because the caregiver is excessively driven to do something, anything that would relieve him or her from having to witness the parent's deteriorated state. The adult child both identifies with the parents' powerlessness and wants it to be wiped out of their awareness because the memory is too painful. This child often experiences guilt for considering setting limits to what they want to do for the good of the parent. While appearing highly motivated to solve whatever is the immediate problem, the goal is escape and avoidance.

Often families with histories of conflict also report to me that the launching stage of family development was fraught with parental ambivalence and particularly intense conflict. I have seen no research that clarifies whether conflicted relationships usually have their roots in difficult launchings, or whether difficult launchings predict difficult transitions toward dependency. I see it often enough, however, that I routinely ask families to describe for me the launching phase and the subsequent relationship between children and parents during adulthood. My goal for this questioning strategy is to identify the family's historical skill at managing transitions in autonomy, and to find out if they ever recovered from any difficulties they experienced during the launching phase. When I hear of cut-offs from the family of origin, whether complete or partial, I become concerned about how the caregiving career will be managed. I presume that families that must use cut-offs to establish separateness and autonomy have not achieved full personal authority among the adults. Thus the process of renegotiating power to empower the midlife family members to act alone or with other members of the parent generation to provide effective care will be complicated. In other words, if adults are not equal in psychological status, their negotiation is obviously not between equals. I must track carefully the power bases among the family members to determine when and how hidden or implicit sources of power might undermine good quality care for the elderly person or reasonable distribution of responsibility among the available caregivers.

For a variety of reasons, the key family members who are most likely to assume the caregiving role may have not matured personally to the point where they can assume personal authority in interaction with their parent. In the Becky Jones case, it appears that Becky needs to step forward to make some decisions that will not be popular with her mother. Before she can assume the responsibility for deciding *for* her mother, she must be able to see herself and her mother as human equals. She must be able to accept her mother as a real person with strengths and weaknesses. Unconscious fantasies that her mother will buffer her from the worst life has to offer, or that her mother will be eternal, must be resolved.

Family caregivers who have not made peace with their parents' or their own mortality struggle significantly to take on the reins. Hagestad (1988) has described this as the acknowledgment that one is becoming a member of the "omega" generation, the final generation that is next in line to die. There is no longer a buffer generation whose wisdom can be sought, or whose time to die precedes your own. When an adult child accepts responsibility for making decisions on behalf of a parent, he or she is inevitably taking a step closer to becoming the omega. This confrontation with one's own mortality and one's senior role in the family lineage requires psychological adjustment.

CASE EXAMPLE

Becky Jones has two siblings, neither of whom will assist her with the daily care of Grammy. According to the reports of all children, Grammy was a narcissistic personality disorder throughout her life. The children had moved away from her for long periods just to protect their own individual and family development. In recent years, Becky felt obligated to take on care of Grammy because it was obvious that Grammy was increasingly unsafe as her own caretaker. The siblings feel absolved of responsibility to provide the hands on care because of the care they provided their father. They have taken their turn, and are ready for Becky to take hers. The fact that Becky insists on doing so much of the care herself mystifies and frustrates her siblings who would prefer that Becky serve more as a case manager of formal services.

In summary, for families that do not step forward easily to take the reins of decision-making and problem-solving on behalf of or collaboratively with the older person, I begin to investigate difficulties in historical and current boundaries and transitions. Once the difficulties are clear, I help the family negotiate safe boundaries that reflect the current status of the older member's capabilities and emotional roles in the family.

TOLERATING POWER OVER PARENTS

Even among families who accept the facts about declining autonomy, and who are prepared to make a commitment to assist, I find some who are reticent to assume the power needed to truly protect the well-being of the older parent. Like Becky Jones, these adult children are good-hearted and kind, even willing to help to the point that their own lives are disrupted. What seems impossible to them, however, is that they could ever make a decision that blatantly goes against the wishes of their parent.

One problem in assuming power is that the adult child is required to tolerate high anxiety as they confront, renegotiate, and claim decision making rights that are new. Adults who are unprepared to tolerate anxiety will struggle with this transition. Certainly, many adults have never looked a parent in the eye and said "I'm sorry, I know this is what you want, but we can't do it." If nothing else, the pity most adults feel for any human being who is forced to accept such a loss of personal autonomy is anxiety provoking. Given that this occurs within the family context ensures that the emotional stakes feel much higher.

Some family members fear that the aging parent will turn on them either legally or personally. If an adult child wants to arrange for a parent to move into an assisted living facility, for example, there is legitimate concern about what will happen if the parent who is legally her own decision maker (i.e., no guardian has been appointed) refuses to move. Many of the important decisions about care of dependent older adults occur in the fuzzy legal context in which the elderly person has severely compromised judgment and decision making capacity, but no guardian has been appointed legally. The family may decide that they can and must go through a guardianship hearing before *forcing* the parent to move, receive medications, accept in home assistance, and so on. This is not an easy decision because the process is financially and emotionally costly for most families. Family members who are not prepared emotionally to take on the decision making power that legal guardianship entails will find the entire procedure to be humiliating and demeaning for the entire family.

Alternatively, the family may decide to proceed with the protective action and trust that the parent will not be capable of implementing a complicated plan to undermine the move. The move may be accomplished by an adult child who simply takes on the task, ignoring the verbal protests of the parent. Few aging parents with diminished capacity will be able to fight the move pragmatically or legally. Perhaps more difficult are the situations like that of Becky Jones who needs to hire formal assistance, but her mother keeps refusing to either pay the bill or simply fires the staff when they arrive. Legal action may simply be needed in such a case to protect Grammy from her own poor judgment which will result in self-neglect.

Another fear family members often express to me about assuming the power is that the final months or years of their parent's life will be dominated by anger and distrust of the adult child following what is perceived as a betrayal by the parent. Again, the adult child is grieving the lost benefits he or she previously received in the relationship. Adult children are understandably distressed by being unjustly attacked by a demented parent who is convinced that the adult child is stealing from him or simply shuffling him off to a poor house. Managing the distress without compromising good judgment about safety and well-being is a challenge. I try to help the adult child identify collaborators who can help take the heat, and whose shared distress is validating and comforting.

Finally, some families struggle to take power because they fear not doing what the parent would have wanted. The classic scenario is one in which a child has promised the parent that he or she would never be placed in a nursing home. Now all other options have been exhausted, and placement is necessary for the well-being of the aging parent. The child may well struggle with breaking a promise, or even simply making a decision that he knows went against the desire of his mother.

In all of these scenarios, the therapist needs to help the family understand their own fears about assuming the necessary power, and move them along to grieve the loss of the parent's capacity that places the child in the position of needing to take control. Most families find it helpful to relate their responsibility in this situation to familiar experiences in their past during childrearing. Most have made an unpopular and difficult decision for the protection of a child (especially an adolescent). An important component of my intervention is to involve the adult child decision maker with others who can either share the load, or at least empathize. Banding together with other children or key members of the family can provide the strength needed to accomplish a very difficult decision. Even attendance at a support group can be amazingly validating while also providing suggestions about how to actually accomplish the next tasks of caregiving.

The most challenging families I see are ones in which the siblings or the siblings and competent parent are conflicted about what decisions should be made, how they should be made (e.g., who should be involved, what options are valid to consider), and how the past difficulties in the family relate to the present challenges.

CASE EXAMPLE

Although Becky was distressed by her mother's excessive demandingness, entitlement, and rageful fits when she didn't get her way, Becky also felt compassion for her mother. Her siblings expressed similar compassion although with less affect. They kept their sense of obligation to a minimum by focusing on formal care networks, and insisting that Grammy simply had to use them. Becky found it much harder to force Grammy into formal care with providers whose care felt intrusive and insulting to Grammy. Her siblings' refusal to provide hands on assistance left Becky feeling dumped on. She was not able to confront her mother's disdain for formal services, so feels trapped to provide the care herself.

My work with Becky Jones and her family focuses on helping Becky set limits, engaging the siblings in shared decision making about appropriate care strategies, and helping the other siblings take some of the heat for the decisions.

Grammy continues to target much of her anger at Becky, but Becky can handle that if her siblings are at least willing to announce decisions to Grammy, for example. Full trust among the siblings was not necessary, nor was full consensus on all decisions. Gradually, Becky is approaching the possibility of legal guardianship to handle the issue of her right to make decisions. Her siblings have advocated this for a while. More challenging was resolution of Becky's guilt that her mother had to exist in an environment that was comfortable for her (no environment was ever sufficient). Explaining the crushing pain that a person with a narcissistic personality disorder will inevitably experience when she loses autonomy was a helpful step in freeing Becky to make decisions that she could predict would evoke rage in response to the pain. The key was not to take the rage personally, but see it as an effort to protest that which seemed intolerable today. Becky learned to hold on to the truth that her mother would never find a tolerable environment because her narcissistic needs were too great to ever be met sufficiently.

The model of intervention I describe here contains the core components of recommended assistance for any caregivers of elderly persons: education, problem-solving, and social support. What I add to the more cognitive-behavioral approaches for working with a single caregiver is a focus on the larger family system. Regardless how many family members actually show up in my office, I conceptualize the problem in terms of necessary development within the relationship. An adult child must do more than simply receive objective information about an illness or disability; he or she must consider how that changes the dynamics of the interaction with the elderly care recipient. I argue that the adult child is forced to conceptualize their role differently, to conceive of their place in the family in a new way, and must renegotiate the fundamental meaning of the generational hierarchy. Certainly, clinicians must be competent to assist with solving particular problems (e.g., what manages wandering effectively, what continence programs work, what legal issues arise when a person has dementia). As I argued above, many families need only this level of assistance. The families that challenge formal delivery systems, however, are those that know the facts and have been shown the strategies, but cannot bring themselves to implement them. For these families, I find family level analysis of the problem to be essential, and family intervention to be most helpful.

REFERENCES

Aneshensel, C.S., Pearlin, L.I., Mullan, J.T., Zarit, S.H., & Whitlatch, C.J. (1995). *Profiles in caregiving: The unexpected career*. San Diego, CA: Academic Press.

Blenkner, M. (1965). Social work and family in later life, with some thoughts on filial maturity. In E. Shanas & G. Streib (Eds.), *Social structure and the family: Generational relations* (pp. 46–59). Englewood Cliffs, NJ: Prentice-Hall.

Boss, P., Caron, W., & Horbal, J. (1989). Alzheimer's disease and ambiguous loss. In C. Chilman, E. Nunnaly, & F. Cox (Eds.), *Families in trouble*. Newbury Park, CA: Sage.

Boss, P., & Greenberg, J. (1984). Family boundary ambiguity: A new variable in family stress theory. *Family Process, 23*(4), 535–546.

Hagestad, G.O. (1988). Demographic change and the life course: Some emerging trends in the family realm. *Family Relations, 37,* 405–410.

Levinson, D.J. (1978). *The season's of a man's life.* New York: Knopf.

Olson, D.H., & Lavee, Y. (1989). Family systems and family stress: A family life cycle perspective. In K. Kreppner & R.M. Lerner (Eds.), *Family systems and life-span development* (pp.165–195). Hillsdale, NJ: Erlbaum.

Olson, D.H., McCubbin, H.I., Barnes, H., Larsen, A., Muxen, M., & Wilson, M. (1983). *Families: What makes them work.* Los Angeles: Sage.

Williamson, D.S. (1982). Personal authority via termination of the intergenerational hierarchical boundary: 2. The consultation process and the therapeutic method. *Journal of Marriage and the Family, 8,* 23–37.

Williamson, D.S. (1991). *The intimacy paradox.* New York: Guilford Press.

CHAPTER 15

Couple Therapy with Long-Married Older Adults

ERLENE ROSOWSKY

Middle age can be defined as that moment of knowing that the life already lived exceeds the life remaining to be lived. One popular definition is that middle age is always five years older than one is presently. It can be heralded by a number on a birthday card or an event that prompts the awareness, the absolute certainty, that life will end. This is the start of the well-known midlife crisis that typically occurs between the early-forties and mid-fifties. While unique to each of us, there are certain conditions that are universal in the lifecourse and which frequently serve as catalysts to this crisis. One's reaction to this moment of knowing, when awareness exceeds denial, depends on the meaning he or she creates. The process of this meaning-making is a dominant psychosocial task at middle age.

DEVELOPMENTAL TASKS AT MIDDLE AGE

Developmentalists conceptualize life stages in terms of tasks to be achieved at each stage. How well the individual is able to negotiate the tasks, and how expectable or "on time" they are, to an extent predicts his or her success at that stage of life. This does not infer a stressless passage. All transitions are, by definition, stressful in that they require change. Successful transition does require that the individual call upon his or her resources to negotiate the passage, and emerge with the self intact. Maturation implies the ability to grow from and be enhanced by the experience. The final step is the individual's ability to integrate the transition into the experience base and repertoire of possible responses to future need for change.

Erikson (1982) has defined the major conflict of younger adulthood as "intimacy versus isolation." The outcome is the capacity for love. For middle adulthood, it is "generativity versus stagnation," the outcome being the capacity to care.

As mature adults, successfully negotiating the middle-age transition means that we move toward the transcendence of self, beyond one's finite lifespan. This is most often achieved through rearing of the next generation. In addition, developmentally successful adults are able in an intimate relationship with another, to take the point of view of another, and to have developed the capacity for mature love.

DEVELOPMENTAL TASKS AT OLD AGE

At old age, the major psychosocial conflict is between integrity versus despair and disgust. Old age is that stage of life during which the individual creates his or her unique life story both to take along and to leave behind. These are the notions of closure and legacy to be discussed later. Successful negotiation at this stage requires that the older adult be able to create a coherent self-story and be able to accept this story as one's own. The outcome of this passage is wisdom, not achieved by every older adult. Many subtasks, including forgiveness, self-acceptance, and reconciliation, are embedded in this overarching task. The process of this work can be observed in the reminiscences that older adults universally do (Parker, 1995).

CHANGE CHALLENGES THE MARRIAGE

Many changes in the marriage can provoke distress in the couple. Joint goals that have given the marriage a common focus or purpose may no longer be viable. For example, child-rearing, the achievement of specific material goals, or joint commitment to career success may have already been achieved. While the achievement of goals can be pleasurable, once they are met, a vacuum in the marital relationship can ensue. A small expression of this is commonly observed in the vacation discomfort experienced by many couples. A sense of disquiet or outright anxiety emerges when the usual frame that supports the relationship is not present and the couple becomes uncomfortable in the vacuum.

At the mid- to late-life shift, spouses reassess their union and, tacitly, may ask "Now what?" This couple evaluation of the dyad occurs concurrently with the self-evaluation, which also informs the couple's relationship.

Consider perceived failure: If a man has not been successful in his work, he may blame his marriage or his wife for his failings. A woman may likewise blame her husband's attitude or the demands of her children for disallowing her to achieve personal goals.

The salient point is that the marriage becomes the repository of blame for failure and disappointment and the inability to accept one's life story.

Consider perceived success: The successful man or woman at this stage re-evaluates both what was accomplished and what was sacrificed in the achievement of goals. The crisis often reflects attempts to correct perceived failures and redress the neglected areas. For example, fathers of second families often are much more involved with their children and less focused on their work than they had been during their first marriage.

The observation of aging in a spouse can be comforting, but it can also be a catalyst to the crisis.

> He looks at her and sees the wrinkles, lines, the passage of time, and life's pain. He feels that perhaps with another partner, someone younger, he can snatch vicarious youth, add more zest in his life, create an illusion of starting over.
>
> She looks at him after the bypass surgery and sees what lies ahead; more years of caregiving. She asks herself "When will it be my time?" Does middle age, marked by the menopause, mean to her the end of her attractiveness and purpose, or the beginning of a liberated, self-actualizing phase? Will post-menopausal zest be a reality or fiction?

And what of the congruence between the spouses? Is one, at this stage, feeling at the brink of new life adventures and possibilities, while the other is winding down, closing up, and waiting?

TASKS FOR COUPLES AT MID-LIFE

Couples' developmental tasks refer to what the couple needs to do to respond to changes that occur in the individual or in the family. Three tasks are central at this stage:

1. Redefining important roles (wife, brother, mother, son, etc.). Frequent events precipitating this include retirement, the children being launched as independent adults, loss of one's parents, and the development of serious illness or physical limitations.
2. Redefining goals for the individual and the marriage.
3. Redefining intimacy. Intimacy between partners can be defined as mutual disclosure, based on trust, that progressively deepens over time. As the couple approaches old age, intimacy reflects their current experience as well as the anticipation of further aging.

THE MID- TO LATE-LIFE SHIFT

This phase is not as well-recognized as the mid-life crisis. It is more subtle and defended against. There is individual work to be done, but it is also an integral part of the couple's work.

Couple therapy at this phase involves the weaving together of both the individual and couple transition into the older individual stage and older married stage. In therapy, a focus is on effective and joining communication, including the recognition of intimacy starters and stoppers. A major intimacy stopper is anything that denies one's experience (the opposite of validation). This includes ridiculing, shaming, intimidating, as well as denying one's own concern with aging and the future.

The work in therapy addresses certain core questions. These sample questions can serve as guide questions for the therapy:

- What age do I expect to live to?
- What do I expect to be like at that age?
- What frightens me most about getting old?
- Who will be there to depend on?
- Do I want that person to be there?
- When would my life not be worth living?
- Who can I trust to understand this?

These are difficult questions. Embedded in them is the reconciliation of life with mortality.

ABOUT OLDER MARRIED COUPLES

Over time, a married couple develops a shared knowledge, whether overt or tacit, of one another's guiding life principles. Their relationship provides a dynamic sounding board for the evolution of these principles. The couple's interdependence and collaboration serves to strengthen the individual's confidence in his or her independence. The long-married partner begins to be experienced as an extension of the self; not fully another.

The elderly individual can often accept help from their spouse without incurring the same degree of narcissistic insult as is experienced in accepting help from outside the dyad.

As roles and relationships that once competed for spousal attention fall by the wayside, each spouse becomes more aware of and more invested in the other; be this by intent, default, or necessity. This is consistent with Carstensen's social selectivity theory (1992).

VICISSITUDES OF OLD AGE

Things that happen in late life are often referred to as the *vicissitudes of old age*. An overarching dynamic of marriage at this stage is to maintain constancy in response to the press for change. The older couple struggles to meet new challenges and re-equilibrate their relationship after each assault in a way that allows them to go on in a way that "feels like them."

Stress can result when the older couple is required to change. Especially stressful are changes in daily routine or living environment. One important aspect of the couple's history that is predicative of the stress they experience is their relationship to change. Understanding this relationship provides the therapist with valuable insight into the couple's overall style of meeting challenges and their experience of distress. A history of the couple's relationship to change should be included in the assessment.

There are three styles of relationship to change:

1. Proactive style describes couples who anticipate possible changes, assess probabilities, plan ahead, and have contingency or alternative plans. Continuing Care and Retirement Communities (CCRCs) accommodate many who evidence this style.
2. Reactive style describes couples who respond to change on an as-needed basis, applying to each challenge the best resources they have available at that time.
3. Resistant style describes couples who resist even the most obvious need for change. They go on as if time holds still for them and always will. Sometimes this can put them at considerable risk, whether through action or inaction, as they try to maintain the illusion of constancy.

Problems for the couple can develop when the partners each have a dissonant relationship to change or when the couple's style is not adaptive to the current challenge.

THE ROLE OF CHANGE IN THERAPY FOR THE COUPLE

- Normalize change
- Identify the couple's historical way of addressing change
- Identify the appropriateness (fit) of their change style to the presenting challenge
- Predict the outcome of applying their usual style to this problem
- Generate (style) options and anticipate responses
- Predict the outcome. What further change could be expected to follow this specific change?
- Select the best response; try it and talk about the experience and the outcome.

MAJOR FUNCTIONS OF MARRIAGE IN OLD AGE

COMMUNICATION

At different times in the marriage, well-practiced communication patterns can be appropriate, while at other times, they can be inadequate or conflict-engendering. There is nothing inherently wrong with flying on automatic; automatic communication patterns in the long-term marriage are comforting and energy efficient. However, the successful couple needs to be able to change their mode of communication when necessary, and to be able to metacommunicate when their usual communication pattern is inadequate (Qualls, 1995).

Overall, marital interactions tend to be more positive in later years. Research has found less negative arousal in older couples; they are better able to manage marital conflict and, indeed, identify fewer areas of conflict (Levinson, Carstensen, & Gottman, 1993; Zeitlow & Sillars, 1988).

COLLABORATION

They both contribute to the task or the recollection. The final product (for example, of a story) is a combined recollection that is (mostly) acceptable to each spouse.

COMPANIONSHIP

Daily togetherness, "the day in and day out of life" (Willi, 1982), is what is most missed with the loss of a spouse. The loss of someone familiar, interested, and being there is at the center of grief. It is not unusual, for instance, for a bereaved spouse to talk to pillows, armchairs, or shadows standing in for the lost mate.

CONTINUITY AND COHESION

Long-married partners have a rich shared history; have been the ultimate fellow traveler and observer. Older couples organize and imbue meaning to their relationship which enables them to experience its continuity and stability (Duck, 1994).

AFFIRMATION

In successful older marriages, each partner is able to affirm the other as having been chosen and committed to. Marriage is not a relationship by birth; it is by choice. The healthy marriage has embedded in it the continued affirmation of that choice.

SUPPORT (INSTRUMENTAL AND EMOTIONAL)

Each couple has a history of the availability, complimentarity, and reciprocity of support. Women generally contribute more into the marriage equity account, but this tends toward greater equity as the couple ages (Hatfield & Rapson, 1993; Van Ypern & Buuk, 1991). Men throughout marriage tend to offer more instrumental support and women emotional support. Both the degree of investment in the marriage and the style of support tend toward the (gender) mean with age, reflecting a shift in men toward becoming more relational and women becoming more assertive (Snell, 1993).

PROTECTION (OF THE PAIRED STATUS)

One partner often comes to seamlessly serve as an auxiliary other with deficits only coming to attention after the loss of the protecting spouse. Research findings support cognitive benefit and real health benefits for couples. This is especially so for men. Women are benefited only if they are in a satisfactory marriage (Levenson et al., 1993).

SEXUALITY AND PHYSICAL TOUCH

There is a Turkish proverb which translates: "Young love is from earth. Mature love is from heaven." There can be earthiness to mature love, too. The aged as asexual is a myth (Kaplan, 1990).

However, this cohort of older adults may not have talked openly about sexual issues. Most couples maintain their sex lives well into their seventies, although there is typically a reduction in the frequency of sexual activity.

Normal, age-related changes and minor illness-related change is usually well accommodated by the couple. However, changes in body-image can lead to withdrawal, and addressing this is frequently part of a therapy.

When sexual decline is more dramatic, it is usually attributed to a change in physical health. Abrupt, poorly understood, and poorly explained illness-related changes can be very hurtful to the couple.

Sexuality tends to maintain the position it has always held in the marriage; the core importance of sexual expression in the marriage is usually maintained (Mancini & Bird, 1985). Therefore, change or loss of sexual expression, from whatever cause, has specific meaning to the couple depending on their history.

The therapist needs to take a sensitive but thorough sexual history and determine if any change in this area is contributing to the couple's distress.

CASE EXAMPLE

Mr. Y was a very vigorous 75-year-old man when he developed prostate cancer. The treatment of choice was a moderately radical surgery. He came through the procedure very well but was left impotent. He had not been warned of this outcome or did not "hear" what information had been provided by his doctor. Rather than address this with his wife, he resigned himself to the sexual part of his life being over. He stopped reaching for his wife or responding to her advances.

Mrs. Y had been told the surgery was a complete success. She had no idea that her husband had been left impotent. They had always had an active sex life; this was an important part of their marriage. She first thought he was perhaps depressed because of his recent health problems. When she saw his energy and spirit revive and return to his favorite activities, but not sexual activity, she began to feel rejected and angry. She became fearful that he had come not to love her. Her worry and general malaise led her primary care physician (PCP) to suggest a mental health consultation. After the initial assessment, Mr. Y was invited in and couple therapy was started.

TOUCH

We never outgrow our need to touch and be touched. Therapy can give permission and increase the value of holding and cuddling, without expectation of sexual performance. Touch, in itself, can be an expression of love and intimacy.

MARITAL SATISFACTION

The individual's self-esteem and the secure knowledge of the spouse's love contribute most to marital satisfaction. Marital satisfaction tends toward greater satisfaction in later life (Orbuch et al., 1996). Generally, marriage is regarded as more "positive." There are a number of ways of understanding this, in addition to the improvement that can be explained in terms of fiscal status, goal achievement, and reduced responsibilities. Consider the following possible contributions:

- Energy conservation. Conflict takes energy, which is reduced in older people.
- There is a narrowing of affective excursions (typically at their peak during adolescence). The affective peaks and valleys are being clipped in older age. As more is learned about the role of neurotransmitters in the expression and regulation of affect, perhaps this narrowing will be explained at a biochemical level. For example, reduced dopamine levels might explain this. From the social learning perspective, the older individual has been there, done that, and survived. Even new events are seldom novel.
- There may naturally occur a truce to old conflicts with the passage of enough time.
- The older person may move toward a more universal position, enabling the letting go of old hurts and injustices. As one approaches the end of life, what once mattered so much may come not to.
- Especially relevant to the older couple is the growing awareness of one's spouse as being the one with whom one will share the process of aging and on whom one may come to rely. There is, in old age, increased value placed on being there.

ROUTES TO COUPLE THERAPY AMONG OLDER ADULTS

I have not encountered in my practice an older couple whose stated reason for coming to therapy was "to work on our relationship." It is likely this will change. There are significant cohort differences including the attitude toward mental health treatment and history of clinical service utilization.

There are four routes to therapy that are frequently observed in older couples:

1. *Returnees.* This route refers to couples who have had therapy or counseling at an earlier point in their marriage. They return to therapy later, again as a response to what they experience as an unsolvable problem. Not infrequently, it was a problem involving a child who led them to therapy initially. Again, in later years, a problem involving this same child may return them to therapy.

CASE EXAMPLE

Sandy W had been a fearful and anxious child, with many problems around separation, including school phobia. He was overly attached to his mother, who joined Sandy against his father. The family went into therapy at a child guidance clinic and had good success. Sandy became healthier, went on to college, developed a career, married, and had a child. As a toddler, Sandy's little boy developed a malignant brain tumor and, after a few difficult months, died tragically before his second birthday.

Mr. and Mrs. W were thrown into terrible grief over the death of their beloved, only grandchild. Rather than come together for mutual comfort and support, they became hostile and adversarial, revisiting the phase of blame and accusation established years before. Mrs.W recognized the tone of their marriage and recalled how in the past professional mental health counseling had been helpful. Her husband, equally distressed, agreed with her suggestion that the couple return to therapy.

2. *Self-referred around a specific problem.* This often is in response to media attention around a specific problem or topic. For example, following media attention about the effect of depression in the family, an older spouse may make an appointment with his or her spouse. Evaluation may reveal that depression is or is not a problem, but its possibility has served as an entree into treatment.
3. Someone else's suggestion. Most often the couple will come in at the suggestion of a physician or an adult child, or grandchild. Primary care physicians (PCPs) most often refer patients for the following reasons:
   • The couple is overwhelmed by the illness and medical management of one of the partners.
   • The caregiving spouse is unable to understand the spouse's condition, or the ill spouse cannot accept the spouse's participation in the care regimen.

- Wanting to establish professional support and connection in anticipation of one partner's serious deterioration or demise.
- The "difficult" patient, where marital conflict is perceived as being at the center of his or her distress.

The suggestion from a middle-aged child that their parents seek counseling is often fraught with important dynamic overtones. The purpose of such a request can be varied, for example:

- Diagnostic clarification. The children may observe a negative change in their parents and are uncertain what it reflects. If the PCP has not diagnosed it, they may encourage their parents to see a mental health professional.
- Problems within the family. The older couple becomes the bellweather for the distress.
- Excessive complaining about one parent by the other parent. The child's response is often: "Mom, I don't know what's going on. Talk to someone about it."
- Conflict between spouses that affects the relationship of the whole family.

CASE EXAMPLE

Nancy and Nate, both in their seventies, have been married for nearly fifty years. They have two daughters and one grandson. Each was, in their youth, a "live wire." They loved a good time; partied, drank, and enjoyed sex. These "ingredients" kept their marriage going. They had very separate career lives and shared few friends. They never developed the art of verbal communication with one another, other than bickering or, with alcohol, "damn good fighting." Usually they would simmer down and smooth things with sex.

After retirement, their time together increased and, predictably, their bickering escalated. But still they were each engaged with their friends and with each other in bed.

Several events conspired to lead them into difficulty and into therapy. Nate had prostate surgery that left him impotent. He also began to show signs of an early dementia. His alcohol consumption increased further compromising his cognitive functioning.

Nancy developed hypertension and gained considerable weight which increased her arthritis pain and decreased her mobility. The final straw was that their daughter refused to bring her son, their grandson, to visit. She told her parents that their fighting was impossible to tolerate, and she was not willing to expose her child to their behavior. Being denied visitation by the grandson was the motivation for Nate and Nancy to seek therapy and to prime their readiness to change.

EVOLVING OUT OF INDIVIDUAL THERAPY

Some of the most creative and productive couple work can be done with one spouse. This work may be through successive approximation or default approximation: One spouse is in individual treatment and, over time, there surfaces a problem within the couple relationship that becomes timely to treat. It then becomes a clinical intervention to invite the spouse into the therapy.

Initially, while clearly a couple problem, one partner may not be willing to come into therapy. However, things happen over the course of couple therapy with one partner that enables the resistant spouse to join in. For example, with the passage of time, there develops adequate *trust* in the process to at least enable the possibility of considering direct participation.

CURIOSITY

The curiosity factor can also be powerful. Over time, what often evolves is that the resistant spouse asks more about the therapy and shows an interest in the process. The missing spouse comes to interact with the therapist (through the present spouse) to challenge, be heard, and provide information to help and support.

This might sound like:

- Next time you see Dr. X, tell her about your screaming at me today.
- Tell the doctor Tuesday that I've lost four pounds and my levels are good.
- Did you tell her how you get a headache every time that Myriam visits?
- I should call Dr. X and thank her. She's right. It's not all my fault.

Sometimes individual work and couple work can alternate, depending on need and willingness. *Flexibility* of modality is a key treatment factor.

DETOXIFY

This cohort of older adults does not hold a positive image of mental health. For them coming of age, there was no mental health, only mental illness. And it was very serious mental illness. Also, they came of age valuing the beliefs and edicts of rugged individualism, don't air your dirty laundry, and depression is a sign of weak character. It is often a desperation move to visit a mental health professional; one couched in shame, distrust, and fear.

CASE EXAMPLE

An 82-year-old woman came into treatment with her husband at the suggestion of her PCP. She was diagnosed with a clinical depression, and treatment was started. She was very frightened, and her husband was not able to calm her. Through the assessment it was discovered that she was worried about the cognitive decline secondary to the depression. She feared this was a progressive dementia and that she and her husband would be evicted from their apartment in subsidized elder housing because of it. "We'll both be shipped off; probably to a nursing home." Early treatment was able to calm and reassure her and model for the husband how to do this as well as heighten his awareness of the core of her anxiety. Her agitation remitted and her cognitive status improved.

DEMYSTIFY AND ORIENT

The process of therapy truly is a mystery, and especially so for older adults. The idea of there being something healing through talking about private matters to a stranger (and one who is usually younger) is foreign to them. At best, they may feel an awkwardness around not knowing what they are expected to do and feel concerned that they might not do therapy right. It is very important that time and patience be used to orient older adults to therapy.

Orientation to therapy includes the following:

- Permission to answer or not answer questions
- Modeling: A stance of attentive and respectful listening; posing questions for clarification and more information; acceptance of the validity of expressed feelings. During the early phase (or a heated phase) of couple therapy, modeling of respectful communication may not be adequate, and direct training and practice may be indicated.
- They can talk about whatever they would like. It can be a serious topic, a worry, something good that is going on, a memory, a dream, a problem that needs to be addressed.
- They can ask the questions; for clarification, feedback, advice.
- Affect display: It is fine to laugh and cry, raise your voice, etc.
- Confidentiality: This is a notion special to and defining of therapy. The limits of confidentiality are to be clearly explained.
- The therapist can hear everything (no topic is taboo): Explain that people can use therapy to talk about topics they cannot talk about anywhere else. For example: sex, religion, hateful feelings, drinking, shameful memories, regrets, and so on.

NORMALIZE

Most older adults take comfort in hearing from a professional that their problems are within the scope of normal experience; tolerable, manageable, and hopeful, in terms of becoming less distressed. During the preparation, always offer the powerful gifts of *faith* and *hope*: faith in the ability of the therapist and therapy to help, and hope that life can feel better.

ASSESSMENT AND TREATMENT PLANNING

The purpose of the assessment of the older couple is:

- To gather information
- To observe the interaction of the spouses, their individual presentation styles, domains of congruence and discrepancy regarding the chief complaint or problem
- To decide if there is need for other referrals for diagnostic refinement, treatment, or other interventions

The end result of the assessment process is clarification of the problem. It is important to determine if/what part of the problem is *new* versus *now and forever* in terms of the specific problem or in terms of the couple's ability to cope with it now (Florsheim & Herr, 1990).

If it is not broken, don't fix it. The older couple's style of being in the world has served them well over the years; it has broken down recently. What might appear to be maladaptive may be very functional for them. They are presenting with a problem, not a style.

The clinical focus needs to be on what they came in for.

HISTORY OF THE MARRIAGE: FORM AND FUNCTION

Taking a full history of a long-term marriage with an old couple can take a long time. The review is not only for assessment purposes. It is inherently part of the therapy. The process needs to be gentle and leisurely, with the stance of the therapist being to *explore* versus to *ask*.

The *marital life review* is a revealing and healing process. This includes:

- How they met
- Their initial attraction
- Why they married
- How they anticipated marriage and what they hoped for
- Their families
- The wedding
- The honeymoon
- The settling down phase
- Major events
- How their spousal roles evolved, changed, remained constant
- How they have been intimate: expressing love, expressing anger, expressing care, concern
- How they anticipate their future

This list is clearly not exhaustive and needs to be customized to suit the couple. The process of the review can be clarifying and healing. It can also model, train, and shape the couple's communication. Along with conflict resolution, problem solving, skill building, validation, and encouragement, communication is the major focus of therapy.

There is a natural tendency to reminisce at this stage. This tendency fits well with the marital history review.

Couple therapy with older adults is both circuitous and focused.

Function

- History of how they have managed other transition points and problems. Identification of what has worked for them (and what has not worked)
- Reminder/validation of their competence in coping and their survivorship as a couple

- Enable them to teach the therapist about them, and engage the therapist to help them achieve their best couple strength (parallel to highest level of functioning in individual therapy).
  (*Note:* When they invest more energy in guiding and teaching the therapist how to help them, and realize that they can often do it themselves, they are often able to end therapy.)
- How they approach challenges now, noting change and conflictual stylistic differences.
- How do they engage help from one another, others? How are they stronger/more competent as a couple than as two individuals?

IDENTIFY THEMES OF THE MARRIAGE

Jacobson and Christensen (1996) and others (Bengston & Kuypers, 1985; Qualls, 1995) suggest that every marriage has an overarching theme that defines the genesis and maintenance of marital conflict. Sometimes these themes are marriage-long, others re-emerge at strategic times. Other themes can appear de novo in older age (as in the next case example). These themes, or operating principles, can be considered in terms of polarities, tensions, or styles. Examples of such themes include:

- Autonomy vs. dependency
- Connectedness vs. separateness
- Conventionality vs. unconventionality
- Idealization vs. disappointment

The clinician needs to determine what is the overarching theme for the couple, historically and at this time. Each polarity can be envisioned as falling along a continuum. Failure to move in the appropriate direction along the specific continuum in response to the press for change, can result in distress. The clinician needs to identify where along the continuum the problem develops, and where the response becomes maladaptive.

CASE EXAMPLE

Mr. and Mrs. Z historically lived quite separate lives during their long marriage. They were respectful of one another but emotionally distant. With the advent of Mr. Z's diabetes, its difficult control, and the need for vigilant attention and management, he has turned to his wife for support and assistance. This degree of mutual interdependence, this closeness, had not been part of their communication and intimacy pattern. She feels very uncomfortable with that degree of intimacy and closeness. She intellectually wants very much to be a good wife, but her anxiety with this change in the marriage has made her behave in an abrupt, sometimes hurtful, way with her husband. She has become more anxious and down on herself. Mr. Z is hurt, angry, and worried that if he remains ill, she will leave him. This stress has contributed to a more brittle presentation of his diabetes, including poor compliance with his diet.

Their themes were connectedness/separateness and autonomy/dependency. The couple needs help to move along the continua to allow more connection and, to a lesser degree, dependency. The therapy will encourage Mrs. Z to know what is expected of her to be a "good wife." She must come to know the limits of what is necessary for his care. She will work toward the goal of reconciling her need to be a good wife with her needs to maintain a sense of separateness and distance that permits the continuity of the marriage. Mr. Z must come to trust that their style, and especially his wife's need for distance, can be consistent with good care and marital commitment.

A challenge to the therapist is to be able to support the continuity and stability of the marriage in response to the press for discontinuity and change.

As Jacobson and Christensen (1996) have suggested, the presenting problem is often what the couple does to neutralize the distress of the core marital conflict. With Mr. and Mrs. Z, the catalyst for therapy was the anxiety engendered by their response to the connectedness/separateness conflict; her withdrawal and his fear of abandonment. The therapy helps to respond in an adaptive way and to consider alternatives.

When something does not work, we tend to do it harder and faster. Therapy can challenge this automatic response.

HOW AGING WAS REGARDED IN FAMILIES OF ORIGIN

It is important to discover how the couple's families regarded aging in general, and marriage in old age in particular. This exploration can develop around central questions, for example:

- Who have been your positive models of aging? Of old age? Why?
- Who have been your negative models of aging? Old age? Why?
- What does a good marriage in old age look like? Have you seen one? Who? What made it good?
- What does a bad marriage look like in old age? Have you seen one? Who? What made it bad?

"Why now?" is a seminal question for clinical assessment. It is especially relevant for the couple in a long-term marriage. What has happened that they cannot cope with, that has led to their seeking professional help now?

Qualls (1995) has suggested that important aspects of a marriage become altered in response to significant change, regardless of the cause of the change. These aspects include:

- How time is structured
- Roles or tasks defining the relationship
- Patterns of communication
- The balance of power over resources or decision making

- The need for nurturance and succorance
- Relationships with children

SPECIFIC PRESENTING PROBLEMS OF THE OLDER COUPLE

EXPECTABLE AGE-RELATED EVENTS

While certain events may be expectable, when they occur, they can jolt the marriage and result in changes in rules and roles that were not anticipated. Among expected events are the children leaving home and retirement. Clinical experience does not support that the time when the children leave home is especially problematic for most couples. At this time (for this cohort), parents are still working and, if the children are basically doing all right, their departure from the nest is well accommodated, even welcomed.

Retirement, however, can throw an enormous curve to the unsuspecting couple. It can precipitate an intradyadic agoraphobia, as they struggle to renegotiate all the aspects of the marriage (Qualls, 1995).

It is often valuable for the couple to do pre-retirement work to anticipate and avoid the more obvious pitfalls. It can help them clarify their needs, goals, and wishes, and identify what may need to be negotiated.

Couple therapy for retirement can be organized around relevant guiding questions to this end including:

- What does the word retirement mean to you? Does it mean the end of purposeful work? The end of not being able to do what you want to do? Or not having to do what you don't want to do?
- When should your spouse retire? The same time as you do? Never?
- What will you do with your time, money, energy, interest after you retire?
- What do you expect of your spouse when you retire? How much togetherness, service, attention?
- What does the ideal marriage look like after retirement?
- What do you expect will be the most difficult adjustment for your spouse to make after you retire?
- At this stage, what gives you the greatest satisfaction in your life? How do you expect this will change/stay the same after you retire?

LOSS OF A FRIEND

Another event that can have a powerful effect on the marriage is the loss of a best friend. Treasured friends mirror and color our lives. They also can serve an integral function of the marriage. When lost, the bereaved spouse may seek from his or her spouse the emotional support provided by the lost friend. This places new demands on the couple relationship.

In answer to the "why now" question during assessment, explore if there have been any recent changes in the friendship network.

Differential Aging

When one partner approaches a certain age or stage, he/she feels that retirement, for example, means waiting for the end. The other partner feels it is a time of freedom, of beginning anew. Clearly this is fertile soil for stress in the marriage. Often this great divide is secondary to illness and physical constraints. It also depends on other factors, such as social learning and personality. Therapy can be organized around the following:

- Matching the presentation to the meaning (intent)
- Negotiating the space in between (difference)
- Contracting for the shared space and noninterference with real differences (degrees of freedom)

For example, they will agree that the more active/dynamic spouse will refrain from being angry with the spouse who wants to take it easy. In exchange, the inactive spouse will agree to go out once a week without moaning, complaining behavior. In other words, an appreciation and normalization of differences in meaning and styles can enhance acceptance and reduce conflict.

The Inadequate Child

It is extremely stressful for the older couple to watch a child fail to become a competent adult. It is experienced as a painful developmental violation. The older parents are trying to achieve closure on their own lives and feel free of the direct responsibilities of parenting. This problem with the children may be long-standing, as in the case where the child has schizophrenia or a developmental disability. Or it can be in response to an acute illness or transient problems, such as financial reversals or marital disruptions. The effect it has on the older couple is:

- To prompt a review of the parenting and reawaken earlier problems, including accusations and guilt
- To complicate the closure task and raise anxiety about how the child will be cared for when the parents are no longer there

The Caregiving Marriage

Illness and disability in a spouse requires that the couple be flexible and make changes within their roles. Flexibility is key as most illnesses do not follow a linear trajectory; functional abilities vary greatly over time and across tasks.

CASE EXAMPLE

Mrs.V was in therapy with her husband, Mr. V while he was undergoing treatment for an especially aggressive cancer. In their late seventies, theirs had been the prototypical traditional marriage, which was comfortable for both of them. His responsibility was to be exclusively in charge of the household finances. Although her name was printed on their personal checks, she never wrote any. While he was seriously ill and debilitated from the effects of the chemotherapy, clearly the business of life did not stop. During these times it fell to Mrs.V take over this responsibility. She was capable and handled it easily. As soon as Mr. V began to feel better, he resumed control over the check book. Initially, neither acknowledged her competence on an "as needed" basis. Over the course of his treatments, this routine became an indicator of when his strength was beginning to return. Mr. and Mrs. V came to acknowledge, and appreciate, their flexibility in the responsibilities of their spousal roles.

The effect of serious illness and disability on couples, and their families, in late life is great (Brown, 1988). Rolland (1994) has discussed illness and disability as having the effect of skewing the couple relationship along several lines. These are the "fault lines" attended to in therapy and include:

- *Ownership of the problem.* Who owns the illness?
- *Boundary of the problem.* How much space in the marital whole does the illness take up?
- *Roles.* How much of the whole role as spouse do the roles of patient and caregiver consume?
- *Togetherness and separateness.* How much togetherness and separateness does the illness require of the couple? How much does the couple require? The greater the differential, the greater the conflict. Attention to this can help avoid caregiver burnout. It can also help avoid conflict emanating from divergent points of view of the patient and caregiver. From the perspective of the spouse patient, the central conflict is abandonment versus control. From the perspective of the spouse caregiver, the conflict is guilt versus rage.

IMPLICATIONS FOR THERAPY

A key is to achieve a working balance so that the patient spouse does not fear abandonment with separateness and the caregiving spouse does not feel guilty. This can be achieved by arriving at a negotiated aloneness/togetherness contract. This usually follows an exploration of worst fears and what ifs.

For example, she will go out and never come back or I will come back and find him dead.

Two illnesses that are frequently involved in couple therapy with older adults are *dementia* and *depression*.

There is a greater burden as the spouse becomes more demented and is less able to relate in meaningful ways to his or her spouse. Naturally occurring antidotes to caregiver burnout include patient responsiveness, cooperation, and expressed appreciation. Dementia caregiving generally covers many years and during this time most care is provided by the family, most often a spouse. Nearly half of caregivers experience clinically significant psychiatric morbidity, anxiety, or depression, or both.

As with dementia, depression can interfere with the ability to participate and show appreciation for care. Clinical depression, especially recurrent depression, is wearing to the spouse and is compounded often in this cohort by denial, shame, and lack of social support afforded other illnesses. A positive marriage has been shown to be a buffer against depression (Salokangas, Mattila, & Joukamaa, 1988). However, depression is often a recurrent illness in old age. Of those who have a first episode after age fifty, 77% go on to develop a recurrent depression. Beyond medical treatment of the depressed individual, the treatment for the couple is largely psychoeducational. It is structured around depression facts, fantasies, and care generally, and depression facts, fantasies, and care that are specific to the patient and couple.

UNFINISHED BUSINESS

One or both partners my revisit old wounds or marital trauma, and that can be a precipitant for conflict in the couple or of one becoming symptomatic. Therapy can enable the stuck spouse to let go of an old injury, make amends, hear regrets, and allow forgiveness. The goals are to heal old wounds and to affect a positive transformation of the current relationship.

RUNNING OUT OF TIME

The goal of the therapy when this is an active theme, typically in advanced old age or when one spouse is seriously ill, is to enable the couple to say goodbye and move on. The following can guide the therapy:

- What I need to say to you
- What I need to hear from you
- Discussing the future of the surviving spouse
- Appreciating the wisdom of age and survival of the marital relationship

The couple relationship often becomes more important and more highly valued as they face the end of the relationship. The goal of the therapy is to reconcile the couple to the end of being a couple.

COUPLE THERAPY AFTER DEATH

The death of a partner in a long marriage leaves a large hole and a long shadow. Time fills the hole. Therapy can help reduce the shadow.

DIFFERENCES IN THERAPY WITH OLDER ADULTS

The clinical work with older couples is more similar than dissimilar to work with couples at any age. It is easier in some ways: They have experience and wisdom to build on, and they are not harboring the delusion that time is infinite. It is more difficult in some ways because old ways of being, doing, and thinking have had a long time to solidify.

Four important differences in doing therapy with older adults, whether individual or couple, are worth noting:

1. *Countertransference issues.* Generally, younger clinicians have more difficulty treating older adults than older adults have in being treated by younger clinicians. (If you are old enough, most people are younger, including your health care providers.)

Countertransference themes in treating older adults include:

- *Futility.* Treating people with a foreshortened future (and a long past)
- *Hopelessness.* Treating people who can be expected to accrue decrements and losses over time
- *Pain.* The difficult feelings that arise in us about our own parents, aged or absent
- *Fear.* Projecting the vision of our aged self into the future

There are special countertransference themes that arise as we treat the older couples, resonating with feelings we harbor about the marriage of our parents, or our own marriage.

2. *Physical concerns.* There is the constant communion of the presence, or specter, of illness, disability, decrement, and loss.
3. *Shifting scene.* Therapy with older adults is always an extended clinical evaluation; the presentation and problem can shift rapidly. Older adults, as a special population, are exquisitely vulnerable to the vicissitudes of aging.
4. *Termination and the therapy contract.* Saying goodbye has special meaning in old age. I have not found termination, in the traditional sense, to be a good fit in the mental health care of older adults. I prefer a position of being an advocate and member of their health care team for whenever there is need of my services, for however long.

   Sometimes planned check-ins can be appropriate. For example, check-ins can comfort the individual who needs an occasional reminder of my availability. An occasional scheduled session can reward the patient's good health and coping, and unlink access to my support from symptoms and distress. It can also be used to monitor status and functional ability, which can change rapidly. It can keep me updated so certain problems can be anticipated and, if a problem does emerge, the patient is more comfortable and more likely to reconnect and re-enter treatment.

If one partner does become terminally ill, both know that I will be there for the course and later for the surviving spouse. Knowing this is comforting to both.

The course of therapy includes time to do a piece of work and time off to savor it. Even in old age, "once and for all" never is.

COUPLE THERAPY: WHEN DOING IT YOURSELF DOESN'T DO IT

The *catalyst* for change comes when an old pattern doesn't work for a new problem.

Older couples may be especially resistant to seek mental health services. They may:

- Believe ageism myths (e.g., "We're too old to change.")
- Resist change ("Even if it's awful, it's mine.")
- Be unaware of therapy as being potentially helpful for their problem
- Carry a bias against psychotherapy

CREATING CHANGE

- Let go of past recriminations (other) and excuses for failures and disappointments (self).
- Communicate openly about interactions with the other that feel good and feel bad.
- Approach change as a possibility and together figure out how you could make change(s) happen.
- Practice negotiating and making decisions. Start with small things, and progress to bigger things. Observe the process. Annotate the process. Discover the traps.
- Talk about what changes are needed now, soon, and later.
- Talk about aging; your own and your spouse's. Talk about the aging of the marriage; what is lost, gained, stays the same.
- Discover acceptance and express it. Self-acceptance is a task in on old age. This extends from the person to the couple. Acceptance means no longer trying to change the other. Acceptance means he or she is okay the way he or she is.

Therapy offers something for now and something (to take home) for later. The therapeutic interventions range from normalizing and supporting to helping the couple access needed resources. They can include short-term or long-term therapy, crisis intervention, and, if necessary, encouraging the separation of one partner from the other and from the home.

GUIDING NOTIONS, METAPHORS, AND ASSIGNMENTS

Certain notions, metaphors, and assignments have been found to be especially useful in conducting therapy with older couples.

Guiding notions include:

- *Notion of anticipated longevity.* Each individual holds an idea of how long he or she will live. It varies from individual to individual, how one arrives at this age, but it is typically highly available information. In addition, each individual usually has an idea, a preconceived notion, of what he or she might be like at that age. The therapist is encouraged to just ask.
- *Notion of self-apportionment.* This refers to the tacit or explicit intention of the individual to personal resources, typically becoming more restrictive with advancing age. These self-resources to be apportioned include energy, interest, and time. A lack of congruence, or even understanding, between spouses can engender considerable stress and conflict.

CASE EXAMPLE

Mr. T, 69 years old, was in the terminal phase of metastatic disease. He and Mrs. T had used couple therapy to support them during earlier phases of aggressive medical and surgical treatment. They returned to therapy for support during this final phase and to work toward a meaningful closure to their marriage. However, it became apparent that Mr. T was choosing to uses his increasingly limited physical energy to wrap up a community service project with which he had been closely affiliated. Mrs. T wanted her husband's limited resources to be spent with her and the focus to be on their love and life together. Rather than coming together, their different agendas seemed to be pulling them apart. In addition to their already heavy emotional burden at this time, she was adding anger and he was adding guilt.

The therapy was able to secure safe space for this couple to explore what was occurring. They ware able to identify that both recognized that his self-resources and time were severely limited, and that they were most precious commodities to both. The choice of how to apportion self-resources was a significant task. Mr. T was encouraged to let his wife in; to help her understand his phenomenology that was the context of this choice. Generativity and altruism were highly involved. But also involved was his absolute conviction that the project of their marriage was solid and had been so well-tended over the years that it could end strong without that last "deposit" of his attention and energy. Mrs. T's anger, and Mr. T's guilt, were reduced and the couple was able to come together at the end. While she did not agree with his choice of self-apportionment ("I wouldn't do it this way"), she did come to understand and respect his position.

After his death, some resentment did remain, but Mrs.T was able to get beyond that and esteem herself for having been open and supportive of her husband, even while their ending was, for her, less than ideal and would not have been her choice.

- *Givens and negotiables.* Givens are those positions and choices to which one is firmly committed. Failure to achieve or maintain these result in a sense of disappointment, failure, or loss. Givens are central to the self. Unlike givens, while preferred, negotiables are not essential. Negotiables can be used in the service of protecting givens and promoting intimacy and mutual caring.
- *Closure and legacy.* To create the final story of one's life, accept it as one's own, accept a mixture of self-responsibility and fate is *closure*. Legacy is the need of another to be in receipt of the story or something left behind to mark the life union. It subsumes the processes of self-divestment and self-investment.

Metaphors useful in therapy include:

- *Elephants under the carpet.* This refers to avoided topics in the marriage.
- *Eggshells.* This refers to topics or behaviors that are glossed-over; addressed only on a subtuse level.
- *Landmines down the road.* This refers to anticipating problems with a likelihood of occurring in the foreseeable future.
- *Boat and baggage.* This refers to the vessel the couple are in, together, negotiating the uncharted waters of old age. The baggage refers to their old resentments and hurts, which they can choose to unload to lighten their load and enhance the safety and the comfort of their passage.

Assignments that can be useful in therapy include:

- Bibliotherapy and videotherapy
- Sharing cognitive behavioral exercises
- The bedtime story (Telling stories/memories from different life stages.)
- *Lists and letters.* Lists are givens and negotiables; ranking and weighting that which is necessary (givens) and that which is desired (negotiables), Letters are to/about; a registered voice
- *Pictures.* To create an album around a specific event or time
- *Future.* Computer programs; for intergenerational and marital projects; serves the purposes of closure and legacy

CONCLUSION

Core concepts for couple therapy with older adults include:

- The couple is a system. The system seeks to maintain its homeostasis. The couple's problems are often what they do to respond to a demand for a change in the system.
- Any change in the system affects on the whole system.
- All therapy (including individual) affects the (couple) system.

- Normal, expectable developmental tasks can challenge the older couple.
- Old age is a time of multiple challenges to the couple. Transitions at later life, predictable or not, require change in the couple's basic ways of interacting, effected through rules, roles, and relationships.
- Older adults are likely to seek problem-focused help, to focus on the individual rather than the system, and to undervalue their experience and wisdom.

Couple therapy in later life is both for the ride now and the bumps ahead along the road.

Jacobson and Christensen's (1996) integrative couple therapy model posits a goal to move the couple from a position of tolerance to acceptance. Sublime acceptance is suggested as the ideal endpoint.

Each partner in the long-lived marriage needs to feel known, and to be esteemed at being known. Each needs to come to accept that life together was an understandable choice, perhaps even a wise one.

It would be truly wonderful if, at the final moment together, each partner could say to the other "It has been a good ride. I would choose you all over again."

REFERENCES

Bengston, V.L., & Kuypers, J.A. (1985). The family support cycle: Psychosocial issues in the aging family. In J. Munnichs, P. Mussen, E. Olbrich, & P. Coleman (Eds.), *Life-span and change in gerontological perspective.* Orlando, FL: Academic Press.

Brown, F.H. (1988). The impact of death and serious illness on the family life cycle. In B. Carter & M. McGoldrick (Eds.), *The changing family life cycle* (2nd ed.). New York: Gardner Press.

Carstensen, L.L. (1992). Social and emotional patterns in adulthood: Support for socioemotional selectivity theory. *Psychology and Aging, 7,* 331–338.

Duck, S. (1994). Steady as (s)he goes: Relational maintenance as a shared meaning system. In D.J. Canary & L. Stafford (Eds.), *Communication and relational maintenance.* San Diego, CA: Academic Press.

Erikson, E. (1982). *The life cycle completed.* New York: Norton.

Florsheim, M.J., & Herr, J.J. (1990). Family counseling with elders. *Generations, 14,* 40–42.

Hatfield., E., & Rapson, R.L. (1993). *Love, sex and intimacy: Their psychology, biology, and history.* New York: HarperCollins.

Jacobson, N., & Christensen, A. (1996). *Integrative couple therapy.* New York: Norton.

Kaplan, H.S. (1990). Sex, intimacy and the aging process. *Journal of the American Academy of Psychoanalysis, 18,* 185–205.

Levenson, R., Carstensen, L., & Gottman, J. (1993). Long-term marriage: Age, gender and satisfaction. *Psychology & Aging, 8,* 301–313.

Mancini, J.A., & Bird, G.W. (1985). Six steps toward a happy midlife marriage. *Medical Aspects of Human Sexuality, 19,* 163–177.

Orbuch, J., House, J., Mero, R., & Webster, P. (1996). Marital quality over the life course. *Social Psychology Quarterly, 59,* 162–171.

Parker, R.G. (1995). Reminiscence: A continuity theory framework. *Gerontologist, 35,* 515–525.

Qualls, S.H. (1995). Marital therapy with later life couples. *Journal of Geriatric Psychiatry, 28,* 139–163.

Rolland, J. (1994). In sickness and in health: The impact of illness on couples' relationships. *Journal of Marriage and Family Therapy, 20,* 327–347.

Salokangas, R.K., Mattila, V., & Joukamaa, M. (1988). Intimacy and mental disorder in late middle age. Report of the TURVA project. *Acta Psychiatrica Scandinavica, 78,* 555–560.

Snell, J.G. (1993). The gendered construction of elderly marriage, 1900–1950. *Canadian Journal of Aging, 12,* 509–523.

Van Ypern, N.W., & Buuk, B.P. (1991). Equity theory and exchange and communal orientation from a cross-national perspective. *Journal of Social Psychology, 131,* 5–20.

Willi, J. (1982). *Couples in collusion.* Claremont, CA: Hunter House.

Zeitlow, P., & Sillars, A. (1988). Life-stage differences in communication during marital conflicts. *Journal of Social & Personal Relationships, 5,* 223–245.

CHAPTER 16

Dynamics and Treatment of Middle-Generation Women: Heroines and Victims of Multigenerational Families

DONNA S. DAVENPORT

Midlife adult children of aging parents have been called the "sandwich generation" (D. Miller, 1981), a term that captures their family roles as responsible caregivers to both their children and their parents. Typically, it is the daughter who assumes the role of the parent's primary caregiver if the other parent is unable or unavailable to provide care (Cantor, 1983; Schwiebert & Myers, 1994). In one of the few studies using national data, women outnumber men more than three to one among adult children caregivers; 77% were women, 23% were sons (Stone, Cafferata, & Sangl, 1987). Although sons often provide some care to ailing parents, daughters are more likely to be *primary* caregivers and "care providers," providing hands-on personal care and daily assistance such as meal preparation and help with household chores (Horowitz, 1985; Stoller, 1983); further, daughters are more likely than sons to provide more hours of care over longer periods (Montgomery & Borgatta, 1987). Sons, in contrast, typically assist parents with transportation needs, home repairs, and financial management. Even when they are the primary caregivers, however, sons commit less time to caregiving tasks and provide less hands-on care than daughters (Coward & Dwyer, 1990; Horowitz, 1985). Among women of color, there is a relatively greater incidence of women caregivers, and these women are seen as being at particular risk because of their multiple roles within the extended family (Montgomery & Datwyler, 1990).

Numerous studies have indicated that, in general, caregiving adult children frequently experience significant emotional, physical, and financial stresses (e.g., King, 1993; Parks & Pilisuk, 1991). A special area of research has been on the challenge that caregivers, particularly women, face in their need to balance multiple roles simultaneously and to resolve conflicts between caregiving and their other roles—such as a spouse, parent, and worker (Myers, 1988). Most women caregivers are mothers, most are married, and about 25% of these women caregivers have minor children living at home (U.S. Select Committee on Aging, 1987). Further, data from the National Long Term Care Survey and the Informal Caregivers Survey found that 44% of all caregiving daughters were employed (Stone et al., 1987).

As noted by Barnett and Baruch (1985), research regarding how women handle such multiple social roles and how much stress they experience has followed one of two models: (1) The scarcity approach, which suggests that multiple roles lead to competing obligations for time and energy, and (2) the expansion hypothesis, which posits that role occupancy provides particular benefits. This split seems to mirror the polorization evident in the early days of gerontology between those who saw aging from a loss-deficit model and those who viewed it as having many positive aspects (Knight & McCallum, 1998). It may be that the two stances regarding women caregivers' stress are more paradox than contradiction. It seems likely that for many caregiving women in some circumstances, such caregiving is especially stressful, but also that for many caregivers—even those especially stressed—the opportunity to provide care is sometimes also experienced as enriching and self-affirming.

Making sense of this paradox requires that we examine some of the sociological, developmental, and possible family dynamics that often affect such women. In this chapter, we consider the contributions of each of these three areas, as well as provide individual, family, and group interventions that counselors working with women caregivers might find helpful.

SOCIALIZATION FACTORS

In general, women are expected to take the primary responsibility for maintaining relationships and caring for others' emotional needs (Lerner, 1983; Matthews & Rosner, 1988; Montgomery & Kamo, 1989; Thompson & Walker, 1989). As Montgomery and Datwyler (1990, p. 37) noted, "Men, in contrast, are socialized to delegate many caregiving tasks . . . to female family members or to purchase such services as necessary." Although there is some evidence that among college-educated, middle-class European Americans attitudes toward women's expected roles may be modifying somewhat, caregiving is still typically considered the woman's responsibility. Women are not only socialized to assume more caregiving responsibility, but also to expect less involvement of male family members; even when men are willing, women often feel uncomfortable in relinquishing such tasks (Montgomery & Datwyler, 1990).

A number of writers have referred to such aspects of women's socialization as the expectation that correct female behavior is "selfless": one should ignore one's own needs and desires on behalf of others (e.g., Davenport & Yurich, 1991). Thus, good wives put their husband's needs ahead of their own; good mothers always consider their children's preferences first; good adult daughters provide caregiving to their parents even when they are exhausted. Although considerable research indicates that such attitudes contribute greatly to women's stress and depression (Vasquez, 1994), the self-expectation of selflessness—and the concomitant fear of being viewed as "selfish"—is a powerful motivation for many women.

Lerner (1983), a feminist grounded in psychodynamic family systems theory, uses a similar but stronger term. She refers to excessive self-sacrifice as "deselfing," a process in which the woman betrays significant aspects of herself to accommodate others. Lerner's belief is that for many women, such a process has its origins in their *socialized* (her emphasis) relationships with their mothers and then carries over to relationships with men and children (Lerner, 1980, 1983, 1985). As Lerner (1983) describes this deselfing process:

> Daughters frequently thwart their own autonomy and growth and sacrifice valued aspects of the self . . . in order to protect a special bond with their mothers, who are unconsciously perceived as unable to tolerate the daughters' moves toward separateness and success. . . . Such difficulties . . . are not inherent or "natural" aspects of the mother-daughter relationship, but rather reflect larger systems issues, including the structuring of gender roles over many generations, and women's subordinate status. (p. 231)

It is no wonder then, if Lerner is at least partially correct, that when women are the caregivers of their aging parents, especially their mothers, they feel that their duty to behave selflessly is nonnegotiable.

Lerner's work, and that of most other writers and researchers of women's caregiving, is primarily based on European American women. The gender socialization of other cultural groups is often even more pronounced in its expectation of women providing the family caregiving, and sometimes quite punishing to women who do not comply (Gelfand & Barresi, 1987). Inasmuch as mental health workers are providing services to increasingly diverse clientele, it behooves us to familiarize ourselves at least minimally with the gender socialization of a variety of cultures. Individuals from any of these groups may have internalized more or less of the injunctions, so we suggest caution in assuming that the following generalizations apply to your particular client. The following brief summary is obviously not a substitute for much more extensive knowledge of culture needed by effective counselors, but provides some initial hypotheses of "what to listen for."

AFRICAN AMERICAN WOMEN

In many African American families, connection with other blood relatives is considered crucial to the individual's survival in a racist society (Boyd-Franklin, 1991; McAdoo, 1988; Sudarkasa, 1988; Turner, 1997). There are variations in the gender socialization patterns in relation to education, socioeconomic level, geographic areas, and so forth, but in general women provide most of the hands-on caregiving of other family members. (An exception to this is that in some families, sons take on parenting responsibilities of younger children.) The pattern of extended family relationships often gives rise to complicated relationships, and children may have several "mamas"—including grandmothers, aunts, and godmothers (Boyd-Franklin, 1991).

Adult women thus have more aging individuals for whom they may potentially provide caregiving, but there are also usually more extended family members to help share the load. According to Beck and Beck (1989), middle-aged African American women take in relatives at twice the rate of White peers. In some families, this pattern is normative and a source of pride among women who may see themselves as the backbone of the family (Yee, 1990). Thus, although they may feel great stress as a result of their multiple caregiving roles, they also feel that what they are doing is appropriate and good.

LATINAS

Latino families also have a very strong extended family orientation, which may include friends and godparents sharing in the family responsibilities and privileges. Traditionally, such families demonstrate strict gender roles, with males clearly the dominant gender, and younger family members subordinate to their elders (Applewhite, 1988; Comas-Dias, 1987). Marianismo is the traditional ideal for women: all-suffering, sweet, and nurturing, like the Virgin Mary (Yee, 1990). The Latina—or female family member—has often "internalized the expectation to nurture, care for, and maintain the family unity and connections . . . and may therefore deny or ignore her needs in order to keep the family intact, even in the face of abuse . . ." (Vasquez, 1994, p. 124).

Younger women, then, tend to be the primary caregivers of ailing parents, but there is an expectation that other women in the family system will help out, and that sons will demonstrate their support and respect. My experience with Texas Latino families is that although the daughters and daughters-in-law do indeed provide much of the hands-on caregiving, many sons show honor and respect to their elderly parents by visiting regularly, giving and receiving emotional support, providing transportation and financial aid, and the like.

WOMEN OF ASIAN AND INDIAN DESCENT

In general, gender roles for women in Asia and the Indian Subcontinent are even more fixed than for other cultures. Bradshaw (1994) traces these strict roles to Confucian social philosophy, which demanded that all relationships be of the subordinate-superordinate type, with women subordinate to men, especially their husbands, and to their elders. In most of these cultures, the needs of the family always take precedence over the needs of a given individual, and being able to adapt to others' expectations and "do what one must do" is a virtue, especially for women. In many of these cultures, not to conform to the strict gender role is to bring shame to one's family—a terrible possibility. Speaking of the

Indian culture, Jayakar (1994, p. 172) says, "The concept of fixed gender roles has made it nearly impossible for many Indian women even to consider the freedom of thinking about, let alone practicing, a more egalitarian attitude." Women were expected to devote themselves to their families (and/or their husband's families) by providing hands-on caregiving, while the men provided the financial support.

First generation Asian American and Indian Americans who immigrated to the United States are more likely to have internalized this way of thinking, with each succeeding generation likely becoming more acculturated to American ways—thereby creating a real gender gap (Osako & Liu, 1986). A first-generation Indian-American elderly woman may well expect her daughter-in-law to quit her job and devote herself to full-time caregiving, an expectation based on the acceptance of interdependency and hierarchical relationships, but that will likely result in considerable internal conflict for the younger woman.

DEVELOPMENTAL ISSUES

The critique during the past two decades of the "male model" of development as normative across genders and cultures has been extensive (e.g., Gilligan, 1982; Jordan, 1997; J. Miller, 1976; Vasquez, 1994). In contrast to theories of development suggested by Erikson, Kohlberg, and Mahler, these opposing voices have emphasized that for most women, as well as for men in many non-European-American cultures, family connection and values are considered much more intrinsic than the Western emphasis on separation-individuation. This process toward mature development is not, they emphasize, pathological or somehow "wrong"; it is merely different.

We have already briefly discussed the cultural differences in gender expectations originating in different socialization experiences. The issue of psychological development is an associated, but separate, issue. Gilligan's (1982) ideas about female development derived from her awareness that prevailing theories of moral development were not applicable to women, but were being used in ways that depicted women as defective or deficient. Not that this was new: Men, writing from men's perspectives and based on research with men as the normative sample, have followed the old "female deficit" tradition captured in Aristotle's statement that "the female is a female by virtue of a certain lack of qualities; we should regard the female nature as afflicted with a natural defectiveness" (Sanday, 1988, p. 58). Regarding moral development, Gilligan emphasized the power of the ethic of caretaking and relationship in women's lives, which were often used as the basis for making moral decisions (in contrast to the more masculine criterion of justice).

Theorists at the Stone Center at Wellesley College have designed what they now refer to as "the cultural relational model" (previously termed the "self-in-relation" theory), which is based in part on Chodorow's and Gilligan's works, as well as on their critiques of the object-relations model of the development of the self. In brief, the theory, as described by Jordan (1997), suggests that young girls do not have the same psychological need as their brothers to separate from their mothers. Unencumbered by fears of being called "sissies," or "mama's girls," they have a much longer pre-oedipal period than males, so their attachments to their mothers can continue uninterrupted. Unlike boys, who must define their self as clearly unlike that of their mothers, girls can continue to identify with their primary caregiver; their self thus evolves within the context of the relationships. In contrast to the rather complete separation-individuation process normative for males, females thus mature with what Chodorow (1978) termed "permeable boundaries." This is not to suggest that daughters do not have sometimes great conflict with their mothers, simply that they do not feel the urgency of breaking away to maintain their identities.

Suggesting that the traditional view of the goal of human growth as the development of a separate, individuated, well-bounded self is simply one perspective, J. Miller, Jordan, Kaplan, Stiver, and Surrey (1997) elaborate on the potential consequences of a more relationally embedded developmental process. From their relational model, they propose that the goal of development is to participate in increasingly empowering relationships that are "growth fostering for all the people involved, . . . mutually empathic and mutually empowering" (p. 28). Further, they suggest that all growth takes place within mutually empathic/empowering relationships, and that the source of most human problems is the disconnection that occurs in nonmutual, dominant-subordinate relationships. Given their developmental histories, women are more likely to act from this perspective than Western males, according to these Stone Center theorists.

In contrast to the previously discussed socialization patterns, then, this theory suggests that women's commitment to relationships is not simply internalized duty, but is often experienced as enlivening, gratifying, and sustaining. Likely, there is some truth in both perspectives; many women provide caregiving out of a sense of duty and obligation, and other women—or even these same dutiful ones—gain a sense of connectedness and vitality that affirms their self and their understanding of connection in the world.

FAMILY ISSUES

In addition to the more generic aspects of socialization and female development, women bring unique factors to their caregiving role. This section briefly highlights two of these. An additional one, the temperament of the woman, is surely also important, but at this point we lack the theory and research to be able to say much about this genetic contribution.

FAMILY ROLE

Family systems literature provides us with another factor that influences the caregiving provided by midlife women to their ailing parents. Women, in addition to being socialized to be the caregivers and to the intrinsic satisfaction they may derive because of their sense of self-in-relation that their development afforded, may flavor this role as a continuation of their historical role in the family of origin.

Birth order often plays a factor in one's relationship with one's parents, especially in some cultures (Bradshaw, 1994). The oldest child, especially if female, may have major caregiving responsibilities for siblings early in life, and this role as "parents' helper" may carry over into later life as feeling specially called on to assist the parents themselves. Regardless of birth order, however, the developing child has unique patterns of expectations, hopes, frustrations, and the like with each parent that influence how the caregiving role is accepted and enacted. The child who always resented what was seen as a parent's arbitrary use of authority will surely feel different than if he or she were providing care for the much-admired parent who had always generated sympathy. Similarly, the child who has been estranged from a parent and is now expected to be a primary caregiver will assume that role with different feelings if the estrangement is viewed as abandonment on the part of the parent, as opposed to believing that it was an unfortunate, enforced separation from which they both suffered.

ATTACHMENT STYLE

Historically, Bowlby's attachment theory grew out of object relations theory (Karen, 1990; Krause & Haverkamp, 1996). Bowlby (1988) suggests that, based on experiences with the parent over time, a child forms "working models" containing beliefs and expectations about whether the caregiver is trustworthy and caring, as well as whether the self is worthy of care and attention. These working models tend to be consistent over time, but can be at least somewhat revised in therapy. Research has confirmed the importance of attachment between children and parents, including between middle-aged children and their parents (Ainsworth, 1989; Cicirelli, 1991). Of even greater significance for the purposes of this discussion, attachment behavior has been found to be related to the maintenance of caregiving to elderly parents—attachment proving more important, in some studies, than feelings of duty (Cicirelli, 1986, 1993).

Several researchers have described the "working models" that form the basis for attachment styles. As summarized by Krause and Haverkamp (1996), these models/styles are secure, anxious/ambivalent, and avoidant. An individual with a secure attachment style is comfortable with closeness, is unworried about being abandoned, and has a good sense of self-worth and self-confidence (e.g., Collins & Read, 1990; Feeney & Noller, 1990). Individuals with anxious styles tend to be characterized by dependence and fear of loss (Dolan, Arnkoff, & Glass, 1993), and avoidant individuals are disinterested or fearful of establishing close attachments, report high levels of hostility, and tend to be highly self-reliant (e.g., Bartholomew, 1990; Dolan et al., 1993).

Relating these models to caregiving of elderly parents, then, suggests that those adult children with secure attachment styles are likely to cope most effectively with stressors and to have the most to offer their parents; anxiously attached caregivers will tend to increase their personal stress by fears of disapproval and/or abandonment, and avoidant caregivers will likely find the forced contact with their parents to be problematic and intrusive.

COUNSELING INTERVENTIONS

When meeting a woman caregiver of her parent in the initial setting, several issues should be remembered—both in regard to content and to process. The goal is to understand what the client is experiencing so that you can provide maximum help to her. To do that, you must address the socialization, developmental, and family issues previously summarized. This can be accomplished by means of specific assessment instruments, by completing a formal intake interview, or by more informal discussion. By the end of the first session, however, counselors should have begun to form some impressions of the client's historical context from which she is presently operating. Information should be obtained regarding the cultural expectations for caregiving that the client absorbed, the developmental history of the parent/daughter relationship, and the family norms and role expectations that the client has internalized. These pieces of the puzzle can be assembled to construct this individual client's "working model" of her caregiving role. No two will be exactly alike, not only because each family and relationship is different, but also because not all socialization is internalized. The rewards and stressors of the caregiving role will thus become illuminated, as well as other relevant aspects of the client's life (e.g., career and family issues, religious influences). The strengths and resources that the woman brings to the role, and the difficulties that add to her stress, all need to be understood.

The process of this session (as well as later ones) may be as important as the content (Jordan, 1997; Krause & Haverkamp, 1996). Sometimes being listened to, having someone who truly understands what she is going through, is all that some clients require (Koile, 1977). The quality of the therapeutic relationship is especially relevant when working with caregivers, since they may not be receiving much care themselves. Resonating affectively may be the most important intervention a counselor can make.

INDIVIDUAL THERAPY

Specific interventions with a client are only helpful when the caregiver can make use of them. Suggestions that are too far outside her cultural, developmental, and/or family context will simply be ignored—or worse, seen as further proof that the mental health professional does not understand. Nonetheless, there are usually degrees of freedom for a stressed midlife caregiver that she does not or cannot claim; even small variations in routine, or in additional support, or in self-talk can be of considerable help. In general, counselors can help caregivers in two ways—either changing the situation somehow, or better adapting to the factors that cannot be changed.

Sometimes caregivers have lost touch with what they need, or feel that such needs are selfish. Others may feel more entitled, but have perhaps been expressing their needs in ways that jeopardize others' positive response (becoming demanding, sulky, histrionic). Helping women caregivers become more self-aware and self-nurturing can be the first step toward possible changes they can make in other aspects of their life. As one client said, "As long as I just did what others expected, I felt taken for granted. When I decided I was part of the equation too, and that I should have a voice, my family started listening better. They couldn't listen until I *spoke*."

Solution-focused therapy offers an approach which asks for the client to consider ways she resolved similar difficulties in the past. The midlife caregiver may not have experienced these particular sets of stressors before, but she has undoubtedly had to cope with stressful situations in the past. Helping her rediscover such coping skills—or perhaps those that she recognizes in individuals in similar situations—may provide some relief for her. These ways of coping may be spiritual (prayer, meditation, etc.), behavioral (better time management, better physical self-care), or relational (e.g., joining a support group, talking to friends).

With some women, a more long-term approach might be appropriate. Especially for those with anxious or detached attachment styles who are having difficulty dealing with the stresses of caregiving, Krause and Haverkamp (1996) suggest an implementation of Bowlby's ideas, including focusing on both affective and cognitive components, in order to revise the caregiver's "working model" of relationships. Another situation in which a longer term approach is indicated is when the client is dealing with existential issues (Remnet, 1987)—possibly arising from the loss of their parent figure, their own role transitions, and the acceptance of mortality. Having someone outside the system to confide in and receive support from may feel more appropriate to such clients than relying on family members for support.

In addition to these therapeutic issues, some writers (e.g., Schwiebert & Myers, 1994; Wasow, 1986) have emphasized the importance of the counselor's providing knowledge of community resources. Knowing what is available in the way of Medicaid, adult day care, home health care, and the like, even if the client doesn't make immediate use of such resources, can ease considerably the feeling that she is trapped and alone with nowhere to turn. Additionally, these writers recommend providing information about the developmental needs of aging parents and midlife caregivers, to validate and provide perspective on some of the possible conflicts.

COUPLES/FAMILY THERAPY

Research on the husbands of caregiving daughters confirms the potential for conflict between caregiving and the wife role. Kleban, Brody, Schoonover, and

Hoffman (1989) found that 46% of sons-in-law reported arguing with their wives as a result of the wives' caregiving. Another 33% reported that the caregiving interfered with vacation plans. Married caregivers with actively antagonistic husbands have special need for intervention (Matthews & Rosner, 1988). Even Walker et al. (1993), in their study of primarily well-educated middle-class White women who felt comparatively little stress in their caregiving and other social roles, nonetheless caution that when their sample of women did feel conflict, it was between providing care to a parent and being a wife.

Couple counseling, if the husband is willing to accompany his wife, is often indicated in such situations. Sometimes, simply having the wife make a list of all of her caregiving and other family responsibilities (and the necessary time to accomplish them) and then negotiating a redistribution of tasks can be helpful. Appealing to the husband's sense of equity may succeed, inasmuch as men in many cultures are socialized to value fairness. Even if he takes on no more responsibilities, hearing her out, and having a chance to express his own concerns, may lead to their adopting a clearer win-win approach in their relationship.

The problem is that many of the caregiving responsibilities the wife feels are necessary may not seem so crucial to the husband. He may not think it is necessary that her mother have a hot meal every night, or that the father's apartment be vacuumed each week, or that she help her parent address holiday cards. As discussed previously, part of their different perspectives originate in gender socialization; part is likely the differences the Stone Center theorists pointed to in women valuing connection and relationships; and part may originate in the wife's unique family dynamics. When the wife is performing caregiving tasks that simply make no sense to the man, an analogy that reverses gender roles may help him understand. Exploring what the husband values because of his *male* socialization that the wife does not (e.g., teaching his son how to hunt, watching televised sports with a buddy, etc.) may help him see that such values and expectations may be somewhat arbitrary but are nonetheless quite deep seated and not subject to easy dismissal. A similar approach is to present him (empathically!) with a trajectory of the future if their relationship patterns remain the same; imagining his wife's having to quit work outside the home, her possible stress-related illness, possible divorce, and the like can be quite sobering. In such situations, a male therapist or cotherapist may be more powerful, inasmuch as such situations involve one male giving another male permission to deviate from traditional masculine expectations of wives.

If children are living at home and the mother-wife caregiver is feeling stress, it is important that family counseling be offered. Such situations typically affect everyone in the family, and if possible, all the family members need to listen to one another and make decisions in as cohesive a family unit as possible.

GROUP COUNSELING

Many communities have support groups for caregivers available but often these are targeted for spouses of Alzheimer's patients (Myers, Poidevant, & Dean,

1991; Wasow, 1986). A support group for women caregivers is theoretically a good idea, but for a woman already stretched to the limit, it is likely to be perceived as an optional luxury she has no time for. Accordingly, some counselors or agencies have decided that time-limited psychoeducational groups may be the treatment of choice.

In their review of the literature of the counseling needs of adult caregivers of aging parents, Schwiebert and Myers (1994) found that three areas are usually pinpointed: (1) knowledge of available community resources and of the aging process; (2) emotional support including catharsis, normalization and diffusion of feelings, and reassurance; (3) skill development in communication, stress reduction, and coping resources. All three variables have been correlated with positive outcomes in caregivers. Their proposed four-session group model targeted each of these areas; participants improved their scores on relevant measures except in the area of skill development. Perhaps a six-session format would allow more time to practice and develop crucial skills.

CONCLUSION

Women traditionally carry the responsibility for providing primary care for their elderly parents. How stressful or rewarding this is depends on factors such as gender socialization provided by their culture, their valuing connection and relationships as a result of their developmental history with their childhood caregiver(s), and specific family dynamics unique to the individual. To understand and support a midlife woman providing care to an ailing parent, each of these areas—and the intertwining of all three—needs to be recognized and respected by the counselor. Individual, couple/family, and group counseling modalities may each be helpful interventions.

REFERENCES

Ainsworth, M.D.S. (1989). Attachments beyond infancy. *American Psychologist, 44,* 709–716.

Applewhite, S.R. (Ed.). (1988). *Hispanic elderly in transition.* New York: Greenwood Press.

Barnett, R.C., & Baruch, G.K. (1985). Women's involvement in multiple roles and psychological distress. *Journal of Personality and Social Psychology, 49,* 135–145.

Bartholomew, K. (1990). Avoidance of intimacy: An attachment perspective. *Journal of Social and Personal Relationships, 7,* 147–178.

Beck, R.W., & Beck, S.J. (1989). The incidence of extended households among middle-aged black and white women. *Journal of Family Issues, 10,* 147–168.

Bowlby, J. (1988). *A secure base: Parent-child attachment and healthy human development.* London: Routledge & Kegan Paul.

Boyd-Franklin, N. (1991). Recurrent themes in the treatment of African-American women in group psychotherapy. *Women and Therapy, 11,* 25–40.

Bradshaw, C.K. (1994). Asian and Asian American women: Historical and political considerations in psychotherapy. In L. Comas-Dias & B. Greene (Eds.), *Women of color: Integrating gender and ethnic identities in psychotherapy* (pp. 72–113). New York: Guilford Press.

Cantor, M. (1983). Strain among caregivers: A study of experience in the United States. *Gerontologist, 23,* 597–604.

Chodorow, N. (1978). *The reproduction of mothering.* Berkeley: University of California Press.

Cicirelli, V.G. (1986). The relationship of divorced adult children with their elderly parents. *Journal of Divorce, 9,* 39–54.

Cicirelli, V.G. (1991). Attachment theory in old age: Protection of the attached figure. In K. Pillemer & K. McCartney (Eds.), *Parent-child relations throughout life* (pp. 25–42). Hillsdale, NJ: Erlbaum.

Cicirelli, V.G. (1993). Attachment and obligation as daughters' motives for caregiving behavior and subsequent effect on subjective burden. *Psychology and Aging, 8,* 144–155.

Collins, N.L., & Read, S.J. (1990). Adult attachment, working models, and relationship quality in dating couples. *Journal of Personality and Social Psychology, 58,* 644–663.

Comas-Dias, L. (1987). Feminist therapy with mainland Puerto Rican women. *Psychology of Women Quarterly, 11,* 461–474.

Coward, R.T., & Dwyer, J.W. (1990). The association of gender, sibling network composition, and patterns of parent care by adult children. *Research on Aging, 12* (2).

Davenport, D., & Yurich, J. (1991). Multicultural gender issues. *Journal of Counseling and Development, 70*(1), 64–71.

Dolan, R.T., Arnkoff, D.B., & Glass, C.R. (1993). Client attachment style and the psychotherapist's interpersonal stance. *Psychotherapy, 30,* 408–412.

Feeney, J.A., & Noller, P. (1990). Attachment style as a predictor of adult romantic relationships. *Journal of Personality and Social Psychology, 58,* 281–291.

Gelfand, D.E., & Barresi, C.M. (Eds.). (1987). *Ethnic dimensions of aging.* New York: Springer.

Gilligan, C. (1982). *In a different voice.* Cambridge, MA: Harvard University Press.

Horowitz, A. (1985). Sons and daughters as caregivers to older parents: Differences in role performance and consequences. *Gerontologist, 25,* 612–617.

Jayakar, K. (1994). Women of the Indian subcontinent. In L. Comas-Dias & B. Greene (Eds.), *Women of color: Integrating gender and ethnic identities in psychotherapy* (pp. 161–183). New York: Guilford Press.

Jordan, J. (1997). A relational perspective for understanding women's development. In J. Jordan (Ed.), *Women's growth in diversity* (pp. 9–24). New York: Guilford Press.

Karen, R. (1990, February). Becoming attached. *Atlantic Monthly,* 35–60.

King, T. (1993). The experiences of midlife daughters who are caregivers for their mothers. *Health Care for Women International, 14,* 410–426.

Kleban, M.H., Brody, E.M., Schoonover, C.B., & Hoffman, C. (1989). Family help to the elderly: Perceptions of sons-in-law regarding parent care. *Journal of Marriage and the Family, 51,* 303–312.

Knight, B.G., & McCallum, T.J. (1998). Adapting psychotherapeutic practice for older clients. *Professional Psychology: Research and Practice, 29*(1), 15–22.

Koile, E. (1977). *Listening as a way of becoming.* Waco, TX: Word Books.

Krause, A.M., & Haverkamp, B.E. (1996). Attachment in adult-child—older parent relationships: Research, theory, and practice. *Journal of Counseling and Development, 75*(2), 83–92.

Lerner, H.G. (1980). Internal prohibitions against female anger. *American Journal of Psychoanalysis, 40*(2), 137–148.

Lerner, H.G. (1983). Female dependency in context. *American Journal of Orthopsychiatry, 53*(4), 697–405.

Lerner, H.G. (1985). *The dance of anger: A woman's guide to changing the patterns of intimate relationships.* New York: Harper & Row.

Matthews, S.H., & Rosner, T.T. (1988). Shared filial responsibility: The family as the primary caregiver. *Journal of Marriage and the Family, 50,* 185–195.

McAdoo, H.P. (Ed.). (1988). *Black families* (2nd ed.). Newbury Park, CA: Sage.

Miller, D. (1981). The sandwich generation: Adult children of the aging. *Social Work, 26,* 419–423.

Miller, J.B. (1976). *Toward a new psychology of women.* Boston: Beacon Press.

Miller, J.B., Jordan, J., Kaplan, A.G., Stiver, I.P., & Surrey, J.L. (1997). Some misconceptions and reconceptions of a relational approach. In J. Jordan (Ed.), *Women's growth in diversity* (pp. 25–49). New York: Guilford Press.

Montgomery, R.J.V., & Borgatta, E. (1987). *Effects of alternative family support strategies.* Final report to the Health Care Financing Administration, Department of Health and Human Services, Baltimore.

Montgomery, R.J.V., & Datwyler, M.M. (1990). Women and men in the caregiving role. *Generations: Quarterly Journal of the American Society on Aging, 14*(3), 34–38.

Montgomery, R.J.V., & Kamo, Y. (1989). Parent care by sons and daughters. In J.A. Mancini (Ed.), *Aging parents and adult children.* Lexington, MA: Heath.

Myers, J.E. (1988). The mid/late life generation gap: Adult children with aging parents. *Journal of Counseling and Development, 66,* 331–335.

Myers, J.E., Poidevant, J., & Dean, L. (1991). Group work with older persons and their caregivers: A review of the literature. *Journal for Specialists in Group Work, 16,* 197–205.

Osako, M.M., & Liu, W.T. (1986). Intergenerational relations and the aged among Japanese Americans. *Research on Aging, 8,* 128–155.

Parks, S.H., & Pilisuk, M. (1991). Caregiver burden: Gender and the psychological costs of caregiving. *American Journal of Orthopsychiatry, 61,* 501–509.

Remnet, V. (1987). How adult children respond to role transitions in the lives of their aging parents. *Educational Gerontology, 13,* 341–355.

Sanday, P.R. (1988). The reproduction of patriarchy in feminist anthropology. In M. Gergen (Eds.), *Feminist thought and the structure of knowledge* (pp. 46–69). New York: New York Universities Press.

Schwiebert, V.L., & Myers, J.E. (1994). Midlife caregivers: Effectiveness of a psychoeducational intervention for midlife adults with parent-care responsibilities. *Journal of Counseling and Development, 72*(6), 627–632.

Stoller, E.P. (1983). Parent caregiving by adult children. *Journal of Marriage and the Family, 45,* 851–858.

Stone, R., Cafferata, G.L., & Sangl, J. (1987). Caregivers of the frail elderly: A national profile. *Gerontologist, 30,* 616–626.

Sudarkasa, N. (1988). Interpreting the African heritage in Afro-American family organization. In H.P. McAdoo (Ed.), *Black families* (2nd ed.). Newbury Park, CA: Sage.

Thompson, L., & Walker, A.J. (1989). Women and men in marriage, work and parenthood. *Journal of Marriage and the Family, 51,* 845–871.

Turner, C.W. (1997). Clinical applications of the Stone Center theoretical approach to women. In J. Jordan (Ed.), *Women's growth in diversity* (pp. 74–90). New York: Guilford Press.

U.S. Select Committee on Aging. (1987). *Exploding the myths: Caregiving in America* (Committee Publication No. 99-611). Washington, DC: U.S. Government Printing Office.

Vasquez, M.J.T. (1994). Latinas. In L. Comas-Dias & B. Greene (Eds.), *Women of color: Integrating gender and ethnic identities in psychotherapy* (pp. 114–138). New York: Guilford Press.

Wasow, M. (1986). Support groups for family caregivers of patients with Alzheimer's disease. *Social Work, 31*(2), 93–97.

Yee, B.W.K. (1990). Gender and family issues in minority groups. *Generations: Journal of American Society on Aging, 14*(3), 39–42.

CHAPTER 17

Family Disruption: Understanding and Treating the Effects of Dementia Onset and Nursing Home Placement

DEBORAH W. FRAZER

TWO FAMILIES, TWO DYNAMICS

MARGE'S FAMILY

Marge is an 83-year-old woman who has been widowed for 20 years. She has lived in her same small Pennsylvania town for most of her life, is active in her church, and has numerous friends. Marge has two children: a divorced daughter, with no children, lives and works on the East Coast; and a married son, with two teenage children, lives and works on the West Coast. Both children visit several times a year.

Marge has been showing increasing signs of memory loss for the past two years. Her children, her friends, and she herself have noticed and remarked on the problem, but no one felt that change or action was warranted. Last week, Marge suffered a stroke, that left her temporarily unable to talk or walk. Although she is recovering some function, she will clearly need rehabilitation services in the short run, and may need assisted living or nursing home placement following rehab. Marge's daughter and son went to her bedside after the stroke. The first few days were emotionally intense, confronting the possibility of their mother's death.

After Marge's survival seemed secure, the son and daughter began discussing next steps: a site for rehabilitation, an assisted living facility, perhaps a nursing home. Marge herself was unable to communicate enough to participate. During these discussions, the son and daughter began to disagree. Marge's son felt that it was of primary importance that she remain in her hometown, surrounded by her friends and minister. Marge's daughter felt that it was of primary importance that she move to her daughter's town, where the daughter could visit daily and oversee her care.

The disagreements between the two children escalated. Each sought out supporting evidence for his or her position. Old disagreements surfaced as elements of the battle: "You've always wanted to center everything around yourself!" and "You're always dictating what should happen, but you're never there to make it happen!" Slowly caring for Marge became secondary to winning the sibling battle. The family is disrupted.

ROBERT'S FAMILY

Robert is an 81-year-old man who has been widowed for four years. Ten years ago, he and his wife moved to a continuing care retirement community (CCRC) that provides three levels of care, as needed: independent, intermediate, and skilled. Robert lives independently in an apartment. Although he suffered with grief and loneliness following the death of his wife, Robert eventually adjusted well. He has many friends in the community, and is a participant in numerous activities. Robert has four children: two live nearby with spouses and children, and two with their families at some distance. He receives a visit from one or more members of his family every few weeks.

Robert has been showing signs of memory loss for over four years. In the last year, he has shown noticeable decline, including episodes of confusion and getting lost. The children, friends, the nurse at the CCRC, and Robert himself, have all noticed and remarked on the recent decline. The facility physician was asked to do a medication review and lab tests, but neither yielded any explanation for the decline. Robert has self-limited his driving: he no longer drives at night, on long trips, or to unfamiliar places. In addition, he is limiting his travel to short stays, always accompanied by a family member. He has arranged for a son to manage the more complicated aspects of his finances. For the most part, Robert is enjoying life, surrounded by friends and remaining physically active. He occasionally gets embarrassed or frustrated by the memory loss, but seems able to brush it aside. He has no memory for the episodes of confusion, and thus is not embarrassed by them.

Robert's children are in close touch by phone. Reports of confused episodes are passed quickly through the informal "phone chain." As the decline has hastened, the children communicate more frequently, and family get-togethers are scheduled with increasing frequency. Although each child asks, "Is there something we can do?" the answer to date has been simply to have as much contact as possible with each other and their father. Both children and father know that the CCRC staff are observing and will intervene if necessary. Being in a CCRC guarantees that intermediate and skilled care are available if needed. The children are rediscovering each other and enjoying their close interactions, finding that they have more free time and emotional energy for each other in middle age. They want to make the best use of the remaining time with Dad. The family is united.

FACTORS IN NURSING
HOME PLACEMENT

Marge and Robert are individuals who are part of families that are part of social networks. Their families' experience of dementia, caregiving, and nursing home placement will be influenced by individual, family, and social characteristics and their interactions. Families are challenged from the first signs of dementia to nursing home placement. To predict whether they will react with disruption or unity will require understanding the characteristics of each element in the system.

Nursing home placement is a critical event in family caregiving. For most families, it is a reluctant choice, the culmination of an agonizing decision-making process. For the larger society, it is an expensive choice. Somewhat more than one third of the population will be admitted to a nursing home at some time during their life (Kemper & Murtaugh, 1991). Ten percent of all health-care dollars for the elderly are spent on nursing home care (Scitovsky, 1994). Because of the enormous cost to society, and the significant disruption it represents for families, the factors that predict a family's decision to place a member in a nursing home have been extensively studied.

INDIVIDUAL FACTORS IN NURSING HOME PLACEMENT

Numerous individual factors have been identified as predictors of nursing home placement. The strongest predictor of placement is age, with advanced age associated with placement at an accelerated rate (Foley et al., 1992; Greene & Ondrich, 1990; Wingard, Williams-Jones, McPhillips, Kaplan, & Barrett-Connor, 1990). Poor health status (Liu, McBride, & Coughlin, 1994; Morris, Sherwood, & Gutkin, 1988) and physical or cognitive impairment (Cohen, Tell, & Wallack, 1986; Jette, Branch, Sleeper, Feldman, & Sullivan, 1992) consistently predict nursing home placement. A combination of physical and cognitive impairments increases risk further (Foley et al., 1992). Living alone is a demonstrated risk factor for placement (Foley et al., 1992; Greene & Ondrich, 1990). However, Freedman, Berkman, Rapp, and Ostfeld (1994) found that men without spouses were at higher risk for placement regardless of contact with other family members; women without spouses reduced the risk for placement through contact with at least one family member. Intense feelings of loneliness (independent of social contact) have been shown to increase the likelihood of nursing home admission and to decrease the time until nursing home admission among rural elderly (Russell, Cutrona, de la Mora, & Wallace, 1997).

FAMILY FACTORS IN NURSING HOME PLACEMENT

High levels of instrumental support from family members are associated with lower risk for nursing home placement (Liu et al., 1994). However, family caregiver stress or the perception of the burden of caregiving increases a family's propensity for nursing home placement (Colerick & George, 1986; McFall & Miller, 1992; Morycz, 1985; Pruchno, Michaels, & Potashnik, 1990). Spouse caregivers are more likely to provide higher levels of care over longer periods of time than caregiving children (Colerick & George, 1986; Horowitz, 1985).

Family structure affects risk for placement, with the presence of a spouse, daughter, or sibling reducing the risk; the presence of a son did not affect risk. Pruchno et al. (1990) tested a two-factor model predicting nursing home placement. First, they identified several significant predictors of the "desire to institutionalize": age and education of caregiver, the spouse's forgetful behaviors, the ADL tasks done by the caregiver, medications taken by the caregiver, services used, and the quality of the relationship with the spouse. Second, they identified predictors of "actual institutionalization": the "desire to institutionalize," the length of time of caregiving, religion, uplifts, and forgetful behaviors.

Ethnic background is predictive of placement, with African American and Latino families using nursing homes significantly less than Caucasian families (Coughlin, McBride, & Liu, 1990; Greene & Ondrich, 1990; Liu et al., 1994). Connell and Gibson (1997), in a review of racial, ethnic, and cultural differences in dementia caregiving, found that non-White caregivers reported lower levels of caregiving stress, burden, and depression; endorsed more strongly held beliefs regarding filial support; and were more likely to use prayer, faith or religion to cope with the stress of caregiving.

SOCIAL FACTORS IN NURSING HOME PLACEMENT

Respite care is the primary community resource that has been studied for effect on nursing home placement. The role of the availability and use of respite care has been controversial. Although some research found little or no effect of respite care on placement decision (Lawton, Brody, & Saperstein, 1989; Montgomery & Borgatta, 1989), reanalysis of data with a different statistical methodology revealed that respite care did achieve an effect of modestly delaying placement (Kosloski & Montgomery, 1995).

FACTORS IN CAREGIVING STRESS

Much research has been devoted to understanding and predicting the community caregiving process. Most long-term care in the United States is provided by family members (McConnell & Riggs, 1994). What factors allow some caregiving families to continue to provide care in the community without undue burden or stress, while others become depleted or disrupted in the caregiving process?

Lawton, Moss, Kleban, Glicksman, and Rovine (1991) proposed a two-factor model of caregiving appraisal and psychological well-being. They investigated the effects of objective stressors, caregiver resources, and subjective appraisals of caregiving (including both satisfaction and burden) on positive affect and depression. For spouses, caregiving satisfaction was a significant determinant of positive affect, but not for children; for adult children, a high amount of caregiving behavior produced both increased satisfaction and also increased burden. Caregiving burden was related to depression for both spouses and children. The authors hypothesized that positive and negative aspects of caregiving contributed to analogous aspects of generalized psychological well-being, but not to opposite-valance outcomes.

Zarit's "stress process model" (Zarit & Whitlatch, 1992) posits primary and secondary effects of caregiving, with institutional placement having a large impact on the primary effects, such as reduction in feelings of overload and tension, and improvement in feelings of well-being. Nursing home placement had a lesser influence on the secondary effects of caregiving, leaving other indicators of stress unchanged.

Looking only at the negative affect side of caregiving, Fingerman, Gallagher-Thompson, Lovett, and Rose (1996) have identified "internal resourcefulness" (as measured by Rosenbaum's Self Control Schedule) as a key factor in protecting caregiving individuals from the effects of stress. Internal resourcefulness is defined as the repertoire of skills and behaviors that individuals employ to deal with negative affective states. The authors investigated the relationship of that factor to the demands of the caregiving situation, the caregiver's self-reported coping behaviors and changes in dysphoric affect over time. They found that internal resourcefulness was the only significant predictor of changes in dysphoric affect over time, with a decrease in dysphoric affect associated with possession of a larger initial set of internal resources to deal with the negative internal experiences of caregiving.

In an analysis of adult child caregivers of institutionalized elders with dementia, Crispi, Schiaffino, and Berman (1997) apply attachment theory to the caregiving process. They questioned whether either attachment traits or states affected either of two aspects of caregiver burden (caregiving difficulty and psychological symptomatology). The authors found that a secure attachment style (trait) is somewhat protective for caregivers from both aspects of caregiver burden. Preoccupation with attachment (state) contributes to psychological symptoms.

Looking at effects on both positive and negative effects of caregiving, Pruchno, Burant, and Peters (1997) studied the mediating effects of coping strategies. They found a differential effect, with personal coping strategies being the best predictors of depression, positive affect, and mastery for women and children; but for husbands, depression was predicted both by personal coping strategies and the coping strategies of their wives. Furthermore, the husbands' positive affect was predicted only by the coping strategy of their wives and children. These results support a complex family systems view of the effects of caregiving.

Recognizing the interdependence of caregivers' well-being and that of care receivers, Pruchno, Burant, and Peters (1997) investigated predictors of well-being of care receivers. They found that contributions made by older care receivers to other family members in a multigenerational household predicted a sense of personal control. The personal control, in turn, predicted psychological well-being of the care receiver. The authors found that the main determinant of being able to contribute to the family was physical health.

MARGE AND ROBERT'S FAMILIES: CLINICAL CONSIDERATIONS

The preceding research helps to identify factors that predict caregiving stress and nursing home placement. These issues sensitize the clinician to risk factors for caregiving families. But the clinician is aware that even if the dementia does not lead to nursing home placement, nor to caregiver stress, the family could suffer.

Let's return to our original example of Marge's family, with her daughter and son having bitter disagreements over her posthospital disposition. One outcome is that she could be fully cared for by her daughter in her daughter's town. This scenario, if executed without further work with the family, would lead to severe disruption of the daughter and son's relationship. Even if nursing home placement were avoided, and the daughter could cope successfully with the stress of caregiving, the unresolved conflict is a negative clinical outcome for the family.

A clinician working with caregiving families needs to analyze the specific factors in that caregiving situation that could lead to family conflict and/or opportunities for strengthening families. Comparing Marge and Robert's experiences with dementia reveals differences on several dimensions. First, *sudden versus gradual onset* of difficulty can influence the extent of family conflict. Although Marge had been exhibiting some cognitive impairment for two years, the stroke presented her family with a sudden-onset, crisis situation. Robert's gradual decline is allowing his family to slowly adjust and adapt, even using the illness to come closer together.

Second, the family's *responsibility for medical and placement decision making* influences the opportunity for conflict. When Marge's son and daughter expected her to die in the hospital from the stroke, they were united in their shock, fear, sadness, and guilt. Their primary responsibility was to be supportive. When her medical prognosis changed, their decision-making responsibilities increased dramatically, and the ambiguity allowed for the reemergence of old family conflicts. Robert's family expects more gradual decline. If a medical crisis should occur, they expect that the CCRC systems, including advance directives, will manage it. Because the CCRC was chosen by their parents, they do not perceive themselves as responsible for decision making. This lack of perceived responsibility allows the children to remain in a primarily supportive, less responsible role.

Third, and related to decision-making responsibility, is the extent to which the family members perceive that the frail member is unsafe. The *perception of parental safety* may be related to the physical environment (neighborhood, stairs, weather, trying to maintain too much house or yard) or to medical/mental condition (driving difficulties, leaving stove on, forgetting medication, fragile medical condition). Family conflicts frequently arise when there is a difference in perception of safety—either among siblings, or between siblings and parent(s). Marge's children felt under more pressure because of her fragile medical condition; Robert's children feel more relaxed because they perceive him to be in a safe environment without medical crisis.

A fourth factor in family conflict is the *adjustment capacity and personal style* of the individual parent. To the extent that the parent is relatively content, regardless of medical/mental condition, the family system remains more stable and free of conflict. A parent who is highly anxious, calling children frequently, depressed, complaining, or giving different information to different family members will destabilize the family system. Robert's generally high morale is more important for his children's well-being than the actual fact of his dementia.

A fifth factor in family conflict is the *historical structure and processes* of the family. Just as there is a great deal of stability to individual personality, family systems exert powerful homeostatic forces. If parents have exerted strong authority in the family, they are likely to continue to do so. If sibling roles were rigidly defined, they are likely to remain so. If conflict and cutoff were historically used as family process, they are likely to be used again. If the parental marriage has been strong, it is likely to remain so. Marge's children, having avoided sibling conflict for years through geographic distance, quickly revert to old patterns when her illness brings them together again. Robert's children find comfort in reestablishing the warm family ties of earlier years. Robert himself has found mechanisms (choosing a CCRC; advance directives) to maintain parental control even with a dementing illness. Through exploring the historical family dynamics, the clinician will quickly receive orientation to the current operating forces. While the diagnosis of dementia or the possibility of nursing home placement may place new stresses on the family, the system is likely to respond by using old roles and processes.

A sixth and final factor for the clinician to consider when working with caregiving families is the *availability of supportive resources.* Although the research on respite care yields mixed results, clinicians are aware that a rich network of support can significantly reduce the burden on caregiving family members, and thus reduce the disruptive pressures. Specific resources that are helpful to families are a wide variety of affordable residential options; medical care that is specific, or at least sensitive to, geriatric concerns; legal help, especially with difficult issues of decision-making capacity for those with dementing illnesses; programs for the elderly including full-service senior centers, adult day health centers, meals and transportation services, educational programs, and dementia support groups; spiritual and religious programs and services; and all the informal supports that neighbors, friends, and extended family might provide. Both the family and the clinician's role are significantly easier when such community supports are available. Conversely, in more rural, isolated, or impoverished areas, the family may have to absorb the caregiving burden with less support, and thus be at greater risk for disruption and conflict. In Marge's hometown, the only alternatives were living at home or going into a nursing home; it was partly this lack of alternatives that stimulated the sibling conflict. Robert's CCRC provides residential alternatives as well as informal and formal support services. This makes it relatively easy to adapt his lifestyle to declining mental function.

INDICATORS OF FAMILY DISRUPTION

Up to this point, we have been discussing the predictors, risk factors, or causes of family disruption related to dementia or nursing home placement. When a family or family member(s) are with the clinician, how does one identify the presence of family distress? What are the signs and symptoms of a family that is not coping well with dementia and its sequelae?

Spouse caregivers are most likely to complain, especially in the early stages of a dementing illness, about the loss of function. The author has heard a wife complaining that her husband no longer discusses "Wall Street Week" to her satisfaction; and children arguing over whether the declining quality of mother's watercolor paintings are the fault of the day center art therapist. Later in the dementing process, families are more likely to argue about bizarre, challenging, or dangerous behaviors.

The signs of a family in distress are dynamics of blaming, accusing, inducing guilt, distancing, and denying the problem. These dynamics can lead to (or exacerbate pre-existing) sibling feuds or couple feuds. Grandchildren may react to a caregiving situation by entering into the situation as problem-solvers and helpers, or by distancing and acting out. Adult child caregivers (usually women) may start having difficulties on the job, as they are increasingly burdened to juggle multiple roles and responsibilities. Spouses of adult child caregivers (usually men) may become resentful of decreasing time and energy spent on the marriage; he may distance or seek other relationships. A caregiving spouse or family may become isolated from the community, especially as challenging or embarrassing behaviors interfere with previous avenues for socialization. Families may resort to substance use (alcohol, sleeping medication, antianxiety medication) to cope with caregiving stress. The substance use can exacerbate other difficulties and induce dependence or addiction.

ASSESSMENT OF FAMILY DISRUPTION

A clinician who perceives signs of family distress should attempt an assessment. As with all family work, it is often difficult to gather all the individual members or to get compliance with an assessment. It is also true with caregiving families, as with many distressed families, that key family members will often refuse to participate in a therapeutic process. Nevertheless, the clinician can take a family *perspective*, even if only one or several family members are actually present.

Any family member who expresses significant distress should be evaluated individually for the presence of a clinical condition, usually depression, anxiety, substance disorder, or a combination. Individual assessment and treatment can proceed concurrently with family treatment.

Family assessment should begin with the current situation, and use appropriate methods from family therapy. Identify each family member's perspective on the problem, the cause, the resources, and possible solutions. Attempt to surface the previously unvoiced hopes and expectations of each member. Set rules prohibiting blaming, accusing, or deriding the contributions of others. Discourage jumping to conclusions or solutions. Use active listening or other communication techniques if family members seem unable or unwilling to listen to each other's perspectives.

The therapist's role is to identify the scope and severity of the problem(s); to identify possible outcomes, both positive and negative, if the problem is/is not addressed; to summarize needs, and to identify additional needs that the family has not identified; to summarize available resources, and to identify additional resources that the family has not identified. Possible solutions can be identified, but should not be extensively discussed or evaluated in the assessment period. In addition to this "public" role, the therapist should be quietly identifying the strengths in the family; the potential obstacles to problem solving; the members who are not present, and why; the family's history of success or difficulty with problem-solving; and any personal or family dynamics that would be threatened by successful resolution of the presenting problems (and would therefore stimulate sabotage of resolution).

Perhaps the most difficult assessment task that the therapist faces is an estimate of what it is possible to change in the family, and what changes the family will resist. As mentioned earlier, family systems include powerful forces to maintain the status quo. The therapist should aim for a strategy that requires the minimum change to accomplish necessary and consensual goals. Using the example of Marge's family, it may be possible to get the son and daughter to agree that Marge needs to be safe and well cared for. They may agree to a trial period while she continues her recuperation from the stroke, but to keep the final decision about hometown versus daughter's town for later. The therapist may assess the sibling relationship as historically contentious and unlikely to change to a positive, cooperative relationship. The goal of therapy will be to keep the son and daughter negotiating well enough, and the decisions small and short-term enough, to avoid a major schism. Not only would a full break represent a negative clinical outcome—in the sense of a family overcome by disruption—but it also potentially leads to increased legal activity and costs. Furthermore, energy expended on sibling battles is energy *not* devoted to Marge and her care.

TREATMENT APPROACHES

Treatment for family members caring for someone with dementia have ranged from formal individual, group or family psychotherapy to informal support groups. Formal therapeutic treatments employ psychotherapeutic modalities to address a diagnosed mental disorder in the caregivers, usually depression or anxiety. Informal support groups, such as those conducted by the Alzheimer's Association, are more typically educational and supportive. There are positive outcomes reported for all of these approaches.

Several intervention models have been developed and tested, usually including a combination of information, stress management skills, problem-solving skills (especially for difficult behaviors), and support. The therapy can be delivered in an individual, family, or group therapy format. A cognitive-behavioral approach developed by Teri and Gallagher-Thompson uses cognitive and behavioral therapy to address depression in the family member with dementia and a comorbid depression. Gallagher-Thompson has reported favorable results with interventions with community caregivers (Gallagher-Thompson & DeVries, 1994; Gallagher-Thompson & Steffen, 1994), while Buckwalter, Maas, and Reed (1997) report on interventions with family and staff during the transition into nursing home placement. Mittelman, Ferris, Shulman, Steinberg, and Levin (1996) describe a randomized controlled trial of a 6-session intervention for family caregivers that consisted of individual and family counseling and support. The authors demonstrated that the family intervention significantly increased the time remaining at home before institutionalization for the treatment group compared with the control group.

In the early stages of dementia, families and the affected elders usually need a great deal of information and support. They need to understand the disease, to come to terms with the prognosis, to think through and act on medical and legal issues, to discuss plans for the future, and to do everything possible to maximize the individual's autonomy and decision making while still capable. Books, videos, support groups, Internet resources, and an exploration of community resources are valuable to most families in the early stages of the disease. Families may struggle with some members who deny that there is a problem—"Mom's always been a little forgetful!" Family disagreements about diagnosis and prognosis can usually be settled with the help of a geriatric multidisciplinary assessment team. Such a team may also provide follow-up care management services. Families may need help with the sensitive issues of exactly what to tell whom about the disease and disease process.

As the dementia progresses, the needs of the family change. Day-to-day care becomes more burdensome. The family caregiver(s) and elder may become more isolated from social supports. More challenging and difficult behaviors may emerge. The family member(s) may become more disturbed as they see their loved one increasingly "slipping away." Family caregiver depression, anger, frustration, and exhaustion may set in. At this stage, the family is likely to need professional help more than in the earlier stages.

Many families who care for dementing elders do so right up to death, and report many "uplifts" as well as "burdens." Therapists should never assume that caregiving leads inevitably to depression or family conflict, although it is not uncommon. In one study (Schulz, Newsom, Mittelmark, Burton, Hirsch, & Jackson, 1997), the authors found that while 80% of persons living with a spouse with a disability provide care, only one-half of the caregivers reported mental or physical strain associated with caregiving.

CONCLUSION

Family caregivers have been perceived in the past as "hidden victims" of dementia, long-suffering and struggling with stress and burden. In a more recent view, they are seen as the heroic solution to the demographic nightmare of Baby Boomer Alzheimer's disease. In both views and in much of the caregiving research, the relationship is usually described as a caregiver-care receiver dyad. This chapter attempts to present a fuller family and social systems view of the care relationship. This systems view can be useful clinically: it is necessary to appreciate the strength of the supportive system surrounding the primary caregiver, and also the dynamic forces that can lead to negative clinical outcomes for spouses, siblings, and grandchildren. It suggests that interventions can be targeted to the primary caregiver, but also to the family system as a whole. The underlying assumption is that strengthening and supporting the entire family will ultimately lead to better outcomes for all its members.

There are social implications of this perspective. Currently, the medical care reimbursement systems in the United States are designed to diagnose and treat individual illnesses. For chronic, progressive, and debilitating diseases like dementia, a system that promotes family health and treats family distress may prove to be the most humane and ultimately the most cost-effective.

REFERENCES

Buckwalter, K.C., Maas, M., & Reed, D. (1997). Assessing family and staff caregiver outcomes in Alzheimer's disease research. *Alzheimer's Disease and Associated Disorders, 11*(Suppl. 6), 105–116.

Cohen, M.A., Tell, E.J., & Wallack, S.S. (1986). Patient-related factors of nursing home entry among elderly adults. *Journal of Gerontology, 41,* 785–792.

Colerick, E.J., & George, L.K. (1986). Predictors of institutionalization among caregivers of patients with Alzheimer's disease. *Journal of the American Geriatrics Society, 32,* 493–498.

Connell, C.M., & Gibson, G.D. (1997). Racial, ethnic, and cultural differences in dementia caregiving: Review and analysis. *Gerontologist, 37,* 355–364.

Coughlin, T.A., McBride, T.D., & Liu, K. (1990). Determinants of transitory and permanent nursing home admissions. *Medical Care, 28,* 616–631.

Crispi, E.L., Schiaffino, K., & Berman, W.H. (1997). The contribution of attachment to burden in adult children of institutionalized parents with dementia. *Gerontologist, 37,* 52–60.

Fingerman, K.L., Gallagher-Thompson, D., Lovett, S., & Rose, J. (1996). Internal resourcefulness, task demands, coping and dysphoric affect among caregivers of the frail elderly. *International Journal of Aging and Human Development, 42,* 229–248.

Foley, D.J., Ostfeld, A.M., Branch, L.G., Wallace, R.B., McGloin, J., & Cornoni-Huntley, J.C. (1992). The risk of nursing home admission in three communities. *Journal of Aging and Health, 4,* 155–173.

Freedman, V.A., Berkman, L.F., Rapp, S.R., & Ostfeld, A.M. (1994). Measuring behavioral disturbance of elderly demented patients in the community and its effects on relatives: A factor analytic study. *Age and Aging, 11,* 121–126.

Gallagher-Thompson, D., & DeVries, H.M. (1994). "Coping with frustration" classes: Development and preliminary outcomes with women who care for relatives with dementia. *Gerontologist, 34,* 548–552.

Gallagher-Thompson, D., & Steffen, A.M. (1994). Comparative effects of cognitive-behavioral and brief psychodynamic psychotherapies for depressed family caregivers. *Journal of Consulting and Clinical Psychology, 62,* 543–549.

Greene, V.L., & Ondrich, J.I. (1990). Risk factors for nursing home admissions and exits: A discrete-time hazard function approach. *Journal of Gerontology: Social Sciences, 45,* S250–S258.

Horowitz, A. (1985). Family caregiving to the frail elderly. *Annual Review of Gerontology and Geriatrics,* 194–246.

Jette, A.M., Branch, L.G., Sleeper, L.A., Feldman, H., & Sullivan, L.M. (1992). High-risk profiles for nursing home admission. *Gerontologist, 32,* 634–640.

Kemper, P., & Murtaugh, C.M. (1991). Lifetime use of nursing home care. *New England Journal of Medicine, 324,* 595–600.

Kosloski, K., & Montgomery, R.J.V. (1995). The impact of respite use on nursing home placement. *Gerontologist, 35,* 67–74.

Lawton, M.P., Brody, E., & Saperstein, A. (1989). A controlled study of respite service for caregivers of Alzheimer's patients. *Gerontologist, 29,* 8–16.

Lawton, M.P., Moss, M., Kleban, M.H., Glicksman, A., & Rovine, M. (1991). A two-factor model of caregiving appraisal and psychological well-being. *Journal of Gerontology, 46,* P181–P189.

Liu, K., McBride, T., & Coughlin, T. (1994). Risk of entering nursing homes for long versus short stays. *Medical Care, 32,* 315–327.

McConnell, S., & Riggs, J.A. (1994). A public policy agenda: Supporting family caregiving. In M. Cantor (Ed.), *Family caregiving: Agenda for the future.* San Francisco: American Society on Aging.

McFall, S., & Miller, B.H. (1992). Caregiver burden and nursing home admission of frail elderly person. *Journal of Gerontology: Social Services, 42,* S73–S79.

Mittelman, M.S., Ferris, S.H., Shulman, E., Steinberg, G., & Levin, B. (1996). A family intervention to delay nursing home placement of patients with Alzheimer's disease: A randomized controlled trial. *Journal of the American Medical Association, 276,* 1725–1731.

Montgomery, R.J., & Borgatta, E.F. (1989). Effects of alternative support strategies. *Gerontologist, 29,* 456–464.

Morris, J.N., Sherwood, S., & Gutkin, C.E. (1988). Inst-risk: II. An approach to forecasting relative risk of future institutional placement. *Health Services Research, 23,* 511–536.

Morycz, R.K. (1985). Caregiving strain and the desire to institutionalize family members with Alzheimer's disease. *Research on Aging, 7,* 329–361.

Pruchno, R.A., Burant, C.J., & Peters, N.D. (1997). Coping strategies of people living in multigenerational households: Effects on well-being. *Psychology and Aging, 12,* 115–124.

Pruchno, R.A., Michaels, J.E., & Potashnik, S.L. (1990). Predictors of institutionalization among Alzheimer disease victims with caregiving spouses. *Journal of Gerontology: Social Sciences, 45,* S259–S266.

Russell, D.W., Cutrona, C.E., de la Mora, A., & Wallace, R.B. (1997). Loneliness and nursing home admission among rural older adults. *Psychology and Aging, 12,* 574–589.

Schulz, R., Newsom, J., Mittelmark, M., Burton, L., Hirsch, C., & Jackson, S. (1997). Health effects of caregiving: The caregiving health effects study: An ancillary study of cardiovascular health study. *Annals of Behavioral Medicine, 19,* 110–116.

Scitovsky, A.A. (1994). "The high cost of dying" revisited. *Milbank Quarterly, 72,* 561–591.

Teri, L., & Gallagher-Thompson, D. (1991). Cognitive-behavioral interventions for treatment of depression in Alzheimer's patients. *Gerontologist, 31,* 413–416.

Wingard, D.L., Williams-Jones, D., McPhillips, J., Kaplan, R.M., & Barrett-Connor, E. (1990). Nursing home utilization in adults. *Journal of Aging and Health, 2,* 179–193.

Zarit, S.H., & Whitlatch, C.J. (1992). Institutional placement: Phases of the transition. *Gerontologist, 32,* 665–672.

CHAPTER 18

Sexual Dysfunction: Using an Interdisciplinary Team to Combine Cognitive-Behavioral and Medical Approaches

Antonette M. Zeiss and Robert A. Zeiss

The effects of normal, healthy aging on sexuality are a mystery to most people, and a rarely contemplated mystery at that. When asked, college students estimate that aging leads to a gradual, but fairly steep, decline in sexual activity over every decade of age after 20 to 30 years (A. Zeiss, 1982). These expectations of decline are even more dramatic when college students consider their parents' decline, rather than their expectations for the average aging couple. Elders, when asked about their own knowledge, report having received little or no information from health care providers, the media, family, or other older adults (Wiley & Bortz, 1996). Many health care providers lack knowledge about sexuality, particularly in relation to age (Hillman & Stricker, 1994).

In the spring of 1998, we all experienced a reversal of the pattern of invisibility of sex among older adults, when the drug Viagra (sildenafil) was released as a treatment for male erection problems. Suddenly the media was full of older men (and occasionally women) championing this therapy and openly discussing its relevance to their lives. A prominent testimonial came from Elizabeth Dole, the wife of Robert Dole, who had been the Republican candidate for President in the 1996 election. She revealed that he had been a participant in one of the drug trials leading to the release of Viagra, and she extolled its effectiveness and importance. Quickly, Viagra became the most successful drug release in U.S. history, and the issues of sexuality and treatment of sexual problems in older adults had come out of the closet. A review of what is currently known about these topics could not be more timely.

PHYSICAL CHANGES IN SEXUALITY WITH AGING

The first and most important thing to understand and constantly remember about sexuality and aging is that aging is a gradual and highly individual process. None of the effects described here can be associated with a specific age; they occur gradually and with great variability. Some women may enter menopause at age 40 and others at 55; some men may have changes in ejaculation at age 50 and others at 80. In addition, all of the changes associated with normal aging to be described are less likely to occur, or occur much less intensely, for those who stay sexually active. The processes described here are intended as guidelines for what a clinician might attend to in working with older people, not a fixed set of norms.

Changes for both women and men are summarized in Table 18.1; most of the evidence for this review is presented in Masters and Johnson (1966) with additions from other more recent sources as relevant (Bachmann & Leiblum, 1991; Schiavi, Schreiner-Engel, Mandeli, Schanzer, & Cohen, 1990; Sherwin, 1991). Some key elements of the table are summarized below.

The marked shift in hormones during menopause may result in changes in sexual response. The most common concern of postmenopausal women is pain with intercourse or any vaginal penetration. Loss of estrogen can result in vaginal walls becoming thinner and decrease their capacity to provide lubrication in response to sexual stimulation. In addition, all changes in response to stimulation become slower with advancing age.

Taking more time for foreplay can compensate for slower sexual response. Estrogen replacement therapy is an option for many women and should be discussed by women and their physicians. Such hormone replacement therapy (HRT) usually improves vaginal wall health and lubrication (although it may pose other risks and should be carefully evaluated for each person). Alternatively, educating women about artificial vaginal lubricants, such as Astroglide or Replens can address problems caused by reduced estrogen. Another source of vaginal pain occurs if the cervix has descended into the vagina—cervical bumping during intercourse can be very painful. Couples can experiment with positions for intercourse that involve less deep penetration. In some cases, surgery may be considered to correct cervical prolapse. Finally, as mentioned earlier, staying sexually active slows and diminishes the problems associated with normal aging, even without HRT.

Many elderly women also find that vaginal penetration is more difficult. One common contributor to this problem is that with advancing age, the vaginal lips, or labia, do not fully elevate during sexual arousal to create the funnel-like entrance toward the vagina seen in younger women. Instead, the labia act as folds of skin covering the vaginal entry, blocking penetration. Most aging women

Table 18.1 Physical changes in sexuality with health aging, by sex.

Types of Changes	Men	Women
1. Basic physical changes	↓ Testosterone	↓ Estrogen & progesterone
	↓ Spermatogenesis	↑ FSH, LH
	↓ Size of testes	↓ Testosterone
	↑ Size of prostate	↓ Thickness & elasticity of vagina
	↓ Strength of prostatic contractions	↓ Vaginal lubrication
	↓ Viscosity & volume of seminal fluid	↓ Size of cervix, uterus, ovaries
2. Impact on the arousal cycle		
a. Excitement phase	Slowed response	Slowed response
	Longer direct penile stimulation required for erection	Genital vasocongestion reduced
	Erection less firm	Reduced lubrication → intercourse may be painful
b. Plateau phase	Longer plateau phase	Reduced uterine elevation
	Decreased preejaculatory fluid	Reduced elevation of the major labia
c. Orgasm phase	Shorter duration	Shorter duration
	Weaker and fewer orgasmic contractions	Weaker and fewer orgasmic contractions
	Reduced amount of semen and ejaculatory force	Clitoral response intact
d. Resolution phase	Increased speed of return to prestimulation state	Increased speed of return to prestimulation state
	Longer refractory period	Multiorgasmic capacity retained

report that clitoral response remains, and clitoral stimulation continues in importance as a prelude to orgasm. Women may report age-related changes in orgasm. Orgasm itself may be shorter, with weaker and fewer vaginal contractions and shorter duration of general body involvement in the orgasmic experience. However, women typically retain multiorgasmic ability.

Although aging men do not experience a marked change like menopause, they do report gradual changes similar to those experienced by women. Men need more direct stimulation of the penis for an erection; they also experience changes in nocturnal erections (Kahn & Fisher, 1969). With age, erection also may take longer, and maximum erection may be less than 100%, compared with younger years. For sex with female partners, reduced erection combined with the woman's reduced lubrication and limited labial elevation may make penetration for intercourse difficult. For most men, whose erection will be around 75% to 90% of maximum, this can be easily solved by using a hand to guide the penis into the vagina and vaginal lubricant for ease and comfort of intercourse.

In older men, stimulation usually must continue for a longer period to reach orgasm (a potential boon for men who had very rapid ejaculation when younger). For men, as for women, orgasm consists of fewer and weaker contractions, as well as reduced general body response. In addition, ejaculatory force and amount of semen may be reduced. Some men believe that a woman feels ejaculate as it spurts into the vagina and that this contributes greatly to her sexual satisfaction, although this is not typically reported by women. Men who believe this can worry about their ability to excite and satisfy a partner.

After ejaculation or orgasm, older men return to the prearoused state more rapidly than when younger. In addition, the refractory period (time period when a man cannot be restimulated to erection) may last hours or even days, whereas in younger men it may be just a few minutes.

As mentioned earlier, all of these changes are less dramatic for men and women who remain sexually active. This is sometimes referred to as the "use it or lose it" phenomenon, a somewhat misleading label, since to some it implies a permanent loss. In fact, after a period of sexual inactivity, these changes will be much more pronounced; however, it is likely that most older adults can regain improved sexual response if they return to consistent sexual activity. As a preventive measure, clinicians may want to advise patients of the sexual health benefits of remaining sexually active. Women over 60 who continue partner sexual activity are likely to experience vaginal lubrication as rapidly as younger women. In addition, postmenopausal women having intercourse three times a month or more are less likely to have a vagina that becomes smaller (shorter and narrower) than their sexually inactive counterparts. Women without a partner who masturbate regularly may also experience fewer physical changes in the vagina and more rapid vaginal lubrication (Bachmann & Leiblum, 1991).

Age-related changes are significant and meaningful, but they do not, in themselves, cause a person's sex life to end. An older adult may need to plan for more time in a sexual encounter, be sensitive to changes in his or her own body and a partner's body, and use aids such as lubricants or vibrators to increase stimulation. An older adult may want to emphasize sexual activities other than intercourse. For example, oral stimulation may be an excellent prelude to intercourse by increasing genital lubrication, or it may be an end in itself, for a woman who has pain during intercourse. Older adults benefit when they can talk about these changes, be flexible in their thinking about the timing and nature of sexual contacts, and be creative in working out activities that fit their own unique pattern of age-related changes.

BEHAVIORAL CHANGES WITH AGING

It is not always easy to be so flexible and to talk so openly about sexual changes and possible adaptations in sexual behavior. Many of us, at all ages, are uncomfortable talking candidly about sex, and few have been encouraged to think creatively and flexibly about sexuality. Strong emotions are generated around sexuality, making it even harder to think clearly and speak openly when changes occur, especially if change results in some failure experiences. It would not be surprising, then, if the actual sexual behavior of older adults showed more change than would follow logically from the previously described physical changes.

Most early research on sexual behavior and aging used a cross-sectional methodology, assessing the sexual activity levels of couples in each decade from their 20s or 30s to their 80s or 90s (summarized in A. Zeiss, 1982). In such research, one pattern was found repeatedly: a gradual but inexorable declining pattern of sexual activity, averaging across all individuals or couples reporting in each decade of life. However, averaging data in this way may obscure the reality for particular individuals or couples. Longitudinal research is needed to learn about patterns of activity over time and to understand events associated with changes in activity over the life span. In the only published longitudinal study to date (George & Weiler, 1981), couples who were initially in late middle age to early old age were followed for 10 years. The most common pattern reported was a level of sexual activity maintained at whatever that couples' baseline level had been (baseline levels, of course, vary greatly across different couples). The second most common pattern was for couples to maintain sexual activity until a point of sudden, dramatic decline or cessation of sexual activity. Other patterns, such as increases over time, or an oscillating pattern of increases and decreases, were reported by a small minority of couples studied. If one looked at these data in the way typically done in cross-sectional research, by averaging over all couples in the study, the inevitable statistical result of the two most common patterns would be a steady, gradually decreasing decline; however, this statistical average would obscure the true patterns: stability for most; a sudden catastrophic decline, at variable time periods, for a subset of older couples.

For those couples who experienced a sharp decline in sexual activity, the precipitating factor was usually a change in the male partner. When men died, their wives usually ceased all sexual activity. When men developed a medical problem that interfered with erections, the couple usually ceased all sexual activity. Reversing the genders did not have the same result. When wives died, their husbands often remained sexually active, either in masturbation or with a new partner. When wives developed medical problems that made sexual activity more difficult, most couples remained sexually active. Thus, both genders acted as if they believed that men must have erections for older adults to have satisfactory sexual lives. When health problems affected erection, many couples apparently did not communicate, plan, or change their behavior; instead they gave up on sex. Medical problems, especially in men, play a major role in sexual function in older couples, but the changes in behavior are also the result of a psychosocial construction of sexuality that emphasizes the passive, receptive role of women and the presumed centrality of intercourse in sexual expression (George & Weiler, 1981; Marsiglio & Donnelly, 1991; Teisler, 1996; Weizman & Hart, 1987).

SEXUAL DYSFUNCTION

The social construction of sexuality turns out to be central to the way in which sexual dysfunction is defined and experienced in older adults, also (Teisler, 1996). A sample case helps to illustrate some basic points (in this case and all others, identities are thoroughly disguised). Brian, 72, and Frieda, 70, have been married for 50 years. Brian has a history of high blood pressure and osteoarthritis. Frieda went through menopause at age 51 and has never been on hormone replacement therapy. Medically, she has a history of diabetes. Brian complains that he cannot get an erection better than about 50%, which rarely allows penetration and only with difficulty. Often he loses his erection after penetration. He says, "I guess I'm just getting too old. Things just don't work the way they used to. This isn't fair to my wife; I'm worried she's missing out on something. Why should she stick around with such a useless husband?" Frieda responds, "My husband thinks about sex all the time. I don't see what the big deal is. Why can't he just understand that I'm not upset with him if he can't get an erection. It's kind of a relief anyway—intercourse is pretty difficult for me these days."

As with Brian, the most frequent complaint of the aging male is erectile dysfunction. Although figures vary considerably depending on age and specific population, the prevalence of this difficulty ranges from 55% to 95% of men over the age of 70 (Feldman, Goldstein, Hatzichristou, Krane, & McKinlay, 1994; Schover, 1986). Current usage advocates avoiding the term "impotence." Much like the old label "frigidity" for female dysfunction, "impotence" is an imprecise, pejorative, and value-laden term. Instead, it is preferable to use more descriptive terms like erectile dysfunction or erectile disorder or, even better, more specific labels, such as difficulty obtaining erection or difficulty maintaining erection.

In older women, as with Frieda, the most common sexual complaint is painful intercourse, a condition called dyspareunia (Schover, 1986). This is a problem for about one in three sexually active women over 65. As with Brian and Frieda, a level of interest in sex discrepant from the partner's is also a common cause for complaint (LoPiccolo & Heiman, 1988). In older adults, this can reflect a change in level of desire for one partner, such that a long-standing equilibrium is destabilized, or it may have been true of the couple throughout their relationship. Sexual desire disorders can represent as many as 50% of sexual complaints, often in conjunction with other problems, such as loss of erection or dyspareunia.

Although less common, older adults may present with other sexual dysfunctions, including rapid ejaculation, delayed ejaculation, lack of orgasm, and orgasm without pleasure, to name a few.

CAUSES OF SEXUAL DYSFUNCTION

Causes of sexual function problems are many and include a wide range of psychological and medical factors, including relationship issues, intrapersonal issues (such as difficulty accepting aging), psychopathologies, grief, adjustment to illness or loss of a partner, medical problems such as diabetes or cardiovascular disease, and treatments such as surgeries and medications. None of these factors are exclusive to older adults, but the prevalence of many of them increases with age. The following sections provide an overview of some of the most prevalent concerns related to sexual dysfunction in the elderly.

PSYCHOLOGICAL ISSUES

Psychological issues are seldom the sole cause of serious sexual dysfunction in elders, particularly those in a stable, long-standing relationship. In a review of 195 men with sexual dysfunction (R. Zeiss, Delmonico, Zeiss, & Dornbrand, 1991), only 10% were identified with solely psychologically caused sexual complaints. Psychological issues, however, do seem to play contributing roles in the development, maintenance, and resistance to treatment of sexual problems in older adults. In the same sample described above, 90% of patients seen had psychological factors that at least contributed to or exacerbated their sexual problems; for 80% there were both medical and psychological factors.

Psychological concerns frequently associated with sexual problems in the elderly include cultural stereotypes, intrapersonal issues, and changes in roles (Feldman et al., 1994; Malatesta, Chambless, Pollack, & Cantor, 1988; Schover, 1986). Ageist stereotypes are widespread, particularly the notions that older adults are not sexually attractive, that older adults are not sexually active or interested, and that there is something wrong with those who are. Stereotypes defining intercourse as the only "normal" sexual activity also have been mentioned. This belief can lead older men with erection problems, who are otherwise healthy, vibrant human beings, to avoid social or romantic relationships and fear that no woman could ever be interested "if I can't have sex the right way." Such pervasive cultural norms interfere with normal sexual interests and desires older adults might experience and seriously impair their abilities to express sexuality or even affection.

Anxiety can have an important negative impact on sex, although research shows that Masters and Johnson's (1966) original formulation of the role of anxiety in disrupting sexual function is too simplistic (e.g., Cranston-Cuebas, Barlow, Mitchell, & Athanasiou, 1993). For example, many men who have one experience of difficulty getting or maintaining an erection develop the fear that this will occur in every future sexual encounter. This creates a self-fulfilling prophecy: it becomes almost impossible to respond with interest and arousal because all attention is diverted to worrisome thoughts (Barlow, 1986; Cranston-Cuebas et al., 1993). Anxiety also affects older individuals, often women, for whom pain is a sexual problem. Fear of pain often develops in response to the pain itself, exacerbating tension in sexual encounters and possibly even increasing the level of pain.

Both sexes experience changes in body image with aging. Some of these coincide with aging, such as wrinkling skin, loss of hair, sagging breasts, or loss of muscle tone. Changes related to disease may be more dramatic, involving function and appearance. Illnesses such as heart disease or lung disease, for example, can lead to loss of stamina, while cancer might necessitate a mastectomy. With the cultural equation of sexuality and youth, it is not surprising that an older person, especially someone medically compromised, would find it difficult to overcome changes in body image and maintain an identity as a sexually active person.

One pattern of erectile dysfunction in older men has been described as "widower's syndrome." Some men still in the grief process after losing a partner feel pressure to be sexually active with a new potential partner, often a long-term personal friend (Morley & Kaiser, 1993). Often this follows a period of sexual inactivity, during the wife's terminal illness or after her death. When a man gives in to pressure to resume sexual activity with a partner before emotionally and physically ready, erectile difficulties can ensue, setting off a vicious cycle in which he defines himself as "impotent," with all the negative connotations of that label.

Another psychological barrier has to do with changes in roles in a long-standing relationship, as a result of changes in health status or the assumption of a patient or caregiver role. The transition from an equal partnership to one of caregiver and patient is never easy and, particularly if there is a lack of communication around sexual issues, sexual relationship changes may never be adequately worked out (Davies, Zeiss, & Tinklenberg, 1992).

Psychological disorders go beyond common sexual worries and self-doubts to reflect more pervasive concerns. In research at one sexual dysfunction clinic for the elderly, 52% of male patients had a psychological disorder that was diagnosable by *DSM-III-R* standards (American Psychiatric Association, 1987; R. Zeiss et al., 1991). Some disorders, particularly depression and alcohol abuse or dependence, were prevalent. However, the prevalence of diagnosable anxiety disorders, severe psychopathology, personality disorders, and dementia was fairly low in this population. These findings are mirrored in those of other sexual dysfunction clinics (Kaiser, 1994).

Considering psychological barriers with the case described earlier, Brian seems to be particularly affected by depression and performance anxiety. His depression is expressed in statements that he is a "useless husband" while his anxiety is expressed in his fear that his wife might not "stick around" because he cannot satisfy her. He holds these beliefs tenaciously, despite her assertion to the interviewers that she is uninterested in sex and glad not to be approached for intercourse. Thus, there also may be some difficulty for this couple in talking openly to each other about sex.

Frieda overemphasizes her husband's concern about sex: "He thinks about sex all the time." This may reflect her acceptance of sexual stereotypes that older people should no longer be interested in sex. In addition, either of them may be having body image problems related to aging and their health problems.

Although psychological considerations are important in this case, as with most older adults experiencing sexual dysfunction, physical problems are of at least equal importance. Sexual problems in older adults almost always result from a combination of factors, both psychological and medical. This is certainly true for the couple in this example, for whom psychosocial factors, menopause, and medical problems all combined to create the final set of sexual complaints. We turn now to a brief consideration of some common physical factors associated with sexual dysfunction in the elderly.

MEDICAL PROBLEMS

Many physical systems are involved in sexual function; thus, a huge array of illnesses and treatments can disrupt it. Despite the association of many medical conditions with sexual dysfunctions, in most cases a direct link between medical problems and the presenting sexual dysfunction cannot be definitively determined. Instead, educated guesses are made, based on the information available. Health care providers need to obtain information about medical problems, surgical history, and medications to identify problems that may contribute to the presenting complaints. It also is helpful to keep in mind that the initial causes of problems may not be the maintaining factors. For example, an erection problem may start with blood pressure medication, but be maintained because of psychosocial problems (e.g., fear of failure or disruption of a sexual relationship) after the initial medication is stopped. In the study cited earlier (R. Zeiss et al., 1991), which examined patterns of etiology for elderly male patients in a sexual dysfunction clinic, only 10% of patients had solely medical problems associated with their sexual dysfunction (mirroring the number who had only psychological problems). As stated earlier, 80% had a combination of both medical and psychosocial problems apparently related to the onset and/or maintenance of the sexual dysfunction.

Cardiovascular diseases, including hypertension, coronary artery disease, arrhythmias, and heart failure are the leading contributors to sexual dysfunction in men and probably in women also, although little research is available with women (Kaiser, 1994). In men, vascular disease can contribute to decreased blood flow to the penis, accounting for as much as a third of erectile dysfunction cases. Sex therapists and researchers assume that the increased blood flow responsible for penile erection is also responsible for vaginal lubrication, but no data are available on the effects of atherosclerosis on women's sexual functioning.

Diabetes is notorious for its link to erectile dysfunction, and problems can occur at any stage of the illness (Kaiser, 1994). Diabetes also may cause semen to be ejaculated into the bladder rather than being expelled out the penis, a condition called retrograde ejaculation. Despite the change in ejaculation, orgasm still occurs for most diabetic men, usually with undiminished pleasure. Rapid ejaculation also can be associated with diabetes, without affecting orgasm. Diabetic men and their partners often do not attribute these sexual side affects to diabetes, and many couples give up reaching sexual satisfaction once erection is inconsistent. Couples who continue to provide each other sexual pleasure to orgasm despite the impact of diabetes have a better prognosis for working out an effective solution to the erection problem.

Diabetes in women may be associated with sexual problems also, including desire disorders, reduced vaginal lubrication, and painful intercourse (Kaiser, 1994). Because these are common problems for older women, the role of diabetes is not clearly understood; the incidence of these problems may be no greater than in the general population. Research into the impact of diabetes on women continues and is much needed to help our understanding of the problems faced by women with this disease.

Decreased amounts of the hormone testosterone are typically associated with diminished sexual desire in both sexes (Schiavi, Schreiner-Engel, White, & Mandell, 1991; Sherwin, Gelfand, & Brender, 1985) and, to some extent, with decreased erections for men and decreased orgasmic capacity for women. While age typically brings a decrease in testosterone for both men and women, the level ordinarily remains within the normal range, and it is uncommon to see older men with testosterone at abnormally low levels. When abnormally low levels are found, testosterone replacement can be a very effective treatment. However, supplementing testosterone in older men can result in a dramatic increase in sexual desire and general well-being, without improvement in erectile capability if other medical or psychosocial problems are present (Korenman, Morley, et al., 1990). Treatment must include other components for these men and their partners.

Testosterone also seems to be responsible for sexual desire in women, and supplementing low levels of testosterone in women can lead to dramatic renewal of interest in sex as well as resumption of preexisting orgasmic responsiveness (Sherwin, 1991). Some practitioners, particularly in Europe, have begun recommending judicious testosterone replacement for postmenopausal women.

For men, the likelihood of developing prostate cancer increases directly with age. Treatment for prostate cancer is likely to have serious sexual effects, including erection and ejaculation problems. Even more common for older men is enlargement of the prostate without cancer, a condition known as benign prostatic hypertrophy. A common surgical treatment, called transurethral resection of the prostate (TURP), involves entering the urethra with a flexible instrument to slice away sections of the prostate. This usually results in ejaculation going back into the bladder rather than out through the urethra. Few men are well prepared for this outcome and many find it very upsetting when not given a forewarning or explanation of why it occurs. Such men need education and reassurance to help them accept this change, since it is irreversible. It is generally argued that this type of surgery should not cause erectile difficulties, but many men and their clinicians believe it sometimes does.

Erectile dysfunction after such surgery may sometimes be psychogenic, but about 4% of men have physically based loss of erectile capacity after such surgery (Bolt, Evans, & Marshall, 1986).

Dyspareunia, or painful intercourse, in the aging woman is most often associated with the postmenopausal changes discussed earlier, such as the vagina becoming smaller and less elastic, delays and decreases in vaginal lubrication, and thinning and impaired elevation of the vaginal lips. It also can be psychologically mediated or associated with medical conditions, including diabetes, endometriosis, pelvic adhesions after surgery, and pelvic tumors (Gupta, 1990).

Many health problems that occur more frequently in the older population do not directly affect sexual organs or function, but they have an indirect effect. Two that are particularly common are arthritis and lung disease. Arthritis, with its stiffness and joint pain, interferes with sexual activity itself, as well as with pleasure and satisfaction. Alternate positions can ease the strain of painful joints. For example, the spoon position allows both partners to lie on their sides, the woman in front of the man, so he can enter her vagina from behind and neither needs to support their weight.

Lung disease, such as emphysema, asthma, and bronchitis, results in shortness of breath and reduced energy, which interferes directly with sexual activity and enjoyment. In extreme cases the healthy partner can take over much of the physical movement, allowing the person with shortness of breath to continue to participate at a level that is physically comfortable.

Whereas all of these medical factors can have important effects as single factors, it would be difficult to overemphasize the importance of the cumulative effect of multiple simultaneous causes for sexual dysfunction in the elderly. It is common to see an older patient with a long history of smoking and lung disease, a history of alcohol abuse, long-standing vascular disease, and obesity who did not lose adequate erectile functioning or, for women, lubrication and sexual desire, until developing an additional disease, such as diabetes. The physical basis of our sexual responses is vulnerable (in that it is dependent on many systems), but it is also resilient. It often takes multiple problems to overcome that innate resilience. Medications are another source of additional pressures on sexual response systems.

Medications

Many medications have a negative impact on sexual function, and, in general, the more medications a person uses, the greater the likelihood of negative effects. Since older adults metabolize medications more slowly and are more likely than younger adults to take multiple medications, the impact on elders is particularly heavy.

While older adults have a lower rate of depression than do most other age groups, there are significant numbers of depressed older adults, and antidepressant medication is the most commonly offered treatment. Each of the three classes of antidepressants in general use has different effects on sexuality. It can be hard to determine whether sexual difficulties are a result of depression itself or a side effect of a drug treatment. A defining symptom of depression, for example, is loss of sexual interest, and loss of interest can also be a result of some antidepressants. In fact, some 10% to 43% of people on tricyclic antidepressants like Elavil say they experience decreased desire, decreased arousal, and/or delayed orgasm. People on the monoamine oxidase inhibitors (MAOIs) such as Nardil and Parnate report even higher rates of sexual dysfunction (Segraves, Madsen, Carter, & Davis, 1985). Another antidepressant, trazodone, has been associated with rare cases of priapism, a painful erection that will not subside, and if untreated, can result in serious and permanent damage to the penis (Balon, Yeragani, Pohl, & Ramesh, 1993).

The newer antidepressants, the selective serotonin reuptake inhibitors (SSRIs), which include Prozac, Zoloft, and Paxil, are associated with reduced desire and a different type of sexual dysfunction: delayed or absent orgasm (Segraves, 1995). Because these medications are new, the exact frequency of orgasm problems is not known, but research has reported anywhere from 10% to 75% of patients with orgasm problems (Walker et al., 1993). Some users say that these sexual side effects dissipate after a few months or when the dose is reduced, but the predictability of improvement is yet unclear.

Many older patients, especially those living in hospitals or nursing homes or whose behavior has been disruptive, receive antipsychotic medications, such as Haldol or Prolixin. Although Thorazine, Mellaril, and Prolixin are the most widely cited culprits, all of the antipsychotic medications can disrupt sexual interest, arousal, and orgasm (Sullivan & Lukoff, 1990). Sometimes a switch to a different drug will result in fewer sexual effects. Prolixin, Trilafon, and Mellaril also cause ejaculatory disturbances in more than 50% of men using them, while effects on orgasm in women are unknown. Occasionally men report priapism when on antipsychotics.

Many of the elderly take at least one high blood pressure medication. Diuretics (e.g., Maxzide) are often used as the first line treatment of elevated blood pressure, but they are associated with erectile dysfunction in men. Less frequently associated with problems are the "alpha-blockers," such as prazosin and terazosin. Finally, newer medications that have not yet been implicated in sexual difficulties include calcium channel blockers and ACE inhibitors (Segraves et al., 1985). While research has only begun to explore the effects of these medications on women, one can suspect comparable problems, for example, reduced vaginal lubrication (Riley, Steiner, Cooper, & McPherson, 1987).

Digoxin, disopyramide (used to treat heart arrhythmias), and clofibrate (for treatment of elevated cholesterol levels) have been associated with erectile dysfunction and decreased interest in sex (Segraves et al., 1985). Tagamet and Zantac, medications used to treat upset stomachs and soothe the effects of other medications on the digestive tract, have been associated with erection problems, decreased sexual interest, breast enlargement, and breast pain. Anticonvulsants are associated with a decrease in sexual interest in men, possibly by reducing testosterone levels, but effects in women are unknown. Estrogens,

antiandrogens, and cancer chemotherapy agents are also associated with reduced desire and arousal.

Drugs of abuse, including alcohol and tobacco, disrupt sexual function,
and their impact increases with age. While small amounts of alcohol may dis-
inhibit men and women, larger quantities lead to reduced response of the
vagina and reduced erection, as well as reduced sex drive and orgasm
(Schuckit, 1986; Segraves et al., 1985). Chronic alcohol abuse has been associated with elevated rates of erection problems, as high as 54% in some studies,
and dysfunction may not be reversible even if the former drinker becomes abstinent (Wein & Van Arsdalen, 1988).

Tobacco use makes it harder to get an erection and possibly harder to have
vaginal lubrication because it reduces blood flow to the genitals. These effects
take time to develop, so they are more likely to be seen in older people who are
lifelong smokers.

TREATMENT OF SEXUAL PROBLEMS

A recent review (Heiman & Meston, 1997) summarizes the empirically supported approaches to psychological treatment of sexual dysfunction. These authors note that well-established treatments are available for primary inorgasmia
in women (women who have never experienced orgasm) and some erection
problems in men. Probably efficacious treatments are available for secondary
inorgasmia in women (women with situational absence of orgasms or who have
lost orgasmic capacity after a period of being orgasmic), vaginismus, and premature ejaculation. For other problems, such as low sexual desire, there are
reports of effective treatments but not enough evidence to conclude that an approach is firmly empirically supported.

Of the empirically supported treatments for sexual dysfunction, all are
based in a cognitive-behavioral treatment model. The most common components of effective treatments are sensate focus and systematic desensitization;
additional important components are interventions to improve interpersonal
and sexual communication, to enhance sensory awareness, and to learn about
one's own sexual experience through masturbation exercises. A model guiding
many cognitive-behavioral therapists in combining these components, the
PLISSIT model, is presented in this chapter.

In the body of evidence supporting a cognitive-behavioral approach to treatment of sexual dysfunction, no studies have provided specific information on
older adults and their responses to therapy. Thus, in the following section, our
own experience in adapting these treatments to work with older adults is included, with appropriate caution about the lack of formal empirical support for
these adaptations. In particular, we emphasize that treatment of sexual dysfunction in the elderly often involves use of a biopsychosocial approach (A. Zeiss,
Zeiss, & Dornbrand, 1992). This interdisciplinary approach includes use of empirically supported brief or intensive individual or couples therapy, in conjunction with medical treatment. In the following section on treatment, we comment
frequently on the relationship between these components.

PSYCHOLOGICALLY BASED INTERVENTIONS: PLISSIT MODEL

A standard model of sex therapy, the PLISSIT model, is especially appropriate for the elderly population (Annon, 1974). The PLISSIT model is a four-level conceptual model that guides the therapist from simple to more complex interventions. If problems are not resolved with a simple intervention, the therapist adds more complex interventions as needed. PLISSIT is an acronym for the four progressive levels of sex therapy: Permission, Limited Information, Specific Suggestions, and Intensive Therapy. At each level, important components of the cognitive-behavioral approach are utilized.

Permission
In the first level, Permission, the therapist acts as an authority, giving endorsement to sexual activities and fantasies and reassuring the person that he or she is normal. For instance, older men may need permission to masturbate as an alternative to intercourse when a wife is uninterested or ill. Older men may associate self-stimulation with adolescence and believe it reflects sexual inadequacy, rather than seeing it as appropriate regardless of age or relationship status. A therapist can give him permission to consider resuming this activity, especially in light of his wife's decreased desire to be sexual.

Limited Information
In the next level, Limited Information, a clinician provides factual information specific to the individual's problem. Such psychoeducational interventions can be quite successful with the elderly (Goldman & Carroll, 1990). People rarely know about normal, age-related changes in sexual function, let alone changes due to illness or medications, so they may misinterpret these changes. For example, we worked with a 52-year-old divorced diabetic man who was experiencing decreased erections, obtaining about 60% of a normal erection. The last two women he dated each believed that his lack of full erections meant he didn't find them sexually desirable. During short-term therapy with an interdisciplinary team, the man began to understand that his decreased erections were physically caused, and that he was not alone in experiencing this problem. As he considered treatment options, he began to feel more confident and started dating again. He also began to discuss in therapy how and when to tell a potential sex partner about the quality of his erections before initiating a sexual relationship.

Specific Suggestions
The third step of the model, Specific Suggestions, involves simple problem-solving interventions. For example, an older couple who used to have sex after romantic evenings out will need to change their pattern if they can no longer drive after dark. Older couples who have always considered the man's erection to be the signal to begin sexual activity will also need specific suggestions on changes in the initiation and orchestration of sex, since the older man will likely need direct penile stimulation to obtain an erection. Couples may need to utilize new positions for sexual intercourse that are less stressful to arthritic

joints or that place fewer energy demands. An excellent pamphlet is available from the Arthritis Foundation for this purpose.

Intensive Therapy

Intensive therapy, the fourth level of intervention, is used when brief therapy is ineffective or when specific suggestions are not carried out because of interpersonal or intrapersonal conflict. A specific program unique to that person's or couple's needs and circumstances is developed. Sensate focus techniques, as described originally by Masters and Johnson (1970), can be as effective with older adults as with younger adults and are a frequent component of Intensive Therapy.

Couples therapy techniques are also appropriate at this level, such as couple communication. Basic to effective communication is managing the anxiety experienced when a partner is anxious, agitated, or upset and managing one's own anxiety while talking with a partner. Various resources for increasing skill in communicating honestly and without miscommunication, defensiveness, or hostility are also available (see, e.g., Gottman, Notarius, Gonso, & Markman, 1978).

MEDICALLY BASED INTERVENTIONS

When a medication-induced dysfunction is suspected, it's important to consult with the patient's primary care clinician, who may choose to discontinue the medication, reduce the dosage, or try an alternate drug. In some cases, the person can be left on the medication and the dysfunction can be treated or an antidote may be available. Periactin or Yocan, for example, may effectively treat lack of orgasm caused by SSRIs (Segraves, 1995). However, geriatric patients with multiple medical problems often have no viable medication adjustments; in such cases it is important to treat the resulting dysfunction rather than manipulating drugs that are otherwise effective.

Hormone replacement therapy (HRT) can increase vaginal lubrication and decrease vaginal dryness and thus, dyspareunia in postmenopausal women (Sitruk-Ware & Utian, 1992). For women unable to use HRT or who choose not to use HRT, artificial lubricants, such as KY Jelly, Astroglide, and Probe, can be recommended. Only water-based lubricants should be used; oil-based lubricants, such as Vaseline, can be harmful and should never be recommended. For aging women with decreased sexual desire, testosterone replacement therapy may be considered by the primary care physician, although little research has been done to confirm its clinical impact.

Surgical treatment for erectile dysfunction includes vascular surgery and penile implants. Less invasive interventions are also available and are usually the treatments of choice. There are four widely used nonsurgical treatments: penile self-injections, insertion of a penile suppository (containing the same chemical used in self-injection), use of sildenafil (Viagra) orally, and vacuum-constriction devices. All have high success rates in creating satisfactory erections for intercourse (Dornbrand, Zeiss, & Zeiss, 1990; Turner & Althof, 1992; A. Zeiss et al., 1992). All have pros and cons; a discussion of them is beyond the scope of this chapter, but additional information is available in A. Zeiss (1996).

Decreased libido, the second most frequently reported sexual problem in older men, can be treated with testosterone enanthate injections when low levels of testosterone are the cause. Men reporting increased sexual desire following a trial of testosterone should be placed on a treatment regimen with regular medical monitoring for potential adverse affects, specifically increased production of red blood cells, which can increase the risk of a stroke, and proliferation of prostate cancer. Testosterone injections don't increase the likelihood of prostate cancer, but may cause it to progress if it develops for other reasons (Morley & Kaiser, 1993).

COMBINING COMPONENTS OF THE PLISSIT MODEL WITH MEDICAL INTERVENTIONS IN AN INTERDISCIPLINARY APPROACH

Even when medical problems initiated a sexual dysfunction, psychological factors may play an important role in the treatment plan. Consider a couple where both partners have difficulty expressing their honest worries and wishes regarding sex. In one such example, Jose was assured that he could express his own interest in continuing a sexual relationship, rather than expressing vague fears that this was something his wife "needed." He was also given permission to express his worries about achieving only a partial erection, as a result of cardiovascular disease. His wife, Maria, was encouraged to express her waning desire since menopause, and it was suggested that she didn't need to be more sexually active than she wanted to be. Both were provided information about normal age-related sexual changes and the impact of medical conditions on their situation. This process helped them to communicate more comfortably about sex as well as to challenge their perceptions that they were "just too old" to care about sex any more.

Maria and Jose also received specific suggestions to begin a series of sensate focus, whole-body stroking exercises to help each focus on pleasure and sensuality. They also began using sildenafil (Viagra) to help Jose get and keep an erection, and received training on using it in a sensual way as part of love-play. Maria received estrogen cream as part of the medical aspect of the interdisciplinary care plan. The couple planned use of the cream in a sensual way as part of foreplay, rather than having Maria apply it on her own before sex.

Intensive therapy was brief in this case, and took the role of coordinating all of the interventions and providing some additional training in sexual communication. For example, both believed that only men discuss sex, only men initiate sex, and men should always be ready for sex. While this had not presented major problems when they were younger, it affected their ability to make flexible adaptations to age-related changes. With therapy, they were able to develop a new pattern in which Jose could express both interest in sex and disinterest if timing was wrong. Maria was able to express interest, which did return with her feeling closer to Jose. Both could talk intimately about the physical aspect of their relationship and how important it remained as they faced other losses with aging.

SPECIAL ISSUES FOR OLDER ADULTS WITH DEMENTIA

A particular problem for older adults is the increased risk of developing a dementing disease. Dementia has serious sexual implications for both patient and caregiver across a wide variety of life experiences. Problems posed by dementia with regards to sexuality are beginning to be understood, although there is still much to learn (A. Zeiss, Davies, & Tinklenberg, 1990). People with Alzheimer's disease frequently experience sexual dysfunction, and caregivers may feel hesitant to have sex with partners who are unable to express either consent or refusal. Yet both may continue to have sexual thoughts, feelings, and desires. Men with early Alzheimer's have a higher than average prevalence of erectile problems. The reasons for this are not well understood, but sex therapy can be helpful in these cases (Davies et al., 1992).

In some cases, it is important to give permission to caregivers to honor their decisions to discontinue sexual activity (e.g., because their partners no longer recognize them) and instead, to satisfy their own sexual desires through self-stimulation. If a demented partner initiates sexual activity, the caregiver can distract the patient or focus him or her on more acceptable sexual contact, such as massage, hugging, cuddling, and kissing. The need for touch by both patient and partner caregiver can also be met through these activities. Caretakers concerned about inappropriate sexual behavior, masturbation in public, for example, can be assured that this is unlikely (A. Zeiss, Davies, & Tinklenberg, 1996). Men with dementia demonstrate little public sexual behavior of any kind, either appropriate or inappropriate. For the occasional patient who does demonstrate this problem, caregivers can be trained to handle the behavior calmly and to provide privacy or distraction.

CONCLUSION

Although aging is associated with a general decline in various factors related to sexual function, sexual satisfaction can, and most typically does, remain stable. Couples who place a high value on sexual intimacy regardless of age are able to make the necessary adjustments that allow them to continue to be sexually active. However, sexuality can be placed at risk in older adults by health issues, by negative stereotypes about aging, or by lack of flexibility for making needed adjustments to age-related changes.

The willingness to experiment with alternatives and the involvement and attitudes of both partners in a sexual relationship are just as important in maintaining sexual activity as are physical changes related to aging. When working with sexual concerns of the elderly, an interdisciplinary approach to evaluating, diagnosing, and treating sexual dysfunction is essential. This approach avoids arbitrary classification of sexual problems as "biomedical" versus "psychogenic" and, instead, recognizes the complex, interrelated roles of both factors in the development of sexual dysfunction and in its successful resolution. Treatment of the psychological components of sexual dysfunction in older adults has generally been based on the cognitive-behavioral treatment model shown to be most empirically supported in outcome research with largely younger adults.

REFERENCES

American Psychiatric Association. (1987). *Diagnostic and statistical manual of mental disorders* (3rd ed., rev.). Washington, DC: Author.

Annon, J. (1974). *The behavioral treatment of sexual problems: Vol. 1. Brief therapy.* Honolulu: Enabling Systems.

Bachmann, G.A., & Leiblum, S.R. (1991). Sexuality in sexagenarian women. *Maturitas, 13,* 43–50.

Balon, R., Yeragani, V.K., Pohl, R., & Ramesh, C. (1993). Sexual dysfunction during antidepressant treatment. *Journal of Clinical Psychiatry, 54,* 209–212.

Barlow, D.H. (1986). Causes of sexual dysfunction: The role of anxiety and cognitive interference. *Journal of Consulting and Clinical Psychology, 54,* 140–148.

Bolt, J.W., Evans, C., & Marshall, V.R. (1986). Sexual dysfunction after prostatectomy. *British Journal of Urology, 59,* 319–322.

Cranston-Cuebas, M.A., Barlow, D.H., Mitchell, W., & Athanasiou, R. (1993). Differential effects of a misattribution manipulation on sexually functional and dysfunctional men. *Journal of Abnormal Psychology, 102,* 525–533.

Davies, H., Zeiss, A.M., & Tinklenberg, J. (1992). 'Til death do us part: Intimacy and sexuality in the marriages of Alzheimer's patients. *Journal of Psychosocial Nursing, 30,* 5–10.

Dornbrand, L.A., Zeiss, R.A., & Zeiss, A.M. (1990). *Treatment outcome for erectile dysfunction in older veterans using the vacuum pump system.* Paper presented at Gerontological Society of America, Boston.

Feldman, H.A., Goldstein, I., Hatzichristou, G., Krane, R.J., & McKinlay, J.B. (1994). Impotence and its medical and psychosocial correlates: Results of the Massachusetts male aging study. *Journal of Urology, 151,* 54–61.

George, L.K., & Weiler, S.J. (1981). Sexuality in middle and late life. *Archives of General Psychiatry, 38,* 919–923.

Goldman, A., & Carroll, J.L. (1990). Educational intervention as an adjunct to treatment of erectile dysfunction in older couples. *Journal of Sex and Marital Therapy, 16,* 127–141.

Gottman, J., Notarius, C., Gonso, J., & Markman, H. (1978). *A couple's guide to communication.* Champaign, IL: Research Press.

Gupta, K. (1990). Sexual dysfunction in elderly women. *Urologic Care in the Elderly, 6,* 197–203.

Heiman, J.R., & Meston, C.M. (1997). In R.C. Rosen, C.M. Davis, & H.J. Ruppel (Eds.), *Annual review of sexuality* (Vol. 8, pp. 148–194). Mason City, IA: Society for the Scientific Study of Sex.

Hillman, J.L., & Stricker, G. (1994). A linkage of knowledge and attitudes toward elderly sexuality: Not necessarily a uniform relationship. *Gerontologist, 34,* 256–260.

Kahn, E., & Fisher, C. (1969). REM sleep and sexuality in the aged. *Journal of Geriatric Psychiatry, 2,* 181–199.

Kaiser, F.E. (1994). Sexuality. In P.D. O'Donnell (Ed.), *Geriatric urology.* Boston: Little, Brown.

Kerfoot, W.W., & Carson, C.C. (1991). Pharmacological induced erections among geriatric men. *146,* 1022–1024.

Korenman, S.G., Morley, J.E., Mooradian, A.D., Davis, S.S., Kaiser, F.E., Silver, A.J., Viosca, S.P., & Garza, D. (1990). Secondary hypogonadism in older men: Its relation to impotence. *Journal of Clinical Endocrinology and Metabolism, 71,* 963–969.

Korenman, S.G., Viosca, S.P., Kaiser, F.E., Mooradian, A.D., & Morley, J.E. (1990). Use of a vacuum tumescence device in the management of impotence. *Journal of the American Geriatrics Society, 38,* 217–220.

LoPiccolo, J., & Heiman, J.R. (1988). Broad spectrum treatment of low sexual desire. In S.R. Leiblum & R.C. Rosen (Eds.), *Sexual desire disorders.* New York: Guilford Press.

Malatesta, V.J., Chambless, D.L., Pollack, M., & Cantor, A. (1988). Widowhood, sexuality, and aging: A life span analysis. *Journal of Sex and Marital Therapy, 14.*

Marsiglio, W., & Donnelly, D. (1991). Sexual relations in later life: A national study of married persons. *Journal of Gerontology: Social Sciences, 46,* S338–S344.

Masters, W., & Johnson, V. (1966). *Human sexual response.* Boston: Little, Brown.

Masters, W., & Johnson, V. (1970). *Human sexual inadequacy.* Boston: Little, Brown.

Morley, J.E., & Kaiser, F.E. (1993). Impotence: The internist's approach to diagnosis and treatment. *Advances in Internal Medicine, 38,* 151–168.

Riley, A.J., Steiner, J.A., Cooper, R., & McPherson, C.K. (1987). The prevalence of sexual dysfunction in male and female hypertensive patients. *Sexual and Marital Therapy, 2,* 131–138.

Schiavi, R.C., Schreiner-Engel, P., Mandeli, J., Schanzer, H., & Cohen, E. (1990). Healthy aging and male sexual function. *American Journal of Psychiatry, 147,* 766–771.

Schiavi, R.C., Schreiner-Engel, P., White, D., & Mandell, J. (1991). The relationship between pituitary-gonadal function and sexual behavior in healthy aging men. *Psychosomatic Medicine, 53,* 363–373.

Schover, L.R. (1986). Sexual problems. In L. Teri & P.M. Lewinsohn (Eds.), *Geropsychological assessment and treatment: Selected topics.* New York: Springer-Verlag.

Schuckit, M.A. (1986). Sexual disturbance in the woman alcoholic. *Medical Aspects of Human Sexuality, 2,* 90.

Segraves, R.T. (1995). Antidepressant-induced orgasm disorder. *Journal of Sex and Marital Therapy, 21,* 192–201.

Segraves, R.T., Madsen, R., Carter, C.S., & Davis, J.M. (1985). Erectile dysfunction associated with pharmacological agents. In R.T. Segraves & H.W. Schoenberg (Eds.), *Diagnosis and treatment of erectile disturbances: A guide for clinicians.* New York: Plenum Medical Books.

Sherwin, B.B. (1991). The psychoendocrinology of aging and female sexuality. In J. Bancroft, C.M. Davis, & H.J. Ruppel (Eds.), *Annual review of sex research* (Vol. 2). Lake Mills, IA: Society for the Scientific Study of Sex.

Sherwin, B.B., Gelfand, M.M., & Brender, W. (1985). Androgen enhances sexual motivation in females: A prospective cross-over study of sex steroid administration in the surgical menopause. *Psychosomatic Medicine, 7,* 339–351.

Sitruk-Ware, R.S., & Utian, W.H. (1992). *The menopause and hormonal replacement therapy: Facts and controversies.* New York: Marcel Dekker.

Sullivan, G., & Lukoff, D. (1990). Sexual side effects of antipsychotic medication: Evaluation and interventions. *Hospital and Community Psychiatry, 41,* 1238–1241.

Teisler, L. (1996). The medicalization of sexuality: Conceptual, normative, and professional issues. In R.C. Rosen, C.M. Davis, & H.J. Ruppel (Eds.), *Annual review of sexuality* (Vol. 7, pp. 252–282). Mason City, IA: Society for the Scientific Study of Sex.

Turner, L.A., & Althof, S.E. (1992). The clinical effectiveness of self-injection and external vacuum devices in the treatment of erectile dysfunction: A six-month comparison. *Psychiatric Medicine, 10,* 283–293.

Walker, P.W., Cole, J.O., Gardner, E.A., Hughes, A.R., Johnston, J.A., Batey, S.R., & Lineberry, C.G. (1993). Improvement in fluoxetine-associated sexual dysfunction in patients switched to bupropion. *Journal of Clinical Psychiatry, 54,* 459–465.

Wein, A.J., & Van Arsdalen, K.N. (1988). Drug-induced male sexual dysfunction. *Urology Clinics of North America, 15,* 23–31.

Weizman, M.D., & Hart, J. (1987). Sexual behavior in healthy married elderly men. *Archives of Sexual Behavior, 16,* 39–44.

Wiley, D., & Bortz, W.M. (1996). Sexuality and aging: Usual and successful. *Journal of Gerontology: Medical Science, 51A,* M142–M146.

Zeiss, A.M. (1982). Expectations for the effects of aging on sexuality in parents and average married couples. *Journal of Sex Research, 18,* 47–57.

Zeiss, A.M. (1996). Sexuality and aging: Normal changes and clinical problems. *Geriatric Rehabilitation, 4,* 11–27.

Zeiss, A.M., Davies, H.D., & Tinklenberg, J.R. (1990). The incidence and correlates of erectile problems in patients with Alzheimer's Disease. *Archives of Sexual Behavior, 19,* 325–331.

Zeiss, A.M., Davies, H.D., & Tinklenberg, J.R. (1996). An observational study of inappropriate sexual behavior in demented male patients. *Journals of Gerontology: Medical Sciences, 51A,* M325–M329.

Zeiss, A.M., Zeiss, R.A., & Dornbrand, L. (1992). *Interdisciplinary treatment of sexual dysfunction in older veterans.* Paper presented at Interdisciplinary Health Care Team Conference, Chicago.

Zeiss, R.A., Delmonico, R.L., Zeiss, A.M., & Dornbrand, L. (1991). Psychologic disorder and sexual dysfunction in elders. *Clinics in Geriatric Medicine, 7,* 133–151.

CHAPTER 19

Preventive Interventions for Older Adults

CANDACE KONNERT, MARGARET GATZ, AND
E.A. MEYEN HERTZSPRUNG

There has been remarkably little overlap between community psychology and the psychology of adult development and aging, despite obvious conceptual reasons that community psychologists should be attracted by dialectic theories of development over the life span and gerontologists should find community psychological viewpoints on intervention particularly compelling for the aged. In this chapter, we will briefly discuss the concept of prevention and present risk and protective factors that are particularly relevant to older adults; discuss some key factors affecting the interaction between older adults and community-based mental health services; and provide an overview of preventive interventions with community-residing older adults and their families, including illustrative examples. Interventions are presented according to indicated, selective, and universal levels of intervention; examples are chosen that have the best empirical evaluation of the interventions.

A few observations should be held in mind while reading this overview of the community intervention literature. First, the bulk of the evaluated interventions are at the individual level. Second, much of the activity in the community on behalf of elders seems to lack a conceptual basis, or is at least described in terms removed from a community psychological theoretical framework. Third, and related to the second point, there is little attention to unintended negative consequences or concern about which interventions might be best for which older adults. Fourth, while independent living is often a stated goal, models of intervention that incorporate considerations of autonomy and empowerment have not strongly influenced practice.

A final guiding thought is to recognize the diversity of older adults. Life-span theorists emphasize the multidimensionality and multidirectionality of development, with individuals as active agents who cope and create meaning (Baltes & Baltes, 1990). The idea of the active agent reflects concepts such as self-efficacy, autonomy, and personal control (Schulz & Heckhausen, 1996). These forces result in a heterogeneous older population. However, overlooking this heterogeneity is dangerously easy; for example, planning programs for older adults as if they were poor simply because poverty is a major issue for some elders, or designing interventions to increase social networks simply because loss of a spouse or friend is common among older adults. Such generalizations overlook that many older adults are quite well-off and feel insulted by programs aimed at low-income persons, or that many elders feel busier than at any other time in their lives.

PREVENTION AND LIFE-SPAN DEVELOPMENT

Preventing mental health problems is important for a number of reasons. First, there are not and never will be sufficient resources to treat all those in need of psychological care, and older adults are particularly underserved. The shortage of resources is exacerbated in managed care systems, which are not equipped for active outreach and casefinding, key features of preventive approaches (Estes, 1995; Knight & Kaskie, 1995). Second, prevention is cost-effective as it reduces long-term disability and the inappropriate use of the medical system to treat psychological disorders (Mrazek & Haggerty, 1994). Prevention programs should be embedded in our economic, political, and social structures; however, concerns about preventive strategies competing for already scarce treatment dollars, the lack of formal training in prevention strategies, and the long-term nature of preventive approaches with fewer immediate rewards, has worked against their development and implementation (Levine & Perkins, 1997).

Recent terminology in the area of mental health emphasizes a *continuum of risk*. Relevant concepts include universal, selective, and indicated preventions (Mrazek & Haggerty, 1994). *Indicated preventions* target high-risk individuals who show some signs or biological markers of a mental disorder, but do not meet full diagnostic criteria. *Selective preventions* target individuals who are at risk but as yet show no signs of the disorder. *Universal preventions* target all individuals without regard to relative risk. While these distinctions are relevant to older adults (Smyer, 1995), few preventive research programs focus specifically on the needs of this age group (Muñoz, Mrazek, & Haggerty, 1996; see Rabins, 1992, for review).

The definition of prevention takes on some unusual aspects when the target group is older adults. First, the prevention of mental health problems in old age is a life-span process (Smyer, 1995). In this chapter, we focus on reviewing interventions where the target group are already aged; nonetheless, it is conceivable that some preventive efforts at much younger ages may actually have their strongest effects in old age. In fact, the best preventive strategies are those that change life trajectories (Levine & Perkins, 1997). Consider that many individuals with troubled developmental histories have, as adults, managed to escape notice of professionals, but encounter obvious problems in their later years when other vulnerabilities have made managing more difficult (Kral, 1968). Similarly, those who experienced difficulties when young—poverty, ill health, or poor health habits, marginal jobs—are more likely to be dependent as elders (Hendricks & Leedham, 1989). Indeed, models of prevention should include both intermediate and long-term outcomes, delineating how early malleable risk and protective factors are related to mental health problems that emerge later in life (Coie et al., 1993; Reiss & Price, 1996).

Second, one must beware of equating prevention of pathology in old age with prevention of old age. Although this warning may sound foolishly simplistic, there is prevalent in this society a paradoxical view that to grow old well is to stay young. We would reject this notion, which is a denial of normal development, in favor of the preventive goal of a fulfilled old age.

A third aspect entails identifying older adults who are at risk of a major intervention into their lives. Unlike younger adults, whose "at risk" status refers to their vulnerability to psychological distress or mental illness, older adults are typically placed in an "at risk" category due to physical frailty that puts them at risk of being placed in a nursing home. In this scenario, risk of mental distress is predominantly secondary to the threat of being placed in a long-term care institution, and a great deal of emphasis is placed on preventing institutionalization.

Developmental theories are important for understanding risk and protective factors. The relative importance of a risk factor is different at different ages, and risk factors are likely to have a cumulative effect over time (Coie et al., 1993). Among older adults, physical, psychological, and social changes may serve to place them at greater risk for mental health problems. The National Institute of Mental Health plan for prevention research (NIMH, 1995) emphasized the importance of focusing preventive efforts on transitional periods or negative life events. Research has indicated that whereas older adults experience fewer life events, those that do occur are often more noxious in nature (Lazarus & DeLongis, 1983) and are often related to the health of an older individual (Karel, 1997), thus providing a window of opportunity for preventive services.

RISK AND PROTECTIVE FACTORS

Aging brings an increased vulnerability to chronic medical conditions, and substantial numbers of older adults have multiple medical conditions (Manton, 1990). Chronically ill older adults are at elevated risk for dependency and mental health problems, especially depression (Karel, 1997), and are an obvious target group for preventive services.

With respect to psychological risk factors it is important to remember that the vast majority of older adults enjoy good mental health. Nevertheless, prevalence rates of psychiatric disorders for those 65 and older have been estimated at 18% to 25% (U.S. General Accounting Office, 1992). The prevalence of moderate to severe dementia has been estimated at 6% for those 65 years and older (Graves & Kukull, 1994). This figure increases markedly with age. Estimated prevalence of mild to severe cognitive impairment in those 85 and older has ranged from 23.8% to over 50% (Bachman et al., 1992; Evans et al., 1989). Dementias have a devastating effect on the individual and a substantial ripple effect that extends to family members involved in their care, and to the health care system, which is ill-equipped for financing long-term care (Kane, 1986).

Epidemiological data suggest that anxiety disorders are more common than affective disorders among the elderly. Data from the Epidemiologic Catchment Area (ECA) survey indicated that, for those 65 years of age and older, prevalence rates across four sites ranged from 1.5% to 2.9% for affective disorders, and 3.0% to 12.1% for anxiety disorders (George, Blazer, Winfield-Laird, Leaf, & Fischbach, 1988). Moreover, many older adults who are not clinically anxious or clinically depressed do endorse symptoms of anxiety or depression (Blazer, Hughes, & George, 1987). Diagnostically, this latter group is challenging as these symptoms may be either overdiagnosed and treated with anxiolytic or antidepressant medication; or mistakenly identified as a natural consequence of the aging process and ignored when, in fact, the individual might well be responsive to psychological intervention.

Life events have become a predominant gerontological concern. In the normal course of development, older adults are likely to experience the illnesses and deaths of friends and relatives. Bereavement leads to greater vulnerability to depression and physical illness (Stroebe, Stroebe, & Hansson, 1993). However, life changes do not inevitably lead to problems in mental health, and older adults may in fact be more resilient in the face of negative events than are younger adults, due to the accumulation of experiences over the life cycle (Murrell, Norris, & Grote, 1988; Norris & Murrell, 1988).

Social support is presented as a moderator variable or as a way of helping those who are faced with stressful events (Dunkel-Schetter & Wortman, 1981). When older adults are in need of support, typically due to illness, family members assume the primary responsibility for care. Often, however, spousal caregivers are in poor health, and adult children have competing demands of parenthood and career. Moreover, sufficient services are seldom available in the community to help these families. Given these factors, caregivers constitute a critical "at risk" group. Indeed, evidence suggests that a disproportionate number of caregivers experience depression (Aneshensel, Pearlin, Mullan, Zarit, & Whitlatch, 1995) and that caregiver fatigue is cited in the decision to institutionalize an elder (Zarit, Todd, & Zarit, 1986). Furthermore, depression related to caregiving can continue long after the death of the impaired relative (Bodnar & Kiecolt-Glaser, 1994).

At a societal level, increases in the elderly population may result in a redistribution of resources benefiting frail elderly and their relatives. These demographic changes have also raised concerns about intergenerational equity, as evidenced by the formation of AGE (Americans for Generational Equity). For example, there have been proposals to cap public expenditures and entitlements for the aged in order to assist other needy groups such as children living in poverty. Thus, recognition of generational interdependence has become part of policy-making (Bengtson, Marti, & Roberts, 1991).

Many risk factors are unique to older adults and their family members. Issues of personal autonomy become highlighted when the older person's health begins to fail or financial resources are limited. The impossibility of curing some of the physical declines or losses, and the interrelationships among areas of change make the problems of older adults especially challenging. There are obvious roles for preventive interventions at all levels.

OLDER ADULTS AND THE MENTAL HEALTH SYSTEM

Provision of preventive interventions must take into account the settings in which older adults reside and can be reached for mental health services. There is considerable evidence that the mental health system has paid little attention to the aged. When older adults do seek help, physicians are the primary gate-keepers to mental health resources (Phillips & Murrell, 1994), and physicians are notoriously unlikely to recognize psychiatric symptoms, far less to consider preventive interventions. For example, Kemp, Staples, and Lopez-Aqueres (1987) surveyed a sample of older individuals of Latino origin. They found that none of the respondents who scored as depressed on the screening questionnaire reported receiving any treatment for depression, although 90% had seen a physician within the past year.

A further potential source of mental health referrals is the extensive network of community programs and information and referral services for the aged that have been developed over the past 25 years, in particular, Area Agencies on Aging (AAA). However, the "aging network" and the mental health system have remained largely independent of one another, despite recognition of the need for interagency cooperation and coordination of service delivery (Grady & Maynard, 1985; Karuza, Calkins, Duffey, & Feather, 1988).

Knight and Kaskie's (1995) analysis of the problem challenges the more traditional view of "lack of coordination of services" or "gaps in the system." They suggest that services available to older adults (i.e., medical, mental health, long-term care, aging network services) operate on different principles and were derived from different historical pressures, without a cohesive and overarching plan to accommodate the diverse needs. Also, failures in coordination often reflect economic pressures which place older adults in competition for services with other special populations. The task, then, is to make preventive services available without being pushed into one or another of these constituencies.

Older adults appear more likely to avail themselves of services offered at sites other than mental health clinics (Waters, 1995). Piggy-backing mental health services on other services is also a feature in these efforts. For example, Pilisuk and Minkler (1980) began by offering free blood pressure screening in the lobby at a single-room occupancy hotel. A review of high-quality community-based mental health programs for older adults found that they all offered the option of having services provided in the recipient's home. Moreover, they emphasized active case-finding and community education, and were interdisciplinary in nature (Knight, Rickards, Rabins, Buckwalter, & Smith, 1995).

Two important trends with respect to mental health services have been the continued growth of the institutional sector and increasing privatization of mental health care (Bickman & Dokecki, 1989). The institutional sector includes mental health facilities, general hospitals, and nursing homes. Nursing homes are and will continue to be a major site for elderly persons. Currently, those alive at age 65 have a 25% chance of being institutionalized in a nursing home at some time before they die.

Older adults receive insufficient community-based mental health services, including preventive mental health services, with psychologists particularly uninvolved. Available funding favors institutional over community treatment, acute care over long-term care, and direct services over prevention, consultation, and programmatic approaches.

OVERVIEW OF INTERVENTIONS

The following section is organized according to indicated, selective, and universal preventive measures. At each level, we attempt to provide the reader with a sense of the scope of the literature and to highlight, whenever possible, conceptually promising community interventions: those that focus on universal prevention or empowerment, and those that have received rigorous evaluation. The major journals devoted to community psychology and gerontological issues were reviewed from 1980 until the present, seeking examples of evaluated programs. There were still remarkably few, and that review is the source of examples cited here. Because space considerations limited our scope, we do not encompass interventions among those elderly who are institutionalized, although theoretically the nursing home can be considered to be a community in which indicated and selective preventive interventions may be appropriate.

INDICATED PREVENTIVE INTERVENTIONS

There is considerable interest in community-based interventions that attempt to prevent institutionalization. Since a primary determinant of institutionalization is the availability of assistance (Radebaugh & Gruenberg, 1985), many programs have targeted older adults living alone and providing them with services such as transportation, meal programs, homemaker services, personal and nursing aid. Evaluations have tended to focus either on large community-based long-term care projects or on one service component (e.g., emergency response systems).

The assumption underlying 30 years of practice is that effective case management, an integral part of most community-based long-term care projects, will increase and facilitate access to services in a more prompt, efficient, and cost-effective manner. Common outcome indicators include nursing home and hospital use, costs, impacts of community care on informal caregiving, quality of life, functioning, and longevity. Wilkinson (1996) reviewed the findings of several large-scale studies that evaluated various approaches, including "expanded" or "skilled" home care and case-managed community-based care. The general conclusion was that evaluations of community-based long-term care projects have shown disappointing results for two reasons. First, these programs tend to serve clients who have a relatively low risk for institutionalization. Of those participants who are at risk, most are at risk for only a short stay within the institution. In part, this has to do with the difficulties associated with identifying and serving those at risk. Some programs such as the National Channeling demonstration attempted to use telephone prescreening processes to identify those at risk; however, these were an added expense and did not identify sufficient numbers of at-risk persons to make the program cost-effective (Weissert, 1985). In general, enrollment in these types of programs has been slow and may reflect low levels of enthusiasm among target persons, barriers to enrollment, or the systematic exclusion of certain types of clients. In the Program of All-Inclusive Care for the Elderly (PACE), barriers to enrollment included clients' unwillingness to attend the Adult Day Health Center for health monitoring (e.g., medications), financial barriers (e.g., unwillingness to contribute a copayment or apply for Medicaid), and loss of freedom of choice of health care providers (Branch, Coulam, & Zimmerman, 1995).

Second, the expense of these community-based programs quickly offsets any potential savings associated with reductions in nursing home use. In addition, home and community-based programs that are of shorter duration (six months to a year) and less expensive are just as effective as those of longer duration. Despite these results, Wilkinson (1996) observed that the level of enthusiasm for case-managed community-based care is high, and more recent efforts have been directed at targeting those in greatest need (Greene, Lovely, & Ondrich, 1993) and integrating these services into traditional acute care delivery systems. In general, models of service-delivery are changing dramatically, with a blurring of distinctions between institutional and community-based care. Cohen (1998) described several experimental programs that integrate community-based and long-term care services into capitated, managed care plans.

Some studies have focused on the effectiveness of just one service component: for example, placing personal emergency response systems in the homes of frail elderly. Roush and Teasdale (1997) examined hospital utilization rates among 207 American and Canadian users, one year before and one year after enrollment in a personal response system. Results indicated that the mean number of hospital inpatient days decreased by about 50% after enrollment in the program. However, as with any intervention, unintended negative consequences must be monitored. For example, Pearson, Seward, and Gatz (1989) found that, although the emergency response system program was generally beneficial, older individuals who did not really want the service, but who acquiesced to their family's wanting it installed, suffered some loss of sense of personal control.

Preventing institutionalization also involves strengthening support systems by providing emotional and instrumental support to caregivers, most often spouses or children. Admittedly, these interventions can be conceptualized as either indicated or selective preventive interventions and we have chosen to include them in the following section.

SELECTIVE PREVENTIVE INTERVENTIONS

Selective interventions often define their targets in terms of having experienced some particular stressful life event. In the gerontological literature, the life events that are most often related to mental distress include death of a spouse and physical health decline (Murrell, Norris, & Hutchins, 1984). Among older adults, preventive interventions based on stressful life events models involve either modifying the social environment or strengthening psychological resources and coping skills (Gesten & Jason, 1987).

Under the heading of modifying the social environment, the fundamental strategy is to increase or strengthen the social support system based on evidence that support may buffer stress (Norris & Murrell, 1984). The most popular types of interventions are friendly visitor programs for isolated elders (e.g., Korte & Gupta, 1991), use of the telephone to overcome isolation (e.g., Heller, Thompson, Trueba, Hogg, & Vlachos-Weber, 1991), and support groups of various sorts (e.g., Thompson, Gallagher, Nies, & Epstein, 1983). Despite the demonstrated relationship between support and well-being, there are remarkably few evaluated studies of support interventions. A meta-analysis of seven interventions designed to promote well-being by providing opportunities for social interaction showed mean effect sizes of .66 (Okun, Olding, & Cohn, 1990). These authors also highlight some of the common problems in studies that attempt to demonstrate the efficacy of support interventions in promoting subjective well-being.

Often these interventions target homebound and isolated elderly persons. Heller et al. (1991) investigated use of the telephone in a well-designed study of 265 community-residing, low-income, elderly women with low perceived social support. Initially, participants were randomly assigned to either a control group or a 10-week program of staff telephone contact. At a second assessment, those in the experimental condition were randomly assigned to continued staff contact, peer telephone contact, or no-contact controls. At a third assessment, participants in the peer condition were encouraged to maintain contact with their partners, while staff contact was discontinued. Results indicated no significant differences on measures of social support and depression between the control and interventions groups, or between the two intervention groups (i.e., staff initiated and peer dyad). In explaining the absence of more effect, Heller et al. (1991) observed, first, that those who initially had more friends, higher levels of perceived support, and better health were more likely to remain in contact with peers; and second, that family members were more important than friends in influencing mental health.

In a particularly well-evaluated study, Buckwalter, Smith, Zevenbergen, and Russell (1991) reported on the Elderly Outreach Program (EOP), which provided a unique combination of mental health outreach services to rural elderly, involving home-based care or existing service delivery mechanisms. A unique aspect of this program was the training and utilization of gatekeepers (e.g., mail carriers, utility workers) to identify at-risk older adults, an approach that is particularly useful in rural communities (Atkinson & Stuck, 1991). The majority of clients served by the program were female, widowed, and living alone, and many were fully functional until the onset of physical deterioration or widowhood. It is likely that these individuals would not have sought out more traditional sources of mental health care (e.g., community mental health centers). Benefits of the program included significant improvements in depression and other psychiatric symptoms in EOP clients and a more cost-effective method of delivering mental health services. Particularly interesting results were reported with respect to need for care. Prior to implementation, need for care was greater in the EOP catchment counties when compared with two matched control counties. These group differences were absent after a 2-year implementation of the EOP program. Furthermore, analyses of change over time indicated no change in the need for care over time in the experimental, EOP group, while there was a significant increase in the need for care in the control groups. This illustrates how early identification and treatment can prevent an increase in need for mental health care.

Widowhood is a stressful life event that has received quite a bit of attention (Lieberman, 1996; Stroebe et al., 1993). There have been studies evaluating support groups for widows, using random assignment to support and control conditions (e.g., Mawson, Marks, Ramm, & Stern, 1981). The elements of intervention may include social support, practical assistance, advice, hope, and new ways of understanding the experience. Wortman and Cohen Silver (1990) have urged attention to individual differences in the experience of bereavement, specifically the risk and protective factors involved, as these have implications for intervention. For example, social ties during adjustment to widowhood are important (Siegel & Kuykendall, 1990); however, support can have both positive and negative consequences (Lehman, Ellard, & Wortman, 1986). Caserta and Lund (1993) found that intrapersonal resources such as self-esteem and perceived competency have a greater impact on outcome than a self-help group intervention. Thus, interventions should focus not only on skill deficiencies but also on strengthening those intrapersonal protective factors that facilitate adjustment to widowhood. Summarizing the literature about widow-to-widow programs leads to the conclusion that they are most effective with women who experience high levels of stress immediately after the death, and that clinical trials should target this group to determine whether depression can be prevented (Mrazek & Haggerty, 1994).

In addition to modifying the social environment, other interventions emphasize strengthening psychological resources as a way of mitigating the negative effects of stressful life events. These include various skill-building interventions such as improving communication skills (Hyde, 1988), assertion training (Franzke, 1987), enhancing performance in educational or work-related endeavors (Braddy & Gray, 1987), and managing stress by anticipating events, altering perceptions of events, and enlarging coping repertoires (Hough, Gongla,

Brown, & Goldston, 1985). Although generally regarded as less effective, some emotion-focused coping strategies such as denial can be effective, particularly in situations where control is limited or nonexistent. Moreover, interventions that promote control must be implemented carefully, taking into account an individual's desire for control, and the physical and sociocultural constraints he or she may be facing (Schulz and Heckhausen, 1996).

Given the uncontrollable nature of many of the stressors associated with old age, stress management interventions may take on some unique characteristics. For example, Schulz and Heckhausen (1996) proposed four control-related processes, including compensatory secondary control strategies that buffer the negative effects of failure or loss. These strategies involve goal reorientation and intrapsychic processes such as strategic social comparison or causal attributions that protect the self and could be conceptualized as ways of managing uncontrollable stress. However, they are beyond the scope of most traditional stress management interventions, which tend to emphasize active approaches over intrapsychic processes.

In general, program planning and evaluation designs in selective prevention would benefit from greater clarity about the target group and intervention strategy. Most of the programs, with the exception of groups for widows, are directed generally toward all older adults. This point is relevant because the same selective prevention strategies can be used for purposes of life enhancement. Although the primary emphasis has been on coping with negative life events, an equally important goal is to promote positive life events that facilitate and enhance psychological growth and well-being.

Selective prevention programs at the family level focus primarily on caregivers of persons who have dementia and include individual behavioral and psychosocial approaches (e.g., Gallagher-Thompson & Steffen, 1994), support groups (see Toseland & Rossiter, 1989, for review), and respite care (e.g., Lawton, Brody, & Saperstein, 1991). A meta-analytic review of interventions for caregivers suggested that respite and individual psychosocial interventions were moderately effective when compared with control groups, while group psychosocial interventions showed smaller positive effects (Knight, Lutzky, & Macofsky-Urban, 1993). Although the data are not entirely consistent (e.g., Pruchno, Michaels, & Potashnik, 1990), one controlled study provided evidence that psychosocial interventions delay the institutionalization of care recipients, particularly if the intervention is intensive (i.e., including individual and family counseling, support groups, and ad hoc consultation) and designed to maximize support (Mittelman et al., 1993). Data also show that increased use of respite services is related to reduced probability of nursing home placement, even after relevant variables were controlled (e.g., age, level of disability, cognitive impairment, other support services).

A major obstacle experienced by caregivers is the unavailability of community resources and, when they exist, a lack of knowledge about how to access them. In a survey of Michigan agencies, Shope et al. (1993) reported that home-delivered meals, and nursing and social work assessments were most available, while respite and adult day care were least available. Moreover, the service delivery network for providing care for dementing elderly is often complex and fragmented, with many systemic and logistical barriers. This problem is most apparent in rural and minority communities (Yeatts, Crow, & Folts, 1992).

Rather than collaborating with and helping family members to better care for older relatives, community agencies may be perceived as taking over and making decisions without the active involvement of family members. The dilemma is how to legitimize the family's asking for assistance and anticipating crises (Radebaugh & Gruenberg, 1985) without treating the family like an "identified patient." In an effort to address this problem, Simmons, Ivry, and Seltzer (1985) designed Family-Centered Community Care (FCCC) for elderly persons. This program strengthens the relationship between formal and informal support systems by increasing family involvement in case management. Participants were randomly assigned to either the FCCC program or to traditional services. Preliminary results suggested that FCCC families were providing more case management and that more services were being provided to the elderly clients in a shorter period of time. Once again, planners need to be sensitive to unintended negative outcomes. Although it is likely that family members who were functioning as case managers would feel more in control, it is also possible that some families perceived serving in this role as just one more responsibility.

The feasibility of economic incentives to encourage families to provide informal care in the community, in order to prevent or delay institutionalization, has become a policy concern in many locales. Incentives most frequently involve direct payments to those with restricted incomes, often limited to family members who live in the same household as the dependent elderly person. Other states have tax incentives. An emerging option for caregivers is family leave, an alternative that until recently has been available only for the care of children.

Evaluations of direct subsidy programs have found substantial savings over the cost of nursing home care, a lower mortality rate, and no lessening of the extent of informal help provided by family and friends (Biegel, Morycz, Schulz, & Shore, 1986). Other writers have emphasized that financial assistance alone will not relieve all of the pressures associated with caregiving and have expressed concern that reimbursement "may change family values" (Arling & McAuley, 1983, p. 306). However, as Brody (1985) has argued, concern about eroding of family responsibility should not be used as justification for failing to provide for genuine monetary needs that will permit the caregiver to secure much needed instrumental support.

When older relatives become physically frail, dependency on family members is inevitable. However, several research and policy questions need to be addressed in models of social care that integrate family members (Cantor, 1991). First, there is little research on the influence of race, culture, and class on the utilization of formal and informal support and their interaction; yet, there is tremendous cultural diversity in the level of need for formal care and its perceived acceptability. Second, if, as is predicted, home-based community care expands significantly and becomes integrated into acute, managed-care systems, how will this influence informal support, if at all? Managed care typically involves less choice in care providers. Will this make elders more re-luctant to accept formal services and increase their reliance on family mem-bers? Third, how is it determined whether kin are "available" and what is an equitable division of responsibility between family members and formal care providers (Cantor, 1991)? Fourth, when should guardianship be obtained and how best to represent the interests of older adults and protect them from po-tential conflicts of interest? The complexity of negotiations between older adults, family, and service providers must be recognized, including the fact that both elders and family have rights to their personal desires, which may be in conflict. Practical help to families—assuming there are family caregivers—thus promotes both interdependence and autonomy.

UNIVERSAL PREVENTIVE INTERVENTIONS

Universal prevention programs target all elders and emphasize the role of helper in promoting wellness; neighborhood network building as a preventive strategy; empowerment strategies; and advocacy.

The role of the elderly as helpers in volunteer and peer counseling programs has received a great deal of notice, and much is made of the potential benefits of helping roles to the helpers themselves. Rates of volunteerism have increased over the past 25 years (Chambré, 1993) and older volunteers are involved in di-verse positions: outreach and case-finding representatives (e.g., Morrow-Howell & Ozawa, 1987), peer counselors in the community and in nursing homes (e.g., Crose, Duffy, Warren, & Franklin, 1987), volunteer mediators (e.g., Cox & Parsons, 1992), advocates for the elderly in long-term care (e.g., Zischka & Jones, 1984), and intergenerational service program providers (e.g., Camp et al., 1997; and see review by Dellmann-Jenkins, 1997). An example of an intergenerational program with benefits to both children and seniors was the "Grandma Please" program, in which senior counselors (including some who were homebound or residents of nursing homes) provided telephone advice and assistance to inner-city children (Szendre & Jose, 1996). Although latchkey children were the identi-fied targets for supportive services, seniors expressed high levels of satisfaction with these interactions. Indeed, promoting the well-being and development of children has often been the focus of these programs.

Most programs are built on volunteerism, and may or may not require a great deal of the older volunteer beyond participation in a training workshop on communication skills (e.g., Hyde, 1988), community resources, and so forth. Occasional programs emphasize the paraprofessional role; these tend to have more extensive training and may pay the older worker.

Losee, Auerbach, and Parham (1988) evaluated a peer counselor hotline and assessed the extent to which technical skills (e.g., identification of client problem and resources, formulation of course of action) and clinical effec-tiveness (e.g., communication of positive regard) contributed to overall client satisfaction with the service and problem resolution. Results indicated that each of these skills are differentially related to outcome, with technical skills leading to more effective problem resolution and clinical skills related to greater client satisfaction. This outcome argues for greater attention to training if the target of the intervention is the client as well as the older adult paraprofessional or volunteer.

Gatz, Hileman, and Amaral (1984) reviewed programs in which older adults were helping other older adults, from peer counselors to indigenous community workers, and reached several conclusions. First, positive effects for helpers are better documented than positive effects for recipients. Second, given that not all responses to people under stress are helpful responses (Dunkel-Schetter & Wortman, 1981), it is important to train peer counselors rather than simply to rely on their natural abilities. Third, although arguments are made that peer programs provide help without stigma and are a cost-effective solution to a scarcity of professional resources, these programs should be seen as supplementing, not replacing, professional help (Morrow-Howell & Ozawa, 1987). Fourth, peer programs represent a community intervention in which there has been explicit attention to cultural differences. Selecting, training, and supervising "natural helpers" has been viewed as a particularly good idea for helping minority elderly (Milligan, Maryland, Ziegler, & Ward, 1987).

Universal preventive interventions also focus on building neighborhood networks of mutual assistance and creating opportunities for empowerment. Rubin and Black (1992) described a Town Meeting for Seniors program designed to empower older adults by providing them with information about medical care (e.g., insurance, advance directives), health promotion and wellness, and legal, ethical, and financial aspects of aging. Other programs have targeted specific cultural groups. For example, the Asian Human Care Centers Senior Empowerment project (Tsukahira, 1987) emphasized getting information about services to older immigrants in the form of fact sheets, videos, and community education forums. Other programs have recruited individuals from religious institutions and retirement communities and trained them as community-based lay health educators (Hale, Bennett, Oslos, Cochran, & Burton, 1997). Some of these educators were from African American churches, facilitating access to a group that are not well served by traditional health care approaches. Market research has suggested that elders may not identify with organizations for seniors because they do not perceive themselves as poor enough, frail enough, or old enough (Gallant, Cohen, & Wolff, 1985).

Most of these interventions do not include control groups, making it difficult to assess their effects. An exception to this was a study by Baumgarten, Thomas, Poulin de Courval, and Infante-Rivard (1988) evaluating the effects of a mutual help network intervention in an age-dense apartment building. A similar setting in the same neighborhood served as the control group. The intervention lasted 16 months and involved matching individuals who needed assistance with those who were willing to help, and planning leisure and cultural group activities. Despite relatively high rates of participation and mutual exchange, results were disappointing. There were no significant differences between the control and experimental groups in the size of social networks or in social support satisfaction. Moreover, subjects in the experimental condition reported higher levels of depression on posttest, whereas those in the control condition had a small decrease. These findings suggest a need for greater sensitivity to the unintended negative consequences of social network interventions, and serve to temper the unbridled optimism often associated with these types of programs. Korte (1991) suggests that mutual aid interventions contradict values of independence and self-sufficiency, and that these programs may be viable only in special circumstances. These situations would include those where money is a more scarce resource than time, or among cultures where mutual aid is more normative.

Some interventions at the community level are designed to provide mental health services, including community education (see review by Knight et al., 1995). Pratt, Schmall, Wilson, and Benthin (1991) developed a community-based education program on depression and suicide for older adults, families, and service providers. In a three-hour workshop, lectures, individual and group activities, and discussions were used to familiarize participants with risk factors for depression and suicide, myths about depression and suicide, and warning signs of suicide. In addition, participants were provided with information about responding to these problems on a personal level and accessing professional help. Compared with a control group, those attending the workshop showed significant gains in knowledge about these conditions and were more inclined to take appropriate action, such as talking directly to the person about his or her depression, or recommending professional help.

In general, neighborhood network building programs emphasize mutual assistance, greater interagency collaboration, education, outreach to at-risk persons (sometimes involving gatekeepers), advocacy, and empowerment. Programs addressing mental health concerns are still rare, as are well-evaluated programs. The roles of the professional in the community empowerment model include advocate, consultant, and facilitator. The professional can aid in identifying common interests and encouraging a collective effort across groups divided by age, race, social class, and gender (Biegel, Shore, & Gordon, 1984). The implementation of community empowerment programs requires a high level of administrative support in the initial stages and may take considerable time to identify and build the necessary grassroots organization. In addition, efforts may be met with resistance, in part because of the novelty of an intervention that places primary control in the hands of the served. Furthermore, empowerment interventions may show few short-term benefits and thus may fail to attract the necessary funding and political support for survival.

Advocacy groups are essentially a cohesive constituency formed to exert political and social influence, and a number are devoted to addressing issues of old age; for example, the American Association of Retired Persons (AARP), the National Council of Senior Citizens, and the Gray Panthers. Other advocacy groups represent subpopulations, including older African Americans (the National Caucus on the Black Aged), older Latinos (Asociación Nacional pro Personas Mayores), and older women (the Older Women's League or OWL).

Advocacy groups have also been formed exclusively at the local level, as was the case with a Chicago coalition of senior groups, Metro Seniors in Action

(Reitzes & Reitzes, 1991). These authors provide several important recommendations for ensuring the survival and efficacy of citywide advocacy groups: (1) continued maintenance in terms of ongoing and active liaisons with key individuals, community groups, and statewide organizations; (2) the need for an experienced and professional organizer, especially in the early stages of development; (3) the necessity of membership dues for enhancing commitment to the organization; (4) an organizing body or board that is sensitive to the needs of its constituents, and (5) the continued use of protest and confrontation to attract media attention to issues of exploitation and inhumane treatment of elderly persons.

Among the issues addressed by advocacy groups is intergenerational equity and inequity. Increasingly, older adults are being recognized by the private sector as an affluent and growing consumer group. Minkler (1989) argues convincingly that economically, older adults have fared better over the past 16 years than their younger counterparts. All older adults, however, have not shared in this increased prosperity. Minority elders and the oldest old continue to be among the poorest segments of the elderly population. A realistic concern is that the current stereotype of the aged as a politically powerful and economically well-off group will jeopardize funding for much needed services for at-risk elderly.

Rosenbaum and Button (1993) suggest that attitudes, beliefs, and stereotypes are often precursors to social change. Their telephone survey data from over 1,000 Florida citizens revealed that about one-third to one-half of younger respondents perceived older adults as an "economic burden, an economically selfish voting block, a generationally divisive influence, or an unconstructive community element" (p. 488). Moreover, these attitudes were strongest in counties with higher proportions of older residents. Due to its large proportion of seniors, Florida may represent the future of many communities across the United States, in which younger adults will coexist with an economically and politically advantaged majority of seniors. The general conclusion is that intergenerational conflict is increasing and will continue to do so.

As a consequence, several authors (e.g., Kingson, 1988; Wisensale, 1988) have encouraged advocacy groups to broaden the politics of aging by placing greater emphasis on themes of generational equity and social justice between rich and poor. Although interest group politics do not generally lend themselves to such an altruistic approach, there are several clear advantages. These include increased legitimacy for the aging lobby, protection of tomorrow's elderly, and reduced intergenerational conflict.

CONCLUSION

It has been said that a society may be judged by the way it treats its youth and its aged. By this standard, application of a community psychology conceptual framework to intervention in the lives of older adults sounds a hopeful note.

Empowerment programs are generally designed to accomplish at least two things: they foster a sense of efficacy in individuals by giving them control over decisions in their lives; and they change the nature of the helping relationship to make it more symmetrical (Gesten & Jason, 1987; Rappaport, 1985). These two perspectives offer direction to program planners and community researchers. However, empowering the older adult is often limited by what is available or possible. Negotiating autonomy in old age requires coming to terms with personal and societal resources. By and large, prevention programs have been neither fundable nor reimbursable (Levine & Perkins, 1997). A chief determinant of decisions regarding programming for older adults is sheer availability: number of rooms in a residence, or funds available to pay for home care. In this respect, perhaps the ecology of empowerment is more clear in old age than at any other life stage.

Nevertheless, a wide range of community interventions have been used with older adults. The frequency of evaluated programs is low, however. The main foci of community programs have been increasing social networks, preventing institutionalization, and supporting family caregivers. Rationales for these goals are obvious and good, yet some conceptual concerns within these foci remain neglected or only superficially addressed. For example, community interventions aimed at increasing social networks often fail to take into account that all support does not equally serve to build competence. In interventions aimed at preventing institutionalization, older adults are rarely involved in decision making or made a partner in their own care, but are often treated as an object of concern. Regarding interventions aimed at supporting family caregivers, although fostering the family's mental health and autonomy sometimes predicts better caregiving (at least the family caregiver continues in the role for longer), such a focus may diminish the perspective and concerns of the older individuals themselves. Cutting across these foci of prevention is the question of the older adult's right to autonomy on the one hand, and the balance of risk and protection as an obligation of the larger environment, including the family, on the other.

Refinement of concepts on which intervention programs are premised, and controlled evaluations of these interventions, could make an enormous contribution to improving the ways in which society is responding to the needs of older adults. Two images of the older adult, both true, must inform program planning for community interventions. One image is of vitality: the older person planning new undertakings, conveying wisdom built up over a lifetime. The other image is of limitation: the older person realistically aware of the inevitable and often limiting changes in the life of an aging individual, particularly changes in physical health. The concept of empowerment—key to many community psychology interventions—has the capacity to encompass both images and to recognize the need to match programs to persons.

REFERENCES

Aneshensel, C.S., Pearlin, L.I., Mullan, J.T., Zarit, S.H., & Whitlatch, C.J. (1995). *Profiles in caregiving: The unexpected career*. New York: Academic Press.

Arling, G., & McAuley, W.J. (1983). The feasibility of public payments for family caregiving. *Gerontologist, 23*, 300–306.

Atkinson, V.L., & Stuck, B.M. (1991). Mental health services for the rural elderly: The SAGE experience. *Gerontologist, 4,* 548–551.

Bachman, D.L., Wolf, P.A., Linn, R., Knoefel, J.E., Cobb, J., Belanger, A., D'Agostino, R.B., & White, L.R. (1992). Prevalence of dementia and probable senile dementia of the Alzheimer's type in the Framingham Study. *Neurology, 42,* 115–119.

Baltes, P.B., & Baltes, M.M. (1990). Psychological perspectives on successful aging: The model of selective optimization with compensation. In P.B. Baltes & M.M. Baltes (Eds.), *Successful aging: Perspectives from the behavioral sciences* (pp. 1–34). New York: Cambridge University Press.

Baumgarten, M., Thomas, D., Poulin de Courval, L., & Infante-Rivard, C. (1988). Evaluation of a mutual help network for the elderly residents of planned housing. *Psychology and Aging, 3,* 393–398.

Bengtson, V.L., Marti, G., & Roberts, R.E.L. (1991). Age-group relationships: Generational equity and inequity. In K. Pillemer & K. McCartney (Eds.), *Parent-child relations throughout life* (pp. 253–278). Hillsdale, NJ: Erlbaum.

Bickman, L., & Dokecki, P.R. (1989). Public and private responsibility for mental health services. *American Psychologist, 44,* 1133–1137.

Biegel, D.E., Morycz, R., Schulz, R., & Shore, B.K. (1986). *Family elder care incentive policies.* Final Report to the Pennsylvania Department of Aging.

Biegel, D.E., Shore, B.K., & Gordon, E. (1984). *Building support networks for the elderly: Theory and applications.* Beverly Hills, CA: Sage.

Blazer, D., Hughes, D.C., & George, L.K. (1987). The epidemiology of depression in an elderly community population. *Gerontologist, 27,* 281–287.

Bodnar, J.C., & Kiecolt-Glaser, J.K. (1994). Caregiver depression after bereavement: Chronic stress isn't over when it's over. *Psychology and Aging, 9,* 372–380.

Braddy, B.A., & Gray, D.O. (1987). Employment services for older job seekers: A comparison of two client-centered approaches. *Gerontologist, 27,* 565–568.

Branch, L., Coulam, R.F., & Zimmerman, Y.A. (1995). The PACE evaluation: Initial findings. *Gerontologist, 35,* 349–359.

Brody, E.M. (1985). Parent care as a normative family stress. *Gerontologist, 25,* 19–29.

Buckwalter, K.C., Smith, M., Zevenbergen, P., & Russell, D. (1991). Mental health services of the rural elderly outreach program. *Gerontologist, 31,* 408–412.

Camp, C.J., Judge, K.S., Bye, C.A., Fox, K.M., Bowden, J., Bell, M., Valencic, K., & Mattern, J.M. (1997). An intergenerational program for persons with dementia using Montessori methods. *Gerontologist, 37,* 688–692.

Cantor, M.H. (1991). Family and community: Changing roles in an aging society. *Gerontologist, 31,* 337–346.

Caserta, M.S., & Lund, D.A. (1993). Intrapersonal resources and the effectiveness of self-help groups for bereaved older adults. *Gerontologist, 33,* 619–629.

Chambré, S.M. (1993). Volunteerism by elders: Past trends and future prospects. *Gerontologist, 33,* 221–228.

Cohen, M.A. (1998). Emerging trends in the finance and delivery of long-term care: Public and private opportunities and challenges. *Gerontologist, 38,* 80–89.

Coie, J.D., Watt, N.F., West, S.G., Hawkins, J.D., Asarnow, J.R., Markman, H.J., Ramney, S.L., Shure, M.B., & Long, B. (1993). The science of prevention: A conceptual framework and some directions for a national research program. *American Psychologist, 48,* 1013–1022.

Cox, E.O., & Parsons, R.J. (1992). Senior-to-senior mediation service project. *Gerontologist, 32,* 420–422.

Crose, R., Duffy, M., Warren, J., & Franklin, B. (1987). Project OASIS: Volunteer mental health paraprofessionals serving nursing home residents. *Gerontologist, 27,* 359–362.

Dellmann-Jenkins, M. (1997). A senior-centered model of intergenerational programming with young children. *Journal of Applied Gerontology, 16,* 495–506.

Dunkel-Schetter, C., & Wortman, C.B. (1981). Dilemmas of social support: Parallels between victimization and aging. In S.B. Kiesler, J.N. Morgan, & V.K. Oppenheimer (Eds.), *Aging: Social change* (pp. 349–381). New York: Academic Press.

Estes, C.L. (1995). Mental health services for the elderly. In M. Gatz (Ed.), *Emerging issues in mental health and aging* (pp. 303–327). Washington, DC: American Psychological Association.

Evans, D.A., Funkenstein, H.H., Albert, M.S., Scherr, P.A., Cook, N.R., Chown, M.J., Hebert, L.E., Hennekens, C.H., & Taylor, J.O. (1989). Prevalence of Alzheimer's disease in a community population of older persons: Higher than previously reported. *Journal of the American Medical Association, 262,* 2551–2556.

Franzke, A.W. (1987). The effects of assertiveness training on older adults. *Gerontologist, 27,* 13–16.

Gallagher-Thompson, D., & Steffen, A.M. (1994). Comparative effects of cognitive-behavioral and brief psychodynamic psychotherapies for depressed family caregivers. *Journal of Consulting and Clinical Psychology, 62,* 543–549.

Gallant, R.V., Cohen, C., & Wolff, T. (1985). Change of older persons' image, impact on public policy result from Highland Valley empowerment plan. *Perspectives on Aging, 14,* 9–13.

Gatz, M., Hileman, C., & Amaral, P. (1984). Older adult paraprofessionals: Working with and in behalf of older adults. *Journal of Community Psychology, 12,* 347–358.

George, L.K., Blazer, D.F., Winfield-Laird, I., Leaf, P.J., & Fischbach, R.L. (1988). Psychiatric disorders and mental health service use in later life: Evidence from the epidemiologic catchment area program. In J. Brody & G. Maddox (Eds.), *Epidemiology and aging* (pp. 189–219). New York: Springer.

Gesten, E.L., & Jason, L.A. (1987). Social and community interventions. *Annual Review of Psychology, 38,* 427–460.

Grady, S.C., & Maynard, C.L. (1985). Building ties: A mental health and aging project. *Gerontologist, 27,* 428–429.

Graves, A.B., & Kukull, W.A. (1994). The epidemiology of dementia. In J.C. Morris (Ed.), *Handbook of dementing illnesses* (pp. 23–70). New York: Marcel Dekker.

Greene, V.L., Lovely, M.E., & Ondrich, J.I. (1993). The cost-effectiveness of community services in a frail elderly population. *Gerontologist, 33,* 177–189.

Hale, W.D., Bennett, R.G., Oslos, N.R., Cochran, C.D., & Burton, J.R. (1997). Project REACH: A program to train community-based lay health educators. *Gerontologist, 37,* 683–687.

Heller, K., Thompson, M.G., Trueba, P.E., Hogg, J.R., & Vlachos-Weber, I. (1991). Peer support telephone dyads for elderly women: Was this the wrong intervention? *American Journal of Community Psychology, 19,* 53–74.

Hendricks, J., & Leedham, C.A. (1989). Creating psychological and societal dependency in old age. In P.S. Fry (Ed.), *Psychological perspectives of helplessness and control in the elderly* (pp. 369–394). North-Holland, The Netherlands: Elsavier Science.

Hough, R.L., Gongla, P.A., Brown, V.B., & Goldston, S.E. (Eds.). (1985). *Psychiatric epidemiology and prevention: The possibilities.* Los Angeles: Neuropsychiatric Institute, University of California, Los Angeles.

Hyde, R.B. (1988). Facilitative communication skills training: Social support for elderly people. *Gerontologist, 28,* 418–420.

Kane, R. (1986). Senile dementia and public policy. In M.L. Gilhooly, S.A. Zarit, & J.E. Birren (Eds.), *The dementias: Policy and management* (pp. 190–214). Englewood Cliffs, NJ: Prentice-Hall.

Karel, M.J. (1997). Aging and depression: Vulnerability and stress across adulthood. *Clinical Psychology Review, 17,* 847–879.

Karuza, J., Calkins, E., Duffey, J., & Feather, J. (1988). Networking in aging: A challenge, model, and evaluation. *Gerontologist, 28,* 147–155.

Kemp, B.J., Staples, F., & Lopez-Aqueres, W.L. (1987). Epidemiology of depression and dysphoria in an elderly Hispanic population: Prevalence and correlates. *Journal of the American Geriatrics Society, 35,* 920–926.

Kingson, E.R. (1988). Generational equity: An unexpected opportunity to broaden the politics of aging. *Gerontologist, 28,* 765–772.

Knight, B.G., & Kaskie, B. (1995). Models for mental health service delivery to older adults. In M. Gatz (Ed.), *Emerging issues in mental health and aging* (pp. 231–255). Washington, DC: American Psychological Association.

Knight, B.G., Lutzky, S.M., & Macofsky-Urban, F. (1993). A meta-analytic review of interventions for caregiver distress: Recommendations for future research. *Gerontologist, 33,* 240–248.

Knight, B.G., Rickards, L., Rabins, P., Buckwalter, K., & Smith, M. (1995). Community-based services for older adults: A role for psychologists? In B.G. Knight, L. Teri, P. Wohlford, & J. Santos (Eds.), *Mental health services for older adults: Implications for training and practice in geropsychology* (pp. 21–29). Washington, DC: American Psychological Association.

Korte, C. (1991). The receptivity of older adults to innovative mutual-aid arrangements. *Journal of Community Psychology, 19,* 237–243.

Korte, C., & Gupta, V. (1991). A program of friendly visitors as network builders. *Gerontologist, 31,* 404–407.

Kral, V.A. (1968). In geriatric psychiatry. In F.C.R. Chalke & J.J. Day (Eds.), *Primary prevention of psychiatric disorders* (pp. 129–139). Toronto: University of Toronto Press.

Lawton, M., Brody, E., & Saperstein, A. (1991). *Respite for caregivers of Alzheimer's patients: Research and practice.* New York: Springer.

Lazarus, R.S., & DeLongis, A. (1983). Psychological stress and coping in old age. *American Psychologist, 38,* 245–254.

Lehman, D.R., Ellard, J.H., & Wortman, C.B. (1986). Social support for the bereaved: Recipients' and providers' perspectives on what is helpful. *Journal of Consulting and Clinical Psychology, 54,* 438–446.

Levine, M., & Perkins, D.V. (1997). *Principles of community psychology.* New York: Oxford University Press.

Lieberman, M.A. (1996). *Doors close, doors open: Widows grieving and growing.* Newark, NJ: Putnam.

Losee, N., Auerbach, S.M., & Parham, I. (1988). Effectiveness of a peer counselor hotline for the elderly. *Journal of Community Psychology, 16,* 428–436.

Manton, K.G. (1990). Mortality and morbidity. In R.H. Binstock & L.K. George (Eds.), *Handbook of aging and the social sciences* (pp. 64–90). New York: Academic Press.

Mawson, D., Marks, I.M., Ramm, L., & Stern, R.S. (1981). Guided mourning for morbid grief: A controlled study. *British Journal of Psychiatry, 138,* 185–193.

Milligan, S., Maryland, P., Ziegler, H., & Ward, A. (1987). Natural helpers as street health workers among the Black urban elderly. *Gerontologist, 27,* 712–715.

Minkler, M. (1989). Gold in grey: Reflections on business' discovery of the elderly market. *Gerontologist, 29,* 17–23.

Mittelman, M.S., Ferris, S.H., Steinberg, G., Shulman, E., Mackell, J.A., Ambinder, A., & Cohen, J. (1993). An intervention that delays institutionalization of Alzheimer's disease patients: Treatment of spouse caregivers. *Gerontologist, 33,* 730–740.

Morrow-Howell, N., & Ozawa, M.N. (1987). Helping network: Seniors to seniors. *Gerontologist, 27*, 17–20.

Mrazek, P.J., & Haggerty, R.J. (Eds.). (1994). *Reducing risks for mental disorders: Frontiers for preventive intervention research.* Washington, DC: National Academy Press.

Muñoz, R.F., Mrazek, P.J., & Haggerty, R.J. (1996). Institute of medicine report on prevention of mental disorders: Summary and commentary. *American Psychologist, 51,* 1116–1122.

Murrell, S.A., Norris, F.H., & Grote, C. (1988). Life events in older adults. In L. Cohen (Ed.), *Life events and psychological functioning: Theoretical and methodological issues* (pp. 96–122). Beverly Hills, CA: Sage.

Murrell, S.A., Norris, F.H., & Hutchins, G.L. (1984). Distribution and desirability of life events in older adults: Population and policy implications. *Journal of Community Psychology, 12,* 301–311.

NIMH Committee on Prevention Research. (1995, May 15). *A plan for prevention research for the National Institute of Mental Health* (A report to the National Advisory Mental Health Council). Washington, DC: Author.

Norris, F.H., & Murrell, S.A. (1984). Protective function of resources related to life events, global stress, and depression in older adults. *Journal of Health and Social Behavior, 25,* 424–437.

Norris, F.H., & Murrell, S.A. (1988). Prior experience as a moderator of disaster impact on anxiety symptoms in older adults. *American Journal of Community Psychology, 16,* 665–683.

Okun, M.A., Olding, R.W., & Cohn, C.M.G. (1990). A meta-analysis of subjective well-being interventions among elders. *Psychological Bulletin, 108,* 257–266.

Pearson, C., Seward, M., & Gatz, M. (1989). Lifeline and other personal emergency response systems. In L.E. Miles (Ed.), *Medical monitoring in the home and work environment* (pp. 317–328). New York: Raven Press.

Phillips, M.A., & Murrell, S.A. (1994). Impact of psychological and physical health, stressful events, and social support on subsequent mental health help seeking among older adults. *Journal of Consulting and Clinical Psychology, 62,* 270–275.

Pilisuk, M., & Minkler, M. (1980). Supportive networks: Life ties for the elderly. *Journal of Social Issues, 36,* 95–116.

Pratt, C.C., Schmall, V.L., Wilson, W., & Benthin, A. (1991). A model community education program on depression and suicide in later life. *Gerontologist, 31,* 692–695.

Pruchno, R.A., Michaels, J.E., & Potashnik, S.L. (1990). Predictors of institutionalization among Alzheimer disease victims with caregiving spouses. *Journal of Gerontology: Social Sciences, 45,* S259–S266.

Rabins, P.V. (1992). Prevention of mental disorder in the elderly: Current perspectives and future prospects. *Journal of the American Geriatrics Society, 40,* 727–733.

Radebaugh, T.K., & Gruenberg, E.M. (1985). Prevention and the helping networks of older people. In R.L. Hough, P.A. Gongla, V.B. Brown, & S.E. Goldston (Eds.), *Psychiatric epidemiology and prevention: The possibilities* (pp. 97–105). Los Angeles: Neuropsychiatric Institute, University of California.

Rappaport, J. (1985). The power of empowerment language. *Social Policy, 15,* 15–21.

Reiss, D., & Price, R.H. (1996). National research agenda for prevention research: The National Institute of Mental Health report. *American Psychologist, 51,* 1109–1115.

Reitzes, D.C., & Reitzes, D.C. (1991). Metro seniors in action: A case study of a city-wide senior organization. *Gerontologist, 31,* 256–262.

Rosenbaum, W.A., & Button, J.W. (1993). The unquiet future of intergenerational politics. *Gerontologist, 33,* 481–490.

Roush, R.E., & Teasdale, T.A. (1997). Reduced hospitalization rates of two sets of community-residing older adults after use of a personal response system. *Journal of Applied Gerontology, 16,* 355–366.

Rubin, F.H., & Black, J.S. (1992). Health care and consumer control: Pittsburgh's town meeting for seniors. *Gerontologist, 32,* 853–855.

Schulz, R., & Heckhausen, J. (1996). A life span model of successful aging. *American Psychologist, 51,* 702–714.

Shope, J.T., Holmes, S.B., Sharpe, P.A., Goodman, C., Izenson, S., Gilman, S., & Foster, N.L. (1993). Services for persons with dementia and their families: A survey of information and referral agencies in Michigan. *Gerontologist, 33,* 529–533.

Siegel, J.M., & Kuykendall, D.H. (1990). Loss, widowhood, and psychological distress among the elderly. *Journal of Consulting and Clinical Psychology, 58,* 519–524.

Simmons, K.H., Ivry, J., & Seltzer, M.M. (1985). Agency-family collaboration. *Gerontologist, 25,* 343–346.

Smyer, M.A. (1995). Prevention and early intervention for mental disorders of the elderly. In M. Gatz (Ed.), *Emerging issues in mental health and aging* (pp. 163–182). Washington, DC: American Psychological Association.

Stroebe, M.S., Stroebe, W., & Hansson, R.O. (1993). *Handbook of bereavement: Theory, research, and intervention.* New York: Cambridge University Press.

Szendre, E.N., & Jose, P.E. (1996). Telephone support by elderly volunteers to inner-city children. *Journal of Community Psychology, 24,* 87–96.

Thompson, L.W., Gallagher, D., Nies, G., & Epstein, D. (1983). Evaluation of the effectiveness of professionals and nonprofessionals as instructors of "Coping and depression" classes for elderly. *Gerontologist, 23,* 390–396.

Toseland, R.W., & Rossiter, C.M. (1989). Group interventions to support family caregivers: A review and analysis. *Gerontologist, 29,* 438–448.

Tsukahira, Y. (1987). Fostering empowerment of older Asians. *Aging Network News, 4,* 6–7.

U.S. General Accounting Office. (1992). *The elderly remain in need of mental health services* (GAO/HRD-B2-112). Gaithersburg, MD: U.S. Government Printing Office.

Waters, E. (1995). Let's not wait till it's broke: Interventions to maintain and enhance mental health in late life. In M. Gatz (Ed.), *Emerging issues in mental health and aging* (pp. 183–209). Washington, DC: American Psychological Association.

Weissert, W.G. (1985). Seven reasons why it is so difficult to make community-based long-term care cost-effective. *HSR: Health Services Research, 20,* 423–433.

Wilkinson, A.M. (1996). Past research on long-term care case management demonstrations. In R.J. Newcomer, A.M. Wilkinson, & M.P. Lawton (Eds.), *Annual review of gerontology and geriatrics* (Vol. 16, pp. 78–111). New York: Springer.

Wisensale, S.K. (1988). Generational equity and intergenerational policies. *Gerontologist, 27,* 773–778.

Wortman, C.B., & Cohen Silver, R. (1990). Successful mastery of bereavement and widowhood: A life-course perspective. In P.B. Baltes & M.M. Baltes (Eds.), *Successful aging: Perspectives from the behavioral sciences* (pp. 225–264). New York: Cambridge University Press.

Yeatts, D.E., Crow, T., & Folts, E. (1992). Service use among low-income minority elderly: Strategies for overcoming barriers. *Gerontologist, 32,* 24–32.

Zarit, S.H., Todd, P.A., & Zarit, J.M. (1986). Subjective burden of husbands and wives as caregivers: A longitudinal study. *Gerontologist, 20,* 260–266.

Zischka, P.C., & Jones, I. (1984). Volunteer community representatives ombudsmen for the elderly in long-term care facilities. *Gerontologist, 24,* 9–12.

CHAPTER 20

Enhancing Mental Health Climate in Hospitals and Nursing Homes: Collaboration Strategies for Medical and Mental Health Staff

KAREN SANDERS, JO ANN BROCKWAY, BEATRICE ELLIS, ELIZABETH M. COTTON, AND JUNE BREDIN

I think making someone feel uncared for and unloved must be the most awful feeling and I feel that even the most confused patients can still sense this.

—A Nurse

J.S. is an 85-year-old retired engineer with Parkinson's disease and non-specific dementia. His wife is 72 and has heart disease. He has two children from an earlier marriage, both of whom live out of state. Mrs. S. cared for her husband at home until she was overwhelmed by his incontinence, wandering, and her own health problems. She recounts:

I looked at all the local nursing homes and put him on two waiting lists, but I just couldn't handle things at home any more and so I brought him to this one, which is a little farther away than I would have liked. It isn't the best place; the facility is wonderful, but there never seem to be enough staff. It's a big problem at night, because my husband wanders into other patients' rooms, and even found his way into the parking lot the other night. They have a Wanderguard on him, but he got out nevertheless.

He has deteriorated so fast since I brought him here. He is very confused much of the time. He's furious with me and accuses me of all sorts of things. I'm here every day, and if I'm not here in the evening he accuses me of being out with other men. I know he's depressed, too. Before he came here I took him to a psychiatrist who started him on a small dose of Paxil, but I don't think it worked. Now I can't take him back to the psychiatrist—it's too much for me—and she won't see him here.

Recently he started hallucinating. I called his primary physician, who came out to evaluate him and stopped about half of his medications. He also requested a mental health evaluation by the nursing home social worker. I wanted them to give him something to sleep at night, but they said he falls too much already and it wouldn't be safe to sedate him. They said it would be better to use behavioral techniques, but I'm not sure what that is. They said they would try to keep him awake all day because he has his nights and days mixed up. But every day when I get here I find him asleep in his chair. I can't be here all the time.

I do as much as I can, but it gets to be too much for me. I tried to keep him at home as long as I could. I thought it would be easier to have him here, but it's still so difficult. I crash and burn, then I pick up and go on, and crash and burn again. My doctor says I need heart surgery to replace a valve. Who's going to take care of me?

Mr. and Mrs. S. find themselves in an increasingly common situation: Both have major health issues and face them with limited resources and few options. The scenario is complicated by staffing problems in the nursing home and fragmentation of care. It may also be complicated by other losses and ongoing family problems.

Problems for Mr. S. include depression, confusion, suspiciousness, sleep disturbance, poor functioning, safety concerns (falling, wandering), and an overall diminished quality of life, in addition to the problems associated with his Parkinson's disease. His wife worries about him, and experiences frustration with doctors and staff related to incomplete knowledge of her husband's condition, prognosis, and treatment, and an unclear sense of which responsibilities are hers and which are not. She also has her own health problems and worries. The providers have their own frustrations as well. The off-site physician is put in the position of making treatment decisions with limited diagnostic and other information. Facility staff may not have been provided with a clear treatment plan, rationale, or means by which to implement it, leaving them with added tasks to solve, such as addressing the consequences of Mr. S.'s wandering, to ensure his safety and that of the other residents, or additional responsibility for keeping him on a regular sleep-wake schedule.

The problems facing the elderly are often complex and multilayered. One patient facing a below-the-knee amputation has been caring for his wife with Alzheimer's disease. Another, the legal guardian of her two young grandchildren whose parents are drug addicted, now has had a stroke with right hemiparesis and aphasia. All of these patients have multiple needs: medical, social, financial, psychological, spiritual, and functional.

Primary care physicians managing patients with these complex needs may be relatively isolated from professional resources that could enhance mental health care and outcomes for patient, family, and staff. Many patients in extended care facilities could greatly benefit by increased contact and collaboration between primary care physicians and mental health and other specialty disciplines.

How do we best care for these patients? In this chapter, we look at the issues impacting mental health of older patients in hospitals and nursing homes from several perspectives, a team approach to treatment, and a proposed model of collaborative care in the nursing home setting. It is our thesis that enhancing mental health climate in hospitals and nursing homes is best done using a patient-centered model of collaborative care.

In our experience the best approach uses an *interdisciplinary, collaborative, dynamic, integrated, patient-centered* model of care. The model is interdisciplinary in that a number of disciplines are involved, depending on the needs of the patient. It is collaborative in that there is on-going communication and exchange of ideas, collegial interactions, mutual respect for the expertise and differences in perspective among team members, and an inclusive biopsychosocial (rather than compartmentalized) approach to the patient arriving at a "whole-person" set of treatment goals. It is dynamic in that the goals are continually reevaluated as the patient's needs change.

The model is also integrated in that each goal may be addressed by several team members. For example, if using memory aids is the goal, a speech pathologist may address this in a formal speech session, and other team members can be taught to complement and reinforce this in the day-to-day environment.

Lastly, the model is patient-centered. The treatment plan is designed with the patient's perspective in mind. Understanding the patient's perspective requires that the members of the treatment team be knowledgeable about the aging process and confront their own attitudes toward aging and the aged. We need to understand our own biases to avoid transferring them to our patients.

THREE PERSPECTIVES

Let us now look at the process of aging and the treatment of older individuals from the perspectives of three health care team disciplines, psychologist, nurse, and physician.

A psychologist who has practiced for 15 to 20 years in various older adult agencies, hospitals and nursing homes, in the capacity of music therapist, neuropsychologist, and psychologist relates, "In these 20 years, I have continually experienced the need to challenge my own attitudes as well as those of my colleagues, patients, and families regarding growing older with grace and dignity. I often ask fellow professionals in Northwest training sessions to draw a picture of themselves at the age of 80. Self drawings ranged from grave stones to climbing Mt. Rainier" (Sanders, personal communication, 1998).

Our attitudes about aging vary, perhaps related to the types of modeling we have had in our own upbringing, perhaps by our own experience with grandparents and parents. Do we expect to be healthy or sick, alone or with others, learning or bored? It is important that health care providers working with older adults be aware of their own biases and how those biases influence their perceptions of their patients and their expectation about their patients potential level of function.

A family physician who attends at a nursing home comments that it is often overwhelming: "Like the case example beginning this chapter, I find myself fielding varied medical, mental health, social and financial concerns, both from family and staff. Often, I address concerns raised only by phone or FAX. Seeing patients only once a month, it is difficult to remain current on the patient's day to day function. There is often limited access to specialty/mental health resources, and even when such resources are available, time for meaningful exchange of information is rare. *Any* collaboration efforts/resources would greatly improve both the care delivered and the stress levels for staff and providers" (Cotton, personal communication, 1998).

The nursing staff of a local inpatient geropsychiatry unit were surveyed regarding their experiences with collaboration. They offered the following comments regarding fruitful interactions, knowledge to be shared, and pitfalls (Highline Nursing Staff, personal communication, 1998).

Interactions among providers and toward patients and family should create an atmosphere of caring, respect, support, and communication. These nurses emphasize collaboration that revolves around patient-focused discussions, in which information is shared among staff and with the family and patient, consistently including the family and patient in the ongoing treatment process. Thorough and accurate reporting by all staff is important.

It is essential for providers to treat all ideas, regardless of source, with respect, to educate staff about how to best meet patient needs, and to educate families about the loved one's problems and how to promote residual function. Slowness and physical limitations require patience on the part of the staff. It is important to demonstrate respect and caring, even when there is conflict with the patient or family.

Nurses need to spend individual time with patients several times in a shift and to note changes. They make every effort to see the patient's viewpoint and be accepting and respectful of realistic and unrealistic requests and convey them to the team. If these requests cannot be met, then it is important to be open about that to the family.

On the topic of collaboration, nurses noted that they spend the most time of any discipline with the patients, and they have valuable input that should be listened to. They are the team members who, on a day-to-day basis, have the most opportunity to integrate biomedical and psychosocial information from patient, family, and providers.

Nurses also noted the importance to them of input from other providers. They rely, for example, on social work for contact with outside sources and information on resources for patient problems: on occupational therapists (OTs) for information about the patient's functional daily living ability and on physical therapists (PTs) for their expertise in assessing potential physical limits and maximizing the patient's mobility. They need input from psychologists regarding psychological test results, cognitive and emotional strengths and weaknesses, and recommendations for strategies to address problems.

Nurses need input from physicians on medical aspects, treatment goals, and rationale (e.g., on the patient's communicable diseases, demonstrations of wound dressings and other procedures, choices in medications, and anticipated outcomes). Being clear about targeted treatment goals helps nurses to determine information they need to report or flag.

THE KNOWLEDGE BASE OF
THE HEALTH CARE TEAM

Each member has an area of expertise, but optimal collaboration requires considerable overlap. As members of the team, each professional needs to stay aware of their own particular biases when approaching the patient's treatment. No one perspective is ideal. It is therefore helpful for all professionals to listen carefully to each other for clues to patient needs and care. For example, based on an interview at admission, a patient was mistakenly diagnosed with depression and Alzheimer's disease. An occupational therapist soon reported that the resident "couldn't put away the dishes." The OT's comments were ignored. It turned out that the patient had had a frontal-parietal stroke, and the dish problem had to do with an apraxia, not memory impairment or lack of motivation or interest.

Three important points should be made concerning the collaborative geriatric team. Anyone working with the geriatric population requires training in normal aging versus pathological symptoms. Minimal training should include academic and clinical experience with gerontology, including social gerontology, economics of aging, pharmacology, psychology, and biology of aging. Knowledge of family intervention and neurocognitive behavioral strategies is also essential. This breadth of training is crucial to understanding the special issues with the older adult. Without this knowledge base, appropriate skill level and clinical experience, the health care team runs may make improper diagnoses, and overlook actual impairment or intact functioning.

Second, mental health providers need increased and continual learning about medical issues, enough to know when an issue can influence psychotherapy progress or when and when not to advise certain approaches (e.g., exercise). Knowing about chronic illness, (e.g., chronic obstructive pulmonary disease, diabetes, and hypertension) is essential in discussing issues of treatment with primary care physicians. Frazer (1995) has suggested that a knowledgeable psychologist and general primary care provider can be an effective collaborative team, as long as one member has adequate knowledge of aging issues and the two providers are able to work together. Preferably both would have knowledge in gerontology. Specialized training in neuropsychology, over and above general psychology training, is essential for comprehensive cognitive evaluation.

Third, further training in creating realistic treatment plans and goals with higher expected gains is important. As Brody and Pawlson (1990) discuss, both medical and mental health care professionals often limit their expectations of older adults. Particularly with severe dementia or medical illness, we tend to feel there is "nothing we can do," which may lead to limited programming. "Nothing we can do" may mean we can't return the patient to "normal," or the person's prior level of functioning. A new perspective regarding quality of life, even if it doesn't involve "total cure" can be far more useful. Funding issues and staff limitations also curtail effective quality of life programming. Is lack of funding also related to "nothing we can do"? Surely, we can't always cure physical issues, but much of our treatment philosophy may need to address these continued psychological, social, and quality-of-life issues. When we don't look at these aspects, people may literally wither, and suffer increased physical and mental health problems.

DECLINE VERSUS GAIN: MYTHS AND REALITIES OF AGING

Understanding the "true facts" of normal aging can educate professionals in how to provide good care. The facts are:

Physically we decline at .8% per year from the age of 25, a non-functional decline. Admittedly, when physical or mental disease become involved, we begin to experience some decline, but even at that, we have limited ourselves, our patients, and families with lowered expectations for improvement and function, because of ageist attitudes. We assume all human development matches physical decline, which is not true. Actually, as health care professionals, we shy away from working with people experiencing chronic physical and mental illnesses, indiscriminate of a patient's age. So, disease and our attitude about disease are the culprits, but we keep blaming age and want to run the other way. Our ability to detect and treat disease, mental or physical, rests on our ability to "look" beyond attitudinal limits and barriers, to the real diagnosis. After all, much of what we see mentally and physically can be improved and sometimes cured. Quality of life can surely be improved with attitude. For the older adult, quality of life, meaning, and intimacy are vital to health, both mental and physical.

It is important to know the facts of normal aging, to compare a patient's complaints accurately with those of the average older adult. Most older adults have the following potentials:

- Physically decline at only 0.8% per year from age 25. This is a nonfunctional decline, in that most activities are not greatly affected.
- Intellectually increase in problem-solving ability and crystallized IQ. Fluid IQ remains the same but overall IQ does not decline unless disease or injury affect the brain.
- Socially, older adults continue to deepen in their capacity to relate to others intimately. Intimacy expands in type and depth.
- Psychologically, men and women "round out" their personality to become naturally androgynous.

We keep growing, despite our tendency to think growing older is a downward walk. In reality, it is more like "invisible gains." It is important to keep normal aging parameters in mind since, as health care professionals, we tend to see primarily those who have cognitive or emotional problems.

ENHANCING MENTAL HEALTH

Many approaches and requirements for maintaining mental health involve promoting basics such as dignity, independence, need for intimacy, and sense of purpose and meaning. The patient-centered facility can enhance mental health by:

- Speaking to patient and family in a respectful, adult manner.
- Fostering independence and self-efficacy.
- Promoting physical and cognitive well-being.
- Maximizing potential by setting goals in conjunction with patient and family.
- Maintaining safety in the least restrictive environment (e.g., minimizing use of physical and chemical restraints).
- Demonstrating concern, taking the initiative to talk with and listen to patients and families.
- Allowing patients as much control as possible (e.g., taking patient preferences into account in sleep-wake schedule, food choices).
- Having a structured but not rigid program including physical, cognitive, and social activities.
- Being alert to changes in physical, cognitive, and emotional status.
- Providing a reasonably consistent schedule for the patient and posting it where patient and family can see it.
- Enhancing patient understanding by presenting information slowly, using short, simple (not childish) sentences, repeating information, and using cues.
- Facilitating connections with family and community.
- Intervening with family and facilitating discussions.
- Assisting patients and families in addressing end-of-life issues.
- Evaluating and treating psychiatric disorders.

THE ESSENTIALS OF COLLABORATION

The most effective models of collaboration are the more egalitarian, where the different providers are viewed as each contributing expertise in a specific area. A case manager, or a provider with frequent contact with the patient, may have as part of their role the responsibility for arranging and coordinating the different care components, and ensuring that the treatment team is functioning consistently, in the service of the same goals.

The quality of the relationship among the providers is probably the most important influence on collaboration. Providers can take specific steps to enhance the quality of the relationships they have with each other.

Seaburn, Lorenz, Gunn, Gawinski, and Mauksch (1996) encourage providers of different disciplines to consider others as belonging to a different "culture." Effective collaboration requires learning something about the other culture, and developing ways to accommodate and work with differences. So, for example, while a strictly biomedical provider might view a patient's depression as a symptom to be managed with medication, a psychosocial provider might focus on how the depression affects the patient's functioning and adherence to recommended treatment (such as taking the medication as prescribed), or the effect on family members. McDaniel, Campbell, and Seaburn (1990) outline areas of the different "cultures" to consider, including language, typical treatment approach or stance (e.g., directive or collaborative), time issues (including how long appointments last, how often they are scheduled, and how long they are expected to be needed, and orientation or focus (biomedical or psychosocial). A provider does not necessarily have to "join" another culture, but, rather, can benefit from being aware of the differences, and clarifying how each can contribute to, and enhance, the work of the others.

Seaburn et al. (1996) outline degrees to which providers work together. "Parallel delivery" entails one provider referring a patient to another provider, to address one or more issues beyond the expertise of the initial provider. Each provider functions fairly separately from the other, and ideally, the two are willing and able to keep each other up to date on their work with the patient.

Consultation can be either informal (also known as the "bump in the hall" or "curbside consult"), where one provider talks briefly with another about a patient issue, or formal, with more structured contact or series of contacts between the provider and a consultant; typically, the initial provider retains responsibility for the patient. In "coprovision of care," multiple providers treat and share responsibility for the patient. They may at times see the patient together. In "collaborative networking," a patient and the providers are involved with a broader network that may include the patient's family and community and other resources.

The crucial difference has to do with the way multiple providers view their respective roles and responsibility for a patient. For example, a consultant may view her role as to simply evaluate a patient and make recommendations to the treating provider or team. The staff who work directly with the patient may feel that these recommendations are imposed on them, without their input as to whether the recommendations may be feasible or realistic. In a collaborative model, if the consultant were to attend a meeting, to present and explain her findings and recommendations in person, the day-to-day staff would have the opportunity to provide information from their perspective. This could be helpful not only in enhancing the sense of input and influence by the staff, but in providing valuable information for the consultant, and ultimately allowing for a richer and more comprehensive basis for the patient's care. The direct communication, between the consultant and actual care providers, permits a more thorough exchange of information than can be obtained from reports alone. Subsequent follow-up by the consultant can also allow for evaluation of the treatment recommendations and progress, with modification if necessary.

Collaboration, then, ideally involves ongoing (rather than one-time) communication, collegial (rather than hierarchical) interactions, mutual respect and accommodation of differences, and an inclusive biopsychosocial (rather than compartmentalized) approach to patient care. Given the complexity and biopsychosocial nature of the functioning and difficulties of a geriatric population, a cooperative integration makes the most sense. Shared information regarding the patient and family and knowledge of current psychoeducational treatments keeps the team effective.

The overall structure of mental health delivery enhances the psychoeducation of patient, family, and staff. The following collaborative model was used with success in a geropsychiatry unit.

This model demonstrates the three essential components of an older adult collaborative model by Knight and Kaskie (1995): assessment (diagnosis), treatment planning, and collaboration.

To illustrate how this collaboration might look, we will discuss one successful program, which emphasized empowerment of all involved, including patients, families, and staff. This was accomplished through shared responsibility, education and reinforcement, and recognition of contributions. This is the Self-Directed Team approach (Orsburn, Moran, Musselwhite, & Zenger, 1990):

- Fostered creative thinking about complex and unique patient problems.
- Honored each staff member's contribution of knowledge, observation of patient needs, behavioral comments and requests.
- Allowed for shared treatment approaches with various tasks shifting among members of the team.
- Ensured continuing education of all disciplines from among staff as well as outside input.

The unit director was a facilitator of the team and not in a hierarchical position with respect to treatment decisions. The director arranged space for meetings and coordinated attendance. The director made sure information was consistently documented and made available to all staff, family, and patient participants.

Meetings, which were clinical, treatment, and systems oriented, were held consistently with all team members, psychiatrists, physicians, psychologists, social work, OT, PT, all nursing staff, and patient and family involved. Meetings involved:

- Family and patient conferences to guide treatment.
- Observations, discussion, and charting of ongoing treatment of the patient by all staff.
- Education on issues by and for all staff members and families.

The initial intake should be thorough, particularly the history, and at this unit a detailed interview was conducted prior to the initial team meeting.

At the initial meeting, when the patient was new to the unit, staff/nursing intake assessment findings were discussed and used to direct/appoint screens: cognitive, emotional, OT, PT. These screens help with determining essential needs in the areas of cognition, emotional status, incontinence, fall history, and other crucial medical history.

In a second meeting, only a few days later, findings of screens were shared and more specific tests were ordered if necessary. Additional assessments might include neuropsychological assessment, extensive personality testing, a full psychiatric evaluation, medical tests such as a CT or MRI, a neurology evaluation, speech testing for swallowing, and aphasia.

At weekly treatment meetings, treatment goals were formed based on the comprehensive evaluations. At the beginning of treatment, specialists performed detailed and careful diagnosis and assessment. Then, the professional language of assessment and treatment was translated into lay language for other staff and families. For example, neuropsychological test results needed for diagnosis and level of dementia were applied to daily needs. A staff member might say "the patient can remember things he sees better than things he hears" (visual memory vs. auditory memory). Or, "repetition of new material helps people learn and remember over time" (repeating data helps consolidation and long-term memory processes). "Mr. S. has apraxia" would be better understood as " Mr. S. can no longer command his body to do well-learned common daily movements."

Regular staff and family meetings mobilized all involved and provided equal opportunity to share insights, observations, and suggestions. For example, an LPN might notice a patient falling asleep during the day or an occupational therapist might observe apraxic behavior. Responsibilities for treatment were divided among staff members depending on their expertise as well as their availability and rapport with the patient. A nurse might become the preferred therapist for a patient and conduct counseling sessions with the guidance of social work or psychology, because the nurse and patient had formed a particularly good alliance. This gave the nursing staff a chance to be involved in another aspect of treatment, remain interested and refreshed with different responsibilities, and offer their own wisdom to the patient and staff. Ideas from each staff member were incorporated into the treatment plan, increasing each member's sense of pride and contribution to the health of the patient and family.

Shared roles, with ongoing training from other professionals, allows for multiple views of the patient, and enhance a feeling of responsibility and contribution by families and staff.

A staff conference log was maintained. All information collected during assessments and conferences was available in a summary statement each week that could be read in between staffings by each discipline to remain updated on changes in behavior and the like. A unit reference list, with names, titles, and contact telephone numbers of all involved providers can help family and staff to be aware—and know how to contact—the entire treatment team.

Families/patients and family conferences were included throughout the patient's stay to help facilitate patient and family involvement in the process.

At the patient's discharge meeting, all staff shared in the input for discharge planning.

An essential aspect of this successful program was staff education. In this program, responsibility for staff education rotated among the disciplines, allowing each discipline to learn and instruct other disciplines on latest findings, techniques, and treatments in gerontology/geriatrics.

This approach was ideal and created a unit where patients and families consistently expressed satisfaction and staff had a high level of high morale. This type of organization is difficult in today's managed care environment, but it is hoped that the overall concept can be used to create as close an approximation as possible in the reader's situation. The future may provide for more flexibility in patient care than we are currently experiencing. The goals and approaches offered here are representative of a possible standard that has worked, rather than a trend influenced by current financial constraints. Quality is still essential in the overall care of patient, and without it care diminishes. One fallout of managed care is that appropriate assessment is often heavily restricted or eliminated altogether.

Sometimes screening fails to detect essential diagnostic issues. A mental status exam can easily miss subtle cognitive and functional deficits of a bright patient with a mild stroke. The KELS (an OT screening tool) can also miss subtle functional problems. Therefore, it is necessary to have an assessment protocol that includes criteria for determining when subtle behaviors or screening results require an in-depth.

The ideal model of care described earlier facilitated enhanced mental health on a geropsychiatry unit. With this foundation in place, it was possible to incorporate the following mental health approaches into a total program.

CASE REVISITED

How could Mr. and Mrs. S.'s situation be addressed in a facility that uses the preceding collaborative model? We can begin by looking at the problem areas depicted in the case and what was done.

ASSESSMENT

In Mr. S.'s case, many behaviors raised questions about possible cognitive and emotional concerns. These concerns would be better understood after neuropsychological testing that emphasized the cognitive and emotional status of the patient. Five neuropsychological findings may have the following implications:

1. Mr. S. may have had trouble understanding verbal input. Often communication with a patient is difficult due to aphasia, even in non-stroke related dementia. Aphasia assessment may help the staff to find alternative ways to communicate with the patient (e.g., modeling to capitalize on visual communication rather than verbal instructions). A nurse who modeled drinking water and taking a pill was able to prevent her patient from becoming agitated and confused by verbal instructions.
2. The staff may understand better how to help Mr. S. when they know the level and extent of memory deficit. The patient may have limited learning, or may learn best through visual prompts. Not all dementias are the same. By understanding the level and type of memory deficit, the staff and family can structure the environment to best suit the patient's needs for adaptation.

3. Mr. S. had no ability to plan or follow more than one-step-at-a-time instructions.
4. Mr. S. may have been apraxic, and possibly needed modeling of adult living skills, dressing, or adaptive devices.
5. Mr. S. was highly suspicious, or showing "paranoia." Is this related to a hearing loss, delirium, medical illness, or gross misunderstandings from a combination of quickly changed environment and limited cognitive capacity? The daily routine may need to be highly structured, with a predictable routine, familiar objects in the patient's room, and full explanation in simple terms to the patient of events, procedures, and so on. When communicating with the patient, caretakers could speak directly with good eye contact, take time, and go over steps slowly. It is important to listen to and acknowledge patient concerns. To keep agitation down, distraction techniques may be useful after acknowledging the patient's emotional state.

Antidepressant medications are often prescribed for older adults. It is hoped that Mr. S. was prescribed antidepressants after a thorough evaluation of symptoms and a complementary program of behavioral treatment and monitoring of behaviors. Families and the patient themselves may need information regarding the purpose of antidepressants and how they work (e.g., they stabilize mood, and don't make people's personality change to constantly "happy" or improve cognitive capacity). Continual monitoring of effectiveness is necessary to assure that the medications work and have no undue side effects.

The primary care physician may be involved in this collaborative model by attending meetings, or if time does not allow the meeting log could be reviewed by a staff member present at the doctor's visit.

A mental health evaluation may be conducted by several professionals but the end result and type of information may vary depending on the specialized training. For general psychosocial history, possible mental status testing with suggestion of diagnosis or screen, a social worker may be appropriate. For comprehensive and more definitive diagnostic workup a neuropsychologist or psychiatrist may offer detail. Often the physician in charge may want more information on the cognitive and emotional functioning of the patient but may not know where to best find it. A specific referral question such as, "Is the patient safe to live at home alone?" is often the most helpful. A referral question, "Does this patient have social support conducive to living alone?" These questions can suggest the appropriate specialty exam. An occupational therapist could answer the question of adult living skills in the home. The social worker could help with social support. The neuropsychologist could assess for level and type of memory capacity and capacity for judgment, problem-solving and decision-making ability needed to live at home. If an evaluation by a psychiatrist is unavailable, psychiatric evaluation could be addressed by both a medical and mental health professional regarding Mr. S.'s "hallucinations." Again, cognitive status, medication review and medical review or delirium are key elements when assessing hallucinations.

Neurocognitive suggestions for treatment are behavioral strategies generated from the neuropsychological evaluation, occupational therapy evaluations and psychiatric evaluations. With detailed information regarding Mr. S.'s strengths and weaknesses, it was possible to arrange an appropriate brain-related behavioral plan. Communication with the patient by staff and family is custom built to facilitate the patient's best adaptation. The techniques for the neurocognitive approach could be taught in staff education sessions and family education sessions.

BEHAVIORAL ISSUES AND TREATMENT

Mr. S. shows behaviors, such as wandering into other patient's rooms and accusing his wife of being with other men, that were problematic for staff and family. The team psychologist set up a behavioral data collection system to determine what pattern of antecedent conditions consistently preceded wandering, and what consequences reinforced or decreased wandering behavior. For example, Mr. S. would often wander when he awakened at night to use the toilet. If a staff member offered him a walk and talked to him a few minutes, he could be redirected back to bed, but if someone called out loudly to him to stop, he became more agitated and confused and continued on. If nighttime urination is frequent, a physician will evaluate medical conditions which could be a factor, such as a urinary tract infection or medication effects, and if appropriate, might prescribe medication to decrease nighttime awakening and wandering. If confusion is a factor, a night-light or means of making Mr. S.'s room more distinct, such as a familiar picture on the door, might help decrease wandering. Wandering that leads to "eloping" from the unit, may be decreased by making doors look like walls (with tapestry) or having a continuous low attractive "fence" around a common area with a patient proof lock on the gate.

The team suggested a fall risk assessment. Mr. S. could have been falling because of visual impairment, dizziness, neglect (brain-related lack of awareness of the right or left side of the body secondary to stroke), lower extremity weakness, impulsivity, sensory deficit, or special perceptual problems, some of which might be amenable to treatment by medication, physical therapy, environmental manipulation, or other means.

Mrs. S. was concerned about her husband's sleeping during the day. It could have been that Mr. S. was bored and needed more stimulation. Initially, keeping a log about the patient's sleep patterns and accumulated sleep time helps the staff develop a flexible approach to sleep habits. A program needs to be flexible, and observations explained to the patient and family, rather than having the patient fit the program.

CAREGIVER ISSUES

Health problems of the caregiver is a common and often overlooked issue. Many caregivers become depressed. Counseling regarding their thoughts and feelings about their loved one and understanding the stress and common feelings associated with caregiving can help them to decide how to provide a healthy lifestyle for themselves. Even a few half-hour visits by the social worker or the nurse seemed to help Mrs. S.

COLLABORATION

In this collaborative model, Mr. and Mrs. S. were seen as a whole with ideas and preferences and with strengths to enhance, not just as problems to be figured out. Whenever possible, Mr. S.'s preferences regarding sleep-wake schedule and food choices are given consideration. When accommodation could be made, an explanation is provided to patient and family. It is well-known that self-efficacy is an important component of mental health. Thus, the encouragement of independence was important. Institutions often reinforce dependency; it is often easier and faster to dress a patient than to wait while he or she does it slowly and independently.

Staff behaved in ways that demonstrated concern about Mr. and Mrs. S. Staff took the initiative to talk with them, and ask how they were doing. Staff actively encouraged and listened to the patient and family's input in a nonjudgmental manner.

Within the facility, it was helpful to have a structured, but not rigid, program that included physical, cognitive, recreational, and social activities. Physical activities, on both an individual and group basis, encouraged mobility, helped maintain range of motion, and provided stimulation. Many activities were multipurpose. Balloon volleyball and chair aerobics provided exercise, social interaction, and simple fun. Bingo, trivia games, or a discussion group combined cognitive stimulation and socialization. Crafts provided social stimulation and assistance with fine motor skills. Music night can be soothing and relaxing, as well as entertaining and stimulating. The staff encouraged patients to design group activities, such as writing songs together, and discussed the benefits of such a group. One discussion group about the topic "What is the benefit of group?" or "Excuses to get out of group" led to an interesting discussion of personal and social interaction.

Staff were trained to be alert to changes in Mr. S.'s cognitive and emotional status as well as to changes in physical status. For instance, Mr. S. may have stopped attending an activity because he was becoming depressed, or because he was having trouble seeing or tracking. Noticing the behavioral change and investigating why it is happening may allow for an earlier intervention.

Mr. S. was given a good idea of what to expect on each day, with a reasonably consistent individual schedule (e.g., bathtime, medications, any therapy time), and schedules of these as well as optional activities should be posted within view. Consistency helps with orientation and new learning.

The slower pace of learning in the elderly may necessitate a slower presentation of information, the use of shorter, simpler sentences, repetition of information, and/or written cues, instructions, and treatment rationales or plans. A memory book helped Mr. S. with orientation and was useful for keeping a log of activities to remind him whether his wife was in to see him, when his doctor visited, and that his granddaughter brought him cookies.

Also important was the availability of mental health professionals, not only to evaluate and treat psychiatric disorders, but also to promote mental *health*. Such providers offered family interventions, and facilitated discussion of issues including coping with changes in function, role reversal, illness, death and dying, or family reconciliation.

CONCLUSION

Including Mr. and Mrs. S. in the treatment team was helpful all around. They felt less isolated and the staff benefited from Mrs. S.'s input. Her inclusion at case conferences reinforced her role as a member of the team. Often, as in the case of more demented patients, the patient and family become involved as a unit on the team.

All players became more comfortable with each other through the collaborative model, and treatment was improved by sharing knowledge and responsibility.

REFERENCES

Brody, S.J., & Pawlson, L.G. (1990). *Aging and rehabilitation: II. The state of the practice.* New York: Springer.

Frazer, D. (1995). Medical issues in geropsychology training and practice. In B. Knight, L. Teri, P. Wohlford, & J. Santos (Eds.), *Mental health services for older adults* (pp. 63–69). Washington, DC: American Psychological Association.

Knight, B.G., & Kaskie, B. (1995). Models for mental health service delivery to older adults. In M. Gatz (Ed.), *Emerging issues in mental health and aging* (pp. 231–255). Washington, DC: American Psychological Association.

McDaniel, S.H., Campbell, T.L., & Seaburn, D.B. (1990). *Family-oriented primary care: A manual for medical providers.* New York: Springer-Verlag.

McDaniel, S.H., Hepworth, J., & Doherty, W.J. (1992). *Medical family therapy: A biopsychosocial approach to families with health problems.* New York: Basic Books.

Orsburn, J., Moran, L., Musselwhite, E., & Zenger, J. (1990). *Self-directed teams: The new American challenge.* Burr Ridge, IL: Irwin.

Seaburn, D.B., Lorenz, A.D., Gunn, W.B., Jr., Gawinski, B.A., & Mauksch, L.B. (1996). *Models of collaboration: A guide for mental health professionals working with healthcare practitioners.* New York: Basic Books.

CHAPTER 21

Environmental Design Features and the Well-Being of Older Persons

M. Powell Lawton

The practice of counseling does not usually make one think of environment. The object of counseling is the individual, with the expectation of change in the feelings, attitudes, and behaviors of the person. One could argue that the person cannot be artificially separated from environment, that person defines environment and environment defines person. This broadest view would thus suggest that all change represents an ecological process, and that the change represents a transaction between person and environment as a system. This chapter argues that the environmental aspect of the total system is unduly neglected and that attention to its significance in the lives of older clients will enhance the effectiveness of the counseling process.

The chapter begins with several general principles that have emerged in the extensive research done on older people and their environments. Although the principles are relatively abstract, it is easy to convert them into procedural measures to use in one-to-one work with individuals. The second major section provides overviews of the two types of environmental issues most likely to affect the quality of everyday life of the older person: The issue of the fit between the older person's home environment and the person's capabilities and needs and the issue of residential location (to move or not to move). Although each of these issues constitutes a major book-length topic, they will be discussed primarily as they might be relevant to the counseling process and the counselor's role.

FIVE MAJOR FACETS OF PERSON-ENVIRONMENT RELATIONS IN OLD AGE

Whether the focus be designing for an older user, creating services for elders, or performing research, the process is facilitated greatly by the ability to call on a theoretical structure to assist in understanding, explaining, and changing behavior. The study of environment and aging has profited over several decades from several such theoretical perspectives. Each is discussed in some detail and illustrated in applied form in the later section of this chapter. First, all human behavior, including the behavior of older people, may be seen as a process of negotiating a dialectic between autonomy and security. Second, the needs and capabilities of people as they become ill or frail result in increased "environmental docility," that is, a tendency to be increasingly influenced by environmental rather than intrapersonal factors. Third, each person retains a sphere of competence in which "environmental proactivity" may be exercised, that is, active searching of the environment for positive needs-fulfilling features. Fourth, congruence between personal needs/competencies and environmental resources/demands is the usual state of affairs but deviations from perfect congruence are frequent and worthy of note. Fifth, outcomes of person-environment transactions must be evaluated for positive features independently of negative features, in light of the evidence that positive and negative affect states are separate, rather than polar states. A recent update of theoretical issues in environment and aging may be of interest (Scheidt & Windley, 1998).

THE AUTONOMY-SECURITY DIALECTIC

Parmelee and Lawton (1990) suggested that environments capable of satisfying needs for both independence and dependence were the goal of most people, but the realities of aging sometimes occasion a new mix of this balance. As research on personal control and intrinsic motivation have demonstrated, the ability to live as one wishes is a primary human need. One's domicile is a major means for achieving the goal of autonomy. Choices of behaviors, times for performing them, with whom one interacts, and the form and maintenance of the domicile are possible in one's own home. Home is, however, also a place for protection from the elements, from intrusion, and a symbolic retreat. For most people, the home's functions in supporting both autonomy and security are mixed relatively effortlessly. Ill health is likely to change that mix, occasioning reconsideration of the results of autonomy-affording and security-providing features of the home. This process is termed a dialectic because it is characterized by continuous accommodation to the primacy of first one need and then another, rather than settling at some point of equilibrium. What must be understood is that the point around which accommodation averages will sometimes be determined by greater acceptance of the pull in one direction and rejection of the other, followed by a reversal. As an example, in the home, maintenance tasks performed by the elder are a source of gratification because they are performed easily, and at times performance of home-related tasks may put a creative mark on the home. Such an autonomy-driven person is probably rarely aware of the protective functions of the home. As frailty ensues, the same physical entity of the home may be used to create a new balance: Maintenance tasks are done less often, perhaps with little risk to the quality of the home, while the person becomes more willing for services to be brought into the home. Thus many people's homes have the capacity to serve differing mixes of autonomy and security while the person's own sense of adequacy remains undisturbed. A single-family home in the community is not the only alternative, however. As the demands of independent residence become more burdensome, the security side may become prepotent, occasioning consideration of a move to a child's home or more protective housing. If this should happen, the pain of forgoing autonomy may be offset by the reassurance provided by the added security.

ENVIRONMENTAL DOCILITY

The environmental docility hypothesis suggested that as personal competence declines, the behavior and psychological well-being of the person become increasingly dependent on environmental factors (Lawton & Simon, 1968). The initial demonstration of this propensity came in these authors' study of friendships in housing for the elderly, where the less-healthy were more dependent on proximate neighbors for their friends; the healthier chose friends from all parts of their high-rise buildings, and therefore had a better chance of matching interests and personal capabilities. Although this principle easily illustrates the risks experienced by the more frail elder in barrier-prevalent housing, high-crime neighborhoods, or residences far from shopping and other amenities, it also illustrates a brighter side. If one can identify and alter favorably an environmental barrier to need satisfaction, the proportionate gain for the less-competent is selectively great. A favorite example is the older home with a single bathroom, located on the upper floor. A major loss of daily life quality is engendered by the disabled person's choice to remain upstairs in a bedroom but in reach of the bathroom all day or be helped to go downstairs where the more life-enriching resources are (kitchen, living room, front door, etc.) but there is no bathroom, at best a commode. Adding a downstairs toilet would elevate the frail person's quality of life markedly, but would have a negligible effect for the fully mobile person.

The docility principle alerts us to think in such terms as compiling a list of present disabilities—in activities of daily living, cognitive function, sensory function, communication, meaningful uses of time, or social behaviors—and adding possible environmental interventions that might counteract the net effect of the disability on the behavior or psychological well-being of the person. Consumer products have been developed in great quantity to help expand the range of competent behavior of disabled people. Low-tech products such as no-drip cups and long-handled bath brushes are available along with more sophisticated devices to remind and track medication use or to signal distress (LaBuda, 1985). A great deal of high-tech development is under way in areas such as robotics and the "smart house." The environmental prosthesis is thus the instrument of intervention relevant to the state of environmental docility.

ENVIRONMENTAL PROACTIVITY

The idea behind environmental docility is simple: Because a person's competence is limited, a prosthesis will help nullify the deficit. In this instance, the person is an object, a passive recipient of the intervention provided by the architect, the product designer, the helpful family member, or service provider. The older person as passive reactor constitutes only half of the picture, however, no matter how badly impaired the person. Research has demonstrated repeatedly that there is always an area where full autonomy can be exercised, choice is still relevant, and the person can shape the environment to fit her needs. Further, as is well known, most elders are not compromised in their competence. It is thus clear that other principles are needed to guide us as we think about both the majority who are fully competent as well as sectors of life where the less-competent may exert competent behavior.

The environmental proactivity hypothesis (Lawton, 1985, 1989) states that the greater the competence of the person, the better able he or she will be to search the environment for, and utilize, the resources for meeting personal needs and preferences. This principle implies that the most competent people require a broader environmental expanse for those resources to be located. In turn, they are more adept at recognizing the resource and finding ways to utilize it. There is no zero point of ability to utilize resources. The least-competent will be able to search and recognize a smaller quantity of resource, but their possibility of benefiting from the appropriate resource is still strong.

The later sections of this chapter detail examples of environmental proactivity, some of which may be mentioned here: making a residential decision, furnishing a home, displaying personal artifacts, travel. In every case, the motivation for experiencing or changing one's environment comes from within the person. The least-competent person with dementia may nonetheless take a seat near the nurses' station, the center of activity in a nursing home, explicitly because there is movement to watch. Many homebound elders create a "control center" in their living rooms (Lawton, 1985). They place their chairs with views of the front door and through the front window. Their connections with the more distant world are assured by telephone, radio, and television at arm's reach. Their resource world is enriched by artifacts, letters, photos, food, and books arrayed on nearby surfaces. The control center is the epitome of a proactively constructed world on a smaller but more manipulable scale.

PERSON-ENVIRONMENT CONGRUENCE

First articulated in this manner by Kahana (1982), this principle encompasses in a single concept much of the rationale for autonomy-security, docility, and proactivity. When the world is in tune with the person and his or her needs and capabilities, wasted energy expenditure is minimized and an even emotional state is more likely. Person-environment congruence is, as noted in discussing autonomy-security, an average, rather than a resting state. Such an average state of equilibrium is attained by a process of active effort by the person that is made increasingly possible by learning over time (i.e., "maturity"). The homes occupied by elders are a case in point. Most people live in a succession of different homes early in their lives, but in the 65+ age range, the homes they are in have usually been occupied for a very long time and about three-quarters of them are owned by the elder. Thus it is likely that the person has had a number of chances to choose a new domicile. Many manage to upgrade the degree to which each successive home approximates her or his ideal. Most homes are not, of course, truly ideal. However, part of the process of adaptation involves, first, learning how to cope with its imperfections and, second, how to ignore what can't be changed. In many ways, the occupant and the home attain a transactional state of congruence.

A benefit of such congruence is that energy may be more available for nonenvironmental goal attainment activity—social relationships, hobbies, health maintenance. The costs of incongruence are obvious. Too strong environmental demands or very diminished congruence are the precursors of perceived stress and nonadaptive behavior. On the other hand, too rich an environment in relation to the competence of the user may mean wasted resources.

As part of their ecological model of aging, Lawton and Nahemow (1973) posited that there were benefits to two types of mild incongruence. When environmental demands are slightly in excess of the person's competence, the person is most likely to feel stimulated, and will experience positive affect and learn new ways of thinking and behaving. They designated this type of environmental incongruence as the "range of maximum performance potential." When environmental demands are slightly lower than the point of total congruence with the person's competence, a state of mild relaxation, an opportunity for respite and reconstitution (the "zone of maximum comfort"), is likely. Congruence as a steady state is neither possible nor desirable. People for the most part find their own ways to increase or decrease demands (proactivity). But informal and formal social support services may have a role in helping adjust person-environment congruence and its deviations.

THE TWO-FACTOR VIEW OF MENTAL HEALTH

The last general principle is that mental health, in this case the outcomes of the person-environment transaction, constitutes not a single continuum ranging from normality to distress, but two continua that are related, but imperfectly correlated. Several decades ago, Bradburn (1969) and, more recently, Watson and Tellegen (1985) provided convincing evidence that people's emotional states could vary on separate scales of positive affect and negative affect (see Lawton, 1997, for an extended discussion with reference to aging). In Bradburn's (1969) seminal research, happiness was related to scales measuring separately positive affect and negative affect, but positive affect and negative affect correlated with each other at 0.00. Although later research has demonstrated that these two dimensions are under most conditions not totally independent, the conclusion is overwhelming that we cannot portray a person's total psychological well-being until we have assessed both the total of positive affects and behaviors and of negative affects and behaviors.

Evidence is building also to identify external engagements as the primary antecedents of positive emotional states and internal factors such as health and self-concept as antecedents of negative states. Lawton (1983) demonstrated that positive environmental cognition contributed to positive affect but did not diminish negative affect. It therefore seems that environment is both a potential source for positive states and a fit object for manipulation toward that end by proactive effort and by professionals. Specifically, change and novelty in modest increments are associated with enjoyment, interest, diversion, and pleasant psychological experience. Stability, predictability, and reduction of pressure are associated with a sense of relaxation or reduction of anxiety. Environmentally based symptom reduction comes through bringing demands back into a tolerable range. Thus in the search for environmental pathways to improved mental health, we do well to consider environmental interventions that may have special capacities to either enhance enjoyment directly or reduce anxiety by way of lowering the excess demand level of the environment.

These five dynamisms are, as has been illustrated, related to one another. They also may be identified in the everyday ways both well and ill older people deal with environmental problems. The remaining portion of this chapter concretizes person-environment transactions and illustrates how they may be relevant to the counseling process.

PERSON-DOMICILE CONGRUENCE

The dwelling unit serves several major functions for the person: attachment, environmental control, competence affirmation, and identity source. Such functions, in turn, are located in four traditional domains studied by psychology: affect, cognition, behavior, and the self.

ATTACHMENT

The home is capable of evoking many emotions, both positive and negative. The function of affective attachment is much more specific than such generalized evaluations, however. Attachment to home may be within temporal frameworks of past, present, or future. Much has been written about the home as a locus of association with earlier periods of life and the people who lived in the home. It is especially the re-evoked affects of such periods as the remembered comfort of childhood, the love of a new spouse, or enjoyable times with one's own children that continue to live in a long-occupied home. Similar expectations for the future may exist as one contemplates the comforts of home in later life. Sometimes the attachment is very concrete, that is, the home is an object that the person has chosen, altered, nurtured, and put one's stamp on. Also related to the identity theme, this investment in the physical object of home is for some people a true love affair. Such attachment may be strongly symbolic, where it is not so much what one has done to the house as what the house, as it is, conveys to the person about her or his achievement in life. The symbolic home is gazed on and savored as a love object that embodies the reflected, achieved self. In the present, the home represents a source of stimulation, a vehicle for the positive affective experiences of interest, aesthetic enjoyment, challenge, and problem-solving. There is often simply more to do in one's own home and therefore it evokes a continuing state of mild arousal in the positive-affect zone.

The longer one lives in a domicile the greater opportunity there is to have experienced significant attachments, to have left more of one's imprint on the home, and to have completed one's task of achieving a personal housing goal. Therefore, it is at least a reasonable hypothesis that the combination of age and housing tenure may increase attachment.

Two other factors moderate this assertion, however. First, not all affect associated with home is positive. Individual examples are not difficult to find of people who decide to move to get away from the negatively emotional associations of a house with a problem child, an unhappy marriage, or a personal failure. The second moderating consideration is that there are very wide individual differences in affective responsiveness to environment in general and to housing in particular. A great deal more research in what might be called "environmental personology" is needed to begin to understand why some people invest so much emotion in their homes whereas others do not.

For some people, the home can be loved for its past, for the person's past, and for the person's present and future. Even if the love is ambivalent, sheer familiarity shades the feeling toward the positive side.

ENVIRONMENTAL CONTROL

To know the world is a first step toward controlling it and moving toward the goal of psychological well-being. The home serves a central role in attaining such controllability of an important segment of the behavioral world. Since from 12 to 22 or so hours of each day are normally spent by older people in their residences (Moss & Lawton, 1982), the cognitive task of establishing order in the environment is located importantly in the home. A stable home affords the opportunity to organize this near environment in a way that enables daily routines to proceed with minimum effort. "Familiarity" is often invoked as an explanation for older people's tenacity in remaining in their homes. Although familiarity has its affective aspects, familiarity also involves a complex set of schemata that orient the person to the living environment, form a template for daily activities, and provide a basis for interpreting new knowledge about the environment. That is, a large part of the activity in and around home is routine. Novel activity (e.g., a stranger at the door, a leak in the roof, a change in land use on one's block) requires vigilance. The baseline cognitive order established over time for the home provides a frame of reference against which to assess the meaning and behavioral implications of new activity. The home also affords the opportunity to make environmental changes in accordance with changing needs. Maintenance of order requires constant adjustment. The amount of control over the environment thus directly flows from having such a domain for oneself about which one knows the rules, customs, limitations, and potentialities. Finally, just as home offers stimulation for affective arousal, home offers learning possibilities consequent to adaptive tasks that can be performed there.

COMPETENCE AFFIRMATION

The choice of the dwelling in the first place is an act that on the whole enhances the ability of the home to lead to goal-achieving competent behaviors. Habitat selection under relatively free conditions where preferences may be exercised maximizes the congruence between personal need and the ability of the environment to fulfill such needs. One facet of such generalized congruence is the freedom to make other choices, as, for example, how one will manage the dialectic between privacy and sociality, as detailed by Altman and Gauvain (1981). Home can be chosen and altered to maximize its closed quality from the outside world, its openness to social engagement, or more likely, some mix of the two, including the zoning of private and public areas. Thus the regulation of social behavior is a major behavioral function of the home. Where such decisions are made by the occupant, the total rhythm of activity is regulated to one's taste: The types of behavior allowed to occur, their location, the times they occur, their frequency, and their social context.

Habitat choice to attain congruity and freedom of choice of activity has another major facet, the maintenance of competent behavior. Highly practiced and competently performed behaviors such as home maintenance, housekeeping, cooking, or gardening become even more expertly performed with long practice. Familiarity with the vagaries of a furnace, the local bus schedules, and the best places to shop nearby are skills that maintain person-domicile congruence. A special case of optimized behavior is that of ensuring security from intruders. It is well documented that behaviors designed to mark one's home territorially may actually harden the home as a target against intrusion (Patterson, 1978); proactive behavior designed to avert crime not only achieves this goal but by its simple enactment reduces anxiety about crime.

Finally, a concrete affirmation of behavioral competence is the financial security represented by the home. Even in the case of a rental unit, there is often a financial advantage to remaining in place, because of rent inflation. For a homeowner the financial advantage is major.

THE DOMICILE AS A SOURCE OF IDENTITY

The function of housing as it relates to the Self is more difficult to define than are the other functions. The identity category may be tentatively thought of as a function of the home that contributes to the person's definition of self, including both uniqueness and shared qualities. Above all else, home is a major medium for the expression of individuality. This imprinting was mentioned in the affective realm. There is general correspondence between the self and the residential choice or the embellishments made on the home. An absence of embellishment or uniqueness may be just as consistent with the occupant's needs as positive occurrences. The stamp of self *may* have an affective or behavioral outcome, but at the identity level, it is existential. One's identity as expressed in the home has been called "autobiographical insideness," by Rowles (1980)—a state where the physical place is a repository for the history of the person and the person in turn has incorporated the place into the self. The distinction between person and environment disappears at this level.

Nonetheless individual differences are evident in people's relationships with their homes. For some their aesthetic is what gets expressed in the home. For others, their ingenuity. For still others, it is sufficient to be different, even if the difference lies only in the color of their door among a sea of identical structures. Individuality is not the only form identity can take, however. What is shared collectively with others is just as often the expression of the identity theme. To have a home as much like that of others as possible expresses a person's need to share social values. Shared norms of the larger society and indicators of one's class may be expressed through the face shown to the world, as in cleanliness or keeping the grass mowed, while cultural values are objectified by the display of religious or ethnic artifacts. All of these indicators of social integration contribute to the definition of who I am. The past as well as the present may be the focus for identity. One's personal history is re-created in microcosm through possessions. Conversely, a break with the past is highly achievable in a change of residence or possessions. Carp (1966) documented the willingness of poor elderly to impoverish themselves by buying new furniture as they embarked on a "new life" in public housing. On the other side, clinging to possessions from the past links oneself to one's origins and departed relatives, often at the same time expressing the continuity of self as cultural symbol bearer. The housing function of identity can express a variation on the Altman dialectic, in the form of individuality versus communality.

THE DOMICILE AS AN ELEMENT OF THE COUNSELING PROCESS

Few are those for whom at least one of these functions is not present. This centrality of the domicile is not always recognized by the person, but the invitation to talk about one's home is often an entrée to the interior of the person. Because most counseling occurs in a professional office setting, it can be very productive to ask the person to describe her home, its history, its furnishings, and the lifespan of activities that have occurred there.

It is our experience that personal themes of great significance for a person's life as a whole are introduced in home-focused discussions. The home is something that many people enjoy discussing. For some, talking about home and its meaning may be relatively nonthreatening, while still indirectly evoking highly personal themes.

The attachment function of home may be an approach path for bereavement counseling. More intrapersonal anxieties are expressed through fears of loss of environmental control (e.g., difficulty with home-maintenance tasks), perceived loss of competence and the threat of loss of identity should the home have to be given up.

HOME ADAPTATION

Both the research and the applied engineering world have begun to recognize the possibilities in adapting homes for the better use of elders whose competences begin to fail. Some technical assistance may be available for such activity. The counselor can usually locate such sources through the local Area Agency on Aging. Such assistance is often not available, however, and the counselor then faces the problem of deciding how far his or her role extends in assisting the client in this somewhat alien task.

It is important to recognize that the home as it is now has evolved under the dominant processes of the proactivity that created the domicile and the congruence that affords the older person's relatively stable residential life. Therefore change is likely to be resisted because some changes involve accepting a turn toward security. Obvious attempts on the part of the counselor to suggest changes in the décor, furnishings, or structure of the home will probably be viewed as affronts to the elder's sense of autonomy. This is one reason a free-flowing discussion of the home and its functions may be useful: the person may voice anxieties or questions about changes that are acceptable because they are self-generated.

Let us assume that the counselor achieves some entrée to the role of assisting the elder in household adaptation. How far should the counselor go? If the person is in active rehabilitation for continued community residence, Medicare will reimburse some in-home services if recommended by an occupational or physical therapist, who are trained to diagnose and suggest improvements on the usability of the home. The counselor may be able to help the client initiate these contacts, or if the person is not Medicare-eligible, the same services may be found on the open market or through lower-cost agencies. The counselor also may play a mediating role with such professionals. Sometimes their expertise is so dominant in their role conceptions that occupational therapists (OTs) or physical therapists (PTs) can underestimate how threatened elders may feel if their competence and ability to control their home environment is questioned. The counselor may on the one hand interpret the OT's suggestions in a less threatening way or discuss with the OT how to offer suggestions in a collaborative rather than prescriptive manner.

In either the mediating role, or sometimes functioning directly as the environmental expert, the counselor should try to elicit suggestions for change from the elder. Changes in such features as the placement of electric cords, adding illumination for focused activities, clearing frequently used pathways, and so on, though simple, are less acceptable when the expert prescribes them (docility) than when the person thinks of them (proactivity).

A real problem in acceptance of adaptive devices is the extent to which they deviate from the usual. Objects with a clear prosthetic or medical design may be rejected because their looks are perceived as demeaning. Many catalogs of such devices are available and one may sometimes find devices with a less clinical look than others.

Some adaptations require extra effort to use or training in their use. The counselor will not usually be the trainer, but he or she may treat the stress of learning and acceptability as a therapeutic topic, supporting early efforts during the time when discouragement is most likely to lead to rejection of the device.

A special role for the counselor may revolve around the aspects of home that involve interest, stimulation, engagement, and positive affect states. Very few professionals in home adaptation are sensitized to the idea that the home is capable of enhancing these positive aspects of mental health. The counselor may play the mediating role in alerting the professional to these possibilities, over and above the safety and accessibility issues with which are most concerned. Or, purely within the counseling setting, it is productive to have the person talk about what is beautiful and interesting in the home and what is boring or depressing. Even while respecting elders' needs for autonomy in the way they arrange their homes, discussion topics may be directed to include possibilities for new paint colors, throw fabrics, pictures, lamps, personal objects, or furniture arrangements. Experience has shown that novelty itself, if it stays within the tolerable zone of deviance from full congruity, and if its institution seems to come from the elder, is likely to be associated with pleasurable feelings.

RESIDENTIAL LOCATION AND RELOCATION

As mentioned earlier, despite the many constraints consequent to poverty, catastrophe, racism, and other negative influences, most older people live in homes that they have chosen and homes onto which they have placed their personal mark. Older people are the least mobile segment of society, and they appear to be extremely reluctant to leave their homes. About 70% own their own homes, which represent the major asset for many of them. Thus in addition to the many psychological reasons for attachment to home, there is often a strong economic basis for wanting to remain in place.

On the other hand, many elders do move. About 8% to 9% of elders now live in various forms of retirement housing. These include for-profit and nonprofit enterprises, luxury and highly subsidized, purchase and rental, and they run the gamut from independent housing with no planned services to full-service continuing-care retirement communities (CCRCs) and high-support assisted living. Another 5% live in nursing homes. In addition, retirement migration most usually does not involve a move to planned housing, but, rather, a move to a community dwelling unit in a location chosen for its weather, recreation, or natural amenities or its low cost of living. Finally, a small number move from their own dwellings to the home of a child or other relative, usually, though not always, in the interest of the increased security afforded by sharing the household.

Thus, despite the potent reasons for staying in place, older people do move. Accomplishing such a move can involve much conflict and an extended period of deliberation. Residential decisions are also made all the time by those who do not move—their outcome is to remain in place. Therefore, the sector of life that includes residential decisions is fertile ground for participation by professionals in a position of counseling for many other purposes.

There is no established subspecialty of housing counseling. Rather, such assistance is usually provided by a generalist counselor who takes on the task of self-instruction regarding the field of housing that seems to be relevant to a specific client. Good beginning sources of local information are the Area Agency on Aging and the American Association of Retired Persons, which provides periodic general updates on the forms of housing available nationally.

Technical knowledge about housing is less important to the counselor, however, than sensitization to the general social and psychological principles introduced earlier. The remainder of this section is devoted to establishing that for the most part older people make rational residential decisions for themselves, but they vary considerably in the extent to which they include future needs in their thinking. As was argued in the previous section, rare is the older person who wants and uses simple advice about what to do in the housing arena. As in all counseling, the professional is only one of many instruments that may be used by the older client to find a suitable residential solution.

Study of older people in the process of residential decision making has shown conclusively that they do not engage in this process either impulsively or irrationally. Unless a crisis demands an immediate change, people are very active in assembling relevant information about the gains and losses associated with a prospective change. Virtually all know age peers who have already made a move, and should be encouraged to seek out such people for reports of their experience. If a client does not succeed in assembling some material that allows financial and service-provision comparisons to be made across alternative housing options, the professional ought to help the client initiate such activity.

It is often said that family, or poverty, or social pressures lead older people to move into age-segregated housing and often with results that run counter to their best interests. In fact, research has failed to confirm this assertion. As far as can be determined from knowledge available now, the elder's own preference is the major contributor to the decision to move. Even service professionals often feel impatient with older people who insist on remaining where they are, despite evidence seeming to indicate that their present home is unsafe or deteriorating. Further, most studies of the outcomes of people's choices suggest that most people's choices succeeded in satisfying their needs. The conclusion is that most elders think autonomously, act proactively, and find a satisfying degree of congruence between their needs and the ability of a new housing environment to satisfy those needs. The degree to which the counselor can influence this process is small, but the amount of assistance such a person can offer to elders in helping them explore their own preferences and balance sheet is great.

One scenario may be more problematic. This is the situation either where the client's competence is clearly declining or where the person seems oblivious to the need to plan for possible future decline in competence. Even here, people often take into account their own needs in such a way as to attain favorable congruence with their housing environments (Lawton, 1976). Nonetheless, not everyone thinks of issues such as the following:

- If your energy declines, would you be willing to accept new housing where eating meals in a common dining room is mandatory?
- If you make a move now, is it important that it be your last move? If so, are there options for partial or full care in the same location?
- Are you willing to pay more now to enter a retirement community in return for the security of knowing that you will have relatively low-cost nursing care later if needed ("life care")?
- If you stay where you are, how easy would it be for you to obtain in-home help?
- If you stay where you are, would it bother you if you could no longer go out easily to visit your friends and relatives (contrasted with a retirement community, with its built-in social opportunities)?
- If you move to a distant location for enjoyment purposes (e.g., Arizona, Florida) while healthy, would it be difficult to return to (here) (the place where relatives live) if your health declined?

Many such questions will arise spontaneously. But because all imply the downside of physical decline, some older clients may avoid thinking about them. Good clinical judgment is required to determine whether and when the counselor should introduce such issues if the client doesn't.

CONCLUSION

The message to counselors is that environmental planning may be an extremely valuable component of the counseling process. Basic human needs drive person-environment relationships. Exploration of these relationships offers a focus for therapeutic interaction that many elders enjoy, thus offering a pathway toward discussion of broader personal themes. The key concepts are autonomy and proactivity. Older people persist in going their own way in making residential decisions. "Their own way" includes the compromises with autonomy and proactivity engendered by increasing frailty. The counselor can perform this role more effectively by learning something about housing and local options. More important, however, is the ability to be a participant and supporter of older people's efforts to find decisions congruent with their needs and competences. Frailty does change the counseling context in the direction of the counselor's taking greater initiative in suggesting the exploration of environmental issues.

By and large, however, most elders in the end will make their own decisions while being reassured because a counselor was willing to think with them.

REFERENCES

Altman, I., & Gauvain, M. (1981). A cross-cultural and dialectic analysis of homes. In L.S. Liben, A.H. Patterson, & N. Newcombe (Eds.), *Spatial representation and behavior across the life span* (pp. 283–320). New York: Academic Press.

Bradburn, N. (1969). *The structure of psychological well-being.* Chicago: Aldine.

Carp, F. (1966). *A future for the aged.* Austin: University of Texas Press.

Kahana, E. (1982). A congruence model of person-environment interaction. In M.P. Lawton, P.G. Windley, & T.O. Byerts (Eds.), *Aging and the environment: Theoretical approaches* (pp. 97–121). New York: Springer.

LaBuda, D.R. (1985). *The gadget book.* Washington, DC: American Association of Retired Persons.

Lawton, M.P. (1976). The relative impact of congregate and traditional housing on elderly tenants. *Gerontologist, 16,* 237–242.

Lawton, M.P. (1980). Environmental change: The older person as initiator and responder. In N. Datan & N. Lohmann (Eds.), *Transitions of aging* (pp. 171–193). New York: Academic Press.

Lawton, M.P. (1983). Environment and other determinants of well-being in older people. *Gerontologist, 23,* 349–357.

Lawton, M.P. (1985). The elderly in context: Perspectives from environmental psychology and gerontology. *Environment and Behavior, 17,* 501–519.

Lawton, M.P. (1989). Environmental proactivity and affect in older people. In S. Spacapan & S. Oskamp (Eds.), *Social psychology of aging* (pp. 135–164). Newbury Park, CA: Sage.

Lawton, M.P. (1996). Quality of life and affect in later life. In C. Magai & S. McFadden (Eds.), *Handbook of emotion, adult development and aging.* Orlando, FL: Academic Press.

Lawton, M.P., & Nahemow, L. (1973). Ecology and the aging process. In C. Eisdorfer & M.P. Lawton (Eds.), *Psychology of adult development and aging* (pp. 619–674). Washington, DC: American Psychological Association.

Lawton, M.P., & Simon, B. (1968). The ecology of social relationships in housing for the elderly. *Gerontologist, 8,* 108–115.

Moss, M., & Lawton, M.P. (1982). Time budgets of older people: A window on four life styles. *Journal of Gerontology, 32,* 115–123.

Parmelee, P., & Lawton, M.P. (1990). The design of special environments for the aged. In J.E. Birren & K.W. Schaie (Eds.), *Handbook of the psychology of aging* (3rd ed., pp. 464–487). New York: Academic Press.

Patterson, A.H. (1978). Territorial behavior and fear of crime in the elderly. *Environmental Psychology and Nonverbal Behavior, 2,* 131–144.

Rowles, G.D. (1980). Growing old "inside": Aging and attachment to place in any Appalachian community. In N. Datan & N. Lohmann (Eds.), *Transitions of aging* (pp. 153–170). New York: Springer.

Scheidt, R.J., & Windley, P.G. (1998). *Environment and aging theory.* Westport, CT: Greenwood Press.

Watson, D., & Tellegen, A. (1985). Toward a consensual structure of mood. *Psychological Bulletin, 98,* 219–235.

CHAPTER 22

Critical Issues and Strategies in Mental Health Consultation in Nursing Homes

MICHAEL A. SMYER AND MAUREEN WILSON

T he same ecological factors that affect the well-being of nursing home residents affect mental health consultation in nursing homes: public policy initiatives that embody public expectations of and commitment to standards of care; underlying demographic and epidemiologic trends that affect the scope and cost of care; and clinical and research efforts that structure approaches to problem identification and treatment. In this chapter, we review each element to highlight its relevance for mental health consultation in nursing homes.

PUBLIC POLICY AS A PREVENTIVE STRATEGY

At first glance, public policy initiatives may seem quite distant from effective mental health consultation strategies in nursing homes. During the past decade, however, there has been an increasing awareness of the interconnections between and among various levels of problem identification and intervention. For example, Susser and Susser (1996a, 1996b) outlined emerging ecological perspectives in epidemiology:

> Systems also relate to one another; they do not exist in isolation. A metaphor may serve to illuminate this ecological perspective. We liken it to Chinese boxes—a conjurer's nest of boxes, each containing a succession of smaller ones. Thus, within localized structures, we envisage successive levels of organization,

each of which encompasses the next and simpler level, all with intimate links between them. . . .

. . . The outer boxes might be the overarching physical environment which, in turn, contains societies and populations (the epidemiological terrain), single individuals, and individual physiological systems, tissues and cells and finally (in biology) molecules. (pp. 675–676)

This ecological perspective echoes Bronfenbrenner's (1979) earlier depiction of the ecology of human development. Bronfenbrenner emphasized the interactions across levels that affect human development, including the public policy level.

More recently, the National Institute of Mental Health (NIMH) has focused attention on the emerging priorities for prevention research (National Advisory Mental Health Council [NAMHC], 1998). The review panel noted gaps in previous theoretical and empirical literature on prevention research. They also noted that prevention efforts must include "all levels of approaches to producing change," including the public policy level.

In emphasizing the importance of systems-level research, the NIMH panel focused attention on three domains: *pre-intervention research* that encompasses basic research on risk and protective factors that affect development, *preventive intervention research* that encompasses the range of research and intervention strategies traditionally associated with prevention efforts (Mrazek & Haggerty, 1994), and *preventive service systems research* which focuses on the organizational ecology of mental disorders.

In defining preventive service system research, NAMHC (1998) stated:

Preventive service systems research is concerned with the study of effective preventive interventions within service systems. The focus of studies in this category is on the interactive effects of preventive interventions with organizational aspects of the service environment, such as system structures, including characteristics and skills of those providing care and of the populations being served, organizational culture and climate, and methods of financing services.

Preventive service systems research can include: (1) studies of policies and procedures that facilitate or hinder the adoption and implementation of effective interventions, and research on the technology of effective interventions, and research on the technology of effective dissemination; (2) studies of the effects of age, gender, ethnicity, or sociocultural factors that affect access to or use of available preventive interventions; and (3) studies of the costs associated with delivery of preventive interventions, as well as methods of financing such interventions. The focus of preventive service systems research is on contextual and system-level outcomes. (p. 19)

Preventive service systems research is the foundation of effective mental health consultation in nursing homes. An understanding of the public policy context of mental health services in nursing homes is essential for identifying critical issues and effective strategies for the setting.

A REVIEW OF PUBLIC POLICY

During 1987, as part of the Omnibus Budget Reconciliation Act of 1987 (OBRA 87), Congress passed the Nursing Home Reform Act (NHRA). The NHRA was designed to use public policy to affect the provision and effectiveness of mental health services in nursing homes (Smyer, 1989). This Act grew out of an earlier, congressionally-mandated study designed to highlight strategies to improve the quality of care in nursing homes (Institute of Medicine, 1986). In contrast to the deregulation efforts of the time, the Institute of Medicine panel called for regulatory reform as a pathway to service improvement.

In this chapter, we highlight three initiatives of the NHRA that affect the provision of mental health consultation in nursing homes: screening and resident assessment; reduction of physical and chemical restraints; and provision of mental health services for those with identified need of such services. For each initiative, we discuss briefly the intent of the legislation and its impact. (See Lichtenberg, 1994 or Smyer & Walls, 1994 for a discussion of the staff-related aspects of the NHRA.)

RESIDENT ASSESSMENT

The NHRA included two major aspects focused on assessment: pre-admission screening and annual resident review process (PASARR) and an annual review of each resident's functioning in numerous domains.

The purpose of PASARR was simple: To exclude those who did not need the intensive physical health services found in nursing homes. PASARR procedures assumed that if the applicant was solely mentally ill, he or she would be diverted to an alternative treatment program or setting. Congress and the regulators *did not* define Alzheimer's and other dementias as mental illness, but as physical (medical) illnesses. Thus, if the applicant was diagnosed with any type of dementia, he or she was presumed to be in need of nursing home care.

The second aspect of the NHRA resident assessment approaches focused attention on the accuracy of the information provided about each nursing home resident. As part of this effort, the Resident Assessment Instrument (RAI) was developed. The RAI is a multidimensional assessment approach, including the minimum data set (MDS) and 18 problem-focused Resident Assessment Protocols (RAPs) (Hawes et al., 1997; Phillips, Hawes, Mor, Fries, & Morris, 1998). The annual resident review was designed to assist in treatment planning, provision, and monitoring by providing a comprehensive assessment approach encompassing medical, social, and behavioral functioning.

For both the initial assessment and the annual resident review, we ask an important question: How has it worked? We can assess the impact of the NHRA in this domain in two ways: Has PASARR affected the characteristics of the nursing population? Has the resident assessment instrument (RAI) provided more accurate information regarding the residents' functioning?

At the outset, many practitioners suggested that the PASARR screening would not significantly alter characteristics of nursing home residents because of the complex combinations of mental and physical disorders that nursing home residents typically have (e.g., Freiman, Arons, Goldman, & Burns, 1990).

Recent national data suggest that the NHRA did not substantially affect the profile of mental illness among nursing home residents. The Medical Expenditure Panel Survey (MEPS) was conducted in 1996 to provide nationally representative depictions of the health and service use of community-dwelling and institutionalized adults (Krauss et al., 1997). Preliminary analyses indicate that a majority of nursing home residents still have a mental disorder, including dementia, in the post-NHRA era: 15% of nursing home residents have Alzheimer's disease; 35% have unspecified dementia; 20% are diagnosed with depression; and 8% have a diagnosis of anxiety disorder (Smyer, Wilson, & Shea, 1998). These rates are comparable to the patterns of mental disorders prior to the NHRA (Burns et al., 1993; Smyer, Shea, & Streit, 1994).

Another analysis of the MEPS data (Table 22.1) focused on a combination of functional limitations and the presence of dementia among nursing home residents (Krauss et al., 1997). The patterns of comorbidity are substantially similar to those prior to the NHRA.

Smaller studies also lead to the conclusion that the NHRA has not substantially affected the rates of mental illness among nursing home residents. For example, in 1989, Tariot and his colleagues (Tariot, Podgorski, Blazina, & Leibovici, 1993) interviewed a randomly selected cohort of 80 residents in a single, public long-term care facility. A geriatric psychiatrist interviewed each of the residents. The results were similar to pre-NHRA patterns: 91% of the sample had at least one psychiatric diagnosis and at least one behavioral problem; 50% had four or more behavioral problems.

Table 22.1 Number and percent of nursing home residents by functional limitations and presence of dementia: 1996.

Limitation	Number	Percent*
Need help with 3 or more ADLs	1,302,200	83.3
Without dementia	643,800	41.2
With dementia	658,800	42.1
Need help with 1-2 ADLs	218,100	14.0
Without dementia	138,900	8.8
With dementia	79,200	5.1
Do not need help with ADLs	43,500	2.8
Without dementia	35,000	2.2
With dementia	8,500	.5

*Percents may not add to 100 due to rounding.
Data source: 1996 Medical Expenditure Panel Survey Nursing Home Component, Round 1.

Tariot and his colleagues' randomly selected sample was 90% White. In contrast, Class and his colleagues (1996) focused on rates among African American nursing home residents. Drawing a sample from six nursing homes in Indianapolis, Indiana, they found that 90% of the residents had at least one primary psychiatric diagnosis, most commonly dementia. In addition, 71% of the sample exhibited at least one behavioral problem and 26% had five or more behavioral problems.

Borson and his colleagues (Borson, Loebel, Kitchell, Domoto, & Hyde, 1997) provide an initial assessment of the impact of the PASARR approach. They assessed all of the residents referred for psychiatric evaluation under the NHRA PASARR implementation in one county of Washington state. Not surprisingly, they found substantial rates of psychiatric illness in this select group: 85% had a primary Axis I disorder or mental retardation and 5% had an adjustment disorder with anxious or depressive symptoms.

Whether the data were gathered in a national sample using structured interviews or in smaller samples using psychiatric examinations, the conclusion was the same: *The PASARR procedures have not substantially altered the psychiatric epidemiology of nursing homes.*

A second aspect of the NHRA resident assessment approaches focuses our attention on the accuracy of the information provided about the medical, social, and behavioral functioning of each resident. The Resident Assessment Instrument (RAI) (Hawes et al., 1997; Phillips et al., 1998) has been in use in nursing homes across the country since 1991. Phillips and his colleagues summarized the impact of the RAI on the quality of information (Table 22.2). Again, there is both good news and bad news. The good news is that the quality of information has improved; the bad news is that it is still far from

Table 22.2   Summary measures for percentage accurate information available for residents before and after mandated use of the RAI.

		Percentage of Residents	
Assessment Area	Percentage of Items Accurate	1990 (Pre-RAI)	1993 (Post-RAI)
All items	0–59	30.6	8.0
	60–89	51.8	43.5
	90–100	17.6	48.6
Functional/continence items (12)	0–59	36.4	15.9
	60–89	37.9	28.2
	90–100	25.7	55.9
Cognitive/psychosocial items (5)	0–59	41.4	14.3
	60–89	29.2	26.1
	90–100	29.4	59.6

Date source: Hawes et al., 1997, p. 981.

perfect in areas important to mental health consultation: functional abilities and cognitive/psychosocial areas.

REDUCTION OF PHYSICAL AND CHEMICAL RESTRAINTS

Concern over inappropriate chemical and physical restraints in nursing homes was part of the context of the NHRA development (e.g., Beers et al., 1988; Buck, 1988; Burns & Kamerow, 1988) after several investigators reported high rates of inappropriate psychotropic medication use. As with resident assessment, we ask the question: What impact has the NHRA had in this area?

Castle and his colleagues (Castle, Fogel, & Mor, 1997) compared physical restraint use patterns prior to and after the implementation of the NHRA in a sample drawn from 268 facilities in 10 states. They found a complicated pattern of stability and change: Overall, there was a 30% reduction in the use of physical restraints following the NHRA implementation. However, the same resident characteristics were predictive of restraint use after the NHRA effort: ADL impairments and cognitive performance impairments. Castle and his colleagues suggest that the same profile requires restraint use, but the threshold for implementation may have risen following the NHRA.

Castle et al. (1997) also focused on the organizational factors that were predictive of continued restraint use. They found three aspects associated with greater restraint use: high nurse aide to resident ratios, high average occupancy, and modest competition for residents. They suggest that a greater presence of registered nurses, as opposed to nurse aides, may affect the setting's flexibility in responding to the increased care needs of residents with functional and cognitive limitations. At the same time, there may be an administrative perception that restraint reduction is costly and, therefore, in settings that are economically competitive, there may be some reluctance to attempt restraint reduction.

This study reflects the complexity of assessing the impact of the NHRA. It is not sufficient to focus solely on rates of restraint use. Castle et al. (1997) provide a more detailed, more complex understanding of the fit between resident characteristics and organizational structure and function that together affects the pattern of restraint use.

A similarly complex picture emerges when the focus shifts to chemical restraints, specifically patterns of psychotropic medication use. For example, Borson and Doane (1997) reviewed the prescription patterns for residents of 39 skilled nursing facilities for a period before and after the NHRA implementation (1989–1992). They found a 14% reduction in the number of residents receiving any psychotropic medication during this period. However, the pattern of use varied across type of medication: a 60% reduction in p.r.n. (as needed) prescription use; a 35% decrease in those receiving antipsychotic agents; a 3% increase in antidepressant use; and a 45% increase in the rate of anxiolytic use (from 5.5% to 8.0%).

Garrard and her colleagues also studied the use of psychotropic medications in Minnesota's 372 nursing homes (Garrard, Chen, & Dowd, 1995). Once again, there were different patterns for different therapeutic classes of drugs: a one-third reduction in antispsychotic use during the four-year period; stable rates of antidepressant and antianxiety use.

Even when the focus is on a single class of drugs, the interaction of resident and institutional factors is apparent. For example, Shorr and his colleagues investigated antipsychotic drug use by 9,432 Medicaid enrollees in Tennessee (Shorr, Fought, & Ray, 1994). They found a 27% reduction in antipsychotic use in a 30-month period prior to and following the NHRA implementation. Importantly, they also found that third-shift staffing patterns were associated with antipsychotic use: above average staffing on the third shift was associated with significant reduction in antipsychotic use.

In short, the impact of the NHRA on physical and chemical restraint use is a function of the residents' characteristics, the facility's structure and organization, and the specific approaches under discussion. These patterns affect the well-being of nursing home residents and the practice of mental health consultation in the setting.

Provision of Mental Health Services

The NHRA also emphasized providing the "best possible" physical and mental health treatment. Prior to the NHRA, estimates were that two-thirds of nursing home residents had a diagnosed mental illness. However, there was very little treatment of those mentally ill residents. For example, Burns and her colleagues (1993) reported that 4.5% of mentally ill nursing home residents received mental health treatment in a one-month period. Smyer and his colleagues (1994) reported that 19% of those in need had received mental health treatment in the prior year.

We are still awaiting national data to assess the impact of the NHRA on provision of mental health treatment for mentally ill nursing home residents. There are preliminary indications of continuing substantial unmet needs. Borson and his colleagues (1997), for example, reported that 55% of nursing home residents who were referred for a psychiatric evaluation had unmet mental health services needs.

Similarly, Hawes et al. (1997) focused on measures of process quality prior to and after the implementation of the Resident Assessment Instrument (RAI) approach. They noted that despite increased attention to mental health problems using the RAI 16% of residents with behavioral symptoms did not receive a behavior management program.

Another indirect indicator of unmet need comes from a recent report from the Office of Inspector General (OIG) of the Department of Health and Human Services (OIG, 1996). Staff members of the OIG were investigating potential fraud and abuse of Medicare funds in the provision of mental health services in nursing homes. While the major focus of their inquiry was on patterns of abuse, they also noted unmet need for mental health services:

> Seventy-eight percent of the nursing facility respondents cite barriers nursing facility residents face in getting needed mental health services. They say there are still areas in the country where providers are not available and providers who do not want to go into nursing facilities since they are not interested in this type of patient. Some say there is a stigma associated with mental health services and patients, or their families refuse needed services. At times, the attending physician reportedly feels this way and refuses to order what nursing facility staff see as needed services. Also noted is a lack of awareness of mental health illness on the part of some of the nursing facility staff working with these patients. Some nursing facility respondents mention that depression is under diagnosed and therefore not treated or sometimes leads to misdiagnosis of dementia. (p. 10)

This anecdotal evidence suggests that there are continuing unmet mental health needs despite the intent of the NHRA. National surveys (e.g., the 1995 national nursing home survey (Strahan, 1997) and the 1996 Medical Expenditure Panel Survey (Krauss et al., 1997) should provide fuller information about the scope and specific nature of the unmet need.

In summary, the NHRA was a major public policy initiative designed to prevent excess disability among nursing home residents by identifying mental disorders among nursing home residents and assuring provision of mental health services to those nursing home residents who need them. As this brief review indicates, although the NHRA has had some effects on the nursing home setting, significant challenges remain. One challenge, the increasing demand for and cost of nursing home services, is discussed next.

DEMOGRAPHIC AND ECONOMIC CHALLENGES

Demographic and economic projections provide information for nursing home services and for funding for mental health consultation. The story line is simple: growth in the number of nursing home residents and growth in the costs associated with their care.

Wiener and his colleagues (Wiener, Illston, & Hanley, 1994) estimate a 60% increase in the nursing home population over the next 25 years. Moreover, the oldest old, those aged 85 and above, will form an increasingly larger share of the nursing home population (Figure 22.1).

Not surprisingly, the costs of nursing home care are also projected to increase substantially over the next 25 years. Again, Wiener and his colleagues (1994) provide an estimate of 134% growth over that time (from $55 billion per year to $128 billion) (Figure 22.2).

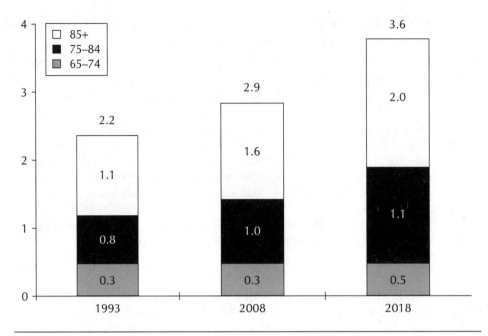

Figure 22.1 Nursing home population, by age, selected periods (in millions). (*Data source:* Weiner, Illston, and Hanley, 1994.)

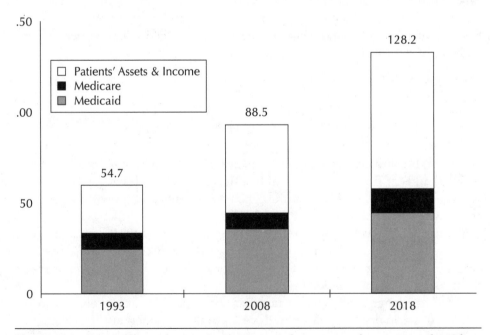

Figure 22.2 Expenditures for nursing home care, by sources of payment, selected periods (billions of 1993 dollars). (*Data source:* Weiner, Illston, and Hanley, 1994.)

We can anticipate continued demand for nursing home care and for mental health consultation in this setting for the foreseeable future. At the same time, the rising costs of long-term care may lead to further restrictions in funding for mental health services.

THE ECOLOGY OF MENTAL HEALTH CONSULTATION IN NURSING HOMES

We end where we began, with a discussion of the ecology of prevention and treatment of mental disorders. Mental health consultants face four types of challenges. We suggest specific strategies for each: public policy changes; institutional characteristics; information resources; and each individual resident's profile.

PUBLIC POLICY CHANGES

Public policy is increasingly being used as an explicit prevention strategy designed to improve mental and physical health care in nursing homes. Thus, mental health consultants must stay informed about the emerging priorities and policies that affect the field. For example, in spring, 1998, the Health Care Financing Administration (HCFA) promulgated a final rule regarding Medicare coverage of services by clinical psychologists and clinical social workers in nursing homes, hospitals, and dialysis facilities. Rosen (1998) summarized the ruling and its potential impact on clinical social workers (CSWs) and residents of skilled nursing facilities (SNFs):

> This rule is a severe setback, particularly in relation to mental health services provided to SNF residents by independent CSWs. CSWs will be excluded from receiving any direct Medicare Part B reimbursement for diagnosing or treating mental illness in residents of SNFs. HCFA's rule specifically states: "We cannot accept the suggestion that CSWs should be paid separate and apart from payment to the SNF for independently diagnosing or treating mental disorders of SNF patients, nor can we accept that psychotherapy services furnished by CSWs to patients who have diagnosis codes indicating mental illness should be covered as CSW services rather than viewed as services that SNFs are required to provide."
>
> This interpretation disregards the fact that significant numbers of SNFs do not employ licensed CSWs, and do not provide mental health therapy as a part of routine SNF care. The rule also disregards a variety of research that links the problem of quality of life in SNFs to the lack of sufficient attention to the mental health needs of SNF residents. (p. 3)

The HCFA ruling exemplifies the direct links among congressional intent, regulatory review, and the challenges of mental health consultation. Each consultant must be aware of the policy and regulatory climate that affects the setting and its practices.

INSTITUTIONAL CHARACTERISTICS

Structural aspects of the nursing home itself may affect both mental health problem identification and treatment approaches. For example, Castle and his colleagues (1997) noted that the RN to resident ratio affected rates of physical restraint use. Similarly, others have noted that the job design (rotating vs. stable assignment of residents to staff) and supervisory style can affect mental health training and job performance of nurses' aides (Smyer, Brannon, & Cohn, 1992; Smyer & Walls, 1994). Others, investigating adoption of innovation in nursing homes (e.g., computerizing the MDS information), have noted that personal demographic characteristics (e.g., job tenure) as well as membership in a nursing home chain affected the innovation process (Castle & Banaszak-Holl, 1997).

The lesson for the mental health consultant is clear: The setting's characteristics can affect the identification of mental health problems and the resources available for their treatment. In initiating a consulting relationship, therefore, it is important to pay attention to a range of information about the setting: size, staff structure (rotating vs. stable assignments, staff ratios (RN/ Nurse Aide/ Resident), physical setting, staff turnover rates, and so on.

INFORMATION RESOURCES

Information gathering is an essential element of any consulting relationship. In nursing homes, two important sources provide both challenges and opportunities: the nursing staff and the resident assessment information.

Nurses are the front-line caregivers in nursing homes: 64% of the workforce are nurses' aides; another 20% are registered nurses (Strahan, 1997). As such, they are key informants on the daily variations in affect and behavior of their residents. Effective mental health consultants must engage the nursing staff as collaborators in problem identification and treatment (Spayd & Smyer, 1996).

A second source of information are the mandated aspects of the PASARR, including the Minimum Data Set (MDS). As indicated earlier, the MDS is not perfect (e.g., Phillips et al., 1998); however, it represents staff perceptions of the individual's functioning. Thus, it offers a common starting point for problem identification. At the same time, the MDS may provide indicators that can be used to pinpoint other diagnostic syndromes not explicitly represented in the MDS (e.g., personality disorders, Rosowsky & Smyer, in press). The challenge for the consultant is how to use the mandated information collection process to assist in problem identification, treatment, and evaluation.

THE INDIVIDUAL RESIDENT'S PROFILE

At its base, the ecology of the nursing home is important for helping the consultant understand the functioning of each resident in the context of the specific demands of a given nursing home setting. In trying to develop an accurate assessment, Cohen's dictum is an important guide: Biography is as important as biology (Cohen, 1993). The challenge is to understand the individual's life experience in a way that will help shape both problem identification and treatment. For many residents, this kind of understanding requires collaboration with not only staff members, but family members—another aspect of the nursing home ecology.

The medical record, the MDS information, formal and informal nursing reports, family reports , traditional geriatric assessment approaches—all combine to depict the current functioning of the nursing home resident. The consultant's challenge is to organize the information in a coherent fashion that will allow for monitoring progress in problem treatment and resolution. This task often requires consulting across various levels of the home (from resident to family to staff to administration), across time (three shifts), and across professions (nurses, nurses' aides, physicians).

CONCLUSION

The effective consultant must attend to all levels—from policy to institution to individual—in assessing the changing challenges and opportunities in mental health consultation in nursing homes. The demographic trends and psychiatric epidemiology are compelling: We anticipate continuing, substantial need for mental health care in nursing homes. The challenges remain: How to use already-existing structure, talent, and information sources to make nursing homes more effective mental health settings.

REFERENCES

Beers, M., Avorn, J., Soumerai, S., Everitt, D., Sherman, D., & Salem, S. (1988). Psychoactive medication use in intermediate-care facility residents. *Journal of the American Medical Association, 260,* 3016–3020.

Borson, S., & Doane, K. (1997). The impact of OBRA-87 on psychotropic drug prescribing in skilled nursing facilities. *Psychiatric Services, 48*(10), 1289–1296.

Borson, S., Loebel, J.P., Kitchell, M., Domoto, S., & Hyde, T. (1997). Psychiatric assessments of nursing home residents under OBRA-87: Should PASARR be reformed? *Journal of the American Geriatrics Society, 45,* 1173–1181.

Bronfenbrenner, U. (1979). *The ecology of human development: Experiments by nature and design.* Cambridge, MA: Harvard University Press.

Buck, J.A. (1988). Psychotropic drug practice in nursing homes. *Journal of the American Geriatrics Society, 36,* 409–418.

Burns, B.J., & Kamerow, D.B. (1988). Psychotropic drug prescriptions for nursing home residents. *Journal of Family Practice, 26,* 155–160.

Burns, B.J., Wagner, R., Taube, H.J.E., Magaziner, J., Permutt, T., & Landerman, R. (1993). Mental health service use by the elderly in nursing homes. *American Journal of Public Health, 83*(3), 331–337.

Castle, N.G., & Banaszak-Holl, J. (1997). Top management team characteristics and innovation in nursing homes. *Gerontologist, 37*(5), 572–580.

Castle, N.G., Fogel, B., & Mor, V. (1997). Risk factors for physical restraint use in nursing homes: Pre- and post-implementation of the Nursing Home Reform Act. *Gerontologist, 37*(6), 737–747.

Class, C.A., Unverzagt, F.W., Gao, S., Hall, K.S., Baiyewu, O., & Hendrie, H.C. (1996). Psychiatric disorders in African American nursing home residents. *American Journal of Psychiatry, 153,* 677–681.

Cohen, G.D. (1993). Comprehensive assessment: Capturing strengths, not just weaknesses. In M.A. Smyer (Ed.), *Mental health and aging: Progress and prospects* (pp. 93–100). New York: Springer.

Freiman, M.P., Arons, B.S., Goldman, H.H., & Burns, B.J. (1990). Nursing home reform and the mentally ill. *Health Affairs, 9*(4), 47–60.

Garrard, J., Chen, V., & Dowd, B. (1995). The impact of the 1987 federal regulations on the use of psychotropic drugs in Minnesota nursing homes. *American Journal of Public Health, 85*(6), 771–776.

Hawes, C., Mor, V., Phillips, C.D., Fries, B.E., Morris, J.N., Steele-Friedlob, E., Greene, A.M., & Nennstiel, M. (1997). The OBRA-87 nursing home regulations and implementation of the resident assessment instrument: Effects on process quality. *Journal of the American Geriatrics Society, 45,* 977–985.

Institute of Medicine. (1986). *Improving the quality of care in nursing homes.* Washington, DC: National Academy Press.

Krauss, N.A., Freiman, M.P., Rhoades, J.A., Altman, B.M., Brown, Jr., E., & Potter, D.E.B. (1997, July). Characteristics of nursing home facilities and residents. *Medical Expenditure Panel Survey, (2),* 1–3.

Lichtenberg, P.A. (1994). *A guide to psychological practice in geriatric long-term care.* New York: Haworth Press.

Mrazek, P.J., & Haggerty, R.J. (Eds.). (1994). *Reducing risks for mental disorders: Frontiers for preventive intervention research.* Washington, DC: National Academy Press.

National Advisory Mental Health Council. (1998). *Priorities for prevention research at NIMH* (NIH Publication No: 98-4321). Washington, DC: National Institute of Mental Health, National Institutes of Health.

Office of Inspector General. (1996). *Mental health services in nursing facilities* (Report no. OEI-02-91-00860). Washington, DC: Department of Health and Human Services.

Phillips, C.D., Hawes, C., Mor, V., Fries, B.E., & Morris, J.N. (1998). Geriatric assessment in nursing homes in the United States: Impact of a national program. *Generations, 21*(4), 15–20.

Rosen, A.L. (1998). New Medicare rule for clinical services. *Dimensions, 5*(2), 3, 6.

Rosowsky, E., & Smyer, M.A. (in press). Personality disorders and the difficult nursing home resident. In E. Rosowsky, R. Abrams, & R. Zweig (Eds.), *Personality disorders in older adults: Emerging issues in diagnosis and treatment.* Hillsdale, NJ: Erlbaum.

Shorr, R.I., Fought, R.L., & Ray, W.A. (1994). Changes in antipsychotic drug use in nursing homes during implementation of the OBRA-87 regulations. *Journal of the American Medical Association, 271*(5), 358–362.

Smyer, M.A. (1989). Nursing homes as a setting for psychological practice: Public policy perspectives. *American Psychologist, 44*(10), 1307–1314.

Smyer, M.A., Brannon, D., & Cohn, M. (1992). Improving nursing home care through training and job redesign. *Gerontologist, 32*(3), 327–333.

Smyer, M.A., Shea, D., & Streit, A. (1994). The provision and use of mental health services in nursing homes: Results from the national medical expenditure survey. *American Journal of Public Health, 84*(2), 284–287.

Smyer, M.A., & Walls, C. T. (1994). Design and evaluation of interventions in nursing homes. In C.B. Fisher & R.M. Lerner (Eds.), *Applied developmental psychology.* Cambridge, MA: McGraw-Hill.

Smyer, M.A., Wilson, M., & Shea, D. (1998, November 23). *Did the nursing home reform act work?* Paper presented at the 51st annual Scientific Meeting of the Gerontological Society of America, Philadelphia.

Spayd, C.S., & Smyer, M.A. (1996). Psychological interventions in nursing homes. In S.H. Zarit & B.G. Knight (Eds.), *A guide to psychotherapy and aging* (pp. 241–268). Washington, DC: American Psychological Association.

Strahan, G.W. (1997). *An overview of nursing homes and their current residents: Data from the 1995 national nursing home survey* (Advance data from vital and health statistics, No. 280). Hyattsville, MD: National Center for Health Statistics.

Susser, M.B., & Susser, E. (1996a). Choosing a future for epidemiology: I. Eras and paradigms. *American Journal of Public Health, 86*(5), 668–673.

Susser, M.B., & Susser, E. (1996b). Choosing a future for epidemiology: II. From black box to Chinese boxes and eco-epidemiology. *American Journal of Public Health, 86*(5), 674–677.

Tariot, P.N., Podgorski, C.A., Blazina, L., & Leibovici, A. (1993). Mental disorders in the nursing home: Another perspective. *American Journal of Psychiatry, 150,* 1063–1069.

Wiener, J.M., Illston, L.H., & Hanley, R.J. (1994). *Sharing the burden: Strategies for public and private long-term care insurance.* Washington, DC: Brookings Institution.

CHAPTER 23

Prevention and Promotion Models of Intervention for Strengthening Aging Families

GREGORY C. SMITH

Despite the reality that contemporary family life frequently includes older family members as sources of gratification and support to younger generations (Cohler & Altergott, 1995), the belief that older adults pose only a burden to family members or are socially isolated from them persists as the primary impetus for practice and applied research with aging families (Troll, 1995). The family caregiving literature, which has dominated the study of aging families to date, exemplifies this tendency by its emphasis on the burden of those family members who provide care and the presumed passivity of the elderly family member who receives that care (Gatz, Bengtson, & Blum, 1990). By focusing so heavily on the problems of aging families, gerontologists have thus ignored the strengths and potentials that exist within these families as well as the appropriate interventions for advancing them.

The purpose of the present chapter is to describe the use of both prevention and promotion models of intervention toward the overall goal of strengthening aging families. I begin by defining prevention and promotion within the context of aging families. This is followed by a consideration of the goals for these interventions with this target population. Next, specific types of intervention are described accompanied by illustrations of their usefulness from the gerontological literature. The chapter ends with a discussion of those factors that make prevention and promotion actually work with aging families.

DEFINING PREVENTION AND PROMOTION

Three general models of intervention exist that are relevant to families at any stage of the family life cycle (Dunst, Trivette, & Thompson, 1991). *Treatment* refers to corrective actions taken to counteract the negative effects of an existing disorder within dysfunctional or seriously troubled families (see Chapter 14, this volume, for a comprehensive discussion of treatment interventions with aging families). *Prevention* involves protective efforts taken on behalf of (still-well) families when stressful family situations are present or impending to forestall otherwise likely negative consequences. Lastly, *promotion* is directed toward the enhancement and optimization of family functioning for the sake of fostering positive outcomes in the absence of existing or impending family stressors. Table 23.1 summarizes pertinent information regarding similarities and differences between the prevention and promotion models of intervention with aging families.

Although both prevention and promotion models of intervention have become increasingly popular in the generic family studies literature, their application to aging families has been primarily limited to the prevention of crises in those situations where families provide care to frail elderly family members (Richardson, Gilleard, Lieberman, & Peeler, 1994). Moreover, these efforts have typically focused on strengthening the one family member who acts as the primary caregiver rather than the entire family unit (Toseland, Smith, & McCallion, 1995). Thus, the present chapter looks beyond the family caregiving literature to consider prevention and promotion within the context of diverse issues that face aging families.

PREVENTION

The concept of prevention is based on the assumption that families at each stage of the family life cycle vary according to how much they are adversely

Table 23.1 A comparison of prevention and promotion models of family intervention.

Characteristics	Prevention	Promotion
Definition	To deter, hinder, or forestall the occurrence of problems or negative functioning	To enhance, bring about, and optimize positive growth and functioning
Major Focus	Avoidance or reduction in the prevalence or incidence of negative outcomes	Development, enhancement, and elaboration of family competencies
Orientation	Protection and defense	Mastery and optimization
Mode of Action	Reactive	Proactive
Primary Objective	Develop family resilience	Achieve family competence
Fundamental Outcome	Family strengthened as functional unit	Family strengthened as functional unit

Note: Adapted from C. Dunst, C. Trivette, and R. Thompson (1991).

affected by the normative and nonnormative events that challenge them. L'Abate (1990), for example, has stated that families of any developmental stage can be trichotomized into three categories regarding potential disruption from major life events, transitions, or crises: (1) families are "at risk" when it is likely that they will eventually be affected by a threatening situation; (2) families are "in need" when the situation has already been encountered, but has not seriously damaged family equilibrium; and (3) families are "in crisis" when the situation has resulted in considerable trouble for family members or the family system as a whole.

The phenomenon of elder abuse may be used to illustrate how this trichotomy pertains to aging families. A family may be at risk for potential abuse or neglect of an elderly relative when such strains as extreme caregiving demands, work and family pressures, or family poverty set the stage for abuse to occur. A family would be in need if sporadic episodes of maltreatment had already occurred, such as verbally abusive arguments with an older parent, but the situation had not yet reached catastrophic proportions. Finally, a family would be in crisis if persistent abuse or neglect, such as when an adult offspring with a drug addiction depletes the finances of a cognitively impaired elder, seriously and continually jeopardizing the elder's physical or emotional wellbeing (Kosberg & Garcia, 1995).

From a preventive orientation, determining whether a family is at risk, in need, or in crisis is critical because it alerts practitioners to how a family heading toward a crisis can escape trouble by taking appropriate steps. Accordingly, three levels of prevention exist that correspond to this trichotomy (Dunst et al., 1991; L'Abate, 1990; Mace, 1983): (1) *Primary prevention* refers to actions taken prior to the onset of a family problem to avert serious difficulties; (2) *secondary prevention* refers to actions taken after a family problem has been identified, but before a serious crisis emerges; and (3) *tertiary prevention* refers to actions taken when a major crisis has already developed within the family, with the goal of preventing negative consequences from escalating any further.

PROMOTION

As stated earlier, promotion involves proactive intervention efforts aimed at the optimization of positive family functioning. In contrast to the defensive posture of prevention, which is aimed at averting negative outcomes or problems, promotion assumes a strengths-based orientation that is directed toward helping families attain such positive outcomes as the enrichment of family roles or increased feelings of mastery and self-efficacy. Promotion models, then, are intended to help families achieve their maximum level of functioning.

PREVENTION VERSUS PROMOTION FOR AGING FAMILIES

There is a controversy within the family studies literature over whether promotion and prevention are basically the same or different. Some family scholars have argued that because the absence of family problems is not necessarily equivalent to the presence of positive family functioning, only promotion and enhancement models increase the likelihood that families will achieve their maximum potential. Thus, the proponents of this view believe that promotion and prevention should be viewed as separate endeavors. An opposing argument, however, has been that promotion and prevention are merely alternative pathways to the same overall goal of strengthening the family (see, for review, Dunst et al., 1991).

Within the context of aging families, it seems that both sides of this controversy have merit. When prevention and promotion are regarded as being the same, a problem orientation is likely to become predominant prompting practitioners to focus on thwarting the various normative crises experienced by aging families (e.g., illness or institutionalization of an elderly family member) rather than on the optimization of family functioning (e.g., enrichment of intergenerational family roles). The legitimacy of this concern is evidenced by the fact that gerontologists have consistently maintained a false misery image of aging despite abundant contradictory evidence (Tornstam, 1992). In contrast, viewing promotion as a distinct model of intervention counters the tendency to equate age with misery as practitioners focus on the potentials as well as the problems of aging families.

Yet, there are also reasons for arguing that a distinction between prevention and promotion is immaterial with respect to aging families. There is no such thing as a mythological problem-free family, which means that every family is likely to need some prevention in the face of normative challenges (Walsh, 1996). This need for prevention seems especially true for aging families where normative events (e.g., reduced income and role involvement due to retirement, or the serious illness and death of loved ones) are likely to jeopardize the equilibrium of even the healthiest families. Some nonnormative challenges that confront aging families, such as the progressive ravages of Alzheimer's disease, are also difficult to cast in the more positive light of promotion, despite growing recognition that the family members may grow from this experience (Farran, 1997).

In reality, then, it may be best for practitioners working with aging families to view the difference between promotion and prevention as one of *degree* rather than of *kind*. For example, the members of an aging family in crisis from the ravages of Alzheimer's disease may seek a primarily preventive-oriented intervention designed to alleviate caregiver stress and avert family conflict. At the same time, however, the more growth-oriented goals of deriving feelings of mastery or satisfaction as a family caregiver may also be achievable (Farran, 1997; Gatz et al., 1990). This orientation is consistent with the belief that crisis is a time of both danger and opportunity, and that successfully coping with a crisis has generalized adaptive value (Cowen, 1985; Walsh, 1996). Conversely, a promotive intervention intending to enhance communication and intimacy within late life marriages might be considered deficient if it did not also prepare older couples for future strains resulting from age-related assaults to the physical well-being of one or both partners (Whitbourne & Cassidy, 1995).

Another reason for viewing the promotion and prevention models of family intervention as more alike than different is that they share the same underlying goal of strengthening the family as a functional unit (Moen & Forest, 1995). An important question to ask in this regard is: What unique characteristics are associated with strong aging families that point to the relevant outcomes for prevention and promotion efforts with this population?

GOALS OF PREVENTION AND PROMOTION WITH AGING FAMILIES

Although gerontologists have virtually ignored the issue of what makes an aging family strong or healthy, the concept of *family resilience* has emerged in the generic family studies literature which informs practitioners of the goals for promotion and prevention at any stage of the family life cycle (Hawley & DeHaan, 1996; Walsh, 1996). Family resiliency has been described as the qualities that enable a family to maintain its equilibrium as it experiences a crisis or hardship, thus revealing a clear focus on wellness rather than pathology (Hawley & DeHaan, 1996). The specific traits associated with resilient families include such processes as cohesion, flexibility, open communication, problem solving, the availability of and willingness to use external resources, and an affirming belief system that allows families to make sense of a crisis and give it meaning (Walsh, 1996).

Interestingly, several of the qualities that characterize resilient families are similar to those included in a rare definition of competence within aging families that was proposed by Kuypers and Bengtson (1984). According to these authors, an aging family functions competently if (1) individual members adequately enact the duties and expectations of family roles; (2) the family's style of coping with challenges involves flexibility, integration with supports and resources outside the family, and the ability to assess the meaning of change and challenge; and (3) family members possess a sense of mastery about their ability to influence important outcomes.

Despite the apparent similarity between Kuypers and Bengtson's (1984) definition of competence for aging families and the generic conceptualization of family resilience, there are some noteworthy differences between these two views as well. Kuypers and Bengtson listed a static set of strengths that presumably define competent aging families regardless of the unique set of circumstances that may confront any one aging family in particular. In contrast, the family resilience perspective assumes that how a given family functions at various points across the life cycle depends more on its unique developmental history than on commonalities between families at a particular developmental stage (Hawley & DeHaan, 1996). This perspective further assumes that attempts to define healthy family functioning are made even more difficult by the increasing diversity of family structure in our society, as well as the fact that normality is a socially constructed phenomenon (for relevance to aging families, see Bengtson, Rosenthal, & Burton, 1990). Thus, the family resilience perspective is unique in encouraging practitioners to avoid a "one size fits all" approach to prevention and promotion with aging families (Walsh, 1996).

It is also worth noting that by including such ideal traits as perceived mastery and optimal performance of family roles in their interpretation of competence within the aging family, Kuypers and Bengtson (1984) implied these as major goals for promotion models of intervention with aging families. On the other hand, because the family resilience perspective has focused more narrowly on those qualities that are used to counteract stress (Hawley & DeHaan, 1996; Walsh, 1996), this view favors prevention models of intervention. Nevertheless, Hawley and DeHaan have commented that resiliency may simply refer to ways that families use their strengths in times of crisis. This reasoning is consistent with the belief that both the prevention and promotion models of intervention aim to develop the same basic composite of family skills and competencies. The key difference is that prevention fosters the development and use of those skills to counteract a stressful situation, whereas promotion interventions provide these skills so that they will radiate positively to adjustment and well-being (Cowen, 1985).

APPROACHES TO PREVENTION AND PROMOTION WITH AGING FAMILIES

There are two overall approaches to strengthening families regardless of whether a prevention or promotion model of intervention is under consideration: Education and environmental engineering. These two approaches are described in the following sections, along with specific examples of how they have been used by gerontologists for the purpose of strengthening aging families.

EDUCATION FOR AGING FAMILIES

The competency of individual family members or the entire family system can be enhanced through educational methods for developing new skills, forming new attitudes, gaining new insights, or obtaining new knowledge. Educational interventions are considered to be especially well suited to aging families because, unlike therapeutic interventions, they offer an approach to family problems that escapes the labeling and stigmatization dreaded by older cohorts (Brubaker & Roberto, 1993; Giordano & Beckman, 1985). Four types of educational programs have been used with aging families: psychoeducational support groups, family life education, guided family reminiscence, and structured family enrichment.

Psychoeducational Support Groups
These interventions provide a blend of factual information and counseling in which the main objectives are enabling participants to (1) develop new coping skills, (2) cognitively reappraise the stressful family situation, (3) ventilate negative affects regarding stressors, and (4) obtain relevant information. In addition to imparting useful facts about important family events, psychoeducational support groups also attempt to improve participants' emotional and behavioral

responses to challenging family situations. In this respect, these interventions emphasize prevention over promotion. As stated by Cowen (1985), "The elements of shared problems, common turf, mutual understanding, and strong motivation that bond group members . . . are all favorable preconditions for event-focused prevention programs" (p. 42).

A psychoeducational support group program for older parents of adults with developmental disabilities reported by Smith, Majeski, and McClenny (1996) demonstrates the usefulness of this approach with aging families. This intervention was deemed necessary because increasing number of elderly parents who are survived by their adult offspring with developmental disabilities face such unique family stressors as a state of "perpetual parenthood," chronic sorrow, age-associated decrements in themselves and their offspring, lack of formal services, social isolation, and the need to plan for their offspring's future (Jennings, 1987; Lefly, 1987).

In developing this program, the authors convened a focus group consisting of relevant professionals and older parents who were given the tasks of (1) developing the goals, content, and format of the intervention; (2) identifying strategies for recruiting participants; and (3) creating evaluation instruments. The major goals were to inform parents about planning for the offspring's future, promote acceptance of the inevitable relinquishment of care to others, foster coping skills, encourage knowledge and use of formal and informal supports, and instill solidarity among the participants. Each group received six 1.5 hour sessions that were led by experienced professionals from the local developmental disabilities service system. At the end of the program, both the group leaders and the older parents judged it to be highly effective in meeting the stated goals.

This particular example reveals several interesting points regarding psychoeducation support groups for aging families. First, it shows that they can be used effectively in situations other than those involving family care to frail elders. Second, by asking older parents to help design the intervention, the target population was empowered and given responsibility for the program's success. Third, although the program was primarily based on the prevention model of intervention, several participants commented that it also validated them as parents and enabled them to see their offspring in a new light. These findings are consistent with the notion that the optimization of family functioning can occur within the context of prevention.

Family Life Education

Although many definitions of family life education exist in the literature, it is often described as a primarily cognitive activity designed to provide useful information to participants about relevant content and skill areas (Hoopes, Fisher, & Barlow, 1984). Such programs may be targeted for either individual family members, family subsystems, or the entire family. Although past family life education efforts have focused rather narrowly on the concerns of younger families (e.g., parent education), family life educators have recently begun to recognize that opportunities exist for family life education at every phase of the family life cycle (see, e.g., Hennon & Arcus, 1993).

Two particular advantages associated with family life education for aging families have been suggested by Brubaker and Roberto (1993). First, it provides a means of reaching out to a cohort that is often hesitant about involvement with either formal services or affectively oriented support groups. Second, family life education may include such diverse methods of imparting information to later life families as workshops, seminars, brochures, pamphlets, and mass media. This range of modalities is important in light of the physical and financial limitations frequently encountered by older family members.

Several important characteristics of older adults must be kept in mind when developing family life education programs for them and their families. First, the tremendous heterogeneity among elderly persons and their families should be addressed, including such factors as urban versus rural participants, as well as differences in functional abilities, financial status, marital status, and ethnicity (Brubaker & Roberto, 1993). Second, because family life education is a cognitive activity, it must be realized that age-related changes in cognition may influence the older adult's ability to retain and process new information (Hennon & Arcus, 1993). Finally, because older persons have a long history as family members, the influence of the past on current family functioning must be considered when developing family-based curriculum (Brubaker & Robeto, 1993).

One promising area for family life education with aging families concerns interventions to help older couples maintain relationship happiness and stability. Although there are numerous examples of interventions like this for couples in their beginning and middle years, family life education programs for older couples have been virtually nonexistent (Dickson, 1996; Gilford, 1997).

An exception to this unfortunate trend, however, involves a brief educational program designed by White and Catania (1982) to inform older adults, their family members, and service providers about normal age-related changes in sexuality. Family members and service providers were included in this novel experimental program for two reasons: (1) to create a permission-giving climate regarding sexuality in old age which is typically denied by these younger age groups, and (2) to provide a potential long-term preventive measure for the future sexuality of the younger participants.

Each group received six hours of lecture-based instruction (supplemented with videotapes, panel discussions, and simulation exercises) on such topics as normative changes related to sex and aging, benefits of sex in old age, psychological and pharmacological factors, "retirement" marriages, and social hindrances to sexual intimacy in old age. Compared with controls, the experimental participants from all three groups demonstrated significant positive changes in knowledge about and attitudes toward sexuality and aging. Most remarkably, though, the older adult participants reported a 400% increase in their sexual behavior at the end of the program.

Inspection of the goals and outcomes of this program reveals an interesting blend of promotion and prevention activities. The enlightened knowledge and attitudes regarding sexuality and aging demonstrated by all three groups, coupled with the dramatic increase in sexual behavior within the older participants, reveal elements of promotion in this intervention. At the same time, however, the goal of preventing future age-related problems in sexuality from emerging when the younger participants reached old age was also present.

Guided Family Reminiscence

De Vries, Birren, and Deutchman (1990) have proposed a guided family reminiscence activity which they describe as "an educational process of bringing up one's understanding of the past into the present in order to integrate the experiences of a lifetime" (p. 4). The specific purposes of this intervention, which includes putting the contradictions of life into perspective, reaffirming one's abilities to meet life's challenges, restoring one's sense of self-sufficiency and personal identity, and educating families about shifting roles, are especially appropriate for use with aging families.

The Biography Project of the University of Minnesota (Caron, 1997) represents an excellent illustration of how guided family reminiscence may be used to assist elders and their families in adjusting to a nursing home placement. In this program, multiple family groups meet together to provide biographical information that captures the life history and personal characteristics of the residents.

This activity not only offers staff a better understanding of what the elder's life was like prior to the nursing home placement, but it also provides a valued role within the institution for family members and helps staff and family to build a constructive relationship. The biography process further results in "a celebration of the elder's life by the family, an act of loyalty and regard that helps balance out the disloyalty of nursing home placement" (Caron, 1997, p. 253).

By conducting the biographies with multiple families present, the program also promotes the development of relationships among families that continue many months after the biographies have been completed. Although this intervention involves a primarily preventive orientation in terms of helping families to survive the crisis of nursing home placement, the element of promotion is also unmistakable in Caron's (1997) pronouncement that "the "problem-saturated" view of the family should be complemented at every turn with the "opportunity-immersed" perspective" (p. 249). Families not only survived the "crisis" of institutional placement, they also derived a sense of purpose, mastery, and family history as a result of this novel program.

Structured Family Enrichment

These programs are grounded in the principle that couples and families have strengths and resources that may be used as the basis of experiences to optimize growth and development within the family (Hennon & Arcus, 1993). The primary intent of structured enrichment programs is to increase the overall quality and intimacy of family life. Thus, these efforts are typically aimed at couples and families who are fairly functional, without crisis, and interested in improving their familial relationships.

The format of structured family enrichment programs involves programmed instruction dealing with interpersonal relations between and among family members. This process emphasizes the systematic structuring of exercises and lessons in a gradual sequence to benefit the family or specific family members (L'Abate & Weinstein, 1987).

The Becoming a Better Grandparent curriculum developed by Robert Strom and his colleagues (Strom & Strom, 1989; Strom, Strom, & Collinsworth, 1990) is an excellent demonstration of structured family enrichment with aging families. In developing their grandparent curriculum, these authors acquired input from over 400 grandparents in small group discussions that were conducted over a two-year period. This mutual sharing of grandparents' satisfactions, problems, and concerns resulted in the following goals being identified for the curriculum: increasing the satisfaction of being a grandparent, improving the performance of grandparent roles, enlarging the sphere of guidance provided by grandparents, decreasing the difficulties and frustrations of grandparenting, and improving grandparents' awareness of personal success (Strom & Strom, 1989).

The efficacy of the curriculum in meeting these goals was later tested experimentally with a sample of 395 grandparents of children between the ages of 7 to 18 (Strom et al., 1990). An experimental group of 210 grandparents received a program consisting of 12 weekly meetings that lasted 90 minutes each. During these sessions, the grandparents shared their views on such topics as peer pressure, drugs, sexuality, gender roles, self-esteem, goals, and schooling; observed videotapes of younger people discussing these same topics; received minilectures on the changes occurring in the lives of family members; and commented on interviews with their family members from the suggested agenda in a guidebook.

To evaluate the program, each grandparent was asked to choose one grandchild and one son or daughter to assess changes in grandparent attitudes and behavior. Grandparents in the experimental group were found to better understand how their role is changing, experience greater mental stimulation, improve their confidence and self-esteem, and experience strengthening family relationships. Moreover, these positive outcomes for grandparents were corroborated by their children and grandchildren alike. In comparison, no improvement was observed for the control group during the project. These positive findings led Strom et al. (1990) to conclude, "The emerging concept of grandparent education deserves to be more widely understood, supported, and implemented" (p. 490).

SOCIAL-ENVIRONMENTAL ENGINEERING FOR AGING FAMILIES

In addition to the educational programs previously described, family prevention and promotion also involves the creation of conditions, settings, and, physical arrangements and facilities that reduce family stress and set the stage for optimal family functioning (L'Abate, 1990). Two major categories of social-environmental engineering, which are typically discussed in the context of younger families (Mace, 1983), are relevant to aging families as well: family support services and advocacy.

Family Support Services
These may be defined as formal services that offer instrumental support to families in meeting the basic responsibilities of family living. The importance

of available community resources and the family's willingness to use them is made abundantly clear by Walsh's (1996) assertion, "Lacking community response to hardship, family disruption may be inevitable no matter how strong the intrafamilial capacities" (p. 273). Although this statement implies that family support services are basically preventive, they also result in more growth-oriented outcomes than the mere diminishment of family stress.

That family support services intended for aging families may yield outcomes other than stress reduction can be seen in the research literature on the impact of respite care on family caregivers to the frail elderly. Although respite care has been found to have little or no impact on such prevention-oriented outcomes as reduced stress and burden or delay of institutionalization, it appears to effect improvement in such areas as socialization, recreation, and positive mood states among family caregivers (see, for review, Chappell, 1990).

Interestingly, these findings have led some to question whether social policy should provide a consistent funding base for respite services (Callahan, 1989). An opposing view, however, has been to put "less emphasis on broad-based social and economic outcome goals, such as prevention of nursing home placements and cost containment, and more emphasis on humane goals such as improving the quality of life of elderly persons . . . and their caregivers" (Wilder, 1993, p. 214). The significance of this controversy will become apparent in the following section on advocacy.

Perhaps the most critical issue regarding support services for aging families, however, is that so few families use these services; and those that do, often fail to use them effectively (Chappell, 1990). Thus, Stephens (1993) compiled a list of reasons why formal services are underutilized by aging families which includes such factors as insufficient knowledge of services; unfamiliarity with accessing them; prohibitive cost; the perception of not needing services; embarrassment over family circumstances; fear of criticism; uneasiness over making decisions for other family members; and negative attitudes toward service providers. Until this widespread lack of service use is better understood and confronted by practitioners, many aging families may be denied the benefits that they would otherwise obtain through proper use of available family support services.

Advocacy

In the context of this chapter, advocacy consists of promoting attitudes, values, and knowledge within the broader society that lead to the strengthening of aging families. Until society recognizes the unique needs and circumstances of aging families, neither the desire nor the resources necessary to develop the types of programs and services previously described will be forthcoming. Some major obstacles confront those professionals who advocate for strengthening aging families.

One factor that thwarts advocacy of this sort is that the overwhelming emphasis within family policy in our society has centered on the concerns of families with young children (Moen & Forest, 1995). In fact, no modern nation has ever interpreted family policy to include the aged as well as children

(Neiderhardt & Allen, 1993). Until older adults are no longer seen as competitors with younger families, prevention and promotion activities that benefit the multigenerational family are not likely to prosper.

Another problem faced by those who advocate on behalf of aging families concerns the ambiguity that is encountered in attempting to define the "aging family." Unlike the conventional view of the young family encompassing parents and their children, a realistic view of the aging family needs to be extremely inclusive to point of considering such influential members as in-laws, fictive kin, and even past family members who are no longer alive (Troll, 1995). Conveying such an expansive definition of "family" to administrators and policy makers who are unfamiliar with the potential structures and functions of aging families can indeed be tricky.

Advocating for promotion and prevention on behalf of aging families is also made difficult because our nation favors a noninterventionist bias when it comes to family matters (Moen & Forest, 1995; Wilcox & O'Keefe, 1991). The overriding sentiment in the United States has been that individuals and families at any stage of the life span should be independent and competitive, and the appropriate role of the government is to intervene only when there is clear evidence of family breakdown or pathology. As a result, family interventions are typically conducted on a case-by-case basis with an emphasis on treatment rather than prevention or promotion (Hobbs et al., 1984).

This bias toward noninterference with family life that pervades our overall society, coupled with the prevailing misery perspective within gerontology (Tornstam, 1992), poses a major obstacle to implementing prevention and promotion interventions with aging families. It is not surprising then that public support of family support services like respite care is jeopardized when they do not appear to alleviate family crisis (Callahan, 1989), despite evidence that they enhance the family's overall quality of life (Chappell, 1990).

MAKING PREVENTION AND PROMOTION INTERVENTIONS WORK FOR AGING FAMILIES

To assure successful implementation of prevention and promotion interventions with aging families, practitioners must be cognizant of guidelines and considerations for the development of effective programs. Bond and Wagner (1988) identified four general orientations that typify successful family prevention and promotion programs: (1) the empowerment of individuals and groups; (2) a multisystem, multilevel perspective; (3) sensitivity to developmental processes; and (4) an emphasis on promoting competence. Each of these orientations is discussed in terms of their relevance to aging families.

Family Empowerment
This orientation is based on the belief that the expert-helper model of intervention should be replaced by one in which program participants are empowered

to deal with family challenges by providing opportunities for growth without continual reliance on professional helpers (Bond & Wagner, 1988). The concept of empowerment further suggests that members of aging families should be instrumental in developing, presenting, and evaluating programs intended for them. In this vein, Brubaker and Roberto (1993) have urged practitioners to view older adults as resources who can serve in such roles as program planners, discussion leaders, or case examples. When families play a role in conceptualizing or implementing a program, they are likely to demonstrate greater commitment to it (Bond & Wagner, 1988).

An innovative program designed by Seltzer (1992) to train older family members to act as case managers for a relative with mental retardation illustrates the empowerment orientation. Not only did this program offset the reluctance of aging families to have their affairs managed by strangers, but it also reduced the caseloads of professionals, helped to ensure continuity of care, and increased the family's sense of mastery. Earlier in this chapter it was noted how Caron's biography project empowered families by giving them a valued role in the nursing home, while both Smith et al. (1996) and Strom et al. (1990) empowered older family members by including them in the development of their programs.

A Multisystem, Multilevel Perspective

Another characteristic of effective family programs according to Bond and Wagner (1988) involves the awareness that individual family members are an integral part of hierarchies of overlapping systems that include both dyads and the entire family system. In turn, these family units are embedded in subcultures and communities that comprise even larger and more complex social, political, and legal systems. Ideally, a family program "should target as many levels of influence as possible in identifying and targeting agents for change, monitoring program implementation, and evaluating program effects" (Bond & Wagner, 1988, p. 344).

This perspective not only points out why family advocacy is such an important component of promotion and prevention, but it also mandates that intervention programs address issues outside the boundaries of the immediate family. Couper and Sheehan (1987) have asserted that family life education programs for caregiving families should provide information on such broad issues as the availability of community resources, how to manage job responsibilities in light of caregiving demands, and the legal ramifications of family caregiving. The importance of a multilevel, multisystem perspective is also evidenced by the inclusion of family members and service providers in White and Catania's (1982) educational program on sexuality and aging to create a permission-giving social climate regarding sexuality among the aged.

Sensitivity to Developmental Processes

Bond and Wagner (1988) have maintained that effective family programs attend to three important aspects of family developmental processes: (1) the chronological age of participants; (2) an awareness of the point of evolution in the family system; and (3) the family's current position with respect to the transition or event at hand. Attention to each of these developmental concerns is especially important for prevention activities with aging families.

In terms of chronological age, it was noted earlier in this chapter that various age-related changes in older adults may influence their ability to participate. Physical adversities may preclude attendance at programs outside the home, while normative changes in learning and memory may make it difficult for older adults to comprehend or retain information presented in educational programs. It was also stated earlier that today's oldest cohorts are often reluctant to use family support services or to attend group-oriented programs. Family practitioners may offset these concerns, however, by arranging transportation for elderly participants, being willing to conduct programs within the family's own home, and developing an educational curriculum that is sensitive to the limitations of older learners.

The practitioner's awareness of the family's evolutionary phase is important because four-generation and even five-generation families are becoming increasingly common in today's society (Bengtson et al., 1990). This points to the need for family programs to encompass a multigenerational perspective (Brubaker & Roberto, 1993). A program for middle-aged caregivers, for example, should include information on how their children are affected by the care that is being provided to a grandparent or great-grandparent (Toseland et al., 1995). It is also important to realize that interventions presented early in the family life cycle should be structured to yield dividends in the later years. Cicirelli (1995), for example, believes that the best way to ensure quality sibling relationships in old age is to enrich them during the earlier periods of childhood and adolescence.

Another relevant developmental issue for prevention and promotion concerns the point the family is at with respect to a given transition or event under consideration. L'Abate and Weinstein (1987) have argued that the ideal time for prevention is just before a family life event occurs. This is when the issues are real enough to seize the family's attention, yet removed enough for family members to stay objective in their outlook toward the future. This "anticipatory stage" may be particularly helpful in enabling family members to accept new roles or to realize modifications in existing roles.

This principle is well illustrated by Smith et al's. (1996) psychoeducational support group program for older parents of adults with developmental disabilities, where the objective was to encourage parents to plan for their offspring's future in view of age-related changes that were making continued caregiving increasingly difficult. Thus, these older parents experienced a need to chart the course for their offspring's future before a crisis situation developed.

An Emphasis on Competence
The purpose of this chapter has been to describe the appropriateness of using prevention and promotion models of intervention in circumstances that strengthen the aging family as a functional unit. The examples presented here reveal not only that prevention and promotion efforts are effective in making aging families more competent, but also that these interventions are

most successful when they draw on the existing strengths and competencies of these families. We must move beyond the prevailing view that focuses so narrowly on the problems faced by aging families to a perspective that also embraces the many potentials and promises of the aging family.

REFERENCES

Bengtson, V., Rosenthal, C., & Burton, L. (1990). Families and aging: Diversity and heterogeneity. In R.H. Binstock & L.K. George (Eds.), *Handbook of aging and the social sciences* (3rd ed., pp. 263–287). New York: Academic Press.

Bond, L.A., & Wagner, B.M. (1988). What makes primary prevention programs work? In L.A. Bond & B.M. Wagner (Eds.), *Families in transition: Primary prevention programs that work* (pp. 343–354). Newbury Park, CA: Sage.

Brubaker, T.H., & Roberto, K.A. (1993). Family education for the later years. *Family Relations, 42,* 212–221.

Callahan, J. (1989). Play it again Sam—There is no impact. *Gerontologist, 29,* 5–6.

Caron, W.A. (1997). Family systems and nursing home systems: An ecosystem perspective for the systems practitioner. In T.D. Hargrave & S.M. Hanna (Eds.), *The aging family: New visions in theory, research, and practice* (pp. 235–258). New York: Brunner/Mazel.

Chappell, N.L. (1990). Aging and social care. In R.H. Binstock & L.K. George (Eds.), *Handbook of aging and the social sciences* (3rd ed., pp. 438–454). New York: Academic Press.

Cicirelli, V.G. (1995). Strengthening sibling relationships in the later years. In G.C. Smith, S.S. Tobin, E.A. Robertson-Tchabo, & P.W. Power (Eds.), *Strengthening aging families: Diversity in practice and policy* (pp. 45–60). Thousand Oaks, CA: Sage.

Cohler, B.J., & Altergott, K. (1995). The family of the second half of life: Connecting theories and findings. In R. Blieszner & V.H. Bedford (Eds.), *Handbook of aging and the family* (pp. 59–94). Westport, CT: Greenwood Press.

Couper, D.P., & Sheehan, N.W. (1987). Family dynamics for caregivers: An educational model. *Family Relations, 36,* 181–186.

Cowen, E.L. (1985). Person-centered approaches to primary prevention in mental health: Situation-focused and competence-enhancement. *American Journal of Community Psychology, 13,* 31–48.

de Vries, B., Birren, J.E., & Deutchman, D.E. (1990). Adult development through guided autobiography: The family context. *Family Relations, 39,* 3–7.

Dickson, F.C. (1996). Aging and marriage: Understanding the long-term. later-life marriage. In W.K. Halford & H.J. Markman (Eds.), *Clinical handbook of marriage and couples interventions* (pp. 255–269). Chichester/New York: Wiley.

Dunst, C.J., Trivette, C.M., & Thompson, R.B. (1991). Supporting and strengthening family functioning: Toward a congruence between principles and practice. *Prevention in Human Services, 9,* 19–41.

Farran, C.J. (1997). Theoretical perspectives concerning positive aspects of caring for elderly persons with dementia: Stress/adaptation and existentialism. *Gerontologist, 37,* 250–256.

Gatz, M., Bengtson, V.L., & Blum, M.J. (1990). Caregiving families. In J.E. Birren & K.W. Schaie (Eds.), *Handbook of the psychology of aging* (3rd ed., pp. 404–426). New York: Academic Press.

Gilford, R. (1997). Marriages in later life. In R.B. Enright, Jr (Ed.), *Perspectives in social gerontology* (pp. 148- 155). Boston: Allyn & Bacon.

Giordano, J.A., & Beckman, K. (1985). The aged within a family context: Relationships, roles, and events. In L. L'Abate (Ed.), *The handbook of family psychology and therapy* (Vol. 1, pp. 284–320). Homewood, IL: Dorsey Press.

Hawley, D.R., & DeHaan, L. (1996). Toward a definition of family resilience: Integrating life-span and family perspectives. *Family Process, 35,* 283–298.

Hennon, C.B., & Arcus, M. (1993). Life-span family life education. In T.H. Brubaker (Ed.), *Family relations: Challenges for the future* (pp. 181–210). Newbury Park, CA: Sage.

Hobbs, N., Dokecki, P.R., Hoover-Dempsey, K., Moroney, R., Shayne, M., & Weeks, K. (1984). *Strengthening families*. San Francisco: Jossey-Bass.

Hoopes, M.H., Fisher, B.L., & Barlow, S.H. (1984). *Structured family facilitation programs: Enrichment, education and treatment*. Rockville, MD: Aspen Publications.

Jennings, J. (1987). Elderly parents as caregivers for their adult dependent children. *Social Work, 32,* 430–433.

Kosberg, J.I., & Garcia, J.L. (1995). Confronting maltreatment of elders by their family. In G.C. Smith, S.S. Tobin, E.A. Robertson-Tchabo, & P.W. Power (Eds.), *Strengthening aging families: Diversity in practice and policy* (pp. 63–79). Thousand Oaks, CA: Sage.

Kuypers, J.A., & Bengtson, V.L. (1984). Perspectives on the older family. In W.H. Quinn & G.A. Hughston (Eds.), *Interdependent aging: Family and social systems perspectives* (pp. 2–21). Rockville, MD: Aspen.

L'Abate, L. (1990). *Building family competence: Primary and secondary prevention strategies*. Newbury Park, CA: Sage.

L'Abate, L., & Weinstein, S.E. (Eds.). (1987). *Structured enrichment programs for couples and families*. New York: Brunner/Mazel.

Lefly, H.P. (1987). Aging parents as caregivers of mentally ill adult children: An emerging social problem. *Hospital and Community Psychiatry, 38,* 1063–1070.

Mace, D.R. (Ed.). (1983). *Prevention in family services: Approaches to family wellness*. Beverly Hills, CA: Sage.

Moen, P., & Forest, K.B. (1995). Family policies for an aging society: Moving to the twenty-first century. *Gerontologist, 35,* 825–830.

Neiderhardt, E.R., & Allen, J.A. (1993). *Family therapy with the elderly*. Newbury Park, CA: Sage.

Richardson, C.A., Gilleard, C.J., Lieberman, S., & Peeler, R. (1994). Working with older adults and their families—a review. *Journal of Family Therapy, 16,* 225–240.

Seltzer, M.M. (1992). Training families to be case managers for elders with developmental disabilities. *Generations, 16,* 65–70.

Smith, G.C., Majeski, R.A., & McClenny, B. (1996). Psychoeducational support groups for aging parents: Development and preliminary outcomes. *Mental Retardation, 3,* 172–181.

Stephens, M.A.P. (1993). Understanding barriers to caregiver's use of formal services: The caregiver's perspective. In S.H. Zarit, L.I. Pearlin, & K.W. Schaie (Eds.), *Caregiving systems: Informal and formal helpers* (pp. 261–272). Hillsdale, NJ: Erlbaum.

Strom, R., & Strom, S. (1989). Grandparents and learning. *International Journal of Aging and Human Development, 29,* 163–169.

Strom, R., Strom, S., & Collinsworth, P. (1990). Improving grandparent success. *Journal of Applied Gerontology, 9,* 480–491.

Tornstam, L. (1992). The quo vadis of gerontology: On the scientific paradigm of gerontology. *Gerontologist, 32,* 318–326.

Toseland, R.W., Smith, G.C., & McCallion, P. (1995). Supporting the family in elder care. In G.C. Smith, S.S. Tobin, E.A. Robertson-Tchabo, & P.W. Power (Eds.), *Strengthening aging families: Diversity in practice and policy* (pp. 3–24). Thousand Oaks, CA: Sage.

Troll, L.E. (1995). Foreward. In R. Blieszner & V.H. Bedford (Eds.), *Handbook of aging and the family* (pp. xi–xx). Westport, CT: Greenwood Press.

Walsh, F. (1996). The concept of family resilience: Crisis and challenge. *Family Process, 35,* 261–281.

Whitbourne, S.K., & Cassidy, E.L. (1995). Achieving intimacy in late-life marriages. In G.C. Smith, S.S. Tobin, E.A. Robertson-Tchabo, & P.W. Power (Eds.), *Strengthening aging families: Diversity in practice and policy* (pp. 158–174). Thousand Oaks, CA: Sage.

White, C.B., & Catania, J.A. (1982). Psychoeducational intervention for sexuality with the aged, family members of the aged, and people who work with the aged. *International Journal of Aging and Human Development, 15,* 121–138.

Wilcox, B.J., & O'Keefe, J.E. (1991). Families, policy, and family support policies. *Prevention in Human Services, 9,* 109–126.

Wilder, D.E. (1993). Evidence of goal achievement: Evaluating respite programs. In L.M. Tepper & J.A. Toner (Eds.), *Respite care: Programs, problems, and solutions* (pp. 213–222). Philadelphia: Charles Press.

Behavior Disorders

CHAPTER 24

The Effect of Personality Disorder on Axis I Disorders in the Elderly

JOEL SADAVOY

The concept of Personality Disorder (PD) brings together an array of etiological theories and descriptive approaches. The richness of these ideas partly derives from the complexity of human behavior and motivations and partly because we do not yet have a satisfactory etiological explanatory model, as we imagine we do for some of the Axis I disorders.

To understand the relevance of Personality Disorders to other psychiatric disorders in the elderly, it is helpful to first review some of the models, theories, and data concerning PD. In this chapter, I focus particularly on psychodynamic models, although there are other equally legitimate models such as learning/behavioral theory and biological models.

The modern theories of PD (as is true for all the psychiatric disorders) began with psychodynamic theory. These theoretical models are useful for conceptualizing the causes of the sometimes bewildering array of behaviors and reactions associated with individuals who have traits or syndromes of PD. Depending on the particular theoretical school, PD may be caused by abandonment, narcissistic assault, failures of basic attachment with attendant failure of differentiation and individuation, early trauma, primal fears of engulfment or uncontrolled destructiveness, and basic failures of ego capacities such as impairments in the capacity to tolerate or modulate affect (Frosh, 1964; Kernberg, 1975; Kohut, 1977; Krystal, 1986; Mahler, Pine, & Bergman, 1975; Silver, 1985; Volkan, 1976).

Developmental theorists convincingly argue that basic psychological change can continue throughout life, and certainly far beyond the first few years of life as originally proposed by classical psychoanalytic models. This suggests a potential degree of plasticity in the dynamic underpinnings of behavior and emotional responses. Interestingly, this position does not always agree with empirical evidence suggesting that most personality traits are unchanged over the course of the life span. The notable exceptions include declines in scores of extroversion, impulsivity, and androgyny (Conley, 1984; Costa & McCrae, 1988; Field, 1991; Finn, 1986; Haan, Millsap, & Hartka, 1986).

More recently, biological models have emerged that suggest a strong interplay between genetics; brain maturation, structure, and neurochemistry; and environmental influences such as loss, interpersonal conflict, and significant psychological trauma such as sexual abuse.

It is therapeutically useful to conceptualize the behaviors associated with categorical diagnoses of PD (e.g., narcissistic schizoid or dependent) as defenses that develop in response to failures of maturation or development of one sort or another. However, a defense model has the advantage of allowing the therapist to see behaviors not as independent symptoms, but rather as a group of manifestations that can be linked to dynamic formulations. As shown in Figure 24.1, a common root can produce a variety of behaviors, each of which may be seen as defensive self-protection against the root dynamic and as components of a categorical diagnosis (see Figure 24.1).

A defensive functioning scale is presented in the *Diagnostic and Statistical Manual of Mental Disorders DSM-IV* (American Psychiatric Association, 1994) as one of the proposed new axes. Five of the seven levels are especially relevant to personality disorders and include both minor and major image-distorting levels, and the levels of action, disavowal, and defensive deregulation.

If behavior is viewed as defensive, then we have a model that explains why the categories of *DSM-IV* do not factor out discreetly (i.e., the behaviors derive from common root causes but manifest in various clusters or categories of PD). Hence, we end up with the odd/eccentric (cluster A), the dramatic/emotional (cluster B), and the anxious/fearful (cluster C), dimensional constructs

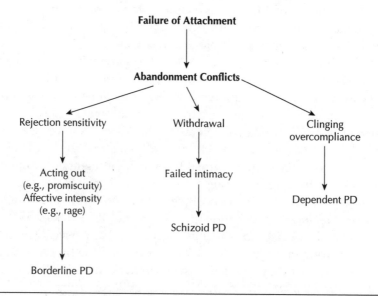

Figure 24.1   Roots to PD diagnosis.

that begin to resemble the dimensional models of the NEO-PI and the five-factor model. Indeed, in *DSM-IV*, there is an explicit recognition that dimensional approaches may be an alternative approach to diagnosis although they are still not formal diagnostic criteria.

Why mention dimensional and psychodynamic models at all? How are they relevant to the discussion of the relationship between PDs and Axis I disorders in the elderly? It seems pretty clear that the elements of dimensional personality constructs (e.g., the five-factor model—McCrae & Costa, 1991), comprising neuroticism, closeness versus openness, antagonism versus agreeableness, and conscientiousness, remain pretty stable and unchanged throughout life. In contrast, we also have convincing data that some behaviors associated with categorical diagnoses often evolve and change over time. Most notably the so-called immature PDs such as antisocial, borderline, and histrionic, that rely on various forms of action oriented and impulsive behaviors, diminish in intensity by middle age (Sadavoy & Fogel, 1992). How can we reconcile these two apparently contradictory findings (i.e., stability of traits vs. plasticity of behavior)? One way is to accept that the psychodynamics (dimensional elements) of personality indeed remain relatively unchanged over the life span but that the expression changes with advancing age (Sadavoy, 1996). There are very few empirical data in this area but clinical descriptions seem to bear out, for example, that the unconscious is timeless (Berezin, 1972) with many elements remaining unchanged from early years to old age. The implication is that elderly who encounter the stresses associated with aging will experience them affectively and at an unconscious level in much the same way that they always have. However, they will respond behaviorally in ways that are often quite different in form from their reaction patterns of younger years.

Why and how does old age assault individuals and what are the special vulnerabilities of those who carry the additional burden of poorly developed personality structures? By asking this question, we open a discourse on the effect that the dynamic etiologies of PD have on the expression of distress in old age and, in particular, the impact that the vulnerabilities associated with PD in old age can have on Axis I disorders.

Table 24.1 presents a list of commonly agreed-on stresses especially associated with old age (although they are not unique to this phase of life) and some associated inner conflicts and responses (see Table 24.1). As impulsive, action-oriented defenses become less prominent in old age, other responses to inner affective states become more evident (Sadavoy, 1987). The expression of these inner states may mimic the symptoms associated with Axis I disorders or may precipitate a full-blown disorder.

Using a psychodynamic perspective, all behaviors may be seen to derive from basic underlying psychodynamic causes that remain stable over time but are expressed in ways that react to environmental and personal changes associated with aging. The stresses of aging promote some reactions more than others, especially depression and dysthymia, anxiety disorders, somatoform disorders, and adjustment disorders leading to a strong interaction between personality-based issues and Axis I expression of disorders. Cognitive disorders

Table 24.1   Stress reactions in old age.

Stresses	Psychological Reactions
Social status and friendship patterns changes	Impotence, lost self-esteem, lost productivity
Physical change: beauty, strength	Narcissistic assault
Illness/infirmity	Dependency conflicts
Cognitive decline	Ego deficits/impaired affect control
Sexual decline	Shame
Bereavement	Abandonment conflicts
Economic stress	Uncertainty/lost control
Loss of stature (e.g., retirement)	Impotence, lost self-esteem, lost productivity
Relocation to institution	Forced intimacy/separation anxiety
Awareness of mortality	Death anxiety
Social status and friendship patterns changes	Separation/individuation
Family changes (e.g., parenting roles)	Dominance and intimacy conflicts

also may be influenced by personality-based factors. Although PD does not appear to alter the course of cognitive disorders per se, preexisting personality-related conflicts and habitual modes of behavior often produce behavioral responses to dementia that are strongly colored by long-standing inner conflicts. This statement is based more on clinical lore than empirical evidence but the clinical cases are often quite convincing. For example, a demented 81-year-old man was repeatedly sexually inappropriate with nurses in a general hospital ward. The consulting geriatric psychiatrist initially attributed the behavior to sexual disinhibition so often seen as part of dementia. On closer inquiry, a lifelong history of sexual impropriety with coworkers in this former professional's office environment was uncovered. His family was not at all surprised at his behavior with hospital staff.

Implied by this example is that the long-standing pattern of personality trait disorder emerged in a somewhat distorted but still recognizable fashion in the context of his Axis I dementia. This is not an uncommon clinical finding although this type of phenomenon needs more careful research before we can draw anything more than tentative conclusions.

In the following sections, I review some of the evidence that PD affects the frequency and mode of expression of Axis I disorders and the mounting evidence that PD also affects outcome of treatment and prognosis. There has been only a little specific investigation of these issues in the elderly population, so it is still necessary to rely on data on younger populations and clinical case studies.

AFFECTIVE DISORDERS

In this section, I explore the data available on the interaction of PD with depression. Especially relevant are questions of whether PD is associated with depression; if so, what form of depression is most affected; and what might be the impact on treatment and outcome.

Nonsyndrome depressive symptoms are common in the elderly (15% of the population), while more narrowly defined syndromes (depressive disorder 1.4% in women and 0.4% in men—Weissman et al., 1988; dysthymic disorder, 2%; and adjustment disorder with depressed mood, 4%—Blazer, Hughes, & George, 1987) are considerably less so. It is interesting to ask why this is so and whether we are seeing different forms of depression that have different etiologies, some of which may be closely associated with the psychological processes associated with PD.

Personality Disorder appears to be closely associated with depression. In a review of 23 studies of PD in patients over the age of 50, Abrams and Horowitz (in press) found an overall rate of 10% for PD. The highest rates by far were among depressed elderly. Abrams, Alexopoulos, and Young (1987) studied recovered depressed elders and compared them with normal controls using the Personality Disorders Examination (PDE). Although limited by its retrospective design, this study found there was significantly more evidence of PD in elders with a history of depression than in normals. Abrams concluded that the data suggest there may be more lifetime PD in depressives than in normal controls. Hirschfeld, Klerman, Clayton, and Keller (1983) showed similar findings in their study of recovered depressed women who showed significantly higher scores on introversion, submission, passivity, and dependence. These findings are similar to other studies (Cofer & Wittenborn, 1980; Klein, Fencil-Morse, & Seligman, 1976). Post (1962) first proposed that personality dysfunction predisposes to, or reflects a vulnerability to geriatric depression. But this global statement does not fully capture the nuances of the data that followed. In a later paper, Post (1972), stated that milder forms of depression are associated more with personality dysfunction than are more severe forms.

In writing about younger patients, Gunderson and Englund (1981) stated that innate and external factors interact to promote the development of concurrent affective and borderline symptoms. External factors may precipitate characterological predispositions that are not readily identifiable under optimal conditions. Based on the formulations proposed for the vulnerabilities of patients with PD, it is a short jump to recognize that individuals already at risk for narcissistic wounds, abandonment, and so on are going to be far more vulnerable to developing depression than those who are better integrated. Data supporting this contention include the studies that suggest when PD is present depression begins earlier in life (Abrams et al., 1994; Fava et al., 1996).

Depressive disorder probably produces symptoms that resemble PD behaviors during the acute phase of the disorder. However, such symptoms seem to generally reflect the depressive process itself rather than core personality features. This is supported by studies such as Thompson, Gallagher, and Czirr (1988) where two-thirds of the sample fulfilled criteria for PD during the depressive episode but only one-third did so after remission of depression.

Equally interesting is the evidence that, in a subset of individuals who have recovered from depression, significant symptoms of PD persist after remission of the depressive disorder. Did the depression itself produce these long-lasting PD-like effects? This is unlikely. A more probable conclusion is that PD in these cases predated the depression. Moreover, we can extrapolate further that PD traits may be markers for predisposition to depression (Abrams et al., 1987).

The idea that underlying deficits in personality development can predispose to depression is supported by Akiskal (1983) who proposed that characterological disturbance may be etiologically related to depression. If this is true, then we may hypothesize that the characterological factors explain the differences between the incidence of depressive symptoms and the incidence of depressive disorders. There is some evidence that PD traits associated with early-onset depressions are also associated with factors of poor emotional support, more life stresses, and frequent separations (Pfohl, Stangl, & Zimmerman, 1984). Schneider, Zemansky, Bender, and Sloane (1992) showed similar findings in a sample of recovered depressed elders. Charney, Nelson, and Quinlan (1981) found that PD traits are more commonly associated with nonmelancholic depressed than melancholic or bipolar.

Taking all these data into account, it is reasonable to conclude, at this stage of our understanding of the interplay of PD traits with depression, that PD is primarily a risk factor for producing that group of depressive symptoms which are most common in the elderly (i.e., nonmelancholic and often subsyndromal). Patients at greatest risk in this sub group are those confronted with tasks of adaptation that overwhelm their defensive capacities such as severe medical illness, institutionalization, bereavement without adequate support, or other situations of abandonment. This position is supported by the fact that the frail, physically ill, and institutionalized elderly have the highest rates of depression and depressive symptoms—30% to 35% in chronic care settings (Weismann et al., 1991) and 30% to 40% in hospitalized medically ill elderly (Koenig et al., 1991). PD is apparently less relevant to the core etiology of more severe depressions (melancholic, psychotic, and bipolar) where the neurochemical and genetic factors seem to predominate. Occasional data support this view, such as Pfohl et al.'s report (1984) that patients in the PD group in their study were significantly less likely to be DST suppressors than the non-PD patients.

Are specific characterological traits more associated with depression? Akiskal (1983) proposed that introversion, interpersonal dependency, orality, and neuroticism were traits associated with depression. Other traits have been proposed as specifically related to depression. The list includes premorbid emotional instability, rigidity, introversion, avoidance, dependency, narcissistic vulnerability, helplessness, and a higher incidence of borderline, histrionic, dependent, and avoidant PDs (Cofer & Wittenborn, 1980; Hirschfeld et al., 1983; Klein et al., 1976; Pfohl et al., 1984; Von Zerssen, 1982).

Most of these studies do not relate specifically to the elderly, but the data on the stability of personality traits throughout life are so strong that we can have some confidence that these findings will be relevant to patients in late life.

Another line of research has helped to clarify the links between personality-related features and depression. It examines the relationship between characterological or personality traits and "well-being" in old age. This research shows a strong relationship between personality traits, life satisfaction, and well-being (Mussen, Honzik, & Eichoon, 1982). For example, McCrae and Costa (1991), found that extroversion is positively related to well-being in the old and very old; Adkins, Martin, and Poon (1996) found that low tension and extroversion scores predicted high morale in centenarians. The importance of extroversion in the maintenance of well-being together with the repeatedly found association of introversion with depression, support the conclusion that the ability to seek out, form, maintain, and take pleasure in relationships in old age is a protective factor against depressive symptoms.

Personality disorder has a specific noxious effect on relationships especially in circumstances of marked stress, such as the forced intimacy of nursing homes, or unaccustomed dependency on adult children with whom conflicted relationships already have made reliable support unlikely. PD often is associated with inability to reach out effectively for desperately needed relationships thereby increasing the likelihood of depression-inducing experiences of empty abandonment, fear, and rage. In its extreme form, the breakdown of necessary caregiving relationships can be malignantly life threatening (Sadavoy, 1992).

The stability of personality traits suggests that they are hard to modify and will be refractory to therapeutic interventions. This certainly is the case for treatment of younger personality-disordered patients. Depression, which is complicated by the significant presence of PD traits or disorders, is also more refractory to treatment. A significant correlation between chronicity and PD has been shown (Devanand et al., 1994), as has a poorer outcome in the brief psychotherapeutic treatment of late-life depression (Thompson et al., 1988). Moreover, there is evidence that the PD component may continue to impair the functioning of recovered depressives during remission. The PD aspect of the patient's symptoms may be key to the residual symptoms so often associated with depression in the elderly (Abrams, Spielman, Alexopoulos, & Klausmer, 1996).

In summary, PD traits and syndromes are commonly associated with depression in the elderly and are an important etiological factor, particularly for chronic, refractory, and subsyndromal types. The presence of a PD diagnosis may be predictive of depressive responses under situations of stress. These traits may also predict a poor prognosis and long-term treatment course. Because the very core of PD is rooted in interpersonal conflict or its avoidance, these depressed patients often present special difficulties for treating staff (Sadavoy & Dorian, 1984) generating strong negative feelings and complicated scenarios between families and professional caregivers. Pharmacotherapy alone may be inadequate and careful attendance to psychotherapeutic approaches is often essential (Sadavoy, 1986).

The following case example illustrates some of the complexity of treating concurrent depression and PD.

CASE EXAMPLE

Mr. E was a 69-year-old man, divorced for many years with two adult sons. He lived alone but had a long-standing relationship with a woman who was also his employee. He presented to a psychiatric emergency crisis service, referred by his family doctor, with the encouragement of his girlfriend, with complaints of "a weak nervous system" and "can't put up with the pressure."

The patient said that his symptoms began about 3 months before seeking help. He attributed the onset to sudden decline in his business, apparently the result of his growing physical inability to keep up with the demands of his work combined with increasing competition and decreasing demand for his services. Consequently, he put his business up for sale but did not know what would happen and was anxious about the future. His anxiety was somewhat unrealistic since he was financially secure, but despite the reality he was obsessed with what would happen.

He described feeling miserable all the time, with decreased interest, poor concentration, impaired appetite, and some mild weight loss. Sleep and energy were undisturbed, and he denied suicidal ideation or substance abuse. However, he strongly endorsed physical symptoms including back "tension," occasional shortness of breath, stomach "tightness" and nausea, and leg weakness. These physical feelings led him to stay home, avoiding crowds and feeling very apprehensive in public. Interestingly, his avoidance symptoms predated his current complaints by several years. There was no evidence of any decline in his cognition or ability to manage activities of daily living. Inquiry about other anxiety-based symptoms, psychosis, or aggressive impulsivity was negative.

These symptoms were familiar to the patient, who had experienced similar feelings about 30 years ago when his wife left him. About 2 years prior to this assessment, he had been put on fluoxetine (dose unknown) and then on fluvoxamine (25 mg) for more than a year, which he thought may have been helpful, although he was not certain. In the year prior to assessment he had seen a psychiatrist for a few sessions with no follow-up. Most recently, he received lorazepam 0.5 mg with partial benefit.

Medical history included remote prostatectomy with no sequelae and mild recent hypertension, which was not treated.

He described his mother and sister as "depressive types" but initially said that they had no formal psychiatric family history. On more careful inquiry into his past, however, a rather deprived and emotionally difficult early life emerged. He reported that his mother had been unavailable to him for months at a time because of emotional breakdowns, and his father was cold, distant, and uncaring of his mother and the rest of the family. His therapist observed that he seemed to have learned from his mother that, to have his needs met, he had to be as emotional as she was. It seemed apparent from his descriptions that he had little basis for a strong and stable sense of self. He struggled often with feelings of betrayal and abandonment that he successfully covered over and dealt with through his young adult years. He married in his homeland at the age of 22, and they had two children. He apparently coped well, although the history of this part of his life is vague. After emigration to North America 10 years after marriage, his wife left him. He managed to "remain strong for the boys" and launched them successfully.

The nature of his relationships is not fully clear but appears to have been characterized by periods of dependant clinging and uncertainty. A key element in his current distress was his fear that if he could not maintain his business he also would lose his girlfriend, who was employed with the firm. He felt, perhaps unrealistically, that her only tie to him was her employment and that if the business went so would she.

Initial mental status revealed somewhat depressed mood, and anxiety. He was excessively preoccupied with worry about work but there was no evidence of delusions or of obsessions or compulsions. Cognition, insight, and basic judgment were all preserved and physical examination was unremarkable.

Initial Axis I diagnosis was Anxiety Disorder NOS and Axis II was "deferred." Shortly thereafter, his diagnosis was revised to major depression as his therapist came to know him better and the extent of his demoralization, agitation, and hopelessness emerged.

On a regimen of fluvoxamine (100 mg), he partially improved. However, as he became more involved in psychotherapy, which was offered concurrently with pharmacotherapy, his transference reactions revealed a clearer picture of his underlying dynamics. For example, as they focused on his abandonment fears (too early in therapy as it turned out), he became more agitated and regressed, saying that he felt "unbearable misery and pain" and began to say that he felt suicidal. Often he would rock back and forth in his chair, moaning like a child. He stabilized somewhat when this exploration stopped and a more supportive focus on his somatized stomach pain was adopted temporarily.

The source of his regression became clearer as his therapist observed his reaction to the changeover that occurred when he left the service and a new therapist took over. His "depression" and anxiety, which had improved considerably under the combined approach of medication and psychotherapy returned full force when he had to deal with a new therapist, despite there being no other change in his treatment. This same pattern of regression occurred again when the next transition became necessary. It was clear that rejection and abandonment were at the root of his reactions and necessitated a move to a more stable long-term therapist.

The results of a structured clinical interview for *DSM-III-R* (APA, 1987) personality disorders (SCID-II) offer more detail about the personality factors at work here. The strongest personality traits revealed were related to interpersonal function. He strongly endorsed seven of nine items on the dependent personality subscale evidencing needs for excessive reassurance, allowing others to make important decisions for him, difficulty initiating projects on his own, feeling uncomfortable when alone, devastated when relationships end, preoccupation with fears of abandonment, and feeling easily hurt by criticism or disapproval.

Beyond dependent traits, he also strongly endorsed more dramatic cluster B characteristics including inappropriate sexual seductiveness, exaggerated emotional expression, self-centeredness, unstable and intense interpersonal relationships, impulsivity, recurrent suicidal threats, affective instability, and frantic efforts to avoid real or imagined abandonment. Overall, he fulfilled formal criteria for both dependent and borderline PD. The SCID was administered at the end of his 1½-year treatment course in the outpatient clinic, prior to his transfer to a long-term therapist. He was stable and his symptoms of both depression and anxiety were in remission.

This case helps to illustrate how personality traits (and in this case, actual disorders) interact to produce a complex clinical picture and treatment course. It demonstrates not only the effect of PD in promoting chronicity, but also helps show the factors that create this prolonged course. Moreover, the patient's history suggests that his symptoms changed and declined somewhat as he began to encounter the age-specific stressors, such as retirement, and feared loss of relationships. The case also shows how dependency in old age may become especially focused on medical and psychiatric practitioners as the patient desperately turns to the system for support that is threatened in his own environment. In this case, the patient had a basic deficit in forming and maintaining relationships that led him to be unable to tolerate elements of the therapeutic process. Any intervention that mobilized his anxiety about abandonment, such as interpretations about his feelings or changes in therapists, promoted immediate regression leading to periods of intense anxiety characterized by frequent inappropriate phone calls to his therapist, emergency room visits, and overreliance on his family. These changes seemed to occur independent of any medication changes, and were always related to interpersonal losses, real or feared. This is not to suggest that he did not need antianxiety medications or antidepressants. On the contrary, these interventions were both necessary and partially helpful. However, in a case like this one, pharmacology alone is not enough. The form of psychotherapy that is often effective is grounded in techniques that pay particular attention to the patient's basic deficits in object constancy and need for a "good-enough" nurturing experience, which he never had in his upbringing. Initially, he required more supportive approaches and could not tolerate interpretation. As time went on, he gradually began to trust that we would not abandon him and that we would ensure that he received the help he needed. In the end, he was able to make the transition to another therapist who did not rotate in the training program and was able to provide consistent long-term intervention. For our part, we recognized that the residency training program is poorly structured to teach residents in psychiatry how to understand this type of patient. Nor is it effective in offering an appropriate treatment environment for such a patient.

ANXIETY DISORDERS

Anxiety disorders are a mixture of fairly discrete entities such as phobia or panic disorder and less well demarcated syndromes such as generalized anxiety disorder (GAD). As with so many disorders in psychiatry, anxiety is a dimensional construct that is expressed in many other disorders. It is a frequent accompaniment of depression, and is present in a wide array of circumstances where negative expectations are at work. The severity of the presentation of anxiety seems dependent on several interacting factors including genetic, neurochemical and other biological predispositions, often interacting with psychological dynamics. Individuals with poorly developed personality structures are likely to be less adaptable to uncertainty and hence, will tend to react with a greater predisposition to anxiety than others. Awareness of danger, real or imagined, is heightened in such individuals who, almost by definition, are overly vigilant, anticipating rejection, abandonment, failure of support systems, and so on.

Does PD exacerbate or produce anxiety in old age? In a study of generalized anxiety disorder, Blazer et al. found that the anxiety symptoms in 50% of their study population had begun within the past 5 years. They concluded that PD is an unlikely cause of GAD in the elderly since one would expect a much longer history in keeping with the lifelong pattern of PD (Blazer, George, & Hughes, 1991).

Studies, such as Blazer's, that rely entirely on categorical diagnoses, probably miss some important aspects of anxiety in old age. Much of the investigation on anxiety in the elderly has focused on worry rather than anxiety disorders per se. Worry may be defined as an involuntary, undesirable process of negatively charged cognitions about a future event that cannot be resolved. Worry creates anxiety or depression but is not as severe as either one (Wisocki, Hunt, & Souza,

1993). Worry may be classified according to external precipitants and content areas—family/interpersonal, illness/health injury, work/school, finances, and miscellaneous (Person & Borkovec, n.d.). In general, worry appears to represent age-appropriate concerns. It is likely, however, that patients with PD are less able to modulate worry and that it easily triggers anxiety in such individuals. This may be particularly true for patients with PD in the context of other problems such as dementia.

Breslau (1986) has described the more dimensional idea of the exaggerated helplessness syndrome. He defines this as behavior and attitudes on the part of an elderly person that highlight in intensified form his or her state of passivity and that are intended to convey to the caretaker an inability to cope with a feared loss of care and self-esteem. He goes on to describe the origin of this behavior as residing in narcissistic vulnerability and fragile adaptive capacities that fail to protect the elderly person from the anxiety-inducing threats of frailty and decline. What results is a behavior pattern characterized by anxious importuning and desperate demanding, proclaiming the patient's helplessness and urgent need for immediate rescue.

Clinging dependency is a familiar pattern of behavior to geriatric therapists that appears rooted in personality-based factors, as shown in the following example.

CASE EXAMPLE

A highly successful businessman retired from his activities in response to very early cognitive decline that mildly, but perceptibly, impaired his previously highly effective abilities. As a younger man, he had easily contained lifelong feelings of deep-seated emptiness and aloneness (despite marrying and having two children) by immersing himself in work and generally avoiding close or intimate interpersonal interactions. With the loss of his key sources of self-esteem and his alternative to relationships (i.e., work), he became much more aware of his long-warded-off sense of emptiness. These feelings had become evident during psychotherapy some years earlier when he had been treated for depressive symptoms associated with a distorted grief reaction to the death of his wife. He improved once he was able to return to work. At this later stage, however, depression was not in evidence. Rather he expressed his underlying vulnerability by desperately calling his daughter or son in apparent panic and demanding that they come to him immediately. His panic was infectious and they unfailingly arrived each time at his door only to find him calm and in good spirits. He seemed to calm almost immediately on learning that one of them was on the way to him.

This vignette demonstrates how anxiety and panic can emerge because of a personality-based inability to defend against age-related decline. Sometimes, as in this case, the anxiety symptom is not only an expression of the abandonment anxiety, but also a largely unconscious method of achieving a form of contact and rescue.

Physical disease states are associated with anxiety just as they are with depression. Anxiety may arise because of impaired mastery resulting from the disease itself, especially when it is seen by the patient as uncontrollable (Penninx et al., 1996).

CASE EXAMPLE

A 75-year-old professional woman sought help for generalized anxiety 2 years after the death of her husband. She had been a self-described workaholic and very successful in her academic career. On her husband's death she immersed herself more fully in her work, recognizing that this was probably a defense against her grief. It was only when she was forced to retire from her clinical/academic position at the university that she abruptly decompensated. She developed symptoms of acute anxiety together with somatic complaints of whole body burning.

She was initially treated with antidepressants, which seemed to successfully improve her symptoms, especially the burning, but gradually her anxiety returned and did not respond to any pharmacological interventions. She denied any other symptoms of depression and showed no evidence of other psychiatric disorders.

In the ensuing period of psychotherapy—an integrated approach, using both cognitive and exploratory interpretive methods—the patient gradually revealed the depth of her fears of being alone and the images of sudden physical impairment such as paralysis from a stroke, which could happen at any moment. Any little change in her physical state was a potent trigger that set off her fears, which at times bordered on panic. With shame and reluctance, she slowly related how dependent she had always been on her idealized relationship with her physician-husband to magically protect her against the dangers of life. Most of this dynamic in the relationship had been unspoken, dealt with through intellectualization, each of them immersed in their work and hobbies, and neither one emotionally reflective or aware of their needs. His death left her feeling nakedly exposed to the long-feared assaults of life, which now, in her old age, took on new power as her lifelong and largely unconscious fears were coupled with the realities of her declining physical state. With the failure of medications to control her symptoms, psychotherapy became the key mode of intervention. Indeed, the patient herself had asked that her prior psychiatrist (primarily a psychopharmacologist) refer her to someone who could provide both psychotherapy and medications, she herself recognizing that she now had to confront her inability to adapt to the death of her husband and her anxiety-filled life of aloneness.

This case helps to clarify some of the common dynamics of anxiety symptoms in old age and their relationship to maladaptive or pathological personality traits. It also reveals why these symptoms may become refractory to therapy: they are sometimes rooted in lifelong unconscious psychodynamics that were successfully defended against in younger years only to be unmasked in late life. Such dynamically based issues may produce symptoms that are only partially responsive to pharmacotherapy and brief interventions. In these circumstances, the patient may have to enter a longer period of psychotherapy. The goal of therapy is to help the patient understand how previously effective defenses and behaviors are now maladaptive, why they were necessary in the first place, and how they now must change in the face of the ineluctable forces of old age. This is the quintessential impact of personality pathology on treatment of symptoms in old age.

SOMATIZATION DISORDERS

Personality-based pathology may be closely tied to somatization disorders in old age. Contrary to frequently held beliefs about the frequency of somatic disorders in old age, the evidence seems clear that the elderly are no more prone to somatization disorders than are the young. The data reveal that there are usually realistic reasons for old persons to be concerned about their physical health and that the elderly do not seek out medical care for "imagined" or feared disorders (see Fogel & Sadavoy, 1996, for a brief review of the data).

When somatization disorder arises de novo in old age, it is most often tied to depressive disorder. However, PD may also promote somatized expression of emotional distress.

CASE EXAMPLE

A 72-year-old widow sought consultation for her anxiety and depressive symptoms that had arisen only in her latter years. A full-blown narcissistic personality disorder with borderline features had characterized her prior adaptation. Her earlier adult disorder was expressed dramatically in grandiose flaunting of her self-perceived importance, lifelong undue reliance on external admiration, shallow relationships, incapacity to mother her children, strife and conflict in her marriage because of her unremitting sense of entitlement, haughty belittling of others, and sexual promiscuity. Despite her evident personality pathology, she functioned adequately when younger and showed no evidence of somatic concerns, panic attacks, or depressive syndrome. Old age changed her life and uncovered her vulnerabilities with a vengeance. Her wealthy husband died, leaving her shockingly financially impoverished. Her children, who had moved far away to escape her, neglected her and wanted little to do with her. Her prior physical beauty deteriorated, and her shallow friendships evaporated when strained by her escalating demands.

In the face of these overpowering external changes she decompensated. Not only did she develop anxious, despairing feelings, she began to turn desperately to doctors for treatment of largely imagined physical problems. At any one time, she would have three or four physicians treating her and several pharmacies filling her prescriptions.

The focus of her psychiatric treatment sessions was her unremitting need for reassurance that she was not ill (and that she would not be disappointed or abandoned by her "ungrateful, hateful" children, friends, and doctors). Not surprisingly, such reassurance was entirely ineffective. She interpreted every small physical sensation as evidence of imminent physical catastrophe—a stroke, heart attack, or cancer. At times, her symptoms resembled depressive disorder, but despite trying almost every medication in the pharmacopoeia during the course of her medical odyssey, she never responded to even the most vigorous and apparently adequate pharmacological regimens. She left cohorts of frustrated physicians in her wake as she plowed through the always-forgiving universal Canadian health care system. In this case, insight-oriented therapy was entirely ineffective, requiring emphasis on behavioral interventions and limit-setting.

Eventually, she stabilized to a degree when her psychiatrist tried to splint her shattered defenses by creating firm controls over her chaotic help-seeking behavior, instituting full-time home care, coordinating all interventions with her physicians and pharmacies and placing strict limits on how and when she could call for help. This form of environmental splinting has been recommended for geriatric patients with similar dynamics in institutional settings (Sadavoy & Dorian, 1983). In the institution, however, there is much more control over the patients' behavior, a form of therapeutic leverage that does not exist to nearly the same extent in the community. Without control, the patient easily can subvert agreements regarding medications, use of pharmacies, desperate manipulation of friends and family and double (or other multiples of) doctoring. Hence, the therapist is best advised to recognize the limitations from the outset and establish realistic goals, both for the patient and for him- or herself.

CONCLUSION

Understanding the dynamics and presentation of personality traits and disorder in the elderly is essential to effective management of both the personality disorders and the often associated Axis I disorder. In addition, such understanding enriches the therapist by providing a much greater degree of fullness and complexity to the work. Personality-based factors have a practical impact on the treatment of Axis I disorders because they are frequently associated with prolonged treatment. Failure to attend to the personality-based issues will lead to lengthy therapy, more frequent treatment failures, and unnecessarily complicated relationships between the therapist, family members, the patient, and other caregivers.

REFERENCES

Abrams, R. (1996). Personality disorders in the elderly: Editorial review. *International Journal of Geriatric Psychiatry, 11,* 759–763.

Abrams, R.C., Alexopoulos, G.S., & Young, R. (1987). Geriatric depression and *DSM-III-R* personality disorder criteria. *Journal of the American Geriatric Society, 35,* 383–386.

Abrams, R.C., & Horowitz, S.V. (in press). Personality disorders after age 50: A meta-analysis. *Journal of Personality Disorders.*

Abrams, R.C., Rosenthal, E., & Card, C., et al. (1994). Personality disorder correlates of late and early-onset geriatric depression. *Journal of the American Geriatric Society, 42,* 727–731.

Abrams, R.C., Spielman, L.A., Alexopoulos, G.S., & Klausmer, E. (1998). Personality disorder symptoms and functioning in elderly depressed patients. *American Journal of Geriatric Psychiatry, 6,* 24–30.

Adkins, G., Martin, P., & Poon, L.W. (1996). Personality traits and states as predictive of subjective well-being in centenarians, octogenarians, and sexagenarians. *Psychology and Aging, 11,* 408–416.

Akiskal, H.S. (1983). Dysthymic disorder: Psychopathology of proposed chronic depressive subtypes. *American Journal of Psychiatry, 140,* 11.

American Psychiatric Association. (1987). *Diagnostic and statistical manual of mental disorders* (3rd ed. rev.). Washington, DC: Author.

American Psychiatric Association. (1994). *Diagnostic and statistical manual of mental disorders* (4th ed.). Washington, DC: Author.

Berezin, M. (1972). Psychodynamic considerations of aging and the aged: An overview. *American Journal of Psychiatry, 128,* 33–41.

Blazer, D., George, L.K., & Hughes, D. (1991). The epidemiology of anxiety disorders: An age comparison. In C. Salzman & B. Lebowitz (Eds.), *Anxiety in the elderly: Treatment and research* (pp. 17–30). New York: Springer.

Blazer, D.G., Hughes, D.C., & George, L.K. (1987). The epidemiology of depression in an elderly community population. *Gerontologist, 27,* 281–287.

Breslau, L. (1986). Exaggerated helplessness syndrome. In J. Sadavoy & M. Leszcz (Eds.), *Treating the elderly with psychotherapy* (pp. 57–173). Madison, CT: International Universities Press.

Charney, D.S., Nelson, J.C., & Quinlan, D.M. (1981). Personality traits and disorders in depression. *American Journal of Psychiatry, 138,* 1601–1604.

Cofer, D.H., & Wittenborn, J.R. (1980). Personality characteristics of formerly depressed women. *Journal of Abnormal Psychology, 89,* 309–314.

Conley, J. (1984). Longitudinal consistency of adult personality: Self-reported psychological characteristics across 45 years. *Journal of Personality and Social Psychology, 47,* 1325–1333.

Costa, P.T., & McCrae, R.R. (1988). Personality in adulthood: A six-year longitudinal study of self-reports and spouse ratings on the NEO personality inventory. *Journal of Personality and Social Psychology, 54,* 853–863.

Devanand, D.P., Nobler, M.S., Singer, T., Kiersky, J.E., Turret, N., Roose, S.P., & Sackheim, H.A. (1994). Is dysthymia a different disorder in the elderly? *American Journal of Psychiatry, 151,* 1592–1599.

Fava, M., Alpert, J.E., Borus, J.S., Nierenberg, A., Pava, J., & Rosenbaum, J. (1996). Patterns of personality disorder co-morbidity in early-onset vs. late-onset major depression. *American Journal of Psychiatry, 153,* 1308–1312.

Field, D. (1991). Continuity and change in personality in old age—Evidence from five longitudinal studies: Introduction to a special issue. *Journal of Gerontology, 46,* 271–274.

Finn, S.E. (1986). Stability of personality self ratings over 30 years: Evidence for an age/cohort interaction. *Journal of Personality and Social Psychology, 50,* 813–818.

Fogel, B., & Sadavoy, J. (1996). Somatoform and personality disorders. In J. Sadavoy, L. Lazarus, L. Jarvik, & G. Grossberg (Eds.), *Comprehensive review of geriatric psychiatry* (Vol. 2, pp. 637–658). Washington, DC: American Psychiatric Press.

Frosh, J. (1964). The psychiatric character. *Psychiatric Quarterly, 38,* 81–96.

Gunderson, J., & Englund, D. (1981). Characterizing the families of borderlines: A review of the literature. *Psychiatric Clinic of North America, 4,* 159–168.

Haan, N., Millsap, R., & Hartka, E. (1986). As time goes by: Change and stability in personality over 50 years. *Psychology and Aging, 1,* 220–232.

Hirschfeld, R.M., Klerman, H., Clayton, P., & Keller, M. (1983). Personality and depression. *Archives of General Psychiatry, 40,* 993–998.

Honzik, M., & Eichorn, D. (1982). Early adult antecedents of life satisfaction at age 70. *Journal of Gerontology, 37,* 316–322.

Kernberg, O. (1975). *Borderline conditions and pathological narcissism.* New York: Jason Aronson.

Klein, D., Fencil-Morse, E., & Seligman, M. (1976). Learning helplessness depression and the attribution of failure. *Journal of Personality and Social Psychology, 33,* 508–516.

Koenig, H.G., Meador, K.G., Shelp, F., et al. (1991). Depressive disorders in hospitalized medically ill patients: A comparison of young and elderly men. *Journal of American Geriatric Society, 39,* 881–890.

Kogan, N. (1990). Personality and aging. In J.E. Birren & K.W. Schaie (Eds.), *Handbook of the psychology of aging* (3rd ed., pp. 330–346). New York: Academic Press.

Kohut, H. (1977). *The restoration of the self.* New York: International Universities Press.

Krystal, H. (1986). The impact of massive psychic trauma and the capacity to grieve effectively: Later life sequelae. In J. Sadavoy & M. Leszcz (Eds.), *Treating the elderly with psychotherapy* (pp. 95–156). Madison, CT: International Universities Press.

Mahler, M.S., Pine, F., & Bergman, A. (1975). *The psychological birth of the human infant.* New York: Basic Books.

McCrae, R.R., & Costa, P.T. (1991). Adding liebe and arbeit: The full five factor model and well-being. *Personality and Social Psychology Bulletin, 17,* 227–232.

Mussen, P., Honzik, M., & Eichoon, D. (1982). Early adult antecedents of life satisfaction at age 70. *Journal of Gerontology, 37,* 316–322.

Penninx, B.W., Beekman, A.T., Ormel, J., Kriegsman, D.M., Boeke, A.J., Van Eijk, J.T., & Deeg, D.J. (1996). Psychological status among elderly people with chronic diseases. *Journal of Psychosomatic Research, 5,* 521–534.

Person, D.C., & Borkovec, T.D. (n.d.). *Anxiety disorders among the elderly: Patterns and issues.* Presented at the 103rd annual meeting of the American Psychological Association, New York.

Pfohl, B., Stangl, D., & Zimmerman, M. (1984). The implications of *DSM-III* personality disorders for patients with major depression. *Journal of Affective Disorders, 7,* 309–318.

Post, F. (1962). *The significance of affective symptoms in old age.* Institute of psychiatry, Maudsley Monographs. London: Oxford University Press.

Post, F. (1972). The management and nature of depressive illness in later life: A follow through study. *British Journal of Psychology, 121,* 393.

Sadavoy, J. (1986). An overview in treating the elderly with psychotherapy. In J. Sadavoy & M. Leszcz (Eds.), *Character disorders in the elderly* (pp. 175–229). Madison, CT: International Universities Press.

Sadavoy, J. (1987). Character pathology in the elderly. *Journal of Geriatric Psychiatry, 20,* 165–178.

Sadavoy, J. (1992). Borderline personality disorders in the elderly. In D. Silver & M. Rosenbluth (Eds.), *The handbook of borderline disorders.* Madison, CT: International Universities Press.

Sadavoy, J. (1996). The symptom expression of personality disorder in old age. *Clinical Gerontologist, 16,* 19–36.

Sadavoy, J., & Dorian, B. (1984). Treatment of the characterologically difficult patient in the chronic care setting. *Journal of Geriatric Psychiatry, 16,* 223–240.

Sadavoy, J., & Fogel, B. (1992). Personality disorders in the elderly. In J. Birren, Sloan, & G. Cohen (Eds.), *Handbook of mental health and aging.* New York: Academic Press.

Schneider, L.S., Zemansky, M.F., Bender, M., & Sloane, R.B. (1992). Personality in recovered depressed elderly. *International Psychogeriatrics, 4,* 177–185.

Silver, D. (1985). The psychodynamics and psychotherapeutic management of the self-destructive character-disordered patient. In A. Roy (Ed.), *The psychiatric clinic of North America* (Vol. 8, pp. 357–376). Philadelphia: Saunders.

Thompson, L.W., Gallagher, D., & Czirr, R. (1988). Personality disorders and outcome in the treatment of late-life depression. *Journal of Geriatric Psychiatry, 21,* 133–146.

Volkan, V. (1976). *Primitive internalized object relations.* New York: International Universities Press.

Von Zerssen, D. (1982). Personality and affective disorders. In E.S. Paykel (Ed.), *Handbook of affective disorders.* New York: Guilford Press.

Weissman, M.M., Bruce, M.L., Leaf, P.J., et al. (1991). Affective disorders in psychiatric disorders in America. In L.N. Robin & D.A. Regier (Eds.), *The epidemiologic catchment area study* (pp. 50–53). New York: Free Press.

Weissman, M.M., Leaf, P.J., Tischler, G.L., Blazer, D., Kaono, M., Bruce, M., & Florio, L. (1988). Affective disorders in five United States communities. *Psychological Medicine, 18,* 141–153.

Wisocki, P.A., Hunt, J., & Souza, S. (1993). *An in-depth analysis of worry and its correlates among elderly chronic worriers.* Unpublished manuscript, University of Massachusetts, Amherst.

CHAPTER 25

Treating Hypochondria in Later Life: Personality and Health Factors

DAMOND LOGSDON-CONRADSEN AND LEE HYER

It is estimated that 20% to 84% of patients presenting to primary care physicians report symptoms for which no significant organic pathology can be attributed (Barsky & Klerman, 1983; Warwick & Salkovskis, 1990). Further, more than a quarter of the patients of this group have no classifiable medical illness whatsoever (Gottlieb, 1989). Perhaps one reason for this involves the lack of clarity of somatoform problems (disorders) and confusion around the interplay of medical and psychological problems. This is especially the case with hypochondriasis, where controversy exists regarding this diagnosis. In fact, so much controversy exists that it is rarely used (Noyes et al., 1993).

It is not uncommon for physical illnesses to increase the occurrence of emotional problems and vice versa. Emotional problems are found between 10% and 30% of hospitalized elderly patients. Ford (1983) reviewed medical use patterns and noted that a sizable percentage of patients who have psychiatric distress seek medical care under the guise of a physical symptom. As a general rule, persons who display somatic behavior are likely to be less educated, have psychiatric disorders, come from a culture that deemphasizes emotional displays but focuses on bodily symptoms, have decreased social support, or have suffered trauma (Blazer, 1998). In general, too, problems eventuate from the illness itself or from attitudes about the physical illness that derive from the basic personality structure. At the least, the personality pattern structures the form of the somatic illness. You might say that the pathogenesis takes one of three forms: illness produces psychological symptoms directly; illness produces symptoms that elicit emotional responses which in turn make physical problems worse; and physical illnesses lead to emotional problems generated to adjust to the physical illness.

It is against this background that we seek to provide some order. Initially, we discuss aging and the context in which hypochondriasis festers. Next, we consider the definition of hypochondriasis and its operative mechanisms, as well as the problems with comorbidity. We argue that hypochondriasis draws its nosological and treatment strength from its conceptual links to other disorders, especially anxiety. We also present traditional hypochondriac models as a way to corroborate this position. We argue further that personality is a way to better understand this disorder and present data explicating hypochondriac patterns. In the last two sections we address assessment and treatment. Finally, we present a case.

AGING

The effects of aging are inescapable. The longer one survives, the longer and more onerous is the burden of cumulative losses and personal physical illness. As Gurian and Miner (1991) stated, "being 85 is clearly different from being 35 because of 50 years of biological change" (p. 33). The average older person has 3.5 diseases and fills 13 prescriptions annually (Blazer, 1998). But common diseases in later life do not start there. A life span developmental perspective is indeed most helpful: An understanding of the person across time is requisite. Chronological age is a most important factor of adjustment, but, as important, is the age of the disease. This applies to chronic diseases as well as psychological stress (Hyer & Associates, 1994).

This inadequate representation of physical problems with psychological influence is a problem for older people, as age and medical illness are related. In a publication by the American Psychological Association, Ables (1997) noted that 10% to 15% of older adults exhibit a marked concern about their health and overestimate their level of physical impairment. Blazer and Houpt (1979) had previously reported that approximately 10% of the elderly report exaggerated concerns about their health. Blazer (1998) also notes that the central feature of the presentation of problems for older people is the somatic theme. Busse (1976) stated that the greatest proportion of hypochondriac patients are elders. In concert, others have reported the mean age of the person diagnosed with hypochondriasis to be 57.1 years, with 76% being women and 51% being married (Barsky, Wyshak, & Klerman, 1990).

Medical illness associated with aging impacts the person (Friedman, 1993). Friedman posited that the advance of time assaults the self-esteem of the elder, and that in the case of a compromised person, the effects of the assault may be extreme. Also, in regard to the normal process of aging, a well-documented neuropsychological change is the disproportionate loss of fluid intelligence relative to crystallized intelligence. Thus, the ability to address and adequately work through novel problems declines as the individual ages. The elder may find the tumult of life more difficult to manage than in the past.

That hypochondriasis has age-specific features seems certain; that we can make sense clinically of this is less clear. Barsky (1993) notes that the elderly are at risk for certain factors likely to foster hypochondriac symptoms. These include social isolation, a high prevalence of psychiatric disorders that commonly have hypochondriac symptoms as secondary features, and increasing medical morbidity and bodily decline. Lyness, King, Conwell, and Cox (1993) evaluated the relationship of somatic worry to age, actual medical illness, and depression severity in 91 psychiatric inpatients, aged 21–89 years, with unipolar major depression. Analyses were used to determine the independent contributions of demographic, psychopathologic, and medical illness variables to the measures of somatic worry. Increased age and higher hypochondriasis scores were significantly and independently associated with greater somatic concern in the sample as a whole, but medical illness was not.

Although hypochondriasis is not more prevalent at later life, it may be unique in certain respects. Aging is after all the season of loss. In the case of the relatively "normal" older patient, the expression of somatic anxiety in response to medical illness is well documented (Cohen, 1991). It is suggested that somatic worry in older patients cannot be conceptualized as just a direct consequence of poor physical health; age and the somatic attitudes play important, though poorly understood, roles. Like peering at a Bonnard painting, something more awaits in the wings.

HYPOCHONDRIASIS: DEFINITION

There remains sizable debate regarding the validity of the diagnosis of hypochondriasis as representing a discrete disorder (i.e., primary hypochondriasis) rather than a constellation of symptoms arising from other illnesses (i.e., secondary hypochondriasis). Primary hypochondriasis is a concept recognized by the *Diagnostic and Statistical Manual of Mental Disorders* (4th ed.) (*DSM-IV*; American Psychiatric Association [APA], 1994). Importantly, hypochondriac symptoms do not reach the level of a somatoform disorder or somatic delusions, but do persist despite medical evaluation and reassurance.

The essential feature of hypochondriasis is a preoccupation with a belief in or fear of having a serious illness. This preoccupation occurs without evidence of significant organic pathology. Also according to the nosology, hypochondriasis represents nonmalingering physical problems and is generally chronic, usually resulting in the overutilization of health care. Above all, however, it is a cognitive disorder, from which behaviors, emotions, and physiological actions (as well as other cognitions) follow. It involves a preoccupation with the fear (phobia) or belief (obsession) that one has a serious disease. The patient is reading signs and symptoms as evidence of physical illness. These symptoms generally remain in evidence for a long period (at least 6 months). Naturally, doctor shopping occurs. And, medical personnel must respect the various presentations for the possibility of a false positive occurrence. It is after all most often a rule-out diagnosis. Interestingly, the victim often leads a productive life.

Schmidt (1994) discusses three types of diagnostic problems with hypochondriasis: (1) the definition of hypochondriasis, including the distinction between hypochondriasis and hypochondriac attitude, the personality aspects of hypochondriasis, and the role of medical findings in the diagnosis; (2) the distinction between hypochondriasis and related disorders, such as somatization disorder and panic disorder; and (3) the measurement of hypochondriasis. We are especially impressed with the "attitude" of hypochondriasis. It is this component (of the disorder), representing the continuum of temporary or permanent beliefs ranging from slight overanxiousness to an almost delusional preoccupation, that underlies the problem. These beliefs are the operative features of the problem and most sensitive to interventions.

There is the other side of the coin, the issue of "healthy" health anxiety. This is not a disease conviction. In the context of aging, it is a natural occurrence to be sensitive to body change and sickness. Critical questions, then, arise: Is a focus on the body excessive in the presence of a serious physical disease? Although "classic hypochondriasis" is perhaps less confusing to the clinician, for many older people these issues are far from settled.

Finally, there are some salient dimensions along which hypochondriasis unfolds. While we cite only a few, they are important because they represent other ways to parse this complex disorder. Barsky (1992a), for example, compared hypochondriasis and obsessive-compulsive disorder. He suggested that hypochondriasis may be divided into two subtypes, one subtype is closer to obsessive compulsive than the other. Similarly, Robbins and Kirmayer (1996) suggested that hypochondriac worry can be divided along the dimension of transient or persistent: persistent clients have more serious medical history and were more likely to have a diagnosis of major depression or anxiety disorder. In addition, Starcevic, Kellner, Uhlenhuth, and Pathak (1992) examined correlates of hypochondriac fears and beliefs (HFBs) in 54 patients with panic disorder. These authors suggested that this group could be divided into groups of clients seeking predominantly treatment or relief from symptoms (treatment-oriented) and those who were searching for a cause of their illness (explanation-seeking). The latter had significantly more HFBs.

Hypochondriasis is not a single problem. It perhaps is best viewed on the dimension of expressiveness. One group is open and emotionally labile, complaining and shows a close connection of emotions and physical status. This is a more hysterical group. Another group is more defensive, unwilling to acknowledge that there are physical/psychological problems. This is a more controlling and obsessive group. The understanding of this dichotomy or any of those previously mentioned is best achieved through an understanding of the person, the personality.

COMORBIDITY

We know two things about hypochondriasis and comorbidity. First, impairment is generally worse the extent to which one has cormorbidity. This is especially so when depression is involved. Second, many have noted the existence of secondary hypochondriasis and expounded on its relationship to other psychiatric symptoms (Busse, 1996). Barsky, Wyshak, and Klerman (1992) found that, in contrast to a control group, there was considerable overlap between the diagnosis of hypochondriasis and the symptoms of mood and anxiety disorders. Blazer (1998) reported that depression is the most common mood disorder to be masked by physical symptoms and that the prevalence of hypochondriasis is quite high among the depressed elderly. Hypochondriac symptoms have also been related to suicidal behavior. Among those persons presenting with hypochondriac symptoms, 24.8% attempted suicide, whereas only 7.3% of those persons free of somatic symptoms attempted suicide (Busse, 1996). Barsky et al. (1992) even proposed transient hypochondriasis as a distinct diagnosis for *DSM-III-R* (APA, 1987) categories and the possibility a frequent player as a secondary feature of another primary psychiatric disorder. Thus, the differentiation between primary hypochondriasis and secondary hypochondriasis remains obscure.

Hypochondriasis has been most associated with depression (Blazer, 1998) and anxiety (Demopulos, et al., 1996). In one study, Noyes et al. (1993) determined the nature and extent of comorbidity among patients with *DSM-III-R* (APA, 1987) hypochondriasis and examined the relationships between this disorder and coexisting psychiatric illness. Fifty subjects with hypochondriasis and 50 matched controls were identified through screening and interviewing. The presence of other psychiatric disorders was determined. More hypochondriac subjects (62%) had lifetime comorbidity than did controls (30%). Major depression, the most frequent comorbid disturbance, was usually current and most often had an onset after that of hypochondriasis. Panic disorder with agoraphobia, the most frequent anxiety disorder, was also current but often began before or at the same time as hypochondriasis. Interestingly, a third of the subjects qualified for a subsyndromal form of somatization disorder and also showed a high prevalence of comorbidity.

In an effort to desegregate the components of anxiety, Starcevic, Fallon, Uhlenhuth, and Pathak (1994) administered illness attitudes scales to 49 patients (mean age 43.67 yrs) with generalized anxiety disorder (GAD) and to 54 patients (mean age 35.46 yrs) with panic disorder (PD), to compare hypochondriac phenomena and to determine the spheres of worry in patients with GAD. Subjects with GAD were significantly less hypochondriac than PD subjects. Additionally, Barsky (1992b) demonstrated the positive relationship between hypochondriasis, depression, and anxiety. He compared a group of hypochondriacs with another heterogeneously diagnosed group and found that those patients diagnosed with hypochondriasis were also more likely to be diagnosed with generalized anxiety disorder, major depression, phobias, and dysthymic disorder. He also reported that those diagnosed with hypochondriasis were given more lifetime diagnoses than a comparison sample.

Busse (1975) noted that anxiety in the elderly may be shunted into high bodily concern and consequently expressed as hypochondriac symptoms. Others note that somatic anxiety may be expressed in the form of gastrointestinal symptoms and may also overlap with hypochondriac symptoms (Johnson, 1991). In fact, if hypochondriasis were an anxiety disorder, Schmidt (1994) argued that its clinical subtypes could be better identified: (1) general hypochondriasis, with a general fear of diseases; (2) illness phobia, with a fear of a particular disease; (3) panic disorder (a fear of fear); and (4) transient hypochondriasis, involving an excessive attitude toward health causing periodic problems.

Salkovskis and Clark (1993) conducted an important study on the intriguing relationship between panic disorder and hypochondriasis. Both result from the enduring tendency to misinterpret bodily changes or variations as indicating catastrophic harm. Differences between the two problems lie in (1) the extent to which the symptoms misinterpreted are capable of being rapidly increased by anxiety; (2) the perceived imminence of the feared catastrophe; (3) the safety-seeking behaviors that are triggered (and that play a part in the maintenance of misinterpretation); and (4) the general beliefs and assumptions on which some of the misinterpretations are based. This is an important study because it outlines similarities with panic attacks. Both misinterpret bodily sensations as a sign of imminent internal catastrophes, possess negative attitudes concerning illness and set off self-triggers that increase a focus on the body, physiological arousal, and checking behaviors, as well as general avoidance. If we can treat panic attacks, can we not apply these methods to hypochondriasis, where the client has an appreciation for relevant interoceptive cues?

Despite some data to the contrary (Barsky, 1992a), hypochondriasis and obsessive-compulsive have shared clinical characteristics and significant structural differences. As principal components, both have an excessive need for control, poor tolerance of uncertainty and ambiguity, and peculiar cognitive styles. The *DSM-IV* (APA, 1994) acknowledged that obsessive-compulsive personality traits often accompany hypochondriasis. Theorists (Barsky, 1992a; Starcevic, 1990) have also noted the relation between obsessive-compulsive traits and hypochondriac symptoms. Starcevic posited that perceptions of excessive threat commingled with notions of vulnerability are at the core of both obsessive-compulsive personality traits and hypochondriasis. Furthermore, he averred that the excessive need for control, and intolerance of uncertainty or ambiguity are attributes of both disorders. Both disorders also contain specific cognitive styles that account for their similar symptom constellations: a high level of preoccupation with detail; decreased ability to withdraw attention from poignant stimuli; and an overall cognitive rigidity. In support of his hypothesis, Starcevic reports that alexithymia is another common phenomenon that is frequently found in both disorders.

Despite the *DSM*, hypochondriasis appears not to represent a uniform nosological disorder. Its essential feature is cognitive, a preoccupation with a fear of having a serious disease. These people are convinced that they are ill or are afraid of becoming ill. But, after this, there are many presentations. In fact, whether one is a psychiatric or medical patient alters the symptom presentation and etiological features (Mabe, Riley, Jones, & Hobson, 1996).

In some important respects, hypochondriasis may be regarded as a nonspecific disorder that has emotional roots but presents in an aging-acceptable way, physical symptoms. In fact, many aspects that apply to other disorders apply to hypochondriasis. The elder who was somatic for much of life, for example, is different from the person who is somatic later in life. More clearly, the former has a somatoform disorder. Whatever the final designation, this disorder possesses many clinical and etiological features of other disorders. It is to this latter issue that we now turn.

CONCEPTUAL MODELS

Psychoanalytic and Psychodynamic

Hypochondriasis evolved from a rich theoretical context. From a psychoanalytic perspective, hypochondriasis may be conceptualized as resulting from the focus of psychic conflict and libidinal energy on the self, which is then expressed somatically. Freud (1950) noted that initially the libidinal investment might be attached to narcissistic fantasies, but that it inevitably became the actual somatic symptoms. Others have focused on and identified the phenomenon of the channeling of unconscious anger into somatic symptoms (Barsky & Klerman, 1983). The unconscious anger explains the prototypical pattern of passive-aggressive rejection of solicited reassurance in the hypochondriac patient.

Other psychodynamic writers propose that the bodily complaints and preoccupations are used as defensive stances against low self-esteem and personal beliefs in one's inadequacy or worthlessness. Additionally, hypochondriac symptoms have been conceptualized as a defense against guilt and a sense of inner badness (Starcevic, 1989). In this case, these defenses take on a more masochistic quality as the physical discomfort and pain associated with the hypochondriac symptoms allow for the atonement or deserved punishment for one's sense of guilt or evil nature.

Diathesis-Stress

Warwick and Salkovskis (1989, 1990) propose a cognitive vulnerability model of hypochondriasis. They suggest that because of past or early experiences with illness or medical interventions, consequent illness represents an exaggerated threat to the hypochondriac's well-being. They assert that hypochondriacs experience anxiety because of their unique perceptions regarding illness. These come from automatic thoughts resulting from the misinterpretation of physical signs and symptoms. If a person believes that he or she will have a serious illness, he or she will interpret any symptoms as support for that conclusion. Hypochondriacs tend to perceive bodily sensations as more dangerous than they truly are, and they often feel that they have a greater probability of contracting a particular illness than other persons without hypochondriasis. According to Warwick and Salkovskis (1989) dysfunctional assumptions typically held by the hypochondriac individual are manifestations of their perceptions of being vulnerable to any illness. Such assumptions might manifest as "If I sneeze that means I'm developing pneumonia and will die. I almost died from pneumonia when I was a child." Such beliefs might be the source of constant anxiety or they may be latent until activated by a critical event, such as the death or serious illness of a significant other.

Starcevic (1989) held that, in most cases, a distinct event activates the problematic assumptions. These assumptions, once energized, beget a state of hypervigilance through which the hypochondriac selectively filters information. This hypervigilance may account for an increase in unfamiliar bodily sensations due to abnormal sensitivity. There appears to be somatosensory amplification, the tendency to experience bodily sensation as intense, noxious, and disturbing (Barsky, 1992b; Haenen, Schmidt, Kroeze, & van den Hout, 1996). Barsky, Brener, Coeytaux, and Cleary (1995) showed that hypochondriac subjects considered themselves more sensitive to benign bodily sensation and reported more functional somatic symptoms than nonhypochondraical patients. Three elements appear operative in amplification: (1) a bodily hypervigilance that includes increased attention to unpleasant sensations; (2) a tendency to focus on certain relatively weak or infrequent sensations; and (3) the tendency to appraise visceral and somatic sensations as abnormal, pathological, and symptomatic of disease (Barsky, 1992b). Amplification is seen then as a pathogenic mechanism in hypochondriasis or may be a more nonspecific concomitant of many psychiatric disorders characterized by prominent somatic features, such as panic disorder and major depression.

Kukleta (1991) investigated defense responses to hypochondriac threat. Many normal bodily sensations or benign symptoms were misinterpreted as signs of serious disease by hypochondriac subjects. Several authors (Blazer, 1998) infer that hypochondriac Ss show a greater fear of criticism and fear of intimacy than normal Ss. Additionally, the proportion of fear, conviction, and bodily preoccupation in a given hypochondriac patient are central treatment elements important in treatment (Fallon, Klein, & Liebowitz, 1993).

Behavioral Learning
This conceptualization suggests that hypochondriacs learn the privileges inherent in being ill, such as being freed from usual responsibilities while concomitantly being nurtured and supported. Furthermore, the person's status as "sick" comes without a loss of self-esteem or failure since the patient cannot be blamed or held responsible for his or her inability to be well. This model asserts that the hypochondriac symptoms are not willful, but rather are learned and reinforced. Indeed, the hypochondriac may have, at one point of time, either personally suffered physical illness or injury, or may have observed another person who was reinforced for taking this position.

Barsky and Klerman (1983) point out that the hypochondriac patient's pursuit for a diagnosis rather than symptom relief is explained by this model. The hypochondriac hopes to find an ailment to support claims of disability. Indeed, these patients are seeking recognition and verification that they are sick and not faking their symptoms. This conceptual model also explains hypochondriac patients' disappointment when not given a diagnosis and their consequent physician-seeking behavior. This perspective illuminates the patients' avoidance of effective treatments as a threat to their perceived role as ill. Importantly, this conceptualization also has implications for the inclusion of the patient's immediate family and significant others in the treatment. Theoretically, family members could be taught to positively reinforce productive and independent behavior while also negatively reinforcing dependent, reassurance-seeking behavior on the patient's part.

PERSONALITY

Differentiation between the true hypochondriac patient and the patient expressing appropriate bodily concern is paramount for the clinician. As with all therapy, relevant interventions lie only to a small extent with the diagnosis. Development of the individually tailored treatment intervention involves a knowledge of the person, the personality (Millon & Davis, 1995). Medical illness that is emotionally driven is filtered through the personality (Friedman, 1993). This may be especially true of older people where the personal meaning of the age-related decline and the way of defending against it are channeled through personological characteristics (Abrams, 1997).

This position is not without some data. Costa and McCrae (1985) found a positive, significant relationship between neuroticism and those who are somatic. Neuroticism as measured by the five-factor model is defined as the propensity to experience negative affect (Costa & McCrae, 1985). Older hypertensives who scored high on measures of neuroticism also endorsed significantly greater somatic complaints than those who scored lower on this index (Costa & McCrae, 1985). In this case, neuroticism is related to exaggerated reports of somatic symptoms.

High levels of the personality trait neuroticism might explain the frequent co-occurrence of hypochondriasis and psychopathological disorders. In support of this hypothesis, Hyer, Gouveia, Harrison, Warsaw, and Coutsouridis (1987) postulated that personality contributes to the symptom formation process, after finding multiple relations between hypochondriasis, anxiety, and depression. These authors evaluated 60 older (age > 55 years) adult geropsychiatric inpatients and found that the correlation between hypochondriasis and anxiety was .64, and that the correlation between hypochondriasis and depression was .53. They further found that hypochondriasis was inversely correlated with life satisfaction. These authors described the unique variance contributed by personality to the symptom formation process, and how symptom expression is a function of one's personality and situational condition.

Data
Data were obtained from 125 combat veterans (both World War II and Korean War) who had participated in a larger study on posttraumatic stress disorder (PTSD) and older veterans (age > 55). Participants were identified prospectively from several selected medical (70%) and psychiatric (30%) outpatient clinics. These were treatment-seeking older men who had been in combat. Participants were administered the Millon Clinical Multiaxial Inventory (2nd Rev.) (MCMI-II), the Minnesota Multiphasic Personality Inventory (2nd Rev.) (MMPI-2), and the Symptom Hopkins Checklist (90 items–Rev.) (SCL-90-R), General Symptom

Index (GSI), a measure of general psychopathology. The Structured Clinical Interview for *DSM* (SCID) was also applied for general diagnostic purposes, current and lifetime. For our purposes, data were dichotomized into two categories: Those participants whose MMPI-2 hypochondriasis scale was at or above a *T* score of 65 were considered high in hypochondriasis (HH) and those whose MMPI-2 hypochondriasis scale was below a *T* score of 65 were considered low in hypochondriasis (LH).

To assess differences in the level of depression a *t*-test was performed. Subjects in the HH group were more depressed than those in the LH group ($t(66)=-5.11$, $p=.001$). Mean base rates for depression of the HH was 73.60 ($SD=15.67$); the LH's mean was 56.57 ($SD=11.63$). The HH group also scored higher on the SCL-90-R GSI than the LH group, ($t(47)=-4.15$, $p=.0001$); HH's mean GSI was 1.4 ($SD=.76$), whereas the LH's mean GSI was .63 ($SD=.51$). Furthermore, chi-square analyses revealed that those in the HH group were more likely to be given a lifetime diagnosis of either dysthymia or major depression than those in the LH group ($X^2 = 3.77$, $p=.0006$).

T-test analyses were also performed using the MCMI-II variables to ascertain personological variables that coincide with hypochondriasis. The HH group was found to be more avoidant $t(123)=1.8$, p=.03. The HH group's mean base rate was 73; LH's mean base rate was 54. The HH group was also found to be less narcissistic, $t(123)=1.9$, $p=.05$. The HH's mean base rate was 52; LH's mean base rate was 68. Finally, the HH group was found to be more Passive-Aggressive ($t(123)=1.8$, $p=.05$); HH's mean base rate was 71, whereas the LH's mean base rate was 53.

Results suggest that older persons who are high in hypochondriasis also tend to be more depressed and distressed, and are likely to possess a concomitant lifetime diagnosis of major depression disorder or dysthymic disorder. This coincides nicely with the data provided by Barsky (1992b), and supports the notion that hypochondriasis is often accompanied by other psychopathology. Those high in hypochondriasis tended to be more avoidant and passive-aggressive than those low in hypochondriasis. This supports the findings of Starcevic, Uhlenhuth, Kellner, and Pathak (1992) reviewed earlier: explanation-seeking hypochondriacs had significantly more fears and worries and tended to be avoidant, histrionic, and borderline (Millon's passive-aggressive) in their personality expression.

The avoidant and passive-aggressive profile suggest a personality profile of conflict and avoidant traits. This dual pattern actually "works" because it mixes the need to be with others and to be alone. This evolves from a conflict between dependent and independent needs. These individuals tend to have low self-esteem and see themselves as inadequate. They are awkward interpersonally. They are both sensitive to others and at the same time sensitive to possible pain, and so avoid. They tend to be moody and resentful. Whether this profile comes before hypochondriasis, after it, or interacts in some way is unclear. What seems more clear is that those high in hypochondriasis are also expert at distancing others while wanting to be a part of things, and to eventually be more depressed.

This is only a modal profile. It does not assist in the description of any one person. For that, we need measures from a personality scale like the MCMI-II, symptom scales, as well as an understanding of the idiosyncratic thinking/ assumptions of the person.

ASSESSMENT

The importance of performing a thorough psychological interview and a solid medical evaluation on the patient cannot be overemphasized. It is time well spent (Blazer, 1998), especially on the symptoms of most concern. The interview in the context of a hypochondriac can be therapeutic. Giving the patient positive feedback for focusing on interpersonal issues rather than on physical symptoms or disease represents a start.

The following represents a precis of necessary components of an interview with a hypochondriac. The initial interview should include a thorough systems review for physical problems, complaints, history of diseases, treatment, surgeries, or hospitalizations. The clinician should not overemphasize the importance of the patient's physical problems. It is during the interview that the clinician should test the patient's flexibility in considering alternative (psychological) explanations for illness. Their cognitive flexibility will be positively related to treatment outcome. The clinician should talk with the patient honestly regarding a possible correlation between emotions or stress and physical symptoms or disease, and should ask the patient to describe his or her perceptions regarding physical problems. The clinician should not argue or confront the patient in the assessment phase. This is unhelpful and may well give rise to defensiveness and resistance.

It is especially important to assess depression in the context of a somatic problem. Depressed hypochondriac patients emphasize the great suffering they have endured. With hypochondriacs who are depressed, social and job-related performance is often compromised. Often, too, tension/anxiety and vegetative symptoms as well as a diurnal rhythm are in effect. Hopelessness and chronicity pervade.

During the interview, the clinician should assist the patient identify stress, anxiety, and related feelings. This will promote the patient's ability to express feelings. Engagement of the patient is important. The clinician can share observations and assessment, and ask for their perceptions about stress, sources of satisfaction and dissatisfaction in their daily life, significant relationships, work, and so forth. If the patient denies experiencing stress or certain emotions, the discussion may need to be less direct. For example, the clinician can point out possible or apparent stresses and ask for feedback.

Finally, if possible, include significant others in the interview process. Corroborating information is never a bad idea as the elder may be a poor historian. The information gained will likely be quite beneficial (e.g., routes of secondary gain may be localized). A thorough interview will define the psychological assessment to follow.

Clients who are hypochondriacs feel that they are not reacted to fairly by professionals. In fact, four areas are especially noted:

1. Did not receive satisfactory explanation.
2. No opportunity to explain problems.
3. Dissatisfied with attitude of health providers.
4. Different agendas than health care provider.

These areas are, then, especially important in the relationship-building features of the assessment.

PSYCHOLOGICAL ASSESSMENT DATA

Various scales of hypochondriasis measure different features of the hypochondriasis syndrome. Many exist; Screening for Somatoform Disorders, the Whiteley Index for Measuring Hypochondria, Illness Attitude Scales (IAS), Illness Worry Scale, Private Body Consciousness Scale, Symptom Interpretation Questionnaire, Nottingham Health Profile, Attitudes Scales, and the Somatosensory Amplification Scale, to name the more popular ones. Like most scales purporting to measure a disorder, solid psychometric data are wanting. The only scale, to our knowledge, that was specifically designed to measure hypochondriasis in an older population is the Hypochondriacal Scale for Institutionalized Geriatric patients (HSIG; Brink, Belanger, & Bryant, 1978). The HSIG assesses health satisfaction, chronic fatigue, sense of wellness, diurnal variation, acceptance of reassurance regarding medical condition, and perception of pain without clearly identifiable sources. The scale includes six questions. A score of 4 out of 6 is indicative of hypochondriasis. This scale can only be considered a gross estimate of health satisfaction.

Alternatively the use of the SCL-90-R, MMPI-2, MCMI-II or III, or the Personality Assessment Inventory (PAI; Morey, 1996) have merit because all have somatic scales along with response styles and other symptoms. But these, too, are limited. The MMPI Hypochondriasis *(Hs)* scale assesses actual awareness of and anxiety about bodily sensations rather than irrational assumptions. In fact, the *Hs* assesses actual somatic awareness. Its use as a measure of hypochondriasis is questionable (Edelmann & Holdsworth, 1993). Hypochondriacal patients' elevations of *HS* will generally fall between *T*-scores of 60–80. Elevations on *HS* beyond 80 *T*-score points will seldom be seen with these patients, and are more indicative of somatic delusion or conversion disorders. Patients with a real medical illness usually show elevations of approximately 60 *T*-score points (Graham, 1993). In regard to the validity scales, clinicians should expect elevations on the *L* and *K* scales because of the defensiveness usually associated with these persons.

Common MCMI-III base rate elevations often include the *H* scale which should extend beyond a base rate score of 75. Anxiety *(A)* and Depression *(D)* scales should also be expected to be elevated beyond a base rate score of 75 if the patient is experiencing comorbid anxiety or depression. As illuminated earlier, the scales measuring passive-aggressive and avoidant personality traits are also expected to be elevated beyond a base rate of 70 on the MCMI-II.

The Structured Diagnostic Interview for the *DSM-IV* (SCID) should be considered. This has been shown to be reliable and to have discriminant validity (Noyes et al., 1993). Another important factor to consider is the need for neuropsychological assessment in older hypochondriac patients who have concomitant complaints of memory disturbance. Evaluation for memory disturbance should be considered when the severity of memory problems is not explained by the presence of any existing mood or anxiety disorder.

Finally, we note this: somatization is a frequent syndrome in primary care and is strongly associated with psychopathology and physical disability. To a study, patients with this disorder have higher levels of medically unexplained symptoms and are more impaired in their physical functioning than patients without the disorder. Often major depressive syndromes are the most frequent among patients with somatic symptoms. Interestingly, hypochondriasis and somatization are somewhat rare conditions in primary care, but, of the two, somatization seems closely intertwined with the more severe depressive syndromes. Escobar et al. (1998) used an abbreviated somatization index, based on specific symptom thresholds. This abridged somatization measure was most usable and predicted unexplained symptoms and subsequent disability and psychopathology. Its use in mental health clinics should be considered, especially for patients at later life.

In a careful understanding of hypochondriasis, the clinician should think factors. One grouping is especially relevant as they reflect a cognitive and behavioral approach: catastrophizing cognitions, intolerance of bodily complaints, bodily weakness, autonomic sensations, and health habits (Hiller et al., 1997). This represents a melding of deviant thought processes, fear of disease, and an overprotective health focus. The information provided by a solid medical evaluation, thorough psychological interview, and empirically validated psychometric instruments will provide the information necessary to identify the various features of the hypochondriac patient. The data obtained will also help the clinician to establish a solid treatment plan.

But, above all, the clinician needs to perform a microanalysis on the cognitive and behavioral targets of somatic problems. This involves (1) discriminative stimuli or triggers, both interoceptive and external cues; (2) cognitive processing, thoughts before, during, and after typical episodes; (3) emotional responses, especially depression; (4) bodily sensations, more overt reactions as sweating; (5) behavioral reactions, those both rewarding and avoidant; and (6) consequences, both positive and negative reinforcement. A macroanalysis of the setting, social relationship, and environment is also requisite.

TREATMENT

Blazer (1998) sets the stage for all-too-often care of the older hypochondriac—treatment falls on the primary care physician as elders are rarely willing to accept assistance from psychiatry. But "once in the door," the recommended treatment strategy results from (1) ruling out a real organic illness through a thorough medical examination; (2) taking a comprehensive biopsychosocial history; and (3) initiating treatment for any prominent comorbid disorder. Almost always, this involves a search for psychiatric comorbidity, a consideration for the use of psychotropic medication, as well as treating the hypochondriasis itself.

Hypochondriac patterns are quite prevalent. Their influence on the formation and etiology of both physical and emotional problems in older people demands careful consideration. The clinician should address this disorder on three fronts. First, treatment should be traditional; the particular features of the disorder that work for all ages are apt. With older people, Busse (1989) took a position that suggested exaggerated physical illness was prevalent and served many purposes. He held that older people apply the four mechanisms that contribute to hypochondriasis (1) as an explanation of failure to social expectations; (2) as a way to isolate and withdraw interest; (3) as a way to shift anxiety from specific anxiety of one psychological conflict to a more comforting one; and (4) as a way to punish self and provide a way of atonement for hostile feelings. The therapist should be sensitive to one or more of these.

In this context, enough cannot be said of the importance of developing a solid therapeutic alliance. Older persons in general and the hypochondriac patient in particular maintain a cautious attitude regarding the use of services for mental health. The clinician forms an alliance with the patient using a vernacular that supports their defenses. The overall disorder should be taken seriously, sufficient time in the beginning stages of treatment being allotted to the patient's ailments. As the course of therapy progresses, the amount of time allocated to a specific complaint should be decreased.

Busse outlined six stock messages for care:

1. Therapist communicates "You are ill. Pain is real."
2. Therapist commits to patient: "I do not know the cause of the problem but I can assist in the understanding of what is happening."
3. Therapist structures the treatment: "I will be responsible for the control of the visits, even though you will feel bad at other times."
4. Therapist is interested in the psychosocial coping and attitudes without stating that there is this component.
5. Therapist thinks out loud about the relative benefits of the medical procedures continually emphasizing the well-being of the patient.
6. Therapist is upbeat on care and neutral in the taking of sides.

And the therapist has these six goals:

1. Decrease the use and control of med services.
2. Decrease the concern and anxiety of the hypochondriac on the availability of health care professionals.
3. Decrease stress on family.
4. Increase capability of family to support patient.

5. Decrease conflict within family.
6. Decrease anxiety within the patient.

The second overall treatment strategy involves the patient being heard slowly. This occurs all along. Little in psychotherapy is straightforward in the equation of care. As a general rule, directive treatments (cognitive therapy) are more effective among patients who have low resistance traits, whereas nondirective treatment (supportive/self-directed) is superior for those who were highly resistant (see Hyer & Associates, 1994). Although there are dissenters regarding the role of reassurance (as only a temporary reduction in anxiety) (Starcevic, 1991), in the case of the hypochondriac patient, much of the treatment should be nondirective. Over time, the work of therapy will drift to appropriate topics, for example, relations with others, marriage, love and sexual concerns, or simply the understanding of the aging process. Treatment will also be directed toward the cognitive work to be outlined. Importantly, the therapist must keep the patient in therapy and create a healing atmosphere for the work of therapy to follow; much of how this happens is reflected through the quality of the relationship.

Friedman (1993) argued for the establishment of a coherent narrative after the therapeutic alliance has been solidified. The narrative allows the clinician to tell a story that outlines the interrelationships among the physical symptoms and the psychological, social, cultural contexts of the symptoms. He noted that by allowing patients to express their experiences, their personal distress can begin to be alleviated. The narrative has also been expounded on by Johnson (1991), who refers to it as the process of reminiscence. Johnson referred to the notion of the Life Review and how this process allows the patient to recognize past achievements and past sources of self-esteem, but also enables to patient identify any "unfinished business."

We have found the narrative to be a powerful tool allowing the patient to feel much closer to the therapist through positive transference. The narrative's information can be explored with familiar themes being brought to the attention of the patient. Existential themes such as isolation, and the loss of others or their own physical health can be addressed. Older people often report feelings of isolation and simply desire to relate to someone who knows them. Male patients, in particular, seek the permission to grieve their losses. The narrative approach allows the therapist to be an active participant in their remembrances and also diminishes the age differential typically found between the elder patient and younger clinician.

The last area of care involves the structured thinking involved in cognitive behavioral therapy. Several poorly designed studies have addressed the treatment of hypochondriasis. These include case studies on the use of cognitive therapy (Visser & Bouman, 1994), behavioral and cognitive therapy (the sequence of behavioral therapy followed by cognitive therapy tended to be more successful than the other way around—Visser & Bouman, 1992), and successful use of the telephone to deliver a course of cognitive psychotherapy (McLaren, 1992).

Barsky (1993) argues for a specific psychotherapy that includes group discussions and cognitive and behavioral exercises. Four factors that amplify somatic distress and hypochondriacal health concerns (attention, cognition, circumstance, and mood) are placed on center stage as treatment issues—patients are encouraged to accept and explore their bodily sensations in a relaxed manner. Avia, Ruiz, Olivares, and Crespo (1996) showed the effectiveness of the Barsky method. So, although the prognosis for treatment of primary hypochondriasis is currently perceived as guarded (Warwick & Salkovskis, 1990), cognitive-behavioral therapy with the hypochondriacal patient has been successfully employed in a small number of cases.

There are learnings from these studies. From the cognitive-behavioral perspective, the treatment process operates because the patient considers an alternative explanation for their discomfort. Again, after the therapeutic alliance has been established, the therapist engages the patient in alternative hypotheses testing. As the client feels validated regarding the existence of the physical symptoms, another perspective is introduced. A cognitive/psychological explanation may satisfactorily account for the symptoms and assist in the alleviation of their intensity. Thus, the patient is not asked to give up beliefs concerning an illness, but to consider and test alternatives, which if they fail, might provide evidence for concerns about an undiagnosed organic illness.

A cognitive behavioral format highlights several features of therapy: *history, physical triggers, thoughts, mood,* and *consequences.* As noted (see "Assessment"), the patient is requested to provide the needed backdrop (history), complete with successes and, of course, failures; a clear rendition of the physical triggers; the negative automatic thoughts that accompany these; the mood state and a rating of its intensity; and a summary of consequences, including the behavior changes, thinking alterations, mood changes, and symptoms.

Once the patient has been engaged, then, therapy consists of gathering and testing evidence for the patient to question the suspected illness. Testing the evidence regarding a certain illness is achieved by having patients rate the extent to which they believe they have an illness. Thereafter they are asked to write down confirmatory and contradictory evidence concerning this belief. During this phase, the clinician and client are working together to discover alternate explanations. If possible, these alternate explanations are tested within the session and the results are also recorded.

Reattribution of thinking, then, becomes central (Warwick & Salkovskis, 1990). Eventually, this is a self-monitoring exercise where the client is taught to record the automatic or negative thoughts that precipitate episodes of reassurance seeking. This allows clients to understand the sequence of events and learn to more accurately identify the cause of the bodily sensations. Eventually, the client may be able to interrupt thoughts leading to bodily sensations with a distraction procedure, thus adverting the bodily sensations and decreasing hypochondriacal complaints.

Similarly, other cognitive behavioral techniques can assist in this process. Those that are especially helpful with this population include mood measurement, scheduling activities, use of coping cards, "responsibility pie charts" for the somatic problem, distraction techniques, and relaxation. Relaxation is best introduced later in the course of therapy. Targeting potential resistance to homework assignments (anticipating problems) also is important (Beck, 1995).

Additionally, an action plan can be helpful. Shapiro (1995) uses this method to identify and process relevant problems, projected situations, personal constraints, medical procedures, and fears. Often this leads to the unearthing of a core memory that is a problem and that can be processed. At this point, she uses EMDR (eye movement desensitization and reprocessing) to process the problem. At the least, these data assist in the identification of positive and negative cognitions, and salient emotions, as well as practical problems.

Finally, we note a formal psychotherapy method applied to cancer patients that has appeal to this population. Nezu and colleagues (Nezu, Nezu, Friedman, Faddis, & Houts, 1998) advocate for a problem-solving procedure for somatic issues as these relate to cancer. The patient with (real) cancer is taught a problem-solving method of coping. What is of interest is that the cancer is considered a major life stressor, that a careful rationale is provided for the need of problem-solving coping, and behavioral methods are applied for treatment. The patient is told that the problem-solving method has been shown to be effective, that the added stress of an emotional problem causes emotional problem solving and not rational problem solving, that added stress causes the "first" problem of the disease to become worse (lower immune system, etc.), and that the disease impacts the whole person. As in other forms of psychosomatic treatment, careful goals are formulated, the patient's beliefs are addressed, and moods are monitored, and outcomes are assessed. The elegance of this approach is its simple structure and patient appeal.

Another treatment approach involves family therapy concurrent with the individual treatment of the patient. Family members and significant others are educated about the importance they play in reinforcing the hypochondriacal symptoms. In particular, education about the concepts of secondary gain and reassurance-seeking behavior is paramount. Family work targets identifying the needs the client (e.g., attention, escape from perceived excess responsibilities, or from stress). Thereafter, work would focus on teaching and enabling the patient to meet these needs in more direct ways, while reducing the benefits of illness as much as possible (e.g., do not allow the patient to avoid responsibilities by voicing somatic discomfort, do not excuse the patient from activities, do not allow special privileges such as staying in bed or dressing in nightclothes).

Blazer (1998) especially advocates for the treatment with the family. Special attention should be paid to ADLs and the role of secondary gain in the family. Often the relationship in the family is based on dependence and hostility. The older somatic patient seems to say "Recognize me: You have a part in my problems." Often, too, there is sibling rivalry competing for attention and expressing hostility (Blazer, 1998).

The combination of these approaches allows the clinician to enlist the help from all sources: what is known about hypochondraisis, older people and medical illness, and learning theory. Effective work often seems to take an indirect path, appearing to take steps toward and, at times, away from the goal of therapy. The following case study illuminates this point nicely.

CASE EXAMPLE

Jenny was a 70-year-old Caucasian, married woman who in her 20s had suffered a serious stroke that left her ambulatory, but without the use of her nondominant hand. She had remained unmarried and quite self-reliant until her 50s when she met her current husband. She presented to therapy due to a referral from her primary care physician. She originally saw her physician many years ago due to continual complaints of diarrhea and constipation, allergies, and generalized stomach upset. Recently, her complaints had become more frequent and pronounced, and occurred along with decreased sleep and appetite. Eventually, the severity of the symptoms increased to a point that her physician decided to consult a psychologist.

Initial interview and consultation with the primary care physician revealed many years of somatic complaints and reassurance-seeking behavior on Jenny's part. Historically, the physician had prescribed multiple medications and diagnoses. Although the treatment initially had the affect of allaying her fears, Jenny typically came back within a month with a different physical complaint.

Psychological data (MMPI-2) suggested that Jenny typically utilized somatization and repression as a defense, and that her present levels of depression and anxiety were interfering with the expression of these defenses. MCMI-III data also suggested increased levels of somatoform, anxiety, and depressive problems in addition to clinically significant personality levels of avoidant and schizoid patterns. In accordance with the MMPI-2 and MCMI-III, BDI and BAI scores indicated moderate levels of depression and anxiety.

Treatment sessions typically began with a host of bodily complaints ranging from sinus trouble to the aches and pains associated with the weather. During particularly stressful weeks, Jenny would become tearful as she spoke of the severity of her pains or the inconvenience of her problems with mobility. Jenny would talk at length about her symptoms and what they might mean.

As therapy progressed, the three stages of therapy were applied. She was respected as a person and listened to. A substantial therapeutic alliance developed. Although the therapist controlled the frequency of the sessions, Jenny controlled the content of the sessions for a period. Eventually, conversation shifted to other "less-important" topics. She related many stories that gave her permission to experience suppressed affect and provide an endless stream of data for the therapist. She admitted that, over the years, her husband had become less and less responsive to her needs, both physical and emotional. She talked of the vicissitudes of her relationships with others and friends who were ill, dying, or dead. But what seemed most important and emotionally laden was her being childless. Her life narrative was especially important here because the process allowed her to draw a direct causative line from her stroke to not marrying until later in life, and consequently having no children. Existential themes of isolation, aloneness, and death added to the poignancy of her emotions. She was very much a person who happened to have problems as therapy progressed.

The therapist saw, too, that the strategies were a way to shift anxiety to a more comforting conflict and a way to control her life with so many unmet needs. She was detached in her personality style and this was met with tolerance, even enthusiasm. She protected herself in her own way and space was given to this. She was never pushed or asked to do things beyond her wishes.

Her thinking was infected with several hypochondriac features including an excessive sensitivity to her heart and arthritic pain. Over time, this was presented to her and the therapist tried miniexperiments to lessen its intensity. She was asked to identify her fears during her "symptom observation time" and to rate these. The therapeutic effort was to highlight the misinterpreted symptoms, the heightened anxiety, the safety-seeking behaviors that are triggered, as well as the general beliefs and assumptions on which some of the misinterpretations are based.

Interestingly, the intensity of her symptoms did not remit for a long time, but her thinking began to change. There was never a point in treatment when Jenny's long-standing defense of bodily complaints fully disappeared. Indeed, at times she would not allow the topic to sway from her ailments. These defenses had taken root early in her life and were established aspects of her persona. But, during these times either other issues were addressed, depression and anxiety were discussed, or other positive stories (narratives) were entertained. Likely, she would have left treatment if her bodily complaints had been confronted.

Her depression and anxiety did wane. BDI and BAI scores at 4 months were at asymptomatic levels. MMPI-2 results also corroborated the decreased anxiety and depression, whereas her level of hypochondriasis and repression did not substantially change. She did report improved relations with her husband and neighbors as well. Soon after the decreases in her depression and anxiety took place, Jenny's attendance to sessions became spotty and eventually she reported having strong doubts as to the continued efficacy of therapy. Prior to termination, she did agree to ask her physician to consult psychology again if any similar problems arose. This suggests that she recognized, to some degree, the importance of the gains achieved.

CONCLUSION

The management of hypochondriac patients is best conceptualized as care, not cure, by helping the patient to cope with and endure his or her symptoms rather than eliminating them. Treatment starts with assessment; assessment as treatment, if you will. We have presented a view of hypochondriasis as a common and difficult later life problem that can be treated. We presented a treatment model based on traditional concepts as well as cognitive behavioral thinking. The main thrust of this work is to enable the patient to reattribute symptoms to psychological explanations. Even if the patient cannot agree with the alternative psychological explanations, a focus directed at the "person of the hypochondriac" in a form of an alliance and narrative listening was advocated.

REFERENCES

Ables, N. (1997). *What practitioners should know about working with older adults.* Washington, DC: American Psychological Association.

Abrams, R. (1997). Assessing personality in chronic care population. In J. Teresi, M. Lawton, D. Holmes, & M. Ory (Eds.), *Measurement in elderly chronic care populations* (pp. 78–89). New York: Springer.

American Psychiatric Association. (1987). *Diagnostic and statistical manual of mental disorders* (3rd ed.). Washington, DC: Author.

American Psychiatric Association. (1994). *Diagnostic and statistical manual of mental disorders* (4th ed.). Washington, DC: Author.

Avia, M., Ruiz, M., Olivares, M., & Crespo, M. (1996, January) The meaning of psychological symptoms: Effectiveness of a group intervention with hypochondriacal patients. *Behaviour Research & Therapy, 34*(1), 23–31.

Barsky, A. (1993). The diagnosis and management of hypochondriachal concerns in the elderly. Scientific Meeting of the Boston Society for Gerontologic Psychiatry, 1992, Boston. *Journal of Geriatric Psychiatry, 26*(2), 129–141.

Barsky, A. (1992a). Amplification, somatization, and the somatoform disorders. *Behavior Research & Therapy, 33*(1), 28–34.

Barsky, A. (1992b). Hypochondriasis and obsessive compulsive disorder. *Psychiatric Clinics of North America, 15*(4), 791–801.

Barsky, A., Brener, J., Coeytaux, R., & Cleary, P. (1995, May). Accurate awareness of heartbeat in hypochondriacal and non-hypochondriacal patients. *Journal of Psychosomatic Research, 39*(4), 489–497.

Barsky, A., & Klerman, G.L. (1983). Overview: Hypochondriasis, bodily complaints and somatic styles. *American Journal of Psychiatry, 140,* 273–283.

Barsky, A., Wyshak, G., & Klerman, G. (1990). Transient hypochondriasis. *Archives of General Psychiatry, 47,* 746–752.

Barsky, A., Wyshak, G., & Klerman, G. (1992). Psychiatric comorbidity in *DSM-III* hypochondriasis. *Archives of General Psychiatry, 49,* 101–108.

Beck, J. (1995). *Cognitive therapy: Basics and beyond.* New York: John Wiley.

Blazer, D. (1998). *Emotional problems in later life: Investigative strategies for professional caregivers.* New York: Springer.

Blazer, D.G., & Houpt, J.L. (1979). Perception of poor health in the healthy older adult. *Journal of the American Geriatric Society, 27,* 330–336.

Brink, T.L., Belanger, J., & Bryant, J. (1978). Hypochondriasis in an institutional geriatric population: Construction of a scale (HSIG). *Journal of the American Geriatric Society, 26,* 557–559.

Busse, E.W. (1975). Aging and psychiatric diseases in late life. In M. Reiser (Ed.), *American handbook of psychiatry.* New York: Basic Books.

Busse, E.W. (1976). Hypochondriasis in the elderly: A reaction to social stress. *Journal of the American Geriatric Society, 24,* 145–149.

Busse, E.W. (1989). Somatoform and psychosocial disorders. In E.W. Busse & D. Blazer (Eds.), *Geriatric psychiatry* (pp. 429–458). Washington, DC: American Psychiatric Press.

Busse, E.W. (1996). Somatoform and psychosexual disorders. In E.W. Busse & D.G. Blazer (Eds.), *The American psychiatric press textbook of geriatric psychiatry* (2nd Rev. ed., pp. 291–311). Washington, DC: American Psychiatric Press.

Cohen, G.D. (1991). Anxiety and general medical disorders. In C. Salzman & B.D. Lebowitz (Eds.), *Anxiety in the elderly: Treatment and research* (pp. 47–62). New York: Springer.

Costa, P.T., & McCrae, R. (1985). Hypochondriasis, neuroticism, and aging. *American Psychologist, 40,* 19–28.

Demopulos, C., Fava, M., McLean, N., Alpert, J.E., Nierenberg, A.A., & Rosenbaum, J.F. (1996, July–August). Hypochondriacal concerns in depressed outpatients. *Psychosomatic Medicine, 58*(4), 314–320.

Edelmann, R., & Holdsworth, S. (1993). The Minnesota Multiphasic Personality Inventory Hypochondriasis Scale: Its relation to bodily awareness and irrational beliefs. *Personality & Individual Differences, 14*(2), 369–370.

Escobar, J., Waitzkin, H., Silver, R., Cohen, M., Gara, M., & Holman, A. (1998). Abridged somatization: A study in primary care. *Psychosomatic Medicine, 60*(4), 466–472.

Fallon, B., Klein, B., & Liebowitz, M. (1993). Hypochondriasis: Treatment strategies. *Psychiatric Annals, 23*(7), 374–381.

Ford, C. (1983). *The somatizing disorders.* New York: Elsevier.

Freud, S. (1950). On narcissism: An introduction. In E. Jones (Ed.), *Collected papers* (Vol. 4, pp. 30–59). London: Hogarth Press. (Original work published 1914)

Friedman, R.S. (1993). When the patient intrudes on the treatment: The aging personality types in medical management. *Journal of Geriatric Psychiatry, 26*(2), 149–176.

Gottlieb, G.L. (1989). Hypochondriasis: A psychosomatic problem in the elderly. In N. Billig & P.V. Rabins (Eds.), Issues in geriatric psychiatric. *Advances in Psychosomatic Medicine, 19,* 67–84.

Graham, J.R. (1993). *MMPI-2: Assessing personality and psychopathology* (2nd Rev. ed.). New York: Oxford University Press.

Gurian, B.S., & Miner, J. (1991). Clinical presentation of anxiety in the elderly. In C. Salzman & B.D. Lebowitz (Eds.), *Anxiety in the elderly: Treatment and research* (pp. 31–44). New York: Springer.

Haenen, M., Schmidt, A., Kroeze, S., & van den Hout, M. (1996). Hypochondriasis and symptom reporting: The effect of attention versus distraction. *Psychotherapy & Psychosomatics, 65*(1), 43–48.

Hiller, M., Rief, W., Elefant, M., Kroyman, R., Leibbrand, R., & Fichter, S. (1997). Dysfunctional cognitions in patients with somatization syndrome. *Zeitschrift fur Klinische Psychologie, 26,* 226–234.

Hyer, L., & Associates. (1994). *Trauma victim: The person of the victim.* Muncie, IN: Accelerated Development.

Hyer, L., Gouveia, I., Harrison, W., Warsaw, J., & Coutsouridis, D. (1987). Depression, anxiety, paranoid reactions, crisis and cognitive decline of later-life inpatients. *Gerontology, 42,* 92–94.

Johnson, F.A. (1991). Psychotherapy of the elderly anxious patient. In C. Salzman & B.D. Lebowitz (Eds.), *Anxiety in the elderly: Treatment and research* (pp. 215–248). New York: Springer.

Kukleta, M. (1991, April). Psychophysiological mechanisms in hypochondriasis. *Homeostasis in Health & Disease, 33*(1/2), 7–12.

Lyness, J., King, D., Conwell, Y., & Cox, C. (1993, Fall). "Somatic worry" and medical illness in depressed inpatients. *American Journal of Geriatric Psychiatry, 1*(4), 288–295.

Mabe, A., Riley, W., Jones, R., & Hobson, D. (1996). The medical context of hypochondriacal traits. *International Journal of Psychiatry in Medicine, 26*(4), 443–459.

McLaren, P. (1992, December). Psychotherapy by telephone: Experience of patient and therapist. *Journal of Mental Health, 1*(4), 311–313.

Millon, T., & Davis, R. (1995). *Disorders of personality: DSM-IV and beyond.* New York: Wiley.

Morey, L. (1996). *An interpretive guide to the personality assessment Inventory (PAI).* Odessa, FL: Psychological Assessment Resources.

Nezu, A., Nezu, C., Friedman, S., Faddis, S., & Houts, P. (1998). *Helping cancer patients cope.* Washington, DC: American Psychological Association.

Noyes, R., Kathol, R., Fisher, M., Phillips, B., et al. (1993) The validity of *DSM-III-R* hypochondriasis. *Archives of General Psychiatry, 50*(12), 961–970.

Robbins, J., & Kirmayer, L. (1996, May). Transient and persistent hypochondriacal worry in primary care. *Psychological Medicine, 26*(3), 575–589.

Salkovskis, P., & Clark, S. (1993, March). Panic disorder and hypochondriasis: Panic, cognitions and sensations [Special issue]. *Advances in Behaviour Research & Therapy, 15*(1), 23–48.

Schmidt, A. (1994, July–August). Bottlenecks in the diagnosis of hypochondriasis. *Comprehensive Psychiatry, 35*(4), 306–315.

Schwenzer, M. (1996, June). Social fears in hypochondriasis. *Psychological Reports, 78*(3, Pt. 1), 971–975.

Shapiro, F. (1995). *Eye movement desensitization and reprocessing: Basic principles, protocols, and procedures.* New York: Guilford Press.

Starcevic, V. (1989). Contrasting patterns in the relationship between hypochondriasis and narcissism. *British Journal of Medical Psychology, 62,* 311–323.

Starcevic, V. (1990). Relationship between hypochondriasis and obsessive-compulsive personality disorder: Close relatives separated by nosological schemes? *American Journal of Psychotherapy, 44*(3), 340–347.

Starcevic, V. (1991). Reassurance and treatment of hypochondriasis. *General Hospital Psychiatry, 13*(2), 122–127.

Starcevic, V., Fallon, S., Uhlenhuth, E., & Pathak, D. (1994). Generalized anxiety disorder, worries about illness, and hypochondriacal fears and beliefs. *Psychotherapy & Psychosomatics, 61*(1/2), 93–99.

Starcevic, V., Kellner, R., Uhlenhuth, E.H., & Pathak, D. (1992, February). Panic disorder and hypochondriacal fears and beliefs. *Journal of Affective Disorders, 24*(2), 73–85.

Starcevic, V., Uhlenhuth, E.H., Kellner, R., & Pathak, D. (1992). Patterns of comorbidity in panic disorder and agoraphobia. *Psychiatry Research, 42*(2), 171–183.

Visser, S., & Bouman, T. (1992). Cognitive-behavioural approaches in the treatment of hypochondriasis: Six single case cross-over studies. *Behaviour Research & Therapy, 30*(3), 301–306.

Visser, S., & Bouman, T. (1994, December). Cognitive behaviour theory with hypochondriasis [Dutch]. *Gedragstherapie, 27*(4), 345–368.

Warwick, H., & Salkovskis, P. (1989). Hypochondriasis. In J. Scott, J. Williams, & A. Beck (Eds.), *Cognitive therapy in clinical practice* (pp. 78–102). London: Croom Helm.

Warwick, H., & Salkovskis, P. (1990). Hypochondriasis. *Behavior Research and Therapy, 28*(2), 105–117.

CHAPTER 26

A Biopsychosocial Approach
to Treatment of Schizophrenia
in Late Life

STEPHEN J. BARTELS, KRISTIN J. LEVINE, AND KIM T. MUESER

Schizophrenia is a severe and often disabling mental disorder that has long presented a challenge to the mental health service delivery system. Schizophrenia affects 1% of the older adult population (Gurland & Cross, 1982), accounts for more beds in psychiatric institutions than any other illness, and is associated with the highest mental health center treatment costs (Cuffel et al., 1996). Although there is substantial literature related to schizophrenia in younger adults, data on treatment of this disorder in late life is scarce. Research findings on the effectiveness of pharmacological treatments of late life schizophrenia are beginning to emerge, yet psychosocial approaches to treatment remain a neglected topic. This is especially important in light of the anticipated increase in numbers of older adults with schizophrenia in the future; high costs of care for this population; and complex needs that are likely to be inadequately addressed by medications alone.

In this chapter, we provide an overview of the treatment of schizophrenia in late life with a specific emphasis on psychosocial approaches to treatment. First we provide a descriptive overview of schizophrenia in older adults. Next we discuss the key factors that affect treatment. Finally, we introduce a biopsychosocial treatment framework, within which we consider the complex needs of this group.

OVERVIEW OF SCHIZOPHRENIA
IN OLDER ADULTS

Schizophrenia was first described by Emil Kraepelin (1919/1971) as "dementia praecox" to characterize a progressive mental deterioration that began in early adult life. Recent data conflict with this overly pessimistic view in that progressive deterioration is not demonstrated by imaging studies (Degreef et al., 1991) or by neuropsychological assessments in older age (Goldberg, Hyde, Kleinman, & Weinberger, 1993). In fact, longitudinal studies suggest that most people with this illness experience gradual improvement in function and symptoms, and that some have full remission later in life (Ciompi, 1980; Harding, Brooks, Ashikaga, Strauss, & Breier, 1987a).

Also contrary to earlier beliefs, the onset of schizophrenia is not limited to young adulthood. Although onset occurs most commonly in late adolescence and early adulthood, the first onset occurs for some in middle age, and for a smaller number, in old age (Castle & Murray, 1993; Harris & Jeste, 1988). Studies of schizophrenia based on age of onset tend to support the identification of two broad diagnostic subgroups: (1) older adults who experienced the onset of the disorder in young adulthood ("early onset schizophrenia") and (2) those who had their first episode in middle or old age ("late onset schizophrenia"). In general, late-onset schizophrenia (LOS) is similar to early-onset schizophrenia (EOS) with several exceptions that have important implications for treatment. Women are more likely than men to develop LOS, especially those who are socially isolated and have hearing deficits (Almeida, Howard, Levy, & David, 1995). In contrast, studies of younger persons with EOS have reported a greater prevalence of males or an equivalent proportion of men to women. Sensory deficits, in general, have been found to be overrepresented in those with late-onset psychotic disorders (Prager & Jeste, 1993), with hearing deficits reported in approximately 40% of those with late-onset paranoid psychosis (Herbert & Jacobson, 1967; Kay & Roth, 1961).

Clinical presentation may also differ depending on age of onset, with positive symptoms largely similar in both LOS and EOS, but decreased likelihood of negative symptoms in LOS. Paranoid delusions and auditory hallucinations are common positive symptoms in LOS, and formal thought disorder is less likely than in EOS. In addition, individuals with LOS are more likely to have had better premorbid functioning including higher rates of marriage, having children, and having held a job than those with EOS (Jeste et al., 1988).

Several conflicting views regarding the relationship of LOS to EOS have been expressed in the literature and the issue of whether LOS should be included in the diagnostic category of schizophrenia remains controversial. Whereas one view supports the classification of LOS as essentially a manifestation of schizophrenia in older age, others suggest that LOS may be a neurobiologically distinct form of schizophrenia or that late paraphrenia differs in etiology, risk factors, and symptoms compared with EOS. Regardless of diagnostic debates, one fact is clear. The complex treatment needs of older persons with late-life psychoses will become an increasing challenge to mental health care, general health care, and social services as this population dramatically increases in number over the coming decades.

TREATMENT OF OLDER ADULTS WITH SCHIZOPHRENIA

The main goals of treatment for schizophrenia are to ameliorate symptoms, reduce risk of relapse, and to improve psychosocial adjustment (Fenton & Mcglashan, 1997). These goals can rarely be accomplished with one isolated treatment modality and require the integration of pharmacological, psychotherapeutic, and community support technologies (American Psychiatric Association [APA], 1997). When applied to those with late-life schizophrenia, treatment and mental health service delivery must also be adapted to the unique biopsychosocial characteristics of this age group. In this section, we describe key factors that are known to be important in defining the treatment needs and outcomes of older persons with schizophrenia, then discuss a biopsychosocial approach to treatment.

KEY FACTORS AFFECTING TREATMENT NEEDS AND OUTCOMES

Factors related to long-term outcomes in schizophrenia are important considerations for assessment and treatment. Key factors include age of onset, cohort, gender, social support, medical and cognitive comorbidity, and depression.

AGE OF ONSET

As previously discussed, individuals with early- and late-onset schizophrenia present with overlapping but different profiles, and may have different treatment needs and outcomes. Individuals with LOS are more likely to be women, and to have experienced successful premorbid occupational and social functioning. As a result, this group is likely to have more financial and social resources available than those who developed schizophrenia in young adulthood. In addition, those with LOS have not lived with the stigma of mental illness, chronic demoralization, and experience of long-term institutional care that may accompany early-onset schizophrenia. The course tends to be chronic for both EOS and LOS; however, the prognosis is thought to be somewhat better for those with LOS (Harris & Jeste, 1995).

COHORT EFFECTS

Among those with early-onset schizophrenia, there are two distinct historical cohorts: those older individuals who entered the treatment system before the mid-1950s, and a younger cohort of middle-aged and older adults who began treatment after 1960. In the 1960s, the use of antipsychotic medication became widespread and mental health care reform resulted in a shift of treatment from long-term mental hospitals to the community. Many elderly state mental hospital patients were transferred to nursing homes, board and care facilities, and public housing facilities. In general, these individuals lacked social and independent living skills, and depended on a structured supervised setting to meet their needs. Little is known about their potential for rehabilitation.

The younger cohort that is reaching old age in the community is more likely to have developed social supports, community living and social skills, and to have experienced rehabilitation programs and modern medications throughout much of their lives. However, they are also more likely to have experienced the negative effects of declining public funds for community mental health services over the past two decades. During this period, there have been high rates of substance use disorder among people with schizophrenia as well as alarming increases in homelessness, victimization and exposure to crime, institutionalization in the criminal justice system, and increased exposure to public health epidemics such as HIV infection. In general, the two groups of older adults with early-onset schizophrenia represent different age and treatment cohorts. They differ substantially in exposure to pharmacological and psychosocial treatment, opportunities for developing independent living skills, and risk factors for adverse outcomes.

GENDER

Women typically have a later onset of schizophrenia, suggesting that there may be intrinsic gender differences in the development of the disorder. Based on a number of studies, men with schizophrenia are at risk for poorer outcomes than women, suggesting a vulnerability factor related to gender itself (Goldstein, 1988). In general, women experience a more benign course of illness, fewer hospitalizations, and better residential status (Seeman, 1986). The etiology of the more positive course experienced by women is uncertain, but may be explained by biological or social factors. Possible biological sources include protective effects of estrogen and other hormones in women or neuroanatomical differences that result in greater vulnerability for men. Relevant social factors include higher levels of social adjustment in women with schizophrenia, lower rates of drug and alcohol abuse, and increased rates of marriage and contact with children.

SOCIAL SUPPORT

Many older persons with schizophrenia do not have available family care providers and are less socially connected than those without mental illness (Semple et al., 1997). They are less likely to be married or to have children and more likely to live alone and have fewer relationships than the general elderly population. Having never been married is one of the key features differentiating those living in nursing homes from those who reside in the community (Bartels, Mueser, & Miles, 1997a). In addition, formerly married older adults may have lost the support of spouses or family members due to the stress and difficulties of caring for a family member with lifelong mental illness. In a retrospective study, Meeks et al. (1990) found that social support was strongly associated with functional status among older persons with chronic mental illness, and appeared to be critical to continued residence in the community. The death of parents (usually mothers) who are key supports for many persons with schizophrenia, frequently leaves a middle-aged individual with a dramatic reduction in social and financial support and at risk for decompensation and loss of residence in the community. In general, older adults with schizophrenia are more functionally dependent and less likely to have needed informal supports than others with mental illness or older adults without mental illness, placing them at increased risk of poor outcomes.

In addition, the outcome of therapeutic interventions may be very different depending on the availability of family support. For example, in a 3-year study of the effectiveness of personal psychotherapy for younger adults with schizophrenia, the intervention had a positive effect on those who lived with family, whereas the rate of psychotic relapse increased in those living independent of family (Hogarty, Kornblith, et al., 1997). The availability of social supports and need to bolster this capacity are important considerations for treatment planning.

DEPRESSION

Depression is also a factor associated with poor outcomes in schizophrenia, including increased relapse rate, longer hospitalizations, and poorer response to pharmacological treatments (Bartels & Drake, 1988). Depressive symptomatology can be secondary to organic factors such as medical disorders, substance abuse, or medication side effects; associated with acute psychosis; or be related to chronic states such as secondary major depression, negative symptoms, or chronic demoralization. The level of depression among community-residing older adults with schizophrenia is approximately one and a half to three times the level of the general elderly population (Cohen, Talavera, & Hartung, 1996). When depressive symptoms are present, identification of the causes and specific subtypes of depression is critical for implementing effective treatment. Based on the association between activity limitations and depressive symptoms, Cohen and colleagues suggest that strategies for preventing depression in older persons with schizophrenia should include comprehensive medical treatment, improved access to transportation, home care assistance, and other services that offset activity limitations.

MEDICAL AND COGNITIVE COMORBIDITY

In contrast to younger adults with schizophrenia who usually present with symptoms that can be attributed to one disorder, symptoms and functional impairments of older individuals typically have several underlying causes.

Schizophrenia is associated with excess mortality and shorter life spans compared with the general population, and the physical health of individuals with schizophrenia is often more typical of much older persons without the disorder (Mulsant et al., 1993). In general, individuals with severe mental illness have high rates of behaviors such as smoking and substance abuse, which damage health, and have difficulty obtaining needed medical care. Because co-occurring medical disorders are common, often undiagnosed, and under-treated in this population, assessment of health care needs and mechanisms to provide medical care are essential.

Cognitive disorders can also complicate diagnosis and treatment of those with schizophrenia and become the primary source of functional impairment. Co-occurring cognitive impairment may be one of the most important factors in determining the level of care needed, and when severe, may necessitate placement in a nursing home where constant care is available. For individuals with comorbid cognitive deficits, the capacity for communication, awareness of a problem, and capacity for retention and carryover should be considered when evaluating the appropriateness of psychotherapy (Zweig & Hinrichsen, 1996).

A BIOPSYCHOSOCIAL TREATMENT APPROACH

The stress-vulnerability model has been proposed to account for the episodic nature of schizophrenia over time and offers a useful approach for understanding treatment needs (Teague, Drake, & Bartels, 1989). In this model, adapted to older adults (see Table 26.1), the presence and severity of schizophrenic symptoms are the result of biological and psychological vulnerability, in combination with biological, psychological, and social stressors. Because the aging process results in age-related changes, treatment of older adults is best accomplished through a biopsychosocial approach that addresses vulnerability and needs in each of these areas. As shown in Table 26.1, the treatment needs may be conceptualized as core services addressing medical, psychiatric, and residential support services, as well as an array of biological, psychological, and social interventions that hold promise in affecting the course and outcome of schizophrenia.

BIOLOGICAL ASPECTS OF TREATMENT

Age-related changes for older adults with schizophrenia include effects on the pharmacokinetics of antipsychotic medications, as well as increased rates of comorbid medical conditions, physical impairment, and cognitive impairment. Treatment, therefore, should address both psychopharmacological and general medical needs.

Psychopharmacological Treatment
Aging is associated with biological changes that directly affect the metabolism and side effects of medication. Antipsychotic medications have long been the

Table 26.1   Biopsychosocial approach for older adults with schizophrenia.

	Biological	Psychological	Social
Age-Related Changes	Increased risk of drug side effects Increased rate of cognitive impairment Increased rate of physical impairment Increased medical comorbidity	Losses Risk of institutionalization Change in residence Decreased functional abilities Stress of medical illness Role changes	Loss of social support and friends due to aging or death of family members or friends, change in residence or decreased mobility Increased need for coordination between organizations providing aging services, psychiatric care, and general medical care Psychiatric and medical health care providers
Needs	Psychopharmacological care & general medical care: Assessment Treatment Maintenance	Geropsychiatric care & psychosocial interventions: Assessment Treatment Maintenance Crisis management	Residential stability Self-care and community living support Social support Service access and coordination
Services/Interventions	Facilitated access to medical care Medical treatment integrated with psychiatric needs Geriatric specialty care	Supportive therapy Personal therapy Cognitive therapy Skills training and other behavioral interventions	Supported housing In-home support services Case management Family/caregiver education, respite, and support Day programs Family therapy

mainstay of treatment for individuals of all ages with schizophrenia. They reduce positive and negative symptoms during an acute exacerbation as well as lowering the risk of relapse when administered in low doses over time (Van Putten & Marder, 1986). However, dosage of antipsychotic medication should be lowered substantially for older adults, and clinicians should be alert to the older patient's high risk of developing tardive dyskinesia and other troublesome side effects (Jeste et al., 1996). Although they have not been evaluated extensively in older adults, atypical antipsychotic agents such as clozapine, risperidone, and olanzapine have reduced risks of motor side effects and may have specific advantages for older adults (Kim & Goldstein, 1997). Clozapine, however, has side effects that may be especially problematic for older adults, including the need to obtain frequent blood tests due to the risk of agranulocytosis (a potentially life-threatening drop in white blood cell count) and an increased risk of postural hypotension and sedation (Thorpe, 1997). In contrast, newer atypical antipsychotics such as risperidone are generally well tolerated in older people and appear to be effective for the treatment of psychosis, including some elderly patients who are not responsive to conventional neuroleptics (Zayas & Grossberg, 1998). Ideally, neuroleptics should be started at low doses, increased slowly, and maintained at the lowest level that is effective. Older adults with LOS generally require lower doses of antipsychotic medications than those with EOS who have taken them for many years. In addition, careful monitoring is important in this age group (including measuring blood levels), and regular attempts to decrease dose should be made over time. Finally, since symptoms decrease with age in over half of those with schizophrenia (Harding, Brooks, Ashikaga, Strauss, & Breier, 1987b), it has been suggested that stable chronic outpatients without a history of antipsychotic discontinuation should be considered for a carefully monitored trial of antipsychotic withdrawal (Jeste, Lacro, Gilbert, Kline, & Kline, 1993).

General Medical Care

In people with schizophrenia, who have more medical problems than the general population even at younger ages, age-related increases in physical problems make access to general medical care crucial. In addition, this medical care should be integrated with psychiatric care, due to the complex interactions between medical and psychiatric illness in this population. Although assessment and treatment of delusional, cognitively impaired, or combative individuals can be challenging, a thorough understanding of comorbid medical illness is crucial for addressing symptoms that may be caused or exacerbated by medication toxicity or medical conditions.

PSYCHOSOCIAL APPROACHES TO TREATMENT OF SCHIZOPHRENIA IN LATE LIFE

For decades, pharmacological treatment and long-term institutional care have been the mainstay of the treatment of older persons with schizophrenia. In many cases, this care is best described as custodial, with little attention to psychosocial interventions. The vast majority of data on psychosocial treatments of schizophrenia is derived from studies on younger adult populations. Though based on younger adults, these approaches may also hold promise for the older person with schizophrenia, particularly among the growing majority of individuals who reside in home- and community-based settings and who are confronted by the daily challenges of living independently.

Psychological Aspects of Treatment
New sources of psychosocial stress may arise for individuals with schizophrenia as they age, including loss of friends and family members due to death or residential change; decreased functional abilities and mobility; the stress of medical illness or chronic disability; increased dependency and role changes. Furthermore, the ability to cope with these stresses may be impaired by secondary neuropsychiatric disorders such as dementia, depression, and delirium, in addition to the effects of schizophrenia (Cohen et al., 1996). Psychotherapeutic and psychopharmacological approaches must be specific to these complex needs and can best be delivered through a geropsychiatric model that integrates geriatric medical and psychiatric specialty services. These specialized services need to address assessment, treatment, maintenance, and crisis management.

Several individual psychological approaches to therapy have been studied extensively in younger adults, including supportive psychotherapy, personal therapy, cognitive therapy, skills training, and other behavioral interventions. In the following overview, we describe this treatment literature. Although largely derived from studies of young adults, these data suggest directions for the treatment of older persons with schizophrenia.

Supportive Psychotherapy
A "reality-adaptive" approach to supportive therapy emphasizing practical "here and now" issues and helping patients deal with day-to-day problems, has demonstrated positive effects on recidivism and role performance (Gunderson et al., 1984). However, other studies suggest that supportive therapy results in worse outcomes than family psychoeducational, major role therapy, and skill training approaches (e.g., Leff, Kuipers, Berkowitz, & Sturgeon, 1985; Tarrier et al., 1989), and that its positive effects may plateau after 12 months (Hogarty, Greenwald, et al., 1997). Nevertheless, supportive therapy resulted in fewer relapses compared with personal therapy for subjects who did not live with their families. This may make it an appropriate approach to consider during stressful periods for those older adults who lack family support.

Personal Therapy
Personal therapy is an approach that is theoretically grounded in the stress-vulnerability model, and includes therapeutic techniques to accommodate the individual needs and preferences of people with schizophrenia. This approach is intended to forestall relapses and to improve personal and social adjustment by identifying and managing the affect dysregulation that precedes relapse or inappropriate behavior (Hogarty, Kornblith, et al., 1997). Therapeutic techniques include building a positive therapeutic alliance, psychoeducation, promotion of self-awareness of internal affective cues associated with stressors, training in self-protective strategies, social skills, and exercises in relaxation and social perception.

A 3-year randomized clinical trial of the effectiveness of personal therapy for young adults with schizophrenia found that it was more effective for reducing relapses than either supportive or family therapy for those individuals who lived with family (Hogarty, Kornblith, et al., 1997). In addition, personal therapy produced extensive improvements in social adjustment and role performance, which continued to improve in the second year with no sign of the plateau effect seen in the supportive and family treatment groups (Hogarty, Greenwald, et al., 1997). Although this study provides support for the efficacy of psychosocial treatments for schizophrenia, personal psychotherapy resulted in an *increased* relapse rate for individuals who lived alone. These recipients were more likely to have unstable housing, higher rates of interpersonal conflict, and difficulty obtaining food and clothing. The researchers conclude that personal therapy might best be delayed until patients are stable in symptoms and residence. It is also important to note that the outcomes of this approach, like most others, have not been assessed in older adults with schizophrenia. Because older adults are more likely to have decreased social support, to lack financial resources, and to experience residential instability, careful consideration of their stability and vulnerability is critical for determining whether individual therapy of this sort is appropriate.

Cognitive Therapy

Cognitive therapy was developed by Beck and colleagues (Beck, Rush, Shaw, & Emery, 1979) and Ellis (1962) primarily for the treatment of depression and anxiety, but has recently gained some empirical support for treating delusions and hallucinations in people with schizophrenia. It is based on the assumption that emotional reactions are filtered through an individual's beliefs, thoughts, and style of processing information. Successfully challenging and modifying dysfunctional beliefs may decrease negative emotions and lead to more adaptive perceptions and beliefs about the world. Although the results of four controlled studies (Drury, Birchwood, Cochrane, & MacMillan, 1996; Garety et al., 1997; Kingdon, 1997; Kuipers et al., 1997; Tarrier, 1997) are encouraging, research is needed to evaluate this approach in older persons with schizophrenia. Cognitive therapy, as described here, is not to be confused with *cognitive rehabilitation* (or *cognitive remediation*). Whereas cognitive therapy focuses on altering the specific content of thoughts and beliefs, cognitive rehabilitation attempts to change specific cognitive processes frequently impaired in persons with schizophrenia, such as memory, vigilance, or abstract reasoning. Only limited evidence supports the effects of cognitive remediation on outcomes for schizophrenia (Penn & Mueser, 1996).

Skills Training and Other Behavioral Interventions

Social skills training is based on the premise that systematic teaching of behavioral components of social skills can result in a decrease in the social impairments associated with schizophrenia (Bellack, Mueser, Gingerich, & Agresta, 1997). Targeted social skills include a wide range of self-care and interpersonal behaviors such as expression of feelings, medication management, and conflict resolution skills. Due to the multiplicity of deficits seen in most individuals with schizophrenia, skills training needs to be embedded in a treatment program to effect major change in functioning (Bellack & Mueser, 1993). Hayes and colleagues (Hayes, Halford, & Varghese, 1995) suggest that social skills training needs to be integrated into ongoing community support to ensure that patients can be engaged in training, that new skills are used and reinforced, and obstacles to effective social behavior can be identified and removed. In addition, Liberman (1992) argues that training in a wide range of skills needs to be incorporated into psychiatric rehabilitation according to individual needs. Suggested skill areas include family psychoeducation, recreation and leisure skills, medication and symptom management, and basic community survival skills as well as social skills. Skills for accessing medical care and residential supports are especially crucial for older adults with schizophrenia.

Because older adults with schizophrenia have significantly greater deficits in self-care skills, community living skills, and social skills compared with older adults who have other psychiatric disorders (Bartels, Mueser, & Miles, 1997b), skills training interventions might also be adapted to focus more extensively on these areas. Behavioral skills training and other behavioral interventions have demonstrated effectiveness for enhancing autonomy and improving self care functions such as bathing, eating, ambulation, and continence in nursing homes where continued reinforcement is available (Ossip-Klein & Karuza, 1996). In addition, behavioral therapy techniques have been used successfully to increase communication, and to decrease wandering and other inappropriate behaviors, including disruptive and assaultive behaviors, in nursing home residents with cognitive impairments. Despite demonstrated effectiveness in institutional settings, this kind of behavioral skills training intervention is utilized infrequently for community-residing older adults. Further research is needed to determine whether these behavioral and skills training interventions can result in lasting changes for older adults if utilized within a comprehensive rehabilitative program.

In general, when considering psychotherapeutic approaches for older adults, it is important to keep in mind that survival needs take precedence over psychological reflection and that cognitive capacity places a limit on what can be learned. Whereas an individual psychotherapeutic approach may be very helpful for older adults with stable circumstances, social support, and relatively few deficits, the same approach may result in destabilizing cognitive overload when misapplied. Current effectiveness studies of individual psychotherapy for younger adults with schizophrenia suggest that several approaches may be effective components of psychosocial care for older adults if adapted to their needs. For many older adults with schizophrenia, however, the first step involves a focus on social aspects of treatment.

SOCIAL ASPECTS OF TREATMENT

Changes that accompany aging may include loss of informal sources of social support; increased need for assistance with activities of daily living and community living skills; changes in social interaction due to residential change or decreased mobility; and an increased need for coordination of services from aging, health, and mental health organizations. Like most older adults in the general population, the majority of older adults with schizophrenia live in the community. Due to increased functional disabilities, however, they are largely dependent on social networks for support, and those without social support live primarily in institutional settings (Meeks & Murrell, 1997). As such, residential and social support are important focuses of mental health treatment for individuals with schizophrenia as they age.

Residential Stability and Support

When family care is unavailable or insufficient for the level of care needed, older adults with schizophrenia living in the community require support services such as home health care, adult day care, respite care, chore services, meals on wheels, and assisted living. These supportive services are needed across the spectrum of residential settings including individual homes, elderly apartment complexes, personal care residences, congregate living, board and care and assisted living facilities, foster care, intermediate care facilities, and nursing homes. In addition, due to the complex multiple problems typically found in older adults with severe mental illness, they require services from organizations that focus on aging, primary care, and mental health. Yet, the current fragmented system of care is hard for them to negotiate, due to limited physical mobility, difficulty finding or using transportation (Bartels et al., 1997b), cost of services, attitudes of health care providers toward older patients, inconvenient service locations, and lack of specialized services for older persons. In general, emphasis on providing outreach services to patients where they live, work, or spend leisure time appears to be necessary for reaching older adults with schizophrenia (Schaftt & Randolph, 1994).

Case management, provided by an individual or team, is also an important component of treatment; it can enhance access to needed services and assist the community-residing person in remaining in a least restrictive environment. Intensive case management is often a key component of assertive community programs, and research has shown that it reduces relapse rates and rehospitalizations, stabilizes housing in younger patients (Mueser, Bond, Drake, & Resick, 1998), and reduces inpatient service utilization in older adults with severe mental illness (Blackmon, 1990).

Family/Caregiver Interventions

The burden of caring for a relative with schizophrenia has been well documented. As needs for care increase with age, services to educate, support, and provide respite for caregivers can be critical for maintaining individuals with schizophrenia in the community. Respite care for older adults with severe mental illness appears to be effective for reducing emotional distress of caregivers (Knight, Lutzky, & Macofsky-Urban, 1993), and many studies have established that family-based interventions can have a significant positive effect on individuals with schizophrenia as well as their relatives. In a review of 14 randomized controlled trial studies of family interventions, Carpenter (1996) noted that relapse rates ranged from 40% to 53% in the control conditions compared with 6%

to 23% in the experimental conditions. In addition, results suggested that these interventions improve functional status and family well-being. These studies, however, involved younger adults with schizophrenia, and implications for older individuals are unknown, particularly as the family and patient dynamic is complicated by the medical deficits of the older adult.

Many family interventions have focused on reducing environmental stress because studies have demonstrated an association between family attitude and rate of relapse (see Kavanagh, 1992 for a review). This may be an important area for reducing stress for older adults with schizophrenia, as well, including the large number who are living with nonfamily caregivers or in institutional settings where negative stimulation and misunderstanding of patient behavior can be high. Attention to environmental stressors is an important considera- tion in assessment, and adaptation of the environment to better fit the individ- ual's needs, strengths, and deficits is a practical treatment goal (Kim & Rovner, 1996). Since the cognitive deficits of older adults with schizophrenia make it difficult for these individuals to adapt to environmental changes, especially when compounded by dementia, it is particularly important to minimize resi- dential changes.

Another focus of family-based interventions is enhancement of coping skills of caregivers. Mittelman and colleagues (Mittelman, Ferris, & Shulman, 1996) conducted a randomized trial of individual and family counseling for spouses of patients with Alzheimer's disease, followed by support groups over 3½ years. The intervention group remained in the community 329 days longer and was less likely to be placed in a nursing home at any point in time. This type of family support intervention may hold promise for older adults with schizophre- nia who may also be difficult to care for in late life.

Finally, educating nonfamily caregivers in residential settings such as board and care and assisted living facilities, residential group and nursing homes is an important treatment component, since most caregivers have little or no med- ical or mental health training. Education about the illness and about use of be- havior management principles for dealing with behavioral disturbances can reduce stress for both patients and caregivers (Tariot, 1996).

CONCLUSION

Although course and long-term outcomes are viewed more positively than in previous years, older adults with schizophrenia continue to utilize a dispro- portionate share of inpatient and community mental health resources. In addi- tion, although they continue to be overrepresented in nursing homes and state psychiatric institutions, the majority live in the community where most receive little or no treatment beyond medication despite continued need. Yet remark- ably little is known about treatment for this growing population. Research on effectiveness of treatments for younger adults with schizophrenia and older adults with dementia and Alzheimer's disease, together with longitudinal studies of characteristics of older adults with schizophrenia, suggest treatment needs of this population. When viewed within a biopsychosocial framework, these include access to general medical care that is integrated with psychiatric care; specialized geropsychiatric care; psychopharmacological and psychosocial interventions that are adapted to the needs of the older adult; residential support and family or caregiver interventions. Further research is needed to clarify which psychosocial and pharmacological treatments are most effective for subgroups of this heterogeneous group of older adults, as well as how psychosocial and pharmacological treatments interact and are best delivered in the community as well as institutional settings.

REFERENCES

Almeida, O.P., Howard, R.J., Levy, R., & David, A.S. (1995). Psychotic states arising in late life (late paraphrenia): The role of risk factors. *British Journal of Psychiatry, 166,* 215–228.

American Psychiatric Association. (1997, April). Practice guideline for the treatment of patients with schizophrenia. *American Journal of Psychiatry, 154*(Suppl.).

Bartels, S.J., & Drake, R.E. (1988). Depressive symptoms in schizophrenia: Comprehensive differential diagnosis. *Comprehensive Psychiatry, 29,* 467–483.

Bartels, S.J., Mueser, K.T., & Miles, K.M. (1997a). A comparative study of elderly patients with schizophrenia and bipolar disorder in nursing homes and the community. *Schizophrenia Research, 27*(2/3), 181–190.

Bartels, S.J., Mueser, K.T., & Miles, K.M. (1997b). Functional impairments in elderly patients with schizophrenia and major affective illness in the community: Social skills, living skills, and behavior problems. *Behavior Therapy, 28,* 43–63.

Beck, A.T., Rush, A.J., Shaw, B.F., & Emery, G. (1979). *Cognitive therapy of depression.* New York: Guilford Press.

Bellack, A.S., & Mueser, K.T. (1993). Psychosocial treatment of schizophrenia. *Schizophrenia Bulletin, 19,* 317–336.

Bellack, A.S., Mueser, K.T., Gingerich, S., & Agresta, J. (1997). *Social skills training for schizophrenia.* New York: Guilford Press.

Blackmon, A.A. (1990). South Carolina's elder support program: An alternative to hospital care for elderly persons with chronic mental illness. *Adult Residential Care Journal, 4*(2), 119–122.

Carpenter, W.T.J. (1996). Maintenance therapy of persons with schizophrenia. *Journal of Clinical Psychiatry, 57*(Suppl. 9), 10–18.

Castle, D.J., & Murray, R.M. (1993). The epidemiology of late-onset schizophrenia. *Schizophrenia Bulletin, 19,* 691–700.

Ciompi, L. (1980). The natural history of schizophrenia in the long term. *British Journal of Psychiatry, 136,* 413–420.

Cohen, C.I., Talavera, N., & Hartung, R. (1996). Depression among aging persons with schizophrenia who live in the community. *Psychiatric Services, 47,* 601–607.

Cuffel, B.J., Jeste, D.V., Halpain, M., Pratt, C., Tarke, H., & Patterson, T.L. (1996). Treatment costs and use of community mental health services for schizophrenia by age cohorts. *American Journal of Psychiatry, 153*(7), 870–876.

Degreef, G., Ashtari, M., Wu, H., Borenstein, M., Geisler, S., & Lieberman, J. (1991). Follow-up MRI study in first episode schizophrenia. *Schizophrenia Research, 5,* 204–205.

Drury, V., Birchwood, M., Cochrane, R., & MacMillan, F. (1996). Cognitive therapy and recovery from acute psychosis: A controlled trial: I. Impact on psychotic symptoms. *British Journal of Psychiatry, 169,* 593–601.

Ellis, A. (1962). *Reason and emotion in psychotherapy.* New York: Lyle Stuart.

Fenton, W.S., & Mcglashan, T.H. (1997). We can talk: Individual psychotherapy for schizophrenia. *American Journal of Psychiatry, 154*(11), 1493–1495.

Garety, P., Fowler, D., Kuipers, E., Freeman, D., Dunn, G., Bebbington, P., Hadley, C., & Jones, S. (1997). London-East Anglia randomised controlled trial of cognitive-behavioural therapy for psychosis: II. Predictors of outcome. *British Journal of Psychiatry, 171,* 420–426.

Goldberg, T.E., Hyde, T.M., Kleinman, J.E., & Weinberger, D.R. (1993). Course of schizophrenia: Neuropsychological evidence for a static encephalopathy. *Schizophrenia Bulletin, 19,* 797–804.

Goldstein, J.M. (1988). Gender differences in the course of schizophrenia. *American Journal of Psychiatry, 145,* 684–689.

Gunderson, J.G., Frank, A.F., Katz, H.M., Vannicelli, M.L., Frosch, J.P., & Knapp, P.H. (1984). Effects of psychotherapy in schizophrenia: II. Comparative outcomes of two forms of treatment. *Schizophrenia Bulletin, 10,* 564–598.

Gurland, B.J., & Cross, P.S. (1982). Epidemiology of psychopathology in old age. *Psychiatric Clinics of North America, 5*(1), 11–26.

Harding, C.M., Brooks, G.W., Ashikaga, T., Strauss, J.S., & Breier, A. (1987a). The Vermont longitudinal study of persons with severe mental illness: Methodology, study sample, and overall status 32 years later. *American Journal of Psychiatry, 144*(6), 718–735.

Harding, C.M., Brooks, G.W., Ashikaga, T., Strauss, J.S., & Breier, A. (1987b). The Vermont longitudinal study of persons with severe mental illness: II. Long-term outcome of subjects who retrospectively met *DSM-III* criteria for schizophrenia. *American Journal of Psychiatry, 144*(6), 727–735.

Harris, M., & Jeste, D. (1988). Late-onset schizophrenia: An overview. *Schizophrenia Bulletin, 14*(1), 39–55.

Harris, M.J., & Jeste, D.V. (1995). Psychiatric disorders of late life: Schizophrenia and delusional disorder. In H.I. Kaplan & B.J. Sadock (Eds.), *Comprehensive textbook of psychiatry* (6th ed., pp. 2569–2571). Baltimore: Williams & Wilkins.

Hayes, R.L., Halford, W.K., & Varghese, F.T. (1995). Social skills training with chronic schizophrenic patients: Effects on negative symptoms and community functioning. *Behavior Therapy, 26,* 433–449.

Herbert, M., & Jacobson, S. (1967). Late paraphrenia. *British Journal of Psychiatry, 113,* 461–469.

Hogarty, G.E., Greenwald, D., Ulrich, R.F., Kornblith, S.J., DiBarry, A.L., Cooley, S., Carter, M., & Flesher, S. (1997). Three-year trials of personal therapy among schizophrenic patients living with or independent of family: II. Effects on adjustment of patients. *American Journal of Psychiatry, 154,* 1514–1524.

Hogarty, G.E., Kornblith, S.J., Greenwald, D., DiBarry, A.L., Cooley, S., Ulrich, R.F., Carter, M., & Flesher, S. (1997). Three-year trials of personal therapy among schizophrenic patients living with or independent of family: I. Description of study and effects on relapse rates. *American Journal of Psychiatry, 154,* 1504–1513.

Jeste, D.V., Eastham, J.H., Lacro, J.P., Gierz, M., Field, M.G., & Harris, M.J. (1996). Management of late-life psychosis. *Journal of Clinical Psychiatry, 57*(Suppl. 3), 39–45.

Jeste, D.V., Harris, M., Pearlson, G., Rabins, P., Lesser, I., Miller, B., Coles, C., & Yassa, R. (1988). Late-onset schizophrenia—studying clinical validity. *Psychiatric Clinics of North America, 11*(1), 1–13.

Jeste, D.V., Lacro, J.P., Gilbert, P.L., Kline, J., & Kline, N. (1993). Treatment of late-life schizophrenia with neuroleptics. *Schizophrenia Bulletin, 19,* 817–830.

Kavanagh, D.J. (1992). Recent developments in expressed emotion and schizophrenia. *British Journal of Psychiatry, 160,* 601–620.

Kay, D., & Roth, M. (1961). Environmental and hereditary factors in the schizophrenias of old age (late paraphrenia) and their bearing on the general problem of causation in schizophrenia. *Journal of Mental Science, 107,* 649–686.

Kim, E., & Rovner, B. (1996). The nursing home as a psychiatric hospital. In W.E. Reichman & P.R. Katz (Eds.), *Psychiatric care in the nursing home* (pp. 3–9). New York: Oxford University Press.

Kim, K.Y., & Goldstein, M.Z. (1997). Treating older adults with psychotic symptoms. *Psychiatric Services, 48*(9), 1123–1126.

Kingdon, D. (1997). *The Wellcome study of cognitive therapy for "treatment resistant" schizophrenia.* Presented at the second International Conference on Psychological Treatments for Schizophrenia, Oxford, England.

Knight, B.G., Lutzky, S.M., & Macofsky-Urban, F. (1993). A meta-analytic review of interventions for caregiver distress: Recommendations for future research. *Gerontologist, 33,* 240–249.

Kraepelin, E. (1971). *Dementia praecox and paraphrenia* (R.M. Barclay, Trans.). New York: Krieger. (Original work published 1919)

Kuipers, E., Garety, P., Fowler, D., Dunn, G., Bebbington, P., Freeman, D., & Hadley, C. (1997). London-East Anglia randomised controlled trial of cognitive-behavioural therapy for psychosis: I. Effects of the treatment phase. *British Journal of Psychiatry, 171,* 319–327.

Leff, J., Kuipers, L., Berkowitz, R., & Sturgeon, D. (1985). A controlled trial of social intervention in the families of schizophrenic patients: Two-year follow-up. *British Journal of Psychiatry, 146,* 594–600.

Liberman, R.P. (1992). *Handbook of psychiatric rehabilitation.* New York: Macmillan.

Meeks, S., Carstensen, L.L., Stafford, P.B., Brenner, L.L., Weathers, F., Welch, R., & Oltmanns, T.F. (1990). Mental health needs of the chronically mentally ill elderly. *Psychology and Aging, 5*(2), 163–171.

Meeks, S., & Murrell, S.A. (1997). Mental illness in late life: Socioeconomic conditions, psychiatric symptoms, and adjustment of long-term sufferers. *Psychology and Aging, 12*(2), 298–308.

Mittelman, M.S., Ferris, S.H., & Shulman, E. (1996). A family intervention to delay nursing home placement of patients with Alzheimer disease: A randomized controlled study. *Journal of the American Medical Association, 276,* 1725–1731.

Mueser, K.T., Bond, G.R., Drake, R.E., & Resick, S.G. (1998). Models of community care for severe mental illness: A review of research on case management. *Schizophrenia Bulletin, 24,* 37–74.

Mulsant, B.H., Stergiou, A., Keshavan, M.S., Sweet, R.A., Rifai, A.H., Pasternak, R., & Zubenko, G.S. (1993). Schizophrenia in late life: Elderly patients admitted to an acute care psychiatric hospital. *Schizophrenia Bulletin, 19,* 709–721.

Ossip-Klein, D.J., & Karuza, J. (1996). Cognitive and behavioral therapy. In W.E. Reichman & P.R. Katz (Eds.), *Psychiatric care in the nursing home* (pp. 209–228). New York: Oxford University Press.

Penn, D.L., & Mueser, K.T. (1996). Research update on the psychosocial treatment of schizophrenia. *American Journal of Psychiatry, 15,* 607–617.

Prager, S., & Jeste, D.V. (1993). Sensory impairment in late-life schizophrenia. *Schizophrenia Bulletin, 19,* 755–772.

Schaftt, G.E., & Randolph, F.L. (1994). *Innovative community-based services for older persons with mental illness*. Rockville, MD: Center for Mental Health Services, Division of Demonstration Programs, Community Support Section.

Seeman, M.V. (1986). Current outcome in schizophrenia: Women vs. men. *Acta Psychiatrica Scandinavica, 73*, 609–617.

Semple, S.J., Petterson, T., Shaw, W.S., Grant, I., Moscona, S., Koch, W., & Jeste, D. (1997). The social networks of older schizophrenic patients. *International Psychogeriatrics, 9*(1), 81–94.

Tariot, P.N. (1996). General approaches to behavioral disturbances. In W.E. Reichman & P.R. Katz (Eds.), *Psychiatric care in the nursing home* (pp. 10–22). New York: Oxford University Press.

Tarrier, N. (1997). *Coping and problem solving in the treatment of persistent psychotic symptoms*. Presented at the second International Conference on Psychological Treatments for Schizophrenia, Oxford, England.

Tarrier, N., Barrowclough, C., Vaughn, C., Bamrak, J.S., Porceddu, K., Watts, S., & Freeman, H. (1989). Community management of schizophrenia: A two-year follow-up of a behavioural intervention with families. *British Journal of Psychiatry, 154*, 625–628.

Teague, G., Drake, R.E., & Bartels, S.J. (1989). Stress and schizophrenia: A review of research models and findings. *Stress Medicine, 5*, 153–165.

Thorpe, L. (1997). The treatment of psychotic disorders in late life. *Canadian Journal of Psychiatry, 42*(Suppl. 1), 19S–27S.

Van Putten, T., & Marder, S.R. (1986). Low-dose treatment strategies. *Journal of Clinical Psychiatry, 47*(Suppl. 5), 12–16.

Zayas, E.M., & Grossberg, G.T. (1998). The treatment of psychosis in late life. *Journal of Clinical Psychiatry, 59*(Suppl. 1), 5–10.

Zweig, R.A., & Hinrichsen, G.A. (1996). Insight-oriented and supportive psychotherapy. In W.E. Reichman & P.R. Katz (Eds.), *Psychiatric care in the nursing home*. New York: Oxford University Press.

CHAPTER 27

Dynamics and Treatment of Narcissism in Later Life

JORDAN JACOBOWITZ AND NANCY A. NEWTON

This chapter focuses on understanding and treating individuals with long-standing narcissistic personality disorders, or features, who develop psychiatric symptoms (usually with affective and/or anxiety components) during the later decades of life. "Narcissism" likely plays some role in the formation and/or reaction to any form of psychopathology during the later years, or for that matter during any period of the life course (Gottschalk, 1990). Nevertheless, reviewing the manifold forms and diverse manifestations of narcissism in the full panoply of psychopathology is beyond the scope of this chapter. Instead, we elucidate the dynamics and suggest a treatment strategy for helping a select, but not uncommon, group of elderly patients who have survived relatively well to become old despite (or perhaps because of) narcissistic defenses and related modes of adaptation until an event, or series of events, undermined their defensive sense of security. These patients possess the central and common characteristics of what Kernberg (1974) called the "narcissistic personality structure," what Kohut and Wolf (1978) termed the "narcissistic personality disorders," and generally, what the *DSM-IV* (American Psychiatric Association [APA], 1994) described as the Narcissistic Personality Disorder (NPD). The goal of this explication of narcissism, particularly as mediated and modified by aging processes, is to aid in the therapy not only of NPD patients, but also of patients with other disorders that have prominent narcissistic features.

This chapter is organized in the following manner. First, a brief history of the concept of narcissism, its multiple meanings and uses, and some key dimensions that define narcissistic personality disorder are presented. Next, the normative and aberrant ways in which the biopsychosocial aspects of aging can undermine the adaptive patterns of NPD individuals are discussed. This discussion is followed by a delineation of treatment possibilities, with particular emphasis on a supportive strategy to help aging NPD individuals reconstitute their narcissistic defenses to restore adaptive competence and self-esteem.

Clinical cases follow to illustrate the techniques of this latter strategy and its consequences, when successful. Finally, the limitations and potentialities of treatment with NPD individuals are considered.

NARCISSISM: HISTORICAL, TERMINOLOGICAL, AND CONCEPTUAL CHARACTERISTICS

Pulver (1970) pointed out about 30 years ago that the term "narcissism" has been used historically in at least four different ways. One way, which is rarely alluded to today, is Freud's description of narcissism as a sexual perversion—a sexual attraction to one's own body (Freud, 1914). A second usage is to denote a specific developmental stage, wherein an infant views itself as the center of the world, or perhaps more precisely, as the world. Nevertheless, the timing and duration of this stage was never clearly delineated by Freud, and it has not been uncommon for theorists to propose an elongated period of narcissism and its transformative transitions to a state of mature object or interpersonal relations (Gottschalk, 1990; Kohut, 1971, 1977; Winnicott, 1965). A third use of the term is to describe narcissism as a mode of relating to others, which broadly includes the perception that others are there exclusively to serve the individual, and that others have no worthy needs of their own. Kohut's idea of the "selfobject" captures this concept best. Finally, the term narcissism has served as a psychoanalytic designation for the construct of "self-esteem." For that matter, many contemporary theoreticians, diagnosticians, and therapists seem to use the term narcissistic as a synonym for the word "self" (Cooper, 1981). Who can state with any certitude what distinctive meaning "narcissistic injury" and "self-injury" have?

The shift in using narcissism as a generic reference for a structural component of the psyche (i.e., "self") instead of as a reference to a specific pathological syndrome has led to both conceptual and terminological confusion (or inconsistency, at best) regarding whether narcissism is "good" or "bad," healthy or pathological, boon or bane for adaptation (Gottschalk, 1990; Miller, 1979; Stolorow, 1975). A core controversy is whether healthy and pathological forms of narcissism originate from a common psychological source, to be differentiated later into their adaptive or maladaptive forms by experience, or whether they represent two qualitatively different courses of development. The former view is taken by Freud (1914) and Kohut (1971) wherein energy is either redirected (or not) from self to object, or infantile narcissistic ways of being are transmuted (or not) to more mature modes of being. The latter view is exemplified by Kernberg (1974) or Erikson (1963): organismic characteristics and interpersonally mediated experiences mold structure into either distinctly healthy and growth-oriented organizations or pathological, vulnerable, and often stagnant ones. One neither transforms or transmutes, in the latter view, but constructs and builds essentially different subjective self-experiences and underlying psychological organizations.

The preceding controversy of whether healthy narcissism is a derivative of infantile—and if unchanged by experience—pathological narcissism, or whether it is nurtured and formed by complex interactions among innate and developmentally mediated dispositions, interpersonal relations, and physical and cultural environmental influences has implications for treatment strategies of narcissistic disorders (Kernberg, 1974). At stake is whether a therapist "merely" has to induce via regressive transference the infantile narcissism and via communicative techniques and attitudes initiate the process of transmutation that went awry in the patients' early development; or whether the therapist must first deconstruct a pathological organization via interpretive or supportive work, and then aid in constructing a healthy organization (Goldstein, 1995). We return to this issue later when discussing treatment strategies for older adults.

Relevant to the issue of what is healthy versus pathological narcissism is the inconsistency with which different authors use the term "narcissistic vulnerability" (Goldstein, 1995; Pearlman, 1993; Sorensen, 1986). At times, the term is used to indicate anyone's sensitivity to potential threats to self-esteem or personal security. At other times, it is used to indicate a particular weakness in an individual, created by past injuries to certain aspects of the self. Finally, sometimes it refers to a certain personality organization that is chronically susceptible to manifold slights to self-worth. In one of the first articles on the psychotherapeutic treatment of the elderly from a self-psychology perspective, Lazarus (1980) identified three types of self-structures and related defensive patterns among aging individuals: the "healthy, integrated self," the "person with self (narcissistic) psychopathology," and "the aging narcissist." The need to differentiate between adaptive and maladaptive reactions to "narcissistic injuries" by individuals with relatively healthy characters, on one hand, and reactions by those with characterologically impaired self-systems and related lifestyles, on the other hand, becomes crucial in understanding and intervening therapeutically with older adults, especially since the latter are normatively confronted with many age-related threats to self-esteem and security (Nemiroff & Colarusso, 1980).

Before considering the particular ways age-related events and experiences can affect characterologically narcissistic individuals who tend to lack healthy narcissism, it is necessary to delineate the defining behavioral and experiential feature of these individuals. While many attempts have been made to characterize them (APA, 1994; Kernberg, 1974; Kohut & Wolf, 1978; Nicholson, 1990), it seems clinically useful to highlight four areas where pathological narcissism is manifest in everyday functioning. These four areas include:

1. *Self-esteem.* Narcissistic individuals are very sensitive to any criticism. When criticized, they tend to denounce the criticizer angrily. Under usual circumstances, these individuals tend to be haughty, consciously self-satisfied, and boastful of their achievements. Unconsciously, they tend to feel insecure, inferior, often to the point of feeling worthless.

2. *Self-Other Relationships.* Individuals with narcissistic characteristics are extraordinarily self-centered and relate to others in a supercilious and essentially exploitative manner. They expect others to recognize their achievements (whether reality based or not), cater to their needs, support their endeavors, and never contravene them. In fact, where possible, they

tend to surround themselves with fawning and subservient followers. They can sponsor, praise, or validate others as long as these others serve their needs. Otherwise, they are quick to disparage their detractors.

3. *Reality Orientation.* Narcissistic individuals can differ in the accuracy of their reality testing, depending on other facets of their personality and pathology. However, as a rule, they will defensively distort their perceptions of self and environment to protect their exaggeratedly positive or grandiose self-image. These distortions can include outright denial of weaknesses, rationalizations and externalizations for any self shortcomings, and projections of faults onto others.

4. *Identity.* Overall, the narcissistic individual possesses an identity characterized by a sense of "specialness." They usually view themselves as particularly talented in some area of endeavor and feel that they are entitled to receive from others constant adulation and service. When thwarted or demeaned in any real or imaginary way, they also feel entitled to vent anger on the perceived culprit. They also tend to depend on outer circumstances to confirm and sustain their sense of specialness.

AGING, NARCISSISM, AND PSYCHOPATHOLOGY

Clinical observations and empirical research have long noted a potential relationship between the aging process and threats to self-esteem and psychological well-being (Cath, 1963; Gatz, Kasl-Godley, & Karel, 1996; Palmore, Cleveland, Nowlin, Ramm, & Siegler, 1985; Pfeiffer, 1977). The threats to self-esteem may develop from external sources, such as retirement, widowhood, death of friends, relatives, or acquaintances, and loss of income or social status. Internal changes may also challenge one's sense of worth and esteem, such as illness, physical and cognitive decline, and the expanding existential realization that time and opportunity for growth, pleasure, achievement, and life itself are contracting rapidly.

Nevertheless, the majority of older adults appear to deal with the negative life stressors of the later years without significant change in self-image, self-esteem, or mental health (Gatz et al., 1996; Ruth & Coleman, 1996). As pointed out in an earlier work (Jacobowitz & Newton, 1990), the relative success of older adults to cope with potentially debilitating life events or psychological changes can be linked to a number of factors. These include (1) intact personalities capable of mourning losses, finding substitutes, maintaining gratifying and supportive relationships developed earlier in life, and altering aims and goals to fit the realities of aging; (2) supportive social frameworks that provide aging individuals with socially satisfying interactions, psychological, physical, and economic support, and an overall sense of belonging to some meaningful social context; and (3) previously developed economic resources, including provisions for health care. These and other resources permit the older adult to actively neutralize and frequently transcend the threats to well-being (Tornstam, 1994).

The ability to deal adaptively with age-normative and even unexpected life events (such as loss of children), however, does not extend to all older adults. There are those who react poorly to the aging process, many of whom develop overt and diagnosable psychopathology. Gatz et al. (1996) point to three categories of such individuals. There are those individuals who developed their pathologies earlier in life and carry their symptoms to the later years. There is a second group who have had various vulnerable dispositions toward psychopathology, but avoided the development of overt symptomatology until one or more of the age-related stressors precipitated a mental illness. Finally, there are essesentially healthy people, probably the minority of cases, who develop psychiatric symptoms for the first time during the later years as a direct result of significant decrements or injuries to biological, social, cognitive, or environmental structures, or some combination thereof.

Our own clinical work with older adults in psychiatric settings (Jacobowitz & Newton, 1990) has led us to examine in detail the history, dynamics, and treatment courses of those patients in the second category. In general, we found that patients prone to develop psychopathology during their later years tended to have childhood histories marked by inadequate, harmful, or painful interactions with parents or significant caregivers. These patients defended against the resultant injuries to self security, esteem, and competence by developing certain defenses and coping styles that became aligned with a lifestyle that they cultivated during the early adult years. There were identifiable defensive patterns of adjustment, including avoiding repetition of early painful relationships by becoming totally independent, unconsciously repeating childhood relationships in adult intimate interpersonal interactions in an effort to change or master the original painful relationships, and nurturing certain skills, talents, or areas of perceived strength to compensate for underlying feelings of inferiority or shame induced originally by parental criticism or rejection. Whatever the particular pattern, each had a rigid quality that closed off certain areas of personal, social, vocational, and economic development during the young and middle adult years. Moreover, individuals employing these defensive strategies never resolved their childhood pains or consequent vulnerabilities. During the later years of life, their defensive structures were undermined by events that disrupted or terminated those elements of their lifestyles that were crucial to the maintenance of self-esteem and cohesion. Not only were they at that point confronted with the long repressed and unresolved issues of childhood, but they also lacked many of the social and environmental supports facilitative of normal adaptation to aging. The combination of threats to internal organization and external support systems seemed to precipitate their late-onset psychopathology.

Among the patients who developed psychopathology during the later years were those who fit the criteria for the Narcissistic Personality Disorder according to the *DSM-IV* (APA, 1994) or who came very close to doing so. Although these patients varied in terms of gender, age (between 60 and 85), marital status, education, severity and kind of psychopathology, and other factors, they possessed some common personality and social characteristics. They all believed they were special in some way (although when they requested therapy, they all felt "broken," disparaged, and angrily discarded by society). They all had interpersonal histories with spouses or partners whom they paradoxically idealized but simultaneously exploited to gratify their sense of specialness. They all demonstrated noteworthy—often dramatic—distortions and exaggerations in describing their achievements and in rationalizing their failures. They all had fairly traumatic childhoods, characterized by one or more of the following: parental instability, death, alcoholism, desertion, severe neglect, or sustained hostility. Finally, despite some adulthood periods of economic or social achievements, they all faced poverty or utter isolation when they sought treatment.

Interestingly, in general, they turned out to be amenable to treatment, or more specifically, as detailed in the next sections, at least to a certain kind of psychotherapeutic treatment.

PSYCHOTHERAPY WITH THE OLDER ADULT NARCISSIST

POSSIBILITIES OF TREATMENT

Older adults with narcissistic personalities rarely come to therapy to change their personalities or major features of them. Their modal presentation is a symptomatic one, usually composed of debilitating depression, which, in their minds, is a reaction to life events that they have experienced as demeaning and insurmountable. They may initially express a sense of personal failure, frequently in the form of maintaining that previous skills, aptitudes, and valued traits have been taken from them by circumstances beyond their control. Sometimes, they will point to age itself as one factor in their downfall. However, noteworthy is their contention that their depression or psychological distress is a consequence of losing their characteristic ways of relating to others, the self, and the world at large; they don't express the thought, or fathom the expression of it by others, that it was *because* of their characteristic ways of relating that their fortunes (real or imagined) declined and disappeared. Their perception of events is dramatically exemplified by Shakespeare's King Lear, who when realizing his loss of power and prestige, ragefully blames his daughters' ingratitude rather than his own vanity and poor judgment for his plight.

The therapist has three choices when constructing a strategy to treat these patients. The first is to treat only the symptom. This may be attempted with either medication or some form of supportive intervention to change the patient's environment or challenge his or her perception of the situation. Such attempts usually do not work well with these character-disordered individuals. Symptomatic relief, if it comes, does not relieve them of their preoccupation with their perceived loss of prestige and power or of their pervasive feelings of shame and anger. In fact, attempts to remove their symptoms quickly often arouse angry feelings directed toward the therapist. These patients usually expect practitioners to invest much time and thought in the treatment process. Any quick solutions are viewed by these patients as disrespect and another slight to their self-esteem.

A second strategy is to attempt to treat the underlying narcissistic personality structure. As mentioned earlier, there are two general approaches to treating such disorders. Both approaches were developed with younger adults. One approach entails mirroring the patient's needs and communicating in an ongoing empathic manner. These techniques are thought to enable the patient to feel safe, to relinquish some of the surface defenses, and, eventually, to regress to infantile narcissism. Once in this state, the patient may develop selfobject transferences that can be interpreted and eventually worked through (Kohut & Wolf, 1978). A second approach (Kernberg, 1974) begins the treatment with interpretation of the patient's narcissistic defenses. Eventually, the repressed or split off bad objects and related aggressive feelings will emerge via the transferences. Recognizing these destructive aspects of the psychological system, gaining insight into their origins and developmental consequences, and working through the psychological conflicts that they engendered can lead to a more healthy and stable psychological organization.

Both these approaches require long periods of time, patient motivation to change, and the availability of interpersonal and instrumental opportunities and potential gratifications in the patient's environment to help develop and sustain reality-oriented sources of self-esteem to replace the pathological ones. These necessary (but by no means sufficient) conditions for significant personality change are more readily extant in the lives of younger than older adults, particularly older adults past the age of 70. As mentioned above, older adults who have successfully employed narcissistic defenses for many decades are generally not motivated to relinquish those traits, which have become a hallmark to their identities. Moreover, they have alienated many people who could have served as realistic sources to their self-esteem as well as depleted the resources to succeed in instrumental or vocational aspirations. The limited social and economic opportunities for older adults contribute to the poor prospects of reality-based achievements commensurate with the narcissistic ambitions. Physical health also restricts the possibilities of many older adults to venture into new areas for development. All these factors, and others, conspire to reduce the chances of success for treating older adult narcissists with long-term psychotherapy aimed at structural change.

A third strategy that we have found useful is to remove the distressing symptoms while reconstituting the narcissistic defenses within an age-appropriate context. Reconstituting the narcissistic defenses means restoring the sense of specialness that the patient had experienced in the past by modifying the way that specialness is achieved and maintained. The patient is helped to reestablish a sense of self-worth by finding a line of continuity to the past (Griffin & Grunes, 1990), by reinterpreting the meaning of events that led to their perceived downfall (Cohler, 1993), by creating a new vision, or story of their current and future lives (Gergen, 1996), and by finding aspects of their current realities that can sustain their newfound grandiosity. This strategy does not aim to restructure the patient's personality but, rather, strives to resuscitate the vitality of the premorbid personality and make it viable under the new circumstances of the aging individual's life. It employs techniques derived from self-psychology (Kohut, 1971) and narrative therapy (Schafer, 1992). These techniques are described in the next section.

PRINCIPLES OF RECONSTITUTION

In this section, we describe what we have found helpful in treating the older adult patient with a narcissistic personality disorder. In the next section, we present short case examples of the techniques and its consequences.

The first principle of treating these patients is to accept their versions of their lives without questioning or challenging the often obvious distortions or exaggerations of their renditions. Even when depressed, these patients characteristically describe their past selves as possessing unique and extraordinary features while frequently demeaning other people. Attempts to question the accuracy of these depictions usually anger these patients, which can manifest in questioning, in turn, the therapist's expertise, or in fleeing treatment. In contrast, accepting their views of self, empathizing with the events they describe as injurious to those views, and relating to the patients in a respectful, caring manner generally will elicit their therapeutic participation. This nonconfrontive acceptance sets the stage for them to express freely both their former prosperous selves and current hurt selves, permitting an eventual dialectical reconstitution of a new-old self.

Once these patients feel accepted and "revered" even, they tend to begin to idealize their therapists. The idealization of the therapist manifests in praise for the therapist's skills in listening, understanding, and comforting. Frequently, these patients imagine that their therapists have great talents extending beyond the therapeutic setting. Principle 2 of treatment is not to challenge these views of the therapist. Narcissistic patients tend to project onto the therapist their own lost sense of greatness. They will later "retake" this greatness from the therapist, using a form of projective identification. Statements, ideas, suggestions, and expressed possibilities by idealized therapists tend to be accepted by these patients as being "correct" and "useful." . . . as long as they don't criticize the patient. Patients frequently are able to feel important once again since they see that a person important to them (whom they made important) believes that they are important. In effect, their idealization rebounds back to them.

The idealization of other and reidealization of self is mediated by another aspect of the therapy. The third principle of the reconstitution therapy is to help the patient find an explanation for the events that precipitated the symptomatology. This "explanation" must protect the patient's self-esteem, and it usually entails externalizing the source of failure. An idealized therapist can introduce or reinforce the idea, for example, that a patient's age is responsible for his or her decline in aptitude, and that compared with other people of that age (and many people even younger), the patient still possesses extraordinary skills. Sometimes, an explanation may be found in "society's attitude" to older people. The explanations will vary from patient to patient, but the key factor of effectiveness is that the patient comes to perceive the source of injury as emanating not from a self-deficiency but from uncontrollable external forces.

The fourth principle of reconstitution is to help these patients find a way to express and maintain their perceived special skills within the context of their life situation. Usually, this requires some modification in what they consider is a valid achievement or recognition of their abilities and status. This modification, sometimes, requires changing their "story line": instead of being the great athlete, they become the great coach or expert critic; instead of being the great lover, they become the writer-or-teller of great love stories. To solidify their modified narcissistic identity, it is necessary to assure that their environment can tolerate (if not facilitate) these new activities. (Sometimes the patient never actually embarks on these new activities . . . but the possibility of beginning them becomes self-sustaining.)

The idealized therapist's crucial role is not only to move the therapeutic process along, but also to serve as the patient's main source of support, or "self-object" experience. Patients will generally rely on the therapist's valuation of them before expanding their audience to include others in the "real world."

Finally, it is difficult to predict the duration of reconstitution therapy. Some patients seem to reconstitute relatively quickly (within 6 months), and others continue therapy interminably. Probably the best rule of thumb for expected duration relates to both past characteristics of the patient and their current circumstances. Patients who have demonstrated in the past the capacity to be instrumentally and/or interpersonally successful have a greater chance of actualizing their modified ambitions (and thus terminating therapy) than those whose past "achievements" were obtained mainly through fantasy distortion and gross exaggeration. Similarly, those patients with relatively intact environmental supports (e.g., stable income, family, supportive friends, etc.) will succeed (and terminate) more quickly than those without such resources. When patients lack the requisite personal or environmental resources, or both, they may develop a dependent reliance on the therapist's sustaining idealized presence for the rest of their lives. Some of these latter patients develop "institutional transferences" if seen in organizational settings and are able to shift from therapist to therapist, while controlling their symptomatic distress.

The following case examples illustrate the variety of patients who present with narcissistic-related pathology. Despite the variety, however, the similarity across these patients demonstrates the underlying dynamics of narcissism well as the generalizability of the reconstituting therapy techniques. The limitations of space permit only highlighting the major diagnostic and therapeutic issues of each case.

CASE EXAMPLE 1

The Rebirth of a Great Salesman (GS)

GS was a 70-year-old white male who was referred by his cardiologist to an outpatient psychiatric clinic for psychiatric treatment. GS was very depressed. He claimed that he felt confused, indecisive, hopeless, dependent, a mere shadow of his former self. He said that he had lost all ability to enjoy leisure activities. These symptoms began after he suffered a heart attack, for which he had received treatment. His physician recommended that he return to work, but the patient had lost all interest, or more specifically, all self-confidence.

At the time of referral, GS was married to a woman 30 years his junior. He had two children with her, one boy of 13 and a girl of 11. This was GS's fourth marriage, and he had two other children who were now adults and married themselves. GS reported that during his adult years he had had many extramarital and intermarital affairs and could always (up until his heart attack) make love "at any moment, for any length of time." Now he felt desireless and impotent.

GS reported feeling "nervous" and "cowardly" these days. For example, when driving, he worried constantly whether he was speeding or in danger of losing control of the car. This nervousness he contrasted with his pre-heart-attack self: he was a former marine with martial arts skills who allegedly felt no fear of any human or circumstance. He had traveled throughout the world, never feeling endangered or ill at ease.

Perhaps, most important, GS felt he had lost his ability to sell. He had always prided himself on being a master salesman, someone who had made millions when and where he wanted. He had never, he said, thought twice about spending money, since he could generate income "at the drop of a hat." Now, however, he was in debt ("medical bills are killing me"), worried about how to support his family, and panicked that he had "lost his touch."

GS reported that his father had been an alcoholic when GS was growing up. When intoxicated at home, his father would often physically abuse GS and his mother. At age 11, GS stood up to his father, "beat him up," and told him never to hit his mother again. His father left home, and GS worked after school to help support his mother and himself.

A psychiatrist attempted to treat GS with antidepressant medication. GS complained of side effects and claimed the medications made him sleepy and interfered with his driving (he still needed to work as a traveling salesman). He stopped taking the medication.

Psychotherapy progressed surprisingly well with this patient. Initially, it was feared that this previously independent, narcissistic, imperious individual would resist being "dependent" or trusting of any other person, either male (whom he felt competitive toward) or female (whom he viewed as weak and needy). To obtain the patient's trust, the male therapist did not challenge GS's stories of prior success and glory. Soon, it became apparent that GS enjoyed telling his stories of yesteryear. The therapist increased the time of each session to encourage the idealized transference. The patient soon came to see the therapist as "nonthreatening," and, in fact, quite empathic and understanding. However, the patient complained that while being understood felt good, it didn't solve "real world problems." In particular, at that time, the patient felt overwhelmed by his medical bills and all the insurance forms he couldn't seem to manage. He felt the burden of owing money and the feeling that he couldn't generate enough income to break even.

At this point in therapy, the therapist decided to demonstrate his "power" by volunteering to help GS organize his insurance papers and medical bills. Week after week, therapist and patient categorized the insurance forms, and calculated precisely how much the patient owed the hospital and physicians. The resultant amount was less than the patient had anticipated. Moreover, the therapist arranged a meeting between the patient and the finance department of the hospital, and a reasonable payback plan was generated that relieved the enormous anxieties of the patient.

This intervention facilitated the idealized transference, and the patient began to perceive the therapist not only as a "man of understanding, but a man of action" who could be depended on. Sensing the patient's growing trust, the therapist suggested that: (1) the patient's lack of confidence had stemmed from his heart attack, and that it was natural to be fearful of it, particularly considering the patient's age and family status; (2) the patient could overcome his physical condition by following his doctor's orders, and dealing with technical issues of his lifestyle, much the way he handled his financial debt; and (3) the patient still had his usual charm and verbal skills, as he demonstrated time and again in therapy, and could return to being a master salesman if he could only accept the limitations that his health placed on him.

Gradually, the patient succeeded in generating enough income to pay off his medical bills. This event seemed to be a turning point in his life, as he claimed he now saw hope. A sense of competency returned to him. He began to feel extraordinarily successful once again, and boasted: "How many seventy-year-olds can do what I can do?" He said he discovered that experience can substitute for vigor, and that he had found his pathway back to the big leagues. He also, though, accepted his physical limitations and thought it was time to let his wife "grow up" and learn to take some responsibility (even though she had been working for many years, he had previously thought she was just "playing at working").

Finally, the patient said that as much as he enjoyed "shooting the breeze" with the therapist, there was no need to continue therapy. He no longer had the time for it.

CASE EXAMPLE 2

The Final Act of a Great Playwright (GP)

GP was an 80-year-old woman when she presented for treatment at a general hospital's outpatient psychiatric clinic. She was Caucasian, a widow, a mother of two adult daughters, and was living alone in a fashionable apartment in a wealthy neighborhood. She complained of severe depression, including suicidal ideation (though she had no plan to carry it out). Initially, she attributed her depression to two events: her 80th birthday (in her words, "I suddenly realized that I was old and finished"), and a significant drop in her savings ("I realized that my money and lifestyle were coming to an end"). Later, it also became known that these two events were preceded by two others: she felt romantically and professionally spurned by a professor of literature, who was 40 years her junior, and with whom she was taking a course at a local college; and she felt ignored by her grandson who recently became engaged and was spending more time with his betrothed than with her. This was the first time in her life that she sought out psychiatric help.

GP described her childhood as difficult. She was the youngest of four sisters and allegedly was "ignored" by them and her parents, the latter being extremely busy making ends meet. She said that even as a child she had exquisite tastes and manners, and, despite the lack of familial support, managed as a young girl to look always fashionable and attractive. She finished high school successfully, but was at that time unaware "of her extraordinary literary talents." A woman, she said, from her poor background had to work and did not have the luxury of time and leisure to pursue intellectual achievements. She worked as a secretary for a lawyer, who quickly marveled at her efficiency and "savoir faire." This lawyer was so struck by her grace and wisdom that he proposed to her within a year. They married, and from that time on she was treated as a "princess."

For the next 40 or so years, she devoted herself to creating and maintaining the most beautiful house—a mansion, really—in a rather exclusive neighborhood, where only the rich and prestigious lived. Her husband was very successful professionally and economically. GP raised her two daughters to acquire the best of social, aesthetic, and educational values and skills to be had. (Despite her efforts, her "heart broke" when her daughters married men "well beneath their status and talent . . ." Her eldest daughter married an alcoholic who eventually divorced her and left her to raise their son alone; and her youngest daughter married an "obnoxious, crude businessman," who lacked the sensitivity, warmth, generosity, and aesthetic tastes of GP's husband.)

When GP was about 60, her husband died after a prolonged illness. Shortly after this time, her eldest daughter had divorced and moved back into GP's home. GP spent time during the next years raising her grandson, while her daughter went out and worked. She described herself as the "best grandmother" a boy could have, and felt that she devoted her life to making her grandson happy. She said his friends were always jealous that they didn't have such an energetic, creative, and devoted caretaker.

By the time she reached age 70, her grandson and daughter had left her household, and GP decided to return to school. She always had an interest in writing, and she began taking classes as a special student at a local college. For one class, she wrote a one-act play, and was praised by her instructor; he thought she had talent. Thereafter, she wrote a three-act play, which eventually was adopted and performed by students in the college's theater department. GP thought that she was on her way to becoming the "Grandma Moses of the theater."

She never did write any more plays, though. She developed back and arthritic problems that limited her freedom of movement. Most of all, though, she had become friendly with a professor who was many years younger than she and was (she believed) flirtatious with her. Fantasies of a romantic liaison developed in her mind. However, he "one day" grew cold to her, and told her was too busy to engage in the long conversations over coffee that they were wont to have. She felt that this rejection by him not only meant that he didn't want her romantically, but also that he believed she was not the talented playwright that she thought she was. She felt crushed. As time progressed, and her savings dwindled (apparently she had always spent money with abandon, never realizing that it was a finite commodity), she grew more and more depressed. She also grew angry, blaming her parents, her sisters, society, and even her husband for having exploited her and having prevented her from developing her writing talents earlier in life. What purpose was there, she asked, to live any longer?

Her therapist accepted and mirrored her anger, her sense of loss of opportunity to write, her belief in her talent, and her concern that the world certainly missed the great literary contributions she could have made. GP requested extra sessions and was granted them. In addition, she frequently phoned the therapist between sessions. She claimed that the therapist was the only one now who lent an ear to her. Her daughters, grandson, and friends were all too busy for her. Ingratitude was her only payment for years of self-sacrifice, she said. But, as she riled against these people, she began to praise the therapist for his great patience and understanding. Within a month, she began to attribute to the therapist many, if not all, the traits she had previously ascribed to her deceased husband: gentleness, wisdom, altruism, sensitivity, and a gift for soothing others.

As this idealization crystallized, the therapist began to suggest that no age was too old to write. Despite the harsh way people and circumstances had treated her, she had lost not an iota of talent. The therapist stated that he was impressed by her knowledge of life and her ability to articulate that knowledge. He encouraged her to use her anger not as an inhibitor of her talent, but as a motivator. She should become a voice for the disenfranchised elderly, for the long-suffering women who were robbed of the opportunity to grow and develop themselves fully.

The patient reacted positively to such suggestions, although she needed recurrent encouragement when her anger and depression were roused by some negative comment by a daughter or relative. She also expressed continuous worry about her financial situation. To deal with the latter concern, the therapist arranged a meeting between her and her youngest daughter in his presence. The patient had been afraid to ask her daughter for financial help, feeling both humiliation and fear. The therapist assured her that he would present her case to her daughter. It turned out that the daughter not only was willing to help her mother (she was quite wealthy herself), but had offered financial help many times to her mother. GP said, "Well, I never thought you really meant it."

The patient continued therapy for another two years. She began working on what she believed would be her greatest play; however, her health began to decline, and she needed, she said, the insightful wisdom and skill of her therapist to keep her spirits high. Eventually though her health compelled her to leave her apartment, and she moved in with her daughter. She terminated therapy, saying, "I have my daughter back. I feel like I'm back home. Perhaps now I can give my play a happy ending."

CASE EXAMPLE 3

The Autobiography of a Great Technician (GT)

GT was a 70-year-old, African American, married (no children), high school educated, and retired man when he presented to an outpatient psychiatric clinic. He complained of depression, particularly a lack of interest in doing anything together with a growing sense of guilt. This depression had seemed to develop over the past year, and allegedly began when his wife of 45 years suffered a stroke. The stroke disabled her and she was confined to a wheelchair. GT devoted almost all his time caring for his wife.

The reason GT felt guilty was that he thought that he had caused his wife's stroke, not directly, but via years of "selfish behavior." This "selfish behavior," he added, was the result of numerous extramarital affairs that he had had since his marriage. (Even on their honeymoon, he said, he managed to sleep with another woman.) He acknowledged that the numerous affairs were not totally his own fault. That was because he was one of the world's greatest lovers, not only an especially handsome man, but also an artist at making love. Consequently, women would compulsively gravitate to him and seduce him mercilessly. He felt, however, that his wife no doubt suffered continually from his infidelities.

Guilt was only part of his explanation for his depression. After his wife's stroke, he decided that he owed it to her to retire to care for her full time. Despite his relative advanced age, his company did not want him to retire, since he was unquestionably the most talented electrical technician that they had. He never understood from where his talent emerged, but he discovered as a young man that he had an extraordinary ability to fix any electrical contraption. He related how his reputation had spread throughout the United States, and how companies would pay his transportation to service their machines, particularly the more complex ones, as only he had that special touch. Anyway, since retiring, he found the life of caretaking to be one of drudgery. Although he was happy that he could be of service to his wife, he seemed to have lost himself in his act of service. He also reportedly had lost his "erotic aura."

GT was generally healthy throughout his life. The one exception he noted was the time he had a "nervous breakdown" during his first year in the armed services. From his description of his symptoms, it sounded as if he had had a panic attack, and possibly a dissociative reaction, during a combat situation. Other than that incident, he reported that he had been a generally optimistic, cheerful, energetic, competent, and intellectually gifted individual.

GT reported that he had a good childhood. His father, like himself, was a talented man and was a great farmer. He and his family lived among White farmers when he grew up. His father was so successful at work that the other farmers relied on his father for help. GT described his mother as a very cultured and intellectually gifted woman who encouraged him to pursue higher education. The family hoped that he would become a physician.

However, GT's father died when he was 11. The family was forced to move to town. It was during high school that GT encountered prejudice against Blacks. He said that this was a difficult time for him because he had always considered himself "an educated White person." He now found it difficult to identify with either the White or Black culture.

After high school, he served in the armed services. After his discharge, he used his "special talents" to succeed financially. He met his wife, who was the most beautiful woman in town. After they married, she opened a fashion boutique. He said they became the "beautiful couple." His wife couldn't conceive and they never had children.

GT reported that it was a pity that circumstances did not permit him to pursue a college education. He said that everyone who met him believed that he must be an intellectual, since he had great knowledge of the world and had a talent for both verbal and written expression.

GT's therapist listened to GT's stories of success in love and work attentively. The therapist expressed understanding and concern about GT's current predicament: both women and the work world had lost a great contributor. As GT unburdened his heart and related self-adulating stories of past triumphs, he began to view the therapist as an "exceptional listener, a veritable artist in the practice of therapy." He praised the therapist's wisdom (even though the therapist did little but validate the patient's sense of specialness). The therapist agreed to extend the time of sessions, as GT had much to tell and the telling seemed to relieve him of the "heaviness that oppressed" him.

Gradually, the therapist suggested that though GT had good intentions in helping his wife, he apparently overdid his self-sacrifice. His sense of having lost his "erotic aura" and vitality was interpreted as a result of this great self-sacrifice he had made. The therapist added, though, that he was certain that GT had not actually lost any of his talents, and that there was no need for him to renounce all his pleasures. There were ways of obtaining help for his wife that would at least free him for some time during the week to pursue activities that could meet his needs.

GT decided that he had "done" enough in his life, and now was the time to help and guide others to do things in their lives. The therapist remarked that given his talents for expression, his knowledge of the world, and the unique experiences of his past life, he should consider sharing his wisdom with others. GT decided that he could do this by writing his autobiography. It would be filled with both "salacious and instructive" material, he said. Who could resist such a work? He arranged through a home health care organization help with caring for his wife, thus freeing him to work on his autobiography.

Soon after, GT terminated therapy, feeling vital once again. He expressed gratitude to the therapist for helping him find a new direction in life.

CONCLUSION

We have tried to demonstrate that it is possible to treat successfully older adults with narcissistic personality disorders, or narcissistic features, with psychotherapy. In our clinical work, we have found that the most effective way of working with these patients is to try to reconstitute their premorbid defenses and self-concepts with certain modifications necessitated by the many physical, financial, social, and psychological correlates of aging. Reconstituting their personalities is a compromise between the therapeutic strategies of merely eliminating symptoms (which is difficult with people suffering from personality disorders, generally, and narcissistic disorders, in particular) and strategies that attempt to alter the underlying structures of personality. We also presented some cases illustrating the technique, dynamics of change, and the consequences of such reconstitution therapies.

Although we had success with the techniques described in this chapter, we don't want to leave the reader with the impression that one can't employ other approaches to treating narcissistic disorder. We are sure that there are individuals who can benefit from more uncovering and restructuring therapies. There are also patients who may respond to symptom relief strategies. It is necessary, though, to conduct a full diagnostic workup, and based on the results, determine the probabilities of each strategy working for that particular individual. In the majority of cases, the reconstituting therapy will be the most appropriate with older adult narcissistic patients, given these patients' long-standing character disorders, established personal identities, and the relative lack of opportunities for change and growth for many older adults.

This approach, however, has certain limitations. For example, many patients with narcissistic features possess other characteristics (such as borderline characteristics) that do not facilitate idealizing transferences. These latter patients may hate or reject the therapist, and additional techniques are required to deal with these negative transferences. Other patients with narcissistic features or disorders may lack the requisite ego or self resources to deal with their narcissistic injuries in even a modified way. These patients may use psychotic, particularly, delusional ways of compensating for their losses. Here, too, other techniques are required.

Nevertheless, many patients can benefit from the treatment approach we described as reconstituting therapy. In particular, it seems suitable to those individuals who in many respects were successful during their adult years in using adaptively their narcissistic defenses and self-concepts. Though these defenses also contributed to their vulnerabilities during the later adult years, they were, paradoxically, their greatest cultivated strengths. Facilitating or reviving these strengths in therapy can alleviate the symptomatic presentation. These patients may remain vulnerable to further injuries to self-esteem, but age-appropriate modifications to the strategies of maintaining self-esteem may reduce the chance of symptomatic recurrences.

Our conclusion: where there's life, at any age, there's still hope for continued "greatness."

REFERENCES

American Psychiatric Association. (1994). *Diagnostic and statistical manual of mental disorders* (4th ed.). Washington, DC: American Psychiatric Association.

Cath, S.H. (1963). Some dynamics of middle and later years: A study in depletion and restitution. In N.E. Zinberg & I. Kaufman (Eds.), *Normal psychology of the aging process* (pp. 21–71). New York: International Universities Press.

Cohler, B.J. (1993). Aging, morale, and meaning: The nexus of narrative. In T.R. Cole, W.A. Achenbaum, P.L. Jakobi, & R. Kastenbaum (Eds.), *Voices and visions of aging: Toward a critical gerontology* (pp. 107–133). New York: Springer.

Cooper, A.M. (1981). Narcissism. In S. Arieti (Ed.), *American handbook of psychiatry* (pp. 297–316). New York: Basic Books.

Erikson, E.H. (1963). *Childhood and society.* New York: Norton.

Freud, S. (1986). *On narcissism: An introduction.* In A.P. Morrison (Ed.), *Essential papers on narcissism* (pp. 17–43). New York: New York University Press. (Original work published 1914)

Gatz, M., Kasl-Godley, J.E., & Karel, M.J. (1996). Aging and mental disorders. In J.E. Birren & K.W. Schaie (Eds.), *Handbook of the psychology of aging* (4th ed., 365–382). San Diego: Academic Press.

Gergen, K.J. (1996). Beyond life narratives in the therapeutic encounter. In J. E. Birren, G.M. Kenyon, J.E. Ruth, J.J.F. Schroots, & T. Svensson (Eds.), *Aging and biography: Explorations in adult development* (pp. 205–223). New York: Springer.

Goldstein, E. (1995). When the bubble bursts: Narcissistic vulnerability in mid-life. *Clinical Social Work Journal, 23,* 401–416.

Gottschalk, L.A. (1990). Origins and evolution of narcissism through the life cycle. In R.A. Nemiroff & C.A. Colarusso (Eds.), *New dimensions in adult development* (pp. 73–91). New York: Basic Books.

Griffin, B.P., & Grunes, J.M. (1990). A developmental approach to psychoanalytic psychotherapy with the aged. In R.A. Nemiroff & C.A. Colarusso (Eds.), *New dimensions in adult development* (pp. 267–283). New York: Basic Books.

Jacobowitz, J., & Newton, N. (1990). Time, context, and character: A life-span view of psychopathology during the second half of life. In R.A. Nemiroff & C.A. Colarussso (Eds.), *New dimensions in adult development* (pp. 306–330). New York: Basic Books.

Kernberg, O.F. (1974). Further contributions to the treatment of narcissistic personalities. *International Journal of Psychoanalysis, 55,* 215–240.

Kohut, H. (1971). *The analysis of the self.* New York: International Universities Press.

Kohut, H. (1977). *The restoration of the self.* New York: International Universities Press.

Kohut, H., & Wolf, E.S. (1978). The disorders of the self and their treatment: An outline. *International Journal of Psychoanalysis, 59,* 413–425.

Lazarus, L.W. (1980). Self-psychology and psychotherapy with the elderly: Theory and practice. *Journal of Geriatric Psychiatry, 13,* 69–88.

Miller, A. (1979). Depression and grandiosity as related to forms of narcissistic disturbances. *International Journal of Psychoanalysis, 6,* 61–76.

Nemiroff, R.A., & Colarusso, C.A. (1980). Authenticity and narcissism in the adult development of the self. *Annual of Psychoanalysis, 8,* 111–129.

Nicholson, A.L. (1990). Narcissism and narcissistic impairments: A perspective from self-psychology. *Psychotherapy in Private Practice, 8,* 99–117.

Palmore, E.B., Cleveland, W.P., Nowlin, J.P., Ramm, D., & Siegler, I.C. (1985). Stress and adaptation in later life. *Journal of Gerontology, 34,* 841–851.

Pearlman, S.F. (1993). Late mid-life astonishment: Disruptions to identity and self-esteem. *Women and Therapy, 14,*(1-2), 1–12.

Pfeiffer, E. (1977). Psychopathology and social pathology. In J.E. Birren & K.W. Schaie (Eds.), *Handbook of the psychology of aging* (pp. 650–671). New York: Van Nostrand-Reinhold.

Pulver, S. (1970). Narcissism: The term and the concept. *Journal of the American Psychoanalytic Association, 18,* 319–341.

Ruth, J., & Coleman, P. (1996). Personality and aging: Coping and management of the self in later life. In J.E. Birrin & K.W. Schaie (Eds.), *Handbook of the psychology of aging* (4th ed., pp. 308–322). San Diego: Academic Press.

Schafer, R. (1992). *Retelling a life: Narration and dialogue in psychoanalysis.* New York: Basic Books.

Sorensen, M.H. (1986). Narcissism and loss in the elderly: Strategies for an inpatient older adults group. *International Journal of Group Psychotherapy, 36,* 533–547.

Stolorow, R.D. (1975). Toward a functional definition of narcissism. *International Journal of Psychoanalysis, 56,* 179–185.

Tornstam, L. (1994). Gero-transcendence: A theoretical and empirical exploration. In L.E. Thomas & S.A. Eisenhandler (Eds.), *Aging and the religious dimension* (pp. 203–225). Westport, CT: Greenwood Press.

Winnicott, D.W. (1965). *The maturational processes and the facilitating environment: Studies in the theory of emotional development.* New York: International Universities Press.

CHAPTER 28

Interpersonal Psychotherapy for Late-Life Depression

GREGORY A. HINRICHSEN

Although depressive disorders are relatively rare in community-dwelling older adults (Weissman, Bruce, Leaf, Florio, & Holzer, 1991), they are usually the most frequent problem treated by mental health professionals. An array of psychotherapeutic modalities may be utilized in the treatment of depression both in earlier and in later life. In recent years, "empirically supported" psychotherapies that have clearly demonstrated their utility in the treatment of specific disorders have been the focus of much professional interest. Several psychotherapies have met empirical tests of their success in treating depression in younger adults. However, fewer studies have documented the efficacy of psychotherapy of late-life depression. Emphasis on understanding the scientific foundation on which health-related interventions are made may also be found in the field of medicine. Advocates of "evidence based medicine" have argued that too often medical interventions are based more on habitual practice than on a contemporary understanding of which interventions have proven efficacy. Although this approach is not without controversy, it reflects recent efforts to provide health care services in the most efficient manner possible, the proliferation of health maintenance organizations, and the need to be responsive to demands by patients for health care interventions that have a reasonable likelihood of success.

In the treatment of depression, Interpersonal Psychotherapy of Depression (IPT; Klerman, Weissman, Rounsaville, & Chevron, 1984) has a well-established record of success. It has been shown to significantly reduce depressive symptoms in the majority of younger adults. There is also evidence that it is successful in treating late-life depression. Its focus on the treatment of interpersonally relevant issues that precede the onset of depression, or that are interwoven with depression, appear especially applicable to concerns of older adults who often confront a variety of changes in their interpersonal worlds. These include loss of loved ones, transitions in their social roles, conflicts with significant others, or the need to acquire new social skills to deal with changing life circumstances.

In this chapter, I review historical concerns by social gerontologists about the social and interpersonal well-being of older adults, research on family relations and the course of psychiatric illness in younger and older adults, the theoretical and empirical origins of IPT, and what I view as the particular suitability of an IPT approach to the treatment of late-life depression. The structure of IPT, specific issues in its application to older adults, and problems that may arise in conducting IPT are reviewed. I draw on the experience of using IPT at our institution and use case material to illustrate its application.

SOCIAL WELL-BEING OF THE ELDERLY

From the very beginning of the field of gerontology, concerns have been expressed about the social well-being of older adults. It was clear to early gerontologists that late life was a time of social change and transition. Sociologists described the loss of social roles that had previously served to integrate older adults, most notably the roles of worker and parent. Social roles define who we are and without them older adults confront what has been characterized as the "rolelessness" and "normlessness" of later life. Social isolation and a lack of meaning were viewed as possible catalysts for reduced morale, anomie, and depression (Rosow, 1966). One facet of social relationships, family relations, has received particular attention. Early gerontological writing expressed concerns that while family relationships played an important role in the lives of older adults, modern life had fractured the nuclear and extended family, further isolating older people. Although research has consistently documented that the state of family relations is on a solid footing (Shanas, 1979), nonetheless, adult children are generally more salient in the social worlds of older adults than they are in their children's. This has been characterized as differences in "generational stake" (Bengtson & Kuypers, 1971). Sharp increases in physical morbidity and mortality among the elderly confront them with many issues. Physical illness in one's self may circumscribe activities including those with friends and family as well as signal the realization that one's physical vehicle is vulnerable and ultimately finite. Physical or cognitive loss in one's partner or spouse may be associated with loss of companionship as it had been known or, in the case of dementia, the incremental loss of the very personhood of the individual with whom one's life has been intimately connected. Death of spouse or friends further circumscribes social opportunities and confronts older adults with feelings of grief as well as larger issues of meaning. These and other social stresses have been tied to a number of indicators of poorer emotional well-being including depression (George, 1994, 1996).

THE IMPORTANCE OF FAMILY
RELATIONS IN PSYCHIATRIC ILLNESS

A large body of research from the field of psychiatry has examined the role of family in the etiology and course of psychiatric disorders. Early literature postulated that problems in family relationships in childhood increased vulnerability to psychiatric difficulties in adult life (Bateson, Jackson, Haley, & Weakland, 1956). Although contemporary perspectives place primacy on biological factors as the most salient factor in the genesis of major psychiatric disorders, early childhood trauma and family dysfunction are thought to increase vulnerability. In the past 25 years, most research has examined how the family's response to psychiatric illness in a relative may increase vulnerability to illness relapse. An impressive body of research has consistently found that criticism, hostility, and emotional overinvolvement of family members toward the psychiatric patient, characterized under the rubric "expressed emotion," greatly increase vulnerability to relapse in schizophrenia and depression (Koenigsberg & Handley, 1986). Interestingly, in one study simply asking depressed individuals how critical they felt a spouse acted toward them was tied to much higher rates of depressive relapse (Hooley & Teasdale, 1989).

A related body of work has examined the impact of depression on social relationships. Weissman and Paykel (1974) found, for example, that depression significantly impaired women's ability to function in their social roles as wife, mother, homemaker, and worker. Even after the episode of depression ended, the adverse impact of depression on relationships with significant others was slow to resolve. Recent work from the National Institute of Mental Health Collaborative Treatment of Depression Research Program documented that over 5 years the psychosocial impact of affective illness was "surprisingly severe, enduring, and pervasive (Coryell et al., 1993, p. 723).

In an especially interesting theoretical piece on depression, Coyne (1976) postulated that the interpersonal dynamics of depression were especially problematic. He argued that an interpersonal downward spiral developed between the depressed person and a significant other, most typically a spouse. Initially, the spouse actively responds to the depressed relative's affective distress with numerous efforts to relieve the distress. Efforts to help may be rejected by the depressed relative or do not seem to bring the desired effect. Eventually, the spouse feels increasing frustration, which is directly or indirectly communicated to the depressed relative. These expressions only confirm the depressed relative's negative evaluation of self as well as engender guilt in the spouse. Redoubled efforts to help the depressed relative bring further frustration, expressions of anger, and greater feelings of distress in the relative. Eventually, the spouse begins to disengage from the relative, further heightening the relative's feelings of isolation, self-loathing, and depression.

RESEARCH ON INTERPERSONAL
ISSUES IN LIFE DEPRESSION

Although a substantive body of work has addressed interpersonal issues in depressed younger adults, relatively little has examined depression in late life. Some have suggested that late-life depression has a contagious quality and have argued that family members of depressed older adults are themselves at risk for developing depressive symptoms (Gurland, Dean, & Cross, 1983). Research at my own institution, Hillside Hospital-Long Island Jewish Medical Center, has longitudinally examined questions pertaining to family members' experience of and response to depression in their older relatives.

In a study of 150 older people hospitalized for major depressive disorder who had spouses or adult children providing care during the episode of depression, family members were asked to report the most important problems they confronted in providing care to the depressed older relative. Seven major problem areas were reported. The most frequently mentioned problem was interpersonal difficulties in contending with the depressed older person; notably, efforts to help the depressed person did not seem helpful or were rejected (Hinrichsen, Hernandez, & Pollack, 1992).

We were interested in understanding what factors were tied to the course of the older person's depression over one year. Patient and family demographic characteristics as well as data on the older person's current and past psychiatric history were measured. Reports by the family member that they themselves were experiencing higher levels of psychiatric symptoms, more reported problems in caring for the patient, and greater strain in the patient-family member relationship were tied to a poorer course of illness over one year (Hinrichsen & Hernandez, 1993; Zweig & Hinrichsen, 1993). These data are consistent with studies of younger depressed persons. Further, in a subset of 54 family members, we examined the influence of expressed emotion on the course of depression in the older depressed patient (Hinrichsen & Pollack, 1997). Adult children who expressed criticism toward the older relative or who were emotionally overinvolved, had parents with a poorer course of depression over one year. In contrast, older patients who had spouses who were critical or emotionally overinvolved with them fared better. Findings suggest that expressed emotion is mediated by the relationship. For example, some older patients may interpret criticism from adult children negatively whereas criticism from spouses may be seen as evidence of concern.

INTERPERSONAL PSYCHOTHERAPY IN THE
TREATMENT OF DEPRESSION

IPT is a time-limited psychotherapy for the treatment of depression. It is manualized and makes explicit the goals and focus of treatment as well as the general issues that are addressed at each phase of treatment. The therapy places primary emphasis on interpersonally relevant issues that may precede depression or are a result of depression. Theoretically, its roots are in the interpersonal school of psychiatry, which emphasizes the interplay of the person and social environment (Sullivan, 1953). Empirically, it is based on research from social psychiatry and studies of the influence of social factors on emotional well-being. The efficacy of IPT has been demonstrated in numerous studies in the acute treatment of major depression (DiMascio et al., 1979; Elkin et al., 1989; Weissman et al., 1979). Maintenance-continuation studies have also demonstrated its utility in the treatment of major depression (Frank et al., 1990; Klerman, DiMascio, Weissman, Prusoff, & Paykel, 1974). In younger patients, IPT has been adapted for the treatment of other depressive disorders (dysthymia), other psychiatric disorders (bulimia), and specific patient groups (HIV infection, primary care, bipolar disorder; Klerman & Weissman, 1993). IPT is listed is an established treatment for major depression by a number of national organizations including an American Psychological Association Division of Clinical Psychology Task Force (Task Force on Promotion and Dissemination of Psychological Procedures, 1995).

IPT is typically conducted over 16 sessions in three phases of treatment. In the initial phase (Sessions 1–3) four major topics are reviewed:

1. A careful assessment of the patient's symptoms is conducted. In the case of older adults, it is particularly important that any medical basis for the patient's depression be ascertained by a physician. Using the *DSM* (American Psychiatric Association, 1994) psychiatric nosology, a name is given to the patient's psychiatric condition. Major depressive disorder is described as a medical illness for which there are treatments including psychotherapy and medication. The patient is told that commonly depressive illness impairs one's ability to function. In view of this, the patient may temporarily reduce daily obligations until feeling better (characterized as giving the patient the "sick role.") The patient is then evaluated for whether antidepressant medication is indicated.

2. Current and past important relationships are reviewed as they might be tied to the depressive symptoms. An "interpersonal inventory" is taken in which the patient reviews the nature of important relationships, differences in expectations within them, satisfying and unsatisfying aspects of the relationships, and what changes the patient would like to make in relationships.

3. An interpersonal problem area is identified from one or two of the four problem areas that are the focus of IPT: Grief, Interpersonal Dispute, Role Transition, and Interpersonal Deficits.

4. The therapist's understanding of the problem is summed up for the patient. Treatment goals are agreed on. The nature of IPT treatment is explained (e.g., the here-and-now focus of IPT, need for the patient to discuss important concerns during treatment hours, and practical aspects of treatment such as session length, fee).

In Phase 2 of treatment (Sessions 4–13), therapeutic treatment strategies are implemented within one or two of IPT's four interpersonal problem areas:

1. *Grief* is complicated bereavement. The major goals within this problem area are to facilitate the process of mourning and then to help the patient to reestablish relationships with others. Specific strategies to achieve goals within this and other interpersonal problem areas have been delineated.
2. *Interpersonal Dispute* refers to conflicts with a person significant in the patient's life. The goals of treatment include identifying and understanding the nature of the dispute, choosing a plan of action to deal with the dispute, and then modifying poor communication or expectations to bring about a satisfactory resolution of the dispute.
3. *Role Transition* is a major change in life circumstances. Goals for this problem area are helping the patient to mourn and accept the loss of the previous role, seeing the new role as more positive than it is currently viewed, and restoring patient self-esteem by developing a greater sense of mastery regarding the new role.
4. *Interpersonal Deficits* is a problem area for individuals who lack the social skills necessary to establish or sustain interpersonal relationships. The goals of treatment are to reduce the patient's social isolation and encourage the development of new relationships.

The final phase of treatment is termination (Sessions 14–16) in which there is explicit discussion of the end of therapy, an acknowledgment that the end of treatment can be a time of grieving, and encouragement of the patient's independence and optimal functioning after the end of treatment. Several treatment techniques are used in IPT including exploration of options, encouragement of affect, clarification, communication analysis, use of the therapeutic relationship, behavior change techniques, directive techniques (psychoeducation, direct suggestions, modeling), and role playing.

IPT IN LATE-LIFE DEPRESSION

One area in which IPT has been adapted is for late-life depression. Early clinical reports suggested that IPT was useful for older adults. In the first research report on use of IPT with a small sample of older adults, it was found to be as effective as nortriptyline in the acute treatment of major depression (Schneider, Sloane, Staples, & Bender, 1986; Sloane, Staples, & Schneider, 1985). Interestingly, older adults receiving IPT had lower rates of dropout from the study than those receiving nortriptyline. The explanation was that side effects of nortriptyline prompted more dropouts from the medication treatment.

The largest study of IPT with the elderly was conducted at the University of Pittsburgh (Frank et al., 1993). The study found that, among elderly persons with recurrent major depression, openly treated with nortriptyline and IPT in the acute and continuation phases of the study, 78.7% achieved full remission from the major depressive episode (Reynolds et al., 1992). Among those elderly persons who had been successfully treated in the acute and continuation phases of the study, but who later experienced another episode of depression during the maintenance phase of the study, 80% evidenced remission from this subsequent episode when treated with both nortriptyline and IPT (Reynolds et al., 1994). Over a three year period, nortriptyline and monthly IPT each reduced rates of recurrence of an episode of major depression. The combination of IPT and nortriptyline was significantly tied to the lowest rates of recurrence of depression in the study (Reynolds et al., 1999). The researchers concluded that in elderly patients with recurrent major depression, combined IPT and nortriptyline treatments should be provided.

In another study, Interpersonal Counseling (IPC), a briefer form of IPT, was provided by psychiatric clinical nurse specialists to elderly people who were hospitalized for medical problems and who evidenced nondiagnosable but clinically significant symptoms of depression (Mossey, Knott, Higgins, & Talerico, 1996). Six months after receiving IPC, older patients had a greater reduction in depression symptoms and better self-rated health than older patients who did not receive the therapeutic intervention.

Initial work on the application of IPT to older adults suggested that adaptations would be needed for the elderly (Sholomskas, Chevron, Prusoff, & Berry, 1983). However, recent work indicates that little or no adaptation is needed. Overall, it appears that IPT can easily be conducted with depressed older adults, is useful in treating symptoms of depression in medically ill elderly, is as effective as nortriptyline in treating acutely depressed older adults, and in combination with nortriptyline, evidences efficacy in treating initial and later episodes of major depression.

USE OF IPT IN A GERIATRIC PSYCHIATRY CLINIC

Based on research on the importance of family interactions and the course of psychiatric illness in younger adults, my own research on family issues in late-life depression, and work demonstrating the utility of IPT in the treatment of earlier and late-life depression, IPT appeared to be a promising approach to the treatment of depressed older patients in the Geriatric Psychiatry Clinic at Hillside Hospital-Long Island Jewish Medical Center. The Clinic is part of a larger Division of Geriatric Psychiatry that includes an inpatient service, day hospital, and liaisons to area nursing homes. The Division also includes a large geriatric psychiatry fellowship, a postdoctoral clinical geropsychology fellowship, and extensive training of clinical and counseling psychology interns and externs. The Clinic has an average census of 450 older patients who present with cognitive, affective, psychotic, and family/marital problems.

Training in IPT was available locally at New York Hospital/Cornell Medical Center which is a prominent research and training site for IPT. This author received approximately one year of supervised experience conducting IPT with older adults. Sessions were videotaped, reviewed by the supervisor, and then discussed on a weekly basis. Subsequently, this author trained a clinical geropsychology colleague. At present, six mental health professionals have received training in IPT at our larger institution and IPT forms an integral part of the outpatient psychotherapy experience for clinical psychology interns who treat younger adults.

At the time of this writing, in the Geriatric Psychiatry Clinic we have provided IPT training to clinical geropsychology fellows and to selected psychology externs. Two psychologists in the Clinic also provide IPT to some depressed older adults. Overall, our experience has been positive. We find IPT is consistent with most older adults' initial expectations for treatment; it is problem-focused, time-limited, with an active therapist. IPT's problem areas generally encompass issues that depressed older adults bring to psychotherapy. Congruent with the observation of others (Miller & Silberman, 1996), we find that IPT requires relatively little adaptation with older adults. Notably, most of the older patients treated with IPT in our Clinic show significant improvement in clinical symptoms.

To date, 16 patients have been treated with IPT in the Geriatric Psychiatry Clinic. Fourteen patients completed the full course of IPT. The most frequent problem areas for focus of treatment have been Role Transition (7 patients) and Interpersonal Dispute (7). Two patients had Grief as the primary problem area and no patients presented with Interpersonal Deficits. Twelve patients had a diagnosis of major depressive disorder, 3 adjustment disorder, and 1 dysthymia. The average initial Hamilton depression rating scale score for patients with major depression was 19, for those with adjustment disorder 7.3, and for dysthymia 11. Of the 14 patients who completed IPT, 7 were receiving antidepressant medication. At the end of treatment, 11 of the 14 (78.6%) patients evidenced at least a 50% reduction of their Hamilton depression rating scale scores from onset of treatment with most no longer meeting criteria for a major depressive episode or adjustment disorder.

These clinical findings do not address the research question of whether IPT is uniquely associated with clinical improvement. Individuals were not randomly assigned to different treatments as in research studies and some received concurrent medication. Findings do suggest that most patients show significant improvement when clinically treated with IPT with and without medication. Why did some patients receive medication and others not? Usually patients themselves were reluctant to take antidepressant medication; or, they wanted to utilize psychotherapy as a first treatment. Our findings on the distribution of IPT problem area is similar to others (Miller & Silberman, 1996) who found that 43.2% of their patients had a primary problem area of Role Transition, 37% Interpersonal Dispute, 18% Grief, and 0.9% Interpersonal Deficits. We have achieved considerable success in retaining the majority of patients for a full course of IPT.

Of the two patients that did not complete treatment, the first patient entered treatment at the time she was deeply conflicted over whether to place her husband with dementia in a nursing home. Within the first few sessions of IPT, she decided to do this and felt that there was no longer any reason to continue psychotherapy. The second patient left treatment when her husband became gravely ill. She did not feel that she could continue treatment for practical reasons.

One patient showed virtually no change in her depressive symptoms at completion of treatment. She was a blind woman in her late 80s with numerous medical problems and a diagnosis of major depressive disorder. On referral, she was characterized as having mild cognitive impairment. After the first few sessions, it became apparent that her cognitive deficits were much more severe. Although we did not view mild cognitive impairment as a necessary bar to receiving IPT, her more severe deficits made it extremely difficult for her to retain the content of sessions. At completion of treatment, efforts were made with a family member to take an active role in changing social and environmental circumstances to improve her mood since she was unable to initiate these efforts herself.

PRACTICAL ISSUES AND PROBLEMS IN CONDUCTING IPT

In providing supervision to colleagues and students, as well as in conducting continuing education workshops, people frequently remark that they already include many of the elements of IPT in their existing psychotherapeutic work with depressed younger and older persons. This reflects that Klerman and colleagues' drew on their own clinical work to use psychotherapeutic approaches to the treatment of depression that seemed most effective in treating depression. IPT seems to make good practical sense to many clinicians since they have learned or identified similar approaches to the effective treatment of depression. However, particularly for individuals who have been trained primarily in longer-term exploratory, psychodynamic psychotherapies, the active stance of IPT may not come easily. In part, this may reflect a general uncomfortableness with brief therapy as a model but also with the IPT therapist's role of active collaborator and patient advocate. In brief therapy, each session is precious and therefore the therapist may need to steer the sessions in the direction of the goals of treatment and within the interpersonal problem area(s). The emphasis of many psychodynamic therapies on therapeutic neutrality and the development of transference within the psychotherapeutic relationship may militate against the kind of active back-and-forth that is evident in IPT. The here-and-now stance of IPT may also be uncomfortable for therapists used to spending considerable time on early childhood experiences that are viewed as critical in the genesis of current problems.

While therapists new to IPT will need to shift gears, so will some patients. If patients have had previous experience in psychodynamic therapies, they may assume that the content of sessions will focus on earlier life experiences. One elderly man in our clinic who had received psychoanalytically informed psychotherapy as a young man, assumed that treatment would focus on unresolved oedipal issues when, in fact, it seemed most useful to focus treatment on the interpersonal precipitants of a recent episode of major depression. In our experience, the majority of older patients easily adapt to the structure of IPT and, as noted earlier, generally find it consistent with their expectations for psychotherapy.

Some key elements in conducting IPT should be emphasized:

- Symptoms of depression are identified and frequently monitored.
- Depressive symptoms are tied to events that appear to be causally linked. These events are examined in detail.
- Options to deal with interpersonally relevant issues are continually explored. Patients are encouraged to experiment with changing their behavior in areas relevant to the interpersonal problem area.
- The therapist takes an active role in the therapy. There is more back-and-forth and give-and-take than in some therapies, particularly psychodynamic therapies.
- The therapy is relatively brief. With the therapeutic clock ticking, there is incentive for both therapist and patient to use sessions productively.
- Although the therapy is brief and has defined goals, there is still latitude to deal with problems that may unexpectedly arise in other areas of the patient's life or to discuss interpersonally relevant issues in some depth.
- Therapeutic gains are identified and attributed to the patient.
- The therapist remains hopeful and encouraging even if the patient is not hopeful.

SPECIFIC ISSUES IN CONDUCTING IPT IN EACH PHASE OF TREATMENT

The initial phase of treatment sets the whole tone for the therapy. It provides the framework for helping to understand the problem as well as the direction that will be taken. It should not be forgotten that the patient will take general clues from the therapist as to how to use the psychotherapy sessions. Not uncommonly, psychologists find IPT's characterization of depression as an "medical illness" uncomfortable. This reflects historical differences between psychology and psychiatry in how human problems are conceptualized. It also reflects the feeling of some that the mental health field has become too "medicalized." The fact remains, however, that biological changes accompany major depression; major depression may result in functional impairment that is as or more severe than many major medical illnesses; and it is a risk factor for suicide. The primary intent of presenting major depression as an illness is to relieve patients of the considerable self-blame they may experience for their own symptoms. Some individuals simply attribute their lack of interest or inability to function in the social or occupational domains as laziness or weakness. Particularly for some elderly people, an illness model makes sense. During treatment, the monitoring of symptoms provides concrete evidence that depression is improving.

During the middle phase of treatment, it is important to keep in mind the goals of therapy. Although IPT affords latitude for discussion of many issues, it is the therapist's responsibility to keep the therapy on track. Given the number of possible concerns that could be discussed in even one hour of psychotherapy, the therapist must selectively attend to issues and facilitate discussion within the agreed on problem area or areas. Events from the previous week become especially valuable material to use in the therapy session. If, for example, a patient had a serious dispute with the spouse, a detailed analysis of the incident provides fruitful material for understanding what happened and how things might go differently next time.

In the final phase of IPT, most patients are doing much better and are often grateful for the therapist's help. It is important to attribute the patient's success to the patient's efforts. The goal is to reinforce the patient's sense of him- or herself as an active agent who has dealt with issues of concern. Some patients feel quite sad about ending therapy, feelings that are normalized and discussed in this phase. Problems anticipated by the patient after the end of therapy can be reviewed, with options explored for dealing with them. Usually options will be gleaned from skills that have been developed or refined in therapy. Some patients may want to continue psychotherapy. Usually this is appropriate if patients have a long history of depressive symptoms (as in the case of dysthymia) or have a partially resolved episode of major depression and it appears that further sessions would be helpful. In fact, there is precedent from the research literature in providing "maintenance IPT." Yet, it is important to formally demarcate the end of the acute phase of IPT before continuing further sessions. What if the patient is not doing better? The patient's disappointment needs to be acknowledged as well as the reality that there are many treatment options. If the patient is not taking antidepressant medication, this option should be considered. If the patient is already taking an antidepressant, the patient might discuss a dosage change with the psychiatrist. Other psychotropic medications might be considered. Other psychotherapies for the treatment of depression are another option.

ISSUES IN CONDUCTING IPT WITH THE ELDERLY

As noted earlier, we find that IPT requires relatively little adaptation for older adults. Some older adults who have no familiarity with psychotherapy may need additional time in the initial phase to discuss the nature and purpose of IPT. As discussed, the therapist must be sure that any medical basis for the depressive episode has been assessed. One issue confronted by some older adults is care for a relative with dementia. For these patients, IPT's interpersonal problem focus is usually Role Transition and/or Interpersonal Dispute. However, there is also a considerable amount of grief over the gradual loss of the impaired relative. Although as originally conceived, IPT's problem area, Grief, refers to feelings of loss over an individual who has died, it may be useful to use elements of the goals and strategies developed for grief to help the caregiver come to terms with the partial or anticipated loss of the person with dementia.

WHERE TO GET TRAINING

It should be emphasized that a major resource in conducting IPT is the original treatment manual published as *Interpersonal Psychotherapy of Depression* (Klerman et al., 1984). This well-written, clinically friendly book describes all the elements for conducting IPT. It includes useful case examples. There is no consensus on whether faithfully applying the book without supervision is adequate for conducting IPT, but it provides a solid foundation. There is also a companion booklet written for patients, *Mastering Depression: A Patient's Guide to Interpersonal Psychotherapy* (Weissman, 1995).

Training opportunities have lagged behind the favorable findings from many of the empirically supported treatments, including IPT. Although IPT is listed as a treatment for major depressive disorder for adults in the American Psychiatric Association's *Practice Guidelines* (Karasu et al., 1993) and the U.S. Department of Health and Human Service's *Clinical Practice Guidelines* for treatment of depression in primary care settings (Depression Guidelines Panel, 1993), only a relatively small cadre of individuals do IPT at present or can provide supervision for persons learning IPT. For established professionals, the presence of academic or clinical research centers where IPT is conducted often dictates whether training is available. Even fewer individuals have experience in conducting IPT with the elderly. John Markowitz, MD in the Department of Psychiatry at New York Hospital-Cornell Medical Center (New York) has compiled a list of mental health professionals with IPT expertise some of whom may be available to provide supervision. Sometimes individuals who have been formally trained in IPT are willing to provide telephone supervision on cases when geography does not permit in-person supervision. Each year, there are continuing education workshops at major professional meetings on IPT or at established continuing education programs. There are current discussions among senior IPT figures as to what might constitute minimal supervision for persons interested in conducting IPT. In most research studies, IPT therapists are required to conduct three complete audio or videotaped IPT cases with ongoing supervision.

Graduate students with interest in IPT may want to review available IPT training through doctoral internships or postdoctoral fellowships. Graduate students might consult the *Directory of Predoctoral Internships with Clinical Geropsychology Training Opportunities and Postdoctoral Clinical Geropsychology Fellowships* distributed by American Psychological Association's (APA) Division 12, Section II (Clinical Geropsychology), a copy of which may be obtained by writing to this author. APA's Division 12, Section III (Society for a Science of Clinical Psychology) also publishes the *Directory of Training Opportunities for Clinical Psychology Interns*, which lists programs that provide didactic and supervisory experiences in empirically-supported treatments.

The following are examples of older adults treated with IPT within the Role Transition and Grief problem areas, respectively. Some information has been changed to disguise the patients' identities.

CASE EXAMPLE: ROLE TRANSITION

NB was an 78-year-old married woman who had enjoyed remarkably good health throughout her life. She characterized herself as a very independent woman with a wide range of interests, many of which she had cultivated and pursued after retirement in her early 70s. Two years previously, she had a seizure following which she was hospitalized and treated with antiseizure medication. She had no prior history of seizures and the cause of the seizure was never identified. By law, she was not permitted to drive an automobile unless she was free of seizures for at least one year. This was a serious disappointment to NB who relied on her car to pursue her many activities. While she circumscribed her activities, she expected that the seizure was an isolated incident and that she would be able to drive again within a year. Eleven months after the first seizure, she had another one. She said she was "devastated" and that it felt like her body was "falling apart." In the next year, she significantly reduced her social involvements and became increasingly depressed. At the onset of treatment, she met criteria for a major depressive disorder with a Hamilton depression rating scale score of 13.

During the initial phase of treatment, NB's depression-related symptoms were reviewed and she was told that she had a major depressive disorder. Her medical condition was reviewed with her physician. NB was not interested in antidepressant medication and acknowledged that she resented taking antiseizure medication. Relationships with important others were reviewed. The fact that the depression followed her second seizure was emphasized. Her difficulties were conceptualized within IPT's Role Transition problem area. That is, she had made a transition from a physically healthy individual to someone with a seizure disorder, a condition that required adaptations in her life. Adjustment had been difficult for NB and with a subsequent major depression, adaptation was even more difficult.

During the middle phase of treatment the patient discussed her anger and disappointment about the seizure disorder. She acknowledged that, at her age, many of her contemporaries had health problems yet she felt she would be the exception. Loss of ability to drive had symbolic as well as practical consequences. She felt she had to ask her husband to take her everywhere. She resented this dependence on her husband and thought that he also resented her increased reliance on him. Her solution had been to significantly reduce activities yet she missed her "old life." Therapy focused on what she wanted from her life now and how she could achieve it despite the possibility of another seizure. Options for resuming previously enjoyed activities and friendships were explored including transportation arrangements. From a discussion with her husband, she learned that he did not resent driving her. She recollected that friends had made frequent offers to drive her to events but stopped after her consistent refusals. She realized that there was a public bus stop near her home. She investigated and learned that the bus line would take her to many of the places she used to frequent. As she began to resume former activities, her mood improved. She expressed more acceptance of the reality of her health problem. She experienced particular satisfaction in mastering the public transportation system, which she had never used.

By the time the patient had entered the final phase of IPT, she had developed a workable way to get to where she wanted, had resumed some of her previous activities, and had a Hamilton depression rating scale score of 3. She no longer met criteria for a major depressive disorder. During the final sessions, the progress she had made was reviewed and her active role in achieving that progress was underscored. The patient expressed some sadness and nervousness about terminating treatment. This was acknowledged by the therapist as a fairly common response to the end of psychotherapy.

CASE EXAMPLE: GRIEF

OC was an 83-year-old married man with an episode of major depressive disorder and a likely lifelong history of a generalized anxiety disorder. On entry into treatment, his Hamilton depression rating scale score was 30. He said that about 1 $\frac{1}{2}$ years prior to beginning treatment, his brother had died. In the following months, two friends whom he had known since childhood died. Following these losses, he became increasingly anxious. Eventually he brought his concerns to the attention of his family doctor, who prescribed benzodiazepines. Although the medication seemed to relieve some of the anxiety, he grew more and more pessimistic. Reluctantly, he acknowledged, "I even thought about ending my life." Review of his symptoms indicated that while anxiety was a prominent part of his clinical picture, so was depression. It appeared that he had symptoms of a clinical depression for about 6 months. The onset of the depressive symptoms were tied to the loss of three persons close to him. He said that he had not made this connection but acknowledged that it was possible that anxiety and depression were tied to these losses. The IPT problem area, Grief, was identified, and the treatment plan and goals were discussed. In addition to IPT, treatment included initiation of antidepressant medication and a change of his antianxiety medication by a psychiatrist.

During the middle phase of treatment, the patient first discussed his relationship with his brother. He discussed how distraught he was to watch his brother's physical deterioration from an extended illness. He described the scene at his brother's deathbed and the moment "when he took his final breath." He experienced guilt over the failure to carry out his brother's funeral services in a manner he felt his brother would have wanted. While initially characterizing his relationship with his brother as loving and amiable, he later acknowledged that he disapproved of many ways in which his brother acted. Later in therapy, he also reviewed different facets of his past relationships with his two deceased friends. He expressed sadness that the long years had ended, yet satisfaction that he had the friendships. OC's life had been organized around visits to his brother's home and outings with his friends. OC said that while his wife had encouraged him to visit with other friends and family, it became harder and harder to do so as he became more depressed. OC's wife joined two sessions to discuss her relationship with him and their social involvements. She voiced frustration over his lack of interest in things and pointed out many activities they could do together. In subsequent sessions, different options for enlarging social involvements were reviewed including increased visits with children, attendance at a senior center, and renewed acquaintance with other friends. OC later made efforts to increase social involvements.

By the final phase of treatment, OC's Hamilton depression rating scale score had reduced to 7. While still experiencing ongoing anxiety, he no longer met criteria for a major depressive disorder. OC's remission from major depression, his efforts to come to terms with his grief, and enlargement of his social life were underscored. OC seemed generally comfortable with the termination of IPT. He continued to see a psychiatrist for evaluation of his medication after the end of IPT.

CONCLUSION

In view of changes in the interpersonal worlds of many older adults, IPT appears to be a particularly well-suited therapeutic modality for this age group. A solid body of research supports its efficacy in the treatment of depression in younger adults and a growing body of work supports it usefulness for older adults. IPT can be conducted with older adults with little adaptation from the original treatment manual. The brevity of therapy and active stance of the therapist are appealing to many older adults we have treated with IPT. Our clinical experience is that almost 80% of elderly people with major depressive disorder and adjustment disorder show significant reduction in their depressive symptoms when clinically treated with IPT alone or in combination with psychotropic medication.

REFERENCES

American Psychiatric Association. (1994). *Diagnostic and statistical manual of mental disorders* (4th ed.). Washington, DC: Author.

Bateson, G., Jackson, D.D., Haley, J., & Weakland, J. (1956). Toward a theory of schizophrenia. *Behavioral Sciences, 1,* 251–264.

Bengtson, V.L., & Kuypers, J.A. (1971). Generational difference and the "developmental stake." *Aging and Human Development, 2,* 249–260.

Coryell, W., Scheftner, W., Keller, M., Endicott, J., Maser, J., & Klerman, G. (1993). The enduring psychosocial consequences of mania and depression. *American Journal of Psychiatry, 150,* 720–727.

Coyne, J.C. (1976). Depression and the response of others. *Journal of Abnormal Psychology, 85,* 186–193.

Depression Guidelines Panel. (1993). *Clinical practice guideline: Depression in primary care: Treatment of major depression* (Agency for Health Care Policy and Research Publication 93–0551). Rockville, MD: U.S. Department of Health and Human Services, Agency for Health Care Policy and Research.

DiMascio, A., Weissman, M.M., Prusoff, B.A., Neu, C., Zwilling, M., & Klerman, G.L. (1979). Differential symptom reduction by drugs and psychotherapy in acute depression. *Archives of General Psychiatry, 36,* 1450–1456.

Elkin, I., Shea, M.T., Watkins, J.T., Imber, S.D., Sotsky, S.M., Colins, J.F., Glass, D.R., Pilkonis, P.A., Leber, W.R., Docherty, J.P., Fiester, S.J., & Parloff, M.B. (1989). NIMH treatment of depression collaborative research program: 1. General effectiveness of treatments. *Archives of General Psychiatry, 46,* 971–982.

Frank, E., Frank, N., Cornes, C., Imber, S.D., Miller, M.D., Morris, S.M., & Reynolds, C.F. (1993). Interpersonal psychotherapy in the treatment of late-life depression. In

G.L. Klerman & M.M. Weissman (Eds.), *New applications of interpersonal psychotherapy* (pp. 167–198). Washington, DC: American Psychiatric Press.

Frank, E., Kupfer, D.J., Perel, J.M., Cornes, C., Jarrett, D.B., Malliner, A.G., Thase, M.E., McEachran, A.B., & Grochocinski, V.J. (1990). Three-year outcomes for maintenance therapies in recurrent depression. *Archives of General Psychiatry, 47,* 1093–1099.

George, L.K. (1994). Social factors and depression in late life. In L.S. Schneider, C.F. Reynolds, B.D. Lebowitz, & A.J. Friedhoff (Eds.), *Diagnosis and treatment of depression in late life* (pp. 131–154). Washington, DC: American Psychiatric Press.

George, L.K. (1996). Social factors and illness. In R.H. Binstock & L.K. George (Eds.), *Handbook of aging and the social sciences* (4th ed., pp. 229–253). San Diego: Academic Press.

Gurland, B.J., Dean, L.L., & Cross, P.S. (1983). The effects of depression on individual social functioning in the elderly. In L.D. Breslau & M.R. Haug (Eds.), *Depression and aging: Causes, care, and consequences* (pp. 256–265). New York: Springer.

Hinrichsen, G.A., & Hernandez, N.A. (1993). Factors associated with recovery from and relapse into major depressive disorder in the elderly. *American Journal of Psychiatry, 150,* 1820–1825.

Hinrichsen, G.A., Hernandez, N.A., & Pollack, S. (1992). Difficulties and rewards in family care of the depressed older adult. *Gerontologist, 32,* 486–492.

Hinrichsen, G.A., & Pollack, S. (1997). Expressed emotion and the course of late life depression. *Journal of Abnormal Psychology, 106,* 336–340.

Hooley, J.M., & Teasdale, D.J. (1989). Predictors of relapse in unipolar depressives: Expressed emotion, marital distress, and perceived criticism. *Journal of Abnormal Psychology, 98,* 229–235.

Karasu, T.B., Docherty, J.P., Gelenberg, A., Kupfer, D.J., Merriam, A.E., & Shadoan, R. (1993). Practice guideline for major depressive disorder in adults. *American Journal of Psychiatry, 150,* 1–26.

Klerman, G.L., DiMascio, A., Weissman, M., Prusoff, B., & Paykel, E. (1974). Treatment of depression by drugs and psychotherapy. *American Journal of Psychiatry, 131,* 186–191.

Klerman, G.L., & Weissman, M.M. (1993). *New applications of interpersonal psychotherapy.* Washington, DC: American Psychiatric Press.

Klerman, G.L., Weissman, M.M., Rounsaville, B.J., & Chevron, E.S. (1984). *Interpersonal psychotherapy of depression.* New York: Basic Books.

Koenigsberg, H.W., & Handley, R. (1986). Expressed emotion: From predictive index to clinical construct. *American Journal of Psychiatry, 143,* 1361–1373.

Miller, M.D., & Silberman, R.L. (1996). Using interpersonal psychotherapy with depressed elders, In S.H. Zarit & B.G. Knight (Eds.), *A guide to psychotherapy and aging* (pp. 83–100). Washington: American Psychological Association.

Mossey, J.M., Knott, K.A., Higgins, M., & Talerico, K. (1996). Effectiveness of a psychosocial intervention, interpersonal counseling, for subdysthymic depression in medically ill elderly. *Journal of Gerontology: Medical Sciences, 51A,* M172–M178.

Reynolds, C.F., Frank, E., Perel, J.M., Imber, S.D., Cornes, C., Miller, M.D., Mazumdar, S., Houck, P.R., Dew, M.A., Stack, J.A., Pollock, B.G., & Kupfer, D.J. (1999). Nortriptyline and interpersonal psychotherapy as maintenance therapies for recurrent major depression: A randomized controlled trial in patients older than 59 years. *Journal of the American Medical Association, 281,* 39–45.

Reynolds, C.F., Frank, E., Perel, J.M., Imber, S.D., Cornes, C., Morycz, R.K., Mazumdar, S., Miller, M.D., Pollock, B.G., Rifai, A.H., Stack, J.A., George, C.J., Houck, P.R., & Kupfer, D.J. (1992). Combined pharmacotherapy and psychotherapy in the acute and continuation treatment of elderly patients with recurrent major depression: A preliminary report. *American Journal of Psychiatry, 149,* 1687–1692.

Reynolds, C.F., Frank, E., Perel, J.M., Miller, M.D., Cornes, C., Rifai, A.H., Pollock, B.G., Mazumdar, S., George, C.J., Houck, P.R., & Kupfer, D.J. (1994). Treatment of consecutive episodes of major depression in the elderly. *American Journal of Psychiatry, 151,* 1740–1743.

Rosow, I. (1966). *Social integration of the aged.* New York: Free Press.

Schneider, L.S., Sloane, R.B., Staples, F.R., & Bender, M. (1986). Pretreatment orthostatic hypotension as a predictor of response to nortriptyline in geriatric depression. *Journal of Clinical Psychopharmacology, 6,* 172–176.

Shanas, E. (1979). Social myth as hypothesis: The case of the family relations of old people. *Gerontologist, 19,* 3–9.

Sholomskas, A.J., Chevron, E.S., Prusoff, B.S., & Berry, C. (1983). Short-term interpersonal therapy (IPT) with the depressed elderly: Case reports and discussion. *American Journal of Psychotherapy, 4,* 552–566.

Sloane, R.B., Staples, F.R., & Schneider, L.S. (1985). Interpersonal therapy versus nortriptyline for depression in the elderly. In G. Burrows, T.R. Norman, & L. Dennerstein (Eds.), *Clinical and pharmacological studies in psychiatric disorders* (pp. 344–346). London: John Libbey.

Sullivan, H.S. (1953). *The interpersonal theory of psychiatry.* New York: Norton.

Task Force on Promotion and Dissemination of Psychological Procedures. (1995). Training in and dissemination of empirically-validated psychological treatments: Report and recommendations. *Clinical Psychologist, 48,* 3–23.

Weissman, M.M. (1995). *Mastering depression: A patient's guide to interpersonal psychotherapy.* Albany, NY: Graywind.

Weissman, M.M., Bruce, M.L., Leaf, P.J., Florio, L.P., & Holzer, C. (1991). Affective disorders. In L.N. Robins & D.A. Regier (Eds.), *Psychiatric disorders in America* (pp. 53–80). New York: Free Press.

Weissman, M.M., & Paykel, E. (1974). *The depressed woman.* Chicago: University of Chicago.

Weissman, M.M., Prusoff, B.A., DiMascio, A., Neu, C., Gohlaney, M., & Klerman, G.S. (1979). The efficacy of drugs and psychotherapy in the treatment of acute depressive episodes. *American Journal of Psychiatry, 136,* 555–558.

Zweig, R.A., & Hinrichsen, G.A. (1993). Factors associated with suicide attempts by depressed older adults: A prospective study. *American Journal of Psychiatry, 150,* 1687–1692.

CHAPTER 29

Cognitive-Behavioral Therapy for the Treatment of Late-Life Distress

DAVID W. COON, KENNETH RIDER,
DOLORES GALLAGHER-THOMPSON, AND LARRY THOMPSON

THE EFFECTIVENESS OF COGNITIVE BEHAVIORAL THERAPY WITH OLDER ADULTS

The effectiveness of cognitive-behavioral therapy (CBT) with adult individuals diagnosed with depression, certain anxiety disorders and substance abuse disorders, and other psychosocial problems continues to be researched and well documented (e.g., Chambless & Hollon, 1998; Chambless et al., 1996, 1998; DeRubeis & Crits-Christoph, 1998; Nathan & Gorman, 1998; Sanderson & Woody, 1995). However, given the divergent sociocultural histories and unique life circumstances of our older clients, we cannot automatically assume that treatments effective with young or middle-aged adults are necessarily effective with today's elders (Gatz et al., 1998). Moreover, older adults who come to our offices have diagnoses and problems that are not as commonly found among other age groups (e.g., dementing illnesses, multiple bereavements, and retirement issues); and furthermore, considerable research and clinical experience supports the need to adapt our intervention protocols to meet the unique situations and needs of these clients (Gatz et al., 1998).

More relevant to the discussion of CBT and its application to older adults is the growing amount of evidence demonstrating the effectiveness and utility of *cognitive therapy* (e.g., Gallagher & Thompson, 1982; Scogin, Hamblin, & Beutler, 1987; Thompson, Gallagher, & Breckenridge, 1987), *behavior therapy* (Gallagher & Thompson, 1982; Scogin et al., 1987; Scogin, Jamison, & Gochneaur, 1989; Thompson et al., 1987), and *combined cognitive-behavioral* interventions (Fry, 1984; Gallagher-Thompson & Steffen, 1994; Steuer et al., 1984) in the treatment of older adults suffering from late-life depression. This evidence includes meta-analyses (Dobson, 1989; Scogin & McElreath, 1994) as well as recent reviews summarizing the empirical literature of older adult psychosocial therapies for treatment of depressed elders (Gatz et al., 1998; Niederehe, 1994, 1996; Scogin & McElreath, 1994; Teri, Curtis, Gallagher-Thompson, & Thompson, 1994; Teri & McCurry, in press). Moreover, several individual difference variables may influence these treatment outcomes, such as major shifts in depressive mood (Thompson, Gallagher-Thompson, & Thompson, 1995), length of time in stressful late-life situations such as caregiving (Gallagher-Thompson & Steffan, 1994), the quality of therapeutic alliance (Gaston, Marmar, Thompson, & Gallagher, 1988), and whether significant endogenous symptom features are present (Gallagher & Thompson, 1983). Future research should help us better understand these influences and learn to more effectively tailor CBT treatment to meet the needs of these clients or in contrast, to refer some of our clients to other forms of therapy found to be more effective for their specific problems, backgrounds, needs, and expectations.

CONCEPTUAL UNDERPINNINGS OF CBT

The abridged CBT intervention protocol described in this chapter, as well as its related intervention strategies and techniques, draws specifically from Beck's theory of the role of cognitions in the origin and maintenance of depression (Beck, Rush, Shaw, & Emery, 1979) and Lewinsohn's theory describing the role that lack of contingent positive reinforcement plays in the development and maintenance of depressive mood states (Lewinsohn, Muñoz, Youngren, & Zeiss, 1986). According to Beck, depression can both result from, and be intensified by, consistently held negative thoughts, attitudes, and beliefs about oneself, one's experiences, and the future—the so-called negative triad. These thoughts or beliefs create a negative lens through which one appraises the world; over time, this leads to the formation of certain errors in thinking that occur relatively automatically and that are self-reinforcing until they are challenged and new data are generated that show how erroneous the original patterns of thinking were. Finally, by systematically challenging negative cognitions and developing more adaptive and flexible ideas in their stead, one's emotional outlook will improve, and this in turn will reduce depression and improve everyday functioning. In contrast, according to Lewinsohn, greater primacy is placed on the interplay between behavior and emotional states: it is believed that depression results when there is repeated lack of contingent positive reinforcement in the person's life, such that the frequency of adaptive behaviors decreases, less positive social interaction occurs, and less pleasure (in general) is present on a daily basis. Over time, this pattern of behavioral withdrawal is itself reinforced, thus creating a vicious cycle whereby the individual does less and feels worse and worse about it. By increasing the rates of engagement in, and enjoyment of, everyday potentially pleasant activities, this pattern can be interrupted, and the person can regain control over his or her mood states by seeing the strong link between engagement in pleasant activities and the maintenance of positive mood.

CBT in our application with elders is a combination of these two theories, based on the rationale that maladaptive cognitions and behaviors (either singularly or in combination) can instigate and sustain late-life depression and related mental health problems. CBT is characterized by a directive, time-limited, structured approach designed to give older adults skills applicable to their daily lives. The cognitive component of CBT implements well-established techniques designed to teach clients to identify, challenge, and modify unhelpful thoughts related to the negative triad that feed their depressed affect (Beck et al., 1979). In contrast, the behavioral component of CBT teaches elders specific methods of behavior management such as tracking their daily activities and reporting subsequent fluctuations in their moods, and then identifying and increasing positive mood-enhancing activities to help alleviate their depression. The behavioral component also frequently incorporates relaxation techniques, assertiveness training, and problem-solving skills, depending on the client's needs.

The next section describes specific ways in which we use the CBT approach with older adults suffering from late-life depression or related disorders. This clinical protocol was developed and implemented successfully over the past decade with hundreds of outpatients at the Older Adult and Family Center (OAFC) of the VA Palo Alto Health Care System and Stanford University School of Medicine. It is described more fully in the current OAFC therapist and client treatment manuals (Dick, Gallagher-Thompson, Coon, Powers, & Thompson, 1996; Thompson, Gallagher-Thompson, & Dick, 1996) and is presented here in an informal style to concretely demonstrate CBT strategies with older adults, and to help bring this material alive.

Some of the material may have a familiar ring for CBT enthusiasts, reflecting our modification and extension of the work of Beck (Beck et al., 1979), Burns (1980, 1989), Lewinsohn (Lewinsohn et al., 1986) and Young (Young, 1990; Young & Klosko, 1993) to effectively meet the needs of older adults. However, space constraints allow us to present only a handful of the diverse array of CBT techniques and strategies we find particularly useful with elderly clients. In the following section, we address dealing with barriers to treatment and performing a comprehensive assessment, eliciting client target complaints, and then subsequently translating those complaints into therapeutic goals. Next, we describe basic CBT methods: introduction of the CB model to clients, how to use "Thinking Tools" to achieve client goals, a brief overview of the use of "Doing Tools," and how to consistently review and evaluate the progress of therapy. We conclude the section with a brief introduction to CBT schema or core belief change processes and a discussion of strategies for termination and relapse prevention. Creative applications are explored next. These include expansion of CBT beyond the basic individual model to meet the needs of a diverse population of elders and adaptation for successful groupwork and psychoeducational classes that address late-life distress. The concluding section offers suggestions for future research.

THE NUTS AND BOLTS OF CBT

BARRIERS TO TREATMENT

A host of factors can make it difficult for older adults to commit to a regular series of therapy appointments. At the OAFC, we generally require participation
in 16 to 20 individual sessions to achieve significant symptom reduction and
improved quality of life. Clients may be reluctant to give informed consent for
this, for several reasons:

1. They may have outmoded beliefs about psychotherapy, thinking that it is
   reserved for persons who are "crazy" or severely mentally ill (which perhaps has some historical truth). Older adults often need education about
   CBT and how its here-and-now, problem-solving orientation can benefit
   them in dealing with their problems in living.
2. Many older adults face significant physical limitations that require the
   therapist to move outside traditional office visits into nursing home and
   hospital or clinic settings. Even when these elders become more mobile,
   physical challenges can discourage them from traveling distances, meeting where parking or building access is difficult, and venturing out in in-
   clement weather. Lack of reliable transportation (e.g., dependence on
   family members), concerns about freeway traffic, and fear of crime or
   travel at night can also dissuade participation by both disabled and able-
   bodied elders.
3. Older clients frequently face many role conflicts and demands on their
   time, ranging from caregiving and grandparenting roles to volunteer
   service and full or part-time work that may be necessary to help make
   ends meet.
4. Cancellations and rescheduling of appointments can result from such realities as competing medical appointments, funerals, short-term illness,
   and caregiving crises or emergencies.
5. Clients with mild to moderate memory impairment will need therapist
   reminder calls and assistance with scheduling by using individualized
   memory cues.
6. Elders with memory or auditory and/or visual impairments can also find
   complex automated telephone instructions difficult to comprehend and
   sometimes overwhelming, leading to frustration and disinterest in beginning therapy.
7. A subgroup of today's elders are resistant to owning answering machines
   or to dealing with therapist voicemail messages and voicemail boxes.

Overcoming these challenges and engaging the elderly in therapy requires
patience, persistence, problem-solving, and advance planning on the part of
both parties to overcome both attitudinal and logistical obstacles.

ASSESSMENT

Before attempting to do CBT with an older adult, it is prudent to know the psychiatric diagnosis as well as to assess such factors as the client's cognitive skills, negative mood states, medical factors, and current alcohol intake. In many settings, a formal intake assessment and/or mental status examination is routinely done so that this information will be available before the first meeting with the client; in other settings, it is routine for the therapist to conduct assessment in the initial session(s). The latter is addressed briefly here; due to space limitations, the reader is referred to other reviews that address these issues in depth (cf. Edelstein, Staats, Kalish, & Northrop, 1996; Futterman, Thompson, Gallagher-Thompson, & Ferris, 1995).

Cognitive Skills

CBT makes several cognitive demands on clients, asking them to read, write, and comprehend concepts and engage in activities requiring memorization, problem-solving, and learning new material. Therefore, older clients should be screened for cognitive impairment. An instrument such as the Mini-Mental Status Examination (Folstein, Folstein, & McHugh, 1975) is efficient for this purpose; however, if time permits, or if there is any reason to suspect a significant cognitive problem, we recommend the COGNISTAT examination using all items (not just the screening ones). This takes about 15 to 20 minutes and if it appears that a cognitive problem does exist, clients should be referred for more detailed neuropsychological testing before engaging in therapy. It is always wise, especially when working with older clients, to be sensitive to even mild or minor changes in cognitive status to facilitate treatment delivery, receipt, and enactment. In our experience, CBT can be used effectively not only with cognitively intact elders, but also with those with mild to moderate dementia (see Teri & Gallagher-Thompson, 1991; Teri, Logsdon, Uomoto, & McCurry, 1997).

Mood

Assessment of various negative mood states is recommended to determine whether depressed mood alone is the target, versus a combination of negative affects, such as depression combined with anxiety and anger. We recommend either the Beck Depression Inventory (BDI) (Beck, Steer, & Garbin, 1988) or the long or short forms of the Geriatric Depression Scale (GDS) (Sheikh & Yesavage, 1986; Yesavage et al., 1983) to assess current level of depression. The GDS has the advantage of containing fewer somatic items and may have more face validity for older people. In addition, we routinely use the State-Trait Anxiety Inventory of Spielberger (STAI; 1983) to assess self-reported anxiety symptoms, and other scales such as the State-Trait Anger Expression Inventory (STAXI; Spielberger, 1988) to assess anger and frustration, all of which are common negative emotions found in older clients.

Medical Factors

With older adults in particular, chronic and/or acute medical illnesses often interact with psychosocial factors in the development and maintenance of affective disorders. Strongly encourage older clients to have a comprehensive physical examination and try to forge a working alliance with the client's physician to understand what medical conditions are present, and how they affect both function and the current medication regimen. Throughout assessment, treatment, and follow-up, one should keep medical factors salient (Haley, 1996).

Substance Use

Always ask older clients about current alcohol intake, as well as current medications (both prescribed and over-the-counter) since abuse or misuse of these substances can complicate treatment. A useful screening measure for alcohol abuse is the Michigan Alcohol Screening Test (MAST; Willenbring, Christensen, Spring, & Rasmussen, 1987). A more detailed discussion of this complex topic can be found in Dupree and Schonfeld (1996).

Interview

Client responses on self-reports measures (particularly for minority elders) can be inaccurate or incomplete, so we recommend a thorough personal interview before accepting a client into CBT. Interviews provide the opportunity to obtain a valuable sociocultural history and to identify other symptoms and situations, such as suicidal ideation, recent bereavement, ongoing caregiver distress, and social isolation, that require specific attention in their own right. For example, suicidal crises require immediate attention; see DeVries and Gallagher-Thompson (1994) for suggestions on handling these situations from a CBT perspective. During the interview, the client's written consent should be obtained so that relevant medical records can be requested and communication can be established with the primary care physician and other relevant service providers.

GETTING THERAPY STARTED

Use the following steps to get started:

1. Elicit target complaints that can be addressed within the CBT model.
2. Teach the CBT model to your client.
3. Elicit the client's cooperation within the context of a developing therapeutic alliance.
4. Engage the client in doing homework as part of treatment.
5. Translate target complaints into goals.
6. Prepare to monitor progress.

Elicit Target Complaints
We employ a six-item checklist to do this:

1. What is the target complaint?
2. In what situations does this occur?
3. What does the client attribute to the cause of this difficulty?
4. Has this problem come up before?
5. What strategies have been used in the past to cope with this problem?
6. The client rates the severity of this problem from 1 (least severe) to 10 (most severe).

Depending on the salience and magnitude of particular target complaints, we try to identify (in collaboration with the client) about three target complaints to address in therapy.

Teach the CBT Model to Your Client
A visual presentation helps clients learn and understand the cognitive model of depression and can be used effectively to build the collaborative therapeutic relationship. Figure 29.1 shows the model that we present on a whiteboard or easel. This simple diagram underscores that there are multiple reciprocal relationships among these four key areas of functioning. Clients are told that in CBT, the emphasis will be on modifying thoughts and behaviors to have impact on emotions, though their physical health and its effects may be involved as well. We find it helpful to personalize this discussion with material that clients present as part of their target complaints.

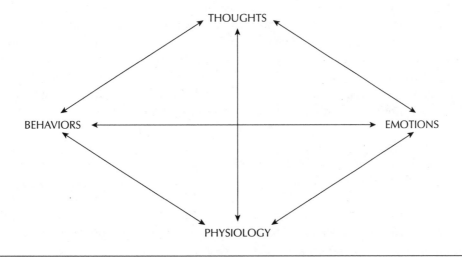

Figure 29.1   CBT model and reciprocal relationships.

Elicit the Client's Cooperation

First, we explore our client's past therapy experiences to help clarify how CBT differs from other therapies. CBT involves a collaborative relationship between therapist and client, also known as collaborative empiricism, in which both parties take an active role in understanding problems, defining goals, and working to achieve those goals. The commitment to actively change is hard work; therefore, help clients identify small rewards to give themselves whenever they complete a step toward each target goal.

Each CBT session is structured by setting an agenda at the beginning, to which the client contributes, followed by review of current mood and homework. The heart of the session is spent developing specific skills, and reviewing and summarizing what was discussed. In the last 10 minutes or so, clients are asked to summarize the session. This provides time for mutual feedback as to what was helpful about the session and what was not, as well as time for positive reinforcement for compliance with the focus of the session. Sessions end with written reminders of homework assignment(s) and confirmation of when to meet next time.

Engage the Client in Homework

Give clients homework at the end of every session and make homework review a priority at the beginning of every session. Doing this reinforces its importance for clients. If they avoid homework, engage them in dialogues around homework tasks, and then work together to find strategies to enhance compliance. Problem-solve rather than label this as resistance. Older adults often have concerns about the "right way versus the wrong way" to do homework, and you can defuse these notions by challenging these unhelpful thoughts in session. Also, work together to help manage distractions and organize specific times to get the homework done. Homework works best if it is related to a theme discussed during the current session and is closely tied to client target complaints and goals. Not all older adults respond well to the term "homework." Homework can bring up unpleasant associations, can be construed as demeaning or even create fear, since some elders have educational and/or sensory limitations that make it very difficult to complete reading and writing assignments. Using alternative terms such as practicing between sessions, working on assignments, and learning new habits can be helpful. It is also important to only assign homework that clients can realistically be expected to complete.

Translate Target Complaints into Goals

We explain to clients that goals are well-defined plans of change that must be realistic to achieve within the bounds of CBT and the time available (e.g., personality reconstruction is not likely to occur in 10 to 20 sessions, nor will major life difficulties be resolved, but a path can be charted and positive change begun in this time frame). Goals also need to be specific, rather than global, and measurable, so that progress can be monitored. Thus, an important part of the first few sessions is translating the client complaints into treatment goals. Many older adults come into therapy with vague goals such as: "I want to be over my depression for good" or "I want to feel more needed by my (adult) daughter and her family." These goals are based on feelings rather than tangible actions and are unrealistic in that they are too global to reasonably achieve. To transform these into goals, therapists can ask questions such as: "How do you know that you are depressed—what are the indicators you look for?" and then develop concrete plans from the responses (e.g., to sleep more through the night; to be out with people again; to be able to concentrate well enough to finish a book). Or to address the second general complaint, the therapist can refocus from the daughter's responses to the client's thoughts and feelings by asking questions like: "What kind of relationship do you have now with your daughter? Do you see one another regularly? Do you participate in caring for her children? What do you mean by 'feeling needed'? Is there a concrete way you will recognize this when it occurs? And what can we do to bring you closer to that ultimate goal?" By setting up intermediate or short-term goals, success experiences can occur, and clients can better maintain motivation to continue in treatment.

Prepare to Monitor Progress

From the very beginning of therapy, help clients avoid thinking that if goals are not reached quickly, "nothing" has been accomplished. Explain that progress on goals rarely occurs at a steady pace, or in a continuous direction, like a smooth curve. Teach clients to recognize and reward themselves for each step made toward achieving a goal and also encourage your client to evaluate the overall process, and not just compare results of only one week against another.

"THINKING" TOOLS—COGNITIVE INTERVENTIONS

Core components of CBT are to demonstrate that unhelpful thoughts create and/or reinforce negative emotions, and to help clients develop more helpful or adaptive thoughts. We use the following sequence to teach these skills: (1) introduce the 3-Column Daily Thought Record (DTR), (2) use it to identify unhelpful thought patterns, (3) help clients challenge these unhelpful thoughts, and (4) use the 5-Column DTR to complete the process and reinforce its continued use.

Introduce the 3-Column Daily Thought Record (DTR)

By using the form depicted in Table 29.1, clients notice thoughts that are associated with stressful events in their lives, gain practice distinguishing thoughts from feelings, and become more aware of how thoughts affect mood. Clients are also encouraged to assign a rating to each thought to show how strongly they believe it. This helps them understand the impact that unhelpful thoughts have on their mood and to identify which thoughts are most difficult to manage and which need immediate attention. These ratings are also useful for monitoring therapy progress. We suggest our clients use the following scale shown in Figure 29.2; it ranges from 0% (not strong at all) to 100% (completely true).

Table 29.1 Daily thought record.

Antecedent (A)	Belief (B)	Consequences (C)
A brief description of the stressful event	A list of the automatic thoughts they had in connection with this event	A list of the emotions that they experienced as a result

It is also important for clients to measure the strength of their emotional responses with a rating scale similar to the one for thought ratings, ranging from 0% (not present at all) to 100% (completely present). Some elders find that a 0-to-100 scale is too broad for them to use comfortably. In these instances, the scale can be modified (e.g., 1 to 10) as long as some kind of intensity rating is used that makes sense to the individual client.

Identify Unhelpful Thought Patterns
The following is a list of several negative thought patterns we find common among depressed older adults. Helping clients identify the patterns they use most frequently is essential so that they can then be examined and challenged:

- *Name calling* attaches a negative label to self or to others. ("I'm a loser," "I was a bad parent," "My husband is a real loser for developing Alzheimer's disease.")
- *Tyranny of the shoulds* are rules one has about the way things *should* be. ("I should or have to have a clean house before I go to the bridge group.")
- *Tune in the negative/tune out the positive* recognizes only negative aspects of a situation and ignores or discounts positive accomplishments.
- *This or that (no in-betweens)* views situations in terms of extreme outcomes. ("I'm either a success or a total failure," or "I never get things right, I am always messing up.")
- *Overinterpreting* is the tendency to blow events out of proportion without all the information and takes the little information provided as the truth without confirming its validity. This type of thinking can occur in three ways—(1) *generalization* draws conclusions with only a few facts; (2) *personalization* assumes that others have negative intentions toward or views of the client; (3) *emotional thinking* uses feelings as the basis for the facts of the situations ("I feel this, then it must be true").

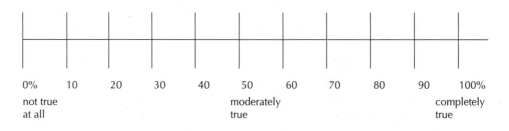

Figure 29.2 Scale for charting progress.

- *What's the use?* Clients believe that their thoughts or behaviors are not ever effective in changing their situations. ("Whenever I plan an outing for myself, it never goes as planned, so why try at all?")
- *If only* means spending time thinking of past events and wishing they had acted or said something differently. A variant of this is the idea: "If only things were the way they used to be, I could be happy again." This is one of the most common patterns observed in depressed older adults who cannot imagine their life being meaningful and enjoyable (at least to some degree) given their present circumstances, yet the circumstances are unlikely to change dramatically (e.g., getting one's career or spouse or health back as it was). It is a particularly "dirty trick."

Challenge Unhelpful Thoughts

To help challenge negative thought patterns, we teach clients one or more of the following techniques:

- *Action*   Clients can engage in specific behaviors to obtain additional information that challenges unhelpful assumptions about situations or people.
- *Language*   Clients change their actual language from negative to positive or harsh to compassionate to replace negative labels and comments with clear, realistic ones.
- *As If*   By changing the tone and language of self talk, clients learn to speak to themselves as if someone whose opinion they greatly respect is talking.
- *Consider Alternatives*   This technique instructs clients to think of a ruler that has 0 inches at one end and 12 inches at another—there are many inches in between as well as even smaller and smaller measurements; clients need to consider the range of alternatives.
- *Scale Technique*   Clients weigh the advantages and the disadvantages of maintaining the particular thought (or emotion, or behavior).
- *Examine Consequences*   Clients examine the specific consequences for each belief, and helps clients find they may have less interest in maintaining the belief.
- *Credit Positives*   This instruction tells clients to spend a few moments thinking of the more pleasant outcomes of events, and positive thoughts, and the positive emotional consequences that result, rather than just dwelling on the negative.
- *Positive Affirmations*   Clients are encouraged to develop some positive, personal statements to say when feeling overwhelmed with negative thoughts and emotions.

Introduce the Five-Column Daily Thought Record

This form adds (beyond A-B-C already described) Column D, which is a list and rating of the more realistic or adaptive thoughts to replace the unhelpful thoughts, and Column E, which is a list and rerating of the prior negative emotions (or new emotions that result). The focus here is on replacing unhelpful thoughts with more realistic ones by using the challenging techniques just covered. After introducing the concepts behind the last 2 columns, take some examples from a recent three column DTR that the client completed, and begin to work through the two new columns *in session.* Then, when the client understands what to do, this is used as homework for subsequent sessions. The following case illustrates this technique.

CASE EXAMPLE

Eloise, a 73-year-old widowed woman with numerous health problems, reported that her 50-year-old daughter Joan, who lives out of state, did not phone her last Sunday evening as she generally did (A, antecedent) and so she was feeling down (85%) and frustrated (75%) about this (C, consequences). This was associated with the thoughts that her daughter did not care for her and was too busy to remember how important these weekly phone calls were (B). Eloise was asked to examine the evidence (her beliefs) that her daughter did not call because she did not care for her: in fact, she usually *did* call, and typically visited at least twice per year, sent gifts on special occasions, and had her teenage children contact their grandmother regularly to tell her about their lives. She also was a very busy professional who traveled frequently all over the world, thus encountering different time zones and phone-calling systems. By discussing these facts, Eloise was able to revise her thoughts (D) to be more adaptive: Joan may have been in Asia again on business and just forgot or was too tired this time to call on schedule; it doesn't mean she doesn't care for me, but rather that something came up and I need to be understanding. Eloise then rerated her emotions and found that both her depression and frustration were reduced (about 45% each). Although they were still present, she decided to wait another week to see if she called before getting upset again. In fact, Joan did call in the interim, thus further improving her mood. Completing this exercise taught Eloise that she needed to "check out" her thoughts before overinterpreting her daughter's behavior, and by doing so, she could keep her negative emotions in check and maintain a better overall quality of life. Because this was helpful, Eloise continued to complete DTRs throughout therapy as part of her homework assignments.

"DOING" TOOLS—BEHAVIORAL INTERVENTIONS

These are drawn from behavior therapy and are based on the rationale that if we can convince depressed clients to increase their level of pleasant activities on a daily basis, then their mood will improve and related symptoms of depression will decrease. A discussion of these tools is beyond the scope of this chapter. But in sum, we use the following sequence to teach these skills: (1) learn to monitor daily mood, (2) identify potentially pleasant events with the Older Person's Pleasant Events Scale, (3) track occurrence of pleasant events, (4) compare mood ratings and pleasant events, and (5) increase the frequency of occurrence of pleasant activities, to achieve a minimum of at least *four* consciously chosen, deliberately done, events each day, to "keep the blues away." Finally, "doing tools" can also include relaxation strategies, guided imagery, assertive communication skills, and anger management techniques as needed for particular clients. All these techniques and strategies are described in more detail in our manuals (Dick et al., 1996; Gallagher-Thompson, Ossinalde, & Thompson, 1996; Thompson et al., 1996).

REVIEWING THERAPY GOALS

This is good to do at about the midpoint of therapy (about session 10 in our 20-session outpatient model). We examine CBT's usefulness by formally evaluating the progress of each treatment goal and determining whether any new goals are now identified as important to the client. This provides an opportunity for clients to consolidate the skills learned thus far and make some decisions about the remainder of therapy. Figure 29.3 shows a set of questions and ratings that can help with this process. In doing this task, clients and therapists may find

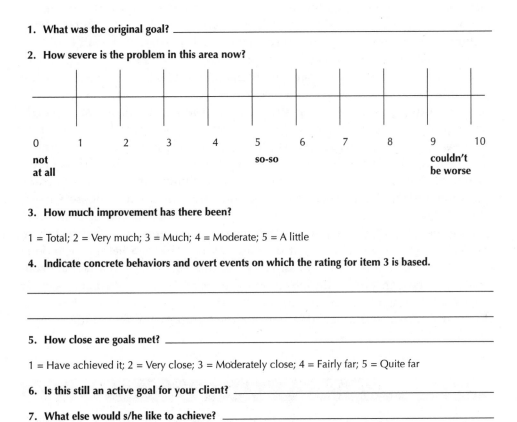

1. **What was the original goal?** _____

2. **How severe is the problem in this area now?**

```
 0    1    2    3    4    5    6    7    8    9    10
not                      so-so                 couldn't
at all                                         be worse
```

3. **How much improvement has there been?**

1 = Total; 2 = Very much; 3 = Much; 4 = Moderate; 5 = A little

4. **Indicate concrete behaviors and overt events on which the rating for item 3 is based.**

_____

_____

5. **How close are goals met?** _____

1 = Have achieved it; 2 = Very close; 3 = Moderately close; 4 = Fairly far; 5 = Quite far

6. **Is this still an active goal for your client?** _____

7. **What else would s/he like to achieve?** _____

Figure 29.3 Goal review—questions and ratings.

that either there is more work to do on each of the original goals or that additional goals have now arisen, which also can be addressed using this same procedure. Goal setting, review, and evaluation involve an "information intensive" process that may need to be spread over two or more sessions. Goal review also offers an opportunity for clients who were initially skeptical (or hopeless) about therapy to have a success experience documenting "real changes" in their lives. Of course, it is possible that original goals will have been met successfully at this point, and no new goals have arisen, so that termination can occur. Whether termination occurs now or later, it needs to be handled with sensitivity because, as discussed later in this chapter, the therapeutic relationship may be one of the only close relationships that the client has presently in his or her life.

Schema Work

Occasionally, interested and motivated clients at the OAFC are offered the opportunity to engage in longer term, more intensive work, focused on identification and modification of long-term core beliefs or schemas that significantly interfere with their functioning and are tied to long-term affective distress. Schemas are categorically and hierarchically organized rules that dominate client information processing and behavior (Beck et al., 1990; Young, 1990). Young defines these dysfunctional schemas as self-perpetuating and enduring themes that are often (though not necessarily) cultivated during childhood, elaborated on across the life span, and then secured as a lens for the processing of additional experiences. Although schemas are change resistant, client problems are often influenced by modification of a few or perhaps even a single schema (Beck et al., 1990; Young, 1990). Among the strategies that can be used to identify dysfunctional schema (Padesky, 1994), we have found two methods to be particularly helpful with older adults: Young's self-report Schema Questionnaire (Young, 1990) and the Down Arrow Technique (a method of Socratic questioning that moves client thinking from the automatic or more surface thought level to a deeper, core schema level). An example of the latter involves asking clients about the meaning of their negative thoughts, so as to direct them to think more deeply about what they are saying. This is a helpful technique when there is a realistically sad situation, so that thoughts and affect are consistent; in those instances, the Down Arrow method allows you to explore other levels of meaning for the individual beyond the surface or automatic level. The following case provides a good example of the Down Arrow Technique.

CASE EXAMPLE

Mary, a 75-year-old woman with chronic and severe pain from arthritis finds it difficult to get things done around the house. She called her son, who lives nearby, to help with an unexpected leak in the bathroom, but he was not able to get there right away. She was, understandably, sad and frustrated about this. By asking what this meant to her, Mary told the therapist she viewed herself as incompetent and was upset that she was dependent on her son for help. Further questioning elicited thoughts that she was a complete failure who could never do anything right; she also believed her son was tired of her asking him for help and would eventually move away so as not to have to keep taking care of her. This in turn, led her to believe that life really wasn't worth living unless she could be the way she used to be: healthy and independent. This core belief was very depressogenic and was underlying many of her more surface negative thoughts as reported on the DTR. By using the Down Arrow technique, the therapist was able to help Mary see how she built negative constructions on top of other negative constructions, so that a relatively straightforward event of everyday life took on many other meanings that had to be addressed if she was going to become less depressed.

Schema Work differs from the brief CBT model in four key ways: (1) treatment is longer in duration (perhaps an additional 6 months to a year); (2) the use of abreactive techniques and the experiencing of affect is more strongly encouraged; (3) the therapeutic relationship becomes more of a direct treatment focus in that thoughts and feelings about the therapist are actively elicited and worked on in sessions; and (4) cognitive and behavioral techniques are used to develop and integrate alternative positive schemas. Schema change techniques we have found especially helpful with older adults include the Historical Test of Schemas (Young, 1984), the continuum concept (e.g., Padesky, 1994), and abreactive techniques, such as the triple role play in which clients role play poignant life situations as the therapist models and coaches them to develop increasingly more effective responses based on positive schema substitution. Case examples of the use of these techniques by OAFC staff are available in the literature (e.g., Coon, 1994; Dick & Gallagher-Thompson, 1995).

Termination

We recommend the following components when terminating with older adults: (1) schedule the ending process, (2) introduce the maintenance guide, (3) teach clients to recognize "danger signals," and (4) establish strategies to handle these danger signals.

Schedule the Ending Process

We find it best to end therapy in a gradual and systematic way (rather than abruptly), helping clients disengage from the therapeutic relationship by spacing out the final few sessions to a biweekly or monthly basis. Typically "Booster Sessions" or check-ins are also scheduled after the last formal session to see how well clients continue to use the skills taught in therapy to combat their negative moods. Generally, boosters at 3, 6, and 12 months following termination give an excellent indication of how the client is doing, and whether additional therapy or referrals to other kinds of services (e.g., ongoing support groups) may be required.

Introduce the Maintenance Guide

The last few sessions focus on developing with your clients a written Maintenance Guide for them that serves as an aid to relapse prevention. It consolidates the client's therapy experiences by reviewing skills learned and preparing for possible setbacks and problems in the future. Start this guide in session; and, then ask clients to add to it for useful homework. Generally, we develop a special notebook or diary just for this aspect of therapy to be added to other materials the client has amassed during treatment. It should contain sections on particular skills that were most beneficial (along with a brief review of exactly what using that skill entails), followed by anticipation of future depressogenic situations that the client can anticipate now, and written information about how he or she expects to deal with those situations based on what was learned in therapy. It is helpful if both therapist and client contribute to this document. We have had clients say, years later, that seeing some comment in their therapist's handwriting brought back positive memories and feelings of attachment that were meaningful.

Recognize Danger Signals

Encourage the client to also write about his or her own danger signals, such as recurrent blue moods, severe anxiety, or problems coping, that signal potential development of more serious problems, and add these to the Maintenance Guide. This way, the signals are more likely to be noticed and responded to quickly.

What to Do When a Danger Signal Is Experienced?

Develop a concrete plan of action to take when certain symptoms resurface. For example, Who can the client call to rally support or engage in pleasant activities? What should clients do if you are no longer in the area, or are unavailable, and they need therapy again? Specific written answers to these and related questions help the client to manage termination more effectively and confidently; this kind of cognitive rehearsal is key to maintenance of success in CBT.

CREATIVE APPLICATIONS: EXPANDING CBT FOR OLDER ADULTS BEYOND INDIVIDUAL PSYCHOTHERAPY

AWARENESS OF DIFFERENCES IN SOCIOCULTURAL CONTEXT

So far in our presentation of CBT with older adults, we have outlined components of a standard protocol; however, powerful sociocultural influences including the elder's immediate family, community, cultural or ethnic background, and country of origin can shape the signs and symptoms of depression, leading some to view their distress as primarily a somatic, mental, or spiritual problem, rather than as a symptom of psychological distress. These sociocultural influences shape older adults' understanding of their feelings, thoughts, and behavior, affect their views of others and the environment in which they live and function, and define acceptable help-seeking behavior and treatment practices

(Gaw, 1993; Purnell & Paulanka, 1998). Therapists must also remember that they, too, bring their own separate sociocultural history into the therapeutic process that shapes their views about client problems, as well as their own expectations for the process and progress of therapy and the evaluation of its outcomes. Effective CBT therapists explore the physical, psychological and social changes of their elderly patients within their sociocultural contexts (e.g., age, gender, sexual orientation, physical disabilities, social support, socioeconomic status, level of acculturation, race, and ethnicity).

Regardless of cultural background and ethnic heritage, the demonstration of respect for elders in therapy is paramount (Jackson, 1988; Sotomayor & Garcia, 1993). We encourage elders to share their personal and family stories using their own descriptors for depression and their feelings of distress. This helps to demonstrate our genuine respect for client differences within and across cultural groups, and helps therapists explore the target complaints of older clients within their given sociocultural contexts (Gallagher-Thompson & Coon, 1996). Although this process is challenging and complex, we have found that CBT provides a compatible conceptual and clinical backdrop for this work. At the same time, little in the background of most psychologists today prepares them to work with clients who also routinely use nontraditional therapies, such as culturally defined healers and helpers (including acupuncturists, herbalists, spiritual advisers, and psychic readers) in conjunction with traditional Western health care practices.

Frequently, we think of tailoring CBT therapy to meet the needs of elders with sensory problems and/or cognitive changes that may make more traditional CBT difficult to implement. These problems can be handled to some extent by adjusting goals and therapeutic strategies or individualizing the length, frequency, and location of sessions beyond the traditional 50-minute office hour. However, many U.S. ethnic, racial, and other minority group members (e.g., the poor, the physically challenged, gay men and lesbians, and non-English-speaking elders) face additional barriers including language barriers, culturally insensitive service providers, and financial constraints that can impede help-seeking behavior and create new challenges for the CBT therapist (e.g., Hatch & Paradis, 1993; Iwamasa, 1993; Miranda & Valdes Dwyer, 1993; Organista, Valdes Dwyer, & Azocar, 1993). Arean and Gallagher-Thompson (1996) address these issues as they apply to ethnic elders in clinical and clinical research settings. Thus, the rich diversity of today's mental health services arena demands that therapists move from mere cultural awareness toward cultural competence. Continued training, supervision, and consultation efforts can help therapists develop and enhance CBT interventions to meet the unique needs of elders based on their histories and sociocultural contexts.

USES OF CBT IN GROUP THERAPY

We and other clinical researchers (e.g., Beutler et al., 1987; Thompson et al., in press; Yost, Beutler, Corbishley, & Allender, 1986) have found that groups can serve as a useful and effective modality to introduce CBT to older adults and reduce their late-life distress. Just as in the case of individual CBT, the psychoeducational approach provides an interactive, learning-focused approach that reduces older adult concerns regarding the stigma associated with more traditional forms of psychotherapy. CBT groups not only afford elders the opportunity to reduce social isolation, share their struggles with peers, and gain new insights and strategies for handling their problems through interactions with one another, but they also can help increase cost-effectiveness and reduce case backlogs for therapists and their agencies. In addition, because of the flexibility of the CB approach, there is considerable potential to tailor such factors as the primary content and the number of sessions to meet the special needs of elders including cognitively impaired older adults or early-stage dementia victims, bereaved elders, frail elders, and those suffering with chronic pain (Thompson et al., in press). We refer the reader to the work of Beutler, Yost, and their colleagues (Beutler et al., 1987; Yost et al., 1986) and our recent chapter (Thompson et al., in press) for additional information on CBT groups with older adults. These contain more discussion on such topics as screening (who is most appropriate for group, rather than individual, treatment?); content areas to focus on; optimal length of treatment; open versus closed-ended groups; sequencing of sessions; handling termination; and related issues.

PSYCHOEDUCATIONAL CLASSES FOR OLDER ADULTS

Psychoeducational interventions differ from "traditional" CBT groups in at least four key ways: (1) classes are always time-limited, with the length depending on the target audience and class goals, (2) they employ a detailed agenda for each meeting that outlines goals for that class and the steps taken in class to achieve those goals, (3) they use a great deal of active in-class participation in role plays and skill demonstrations to learn and practice the CBT-based material, and (4) they extensively use homework assignments to encourage practice of new skills outside the classroom (Gallagher-Thompson, Coon, Rivera, Powers, & Zeiss, 1998). Here at the OAFC, we have developed several 10-session psychoeducational classes for small groups of 8 to 10 individuals that are based on CBT change strategies designed to reduce depression in older adults (Thompson, Gallagher-Thompson, & Lovett, 1992) and to reduce distress in family caregivers of impaired elders (Gallagher-Thompson et al., 1992, 1996). For example, our current "Coping with Caregiving" class is designed to teach mood management skills through two principal approaches: (1) an emphasis on reducing negative affect by learning how to relax in the stressful situation, appraise the care-recipient's behavior more realistically, and communicate assertively; and, (2) an emphasis on increasing positive mood through acquisition of such skills as seeing the contingency between mood and activities, developing strategies to do more small, everyday pleasant activities, and learning to set self-change goals and reward oneself for accomplishments along the way (Coon, Schulz, & Ory, 1999; Gallagher-Thompson et al., 1996). In general, these psychoeducational approaches have been found to be effective in reducing caregiver distress and increasing caregiver self-efficacy (e.g., Lovett & Gallagher, 1988; Steffen, Gallagher-Thompson, Zeiss, & Willis-Shore, 1994). Zeiss and Steffen (1996) also review other effective uses for psychoeducational CBT approaches, such as treatment of anxiety disorders, insomnia, and sexual dysfunctions of later life.

CONCLUSION

This chapter provided a brief overview of a CBT protocol used successfully with depressed older adults, and very briefly discussed ways to extend some key intervention techniques and strategies into group therapy and psychoeducational classes designed for depressed elders and family caregivers. However, we have not gone into depth about several topics that are also relevant and that need to be considered when working with older adults—partly because of the dearth of research data about the effectiveness of CBT with these particular subgroups of depressed elders. The first of these is the medically frail elderly, who often have several chronic illnesses that interfere with their everyday functioning and quality of life. As Haley (1996) has pointed out, we need to become more sensitive to the medical context of psychotherapy and to increase our knowledge of the common illnesses and functional impairments of older adults. More emphasis on teamwork, greater flexibility in where and when to meet with clients, and presentation of key concepts in more simplified forms seem to be essential ingredients in the application of CBT with these individuals. Grant and Casey (1995) provided a clinically rich array of suggestions for how to modify CBT to meet the needs of frail elderly, but caution that these are really recommendations based on clinical experience, not on research data.

The second group with which more empirical research is needed to demonstrate the effectiveness of CBT is with the cognitively impaired elderly. As with the medically frail elderly, much of what is known is based on the experience of clinicians working in such settings as nursing homes and long-term care facilities (see, e.g., the work of Burgio, Cotter & Stevens, 1996; Hartz & Splain, 1997; Lichtenberg, 1998; Meador, Ray, Taylor, Gallagher-Thompson, & Thompson, under review, which present various forms of behavioral interventions that have been used in residential care homes and that show great promise for improving mood and function in these patients). On an outpatient basis, the work of Teri and colleagues (Teri et al., 1997) demonstrated that depressed mood could be improved, both in dementia patients and their primary caregivers, through behaviorally based interventions such as increasing shared everyday pleasant activities. However, compared with the much larger empirical literature on CBT for outpatient depression, relatively few controlled studies have been done with this population. Furthermore, the use of cognitive interventions with early-stage dementia victims and their families has been recommended in the literature (Teri & Gallagher-Thompson, 1991), but no empirical studies have been reported to document its effectiveness, or how the "typical" kind of CBT described in this chapter would need to be modified to make it more effective with this ever-increasing group.

As Gatz and her colleagues note (Gatz et al., 1998), the time has come for clinical outcome studies with larger samples of depressed older adults to further substantiate individual and group CBT treatment efficacy and effectiveness with these elders, and provide more consistent demonstration of its performance relative to other psychosocial treatments. This is particularly true for ethnic elders about whom little is known on an empirical level, since until recently, their participation in clinical outcome research has been minimal. This should change with the establishment of several centers for minority research and the continued development of the field of ethnogerontology (see Yeo & Gallagher-Thompson, 1996, for discussion of how ethnic and cultural issues affect dementia research and interventions for family caregivers). In the meantime, therapists, clinical researchers, and mental health program teams interested in the individual and group application of CBT with older adults need to be creative in practice and innovative in the development of CBT research protocols designed to meet the needs of our society's diverse elders who suffer from depression and related late-life disorders.

REFERENCES

Arean, P., & Gallagher-Thompson, D. (1996). Issues and recommendations for the recruitment and retention of older ethnic minority adults into clinical research [Invited paper]. *Journal of Consulting and Clinical Psychology, 64,* 875–880.

Beck, A.T., Freeman, A., Pretzer, J., Davis, D.D., Fleming, B., Ottaviani, R., Beck, J., Simon, K.M., Padesky, C., Meyer, J., & Trexler, L. (1990). *Cognitive therapy of personality disorders.* New York: Guilford Press.

Beck, A.T., Rush, A.J., Shaw, B.F., & Emery, G. (1979). *Cognitive therapy of depression.* New York: Guilford Press.

Beck, A.T., Steer, R.A., & Garbin, M.G. (1988). Psychometric properties of the Beck depression inventory: Twenty-five years of evaluation. *Clinical Psychology Review, 8,* 77–100.

Beutler, L.E., Scogin, F., Kirkish, P., Schretlen, D., Corbishley, A., Hamblin, D., Meredith, K., Potter, R., Bamford, C.R., & Levenson, A.I. (1987). Group cognitive therapy and alprazolam in the treatment of depression in older adults. *Journal of Consulting and Clinical Psychology, 55,* 550–556.

Burgio, L., Cotter, E.M., & Stevens, A.B. (1996). Treatment in residential settings. In M. Hersen & V.B. Van Hasselt (Eds.), *Psychological treatment of older adults: An introductory text* (pp. 127–145). New York: Plenum Press.

Burns, D.D. (1980). *Feeling good: The new mood therapy.* New York: Signet.

Burns, D.D. (1989). *The feeling good handbook: Using the new mood therapy in everyday life.* New York: Morrow.

Chambless, D.L., Baker, M.J., Baucom, D.H., Beutler, L.E., Calhoun, K.S., Christoph, P.C., Daiuto, A., DeRubeis, R., Detweiler, J., Haaga, D.A.F., Johnson, S.B., McCurry, S., Mueser, K.T., Pope, K.S., Sanderson, W.C., Shoham, V., Stickle, T., Williams, D.A., & Woody, S.R. (1998). Update on empirically validated therapies II. *Clinical Psychologist, 51*(1), 3–21.

Chambless, D.L., & Hollon, S.D. (1998). Defining empirically supported therapies. *Journal of Consulting and Clinical Psychology, 66*(1), 7–18.

Chambless, D.L., Sanderson, W.C., Shoham, V., Johnson, S.B., Pope, K., Crits-Christoph, P., Baker, M., Hohnson, B., Woody, S.R., Sue, S., Beutler, L., Williams, D., & McMurry, S. (1996). Update on empirically validated therapies. *Clinical Psychologist, 49*(2), 5–15.

Coon, D.W. (1994). Cognitive-behavioral interventions with avoidant personality: A single case study. *Journal of Cognitive Psychotherapy: An International Quarterly, 8*(3), 243–253.

Coon, D.W., Schulz, R., & Ory, M. (1999). Innovative intervention approaches with Alzheimer's disease caregivers. In D. Biegel & A. Blum (Eds.), *Innovations in practice and service delivery across the lifespan* (pp. 295–325). New York: Oxford University Press.

DeVries, H., & Gallagher-Thompson, D. (1994). Crises with geriatric patients. In F. Dattilio & A. Freeman (Eds.), *Cognitive-behavior therapy and crisis intervention* (pp. 200–218). New York: Guilford Press.

DeRubeis, R.J., & Crits-Christoph, P. (1998). Empirically supported individual and group psychological treatments for adult mental disorders. *Journal of Consulting and Clinical Psychology, 66*(1), 37–52.

Dick, L., & Gallagher-Thompson, D. (1995). Cognitive therapy with the core beliefs of a distressed, lonely caregiver. *Journal of Cognitive Psychotherapy: An International Quarterly, 9*, 215–227.

Dick, L., Gallagher-Thompson, D., Coon, D., Powers, D., & Thompson, L.W. (1996). *Cognitive-behavioral therapy for late-life depression: A patient's manual.* Stanford, CA: VA Palo Alto Health Care System and Stanford University.

Dobson, K.S. (1989). A meta-analysis of the efficacy of cognitive therapy for depression. *Journal of Consulting and Clinical Psychology, 57*, 414–419.

Dupree, L., & Schonfeld, L. (1996). Substance abuse. In M. Hersen & V.B. Van Hasselt (Eds.), *Psychological treatment of older adults: An introductory text* (pp. 281–297). New York: Plenum Press.

Edelstein, B., Staats, N., Kalish, K., & Northrop, L. (1996). Assessment in older adults. In M. Hersen & V.B. Van Hasselt (Eds.), *Psychological treatment of older adults: An introductory text* (pp. 35–68). New York: Plenum Press.

Folstein, M.F., Folstein, S.E., & McHugh, P.R. (1975). 'Mini-mental state': A practical method for grading the cognitive state of patients for the clinician. *Journal of Psychiatric Research, 12*, 189–198.

Futterman, A., Thompson, L.W., Gallagher-Thompson, D., & Ferris, R. (1995). Depression in later life. In E. Beckham & R. Leber (Eds.), *Handbook of depression: Treatment, assessment and research* (2nd ed., pp. 494–525). New York: Guilford Press.

Fry, P.S. (1984). Cognitive training and cognitive-behavioral variables in the treatment of depression in the elderly. *Clinical Gerontologist, 3*, 25–45.

Gallagher, D.E., & Thompson, L.W. (1982). Treatment of major depressive disorder in older adult outpatients with brief psychotherapies. *Psychotherapy: Theory, Research, and Practice, 19*, 482–490.

Gallagher, D.E., & Thompson, L.W. (1983). Effectiveness of psychotherapy for both endogenous and non-endogenous depression in older adult outpatients. *Journal of Gerontology, 38*, 707–712.

Gallagher-Thompson, D., & Coon, D.W. (1996). Depression. In J. Sheikh (Ed.), *Treating the elderly* (pp. 1–44). San Francisco: Jossey-Bass.

Gallagher-Thompson, D., Coon, D.W., Rivera, P., Powers, D., & Zeiss, A.M. (1998). Family caregiving: Stress, coping and intervention. In M. Hersen & V.B. Van Hasselt (Eds.), *Handbook of clinical geropsychology* (pp. 469–493). New York: Plenum Press.

Gallagher-Thompson, D., Ossinalde, C., & Thompson, L.W. (1996). *Coping with caregiving: A class for family caregivers.* Palo Alto, CA: VA Palo Alto Health Care System.

Gallagher-Thompson, D., Rose, J., Florsheim, M., Jacome, P., DelMaestro, S., Peters, L., Gantz, F., Arguello, D., Johnson, C., Moorehead, R.S., Polich, T.M., Chesney, M., & Thompson, L.W. (1992). *Controlling your frustration: A class for caregivers.* Palo Alto, CA: VA Palo Alto Health Care System.

Gallagher-Thompson, D., & Steffen, A.M. (1994). Comparative effects of cognitive behavioral and brief psychodynamic psychotherapies for depressed family caregivers. *Journal of Consulting and Clinical Psychology, 62,* 543–549.

Gaston, L., Marmar, C., Thompson, L.W., & Gallagher, D. (1988). Relationship of patients' pretreatment characteristics to therapeutic alliance in diverse psychotherapies. *Journal of Consulting and Clinical Psychology, 56,* 483–489.

Gatz, M., Fiske, A., Fox, L.S., Kaskie, B., Kasl-Godley, J.E., McCallum, T.J., & Wetherell, J.L. (1998). Empirically validated psychological treatments for older adults. *Journal of Mental Health and Aging, 4*(1), 9–46.

Gaw, A. (Ed.). (1993). *Culture, ethnicity, and mental illness.* Washington, DC: American Psychiatric Press.

Grant, R.W., & Casey, D.A. (1995). Adapting cognitive behavioral therapy for the frail elderly. *International Psychogeriatrics, 7*(4), 561–571.

Haley, W. (1996). The medical context of psychotherapy with the elderly. In S. Zarit & B. Knight (Eds.), *A guide to psychotherapy and aging* (pp. 221–239). Washington, DC: American Psychological Association.

Hartz, G.W., & Splain, D.M. (1997). *Psychosocial intervention in long-term care: An advanced guide.* New York: Haworth Press.

Hatch, M.L., & Paradis, C. (1993). Panic disorder with agoraphobia: A focus on group treatment with African Americans. *Behavior Therapist, 16*(9), 240–241.

Iwamasa, G.Y. (1993). Asian Americans and cognitive behavioral therapy. *Behavior Therapist, 16*(9), 233–235.

Jackson, J. (Ed.). (1988). *The Black American elderly: Research on physical and psychosocial health.* New York: Springer.

Lewinsohn, P., Muñoz, R., Youngren, M.A., & Zeiss, A. (1986). *Control your depression.* Englewood Cliffs, NJ: Prentice-Hall.

Lichtenberg, P.A. (1998). *Mental health practice in geriatric health care settings.* New York: Haworth Press.

Lovett, S., & Gallagher, D. (1988). Psychoeducational interventions for family caregivers: Preliminary efficacy data. *Behavior Therapy, 19,* 321–330.

Meador, K., Ray, W., Taylor, J.A., Gallagher-Thompson, D., & Thompson, L.W. (under editorial review). *Application of a behavioral model using care providers for the treatment of depression in nursing home residents: A feasibility study.*

Miranda, J., & Valdes Dwyer, E. (1993). Cognitive behavioral therapy for disadvantaged medical patients. *Behavior Therapist, 16*(9), 226–228.

Nathan, P.E., & Gorman, J. (Eds.). (1998). *A guide to treatments that work.* New York: Oxford University Press.

Niederehe, G. (1994). Psychosocial therapies with depressed older adults. In L.S. Schneider, C.F. Reynolds, & B.D. Lebowitz (Eds.), *Diagnosis and treatment of depression in late life: Results of the NIH consensus development conference* (pp. 293–315). Washington, DC: American Psychiatric Press.

Niederehe, G. (1996). Psychosocial treatments with depressed older adults: A research update. *American Journal of Geriatric Psychiatry, 4,* S66–S78.

Organista, K.C., Valdes Dwyer, E., & Azocar, F. (1993). Cognitive behavioral therapy with Latino outpatients. *Behavior Therapist, 16*(9), 229–233.

Padesky, C.A. (1994). Schema change processes in cognitive therapy. *Clinical Psychology and Psychotherapy, 1,* 267–278.

Purnell, L., & Paulanka, B.J. (Eds.). (1998). *Transcultural health care: A culturally competent approach.* Philadelphia: Davis.

Sanderson, W.C., & Woody, S. (1995). Manuals for empirically validated treatments. *Clinical Psychologist, 48,* 7–11.

Scogin, F., Hamblin, D., & Beutler, L. (1987). Bibliotherapy for depressed older adults: A self-help alternative. *Gerontologist, 27,* 383–387.

Scogin, F., Jamison, C., & Gochneaur, K. (1989). Comparative efficacy of cognitive and behavioral bibliotherapy for mildly and moderately depressed older adults. *Journal of Consulting and Clinical Psychology, 57,* 403–407.

Scogin, F., & McElreath, L. (1994). Efficacy of psychosocial treatments for geriatric depression: A quantitative review. *Journal of Consulting and Clinical Psychology, 62,* 69–74.

Sheikh, J.I., & Yesavage, J.A. (1986). Geriatric depression scale: Recent evidence and development of a shorter version. *Clinical Gerontologist, 5*(1) 165–173.

Sotomayor, M., & Garcia, A. (Eds.). (1993). *Elderly Latinas: Issues and solutions for the 21st century.* Washington, DC: National Hispanic Council on Aging.

Spielberger, C. (1983). *Manual for the state-trait anxiety inventory.* Palo Alto, CA: Consulting Psychologists Press.

Spielberger, C. (1988). *State-trait anger expression inventory: Research edition professional manual.* Odessa, FL: Psychological Assessment Resources.

Steffen, A.M., Gallagher-Thompson, D., Zeiss, A.M., & Willis-Shore, J. (1994, August). *Self-efficacy for caregiving: Psychoeducational interventions with dementia family caregivers.* Presented at American Psychological Association, Los Angeles.

Steuer, J.L., Mintz, J., Hammen, C.L., Hill, M.A., Jarvik, L.S., McCarley, T., Motoike, P., & Rosen, R. (1984). Cognitive-behavioral and psychodynamic group psychotherapy in treatment of geriatric depression. *Journal of Consulting and Clinical Psychology, 52,* 180–189.

Teri, L., Curtis, J., Gallagher-Thompson, D., & Thompson, L. (1994). Cognitive behavior therapy with depressed older adults. In L.S. Schneider, C.F. Reynold, B.D. Lebowitz, & A.J. Friedhoff (Eds.), *Diagnosis and treatment of depression in late life: Results of the NIH consensus development conference* (pp. 279–291). Washington, DC: American Psychiatric Press.

Teri, L., & Gallagher-Thompson, D. (1991). Cognitive-behavioral interventions for treatment of depression in Alzheimer's patients. *Gerontologist, 31*(3), 413–416.

Teri, L., Logsdon, R.G., Uomoto, J., & McCurry, S.M. (1997). Behavioral treatment of depression in dementia patients: A controlled clinical trial. *Journal of Gerontology: Psychological Sciences, 52B,* 159–166.

Teri, L., & McCurry, S. (in press). Psychosocial therapies with older adults. In C.E. Coffey & J.L. Cummings (Eds.), *Textbook of geriatric neuropsychiatry* (2nd ed.). Washington, DC: American Psychiatric Press.

Thompson, L.W., Gallagher, D., & Breckenridge, J.S. (1987). Comparative effectiveness of psychotherapies for depressed elders. *Journal of Consulting and Clinical Psychology, 55,* 385–390.

Thompson, L.W., Gallagher-Thompson, D., & Dick, L. (1996). *Cognitive-behavioral therapy for late-life depression: A therapist's manual.* Stanford, CA: VA Palo Alto Health Care System and Stanford University.

Thompson, L.W., Gallagher-Thompson, D., & Lovett, S. (1992). *Increasing life satisfaction class leaders' and participant manuals* (revised version). Palo Alto, CA: Department of Veterans Affairs Medical Center and Stanford University.

Thompson, L.W., Gantz, F., Florsheim, M., DelMaestro, S., Rodman, J., Gallagher-Thompson, D., & Bryan, H. (1991). Cognitive-behavioral therapy for affective disorders in the elderly. In W.A. Myers (Ed.), *New techniques in the psychotherapy of older patients* (pp. 3–39). Washington, DC: American Psychiatric Press.

Thompson, L.W., Powers, D., Coon, D., Takagi, K., McKibbin, C., & Gallagher-Thompson, D. (in press). Group cognitive behavioral therapy with older adults. In A. Freeman & J. White (Eds.), *Cognitive behavioral group therapies for older adults*. Washington, DC: American Psychological Association Press.

Thompson, M., Gallagher-Thompson, D., & Thompson, L.W. (1995). Linear and nonlinear changes in mood between psychotherapy sessions: Implications for treatment and outcomes and relapse risk. *Psychotherapy Research, 5,* 327–336.

Willenbring, M.L., Christensen, K.J., Spring, W.D., & Rasmussen, R. (1987). Alcoholism screening in the elderly. *Journal of American Geriatric Society, 35*(9), 864–869.

Yeo, G., & Gallagher-Thompson, D. (Eds.). (1996). *Ethnicity and the dementias.* Washington, DC: Taylor & Francis.

Yesavage, J.A., Brink, T.L., Lum, O., Huang, V., Adey, M.B., & Leirer, V.O. (1983). Development and validation of a geriatric depression rating scale: A preliminary report. *Journal of Psychiatric Research, 17,* 37–49.

Yost, E.B., Beutler, L.E., Corbishley, M.A., & Allender, J.R. (1986). *Group cognitive therapy: A treatment approach for depressed older adults.* New York: Pergamon Press.

Young, J.E. (1984, November). *Cognitive therapy with difficult patients.* Workshop presented at the meeting of the Association for Advancement of Behavior Therapy, Philadelphia.

Young, J.E. (1990). *Cognitive therapy for personality disorders: A schema-focused approach.* Sarasota, FL: Professional Resource Exchange.

Young, J.E., & Klosko, J.S. (1993). *Reinventing your life: How to break free from negative life patterns.* New York: Dutton.

Zeiss, A., & Steffen, A. (1996). Behavioral and cognitive-behavioral treatments: An overview of social learning. In S. Zarit & B. Knight (Eds.), *A guide to psychotherapy and aging* (pp. 35–60). Washington, DC: American Psychological Association.

CHAPTER 30

Strategies for Treating
Generalized Anxiety in the Elderly

MELINDA A. STANLEY AND PATRICIA M. AVERILL

Epidemiological data have attested to the notion that anxiety disorders pose a significant public health concern for the elderly. In fact, prevalence rates suggest that anxiety disorders are more than twice as frequent as affective disorders in this segment of the population (Weissman et al., 1985), and it already is clear from available data that late-life depression is a serious health issue (Reynolds, Lebowitz, & Schneider, 1993). Nonetheless, the study of anxiety among older adults has been neglected, and there is a need for continued work in this area (e.g., Salzman & Lebowitz, 1991). Of particular relevance is further investigation into the nature and treatment of generalized anxiety disorder (GAD), a chronic and pervasive syndrome with high prevalence rates among older adults (Blazer, George, & Hughes, 1991). In this chapter, we begin with a brief description of GAD in late life, then provide an overview of the relevant psychosocial treatment literature, the majority of which focuses on cognitive-behavioral approaches. Several relevant issues of service utilization then are reviewed, and a discussion of therapeutic techniques from an ongoing clinical trial of cognitive-behavioral therapy (CBT) for older adults with GAD is presented. Finally, potential psychosocial alternatives or adjuncts to CBT for GAD in late life are mentioned briefly.

DESCRIPTION OF GENERALIZED
ANXIETY IN THE ELDERLY

Current diagnostic criteria for GAD call for the presence of unrealistic or excessive worry accompanied by at least three physiological sensations representative of motor tension, autonomic hyperactivity, and/or vigilance (American Psychiatric Association [APA], 1994). Symptoms must have occurred more days than not over a period of at least 6 months, and significant distress and/or interference in life function must be reported. At present, these criteria are used to diagnose GAD in both younger and older adults, although research has recently begun to examine areas of both similarity and divergence between older and younger patients with GAD. In one of the earliest studies designed to examine GAD in late-life, 44 older adults with the disorder were compared with a control sample matched for age, gender, level of education, and ethnicity (Beck, Stanley, & Zebb, 1996). In this study, GAD was associated with elevated levels of worry, anxiety, social fears, and depression, with mean scores comparable to those reported in previous studies of younger GAD patients.

Despite these apparent similarities, however, other data have suggested some potentially important phenomenological differences in the experience of worry and related symptoms for younger and older individuals. In studies with community volunteers, for example, the content of worry appears to vary across the life span. Person and Borkovec (1995) reported that older adults (aged 65 and over) worried most about health and least about work, whereas younger individuals (aged 25–64) were most concerned about family and finances. Powers, Wisocki, and Whitbourne (1992) also reported that older adults worried less about social events and finances than a college-age comparison group. Moreover, older adults typically report fewer worries overall than their younger counterparts (Person & Borkovec, 1995; Powers et al., 1992), and descriptive data from carefully selected nonpsychiatric samples of older adults highlight the need for age-appropriate norms to interpret measures of anxiety symptoms (Stanley, Beck, & Zebb, 1996). Finally, there appears to be some variation in the structure and prevalence of affect in general across the life span. Specific to the experience of anxiety, affect terms assessing guilt (e.g., ashamed, guilty, worried, blamed) seem to be more relevant for younger adults (aged 18–30) than older individuals (aged 60 and over) (Lawton, Kleban, & Dean, 1993). It is unclear, however, whether these differences reflect differential meanings of affect terms and/or variations in the actual experience of anxiety.

In addition to potential experiential differences across the life span, important differential diagnostic issues are particularly salient for establishing the presence of GAD in elderly patients. Probably of central importance is the need to distinguish between anxiety symptoms and medical illness (Blazer, 1997). It is well known that many medical conditions (e.g., cardiovascular disease, hyperthyroidism) can create anxietylike symptoms, and that severity of physical complaints correlates positively with anxiety (Stanley & Beck, 1998). In addition, older adults often are reluctant to report psychological difficulties, tending instead to attribute the signs of anxiety to physical illness (Gurian & Miner, 1991). Thus, differentiating between anxiety disorders and medical disease among older adults is of major importance and an issue to be considered carefully by both medical practitioners and mental health professionals.

Differentiating anxiety disorders from depression among the elderly also is a significant concern. High rates of coexistence have been reported for both disorders and symptoms in the anxiety and affective domains (Stanley & Beck, 1998), and this issue is of particular importance for GAD wherein a notable amount of symptom overlap is evident when reviewing diagnostic criteria

(APA, 1994). Other issues of particular concern for the differential diagnosis of anxiety disorders in late life include high rates of coexistence between anxiety and sleep difficulties, along with some evidence of increased cognitive dysfunction associated with anxiety (Stanley & Beck, 1998). Clear decision-making rules are not available for evaluating these areas of overlap, but clinicians working with older anxious patients should remain aware of potential alternative explanations for anxiety symptoms.

CASE EXAMPLE

Mr. A is a 68-year-old African American, married male who reported that throughout his life he had always been overly "concerned" about various topics (he preferred this word to "worry"). These concerns became even more excessive approximately one year prior to interview when he experienced a number of deaths in his family and had to assist his mother in moving to a nursing home. He reported primary concerns about his own and his wife's health, numerous minor matters (e.g., being on time, repairs to his home and farm), and his children's well-being (e.g., their relationships with their spouses, his son's business). Mr. A indicated that he had difficulty controlling his thoughts surrounding these issues, and reported that he was concerned at least 75% of the time. He also endorsed less severe concerns regarding financial matters (although he was experiencing no real financial difficulties) and his own business. Mr. A acknowledged difficulty concentrating, muscle tension, sleeping disruption, and irritability associated with his concerns. He also indicated that he procrastinated significantly in making decisions and was experiencing significant interpersonal difficulty with his wife as a result of his worrying. In addition to these anxiety symptoms, Mr. A reported feelings of depressed mood and loss of interest in pleasurable activities, feelings of guilt, and decreased energy. He readily acknowledged, however, that these feelings of depression postdated his problems with worry and were not overwhelming for him. He noted that he had always been anxious, but only began to experience depression in the previous year. Mr. A acknowledged minor specific fears of snakes and heights, but these did not interfere in any meaningful way with his life. During the initial interview, Mr. A was fidgety and had difficulty sitting still. A full medical evaluation indicated no serious medical conditions that might account for his anxiety symptoms. His symptoms were assigned a principal diagnosis of GAD, with coexistent major depression.

OVERVIEW OF PSYCHOSOCIAL TREATMENT LITERATURE

The earliest empirical trials of psychosocial interventions for anxiety in older adults focused on the utility of cognitive-behavioral therapy (CBT) in nondiagnosed community volunteers. In an initial study, DeBerry (1982) compared two variants of relaxation training (RT) with a "pseudo-relaxation control" condition in a group of 36 women reporting complaints of anxiety, nervousness, tension, fatigue, insomnia, and somatic complaints. Both relaxation conditions were effective relative to the control group on measures of state and trait anxiety. In a subsequent comparison, DeBerry, Davis, and Reinhard (1989) compared the efficacy of RT, CBT including both cognitive restructuring and assertiveness training, and a control condition for 32 adults, aged 65 to 75 years, who reported a range of anxiety symptoms. Only RT was effective in reducing state anxiety, although improvements in both trait anxiety and depressive symptoms were evident across all treatment conditions.

In a separate trial, Sallis, Lichstein, Clarkson, Stalgaitis, and Campbell (1983) administered anxiety management training, CBT for depression, and a discussion control condition to small groups of adults over age 60 who met cutoff criteria on measures of anxiety and depression. Significant improvements were noted in both types of symptoms across all groups, although the total sample size was small ($n = 38$) and dropout rates were high in all three conditions (33–38%). In a more recent study with a larger group of older anxious adults ($n = 71$), two variants of RT were compared with a wait-list control condition (Scogin, Rickard, Keith, Wilson, & McElreath, 1992). Significant improvements on measures of state anxiety and general psychiatric distress were apparent following both types of RT relative to the control condition, and the dropout rate from active treatment was only 19%. In a follow-up evaluation of 27 participants from this study, data suggested the maintenance of treatment gains over one year (Rickard, Scogin, & Keith, 1994).

Overall, these studies provide preliminary evidence for the utility of cognitive-behavioral interventions in the treatment of late-life anxiety. Generalizability of the data are limited, however, given that participants were not evaluated for the presence of diagnosable anxiety disorders. Only recently has research begun to address the potential efficacy of CBT for well-diagnosed anxiety disorders among older adults. The majority of work in this area has been directed toward evaluation of treatments for GAD, given the high prevalence and pervasiveness of this disorder in late life.

In an initial controlled trial, the efficacy of CBT was evaluated relative to nondirective supportive psychotherapy (SP) for 48 older adults with a principal diagnosis of GAD (Stanley, Beck, & Glassco, 1996). CBT in this study was based on an approach described by Craske, Barlow, and O'Leary (1992) that included progressive deep muscle relaxation, cognitive therapy, and graduated exposure practice in worry-producing situations. SP involved nondirective discussions of anxiety symptoms and experiences. Both treatments were conducted in a group format over a period of 14 weeks. Posttreatment evaluations revealed significant decreases in both treatment conditions on self-report and clinician-rated measures of worry, anxiety, and depression. Follow-up data suggested maintenance of improvement over six months, with some continued reduction in severity of worry. In general, data from this trial suggested the potential utility of psychosocial interventions in the treatment of late-life GAD. However, design limitations, most notably the omission of a no-treatment or wait-list control condition, seriously restricted the conclusions that can be drawn from this report.

At least two other clinical trials currently are under way to examine further the utility of psychosocial interventions, in particular, CBT, for the treatment of GAD in later life. In one of these, the efficacy of CBT is being compared with a minimal contact control condition (MCC). Preliminary results suggest potentially meaningful decreases in worry, anxiety, and depression following CBT, as well as increases in life satisfaction and quality of life. Although no statistical analyses have yet been conducted, patterns suggest no meaningful changes in these same variables following MCC (Stanley, Beck, Novy, Averill, & Swann, 1997). The program of CBT under investigation in this trial is described in some detail later in this chapter.

In another ongoing trial, the impact of CBT for late-life GAD is being investigated in a sample of patients taking benzodiazepines on a regular, prescribed basis (Gorenstein, Papp, & Kleber, 1997). Patients are assigned randomly to CBT plus medical management (CBT-MM), the goal of which is to reduce benzodiazepine use, or medical management alone (MM). Preliminary results suggest potentially greater decreases in various measures of worry and anxiety following CBT-MM than MM, although sample sizes at present are too small to permit statistical analyses. Of particular interest, however, are data suggesting that improvement following CBT occurs despite meaningful reductions in benzodiazepine use that are not apparent in the MM condition.

Available data suggest the potential utility of CBT for the treatment of late-life anxiety. However, firm conclusions await completion of ongoing and subsequent clinical trials designed to evaluate outcome in well-diagnosed patient groups.

SERVICE UTILIZATION

Although preliminary evidence suggests that mental health services can be effective for older adults, these individuals are less likely to receive formal treatment for mental illness than their younger counterparts. In fact, they represent only 2% to 3% of the patients seen in private practices and hospital outpatient clinics (Butler & Lewis, 1982); and only 4% to 5% at community mental health centers are 65 or older (Redick & Taube, 1980). Suggested reasons for the lack of service utilization generally have fallen into three categories; client issues, professional issues, and practical issues. A variety of cultural issues, however, also have impeded mental health utilization, and these are reviewed also.

CLIENT ISSUES

Many older adults are reluctant to seek assistance for psychological disorders (Lasoski, 1986), and several possible reasons have been reported. For some, psychological problems are associated with a fear of being "crazy" or a sign of weakness (Small, 1997). Others may fear long-term institutionalization. Yet others may be concerned that cognitive symptoms, such as difficulty concentrating and memory deficits, are due to a dementing process. Such fears may be particularly likely among those with GAD, for whom memory deficits and difficulty concentrating are common. Also, catastrophizing is a common symptom of GAD, and individuals with this disorder may be more likely to suspect the worst and, therefore, avoid seeking a cause for their symptoms.

Finally, although the symptoms of GAD can be debilitating, many older adults, particularly those who have experienced these symptoms for most of their lives, see some value in their worry because it has helped them prevent "catastrophes" through the years. For all these reasons, older anxious adults may avoid seeking mental health services, despite the potential benefits.

Even those older adults who might be open to mental health services may lack sufficient information to access available treatment (Lasoski, 1986). First, they may lack knowledge of symptoms associated with psychological disorders and instead may interpret these symptoms as having a physical cause. Indeed, the physiological symptoms of GAD and other anxiety disorders often are perceived by older adults as evidence of a physical problem (Small, 1997). As such, they tend to seek help from primary care physicians who usually treat with psychotropic medication. Second, even if they recognize their symptoms as due to anxiety, older adults may not be aware that effective nonmedication treatments are available. Since older adults often are taking several medications for physical problems, many might prefer to seek nonmedication forms of treatment if they knew these were available. Interestingly, research on older individuals participating in psychotherapy suggests that, although they are more difficult to recruit for treatment, they are more likely to continue in treatment once they have committed to it (Bullard, Nash, Raiford, & Harrell, 1993).

Many of the preceding concerns can be addressed by providing older adults with more information about mental disorders and available treatment. First, mental health professionals can contact local organizations (e.g., community centers, church groups, and residential facilities) that provide special services for the elderly and arrange to speak about relevant topics at group meetings. Second, providing handouts or brochures directed toward the specific concerns of older adults can be useful. Such material should reflect the terminology preferred by many older adults (e.g., concern or fret rather than worry or anxiety). Printed material has the additional advantage of serving as a reminder to older adults, following educational presentations. In addition, handouts can be made available to primary care physicians in neighborhoods adjacent to the clinician's practice. The media also are a useful way of disseminating information to older adults, particularly through publications targeted toward older individuals.

PROFESSIONAL ISSUES

To some extent, the lack of utilization of mental health services by the elderly may be due to the types of services that traditionally have been available. Primary care physicians are less likely to refer older than younger patients for mental health services, and there has been an overreliance on drug treatment for late-life mental health issues (Ford & Sbordone, 1980). Relatedly, there has been little recognition that the elderly are capable of benefiting from psychotherapy (Lasoski, 1986). Primary care physicians also may be hesitant to refer older patients whose mental and physical illnesses have overlapping symptoms.

Even when primary care providers are willing to refer elderly patients, they may have difficulty finding an appropriate resource, since relatively few mental health professionals have specialized in geriatric care until recently. Several reasons have been posited for the lack of interest in geropsychology specialization, including a tendency to attribute symptoms in the elderly to the irreversible aging process and concerns that the problems of the elderly are too complex to treat. Even if older clients improve, there may be a tendency to believe that the effort may not be as valuable for older adults since they have fewer years during which to benefit from treatment. Also, despite evidence to the contrary (see Overview of Psychosocial Treatment literature), there has been a tendency to believe that older adults are "set in their ways" and resistant to change. Elderly clients may trigger clinicians' own concerns about aging or about problems in their relationships with aging parents. In addition, working with the elderly has not been considered glamorous work, and therapists may be concerned about their own perceived low professional status if they specialize in this population (Lasoski, 1986).

PRACTICAL ISSUES

Many older adults might be open to receiving services from mental health specialists if there were fewer practical barriers. One such barrier is insufficient insurance coverage for mental health visits (Lasoski, 1986). Whereas older adults can have virtually unlimited visits to their primary care physicians with minimal copay, their mental health coverage typically requires a more substantial copay and allows fewer sessions. Many older adults also have transportation problems. They may need to depend on public transportation or the availability of family members to drive them to their appointments. Those who drive themselves to appointments often prefer daytime appointments, when visibility is clearer and traffic is lighter. Transportation difficulties may be of particular concern to anxious older adults who are fearful of driving, getting lost, and so on. To reduce these fears, appointments can be scheduled at off-peak hours and detailed maps to clinic sites can be provided. A third practical barrier to treatment can include physical limitations that make it difficult for older adults to attend sessions. These limitations are relatively easy to address in residential facilities, where the clinician can travel to the site and provide services. However, it is more difficult to provide services for older adults who live alone and whose physical limitations prevent them from traveling independently. In such situations, it may be possible to arrange special public transportation services, particularly if sessions are scheduled at off-peak times. Also, it may be beneficial for clinicians servicing older populations to consider accessibility when choosing office space.

CULTURAL ISSUES

In general, research suggests that older adults from ethnic minority groups appear no less likely to engage in treatment than their nonminority age peers (Arean & Gallagher-Thompson, 1996). However, there are treatment barriers specific to minority populations, in addition to those described earlier. In particular, many minority older adults may have experienced overt discrimination as younger adults, before the civil rights movement of the 1960s (Yeatts, Crow, & Folts, 1992). As such, they may harbor considerable distrust toward majority clinicians. In addition, some older adults may not speak English and therefore are excluded from available services. Both of these barriers can be addressed by efforts to train more minority clinicians (e.g., Yeatts et al., 1992). In addition, majority clinicians may need to take advantage of workshops and seminars addressing cultural differences as well as courses in other languages. Another issue for some ethnic minority groups is the importance of involving the family and other important community figures in the decision-making process (Arean & Gallagher-Thompson, 1996). In fact, research suggests that almost one-third of ethnic minority older adults refused to participate in mental health services because their families or physicians discouraged them (Carter, Elward, Malmgren, Martin, & Larson, 1991). As such, these important figures need to be informed about the nature of mental health treatment early in the process.

COGNITIVE-BEHAVIORAL TECHNIQUES

Given the current state of the literature, the use of CBT for late-life GAD seems particularly promising. Thus, we describe here the components of one such CBT program currently under investigation in an ongoing clinical trial (Stanley, Beck, Averill, & Novy, 1997), the preliminary results of which were described earlier (Stanley, Beck, Novy, Averill, & Swann, 1997). Treatment is based on approaches outlined by Craske et al. (1992) and Borkovec and Costello (1993). Weekly sessions are provided over a period of 15 weeks. Although the literature documenting the efficacy of CBT for GAD in younger adults is based on treatment administered during individual sessions, a small group format was selected based on recommendations that older adults may benefit from increased social contact (Arean, 1993; Yost, Beutler, Corbishley, & Allender, 1986). The CBT program includes four major components: (1) education and self-monitoring; (2) relaxation training; (3) cognitive therapy; and (4) graduated behavioral practice. At the end of each session, homework is assigned to facilitate practice with CBT skills. Participants are asked to allot at least 20 minutes, twice per day, for the completion of homework assignments.

EDUCATION AND SELF-MONITORING

In the initial session, a description of generalized anxiety is presented, with attention to the differences between "normal" and "abnormal" anxiety. Three components of generalized anxiety are discussed (i.e., physiological sensations, worry, and avoidance or escape behaviors). After educational material is presented for each symptom domain, group participants are asked to provide examples of the symptoms from their own experience. Each group member is encouraged to share at least some aspect of his or her experience with anxiety. During this discussion, care is taken to utilize synonyms for "worry" that may be preferred by older adults, with particular inclusion of terms that were used by group members during their pretreatment assessments. An overview of the treatment program then is provided, with attention to the utility of relaxation training, cognitive therapy, and graduated practice for reducing the three types of anxiety-related symptoms. During this review, an attempt is made to deemphasize terms such as "disorder," "therapy," and "treatment" because older adults generally have some reluctance to define their difficulties and needs for assistance in this way. Homework following this session involves daily records of physical sensations, thoughts, and behaviors associated with anxiety experienced during the upcoming week.

Although much of the material covered in this session is similar to treatment protocols utilized with younger adults, a number of procedures have been modified in an attempt to meet the special needs of an older population. In particular, information is presented at a somewhat slower pace, and there is increased use of visual and written aids to match potential differences in learning strategies and sensory function between younger and older adults (Gallagher-Thompson & Thompson, 1995). At the beginning of the session, an outline of the material to be covered is presented on a chalkboard. This outline is then referenced as the therapist covers each of the essential topics. Group members also receive notebooks containing copies of this outline that they take home for easy reference during the week. When homework is assigned, an enlarged copy of the form to be completed is posted on a board as the therapist explains the instructions. Group members are asked to participate in completing some entries on the sample homework form to ensure that they understand all procedures. Written homework instructions and forms are included in the notebooks previously mentioned. As such, group participants have easy access to session materials throughout the week.

At the end of the first session, the therapist is careful to query each participant about any questions he or she might have about the material covered or the homework assigned. The therapist also states that she is available to answer any questions about the session that might arise during the week. Her name and phone number are provided on notecards for each participant.

RELAXATION TRAINING

Sessions 2–5 focus on training in Progressive Deep Muscle Relaxation (PDMR) based on procedures outlined by Bernstein and Borkovec (1973). The rationale for relaxation training is reviewed in some detail, and participants initially are taught to alternately tense and relax 10 muscle groups. The therapist begins by explaining the procedure in detail, being careful to note that participants should not tense areas of the body where they experience pain. A full relaxation practice then is completed, after which group members are given the opportunity to discuss any reactions, problems, or questions related to the procedure.

During sessions 3–5, the number of muscle groups is progressively reduced, with procedures included to address discrimination training, cue controlled relaxation, and relaxation by recall. Homework during this phase of treatment includes continued self-monitoring of anxiety symptoms, as well as twice-daily practice of relaxation procedures. Following sessions 2–4, audiotapes are provided to assist with home relaxation practice.

At the beginning of each relaxation session, homework forms are reviewed, and group members discuss specific examples from their monitoring forms. As examples are presented, the therapist writes them on an enlarged sample homework form to clarify any continued misunderstandings. Practice with relaxation procedures also is reviewed, with discussion of any relevant problems. Session outlines always are presented at the beginning of the session; an enlarged version is printed on a chalkboard, and group members receive written copies for their homework notebooks. At the end of each session, homework instructions are reviewed and examples are completed with the use of an enlarged form. Instructions and homework forms also are added each week to group members' notebooks, again for easy reference during the upcoming week.

Cognitive Therapy

Cognitive therapy occurs during sessions 6–10 using a format similar to all earlier sessions. Each meeting begins with presentation of an outline of topics to be covered, followed by a discussion of completed homework, which includes both continued self-monitoring of anxiety symptoms and practice with cognitive therapy techniques. Specific examples from each group member's homework forms are written on a board and discussed. In this manner, participants are given very concrete, specific feedback to optimize their use of anxiety-reducing skills. New skills then are taught and practiced, and homework is assigned. To optimize understanding of new homework assignments, specific examples using group members' experiences are completed using an enlarged, sample homework form. At each session, members receive copies of the session outline, homework instructions, and homework forms for their project notebooks.

The content of cognitive therapy sessions follows procedures outlined by Craske et al. (1992) and begins with a thorough explanation of the rationale for this component. Participants then are instructed in the use of alternative explanations, examination of logical errors (e.g., polarized thinking, overgeneralization), decatastrophizing, reattribution, self-statements, and thought-stopping. In the discussion of these topics, an attempt is made to deemphasize psychological jargon and utilize simple explanations. The therapist presents numerous examples associated with each skill, and each group member is asked to participate in the discussions using examples from his or her own experience. Therapists are careful to query participants about any issues they may find confusing, and they repeatedly remind group members to call during the week with any questions that arise.

GRADUATED BEHAVIORAL PRACTICE

At the end of cognitive therapy, group participants begin to construct a hierarchy of anxiety-producing situations. They list at least 10 situations that create anxiety, noting the physiological sensations, thoughts, and avoidance or escape behaviors associated with each. Situations then are rated according to level of distress experienced, on a scale ranging from 0–100. An attempt is made to create a list of specific situations for each group member that includes a range of distress levels.

Graduated behavioral practice occurs during sessions 10–14 and includes both imaginal and in vivo practice using previously learned skills. Initially, a rationale for graduated practice is provided, as well as some preliminary imagery training. Participants then create a scenario for an initial practice session, writing out on an index card the physiological symptoms, thoughts, and behaviors associated with the situation lowest on the hierarchies. Significant individual attention often is needed at this stage, with therapists providing specific feedback to each group participant as the scenes are being created in session. Once all scenes are complete, participants select a relaxation and/or cognitive coping skill that they would like to practice. They are then asked to close their eyes and imagine the scenario they have just written. Participants indicate via raised fingers when the scenes are vivid; at this point, instructions are given to utilize a coping skill until a 50% reduction in anxiety is experienced. The session is ended when all participants indicate that they have achieved this degree of anxiety reduction.

Homework following sessions 10 and 11 involves twice-daily practice of imaginal scenes. Participants are instructed to move up the hierarchy when a scene creates a distress level of no more than 20 during two successive practices. In session 12, imaginal procedures are continued, but in vivo practice also is initiated for hierarchy items already mastered imaginally. In this domain, avoidance or escape behaviors are targeted (e.g., safety checks, procrastination) and participants identify situations for the upcoming week wherein they can prevent these behaviors and use coping skills. Homework at this point involves one imaginal and one in vivo practice per day.

As with other phases of the CBT program, session outlines and enlarged homework forms are used to facilitate group discussion and understanding of concepts during graduated practice. Homework notebooks regularly are updated with session outlines, as well as homework instructions and forms.

As the treatment program nears a close, group members are asked to review progress and discuss strategies for maintaining gains when the group is no longer available for "check in." Participants' feelings about the program are elicited, as well as suggestions for enhancing the group experience. Generally, group members choose to celebrate their "graduation" from the program with a party held at the end of the final session. At this time, graduation certificates are presented, and the therapist emphasizes with each participant the gains that have been made.

CASE EXAMPLE

Mr. A attended 14 of 15 scheduled group treatment sessions that followed the preceding protocol. In general, he participated actively in group discussions and completed daily homework assignments. At one point during the treatment protocol, Mr. A began to experience increased symptoms of depression. Although his level of participation in session discussions decreased somewhat during this time, he continued to complete homework assignments and practice new coping skills. As a result, Mr. A reported significant improvements in worry and anxiety from pre- to posttreatment. In particular, clinician-rated severity of GAD dropped from a 7 (indicated severe worry and physiological symptoms) on a 0–8 scale to a 4 (indicated moderate symptomatology) following treatment. Severity of anxiety and depressive symptoms also decreased according to the Hamilton anxiety and depression scales, with scores of 32 and 35, respectively, at pretreatment and scores of 19 on each instrument at posttreatment.

ALTERNATIVE PSYCHOSOCIAL APPROACHES

In addition to CBT procedures such as those previously described, other treatments have potential utility for treating late-life anxiety. For example, in one study reviewed earlier (Stanley, Beck, & Glassco, 1996), supportive psychotherapy (SP) appeared to be equally effective to CBT in treating late-life GAD. Despite significant methodological limitations, these data suggest that older adults may benefit from sharing their anxiety-provoking experiences with other adults and receiving support and validation, without being taught new coping skills. However, additional studies need to be conducted comparing these treatments, particularly since studies with younger adults have found SP less effective than CBT for the treatment of GAD (Borkovec & Costello, 1993). It is possible that the group format used with older adults was particularly effective such that any specific treatment differences were undetectable.

Other alternative interventions also warrant future consideration in the treatment of generalized anxiety among older adults. In particular, treatments with demonstrated efficacy for the treatment of late-life depression deserve attention given the significant overlap between anxiety and affective symptoms in older adults. For example, some data have suggested the utility of reminiscence therapy for the treatment of depression in older adults (e.g., Arean et al., 1993), and at least one study with community volunteers suggested significant reductions in state anxiety following this type of treatment (Harp-Scates, Randolph, Gutsch, & Knight, 1985–1986). As such, the potential benefits of reminiscence therapy for reducing generalized anxiety may warrant empirical attention with well-diagnosed, older anxious patients. To our knowledge, however, no empirical work has yet addressed this issue. (See Chapter 9 of this volume for a general description of reminiscence therapy.)

In a similar vein, insight-oriented and interpersonal psychotherapies also may prove useful in the treatment of late-life GAD. These approaches have demonstrated utility for the treatment of late-life depression, with effects comparable to cognitive behavioral and pharmacological interventions (Niederehe, 1994; see also Chapters 28, 29, and 33 of this volume). Again, given the extensive overlap between affective and anxiety symptoms and disorders among the elderly, these approaches are worth examination in the treatment of older adults with GAD. Future research will need to address this issue.

CONCLUSION

The anxiety disorders, in particular, GAD, pose a significant and seriously understudied public health problem for older adults. Research has only begun to address issues related to the nature and treatment of GAD in late life, although preliminary data strongly suggest the utility of psychosocial interventions. The majority of studies have examined the efficacy of cognitive-behavioral approaches, in particular, and specific techniques in this domain have been reviewed in this chapter. Alternative psychosocial interventions, however, deserve further attention, as the specificity of CBT effects has not yet been demonstrated.

REFERENCES

American Psychiatric Association. (1994). *Diagnostic and statistical manual of mental disorders* (4th ed.). Washington, DC: Author.

Arean, P.A. (1993). Cognitive behavioral therapy with older adults. *Behavior Therapist, 16,* 236–239.

Arean, P.A., & Gallagher-Thompson, D. (1996). Issues and recommendations for the recruitment and retention of older ethnic minority adults into clinical research. *Journal of Consulting and Clinical Psychology, 64*(5), 875–880.

Arean, P.A., Perri, M.G., Nezu, A.M., Schein, R.L., Christopher, F., & Joseph, T.X. (1993). Comparative effectiveness of social problem-solving therapy and reminiscence therapy as treatments for depression in older adults. *Journal of Consulting and Clinical Psychology, 61,* 1003–1010.

Beck, J.G., Stanley, M.A., & Zebb, B.J. (1996). Characteristics of generalized anxiety disorder in older adults: A descriptive study. *Behaviour Research and Therapy, 34,* 225–234.

Bernstein, D.A., & Borkovec, T.D. (1973). *Progressive relaxation training.* Champaign, IL: Research Press.

Blazer, D.G. (1997). Generalized anxiety disorder and panic disorder in the elderly: A review. *Harvard Review of Psychiatry, 5,* 18–27.

Blazer, D.G., George, L.K., & Hughes, D. (1991). The epidemiology of anxiety disorders: An age comparison. In C. Salzman & B.D. Lebowitz (Eds.), *Anxiety in the elderly: Treatment and research* (pp. 17–30). New York: Springer.

Borkovec, T.D. & Costello, E. (1993). Efficacy of applied relaxation and cognitive-behavioral therapy in the treatment of generalized anxiety disorder. *Journal of Consulting and Clinical Psychology, 61,* 611–619.

Bullard, E.L., Nash, F., Raiford, K., & Harrell, L.E. (1993). Recruitment of black elderly for clinical research studies of dementia: The CERAD experience. *Gerontologist, 33,* 561–565.

Butler, R., & Lewis, M. (1982). *Aging and mental health* (3rd ed.). St. Louis, MO: Mosby.

Carter, W.B., Elward, K., Malmgren, J., Martin, M.L., & Larson, E. (1991). Participation of older adults in health programs and research: A critical review of the literature. *Gerontologist, 31,* 584–592.

Craske, M.G., Barlow, D.H., & O'Leary, T. (1992). *Mastery of your anxiety and worry.* Albany, NY: Graywind.

DeBerry, S. (1982). The effects of meditation-relaxation on anxiety and depression in a geriatric population. *Psychotherapy: Theory, Research and Practice, 19,* 512–521.

DeBerry, S., Davis, S., & Reinhard, K.E. (1989). A comparison of meditation-relaxation and cognitive behavioral techniques for reducing anxiety and depression in a geriatric population. *Journal of Geriatric Psychiatry, 22,* 231–247.

Ford, C., & Sbordone, R. (1980). Attitudes of psychiatrists toward elderly patients. *American Journal of Psychiatry, 137,* 571–575.

Gallagher-Thompson, D., & Thompson, L.W. (1995). Efficacy of psychotherapeutic interventions with older adults. *Clinical Psychologist, 48,* 24–30.

Gorenstein, E.E., Papp, L.A., & Kleber, M.S. (1997, November). Psychosocial treatment of benzodiazepine dependence and anxiety in later life. In C. Morin (Chair), *Treatment of insomnia, anxiety, and benzodiazepine dependence in late life.* Miami Beach, FL: Association for Advancement of Behavior Therapy.

Gurian, B.S., & Miner, J.H. (1991). Clinical presentation of anxiety in the elderly. In C. Salzman & B.D. Lebowitz (Eds.), *Anxiety in the elderly: Treatment and research* (pp. 31–44). New York: Springer.

Harp-Scates, S.K., Randolph, D.L., Gutsch, K.U., & Knight, H.V. (1985–1986). Effects of cognitive-behavioral, reminiscence, and activity treatments on life satisfaction and anxiety in the elderly. *International Journal of Aging and Human Development, 22*(2), 141–146.

Lasoski, M.C. (1986). Reasons for low utilization of mental health services by the elderly. *Clinical Gerontologist, 5*(1/2), 1–18.

Lawton, M.P., Kleban, M.H., & Dean, J. (1993). Affect and age: Cross-sectional comparisons of structure and prevalence. *Psychology and Aging, 8,* 165–175.

Niederehe, G.T. (1994). Psychosocial therapies with depressed older adults. In L.S. Schneider, C.F. Reynolds, B.D. Lebowitz, & A.J. Friedhoff (Eds.), *Diagnosis and treatment of depression in late life.* Washington, DC: American Psychiatric Press.

Person, D.C., & Borkovec, T.D. (1995, August). *Anxiety disorders among the elderly: Patterns and issues.* Paper presented at the annual meeting of the American Psychological Association, New York.

Powers, C.B., Wisocki, P.A., & Whitbourne, S.K. (1992). Age differences and correlates of worrying in young and elderly adults. *Gerontologist, 32,* 82–88.

Redick, R., & Taube, C. (1980). Demography and mental health care of the aged. In J.E. Birren & R.B. Sloane (Eds.), *Handbook of mental health and aging.* Englewood Cliffs, NJ: Prentice-Hall.

Reynolds, C.F., Lebowitz, B.D., & Schneider, L.S. (1993). The NIH consensus development conference on the diagnosis and treatment of depression in late life: An overview. *Psychopharmacology Bulletin, 29,* 83–85.

Rickard, H.C., Scogin, F., & Keith, S. (1994). A one-year follow-up of relaxation training for elders with subjective anxiety. *Gerontologist, 34,* 121–122.

Sallis, J.F., Lichstein, K.L., Clarkson, A.D., Stalgaitis, S., & Campbell, M. (1983). Anxiety and depression management for the elderly. *International Journal of Behavioral Geriatrics, 1,* 3–12.

Salzman, C., & Lebowitz, B.D. (1991) *Anxiety in the elderly: Treatment and research.* New York: Springer.

Scogin, F., Rickard, H.C., Keith, S., Wilson, J., & McElreath, L. (1992). Progressive and imaginal relaxation training for elderly persons with subjective anxiety. *Psychology and Aging, 7,* 419–424.

Small, G.W., (1997). Recognizing and treating anxiety in the elderly. *Journal of Clinical Psychiatry, 58*(3), 41–47.

Stanley, M.A., & Beck, J.G. (1998). Anxiety disorders. In B. Edelstein (Ed.), *Clinical geropsychology* (Vol. 8). New York: Elsevier Science.

Stanley, M.A., Beck, J.G., Averill, P., & Novy, D. (1997). *Manual: Cognitive behavioral treatment for generalized anxiety disorder in older adults.* Unpublished manuscript.

Stanley, M.A., Beck, J.G., & Glassco, J.D. (1996). Treatment of generalized anxiety in older adults: A preliminary comparison of cognitive-behavioral and supportive approaches. *Behavior Therapy, 27,* 565–581.

Stanley, M.A., Beck, J.G., Novy, D.M., Averill, P.M., & Swann, A.C. (1997, November). In C. Morin (Chair), *Treatment of insomnia, anxiety, and benzodiazepine dependence in late life.* Miami Beach, FL: Association for Advancement of Behavior Therapy.

Stanley, M.A., Beck, J.G., & Zebb, B.J. (1996). Psychometric properties of four anxiety measures in older adults. *Behaviour Research and Therapy, 34,* 827–838.

Weissman, M.M., Myers, J.K., Rischler, G.L., Holzer, C.E., Leaf, P.J., Orvaschel, H., & Brody, J.A. (1985). Psychiatric disorders *(DSM-III)* and cognitive impairment among the elderly in a US urban community. *Acta Psychiatrica Scandanavia, 71,* 366–379.

Yeatts, D.E., Crow, T., & Folts, E. (1992). Service use among low-income minority elderly: Strategies for overcoming barriers. *Gerontologist, 32,* 24–32.

Yost, E.B., Beutler, L.E., Corbishley, M.A., & Allender, J.R. (1986). *Group cognitive therapy: A treatment approach for depressed older adults.* New York: Pergamon Press.

CHAPTER 31

Treating Obsessive-Compulsive Disorder in Older Adults: A Review of Strategies

JOHN E. CALAMARI AND KAREN LYNN CASSIDAY

Obsessive-compulsive disorder (OCD) was once considered a rare and severely treatment refractory form of psychopathology. During the past three decades of intensive study, dramatic gains have been made in understanding OCD and in the treatment of what is now known to be a highly prevalent type of anxiety disorder. These dramatic changes have come late in the life of many older adults who have endured a typically early-in-life onset of OCD, and a history of misdiagnosis or involvement in what is now known to be ineffective treatment. Such a treatment history complicates late life intervention for the older adult. Many fear they suffer alone and believe little can be done to relieve their suffering.

In this chapter, the limited information available on the presentation and treatment of OCD in older adults is reviewed. The characteristic symptoms of this condition including the specific types of obsessions or compulsions that may occur in this age group are examined. Challenges to assessing older adults suspected of having OCD are described and detailed treatment intervention is reviewed through case examples illustrating how treatment approaches may need to be modified with this age group.

Although anxiety disorders appear to occur less often in older adults (see G. Beck & Stanley's, 1997, review), older adults may be inclined to under report psychological problems (e.g., Lasoski, 1986). Lifetime prevalence estimates for OCD in the population have been between 1.9% and 3.3% (Karno, Golding, Sorenson, & Burman, 1988). In a recent report where assessment was conducted by skilled clinicians (Stein, Forde, Anderson, & Walker, 1997), rates were lower. For persons over age 65, a 1-month prevalence rate of OCD of 0.8% (Regier et al., 1998) and 6-month prevalence rate of 1.5% (Bland, Newman, & Orn, 1998) have been reported. The prevalence rate of OCD in older adults living in institutional settings may be significantly higher (Bland et al., 1998), although study has been very limited. Juninger, Phelan, Cherry, and Levy (1993) reported rates of structured clinical interview determined anxiety disorders almost three times higher in nursing home residents compared with community residents. The rate of OCD was five times greater in the nursing home sample, although the sample size was small.

The typical age of onset of OCD has consistently been approximately 19 to 25, although earlier onset of different types of OCD symptomatology may not always have been thoroughly investigated in these studies (Steketee, 1993, p. 11). Fewer than 15% of individuals with OCD develop symptoms for the first time after age 35 (Goodwin, Guze, & Robins, 1969; Rasmussen & Tsuang, 1986). Onset after age 65 has been reported (Austin, Zealberg, & Lydiard, 1991; Bajulaiye & Addonizio, 1992). Possibly life-long subclinical OCD is exacerbated for some individuals following significant late life stressors (e.g., retirement, physical illness, death of a spouse; Calamari, Faber, Hitsman, & Poppe, 1994). The majority of individuals with OCD experience chronic or deteriorating symptoms over their life span, although periods of partial remission are occasionally observed (Steketee, 1993, p. 12).

OBSESSIVE-COMPULSIVE DISORDER SYMPTOMS

Obsessions are defined in contemporary psychiatric taxonomy as persistent ideas, thoughts, impulses, or images experienced as intrusive and inappropriate, and which cause marked anxiety or distress (American Psychiatric Association [APA], 1994). Compulsions are repetitive behavior or mental acts intended to prevent or reduce anxiety or distress (APA, 1994). Compulsive behavior or compulsive thoughts (e.g., canceling a harming thought by thinking a "good" thought) are understood to function to neutralize the anxiety or distress caused by obsessions (e.g., Salkovskis, 1989). There is no reason to believe that the diagnostic criteria for OCD in the Fourth Addition of the Diagnostic and Statistical Manual of Mental Disorders (*DSM-IV*; APA, 1994) are not equally applicable to the elderly (Pollard, Carmin, & Ownby, 1997).

Historically, persons with OCD have been characterized as maintaining insight into the excessive or unreasonable nature of their obsessions and compulsions. In the *DSM-IV*, greater variability in this characteristic is acknowledged and clinicians are asked to specify OCD with poor insight if for most of the time during the current episode the individual does not recognize that the obsessions or compulsions are unreasonable. Some researchers and clinicians contend that insight into the unreasonable nature of obsessions or compulsions can be best understood as existing along a continuum (e.g., Riggs & Foa, 1993, p. 191). For example, one patient with contamination obsessions about contracting the AIDS virus may present with severe obsessions and washing rituals lasting over four hours each day and report avoiding the use of any public restrooms, though readily acknowledge the complete unreasonableness of his behavior (but gain no relief from this insight). Another patient with identical concerns and similar symptom severity may express less insight (e.g., point out that all the means by which the virus can be contracted are not known and suggest that avoiding public restrooms may be a wise precaution). Yet a third patient with identical concerns and similar symptom severity may argue vehemently that the AIDS virus can be contracted by sitting in a chair that someone with the virus has used. Individual's level of insight into the reasonableness of their OCD symptoms may affect their willingness to consider important treatment options including behavior therapy procedures that involve directly confronting obsessional fears. Although there is no systematic data available, it has been our clinical experience that many older adults with OCD function with less than full insight. It remains unclear whether insight is adversely affected by the duration of their clinical condition or by the nature of the obsessional worries that some older adults experience. Some of the obsessional concerns described in the case examples that follow may more often be associated with poorer insight (e.g., scrupulosity, hoarding) regardless of age.

Obsessions and compulsions can take many different forms. Commonly occurring presentations involve contamination obsessions with washing compulsions, doubting obsessions associated with checking, and harming obsessions associated with checking, repeating behavior and reassurance-seeking compulsions (e.g., Baer, 1994; Hodgson & Rachman, 1977; Leckman et al., 1997). These more typical presentations have been reported to occur in older adults (Pollard et al., 1997), but there has also been suggestion that atypical symptoms or unusual co-morbidities may occur more often in this age group (Calamari et al., 1994). This issue has not been systematically studied. Ego-syntonic moral and religious scrupulosity has been reported in patients over 65-years-old (e.g., Fallon et al., 1990). Overlapping obsessional and hypochondriacal concerns have been observed in older adults (e.g., Fallon, Javitch, Hollander, & Liebowitz, 1991), including cases where the obsessional focus centered on bowel function (Hatch, 1997; Jenike, Vitagliano, Rabinowitz, Goff, & Baer, 1987; Ramchandani, 1990). Co-morbidity with bipolar illness (Grodon & Rasmussen, 1988) and psychotic symptomatology (Deckert & Malone, 1990) has been reported in the older adult literature, also, although such co-morbidities occur in other age groups as well. Because none of these presentations are unique to older adults, there is no convincing evidence at this time that unique or atypical symptoms are strongly associated with OCD in older adults (Pollard et al., 1997).

EFFECTIVE TREATMENT FOR OBSESSIVE-COMPULSIVE DISORDER

At present, there are two treatment interventions for OCD with definitive empirical support: pharmacologic strategies involving the selective serotonin reuptake inhibitors (SSRIs), and a specific form of behavior therapy, exposure and response prevention (see Stanley & Turner's, 1995, review). There is also growing evidence for the utility of cognitive therapy approaches (Emmelkamp & Beens, 1991; Emmelkamp, Visser, & Hoekstra, 1988; Freeston et al., 1997; Van Oppen et al., 1995).

PHARMACOLOGIC INTERVENTION

Contemporary medication intervention for OCD most often entails administration of SSRIs (Jenike, 1996; Stanley & Turner, 1995), an antidepressant medication. Improvement at post-treatment is observed for medication trial completers in 30% to 40% of patients and involves reductions in symptoms of 40% to 60% (Stanley & Turner, 1995). Clomipramine appears to be the most efficacious of these medications (Stanley & Turner, 1995), but clomipramine may not be the drug of choice in treating older adults with OCD because of side effects more frequently associated with this medication (Jenike, 1991). In general, though, the SSRIs are well tolerated by elderly patients. Rates of more serious cardiovascular complications are low (Jenike, 1996). More common side effects involve agitation, anorexia, nausea, gastrointestinal discomfort, and sexual dysfunction (Jenike, 1996).

Initiation of pharmacotherapy with older adults warrants several important considerations (Pollard et al., 1997). Dosing level and scheduling must allow for the possible diminished ability of older adults to metabolize medication. Additionally, older adults may be more sensitive to the cognitive side effects of these drugs and be at greater risk for adverse drug interactions because of taking many other medications. Pollard and colleagues suggested that fluoxetine may be the initial drug of choice with elderly OCD patients. They recommend starting with low dose trials (10 mg/day or lower) and very gradually increasing dose while evaluating the medical status of the older adult. Effective OCD treatment with fluoxetine may require dosages higher than levels required for the treatment of depression (Pollard et al., 1997).

BEHAVIOR THERAPY

Exposure therapy consists of graduated involvement in obsession precipitating experiences carried out in the context of the patient's commitment to response prevention, a resolution to not engage in anxiety neutralizing compulsive behavior. (See Steketee, 1993, or Riggs & Foa, 1993, for detailed descriptions of this treatment procedure.) Exposure therapy may involve imaginal exposure initially (e.g., imagining touching a contaminated doorknob), but progress to later in vivo exposure. Critical to the success of exposure therapy is the continuation of the exposure experience until the patient undergoes a perceptible decrease in their anxiety, that is, habituation (e.g., Riggs & Foa, 1993). For example, a patient with contamination obsessions and washing compulsions might initially be asked to touch a table top in a public area while committing to not washing her hands. Following successful habituation with the table touching exercise, the patient might be guided to touch the seat of a chair and then the floor. Each exercise is first modeled by the therapist. Typically, exposure and response prevention activities are structured to forcefully challenge the OCD, and therefore, often involve activities that go beyond normalized living. In the case of contamination obsessions, the end points on the exposure hierarchy might involve touching toilet seats in public restrooms and a commitment to refrain from all forms of washing for three days in a row during intensive treatment (e.g., Riggs & Foa, 1993, p. 215). It is essential that the rationale for such activities be clearly explained to the patient if their cooperation is to be obtained. Patients will need to be prepared for the initial increases in anxiety that exposure therapy produces. Didactic intervention involving making the individual aware that short-term increases in anxiety will not produce deleterious physical or psychological side effects are often necessary. The advisability of anxiety-increasing exposure therapy procedures for elderly patients must be carefully reviewed, and consultation with the patient's primary care physician is necessary. It has been our clinical experience that older adults tolerate exposure therapy well, although the intervention may need to be more gradual with this age group. Additionally, it may be necessary to repetitively review the rationale behind this approach to anxiety reduction with older adults (e.g., beginning each session with a brief review of the necessity of directly confronting feared experiences until habituation occurs).

Treatment outcome has been very favorable with exposure and response prevention, although controlled study of the response of older adults has not occurred. There have been a small number of favorable case reports of treating OCD in elderly patients with exposure and response prevention (e.g., Calamari et al., 1994; Colvin & Boddington, 1997). In controlled studies with general adult samples, approximately 30% of patients with OCD refuse or fail to complete behavior therapy (Stanley & Turner, 1995). Approximately 36% of patients who complete therapy will show at least a 70% reduction in symptoms, 27% will experience a 31% to 69% improvement in symptoms, while 7% will fail to benefit. Thus, if dropouts and treatment refusers are considered, 63% of OCD patients can be expected to respond favorably to exposure and response prevention (Stanley & Turner, 1995). O'Sullivan and Marks (1991) reported that the majority of patients treated with exposure and response prevention remained much improved at 1- to 6-year follow-up. Further, the degree of the patients' involvement in exposure and response prevention therapy has been found to predict the maintenance of treatment gains (O'Sullivan, Noshirvan, Marks, Monteiro, & Lelliott, 1991).

COGNITIVE THERAPY

A. Beck, Emery, and Greenberg (1985) described over a decade ago the utility of cognitive therapy approaches for the treatment of anxiety disorders including

OCD. Although initial evaluations of cognitive therapy treatment of OCD have been favorable (Emmelkamp & Beens, 1991; Emmelkamp et al., 1988; Van Oppen et al., 1995), the approach had not been broadly used until recently. Developments in the cognitive theory of OCD (Salkovskis, 1985, 1989; Rachman, 1993) and advances in OCD specific cognitive therapy (e.g., Freeston, Rheaume, & Ladouceur, 1996) have precipitated much greater interest in cognitive interventions for OCD in general, and in applications of cognitive therapy for specific OCD subtypes or with patients with less than full insight. In cognitive model of OCD, clinical obsessions are understood to result from the extreme reactions of patients to negative intrusive thoughts, thoughts that are in fact universally experienced (e.g., Rachman & DeSilva, 1978; Salkovskis & Harrison, 1984). OCD patients are distinguished by their appraisal of intrusive thoughts as highly significant events and this tendency is driven by dysfunctional beliefs involving excessive responsibility for preventing negative events (Salkovskis, 1985, 1989). Yet more specific dysfunctional beliefs relevant to some OCD patients have been described. Freeston et al. (1996) suggested that OCD patients' cognitive processing can be characterized by five broad groupings of faulty beliefs: Over estimations of the importance of thought and related magical thinking (e.g., thinking it makes it likely to happen), exaggerated responsibility for events beyond their control, a need to seek perfect states such as absolute certainty or completeness, overestimation of the probability and severity of negative outcome, and beliefs that the anxiety caused by their thoughts is unacceptable or dangerous. Intervention for these problems involves clarification of patients' specific beliefs, examination of evidence that supports or refutes beliefs, and completion of specific types of behavioral experiments. For example, the overestimation of the importance of thoughts might be approached through a thought suppression exercise (Freeston et al., 1996). The patient might be asked to force any thoughts about the color green from consciousness during the next five minutes and carefully monitor their success. This exercise often serves to demonstrate that effortful attempts to not think about something and hypervigilant monitoring for the occurrence of specific thoughts results only in a dramatic increase in the thought.

Freeston and colleagues described additional approaches to other obsession. Thought-action fusion, the belief that thinking a negative thought makes the event more likely, might be approached through examination of the effects that a range of thoughts have on outcome in the world. Behavioral experiments involving attempting to increase positive events by thinking about specific outcomes are sometimes used to explore this issue (e.g., thinking about winning the lottery). Excessive responsibility and guilt for negative events might be approached by having the patient take on the roles of both prosecuting and defense attorneys and presenting the evidence supporting the patient's culpability. It is typically difficult for the patient to function as the prosecuting attorney with this issue as often the only evidence for the patient's responsibility results from their emotional reasoning (i.e., I feel guilty, therefore, I have done something wrong; Freeston et al., 1996).

EXAMPLES OF OBSESSIVE-COMPULSIVE DISORDER IN OLDER ADULTS

Described next are two clinical case examples of older adults with OCD who have presented for treatment at one of two anxiety disorders specialty clinics in a large metropolitan area. One of these clinics was a community-based private practice and the other a university training and research clinic. Although over 250 patients meeting diagnostic criteria for OCD have been treated at these two clinics during the past seven years, less than 10 patients over age 60 have presented for treatment. Additionally, over half of the older adults seeking treatment only pursued intervention following the persistent insistence of a family member.

CASE EXAMPLE

Hoarding and Checking

Mrs. M was a widowed 77-year-old Caucasian woman who lived on her own and was referred for behavioral treatment by her daughter's psychiatrist. Her daughter had been receiving pharmacotherapy for panic disorder with agoraphobia, during which time she had discussed with the psychiatrist her mother's symptoms of anxiety attacks, fear of traveling, hoarding and checking. Mrs. M had reluctantly met with the psychiatrist while accompanied by her daughter and begun pharmacotherapy with clomipramine. Severe side effects resulted in the discontinuation of clomipramine and a trial of fluoxetine with alprazolam was initiated. This intervention decreased her panic attacks but left the patient nauseated, "jittery," and with sleep maintenance difficulties.

Mrs. M was assessed using a structured clinical interview (Brown, DiNardo, & Barlow, 1994). Both she and her daughter provided information. She met diagnostic criteria for OCD-moderate severity, major depression-recurrent, moderate severity, and panic disorder with agoraphobia-mild severity.

Mrs. M expressed great doubt about initiating behavioral treatment during the first and subsequent interviews. She revealed a history of multiple hospitalizations and trials of medications during her thirtys and fortys for "nervous breakdowns." She had also been treated with electroconvulsive therapy and psychoanalytic psychotherapy. Review of her apparent symptoms during this time suggests that she suffered from major depression, panic attacks, and harming obsessions (intrusive thoughts about harming her only child) along with checking and hoarding compulsions. She reported that her symptoms decreased somewhat once her daughter went away to college. Since then and until consulting with her daughter's psychiatrist, she had received all of her mental health care in the form of various anxiolytics and antidepressants prescribed by her general physician.

Mrs. M expressed a desire to rid herself of her anxiety and to live in a less cluttered space, but was reluctant to attempt behavioral treatment for fear of making her symptoms worse. Since Mrs. M seemed more motivated to please her daughter than to help herself, emphasis was placed on the pleasure that Mrs. M would feel at knowing her daughter's relief over her mother's recovery. Mrs. M freely talked of her death and this discussion was used to frame therapy in terms of allowing her and her daughter to spend their last years together in happy pursuits, rather than in conflict over OCD and panic. Mrs. M acknowledged that she hoarded unneeded items but justified her behavior by stating that "I lived through the depression. We had to save things." The only item that she could comfortably discard was kitchen trash or "dirty things" (e.g., used tissues). Her daughter was eager to commence exposure-based therapy and the two of them agreed to work together with the daughter serving as coach. We also agreed to start anxiety-modulation therapy involving diaphragmatic breathing retraining and relaxation training to help Mrs. M modulate her severe anxiety and to control bodily sensations she feared. Both the patient and her daughter learned relaxation techniques well enough to be able to coach each other to use them effectively to manage episodic anxiety attacks. These approaches also allowed the therapist to develop rapport with the patient and provided a context for repeatedly explaining the rationale for treatment. Additionally, these interactions with the patient helped the therapist determine which cognitive reframes were likely to be most motivating (e.g., "I want my house to be clean and tidy when I die so that my daughter does not have to deal with the clutter.")

Exposure-based therapy focused on planning graduated tasks for the patient and daughter to complete at home. Bags of hoarded items were brought into the therapist's office so that the therapist could role-model coaching the patient to manage her anxiety while completing exposure work. Unlike typical exposure therapy in which the patient's anxiety is allowed to subside of its own accord, the patient employed diaphragmatic breathing to help manage and decrease within session anxiety because of the co-morbid panic disorder symptoms. At the end of sessions, homework assignments were structured in which the patient and her daughter determined items that needed to be discarded next. The daughter was instructed to avoid critical comments and any pressuring of Mrs. M to discard items that had not been agreed upon in advance. Between sessions, the patient and daughter met to complete assignments and were encouraged to end their "sessions" by engaging in pleasant activities together, such as going out to dinner. Over the course of treatment, the patient experienced between-session decreases in anxiety to the point at which she no longer felt the need to use diaphragmatic breathing as an aid to exposure. She was also able to follow a set of anti-hoarding guidelines sufficiently well such that she was not continually adding to the existing clutter in her house. The patient was unwilling to address checking compulsions (doors, windows, stove, locks, and the location of her purse), describing this behavior as something that she had "just gotten used to." Mrs. M and her daughter also attended an OCD support group, which seemed to benefit the daughter more than the mother by improving the daughter's motivation to help and knowledge about OCD.

Treatment consisted of eight sessions that took place every 2 to 3 weeks to accommodate the daughter's work schedule since the patient could not comfortably drive outside her own neighborhood. Both the patient and daughter felt unconcerned about the mother's agoraphobic avoidance, believing that "at my age, who needs to drive farther?" At the end of eight sessions, the patient's home environment was sufficiently improved to allow both the daughter and patient to be pleased. Mrs. M and her daughter felt able to maintain this level of tidiness on their own with the backup of the OCD support group or through only periodic contact with the therapist. Follow-up conversations with the psychiatrist during the subsequent three years suggested that Mrs. M and her daughter had maintained a less cluttered home and felt that the OCD was no longer a significant problem, however recurrent depression, panic attacks, and medication side effects continued to distress the patient.

CASE EXAMPLE

Scrupulosity and Doubting

Mrs. S was an 86-year-old Caucasian widow who was referred for treatment by her son. His mother's retirement home staff had been complaining of his mother's unusual behavior and risk for bladder infections due to avoidance of urinating until the last possible moment. Her son noted that she had recently begun constant listening to religious songs, ate only corn flakes, and was repeatedly cleaning her dentures and hands.

Mrs. S was assessed using a structured clinical interview (Brown et al., 1994). She met criteria for OCD-severe. She took fluoxetine and doxepine at the time of evaluation which was prescribed by her psychiatrist.

Discussion with both the son and the patient revealed a lengthy history of intrusive thoughts, scrupulosity, superstitious thoughts, superstitious compulsions, and hand washing that the patient reported began at age 5. The patient described her need to recall "good thoughts" and avoid "bad thoughts" and that this concern had begun prior to beginning elementary school. Mrs. S reported undergoing multiple involuntary hospitalizations in which her family had called the police who then escorted her to the psychiatric hospital. These hospitalizations were precipitated by incidents involving begging family members to pray with her, repetitive hand washing until her hands were raw, extensive checking rituals, and ritualistic praying that prevented her from attending to household duties. She reported undergoing multiple treatments, including medication, spiritual counselling, psychotherapy, and electroconvulsive therapy. She was not formally diagnosed with OCD until 1985. Her son recalled early incidents involving his mother weeping and begging him to pray with her so that she might "think good thoughts." He also recalled his mother repeatedly checking the pilot lights on the stove. Neither the son nor the patient had heard about exposure in vivo with response prevention for the treatment of OCD.

The patient's current symptomatology focused on trying to avoid thinking about God while engaging in "dirty" activities (e.g., urinating and eating). Other compulsions included repetitively and excessively cleaning her dentures and trying to avoid blasphemous thoughts. The patient also compulsively made religious vows about forgoing pleasurable activities to rid her mind of intrusive thoughts, thus the diet of corn flakes. She compulsively bathed and washed her hands after using the bathroom. Additionally, she repeatedly checked to make sure that faucets and stoves were turned off in her retirement home.

Mrs. S agreed to attempt exposure therapy but did not want to involve any support persons in treatment because of embarrassment over her symptoms. Accordingly, she did not attend an OCD support group, although we strongly recommended this because a nearby support group had many members who suffered from symptoms similar to hers. Her son, however, attended support group meetings and found it helpful in increasing his tolerance and compassion for his mother's past and current behaviors; behaviors that he had experienced as very hurtful. Mrs. S also denied permission to the therapist or her son to discuss her OCD with the retirement home staff.

Before exposure in vivo with response prevention, extensive education and motivation enhancement was conducted because Mrs. S believed her case to be hopeless. She also had limited insight and believed that she would feel better if only she could develop the proper spiritual attitude. Helpful strategies involved the use of lists of the pros and cons for entering treatment and emphasizing that the chance of symptom relief was worth the risk after having suffered for so many years. Exposure sessions were conducted weekly over a two-month period after consultation with her physician who felt that an intensive exposure protocol of multiple sessions per week would be too physically challenging to her hypertension. During sessions, exposure to blasphemous thoughts while engaging in feared activities (e.g., urinating while thinking about Jesus) was completed. Additionally, imaginal exposure involving the production of images of Jesus, the Virgin Mary, and the clergy paired with sexual or body-function related thoughts. She experienced both within and between session decreases in anxiety that accelerated after she consulted with a priest to receive her church's official sanction for exposure therapy. Reading the Scrupulous Anonymous Newsletter (Redemption Press, 1997), a support group newsletter for Catholics with scrupulosity, also improved her motivation and willingness to participate in exposure therapy. The patient was unwilling to allow home visits by the therapist, thus we were unable to effectively practice exposure for checking and bathing rituals. The patient gradually reduced her denture cleaning compulsions by following a prearranged schedule for reducing cleaning. Therapy ended after nine sessions when Mrs. S felt able to eat, urinate, and do daily activities with a minimum number of vows and canceling of "bad thoughts." Although she continued to have significant symptoms of OCD, she felt pleased with her progress and felt that her OCD symptoms were less severe than at any other time in her life.

SPECIAL CONSIDERATIONS IN THE TREATMENT OF OLDER ADULTS

Motivation enhancement for treatment is often necessary for older adults. Many older patients will have suffered with symptoms for many years and have a history of involvement in ineffective treatment. Older patients may also believe that mental health treatment is only for psychotic disorders or is for the neurotic wealthy. They may also believe that discussion of problematic thoughts and feelings is somehow shameful. As stated by one older patient, "You just don't talk about things like that." Our experience has taught us the need to use a combination of basic education and cognitive therapy to alter these beliefs.

Additionally, providing written handouts explaining the nature of OCD in easy-to-read print is helpful. Frequent repetition of key points is important in overcoming the normal decrements in short-term memory that may occur in older adults. Frank discussion of the patient's motivation for treatment and elicitation of reasons to attempt treatment are necessary to address skepticism and pessimism. Asking the patient to attempt several treatment sessions as an experiment to see if they can reduce their anxiety may be helpful.

Support groups may be an invaluable aid to the families of older patients with OCD, although older adults appear more reluctant to use this resource themselves. Perhaps this is because older adults have not been raised in a culture in which support groups and self-disclosure are understood as therapeutic. Nevertheless, several of our older patients have found support and inspiration within an OCD support group.

CONCLUSIONS AND FUTURE DIRECTIONS

OCD remains a significantly understudied problem in older adults. Although the available prevalence data suggest that OCD may occur less often in older adults, the condition appears likely to be one of the most frequently occurring psychiatric conditions in this age group. The problem may be significantly under-recognized in older adults with diagnosis complicated by co-occurring medical conditions or the cognitive impairment seen in some older adults. Older adults' apparent unwillingness to discuss psychiatric symptomatology further complicates diagnosis. OCD may be more prevalent and more significantly under-recognized in supported living environments such as retirement communities and nursing homes. Under-recognition of this problem in older adults is especially tragic because effective treatment is available. Although not all older adults will be responsive to cognitive-behavioral or pharmacologic intervention, it appears that these interventions, with minor modifications, may be efficacious with the majority of this age group. Positive treatment response rates may be equivalent to treatment outcomes observed in other age groups, although definitive conclusions await the initiation and completion of controlled studies.

REFERENCES

American Psychiatric Association (1994). *Diagnostic and statistical manual of mental disorders* (4th ed.). Washington, DC: Author.

Austin, L.S., Zealberg, J.J., & Lydiard, R.B. (1991). Three cases of pharmacotherapy of obsessive-compulsive disorder in the elderly. *Journal of Nervous and Mental Disease, 179*, 634–635.

Baer, L. (1994). Factor analysis of symptom subtypes of obsessive-compulsive disorder and their relationship to personality and tic disorders. *Journal of Clinical Psychiatry, 55*, 18–23.

Bajulaiye, R., & Addonizio, G. (1992). Obsessive compulsive disorder arising in a 75-year-old woman. *International Journal of Geriatric Psychiatry, 7*, 139–142.

Beck, A.T., Emery, G., & Greenberg, R. (1985). *Anxiety disorders and phobias: A cognitive perspective.* New York: Basic Books.

Beck, G., & Stanley, M. (1997). Anxiety disorders in the elderly: The emerging role of behavior therapy. *Behavior Therapy, 28*, 83–100.

Bland, R.C., Newman, S.C., & Orn, H. (1998). Prevalence of psychiatric disorders in the elderly in Edmonton. *Acta Psyciatric Scandanavia, 338*(Suppl.) 57–63.

Brown, T.A., DiNardo, P.A., & Barlow, D.H. (1994). *Anxiety disorders interview schedule for DSM-IV.* New York: Graywind.

Calamari, J.E., Faber, S.D., Hitsman, B.L., & Poppe, B.A. (1994). Treatment of obsessive-compulsive disorder in the elderly: A review and case example. *Journal of Behavior Therapy and Experimental Psychiatry, 25*, 95–104.

Colvin, C., & Boddington, S. (1997). Case report: Behaviour therapy for obsessive-compulsive disorder in a 78-year-old woman. *International Journal of Geriatric Psychiatry, 12*, 488–491.

Deckert, D.W., & Malone, D.A. (1990). Treatment of psychotic symptoms in OCD patients. *Journal of Clinical Psychiatry, 51,* 259.

Emmelkamp, P., & Beens, H. (1991). Cognitive therapy with obsessive-compulsive disorder: A comparative evaluation. *Behaviour Research and Therapy, 29,* 293–300.

Emmelkamp, P., Visser, S., & Hoekstra, R. (1988). Cognitive therapy vs. exposure in vivo in the treatment of obsessive-compulsives. *Cognitive Therapy and Research, 12,* 103–114.

Fallon, B.A., Javitch, J.A., Hollander, E., & Liebowitz, M.R. (1991). Hypochondriasis and obsessive-compulsive disorder: Overlaps in diagnosis and treatment. *Journal of Clinical Psychiatry, 52,* 457–460.

Fallon, B.A., Liebowitz, M.R., Hollander, E., Schneier, F.R., Campeas, R.B., Fairbanks, J., Papp, L.A., Hatterer, J.A., & Sandberg, D. (1990). The pharmacotherapy of moral or religious scrupulosity. *Journal of Clinical Psychiatry, 51,* 517–521.

Freeston, M.H., Ladouceur, R., Gagnon, F., Thibodeau, N., Rheaume, J., Letarte, H., & Bujold, A. (1997). Cognitive-behavioral treatment of obsessive thoughts: A controlled study. *Journal of Consulting and Clinical Psychology, 65,* 405–413.

Freeston, M.H., Rheaume, J., & Ladouceur, R. (1996). Correcting faulty appraisals of obsessional thoughts. *Behavior, Research and Therapy, 34,* 433–446.

Goodwin, D.W., Guze, S.B., & Robins, E. (1969). Follow-up studies on obsessional neurosis. *Archives of General Psychiatry, 20,* 182–187.

Grodon, A., & Rasmussen, S.A. (1988). Mood-related obsessive-compulsive symptoms in a patient with bipolar affective disorder. *Journal of Clinical Psychiatry, 49,* 27–28.

Hatch, M.J. (1997). Conceptualization and treatment of bowel obsessions: Two case reports. *Behaviour Research and Therapy, 35,* 253–257.

Hodgson, R.J., & Rachman, S. (1977). Obsessional-compulsive complaints. *Behaviour Research and Therapy, 15,* 389–395.

Jenike, M.A. (1991). Obsessional disorders in the elderly. In J.R.M. Copeland, M.T. Abou-Saleh, & D. Blazer (Eds.), *The psychology of old age.* New York: Wiley.

Jenike, M.A. (1996). Psychiatric illness in the elderly: A review. *Journal of Geriatric Psychiatry and Neurology, 9,* 57–82.

Jenike, M.A., Vitagliano, H.L., Rabinowitz, J., Goff, D.C., & Bear, L. (1987). Bowel obsession responsive to tricyclic antidepressants in four patients. *American Journal of Psychiatry, 144,* 1347–1348.

Juninger, J., Phelan, E., Cherry, K., & Levy, J. (1993). Prevalence of psychopathology in elderly persons in nursing homes and in the community. *Hospital and Community Psychiatry, 44,* 381–383.

Karno, M., Golding, J.M., Sorenson, S.B., & Burnam, M.A. (1988). The epidemiology of obsessive-compulsive disorder in five US communities. *Archives of General Psychiatry, 45,* 1094–1099.

Lasoski, M.C. (1986). Reasons for low utilization of mental health services by the elderly. In T.L. Brink (Ed.), *Clinical gerontology: A guide to assessment and intervention* (pp. 1–18). New York: Haworth Press.

Leckman, J.F., Grice, D., Boradman, J., Zhang, H., Vitale, A., Bondi, C., Alsobrook, J., Pererson, B., Cohen, D., Rasmussen, S., Goodman, W., McDougle, C., & Pauls, D. (1997). Symptoms of obsessive-compulsive disorder. *American Journal of Psychiatry, 154,* 911–917.

O'Sullivan, G.O., & Marks, I. (1991). Follow-up studies of behavioral treatment of phobic and obsessive compulsive neurosis. *Psychiatric Annals, 21,* 368–373.

O'Sullivan, G.O., Noshirvani, H., Marks, I., Monteiro, W., & Lelliott, P. (1991). Six-year follow-up after exposure and clomipramine therapy for obsessive-compulsive disorder. *Journal of Clinical Psychiatry, 52,* 150–155.

Pollard, C.A., Carmin, C.N., & Ownby, R. (1997). Obsessive-compulsive disorder in later life. *Annals of Psychiatry, 3,* 57–72.

Rachman, S. (1993). Obsessions, responsibility and guilt. *Behavior, Research and Therapy, 31,* 149–154.

Rachman, S., & DeSilva, P. (1978). Abnormal and normal obsessions. *Behaviour, Research and Therapy, 16,* 233–248.

Ramchandani, D. (1990). Trazadone for bowel obsession. *American Journal of Psychiatry, 147,* 124.

Rasmussen, S.A., & Tsuang, M.T. (1986). Epidemiological and clinical findings of significance to the design of neuropharmacologic studies of obsessive-compulsive disorder. *Psychopharmacological Bulletin, 22,* 723–733.

Redemption Press. (1997). *Scrupulous Anonymous Newsletter.* Liguori, MO: Author.

Regier, D.A., Boyd, J.H., Burke, J.D., Rae, D.S., Myers, J.K., Kramer, M., Robins, L.N., George, L.K., Karno, M., & Locke, R.Z. (1998). One-month prevalence of mental disorders in the United States: Based on five epidemiologic catchment area sites. *Archives of General Psychiatry, 45,* 977–986.

Riggs, D.S., & Foa, E.B. (1993). Obsessive-compulsive disorder. In D.H. Barlow (Ed.), *Handbook of clinical disorders* (2nd ed., pp. 189–239). New York: Guilford Press.

Salkovskis, P.M. (1985). Obsessional-compulsive problems: A cognitive-behavioural analysis. *Behavior, Research, and Therapy, 23,* 571–583.

Salkovskis, P.M. (1989). Cognitive-behavioral factors and the persistence of intrusive thoughts in obsessional problems. *Behavior, Research and Therapy, 6,* 677–682.

Salkovskis, P.M., & Harrison, J. (1984). Abnormal and normal obsessions: A replication. *Behavior, Research, and Therapy, 22,* 549–552.

Stanley, M.A., & Turner, S.M. (1995). Current status of pharmacological and behavioral treatment of obsessive-compulsive disorder. *Behavior Therapy, 26,* 163–186.

Stein, M.B., Forde, D.R., Anderson, G., & Walker, J.R. (1997). Obsessive-compulsive disorder in the community: An epidemiologic survey with clinical reappraisal. *American Journal of Psychiatry, 154,* 1120–1126.

Steketee, G.S. (1993). *Treatment of obsessive compulsive disorder.* New York: Guilford Press.

Van Oppen, P., De Haan, E., Van Balkom, A., Spinhoven, P., Hoogduin, K., & Van Dyck, R. (1995). Cognitive therapy and exposure in vivo the treatment of obsessive-compulsive disorder. *Behaviour Research and Therapy, 33,* 379–390.

CHAPTER 32

The Effects of Trauma: Dynamics and Treatment of PTSD in the Elderly

Lee Hyer

The study of trauma has become so popular that it has been labeled "the soul of psychiatry" (van der Kolk & McFarlane, 1996). During the past decade, it has been the most intriguing and studied construct to evolve in mental health. Trauma is everywhere. It is now unreasonable to expect that victims of trauma, any trauma, are able to walk away from the experience as whole people (Hyer & Associates, 1994). Trauma symptoms are sufficiently prevalent and intrusive as to become a major concern for mental health practitioners, giving rise to a variety of disorders, some of which may affect the victim at a subclinical level; whereas others are full-blown and more seriously affect psychological adaptation. The most noxious disorder resulting from trauma is posttraumatic stress disorder (PTSD).

The study of trauma in older people, especially PTSD, is fraught with problems related to developmental issues and life-span patterns. Uncontaminated facts are hard to come by. It is conventional to argue (Green, 1991) that the trauma response is a function of the individual (personality variables), considerations of the trauma itself, and the mediating influences of the recovery process. But, when the aging process is added to the mix, the trauma response is not so easily separated. Disruptions of the life-span transitions result and alter the acquisition and integration of developmental competencies (Pynoos, Sternberg, & Goenjian, 1996). In fact, trauma influences development, disrupts expectancies and competencies, juggles transition points, and disturbs normal biological maturation. The person must adjust developmentally.

Complications related to the nature of trauma and aging decline, to cohort issues and the natural transition from an acute to a chronic status (of trauma) are also present. In fact, it is at the interface of aging and trauma that issues of trauma unfold. Over time, we know that trauma-related problems may be reactivated when reminders of the war occur, perhaps also when events associated with aging occur, as in retirement and medical illness. But, while these events are stock occurrences, for most they are not stressful (Schnurr, 1996). We are just now asking the right questions about whether dormant triggers of past conflict are more accessible when aging occurs, when an organ insult is in process, or when a role jolt happens (as in a retirement). We will never know the exact prevalence of PTSD of these or other older victims when they were younger because longitudinal data do not exist. We must rely on retrospective accounts of the experiences.

At the risk of iconoclasty, PTSD is not the only disorder specific to a poor trauma response. Trauma is like a deathbed confession: It needs to be heard and is not very poetic in its expression. But how it is heard is open. The traditional way to categorize trauma, the criteria for PTSD (APA, 1994), may not serve the study of trauma (Green, 1991) or older people (Summers & Hyer, 1991) well. With old people, this formulation does not represent well how fear memories depict erroneous messages that generalize to behavior in life (Hyer & Summers, 1994). That trauma is a risk factor for a later mental disorder seems accepted; that it represents an etiologic factor is not corroborated (Maughan & Rutter, 1997). In fact, factors that initiate psychopathology are generally not the same as those that maintain its persistence into older age (Rutter & Maughan, 1997). The myriad factors related to the parameters of abuse (nature of the trauma), the balancing of risk and resilient components, extant cognitive schemas, the social network, and predisposing factors interact to "produce" a response to trauma, most often one that results in adequate adjustment (Paris, 1997). In effect, the trauma response is more (or less) than PTSD.

All things being equal, however, the "continuity position" of treatment is most apt: operative concerns are more a function of PTSD-specific factors than aging-specific ones. The issues that apply to younger trauma groups apply to older ones for the most part. This said, just as in therapy the more the person knows about the therapy, the better the chances for success, so too, the more the therapist knows the concatenations of aging and trauma, the better the chances for success in therapy. An understanding of the care of an older victim of trauma rests, then, to some extent on chronological status and to some extent on an understanding of psychiatric disorders or disordered responses to life (trauma response). Also it is important to say that this understanding at older ages is just beginning (Gurian & Miner, 1991).

In this chapter, we discuss several issues. First, we consider stress as it applies to older people. Second, we present the research data on the general curative factors of trauma and address issues of the care of older victims. Next, we present a treatment model for older trauma victims. Last, we present a case outlining the features of the model.

STRESS

Stress is not an understudied area: Over 10,000 studies exist from the past decade. Studies of trauma and PTSD indicate that on average about a quarter of the individuals who are exposed go on to develop PTSD (lifetime). This appears to apply to older victims. Prevalence rates of lifetime PTSD vary as a function of the sample assessed, methods used, and the definition of trauma. Current rates of PTSD exposed to traumatic events in general range from about 5% to 11% (Norris, 1992). Norris found the lifetime exposure rate to at least one major stressor event of 69%. And stress is plentiful at later life. Ensel (1991) showed that most older community-dwelling adults (74%) had at least one major life event during the past six months that produced a negative impact. Considering combat trauma of older victims as a marker, prevalence rates are low (at times < 2%) when community samples are used (Hankin, Abueg, Gallagher-Thompson, & Laws, 1996; Schnurr, Aldwin, Spiro, Stukel, & Keane, 1993; Spiro, Aldwin, Levenson, & Schnurr, 1993), higher when medical subjects are studied (Blake et al. 1990), higher still among psychiatric outpatients (Garfein, Ronis, & Bates, 1993), and most high among psychiatric inpatients (Goldstein, van Kammen, Shelly, Miller, & van Kammen, 1987; Hovens et al., 1994; Rosen, Fields, Hand, Falsettie, & van Kammen, 1989; Zeiss & Dickman, 1989) or prisoners of war (Tennant, Goulston, & Dent, 1993). This is accurate even when the effects due to aging are accounted for (e.g., sleep disturbance and memory impairment) (Zeiss & Dickman, 1989).

The research on PTSD informs us that, if the trauma is sufficiently intense, that this is correlated with the extent of symptoms in almost all studies. So exposed, most elderly are likely to experience psychological consequences (see Hyer & Associates, 1994). G. Elder and Clipp's (1989) longitudinal study, however, presents evidence that, overall, symptoms decrease over time. In general, it appears that, although older people experience both minor (Ensel, 1991) and major (Hyer & Summers, 1994) negative life events, often are bothered by these (Falk, Hersen, & Van Hasselt, 1994; Tait & Silver, 1984), and underrepresent or alter (e.g., somaticizing) problems (Hankin et al., 1996), or have a more closed view of mental problems (Bortz & O'Brien, 1997; Logsdon, 1995), older victims are not worse off as a result of trauma. Older age may not be just a continuation of earlier ages, not just mature resilience of coping or improved stress inoculation. It is the time to see life as it is (Baltes & Staudinger, 1993) and to appreciate universal and cosmic properties (Chinen, 1984). The last tasks of life—love, care, and wisdom—are different in kind (Erikson, 1975), and present themselves with the hope that a sense of integrity can be achieved.

Studies on major life events have noted that the aged experience fewer life events, although they experience more loss, including those associated with declining health, work role, and loved ones (Chiriboga & Cutler, 1980). Development is compromised when trauma occurs. The integration of information is affected not just by the trauma, or the adaptation and adjustments to the trauma, but by the age at the time of trauma. Different symptoms may represent the reaction to traumatic exposures at different points in development. Other influences of subsequent adjustment include caretaking, disturbances in developmental expectations in the acquisition and integration of development competencies, the disruption of developmental transitions, disturbances in normal biological maturation, and the expression of traumatic expectations and interfering fantasies (Pynoos, Steinberg, & Groetjin, 1995).

To be complete, moderating (at times mediating) influences of trauma differentially affect older people. If we are saying anything here, it is that the mixture of the life transition process and the trauma adjustment make for an interesting interaction (L. Elder & Caspi, 1990; McAdams, 1993). In Table 32.1, five variables are highlighted, but others exist. Older people are vulnerable to the effects of different stressors, compromised health status, comorbidity, inadequate social support, and cognitive decline. And, even these variables that affect the adjustment differ over time, those directly influential after the trauma differing from those 30 or 50 years later (Schnurr & Aldwin, 1993). The trajectory of the (mental) health of war trauma victims, for example, varies over the life span (Mellman, Randolph, Brawman-Mintzer, Flores, & Milanes, 1992).

TREATMENT

The efficacy of PTSD treatment is suspect. The alteration of the trauma memory remains the key work of therapy in PTSD. Standard treatment of trauma is often discussed in phase language. In fact, it seems that we are forever iterating Freud's ideas of stimulus barrier and repetition compulsion, and later Horowitz's phase model (Hyer & Associates, 1994). Trauma occurs when the intrusion and avoidance phases are out of control, when the oscillation is out of sync. After a reasonable alliance, the therapist assures him/herself of the client's tolerance for treatment, often based on the client's history interpersonally. Here, baseline anxiety levels must be reduced to at least tolerable levels. Soon the treatment components of encouraging action (social support, reduce

Table 32.1   Stress "facts" at later life.

1. Older victims are not worse off as a result of stress.
2. There are positive effects of stress.
3. Stress at later life has a generativity filter: it is mediated.
4. Victims at later life often react to stress "better" than other age groups.
5. Cognitive complexity of the person who experiences trauma is important.
6. Stress is a subjective experience.
7. Stress is hard to measure.
8. The best treatment method for older patients with PTSD is unknown.

Moderators

1. Older people are vulnerable to the effects of multiple past and current stressors.
2. Compromised health status covaries with PTSD.
3. Psychiatric comorbidity, especially depression, may be addressed.
4. Social support must be addressed.
5. Cognitive decline influences the processing of information.

avoidance, etc.) are activated. Compensatory skills are always in place before exploration. Eventually the revision of the trauma is addressed. By repeatedly redoing the trauma event, the inner and outer worlds of the client are revisited and an appreciation of cognitive and emotional meanings can unfold. Eventually the person is encouraged to practice new skills, experience and recognize the provoked emotions and thoughts, and alter these. In a manual to treat younger combat veterans, Smyth (1995) framed these ideas, endorsing the activation of the target memory with the autonomic nervous system at a moderate range and the concomitant use of the assimilation process. These ingredients, along with the therapeutic relationship, constitute the curative agents for trauma victims.

Psychotherapy at later life is not suspect: It works (Gallagher-Thompson & Thompson, 1995; Gatz, 1994) on a wide variety of pathological areas (Zeiss & Steffen, in press), combined with medication (Thompson, Gallagher, Hansen, Gantz, & Steffen, 1991), or applied to difficult problems (Hanley-Peterson et al., 1990; Thompson, Gallagher, & Czirr, 1988). Some adjustments to traditional therapeutic techniques, such as being more active or task focused with a few clearly outlined goals and using a psychoeducational model and collaborative approach (Zeiss & Steffen, in press), are often required. As early as 1973, "special psychologic needs of the elderly" requiring distinctive themes (e.g., loss, increased dependency, existential approach of death), age-specific reactions (e.g., survivor guilt at having outlasted others), and "aging" therapy needs (e.g., symbolic giving, more limited goals, greater amount of positive benefit, as well as a slower pace and lack of termination), were noted (Pfeiffer & Busse, 1973).

While other forms of therapy have been addressed in the literature, notably problem-solving therapy (Nezu, Nezu, Friedman, Faddis, & Houts, 1998) and interpersonal psychotherapy (Hinrichsen, 1997), two forms have received most attention, cognitive behavioral therapy (CBT) and reminiscence. Both relate to trauma therapy. During the past 15 years, the use of the CBT has proved effective with later life depression (Beutler et al., 1987; Gallagher & Thompson, 1981, 1982; Hyer, Swanson, et al., 1990; Hyer, Swanson, & Lefkowitz, 1990; McCarthy, Katz, & Foa, 1991; Thompson, Gallagher, & Breckenridge, 1987) and anxiety (Scogin, Rickard, Keith, Wilson, & McElreath, 1992). The application of CBT is also responsible for the maintenance of treatment gains (Gallagher-Thompson, Hanley-Peterson, & Thompson, 1990).

Reminiscence has not received the methodological rigor that CBT has. Nonetheless, it has a long history and has been used almost exclusively with older people (Butler, 1963; Parker, 1995). Overall results of its efficacy are inconclusive (Parker, 1995), but show it to be enjoyable, natural, informative, often social, and to end in improved outcomes like increased self-esteem (Kovach, 1990). In one study, Sherman (1991) showed that older people change through an active process of reminiscing—a conscious attempt to pull together positive and negative features into a cohesive pattern. Victims responded best when they were engaged, when they had developed a reasonable level of experiencing of the memory (exploratory or elaborated experience), and when they reached a level of "life review reminiscing." In this form of reminiscing, the person brings older memories to life and feels and experiences them in the "now," bolstered by the ongoing processing of information (reconstruction).

There are no carefully controlled studies of the treatment of trauma on older victims. So we must look to components of care. In a review, Solomon, Gerrity, and Muff (1992) identified only 11 outcome studies that utilized random assignment to treatment and control groups. Although none applied to older victims, the active therapeutic ingredients for the treatment of PTSD were of interest. They included systematic desensitization and cognitive-behavioral therapy (Frank et al., 1988; Resick & Schnicke, 1992), exposure therapy (Boudewyns & Hyer, 1990; Cooper & Clum, 1989; Foa, Rothbaum, Riggs, & Murdock, 1991; Keane, Fairbank, Caddell, & Zimering, 1989), and several general factors, including support and skills training (Resick, Jordan, Girelli, Hutter, & Marhoefer-Dvorak, 1988). The combination also of Anxiety Management Training (AMT) or Stress Inoculation Training (SIT), along with prolonged exposure (Foa et al., 1994; Resick & Schnicke, 1992), constitutes the treatments of choice for PTSD. These findings have been endorsed in other review papers (Shalev, Boone, & Eth, 1996).

These findings apply to older trauma victims. Intensive exposure methods are not productive with older people, tending to increase the level of autonomic arousal with adverse effects on cognitive performance (McFarlane & Yehuda, 1996). AMT and SIT do not do this: The former seeks to manage the anxiety as it occurs, due less to fear activation and more to necessary coping tools; and SIT addresses the perception of control to tolerate trauma memories and the belief (and tools) that one can cope. Gradual exposure is implied in both methods. AMT provides a user-friendly atmosphere, where the client feels in control.

In one of the few studies that included stressor victims, Hyer and colleagues (1990) evaluated two groups of older clients, chronic PTSD or recent stress reactions due to loss, as well as a no-treatment control group. Two CBT components were identified and practiced—cognitive schemas/irrational beliefs and relaxation/anxiety management training (AMT). Each group received a 12-session CBT program and was evaluated on several psychological and behavioral outcome measures. Although objective repeated measures showed no differences among the groups, subjective measures of outcome and individual change supported the treatment package. All subjects believed they benefited from the cognitive therapy and the relaxation training along with the AMT.

Eye movement desensitization and reprocessing (EMDR) acts in a similar way. Despite critical reviews (e.g., Acierno, Hersen, Van Hasselt, Tremont, & Meuser, 1994), this procedure provides a dosed exposure that targets state-specific information related to the trauma (Boudewyns & Hyer, 1997) and has applicability with older victims (Hyer, 1995). Like standard CBT, EMDR employs all treatment modalities—emotions, sensations, cognitions, images—to unearth the trauma paced by the client. Like AMT and SIT, EMDR provides both exposure and assimilation components. Unlike these other methods, EMDR is more active and guides the client when information is blocked (Hyer & Brandsma, 1997).

Both AMT and EMDR allow for several positive features of change. The exposure is dosed at the direction of the client. Additionally, the autonomic nervous system is activated at a moderate range and new and incongruent data are added. Anxiety then is managed within the treatment context and coping techniques are suggested. Just as exposure is provided in a dosed way, altered cognitions or behavior interventions are introduced when the naturalness of the intervention is not effective. The stuck story of the trauma is reframed or repaired, then, with a considerable assist of cognitions.

From another perspective, the assimilation methods used by these methods are similar to those employed by the narrative (Hyer & Associates, 1994). With trauma, information processing is compromised, maintaining the status quo (Litz & Keane, 1989). There is some consensus that the more the trauma memory is simply disclosed (Pennebaker, 1989) and validated (Murray & Segal, 1994), the more improvement occurs. The more organized (Foa, Molnar, & Cashman, 1995), placed into explicit memory (van der Kolk & Fisler, 1995), elaborated (Harvey, Orbuch, Chivalisz, & Garwood, 1991; Sewell, 1996), moved (Shapiro, 1995), or retrieved as less summary and more positive (McNally, Lasko, Macklin, & Pitman, 1995), the more improvement occurs. Interventions used with older people, as in reminiscence (expose the story, unearth obvious distortions, and foster alternative beliefs) or CBT (surface and core construals) naturally challenge cognitive distortions unique to trauma. In effect, they reorganize stories. In the narrative context, they repair the story and rewrite the biography of the person. It is in this context that the story is a rediscovery and healing occurs.

TREATMENT MODEL

Building on the preceding research, a treatment model for trauma victims applicable to older people is presented. It is intended to provide structure with flexibility: first treat perturbation, then coping/social supports, then issues specific to trauma. It has six parts (Table 32.2).

First, the task is to stabilize symptoms, including the treatment of comorbid disorders and current stressors (including health). Symptoms must be treated initially both because they are important by themselves and because

Table 32.2 Treatment model.

1. Stabilize symptoms. Treat comorbid disorders or stressors (including health).
2. Relationship building. Build trust, the ability to confront combat trauma with a trusted therapist. Respect the narcissistic alliance (what he needs to have stroked).
3. Attend to necessary developmental and treatment and education (normalization) factors.
4. Reduce avoidance/other symptoms. Use tactics of personality style.
5. Build on positive memories. Foster a renarration of self with core memories that can generalize to current life situations. This is often a core life story, the person's identity that can assist in the balance of his or her life.
6. Overcome intrusion. Decondition trauma memories. Apply AMT or EMDR.

only by a reduction of symptoms can later components of care be provided (Cummings & Sayama, 1995). Often all that is required is a reduction of severity level to a level at which the older client feels progress is possible and that life is tolerable. This communicates progress. Howard et al. (1993) found that just the changed subjective well being of the patient in the first few sessions was enough to assure compliance.

Depression is a special problem (Fry, 1983) and may require a focused dose of CBT or medication or both (see Gallagher-Thompson & Thompson, 1995; Hyer & Stanger, 1997). Our clinical rule of thumb is that, when depression is but part of PTSD (subthreshold), then treat the PTSD; if it is a distinct syndrome, then treat the depression. If the person meets criteria for clinical depression (Major Depressive Disorder), then treat this with CBT or medication or both. Depression reduces the ability to be active in therapy and in accessing memories (Shapiro, 1995).

Information on two other areas is relevant at the gate. Information on cognitive functioning assists in designing an appropriate treatment plan because both the in-session work and homework rely heavily on the person's ability to comprehend, remember, and produce material in oral and written formats. Some clinicians (Gallagher-Thompson & Thompson, 1996) routinely administer the Mini-Mental State Examination (MMSE; Folstein, Folstein, & McHugh, 1975). Cognitive changes may be similar in people with a specific disorder (e.g., Alzheimer's disease), but each person loses abilities at different rates and along sometimes different dimensions, and each responds differently to interventions.

Also, information on the older client's physical health status and medication regimen is a necessity for psychotherapy. These affect everything, including masking and "dulling" the processing of trauma. Because of cohort effects (e.g., social and historical), there is greater variability in educational level, interests, current life situations, and physical and intellectual functioning (Seigler, 1994). Thus, the clinician should conduct a thorough psychological and social assessment, obtain a medical history, and confer with the patient's primary physician about current health status and medications. Information from family and caretakers is vital to assess compliance with medications and other treatments.

The second treatment component involves the relationship itself. No other component of therapy is more accepted than this (Bugental, 1987). For some, this is the therapy (Kahn, 1991). How does the therapist let the client know that he/she is doing the best possible to understand the way the situation looks to the client (Yehuda et al., 1995)? Referencing trauma, this task involves safety (Weiss, 1971), as well as needed psychological components of psychological mindedness, affect tolerance, and the ability to self soothe (Hyer & Stewart, in press). Reflection and unconditional positive regard are rarely overused in an environment of dosed exposure. Referencing the clinician, Egendorf (1995) says:

> Whatever else we can say about it hearing people through their pain is most of all privilege. On the way we may fall into self inflation ("look at what I can do!")

or skirt the challenge out of fear ("I can't bear this!"), callousness ("better him than me!"), counterprobia ("what a wonderful challenge!"), guilt ("how awful of me to get off on someone else suffering!"), and the various ways of erring by blurring or emerging ("he is me!"), rescuing ("she needs me!"), and romantic or pseudospiritual fusion ("we are one and our love is all"). But what path to this sublime is not paved with pitfalls. p. 9

The essence of trauma is that the person loses faith that there is order and continuity in life. Eventually there is no safety except in the extreme caverns of life. Eventually learned helplessness evolves: You have no say in your life. Empathy is a natural for this disorder. Brandt (1981) distinguished between "technical" and "hermeneutic" psychologies. The former attempts to change others by interfering with observable behaviors; the latter seeks new meanings involving different perspectives and different reference systems. "Whereas technical psychology aims at power through controlling others, hermeneutic psychology aims at power through questioning the taken-for-granted" (p. 64). The key difference between the technical and hermeneutic approaches is in the implicit equivalence of therapist and client. Better trauma repair involves a hermeneutic stance for care.

This section of the model is really "socialization" (Gallagher-Thompson & Thompson, 1996). Preparation of the older client for therapy is the most important component of therapy (McNally et al., 1995). This is the slow process of a mutual determination of treatment goals, as well as the education and needed commitment that normalize and place perspective on trauma. It is the essence of positive treatment expectations. Often the therapeutic tasks are basic; keeping the trauma victim in treatment, being supportive during difficult periods, maintaining appropriate arousal levels, and in general assuring commitment to the goals of therapy. In effect, the relationship sets the stage for the work of trauma, the necessary invalidation process after requisite validation. In this way, the relationship is both an epiphenomenon and the phenomenon of care (Kahn, 1991). Brandsma and Hyer (1994) saw this as a covenant, a contract beyond the medical/legal commitment of mutual care, allowing for both bonding and problem solving.

The third task of trauma therapy then is to attend to aging-related and treatment, as well as lifestyle, factors. In Tai Chi, balance is important. "All things in moderation," goes another saying. Despite its obvious message, this stage of the model is perhaps the most important one. If older people can practice a healthy lifestyle both internally and externally, the disease process will be less intense, occur less frequently or wane. About PTSD, we know that the disorder progresses and aspects become functionally autonomous. At later stages, individuals have organized their lives around avoidance of triggers of trauma and often have downwardly adapted. Multiple triggers of traumatic intrusions have given way to helplessness, withdrawal, low grade suspicion, cynicism, and interpersonal problems. When this is the case, the primary attention needs to be paid to the stabilization of the social realm (van der Kolk & McFarlane, 1996). Even when this has not occurred, the issue of balance is important.

The chief aging-related factors include social supports, daily coping, and social skills, as well as treatment compliance. If the trauma is intense and if social supports (and coping mechanisms) are inadequate following the trauma, for example, the "total" resources of victims (social roles, possessions, self and worldviews, and energy) become depleted (Freedy, Shaw, Jarrell, & Masters, 1992). Most diseases have age distributions that are unique (Seigler, 1994). Behavioral risk factors tend to increase with age and all have age by sex interactions. The behavioral risk factors most amenable to change are smoking, alcohol use, obesity, cholesterol level, Type A behavior pattern, job strain, psychosocial stress, and sexual behavior. Modification of risk factors are worth the effort. To these we can add healthy life styles related to sleep, vacations, relaxation, meditation, entertainment, hobbies, sex, sharing, and friends. Even though age increases risk for all, those individuals who abuse these areas the most, have greater number and amount of problems (Seigler, 1994).

Therapeutically, the older person must come to know what to do, and have sufficient internal (coping and social skills, as well as treatment compliance) and external (social supports) skills for change. The target is to keep people committed to therapy (and with appropriate skills) and live a balanced and reasonably healthy life. These issues are assessed and addressed early in treatment. Simply assessing the person's day-to-day activities, with a special focus on coping and social supports, is often all that is required (Gallagher-Thompson & Thompson, 1996). The implication here is that older people do better if they are proactive in regards to their lifestyle. This means that they have the requisite social skills, practice balanced habits of living, and have a complete repertoire of coping skills (Hobfoll et al., 1991). When a person represses any one emotion, they tend to do so with others; when they live less in one area, they live less in time and quality everywhere. For later narrative components of care to be effective, the self-management components must be in place.

The fourth task is more complicated to explain but simple in intent: An analysis of personality is the best vehicle available to improve the outcomes of psychotherapy, to understand entrenched patterns of coping (Ruegg & Frances, 1995), even with PTSD (Fontana & Rosenheck, 1994; Frueh, Turner, Beidel, Mirabella, & Jones, 1996). If PTSD in older combat veterans is chronic and relapsing, a knowledge of personality is helpful in the understanding of the whole trauma response (Millon & Davis, 1995).

The clinician addresses the personality pattern *and* its logical unfolding of the trauma (Horowitz et al., 1984; Hyer & Associates, 1994; McAdams, 1990; Ulman & Brothers, 1988), even with problems of the elderly (Abrams, 1997; Costa, 1994). One model of personality is that provided by Millon (Millon & Davis, 1995). On the basis of reinforcement theory and on a knowledge of the salient domains specific to each person, those features of the personality style that most represent the patterned problems of the person, the therapist can attempt a harmonic balance of the care process. Like an orchestra conductor the maestro therapist understands the full piece and in this context makes an effort to find a harmonized balance of the performance. For the avoidant personality, the targets would be self-image and behavioral acts. The clinician would want to assist the avoidant person in developing a better self-view and in acting interpersonally with less anxiety. They represent the best fit of how to treat that individual. Treatment techniques, then, are only tactics or strategies to achieve integrated goals. The goal is to reduce imbalances of deficient polarities by techniques that are optimistically suited to modify the expression of these problems.

Therapy works at the level of the techniques but is defined at the level of conceptualization. It is a model of care that has rules. In clients where personality is an issue, it is often the case that the "head" changes before the gut. To translate this into the real world of the client, he or she must experience the "sensation of the personality pattern" and agree that these are issues of relevance and are workable in therapy. As a general rule, the clinician attacks the overall rigidity in the PD, to increase flexibility and decrease self-defeating patterns. The Millon model allows for this.

The last two components of the model center on memories. Both apply after other issues have been considered and both can occur at the same time. Component 5 represents the positive side of the treatment process. It involves positive memories. Here, therapists work with existing life stories (positive ones), to help the client develop new perspectives on current issues or to facilitate the integration of unresolved past events and choices. The therapist highlights positive aspects of the individual's life story, focusing on the past exclusively. Subjects who participate in this form of recall often show a reduction in anxiety and a positive change in appraisal of coping abilities and resources (Rybarczyk & Bellg, 1997). Narrative therapists speak of changing or "rewriting" dysfunctional stories about the self. This has been applied in several studies but is best defined as a self-defining memory (SDM), a core representation of the self in the form of autobiographical memories (Singer & Salovey, 1993).

No taxonomy of memories exists (McAdams, 1996). But the victim is more than a series of problem-saturated memories. In Stage 5, the victim tells an important defining event other than the trauma. The therapist validates the stability of the self, accentuates agency, endorses positive actions, and challenges growth as well as several other features of self-referenced components or change (Hyer & Sohnle, in press). This is almost always helpful because it gives the person permission to evaluate the self differently, to see self compassionately and more realistically. In approaching this, it is important to remember that we can change memories, especially at later life, through words. The "unsaid" is something that already exists. It is not lying hidden in the unconscious or waiting, fully formed, to be noticed and described in the cybernetic structures of family interactions. It is ready to be reconstructed. Hyer and Sohnle (in press) provide rubrics for its expression and unearthing.

The last component involves the trauma memory—desensitize trauma memories by the application of AMT or EMDR. Whichever one is used, a standard EMDR evaluation, pretherapy procedure for clients, is applied (see Shapiro, 1995). This is an excellent and efficient method to acquire data on the target memory, its intensity, negative and positive cognitions, emotions, salient sensations, and safety cues. After this, we apply several sessions of a relaxation procedure that is eventually cued to trauma memories. This is initially learned so that the client can control the anxiety associated with the traumatic event. An audiotape is used and the person is instructed to practice at least once daily (Hyer & Associates, 1994; Suinn, 1990). Older people respond well to relaxation.

Following this, standard AMT or EMDR is used. Both appear effective and can actually be used interchangeably. In both, the trauma memory is initially the target. In AMT, the desensitization process is applied (Suinn, 1990) with some modifications (Smyth, 1995). The principal alteration is to have the client initially target a scene that has already occurred and is at a moderate level of distress. As with psychiatric medications with older people, the rubric is to start low (in target memory perturbation) and go slow (Gatz, 1994). Commonly, failure results in an underresponse, where avoidance is occurring (here the clinician becomes active finding out and targeting the cause), or in an overresponse (here the therapist can do any number of AMT responses, usually backing up and finding a memory lower in intensity). Success must occur before more difficult issues can be addressed. Sessions are taped and used as homework.

EMDR is the other option. We have noted that this method maximizes sound psychotherapy principles, especially CBT (Hyer & Brandsma, 1997). It is fast paced, equal to other treatments, and user friendly. It requires a set procedure, a process in which the client experiences the target at his/her own pace. EMDR utilizes the power of treatment expectations, accesses associative networks unique for each person, uses "clean language" (language of the client), employs traditional cognitive techniques, especially the identification of positive and negative cognitions, challenges evidence, and applies affect and necessary sensory experiencing of past targets (Hyer & Brandsma, 1997). In EMDR also the mixture of both experiencing and meta-communication on the client-governed content is paramount: Experience, then comment on the target. This process of self reporting on one's experiencing increases the "now" experiencing and the consolidation of this. In sum, EMDR has evolved into a sophisticated technique that blends exposure with a nondirective, free associative processing and other treatment components common to good "traditional" therapy: EMDR applies the active treatment ingredients of exposure in a patient-acceptable manner.

AFTERCARE

The journey of aging is played out in a family context. Two research trends have addressed this. Caregiving with dementia or mental illness (see Zarit & Edwards, 1996), where the consensus is that caregivers are at risk, that social support is important for mental and physical health, that marital happiness affects outcomes for the better, that containing stress is important or it will proliferate into life and cause secondary role strain; and the problems of caretaking with a PTSD victim over time, where women (generally) in long-term relationships with veterans suffer from PTSD-related symptoms.

Our procedure is simple and surprisingly appealing to older people. We schedule a booster session, usually three months later. This involves a check-in, made popular by CBT, but also discussion about relapse prevention. We schedule it because it cements the learnings of therapy and communicates commitment over time as well as attends to the issues just raised.

This final task of psychotherapy is largely an educational exchange and then a reinforcement of learnings about possible lapses and setbacks (Stages 3 and 4). Relapse prevention is really a method to convince clients that they can be their own therapist. The therapist works with the client to ensure that the re-experiencing of symptoms (lapses) does not lead the client back to the pretreatment level of adjustment (relapse). The client learns how to anticipate, accept, and cope with possible lapses and setbacks. A discussion that PTSD symptoms may reoccur when the client is stressed or under specific conditions (e.g., anniversary date) is always helpful.

CASE EXAMPLE

AB is a 76-year-old white male who has had problems of depression since his daughter died of cancer a few years back. He has been in a supportive marriage for 50 years and has three other adult children, also supportive. He has a 10th-grade education and has worked as a farmer all his life. He is still active. Currently, he has no compromising medical problems.

He was in the service between 1942 and 1945. He was in combat in World War II for 32 months. He is able to identify several combat experiences that continue to haunt him. AB noted that he has always had problems with these issues but that they have gotten worse. In fact, PTSD-related problems were worst in 1946, shortly after discharge, and again after his daughter died. Over the years, he has been depressed on various occasions, has avoided public events, and has always had sleeping problems. He related that depression has always been a problem.

He describes a typical day as one where he gets up early due to poor sleep habits, remains in the house, and (in recent months) broods over the past. He relates that he is now eating too much because he is nervous all the time, and that he feels useless. He has few friends and rarely calls his children. He is now angry at himself.

Tests revealed that he was depressed and scored in the PTSD ranges on all scales. Noteworthy for depression was a negative self-view and a global discouragement regarding the future. His cognitive tests were normal as were scales sensitive to other comorbid conditions. He denied major medical problems but believed that he needed more social support. Personality scales revealed Avoidant and Passive-Aggressive styles. He has also experienced heavy combat. Such patients are characterized by a mistrust of others, emotional confusion as well as interpersonal testiness in an overreporting response style. As a result of his history and these data, he appears to have PTSD, Chronic and Major Affective Disorder, Recurrent, as Axis I diagnoses, and has personality traits consistent with Avoidant and Passive-Aggressive styles.

Treatment followed the model. First, symptoms were stabilized (Stage 1). Depressive symptoms of sleep, agitation, and inactivity were addressed with an antidepressant as well as a behavioral program targeting negative cognitions and activity. His wife agreed to assist in the latter. He had no outstanding current stressors. The treatment relationship (Stage 2) allowed for a balance between empathy and interpretation. He was easy to engage, reasonably psychologically minded, and could be confronted on issues. He was able to tell his story. His role as a client and his ability to take an observing ego position were also fostered, again in a slow Socratic process. The therapist also assured that the patient was active, and that he understood what PTSD was and how it was affecting his life. He was also given data suggesting that he was "bigger than his problem and that now he was allowing himself to experience change." These other treatment factors (Stage 3) were generally low key, including education (normalization), social supports, daily coping, social skills, as well as aspects of treatment compliance. This took 3 to 5 sessions.

Next, the focus was on the predominant styles or symptoms exclusive of intrusions (Stage 4). As with many other older individuals, AB had organized his life around avoidance. He had detached (Avoidant) and ambivalent (Passive-Aggressive) styles. Regarding overall strategies for the Avoidant style, the goal was to enhance pleasure and reduce the expectation of pain, as well as reduce his clinging to others. For the Passive-Aggressive style, the goal was to diminish self-other conflict and stabilize erratically changing actions. With AB, the therapist chose to develop behavioral and cognitive interventions that addressed the most salient features of the personalities, alienated self-image ("I am no good") and behavioral avoidance, as well as the dysphoric moods. These were the personality-based strategies and tactics most apt for the two personalities. Miniexperiments were devised for these. He was also requested to monitor the influence of his mood and over time challenge this. These tasks were ongoing and took the better part of 20 sessions.

In Stage 5, a life review was undertaken and the acquisition of several core memories were obtained. With AB, one core memory was an early memory of being in his neighborhood and protecting friends from bullies. He was the central figure, one who was both assertive and loving. This served as a template (metaphor) for action in his life, to be active and helpful to others. This provided a new reality that allowed for a reauthoring of his identity. So, with the use of the personality styles assisting in the forming of new behaviors/cognitions/feelings, and the use of the core memories in the forming of a new self reality, therapy moved the point of the trauma.

Finally, a course of EMDR was applied. Trauma work is done last. With AB, 10 sessions of EMDR were applied. Initially, he was taught to relax. Some therapy time was devoted to the purpose of trauma work—"We will take this at your pace, you will not fall apart, you will not forget the event, and it will allow you to have a sense of mastery over it." As with many combat veterans, AB had several identified trauma memories. We selected the most traumatic one. The EMDR procedure calls for a negative cognition. AB's was "I cannot make a mistake or bad things will happen." A positive one, "I do the best I can," was also installed (as part of the procedure). His emotion was fear and his expressed sensation was a tight chest (other EMDR components). All these person features were processed in EMDR.

He had an initial subjective distress level (SUDS) at 10 in his first session. He processed the memories, reducing his initial and ending SUDS over the 10 treatment sessions. During the last session, he reached a SUDS of 3. He had never been this low in the past. As is usual with this procedure, he saw many elements of the trauma that he had forgotten and saw what he was doing to himself with self-blame and feelings of uselessness. Uselessness was grounded in negative cognition and was targeted as a special problem. At one point, it was reframed as necessary for him, as his way to remain in control of his life.

Therapy took 26 sessions. At the end, he was less depressed and more hopeful. He was also able to deal with people better. The intrusions of his PTSD were less in evidence and he had been sleeping for the first time in over 30 years. Interestingly, he felt more loving and attached to his wife and was a volunteer in an aging center.

CONCLUSION

In typical published reviews of geriatric psychiatry (Blazer, 1998), no reference to PTSD appears, although these volumes contain chapters on anxiety disorders, sleep disorders, and the epidemiology of psychiatric disorders in the elderly. Despite early reports, then, of increased negative outcomes and consistent findings of increased risk for physical harm among the elderly, the data of the past two decades do not support the hypothesis that older adults are at greater risk than younger adults for negative psychosocial outcome following exposure to natural disasters. Much available data suggest that the elderly cope as well and at times better than younger adults. If anything, data suggest that age contributes minimally to the prediction of psychosocial outcomes and that variables, such as preexisting physical and mental health, severity of trauma, and availability of specific resources, are of greater predictive value.

Is there a model of change common to human growth and development and to psychological intervention? Because the existential issues of trauma—loss, meaning-making, accepting reality, achieving ego integrity—are very close to those of aging, the treatment of trauma at later life seems to meld almost naturally with age. Again, any quick-fix mentality of earlier ages may not be appropriate here. The longitudinal course of PTSD is really a total person response: There is a rhyme and reason for change around the person's own stability. Any reaction to trauma then is the story of a human being, who represents a smorgasbord of resilience and vulnerability factors. If this process of (trauma) decline is impacted unduly at first by fearful and intrusive experiences and accommodated to by a symphony of poor adaptation, maybe the strengths of later life are the only ones that redress this frozen self.

We have also advocated for an integrated therapy with our model. The goal of trauma therapy is to be able to cooperate and problem solve in the observation and evaluation of experiences related to the trauma in the ongoing drama of the therapy. The wise clinician "treats" the person of the trauma victim in later life; ready to manage the victim or to facilitate a change of the trauma itself, or both. Not surprisingly then, with many older trauma victims, other issues of therapy are equally important to those of the trauma itself—a supportive social system, an empowered problem-solving focus, ability to cope in ongoing (and past) stress situations.

In this chapter, we have ignored many "critical" questions. Research on the organization, decision rules and best exemplars of PTSD at later life have been left behind. What really is PTSD at later life? If an older victim has a few intrusion and arousal symptoms, but no evident avoidant problems, what does that mean? We do not know either what potentiates problems for the most common variety of the aging person, the appearance of PTSD symptoms after remitted periods: Do trauma symptoms occur as a result of age-related coping decline, recent stressful events, or is it just the nature of the disorder? Also, how are narratives defined—in terms of textual structures, social interactions, or cultural issues? Indeed, what is the best developmental framework to understand the core issues of the older person? And with regret, we simply assume that the *DSM* is the best model for the categorization of a person who experiences trauma.

The study of the response to trauma is really an illusion, a coterie of variables that hang together in psychological space. Trauma symptoms represent only memory markers that capture moments of traumatic schemes of helplessness, terror, horror, and utter ineffectiveness. The *DSMs* create order, but imperfect ones and ones that do not provide clear treatment rules. The value or meaning of a symptom in the context of PTSD for an older person requires something simple, a clinical ear. Therapy will always depend on the therapist and will always be something more (Bugental, 1987).

REFERENCES

Abrams, R. (1997). Assessing personality in chronic care populations. In J. Teresi, M.P. Lawton, D. Holmes, & M. Ory (Eds.), *Measurement in elderly chronic care populations.* New York: Springer.

Acierno, R., Hersen, M., Van Hasselt, V.B., Tremont, G., & Meuser, K.T. (1994). Review of the validation and dissemination of eye-movement desensitization and reprocessing: A scientific and ethical dilemma. *Clinical Psychology Review, 14*, 287–299.

American Psychiatric Association. (1994). *Diagnostic and statistical manual of mental disorders* (4th ed. Rev.). Washington, DC: Author.

Baltes, P.B., & Staudinger, U.M. (1993). The search for a psychology of wisdom. *Current Directions in Psychological Science, 2*, 75–80.

Beutler, L.E., Scogin, F., Kirkish, P., Schretlen, D., Corbishley, A., Hamblin, D., Meredith, K., Potter, R., Bamford, C.R., & Levenson, A.I. (1987). Group cognitive therapy and alprazolam in the treatment of depression in older adults. *Journal of Consulting and Clinical Psychology, 55*, 550–557.

Blake, D.D., Weathers, F.W., Nagy, L.M., Kaloupek, D.G., Klauminzer, G., Charney, D.S., & Keane, T.M. (1990). A clinician rating scale for assessing current and lifetime PTSD: The CAPS-1. *Behavior Therapy, 13*, 187–188.

Blazer, D. (1998). *Emotional problems in later life.* New York: Springer.

Bortz, J., & O'Brien, K. (1997). Psychotherapy with older adults. In P. Nussbaum (Ed.), *Handbook on the neuropsychology of aging* (pp. 341–351). New York: Plenum Press.

Boudewyns, P., & Hyer, L. (1990). Changes in psychophysiological response to war memories among Vietnam veteran PTSD patients treated with direct therapeutic exposure. *Behavior Therapy, 21*, 63–87.

Boudewyns, P., & Hyer, L. (1997). Eye movement desensitization and reprocessing (EMDR) as treatment for post-traumatic stress disorder (PTSD). *Clinical Psychology and Psychotherapy.*

Brandsma, J., & Hyer, L. (1995). The treatment of grief in PTSD. *NCP: Clinical Newsletter, 5.*

Brandt, L.W. (1981). *Psychologists caught: A psycho-logic of psychology.* Buffalo: University of Toronto Press.

Bugental, J. (1987). *The art of the psychotherapist.* New York: Norton.

Butler, R.N. (1963). The life review: An interpretation of reminiscence in the aged. *Psychiatry, 26*, 65–76.

Chinen, A.B. (1984). Modal logic: A new paradigm of development and late life potential. *Human Development, 27*, 52–56.

Chiriboga, D.A., & Cutler, L. (1980). Stress and adaptations: Life span perspectives. In R.W. Poon (Ed.), *Aging in the 1980s* (pp. 347–362). Washington, DC: Gerontological Society.

Cooper, N.A., & Clum, G.A. (1989). Imaginal flooding as a supplementary treatment for PTSD in combat veterans: A controlled study. *Behavior Therapy, 20*, 381–391.

Costa, P. (1994). Personality continuity and the changes of adult life. In M. Storant & G. VandenBos (Eds.), *The adult years: Continuity and change* (pp. 41–78). Washington, DC: American Psychological Press.

Cummings, N., & Sayama, M. (1995). *Focused psychotherapy: A casebook of brief, intermittent psychotherapy throughout the life cycle.* New York: Brunner/Mazel.

Egendorf, A. (1995). Hearing people through their pain. *Journal of Traumatic Stress, 8,* 1–10.

Elder, G.H., & Clipp, E.C. (1989). Combat experience and emotional health: Impairment and resilience in later life. *Journal of Personality, 57,* 311–341.

Elder, L., & Caspi, A. (1990). Studying lives in a changing society: Sociological and personological explanations. In A. Rabin, R. Zucker, R. Emmons, & S. Frank (Eds.), *Studying persons and lives* (pp. 201–247). New York: Springer.

Ensel, W.M. (1991). "Important" life events and depression among older adults: The role of psychological and social resources. *Journal of Aging and Health, 3,* 546–566.

Erikson, E. (1975). *Life history and the historical movement.* New York: Norton.

Falk, B., Hersen, M.H., & Van Hasselt, V. (1994). Assessment of post-traumatic stress disorder in older adults: A critical review. *Clinical Psychology Review, 14*(5), 383–415.

Foa, E.B., Freund, B.F., Hembree, E., Dancu, C.V., Franklin, M.E., Perry, K.J., Riggs, D.S., & Molnar, C. (1994, November). *Efficacy of short term behavioral treatments of PTSD in sexual and nonsexual assault victims.* Paper presented at the annual meeting of the Association for Advancement of Behavior Therapy, San Diego, CA.

Foa, E.B., Molnar, C., & Cashman, L. (1995). Change in rape narratives during exposure therapy for posttraumatic stress disorder. *Journal of Traumatic Stress, 8*(4), 675–690.

Foa, E.B., Rothbaum, B.O., Riggs, D.S., & Murdock, T.B. (1991). Treatment of posttraumatic stress disorder in rape victims: A comparison between cognitive-behavioral procedures and counseling. *Journal of Consulting and Clinical Psychology, 59,* 712–715.

Foldstein, M., Foldstien, S., & McHugh, P. (1975). "Mini-Mental State": A practical method for grading the cognitive state of patients for the clinician. *Journal of Psychiatric Research, 12,* 189–198.

Fontana, A., & Rosenheck, R. (1994). Traumatic war stressors and psychiatric symptoms among World War II, Korean, and Vietnam War veterans. *Psychology and Aging, 9*(1), 27–33.

Frank, E., Anderson, B., Stewart, B.D., Dancu, C., Hughes, C., & West, D. (1988). Efficacy of cognitive behavior therapy and systematic desensitization in the treatment of rape trauma. *Behavior Therapy, 19,* 403–420.

Freedy, J.R., Shaw, D.L., Jarrell, M.P., & Masters, C.R. (1992). Towards an understanding of the psychological impact of natural disasters: An application of the conservation resources stress model. *Journal of Traumatic Stress, 5,* 441–444.

Frueh, B.C., Turner, S.M., Beidel, D.C., Mirabella, R.F., & Jones, W.J. (1996). Trauma management therapy: A preliminary evaluation of a multicomponent behavioral treatment for chronic combat-related PTSD. *Behavioral Research Therapy, 34*(7), 533–543.

Fry, P.S. (1983). Structured and unstructured reminiscence training and depression among the elderly. *Clinical Gerontology, 1,* 15–37.

Gallagher, D., & Thompson, L.W. (1981). *Depression in the elderly: A behavioral treatment manual.* Los Angeles: USC Press.

Gallagher, D., & Thompson, L.W. (1982). *Elders maintenance of treatment benefits following individual psychotherapy for depression*. Results of a pilot study and preliminary data from an ongoing replication study. Paper presented at the annual meeting of the American Psychological Association, Washington, DC.

Gallagher-Thompson, D., Hanley-Peterson, P., & Thompson, L.W. (1990). Maintenance of gains versus relapse following brief psychotherapy for depression. *Journal of Consulting and Clinical Psychology, 58,* 371–374.

Gallagher-Thompson, D., & Thompson, L.W. (1995). Psychotherapy with older adults in theory and practice. In B. Bonger & L. Beutler (Eds.), *Comprehensive textbook of psychotherapy* (pp. 357–379). New York: Oxford University Press.

Gallagher-Thompson, D., & Thompson, L.W. (1996). Applying cognitive-behavioral therapy to the psychological problems of later life. In S.H. Zarit & B.G. Knight (Eds.), *A guide to psychotherapy and aging*. Washington, DC: American Psychological Association.

Garfein, A.J., Ronis, D.L., & Bates, E.W. (1993). *Toward a case-mix planning model for the VA mental health outpatient system: Factors affecting diagnostic case-mix*. Ann Arbor, MI: Great Lakes HSR&D Field Program.

Gatz, M. (1994). Application of assessment to therapy and intervention with older adults. In M. Storandt & G.R. VandenBos (Eds.), *Neuropsychological assessment of dementia and depression in older adults: A clinician's guide*. Washington, DC: American Psychological Association.

Goldstein, G., van Kammen, W., Shelly, C., Miller, D.J., & van Kammen, D.P. (1987). Survivors of imprisonment in the Pacific Theater during World War II. *American Journal of Psychiatry, 144,* 1210–1213.

Green, B. (1991). Evaluating the effects of disasters. *Psychological Assessment: A Journal of Consulting and Clinical Psychiatry, 3,* 538–546.

Gurian, B., & Miner, J. (1991). Clinical presentation of consulting in the elderly. In C. Salzman & B. Lebowitz (Eds.), *Anxiety in the elderly: Treatment and research* (pp. 31–40). New York: Springer.

Hankin, C.S., Abueg, F.R., Gallagher-Thompson, D., & Laws, A. (1996). Dimensions of PTSD among older veterans seeking outpatient care: A pilot study. *Journal of Clinical Geropsychology, 2*(4), 239–246.

Hanley-Peterson, P., Futterman, A., Thompson, L., Zeiss, A.M., Gallagher, D., & Ironson, G. (1990). Endogenous depression and psychotherapy outcome in an elderly population [Abstract]. *Gerontologist, 30,* 51A.

Harvey, J., Orbuch, T., Chivalisz, K., & Garwood, G. (1991). Coping with sexual assault: The roles of account making and confiding. *Journal of Traumatic Stress, 4,* 515–532.

Hindrichsen, G. (1997). Interpersonal therapy for depressed older adults. *Journal of Geriatric Psychiatry, 30,* 239–257.

Hobfoll, S., Spielberger, C., Breznitz, S., Figley, C., Folkman, S., Lepper-Green, B., Meichenbaum, D., Milgram, A., Sandler, I., Sarason, I., & van der Kolk, B. (1991). War related stress: Addressing the stress of war and other traumatic events. *American Psychologist, 46,* 848–855.

Horowitz, M.J., Marmar, C., Krupnick, J., Wilmer, N., Kaltreider, M., & Wallestein, R. (1984). *Personality styles and brief psychotherapy*. New York: Blair Book.

Hovens, J.E., van Der Ploeg, H.M., Klaarenbeek, M.T., Bramsen, I., Schreuder, J.H., & Rivero, V.V. (1994). The assessment of posttraumatic stress disorder with the clinician administered PTSD scale: Dutch results. *Journal of Clinical Psychology, 50*(3), 325–336.

Howard, K., Lueger, R., Maling, M., Martinovich, & Lutz, W. (1993). A phase model of psychotherapy outcome: Causal mediation of change. *Journal of Consulting and Clinical Psychology, 61,* 678–685.

Hyer, L. (1995). Use of EMDR in a "dementing" PTSD survivor. *Clinical Gerontologist, 16,* 70–74.

Hyer, L., & Associates. (1994). *Trauma victim: Theoretical issues and practical suggestions.* Muncie, IN: Accelerated Development.

Hyer, L., & Brandsma, J. (1997). EMDR minus eye movements equals good psychotherapy. *Journal of Traumatic Stress.*

Hyer, L., & Sohnle, S. (in press). *The expression and treatment of trauma at later life.* New York: Guilford Press.

Hyer, L., & Stanger, E. (1997). The interaction of posttraumatic stress disorder and depression among older combat veterans. *Psychological Reports.*

Hyer, L., & Summers, M. (1994). *PTSD among older combat veterans: A validation study.* VA Merit Review Grant.

Hyer, L., Swanson, G., Lefkowitz, R., Hillesland, D., Davis, H., & Woods, M. (1990). The application of the cognitive behavioral model to two older stressor groups. *Clinical Gerontologist, 9*(3/4), 145–190.

Kahn, M. (1991). *Between therapist and client: The new relationship.* New York: Freeman.

Keane, T.M., Fairbank, J.A., Caddell, J.M., & Zimering, R.T. (1989). Implosive (flooding) therapy reduces symptoms of PTSD in Vietnam combat veterans. *Behavior Therapy, 20,* 245–260.

Kovach, C. (1990). Promise and problems in reminiscence research. *Journal of Gerontological Nursing, 16*(4), 10–14.

Litz, B.T., & Keane, T.M. (1989). Information processing in anxiety disorders: Application to the understanding of post-traumatic stress disorder. *Clinical Psychology Review, 9,* 243–257.

Logsdon, R.G. (1995). Psychopathology and treatment: Curriculum and research needs. In B.G. Knight, L. Terri, P. Wohlford, & J. Santos (Eds.), *Mental health services for older adults: Implications for training and practice in geropsychology* (pp. 41–51). New York: Springer.

Maughan, B., & Rutter, M. (1997). Retrospective reporting of childhood and adult psychopathology. *Journal of Personality Disorders, 11,* 19–33.

McAdams, D. (1990). Unity and purpose in human lives: The emergency of identity as a life story. In I. Rabin, R. Zucker, R. Emmons, & S. Frank (Eds.), *Studying person and lives* (pp. 148–200). New York: Springer.

McAdams, D. (1996). Personality, modernity, and the storied self: A contemporary framework for studying persons. *Psychological Inquiry, 7*(4), 295–321.

McAdams, D.P. (1993). *The stories we live by: Personal myths and the making of the self.* New York: Morrow.

McCarthy, P., Katz, I., & Foa, E. (1991). Cognitive-behavioral treatment of anxiety in the elderly: A proposal model. In C. Saltzman & B. Lebowitz (Eds.), *Anxiety in the elderly: Treatment and research* (pp. 197–214). New York: Springer.

McFarlane, A.C., & Yehuda, R. (1996). Resilience, vulnerability, and the course of posttraumatic reactions. In B.A. van der Kolk, A.C. McFarlane, & L. Weisaeth (Eds.), *Traumatic stress: The effects of overwhelming experience on mind, body, and society* (pp. 155–181). New York: Guilford Press.

McNally, R.J., Lasko, N.B., Macklin, M.L., & Pitman, R.K. (1995). Autobiographical memory disturbance in combat-related posttraumatic stress disorder. *Behavior Research Therapy, 33*(6), 619–630.

Mellman, T.A., Randolph, C.A., Brawman-Mintzer, O., Flores, L.P., & Milanes, F.J. (1992). Phenomenology and course of psychiatric disorders associated with combat-related posttraumatic stress disorder. *American Journal of Psychiatry, 149,* 1568–1574.

Millon, T., & Davis, R. (1995). *Disorders of personality:* DSM-IV *and beyond.* New York: Wiley.

Murray, E.J., & Segal, D.L. (1994). Emotional processing in vocal and written expression of feelings about traumatic experiences. *Journal of Traumatic Stress, 7,* 391–405.

Nezu, A., Nezu, C., Friedman, S., Faddis, S., & Houts, P. (1998). *Helping cancer patients cope.* Washington, DC: American Psychological Association.

Norris, F.H. (1992). Epidemiology of trauma: Frequency and impact of different potentially traumatic events on different demographic groups. *Journal of Consulting and Clinical Psychology, 60,* 409–418.

Paris, J. (1997). Introduction: Emotion and empiricism: Research on childhood trauma and adult psychopathology. *Journal of Personality Disorders, 11,* 1–4.

Parker, R.G. (1995). Reminiscence: A continuity theory framework. *Gerontologist, 35*(4), 515–525.

Pennebaker, J.W. (1989). Confession, inhibition, and disease. In L. Berkowitz (Ed.), *Advances in experimental social psychology* (Vol. 22, pp. 211–244). Orlando, FL: Academic Press.

Pfeiffer, E., & Busse, E.W. (1973). Mental disorder in later life: Affective disorders; paranoid, neurotic, and situational reactions. In E.W. Busse & E. Pfeiffer (Eds.), *Mental illness in later life* (pp. 107–144). Washington, DC: American Psychiatric Association.

Pynoos, R., Sternberg, A., & Goenjian, A. (1995). Traumatic stress in childhood and adolescence: Recent developments and current controversies. In B.A. van der Kolk, A.C. McFarlane, & L. Weisaeth (Eds.), *Traumatic stress: The effects of overwhelming experience on mind, body, and society* (pp. 331–358). New York: Guilford Press.

Resick, P.A., Jordan, C.G., Girelli, S.A., Hutter, C.K., & Marhoefer-Dvorak, S. (1988). A comparative outcome study of behavioral group therapy for sexual assault victims. *Behavior Therapy, 19,* 385–401.

Resick, P.A., & Schnicke, M.K. (1992). Cognitive processing therapy for sexual assault victims. *Journal of Consulting and Clinical Psychology, 60*(5), 748–756.

Rosen, J., Fields, R.B., Hand, A.M., Falsettie, G., & van Kammen, D.P. (1989). Concurrent posttraumatic stress disorder in psychogeriatric patients. *Journal of Geriatric Psychiatry and Neurology, 3,* 65–69.

Ruegg, R., & Frances, A. (1995). New research in personality disorders. *Journal of Personality Disorders, 9*(1), 1–48.

Rutter, M., & Maughan, B. (1997). Psychosocial adversities in childhood and adulthood. *Journal of Personality Disorders, 11,* 4–19.

Rybarczyk, B.D., & Bellg, A. (1997). *Listening to life stories: A new approach to stress intervention in health care.* New York: Springer.

Schnurr, P.P. (1996). Trauma, PTSD, and physical health. *PTSD Research Quarterly, 7*(3), 1–3.

Schnurr, P.P., & Aldwin, C.M. (1993). Military service: Long-term effects on adult development. In R. Kastenbaum (Ed.), *Encyclopedia of adult development.* Phoenix, AZ: Onyx Press.

Schnurr, P.P., Aldwin, C.M., Spiro, A., Stukel, T., & Keane, T.M. (1993). *A longitudinal study of PTSD symptoms in older veterans.* Poster session for the Symposium on The Future of VA Mental Health Research, Department of Veterans Affairs Office of Research and Development and National Foundation for Brain Research, Washington, DC.

Scogin, F., Rickard, H.C., Keith, S., Wilson, J., & McElreath, L. (1992). Progressive and imaginal relaxation training for elderly persons with subjective anxiety. *Psychology and Aging, 7*, 419–424.

Seigler, I. (1994). Developmental health psychology. In M. Storant & G. VandenBos (Eds.), *The adult years: Continuity and change* (pp. 115–143). Washington, DC: American Psychological Press.

Sewell, K. (1996). Constructional risk factors for a post-traumatic stress response following a mass murder. *Journal of Constructivist Psychology, 9*.

Shapiro, F. (1995). *Eye movement desensitization and reprocessing: Basic principles, protocols, and procedures.* New York: Guilford Press.

Shalev, A., Bonne O., & Eth, S. (1996). Treatment of posttraumatic stress disorder: A review *Psychosomatic Medicine, 58*(2), 165–182.

Sherman, E. (1991). *Reminiscence and the self in old age.* New York: Springer.

Siegel, D.J. (1995). Memory, trauma, and psychotherapy: A cognitive science view. *Journal of Psychotherapy Practice and Research, 4*(2), 93–122.

Singer, J.A., & Salovey, P. (1993). *The remembered self: Emotion and memory in personality.* New York: Free Press/Macmillan.

Smyth, L. (1995). *Clinicians's manual for the cognitive-behavioral treatment of post traumatic stress disorder.* Harve de Grace, MD: RTR.

Solomon, S., Gerrity, E.T., & Muff, A.M. (1992). Efficacy of treatments for posttraumatic stress disorder. *Journal of the American Medical Association, 268*, 633–638.

Spiro, A., Aldwin, C.M., Levenson, M.R., & Schnurr, P.P. (1993). *Combat-related PTSD among older veterans.* Poster session for the Symposium on The Future of VA Mental Health Research and Development and National Foundation for Brain Research, Washington, DC.

Suinn, R.M. (1990). *Anxiety management training: A behavior therapy.* New York: Plenum Press.

Summers, M., & Hyer, L. (1991). *Measurement of PTSD among older combat veterans.* VA Merit Review Grant.

Tait, R., & Silver, R. (1984, August). *Recovery: The long term impact of stressful life experience.* Paper presented for the 92nd Annual Convention of the American Psychological Association, Toronto.

Tennant, C.C., Goulston, K., & Dent, O. (1993). Medical and psychiatric consequences of being a prisoner of war of the Japanese: An Australian follow-up study. In J.P. Wilson & B. Raphael (Eds.), *International handbook of traumatic stress syndromes* (pp. 231–240). New York: Plenum Press.

Thompson, L.W., Gallagher, D., & Breckenridge, J.S. (1987). Comparative effectiveness of psychotherapies for depressed elders. *Journal of Consulting and Clinical Psychology, 53*, 385–390.

Thompson, L.W., Gallagher, D., & Czirr, R. (1988). Personality disorder and outcome in the treatment of late-life depression. *Journal of Geriatric Psychiatry, 21*, 133–146.

Thompson, L.W., Gallagher, D., Hanser, S., Gantz, F., & Steffen, A. (1991, November). *Comparison of despramine and cognitive/behavioral therapy in the treatment of late-life depression.* Paper presented at the meeting of Gerontological Society of America, San Francisco.

Turner, S., McFarlane, A., & van der Kolk, B. (1995). The therapeutic environment and new explorations in the treatment of posttraumatic disorder. In B.A. van der Kolk, A.C. McFarlane, & L. Weisaeth (Eds.), *Traumatic stress: The effects of overwhelming experience on mind, body, and society* (pp. 3–23). New York: Guilford Press.

Ulman, R.B., & Brothers, D. (1988). *The shattered self: A psychoanalytic study of trauma.* Hillsdale, NJ: Analytic Press.

van der Kolk, B.A., & Fisler, R. (1995). Dissociation and the fragmentary nature of traumatic memories: Overview and exploratory study. *Journal of Traumatic Stress, 8*(4), 505–525.

van der Kolk, B.A., & McFarlane, A.C. (1996). The black hole of trauma. In B.A. van der Kolk, A.C. McFarlane, & L. Weisaeth (Eds.), *Traumatic stress: The effects of overwhelming experience on mind, body, and society* (pp. 3–23). New York: Guilford Press.

Weiss, J. (1971). The emergence of new themes: A contribution to the psychoanalytic theory of therapy. *International Journal of Psycho-Analysis, 52,* 459–467.

Yehuda, R., Kahana, B., Schmeidler, J., Southwick, S.M., Wilson, S., & Giller, E.L. (1995). Impact of cumulative lifetime trauma and recent stress on current posttraumatic stress disorder symptoms in Holocaust survivors. *American Journal of Psychiatry, 152,* 1815–1818.

Zarit, S., & Edwards, A. (1996). Family caregiving: Research and clinical intervention. In R.T. Woods, et al. (Eds.), *Handbook of the clinical psychology of aging* (pp. 331–368). Chichester, England: Wiley.

Zeiss, R.A., & Dickman, H.R. (1989). PTSD 40 years later: Incidence and person-situation correlates in former POWs. *Journal of Clinical Psychology, 45,* 80–87.

Zeiss, R.A., & Steffen, A.M. (in press). Interdisciplinary health care teams: The basic unit of geriatric care. In L.L. Carstensen, B.A. Edelstein, & L. Dornbrand (Eds.), *The handbook of clinical gerontology.* Newbury Park, CA: Sage.

CHAPTER 33

A Guide to Current Psychopharmacological Treatments for Affective Disorders in Older Adults: Anxiety, Agitation, and Depression

IRIS R. BELL

The elderly are a growing and vulnerable subset of the population. They often experience an accumulating burden of medical problems, some of which contribute to or interact with the initial onset of psychiatric disorders late in life (Alexopoulos, Meyers, Young, Mattis, & Kakuma, 1993; Busse & Blazer, 1996; Jenike, 1996; Katz, Beaston-Wimmer, Parmelee, Friedman, & Lawton, 1993; Penninx et al., 1998; Simon, Ormel, VonKorff, & Barlow, 1995; Zubenko, Mulsant, Sweet, Pasternak, & Tu, 1997). Many milder forms of psychological distress are well addressed with psychotherapeutic and behavioral therapies. However, patients with poor motivation or insight or those with cognitive problems, which are increasingly common with age, can add to the complexity of the clinical picture. In such cases, the usefulness of nonpharmacological interventions for concomitant anxiety, agitation, or depression is limited, and judicious use of psychopharmacological treatments is indicated. At the same time, appropriate psychopharmacological interventions in older patients can increase risks of medical morbidity and even mortality from falls and fractures (Thapa, Gideon, Fought, & Ray, 1995), adverse drug reactions, and drug interactions. The purpose of this chapter is to introduce the non-physician professional to clinical approaches of geriatric psychiatrists to the psychopharmacological treatment of common psychiatric disturbances in the elderly. Despite many reviews on the topic (Jenike, 1996; Kamath, Finkel, & Moran, 1996; Lebowitz et al., 1997; Sheikh & Nguyen, 1997; Solomon & Pendlebury, 1997), systematic research studies on issues of using specific drugs in the elderly for these conditions are only now emerging, and geropsychiatrists currently rely a great deal on clinical consensus and experience to implement a treatment plan (Lebowitz et al., 1997; Small et al., 1998). The goal here is not to provide an exhaustive discussion of all possible agents for each condition, but rather, to make the reader aware of representative issues in the field.

Geriatric psychopharmacology involves several basic principles of management, regardless of the diagnostic condition. First, it is essential to identify and treat any possible medical causes for a psychiatric disorder before adding medications just for symptom control. Second, it is crucial to remove or replace medications for medical conditions that may be causing the psychiatric symptoms. Third, when they are necessary, psychotropic medication programs should be as simple as possible to minimize the risk of medication interactions. Finally, one of the most well-known points is to "start low and go slow." Older individuals have metabolic changes from aging that increase the impact of a given drug dose. Drugs can accumulate more readily in the elderly and cause severe toxicity. A common rule of thumb is to give geriatric patients no more than ⅓ to ½ or less of the typical adult dose.

The elderly rarely seek out psychiatric treatment on their own. More likely, they will go to their primary care provider with their concerns. Although geriatricians usually are aware of these management issues, other physicians and health care providers may be less familiar with the many pitfalls involved in geriatric psychopharmacology (Gelenberg & Bassuk, 1997; Schatzberg, Cole, & DeBattista, 1997).

ANXIETY

DIFFERENTIAL DIAGNOSIS

All of the common *DSM-IV* (APA, 1994) anxiety disorders can occur or persist into old age (e.g., agoraphobia, other phobias, generalized anxiety disorder, obsessive-compulsive disorder, posttraumatic stress disorder, panic disorder). Differential diagnosis of anxiety in older individuals can be difficult. For example, the elderly often have a fear of seeing a psychiatrist and of being diagnosed as "out of my mind." On direct questioning, they may deny feeling anxious or nervous. As a result, many present with a focus on somatic complaints, leading to costly and unnecessary medical tests. At the same time, it is essential to perform some medical evaluation to avoid missing important etiologies. Table 33.1 gives a list of the clinically more common medication and medical problems in which patients may experience prominent anxiety or nervousness (see also Sheikh & Nguyen, 1997).

The number of widely used prescription and nonprescription drugs that can cause anxiety is notable, ranging from hormones such as excessive thyroid or insulin to self-medication with alcohol or caffeine. Thus, even in the setting of obvious psychosocial stressors, it is still important to investigate the potential contribution of nonpsychological factors to the psychological state.

Table 33.1   Drugs and medical conditions associated with prominent anxiety states or agitation in older persons.

Medication or Medical Condition
Akathisia (restlessness) from neuroleptic (antipsychotic) drugs
Respiratory medications such as theophylline
Over-the-counter decongestant medications containing pseudoephedrine
Hyperthyroidism from endogenous condition or excess thyroid hormone replacement
Alcohol or sedative-hypnotic withdrawal
Excessive caffeinated beverage use (coffee, tea, colas)
Excessive insulin effects in diabetics (low blood sugar reactions)
Various heart conditions
Poor oxygenation of blood from lung diseases
Temporal lobe epilepsy (terror attacks from limbic nervous system focus)

MEDICATION OPTIONS

Once it is clear that the patient will require medications for anxiety, the primary options involve three classes of drugs: benzodiazepines, buspirone, and certain antidepressants (Sheikh & Nguyen, 1997). Table 33.2 lists the names of frequently prescribed agents and their major characteristics. The preferred benzodiazepines for the elderly are lorazepam (Ativan) and oxazepam (Serax). Useful lorazepam doses may range from 0.5 mg three times a day to 1 mg four times a day. The rationale for this preference is that, in contrast with most other medications, age does not impair the metabolism of these two drugs. They last about 4 hours per dose and do not build up in the body. On the one hand, this profile of action is desirable to minimize adverse effects. However, in practice, a number of patients have problems between doses as the drugs wear off, e.g., with interdose rebounds of anxiety or insomnia. If the latter problem develops, geropsychiatrists often then choose a benzodiazepine with an intermediate duration of action such as clonazepam, as the best compromise. Benzodiazepines are useful in the treatment of generalized anxiety disorder and panic disorder in particular. Evidence suggests that the benefits of benzodiazepines for insomnia dissipate after approximately 1 to 2 weeks of treatment; thus, it is inappropriate to continue these drugs solely for treating insomnia over extended periods (Schatzberg et al., 1997).

Accumulating evidence indicates that benzodiazepines, even in modest doses, cause mild cognitive impairment. The most common side effect is daytime drowsiness, which can lead to accidents at home or while driving (Ray, Fought, & Decker, 1992). Benzodiazepines with longer half-lives (i.e., more likely to accumulate in the body over time) significantly increase the risk of falls and thus fractures, which can be terminal events in older persons. All benzodiazepines have the potential for inducing tolerance and addictive processes;

Table 33.2   Medications commonly used in the treatment of geriatric anxiety states

Generic Name	Trade Name	Geriatric Dose Range (Total Milligrams/Day)	Accumulation Risk in Elderly	Comments
Lorazepam	Ativan	0.5–4	Low	Preferred benzodiazepine in elderly
Oxazepam	Serax	10–45	Low	Preferred benzodiazepine in elderly
Alprazolam	Xanax	0.25–4	Moderate	Difficult to withdraw; seizure risk high with abrupt discontinuation
Clonazepam	Klonopin	0.25–4	Moderate	Useful in situations when shorter half-life drugs wear off too quickly
Diazepam	Valium	2–20	High	Avoid because of risk of respiratory depression
Chlordiazepoxide	Librium	10–50	High	Avoid because of risk of respiratory depression
Buspirone	BuSpar	10–45	Low	Well-tolerated; but does not cover benzodiazepine withdrawal symptoms
Clomipramine	Anafranil	50–200	High	Most effective for obsessive-compulsive disorder; poorly tolerated by most elderly because of anticholinergic and orthostatic effects

hence, they have a limited role in treating anxiety of individuals with histories of substance abuse. It is also a risk that some patients may experience paradoxical reactions to benzodiazepines and become more rather than less agitated. Consequently, although benzodiazepines are a mainstay of treatment for anxiety and insomnia, practitioners ideally strive to limit the dose and duration of treatment and to seek alternative approaches whenever feasible.

One nonaddictive, nonbenzodiazepine alternative for treating anxiety is buspirone (BuSpar). Older patients tolerate this drug well without oversedation in doses from 5 mg three times a day up to 15 mg three times a day. Dizziness is the most common side effect at the higher doses. Controlled trials of buspirone have shown that it is effective in generalized anxiety disorder, but not in panic disorder. Notably, it cannot prevent withdrawal symptoms from benzodiazepines; therefore, benzodiazepine withdrawal should be done gradually on its own without relying on buspirone for symptom relief at first. Also, it takes approximately 3 weeks for the effects of buspirone to occur, making the timing of any transition from one drug program to another a crucial consideration in an anxious patient. The best approach may be to introduce the buspirone for 3 weeks before even beginning a slow taper of benzodiazepines. In clinical practice, many geropsychiatrists question buspirone's usefulness for generalized anxiety disorder but have found the drug very helpful as a primary or adjunctive medication for agitation in dementia or depression (discussed later in this chapter).

Drugs labeled as "antidepressants" have emerged as a valuable psychopharmacological tool in the long-term treatment of anxiety. These agents do not offer the immediate symptom relief possible from benzodiazepines, but antidepressants can reduce background anxiety in a number of conditions and lower the tendency to have panic attacks. Antidepressants are nonaddictive and thus a preferable choice under many circumstances. Agents with potential benefits in various anxiety disorders include the selective serotonin reuptake inhibitors (SSRIs) such as fluoxetine (Prozac), sertraline (Zoloft), or paroxetine (Paxil) and the 5-HT$_2$ (a specific serotonin receptor) antagonist nefazodone (Serzone). For obsessive-compulsive disorder, SSRIs and the older tricyclic antidepressant clomipramine (Anafranil) are specifically helpful. Elderly patients tend to tolerate SSRIs better than they do tricyclics in terms of side effects (see "Depression" later in this chapter). All these medications have side effects and characteristics that can complicate their management. It is risky to stop any antidepressant abruptly without tapering, and some of the SSRIs with shorter durations of action such as paroxetine actually have unpleasant withdrawal syndromes. SSRIs can also indirectly affect dopamine status in the brain and cause some of the same adverse reactions seen with the older neuroleptic (antipsychotic) drugs such as haloperidol (Haldol): extrapyramidal syndromes (EPS), neuroleptic malignant syndrome (NMS), and even rarely, tardive dyskinesia (TD).

EPS is a general term for the motor side effects of dopamine-blocking drugs, which can include akathisia or restlessness as well as cogwheeling rigidity of muscles, gait disturbance, and masklike facies. NMS is a rare but potentially fatal complication of dopamine-blocking drugs involving fever, muscular rigidity and breakdown, and autonomic nervous system instability. TD is a long-term, often irreversible side effect of dopamine-blocking drugs involving involuntary motor movements, such as tongue thrusting and chewing motions. Elderly patients, especially those with diabetes mellitus or affective disorders, are especially susceptible to developing TD from dopamine-blocking drugs.

Other options for short-term anxiety or insomnia treatment in younger patients may include antihistamines such as diphenhydramine (Benadryl) or hydroxyzine (Atarax). These drugs carry undesirable side effects for the elderly, including blurry vision, urinary retention, constipation, and confusion from their anticholinergic properties. Patients develop tolerance and lose the sedative benefit after 2 or 3 weeks. In certain situations, such as treating hives or other allergic reactions, antihistamines may be necessary; but they are not a good solution for anxiety per se in geriatrics.

Finally, many patients resort to complementary and alternative medicine self-treatment without telling their primary care providers (30–40% of the U.S.

population overall—Eisenberg, 1997; Eisenberg et al., 1993). While many of these agents can be safe and effective, older persons may start these treatments at too low or too high a dose, using products that are not standardized in content, and not realizing the risks for drug interactions with their prescription medications (Crone & Wise, 1998). For example, one over-the-counter botanical substance for anxiety is Kava-Kava (Volz & Kieser, 1997), which can lead to serious oversedation and even coma in combination with benzodiazepines or other sedating medications (Almeida & Grimsley, 1996). St. John's Wort, which may help some cases of depression (Linde et al., 1996) and perhaps anxiety, can cause a life-threatening serotonin syndrome in combination with SSRIs. Many patients prefer and tolerate botanical products for particular problems better than they do prescription drugs. The main caveat is simply that they need to work together with their primary care provider and pharmacist to adjust their total treatment program for safety and effectiveness (Eisenberg, 1997).

AGITATION

DIFFERENTIAL DIAGNOSIS

Agitation is a nonspecific term that crosses diagnoses and encompasses behaviors ranging from manifest anxiety to violence toward self or others. Agitation is a feature of anxiety disorders, depressions, psychoses, dementias, medication side effects, and delirium from medical or medication causes. For example, researchers have found that delusions may constitute a greater risk for violence than do hallucinations in patients with Alzheimer's disease (Gilley, Wilson, Beckett, & Evans, 1997). The first goal of treatment is to maintain safety, reduce environmental overstimulation, and provide a reassuring context for the patient. Many times, it is necessary to give acute symptomatic treatment to reestablish some control and comfort for the elderly patient and those around the patient, with neuroleptics such as haloperidol (Haldol). However, clinical diagnosis of the underlying condition is the next step. Selection of the proper psychopharmacological treatment will depend on the source of the agitation. In some cases, the prescribed medications, notably agents like haloperidol, are the source of the problem and need to be lowered in dose or stopped rather than increased. For agitation and violence in the elderly, geropsychiatrists rely on an ever-expanding set of medication choices, chosen by the overall clinical picture more than by the category from which the drug derives (American Psychiatric Association [APA], 1997; Jenike, 1996). Thus, older (typical) and newer (atypical) antipsychotic drugs (Berman et al., 1996), anticonvulsants such as valproate (Depakote) (Lott, McElroy, & Keys, 1995), carbamazepine (Tegretol) (Lemke, 1995), and gabapentin (Neurontin), buspirone (Cantillon, Brunswick, Molina, & Bahro, 1996), antidepressants such as the SSRIs (Karlsson, 1996) or trazodone (Solomon & Pendlebury, 1997; Sultzer, Gray, Gunay, Berisford, & Mahler, 1997), and beta-blocking drugs such as propranolol or atenolol are often prescribed alone or, if necessary, in combination.

MEDICATION OPTIONS

Many people, including medical personnel, overlook (Rockwood et al., 1994) or mistake the acute change (in hours to days) in mental status with fluctuating confusion that marks delirium, a life-threatening medical condition, as evidence of new onset "dementia." Dementia is a much slower process, in most cases developing over periods of years. Dementia patients are more vulnerable to delirium than are normal elderly, but anyone can have a delirium when ill. Delirium can result from acute infections such as pneumonia or urinary tract infection, dehydration, blood chemistry disturbances, low oxygen in the blood from lung diseases, medication side effects (especially anticholinergic, including blurry vision, dry mouth, urinary retention, constipation), and many other causes. It has up to a 25% mortality rate, and proper medical evaluation early in its course is essential for optimal outcome. Usually, medications such as haloperidol are the appropriate short-term symptomatic approach for delirium to calm the patient and permit the necessary specific medical treatment. An advantage of haloperidol in this situation is that it is available in liquid and injectable forms for poorly compliant patients; it also has fewer autonomic nervous system side effects that might complicate medical care. Once the underlying cause is treated, patients generally do not require continued use of the haloperidol.

Another classic mistake in using psychopharmacology is to increase the dose of a drug such as haloperidol in response to increasing agitation in the patient. Often, but not always, it is the ability of the haloperidol to cause intense restlessness and agitation as a side effect (akathisia) when used in excessive doses that is responsible for the agitation. Again, if every dose increase worsens rather than improves the situation, it is time to reassess and probably stop the neuroleptic medication program, manage briefly with a benzodiazepine such as lorazepam or a beta-blocker to reduce restlessness, and find an alternative drug for the original agitation.

If an anxiety disorder or depression is the source of agitation, benzodiazepines or buspirone may be helpful, as outlined above under "Anxiety." However, if psychosis derives from a psychotic depression, a late-life delusional disorder, or dementia (at least 30% of dementia patients experience psychosis), then neuroleptic (antipsychotic) medications are usually needed (Table 33.3). Perphenazine (Trilafon) is one of the older, typical antipsychotic drugs that many geriatric psychiatrists prefer to prescribe, in doses ranging from 2 to 16 mg per day. These types of neuroleptics act by blocking the neurotransmitter dopamine. Perphenazine has the advantage of having moderate side effects in terms of causing stiffness or other common extrapyramidal symptoms otherwise common with haloperidol and in terms of causing anticholinergic problems such as confusion, urinary retention, or constipation symptoms common with thioridazine (Mellaril) or chlorpromazine (Thorazine). In recent years, however, the availability of newer neuroleptic drugs with better profiles of tolerability and lower long-term risks of tardive dyskinesia (Schatzberg et al., 1997; Yassa, Nastase, Dupont, & Thibeau, 1992) have led to shifts in practice for patients needing long-term medications.

Table 33.3   Representative typical and atypical antipsychotic medications for psychoses and agitation.

Generic Name	Trade Name	Geriatric Dose Range (Total Milligrams/Day)	Typical (Older) or Atypical (Newer) Type	Comments*
Haloperidol	Haldol	0.25–4	Typical	Marked stiffness and other Parkinsonian-like side effects
Perphenazine	Trilafon	2–16	Typical	Moderate in both Parkinsonian-like and anticholinergic side effects
Thioridazine	Mellaril	25–200	Typical	Marked sedative, anticholinergic, and orthostatic side effects
Risperidone	Risperdal	0.25–4	Atypical	Parkinsonian side effects at higher doses
Olanzapine	Zyprexa	2.5–20	Atypical	Orthostatic side effects
Quetiapine	Seroquel	150–500	Atypical	Gastrointestinal side effects
Clozapine	Clozaril	12.5–200	Atypical	Orthostasis and drooling common; life-threatening loss of white blood cells is a side effect; needs regular blood tests; other options preferable

*Parkinsonian and extrapyramidal side effects can include muscle stiffness, restlessness, tremor, slowed movements.

Many newer (atypical) neuroleptics have more selective blocking effects on specific dopamine and serotonin receptors. An important benefit of the atypical over the typical neuroleptics is the newer drugs' ability to reduce both the negative (e.g., social withdrawal) and the positive (e.g., hallucinations) symptoms of schizophrenia. At this point, many geropsychiatrists are prescribing the newer neuroleptic risperidone in doses of 0.25 to 4 mg per day. The most common side effect in that dose range may be drowsiness, which can be used to advantage by dosing at bedtime and avoiding an additional sedative drug. At doses above 2–4 mg/day, patients will experience extrapyramidal side effects and sometimes paradoxical worsening of agitation, even to the point of mania. Most older patients do not need these higher doses, making risperidone a valuable, well-tolerated choice in many cases. The newer atypical antipsychotics are also preferred in elderly with Parkinson's disease, because of the far lower risk of worsening the neurological condition's movement disorder with drug side effects than used to occur with the older neuroleptics.

As noted earlier, medication side effects are a major potential source of not only anxiety, but also agitation (see also Table 33.1). One clinical approach to determining whether medications may be involved is to take a careful history from the patient and caregivers about any changes in medications within the week or so prior to the appearance of the agitation. If a patient has been on a stable doses of medications for many months, then drugs may not be contributing to an acute increase in agitation.

However, adding another drug sometimes leads to interference in clearance of other drugs that had been stable and thus side effects or even toxicity from those agents. One common example in geropsychiatry would be the addition of fluoxetine, which can drastically raise levels of a number of medical and psychiatric drugs. Even some antibiotics may impede the clearance of other agents such as phenytoin (Dilantin) or carbamazepine (Tegretol) and elevate levels of the other drug in a short period of time.

In many dementia patients, antipsychotics do not provide sufficient control of the agitation short of overdrugging to the point of falls and daytime sedation. For this common problem, geropsychiatrists have resorted to classes of agents other than antipsychotics to treat the agitation. In cases in which loss of behavioral inhibition from brain cell death is likely (e.g., as in vascular dementia or Alzheimer's disease), the anticonvulsant valproate (Depakote) has emerged as a leading choice. The rationale is that these problems reflect neurological damage and lowered thresholds for neuronal firing and irritability, problems that anticonvulsants may attenuate, even without an overt seizure disorder. Blood tests provide a target to assist in using only the amount of medication needed to achieve therapeutic benefit; many elderly respond to blood levels at the lower end of the target range (e.g., around 50 micrograms/ml). Notably, valproate can exacerbate tremors in predisposed patients. Anticonvulsants such as carbamazepine (Tegretol) are also helpful in agitation, but this drug is especially problematic to manage because of its ability to induce metabolism of itself and of other drugs.

Buspirone (BuSpar) is another agent reported to lessen agitation and/or violence, especially in dementia, without causing oversedation. Furthermore, by itself, studies have shown buspirone can be effective in doses around 45 mg/day in the treatment of agitated depression. An obvious possible indication then could be when the agitation of a dementia patient includes episodic tearfulness or despair over his or her condition, hinting at some degree of depression as a source. Other clinicians have reported that the SSRI antidepressants and trazodone, which have a nonspecific antiaggression effect, also may reduce agitation and violent behaviors in dementia apart from depression. Finally, in situations in which other approaches fail, especially when hypertension or cardiac problems would also indicate their use, beta-blocking drugs (which inhibit sympathetic nervous system responses, i.e., fight or flight) such as atenolol or propanol may reduce violent behaviors. A major disadvantage of the latter agents in persons with normal blood pressure is the risk of lowering blood pressure excessively and causing fainting and falls. Moreover, beta-blockers can cause depression. Beta-blockers are also problematic in patients with asthma, who need sympathetic nervous system activation to open bronchial airways, or with diabetes mellitus, who must rely on the symptoms of sympathetic nervous system activation (e.g., anxiety, sweating, racing heart) to cue them about incipient low blood sugar episodes from their insulin or oral hypoglycemic medications.

DEPRESSION

DIFFERENTIAL DIAGNOSIS

Depression is the most common psychiatric problem treated in the geriatric population (Lebowitz et al., 1997). As with anxiety and agitation, providers must first assess medical and medication issues in the etiology of the affective disorder (Table 33.4) (see also Gelenberg & Bassuk, 1997). Common blood tests in the workup of geriatric depression include serum TSH and free T_4 for thyroid status and serum B_{12} and folate for B vitamin status. Many opiate drugs for pain control can have profound depressogenic effects, in addition to the association of chronic pain with depression. Occult alcoholism is also a consideration, and sometimes testing blood alcohol levels may be necessary. Depression is a common comorbidity in many medical conditions, including heart disease, cancer, and diabetes mellitus. Even subclinical depression is associated with increased health care service utilization and costs as well as poorer medical outcomes. In heart attack patients, depression is a risk factor for subsequent mortality. Studies have shown that the depressions associated with stroke and with Parkinson's disease are part of the disease processes rather than from psychological maladjustment to disabling physical impairment. Late-onset depression, even when the depression-related cognitive problems are reversible with antidepressant treatment, is often the precursor of subsequent irreversible dementia (Alexopoulos et al., 1993).

MEDICATION OPTIONS

Table 33.5 summarizes commonly prescribed medications for depression in the elderly. Current standards of practice converge on the use of newer antidepressant agents rather than the tricyclic antidepressants. Thus, drugs such as SSRIs, especially sertraline and paroxetine, are first-line choices for pharmacological

Table 33.4   Drugs and medical conditions associated with prominent depressive states in older patients.

Medication or Medical Condition
Antihypertensive drugs such as propranolol or methydopa
Analgesic drugs such as morphine, meperidine, propoxyphene
Sedative-hypnotic drugs such as benzodiazepines or barbiturates
Excess alcohol
Steroids such as dexamethasone or prednisone
Hypothyroidism
Stroke
Parkinson's disease
B vitamin deficiencies such as B_6 or folate

Table 33.5   Medications commonly used in the treatment of geriatric depression.

Generic Name	Trade Name	Geriatric Dose Range (Total Milligrams/Day)	Class*	Comments
Fluoxetine	Prozac	10–40	SSRI	Variably tolerated; raises levels of other drugs; often poor choice in the elderly
Sertraline	Zoloft	25–100	SSRI	Reasonable SSRI choice for elderly; some drug interactions
Paroxetine	Paxil	10–20	SSRI	Useful in anxious depressions; withdrawal syndrome possible on abrupt discontinuation
Nortriptyline	Pamelor	35–75	Tricyclic	Dry mouth, urinary retention, constipation, some orthostasis are side effects
Desipramine	Norpramin	100–200	Tricyclic	Somewhat more activating for retarded depression; see nortriptyline for side effects
Bupropion	Wellbutrin	150–300	NE-DA	Activating drug; no sexual side effects
Venlafaxine	Effexor	75–225	5-HT & NE reuptake inhibitor	Fewer drug interactions
Nefazodone	Serzone	100–400	5-HT$_2$ antagonist	Useful in anxious depressions; fewer sexual side effects
Methylphenidate	Ritalin	2.5–10	Stimulant	Useful in apathetic medically ill patients; can cause agitation

*SSRI is selective serotonin reuptake inhibitor; 5-HT is serotonin; NE is norepinephrine; DA is dopamine (all brain neurotransmitters).

treatment of many geriatric depressives. SSRIs are generally well-tolerated in the elderly population. The most common side effects can include nausea, diarrhea, and sexual dysfunction. Their greatest drawbacks are their tendency to interact with the metabolism and clearance of other drugs. Sertraline can increase the levels and anticoagulant effects of Coumadin (warfarin), a common drug to prevent blood clots in the elderly, but the interaction can potentially cause serious bleeding complications. Paroxetine can elevate digoxin levels, leading to toxicity and cardiac complications in patients on the latter drug for atrial fibrillation. Most SSRIs can raise levels of tricyclic antidepressants into the toxic range. Fluoxetine is less useful than the others in older patients because of these drug interaction risks and because of its extremely long half-life (it can take up to 10 weeks to clear all fluoxetine metabolites from the system of the older person).

However, tricyclics still have an important place in the treatment armamentarium. For example, studies have demonstrated an advantage for tricyclics over

SSRIs in melancholic depression and in certain types of chronic pain (e.g., diabetic neuropathy). The side effect problems with tricyclics include dry mouth, blurry vision, urinary retention, constipation, and orthostasis (tendency for blood pressure to fall too far on rising from a lying or sitting position). Tricyclics can cause cardiac arrhythmias in patients with conduction defects, accentuating the need for careful medical evaluations prior to and during treatment. Nortriptyline is the preferred tricyclic in the elderly because of its lower degree of anticholinergic and orthostatic side effects and the ability to measure its blood levels and titrate doses to achieve a therapeutic "window" of 50–150 mg/ml. Although many doctors still prescribe amitryptyline (Elavil) in low doses for pain in older patients, this drug has among the worst side effect profile of the tricyclics. Nortriptyline or another tricyclic, desipramine, have effects comparable to amitryptyline without the same level of risks.

Another newer antidepressant with useful applications for treating retarded depressions in the elderly is bupropion (Wellbutrin), an activating drug that potentiates neurotransmitters norepinephrine and dopamine. A slow-release form of bupropion is also approved for use in smoking cessation. Clinical lore suggests that this drug may be the preferred agent for patients with anergic depressions common in bipolar disorder. Most elderly, including those with cardiac conditions, tolerate it well in doses of 150–300 mg/day (divided). It has an advantage over SSRIs in that bupropion does not cause sexual side effects. Unlike most other antidepressants, however, bupropion is not helpful in reducing the rate of panic attacks in panic patients. At higher doses and in patients with preexisting seizure disorders or bulimia, bupropion has an increased risk of inducing seizures.

Venlafaxine (Effexor) is a newer antidepressant with a broader spectrum of action on neurotransmitters in the brain (e.g., serotonin and norepinephrine reuptake inhibitor) than the SSRIs. Its advantage over SSRIs is that it has less potential for drug metabolism interactions. Its main disadvantage is the risk that a small percentage of patients develop blood pressure elevations in a dose-related manner. However, this blood pressure elevating effect may favor its use in patients with preexisting problems with low blood pressure or orthostasis. Other common side effects include nausea, dizziness, sleepiness, sweating, dry mouth, and sexual dysfunction.

An alternative to the tricyclics for severe depressions or for agitated depression may be nefazodone, another newer drug with the capacity to block a specific serotonin receptor (5-HT$_2$) (Goldberg, 1997). Nefazodone causes less nausea than do the SSRIs, but it can lead to dizziness and orthostasis in the elderly. Like bupropion, nefazodone may have a low rate of sexual side effects. However, nefazodone can elevate levels of some drugs such as alprazolam, carbamazepine, and some newer antihistamines into a dangerous range. In the elderly, doses can start at 25 mg twice a day and may reach 400 mg/day total.

Other medications can play a role in the treatment of depression as well. These include buspirone (BuSpar), mirtazapine (Remeron), and trazodone. Both buspirone and mirtazapine may have a place in the treatment of anxious or agitated depressions. Trazodone is difficult to use in the elderly at the higher doses needed for antidepressant effects, because of extreme sedation and orthostasis. However, many geropsychiatrists use trazodone in very low doses such as 25–100 mg once a day at bedtime to help with sleep problems in patients with insomnia from various causes. Trazodone's most common side effect is orthostasis, with the additional relatively rare risk of priapism in men (painful sustained erections requiring emergency medical treatment).

In situations in which a medically ill elderly patient is apathetic, stimulant drugs such as methylphenidate (Ritalin) in doses of 2.5–10 mg/day can play a valuable role in mobilizing participation in rehabilitation and treatment. Stimulants have the advantage of rapid onset of action within hours to days rather than weeks. In rare cases with highly intact and compliant patients, monoamine oxidase inhibitors (e.g., phenelzine, tranylcypromine) may be necessary, especially in treatment-resistant anxious depressions or anergic bipolar depressions. However, the risk of life-threatening hypertensive or other medical crises from dietary (e.g., aged cheese, red wine) or medication (e.g., pseudoephedrine in decongestants, epinephrine for allergic reactions, meperidine [Demerol] for pain) interactions with MAOIs has limited their clinical usefulness. MAOIs must be stopped for at least 2 weeks to allow their effects to clear the system before starting many other types of antidepressant agents, to avoid life-threatening interactions.

Electroconvulsive therapy (ECT) remains a safe and effective treatment for elderly patients with depression who fail to respond to medications, refuse to eat or drink and thus threaten their own life with dehydration, or express active, acute suicidal ideation with an accessible plan. Primary risks are those of undergoing brief general anesthesia. Follow-up research has shown only short-term memory impairment post-ECT, which resolves over a period of weeks to months. One study demonstrated lower long-term mortality rates in patients treated with ECT than with medications for depression (Philibert, Richards, Lynch, & Winokur, 1995).

Clinical research suggests that patients with melancholic depression may benefit from supplementation with the B vitamin folic acid (folate) to improve medication responsivity (Fava et al., 1997). To augment medication effects, geropsychiatrists sometimes add low dose lithium (e.g., 300 mg/day) to improve on the partial antidepressant effects of the previously listed antidepressants. The lithium can be useful not only in patients with bipolar disorder, but also simply in those with incomplete antidepressant drug responses. It is important to note that some elderly can become lithium toxic, however, even at seemingly normal serum levels (1.0 mEq/L or below). Kidney failure, dehydration, and some diuretic drugs for heart failure or hypertension as well as certain analgesics (e.g., nonsteroidal medications such as ibuprofen) can elevate lithium levels. Overall, lithium, valproate, and carbamazepine are still the leading mood-stabilizing agents for bipolar patients of all ages.

Finally, it is important to note that all antidepressants can take at least 3 weeks and sometimes up to 12 weeks to begin working in older persons. People around the patient may notice behavioral improvements such as greater animation, better sleep and appetite, and enhanced interest in activities before the individual notices any internal sense of elevation of mood in themselves. Patience is essential in psychopharmacological treatment of depression to avoid premature and unnecessary dose increases. Supportive nonpharmacological interventions are crucial in this phase. For patients who can take advantage of psychotherapeutic treatment, their long-term course in general may be better than in those treated with medications alone.

CONCLUSION

The use of psychopharmacological agents in geriatric individuals is complex. It requires a highly trained and knowledgeable physician with experience in dealing with the interaction of medical and psychiatric problems and medications. At the same time, the practice of geriatric psychopharmacology is likely to improve as more systematic studies become available to guide clinical practice. Especially because of the difficulties that many impaired elderly have in describing symptoms, it is crucial to assist patients and caregivers with straightforward information about the indications for and risks, benefits, and alternatives of each medication. The medication program is often only as good as the quality of the observations of people around the patient. Geriatric psychopharmacological treatment is a team effort led by a physician, in which the team must include the patient and caregivers and should include pharmacists, nurses, and other allied health professionals.

REFERENCES

Alexopoulos, G.S., Meyers, B.S., Young, R.C., Mattis, S., & Kakuma, T. (1993). The course of geriatric depression with "reversible dementia": A controlled study. *American Journal of Psychiatry, 150,* 1693–1699.

Almeida, J.C., & Grimsley, E.W. (1996). Coma from the health food store: Interaction between kava and alprazolam. *Annals of Internal Medicine, 125,* 940–941.

American Psychiatric Association. (1994). *Diagnostic and statistical manual of mental disorders* (4th ed.). Washington, DC: American Psychiatric Association.

American Psychiatric Association. (1997). Practice guideline for the treatment of patients with Alzheimer's disease and other dementias of late life. *American Journal of Psychiatry Supplement, 154,* 1–37.

Berman, I., Merson, A., Rachov-Pavlov, J., Allan, E., Davidson, M., & Losonczy, M.F. (1996). Risperidone in elderly schizophrenic patients. An open-label trial. *American Journal of Geriatric Psychiatry, 4,* 173–179.

Busse, E.W., & Blazer, D.G. (Eds.). (1996). *Textbook of geriatric psychiatry* (2nd ed.). Washington, DC: American Psychiatric Press.

Cantillon, M., Brunswick, R., Molina, D., & Bahro, M. (1996). Buspirone vs. haloperidol. A double-blind trial for agitation in a nursing home population with Alzheimer's disease. *American Journal of Geriatric Psychiatry, 4,* 263–267.

Crone, C.C., & Wise, T.N. (1998). Use of herbal medicines among consultation-liaison populations. A review of current information regarding risks, interactions, and efficacy. *Psychosomatics, 39,* 3–13.

Eisenberg, D.M. (1997). Advising patients who seek alternative medical therapies. *Annals of Internal Medicine, 127*, 61–69.

Eisenberg, D.M., Kessler, R.C., Foster, C., Norlock, F.E., Calkins, D.R., & Delbanco, T.L. (1993). Unconventional medicine in the United States. Prevalence, costs, and patterns of use. *New England Journal of Medicine, 328*, 246–252.

Fava, M., Borus, J.S., Alpert, J.E., Nierenberg, A.A., Rosenbaum, J.F., & Bottiglieri, T. (1997). Folate, vitamin B_{12}, and homocystine in major depressive disorder. *American Journal of Psychiatry, 154*, 426–428.

Gelenberg, A.J., & Bassuk, E.L. (1997). *The practitioner's guide to psychoactive drugs* (4th ed.). New York: Plenum Medical Books.

Gilley, D.W., Wilson, R.S., Beckett, L.A., & Evans, D.A. (1997). Psychotic symptoms and physically aggressive behavior in Alzheimer's disease. *Journal of the American Geriatrics Society, 45*, 1074–1079.

Goldberg, R.J. (1997). Antidepressant use in the elderly. Current status of nefazodone, venlafaxine, moclobemide. *Drugs and Aging, 11*, 119–131.

Jenike, M.A. (1996). Psychiatric illnesses in the elderly: A review. *Journal of Geriatric Psychiatry and Neurology, 9*, 57–82.

Kamath, M., Finkel, S.I., & Moran, M.B. (1996). A retrospective chart review of antidepressant use, effectiveness, and adverse effects in adults age 70 and older. *American Journal of Geriatric Psychiatry, 4*, 167–172.

Karlsson, I. (1996). Treatment of non-cognitive symptoms in dementia. *Acta Neurologica Scandinavica , 168*(Suppl.), 93–95.

Katz, I.R., Beaston-Wimmer, P., Parmelee, P., Friedman, E., & Lawton, M.P. (1993). Failure to thrive in the elderly: Exploration of the concept and delineation of psychiatric components. *Journal of Geriatric Psychiatry and Neurology, 6*, 161–169.

Lebowitz, B.D., Pearson, J.L., Schneider, L.S., Reynolds, C.F., Alexopoulos, G.S., Bruce, M.L., Conwell, Y., Katz, I.R., Meyers, B.S., Morrison, M.F., Mossey, J., Neiderehe, G., & Parmelee, P. (1997). Consensus statement. Diagnosis and treatment of depression in late life. *Journal of the American Medical Association, 278*, 1186–1190.

Lemke, M.R. (1995). Effect of carbamazepine on agitation in Alzheimer's inpatients refractory to neuroleptics. *Journal of Clinical Psychiatry, 56*, 354–357.

Linde, K., Ramirez, G., Mulrow, C.D., Pauls, A., Weidenhammer, W., & Melchart, D. (1996). St. John's wort for depression—an overview and meta-analysis of randomized clinical trials. *British Medical Journal, 313*, 253–258.

Lott, A.D., McElroy, S.L., & Keys, M.A. (1995). Valproate in the treatment of behavioral agitation in elderly patients with dementia. *Journal of Neuropsychiatry and Clinical Neurosciences, 7*, 314–319.

Penninx, B.W.J.H., Guralnik, J.M., Ferrucci, L., Simonsick, E.M., Deeg, D.J.H., & Wallace, R.B. (1998). Depressive symptoms and physical decline in community-dwelling older persons. *Journal of the American Medical Association, 279*, 1720–1726.

Philibert, R.A., Richards, L., Lynch, C.F., & Winokur, G. (1995). Effect of ECT on mortality and clinical outcome in geriatric unipolar depression. *Journal of Clinical Psychiatry, 56*, 390–394.

Ray, W.A., Fought, R.L., & Decker, M.D. (1992). Psychoactive drugs and the risk of injurious motor vehicle crashes in elderly drivers. *American Journal of Epidemiology, 136*, 873–883.

Rockwood, K., Cosway, S., Stolee, P., Kydd, D., Carver, D., Jarrett, P., & O'Brien, B. (1994). Increasing recognition of delirium in elderly patients. *Journal of the American Geriatrics Society, 42*, 252–256.

Schatzberg, A.F., Cole, J.O., & DeBattista, C. (1997). *Manual of clinical psychopharmacology* (3rd ed.). Washington, DC: American Psychiatric Press.

Sheikh, J., & Nguyen, C. (1997). Psychopharmacologic treatment of anxiety disorders in older patients. *Essential Psychopharmacology, 1,* 377–390.

Simon, G., Ormel, J., VonKorff, M., & Barlow, W. (1995). Health care costs associated with depressive and anxiety disorders in primary care. *American Journal of Psychiatry, 152,* 352–357.

Small, G.W., Rabins, P.V., Barry, P.P., Buckholtz, N.S., DeKosky, S.T., Ferris, S.H., Finkel, S.I., Gwyther, L.P., Khachaturian, Z.S., Lebowitz, B.D., McRae, T.D., Morris, J.C., Oakley, F., Schneider, L.S., Streim, J.E., Sunderland, T., Teri, L.A., & Tune, L.E. (1998). Diagnosis and treatment of Alzheimer disease and related disorders. Consensus statement of the American Association for geriatric psychiatry, the Alzheimer's association, and the American geriatrics society. *Journal of the American Medical Association, 278,* 1363–1371.

Solomon, P.R., & Pendlebury, W.W. (1997). Pharmacotherapy of Alzheimer's disease. *Essential Psychopharmacology, 1,* 217–242.

Sultzer, D.L., Gray, K.F., Gunay, I., Berisford, M.A., & Mahler, M.E. (1997). A double-blind comparison of trazodone and haloperidol for treatment of agitation in patients with dementia. *American Journal of Geriatric Psychiatry, 5,* 60–69.

Thapa, P.B., Gideon, P., Fought, R.L., & Ray, W.A. (1995). Psychotropic drugs and risk of recurrent falls in ambulatory nursing home residents. *American Journal of Epidemiology, 142,* 202–211.

Volz, H.P., & Kieser, M. (1997). Kava-kava extract WS 1490 versus placebo in anxiety disorders—a randomized, placebo-controlled 25-week outpatient trial. *Pharmacopsychiatry, 30,* 1–5.

Yassa, R., Nastase, C., Dupont, D., & Thibeau, M. (1992). Tardive dyskinesia in elderly psychiatric patients: A 5-year study. *American Journal of Psychiatry, 149,* 1206–1211.

Zubenko, G.S., Mulsant, B.H., Sweet, R.A., Pasternak, R.E., & Tue, X.M. (1997). Mortality of elderly patients with psychiatric disorders. *American Journal of Psychiatry, 154,* 1360–1368.

CHAPTER 34

Reaching the Person behind the Dementia: Treating Comorbid Affective Disorders through Subvocal and Nonverbal Strategies

Michael Duffy

Some time ago I was in conversation with several colleagues who work in the area of clinical geropsychology. They expressed the opinion that the Health Care Financing Administration would be correct in refusing Medicare reimbursement for psychotherapy for older adults with Alzheimer's disease. This opinion was based on the straightforward logic that since mid- and late-stage Alzheimer's patients lose language capacity, there would be no medical necessity to justify verbal psychotherapy. My own view of this situation is considerably at odds with this position; in psychotherapy with any client, language is a multidimensional event that cannot be merely described linguistically nor in its logical structure but rather in a series of levels of meaning that exist in both cognitive and affective domains. While disagreeing vehemently, I did, however, understand my colleagues' viewpoint, which is in accord with the assumption that when language is no more, then communication and relationship are virtually at a standstill. This is a perfectly natural and intuitive position; however, as in so many facets of life and certainly in the world of psychotherapy, the truth follows not the intuitive or obvious position but is often best expressed in counterintuitive terms. Intuitively, family members, personal friends and even professionals become somewhat detached from a person who has lost language, whether it be through stroke or through the onset of a dementing disease. I have been present in situations where a spouse was going through an intensely emotional bereavement reaction for her husband when in fact he had a stroke, which had temporarily impaired his speech. Such was her intuitive dependence on language as a sign of emotional connection that she felt bereaved at that moment when she could no longer be connected to him through language. Similarly, in the case of Alzheimer's disease, it is common for family members and friends and, indeed, even professionals to become detached emotionally from the Alzheimer's victim. Metaphorically and really, it is as if everyone is leaving the room of the Alzheimers' patient one by one, with the poignant message, "Would the last one out, please turn off the light?" Although this reaction is naturalistic and understandable, what has actually occurred is an emotional abandonment of the stroke victim or person with dementia. Another metaphor comes to mind to describe the predicament of patients who are language deprived either through stroke or the onset of dementia. It is almost as if they were in a glass coffin, able to see and take in completely their environment, eager to reach out and touch, eager to be an emotional connection with those around them and yet completely cut off and alone. It is not surprising that in such a condition a comorbid depression is frequently found.

Language, of course, is not the whole of our internal experience. Nor is the logical structure of language the only dimension in which language communicates. Speech communication theorists, often more expertly than mental health workers or psychologists, have a sophisticated classification in understanding the various ways in which human beings communicate. They consider that all behaviors are potentially communicative and use a classification schema for communicative behaviors as follows: within the vocal area we can have *linguistic* and *paralinguistic* expressions. There is also a *kinesic* dimension, which includes both overt bodily movements, including facial expressions, an *autonomic* bodily signals including skin color, pupil dilation, visceral activity, and posture. Finally, *tactile* dimensions give important communicative signals in dress, cosmetics, ornamentation, and touch itself. Psychology is relatively aware of the nonverbal dimensions of communication and sometimes, somewhat simplistically, uses these dimensions instrumentally to affect client behavior. So, for example, counselors are taught to sit forward in the chair in an "interested" manner or take a position close to the client to signal intimacy. Psychologists, however, are strongly influenced by empirical views of human behavior, and are little aware of what can be called *subvocal* aspects of communication. In a verbal communication, a linguistic structure of words is connected in sentences with an overt associated meaning, but we all know through daily experience that the actual intended communication in a particular sentence can be far different from the words themselves. It is in this subvocal area that we very often communicate the true emotional message of our language; it is in the subvocal domain that we send signals to one another within the words we use. Language, in other words, mediates emotions through the surface structure. There is perhaps no better example of this than in the early language between mother and child where the overt structure and content of the language could be said to be logically meaningless. Few of us, however, would suggest that there is not a meaningful emotional exchange going on between parent and child in such a situation (Papoušek, 1995). The parent does not cease to use language because of the limitations in logical exchange. Indeed, language becomes a vehicle to communicate several different dimensions within the exchange. This form of nonrational language communicates many things including affirmation, affection, approval, reinforcement, and at the same time also provides the context in which the emotional bond between parent and child is increasingly stabilized and nourished. It is perhaps a less than happy result of maturity and aging that we lose this childlike capacity to communicate without complete reliance on logical structure. As a result, it becomes a difficult and onerous task to maintain verbal communication with an older adult when logical structure is diminished and eventually completely absent. Is it not possible, therefore, to learn to reinstate this type of poignant communication between family members and their demented relatives and, in the case of therapy, between the psychotherapist and the older client? This is not to infantilize the relationship between therapist and older client but rather to restore some of the emotional vibrancy in the communication that has been lost or obscured as adults become increasingly dependent on structural logical language. To be able to continue talking, not just nonverbally, to our demented patients allows us to nourish and continue their still existing rich emotional life.

The truth is that the loss of language does not denote the loss of emotional life; a full emotional life seems still to exist. This should not surprise us since increasing knowledge of neuropsychological midbrain activity suggests that while working and long-term memory may be compromised in the dementing disorders, the "emotional memory" seems to be preserved intact within midbrain structures. Research on posttraumatic stress suggests an explanation for the loss of memory of trauma; frontal cortex memory functions block memory of the trauma for self-protective reasons. However, memory traces still seem to exist in the midbrain structure that are available for retrieval at an opportune time (van der Kolk & McFarlane, 1996). This preservation of midbrain memory is consistent with the general pattern of neurological damage in Alzheimer's which, in an apparent reversal of phylogenetic development (Feyereisen, 1991), appears to commence in the frontal areas and then eventually progress downward through midbrain and brainstem structures. So it is that an Alzheimer's patient will commonly not be able to identify the name or correct relationship of a close relative but may well be able to recognize this same relative as personally and emotionally familiar. Although this may be of little comfort when a demented parent misidentifies a disconsolate adult child, it suggests that the patient holds an "emotional memory" of their past relationship without being able to precisely identify it.

Magai and Cohen (1988) have conducted a study, which gives interesting confirmation to the consistency and continuity of emotional life in Alzheimer's patients. They found that the premorbid attachment patterns (secure, avoidant, ambivalent) of these elderly patients continued in later life after the onset of dementia. This is evidence of the continuity of emotional life even alongside the decrement in logical thinking and language. It is noteworthy that they found fewer cases of ambivalent attachment in this older population than they would expect in the general population. Their interpretation of this result pointed to supposed methodological characteristics of this study. In my clinical experience, however, this could well be explained by the gradual development (or regression) of ambivalent, anxiety-related conditions to a more avoidant position later in life. Generally, they found that ambivalent patients had more depression and anxiety than secure and avoidant patients. The avoidant patients experienced more activity disturbance than the ambivalently attached individuals and were higher on paranoid symptomatology than securely attached persons. Premorbid securely attached persons seem to do better in later life even under the conditions of dementia.

For those of us who work directly with Alzheimer's patients, the continued existence of an affective life is pointedly demonstrated in the capacity of the Alzheimer's patient to still feel the emotions of embarrassment and shame at their predicament. The continuance of emotional life within the condition of dementia and the continued capacity to have meaningful emotional relationships should not surprise us. We know from our daily experience that, as our significant relationships develop, logical language becomes less and less important. A characteristic of intimacy within a significant relationship is the capacity to tolerate silence. When we communicate, we frequently communicate without words. We also communicate subvocally as when we signal many intentions and meanings within our words: "Don't you know that I love you? Don't I tell you all the time? . . ."

THE CONTRIBUTION OF THE COMMUNICATION SCIENCES

While psychology was overly concerned with outcome indicators of the efficacy of psychotherapy, communication science was utilizing process research methods in their detailed studies using discourse analysis. The moment-to-moment and reciprocal interactions of human conversation, including therapeutic conversation (Grossen & Apolheloz, 1996) was of significant interest to them. Human conversation and communication is perceived in communication science as a multidimensional and complex affair full of meaning. Scheflen (1980) in the article on systems in human communication gives a humorous but telling vignette describing the influence of culture on the communication pattern through a variety of channels: " If, for instance, we come from a certain region in the midwest we will not only speak midwestern but move, sit, walk, gesture, grimace, eat, work, court, and cut grass like people of this region have learned to do." In this sense, all behaviors are communicative and paint a complex portrait defining a particular interaction. We are communicating constantly, implicitly, without specific intent but with great impact.

This process of multidimensional communication contributes a subtle, formative influence on our development, mental health, and personality style. This kind of pervasive communication is present in the lives of even patients with dementia with good or bad effect, providing either a positive climate and psychological presence or a psychological climate that is at best detached and at worst toxic. Recently, I provided psychotherapy for an 83-year-old man who was dying of bone cancer. As we worked through initial reactive depression and later preparation for death, I reminded his family to keep talking to him even if he seemed not to understand, either through inability to respond or actual cognitive decline. After his death, they called especially to thank me for my advice. Rather than follow their natural instincts and withdraw, they had continued to talk to him and felt close to him and comforted until the end. I knew, by the use of signals, that he understood most of what they said and felt greatly comforted by their presence.

Kendon (1980) gives further specification to the variety of channels that this pervasive communication takes. He distinguishes between *linguistics* (language), *kinesics* (body motion), *proxemics* (spacing and orientation), and *tacesics* (touch). Thus, we get some sense of the complexity of communication science, which essentially breaks up into several subdisciplines. When taken together, these subdisciplines provide a comprehensive view of any given interaction or conversation. Even further definition can be given to the linguistic area. Labov and Fanshel (1977), for example, emphasize not only verbal but *paraverbal* cues to include temporal, volume, pitch, breathiness, and whine. These, together with the subvocal meaning dimension of the conversation, comprise a *subtext* to the conversation that, incidentally, often contains the central theme or message of the communication. Given the existence of a subtext in most human conversations it should not surprise us that this subtext can exist intact even when the linguistic logic of a conversation is impaired as in Alzheimer's disease. These elements of communication behavior are certainly capable of carrying a clear psychological and emotional message to each party in the interaction even in the case of dementia. It is frequently in the subtext of our conversations that we signal our *meaning* and *intent* to one another. Communication science labels this communication of meaning as *semiotics* (Kendon, 1980) which is, essentially, the study of signs. While the narrative language of a conversation may be seemingly simple and unambiguous, the meaning of the conversation often contained in subtext can be various. Even overt behavior is rarely unambiguous in its meaning. Scheflen (1980) gives an amusing example of multiple meaning. He describes a situation where something is going on in Mr. Smith's garden. It may be stated that Mr. Smith is "mowing the lawn," "beautifying the garden," "engaging in physical exercise," "avoiding his wife," and the like. Each of these elements might legitimately describe the purpose, meaning, and intentionality of seemingly straightforward behavior.

CORRECTIVE THERAPEUTIC STRATEGY

Given the complexity of human conversation and communication even in the case of a dementing disorder that incapacitates language and logical process, many channels remain open to provide psychological presence, emotional support, and meaningful communication with our clients. In this section, we discuss therapeutic approaches, attitudes, and strategies that attempt to maintain a rich discursive relationship with the victim of Alzheimer's disorder and avoid the frequent communicative isolation that surrounds demented patients.

What follows, then, is a series of specific practice suggestions and guidelines drawn from both pertinent research and from my own direct clinical experience in working with older clients with cognitive impairment (Duffy, 1999).

AVOIDING "CLINICAL DETACHMENT"

The general intuitive-level reaction to withdraw both physically and psychologically when confronted with a loss of logical language occurs not only among people in general, but also with health and mental health professionals. Under the rubric of "clinical detachment," we frequently create physical and emotional distance from our patients (Duffy, 1988). In acute care hospitals where care is short term, this may have limited effect, but in long-term care settings this clinical detachment can have greater negative impact. For the dementia patient, it may be catastrophic in its effects. Clinical detachment, a pleasant but emotionally distant connection, is defended as necessary to "keep perspective." However, true empathy for the older client can only be obtained by an intimate, phenomenological connection with this person's feelings and experiences of the surrounding world. In fact, experienced psychotherapists learned to both maintain perspective and objectivity, and also stay within the client's emotional world.

CONTACTING THE PERSON BEHIND THE DEMENTIA

In health care, there is a constant critical danger of the depersonalizing the patient. It is the illness that is the prominent subject of discussion; we even name people for their illness, referring routinely to "schizophrenics," "manic-depressives," and so on. This again tends to remove the caregiver emotionally from the client (the term "patient" itself tends to denote a more distant and unilateral relationship with the person. The Latin root of the word patient denotes passivity). To be therapeutically helpful to older clients who suffer from dementing illnesses, it helps to deliberately set out to discover, and to be curious, and even fascinated, by the rich idiosyncratic character of this unique human being. And, the more we look for, the more we find. One of the most gratifying aspects of psychotherapy in any context is the fascinating world of individual differences and the rich portraits that individuals portray. Behind the seemingly innocuous and homogenized face of aging, there lies a complete and vibrant person who has lived through a rich and sometimes painful array of life experiences that are belied by the ordinariness of the setting and the leveling effects of aging. As therapists, we have to allow ourselves to discover that older clients and even clients with dementia, have internal emotional lives that are at least as rich, complicated, idiosyncratic, mixed up, childlike, and fascinating as any of the younger clients we work with. Logic must outwit intuition here; surely we do not assume that when we ourselves age, we lose the life histories, complexities, problems, and fascinating personality that we currently possess. When working with cognitively confused patients, it is important to gain as much insight as possible into the person's personality style and structure, both by retrospective accounts through family members of this person's premorbid personality and, most importantly, by sensing the personality as it exists now within the person's overall character.

MAKING STRONG PSYCHOLOGICAL CONNECTIONS

One of the most central and perhaps most critical aspects of psychotherapy is the degree and quality of the psychological connection we forge with our clients. Although this seems a rather abstract and ephemeral concept, it is highly concrete and visceral; we all know within seconds of meeting another person the degree to which he or she is in contact with us, paying attention, focused on us, "tuned in." The clues to this phenomenological experience are often subtle microbehavioral signals that we pick up implicitly in our day-to-day lives and follow many of the paralinguistic elements that we have described including eye contact, movement, posture, and breathing. It is not too extreme to say that unless an intense psychological connection is made, no intimate relationship can proceed either in the realm of day-to-day intimacy or in the context of psychotherapy where intimacy is a central therapeutic vehicle. Interestingly, a growing body of clinical opinion and research suggests that it is this psychological connectedness that offsets the possibility of burnout among mental health workers and psychotherapists. The more we are intimately attuned to the people with whom we work, the less are the relationships experienced as burdensome and psychologically straining. It is therefore, paradoxical that the clinical detachment urged by heath care trainers, to protect psychological stability, in fact, works in the precise reverse direction. It is emotional detachment that creates psychological strain and burnout in relationships. When we are interested, curious, engaged, then we will frequently find intense relationships to be refreshing rather than wearying. Again, the evidence for this session is naturalistic; in our day-to-day lives, how often we say that we do not notice time passing when we spend it with those we love.

EMPHASIZING DECISION VERSUS FEELING

These psychological dispositions necessary for strong therapeutic relationships with clients, including those with dementing illnesses, are not necessarily "heaven sent." Whereas the intense psychological engagement we feel with a lover may require little conscious decision, the connection we make with our clients with whom we may have little motive or incentive to connect, must be a matter of *will* and *decision*. Again, the naturalistic equivalents help us to understand this principle; it is rare that even the parent enjoys getting up at 3:00 A.M. to change a soiled diaper. Loving the child in situations like this consists of the will and decision to care rather than the feeling or desire to be of assistance.

Feelings, while of inestimable value, are not a good guideline or prelude to all important behaviors. We do good, we love people in an instrumental way, because we choose to rather than we feel like being kind and generous. In fact, positive feelings frequently follow decisions and choices to be kind. This principle is particularly important in working with debilitated older clients. Illness, physical, as well as psychological, is not a pretty sight, and it is only through our decision to be "present" with this person that we can begin to move past the ephemeral aspects of the physical disorder and meet the person and the rich personality behind the face of illness. This principle of choosing to be psychologically present and helpful is of great importance in training students to work in long-term care settings. Initial reactions of distaste can only be overcome with a steadfast determination to stay in place and to remain psychologically connected. When students maintain this attitude and behavior, most people adjust to working in nursing homes quite rapidly and the ugliness of illness and disorder begins to fade in the background and take a backseat to the fascinating world of personalities that exist in any community setting.

"APPROACHING" VERSUS "ESCAPING"

I have frequently had referrals from experienced therapists of older adults with dementia. They seem more than willing to "pass on" these clients. My guess is that the therapists had not been able to find a psychological connection with older or demented clients. Working with this group certainly requires at least temporary suspension of our own narcissistic need for gratification in the therapeutic process. Such efforts are eventually well rewarded when we "break through" to the vibrant personality that lies behind the disorder. It is not unusual that caregivers and health care professionals are in a psychological "escape mode" with regard to the elderly and especially those with dementing illness. This can even be observed among professionals who routinely work with older adults, for example, in nursing homes. A not infrequent scenario in a nursing home corridor is the situation of a resident who is routinely, annoyingly, somewhat whiningly calling out for assistance and is met with a response from a health care professional that is pleasant, distant, but avoidant of psychological and physical contact through such typical phrases as "All right dear, I'll be with you in a moment as soon as I can . . ." And when contact is eventually made, it is fleeting, without providing a true psychological presence or connection with the person and one has the sense that the health care provider is looking for an opportunity to seize on a moment for escape at the earliest possible opportunity. This everyday situation captures an important psychological dimension in caregiving: the choice to deal with difficult and demanding patients through psychological "approach" behavior or "escape" behavior. Counterintuitively, it can take 20 minutes to escape the clutches of a demanding patient, but it can take just 20 seconds to make intense psychological contact and satisfy the patient's need for affiliation. Learning to listen and attend intensively can be more time-efficient, in fact, than pursuing a pervasive pattern of psychological avoidance. Psychotherapists are generally well skilled in listening and attending skills and recognize their importance in the development of empathy. However, working with demented older adults is a particular challenge and even therapists need to focus clearly and decisively on their psychological posture toward older clients.

BEING ATTENTIVE TO SUBVOCAL SIGNALS

When working with patients who are cognitively impaired, the lack of logically structured language can be a significant distraction in the attending and listening process. It frequently naturally engenders the feeling of needing to escape and this is precisely what occurs even among health care professionals. What is required here is for the therapist to stay composed and nonreactive to the discordant connections that exist in the language area and to focus their attention intensively on the subvocal aspects of the interaction. It is important in any therapeutic conversation, including with cognitively impaired elderly, to focus clearly on the meaning, purpose, and intent of the client, as well as to detect sensitively the affective messages contained in the communication. Again, the naturalistic equivalent is helpful here; we precisely, if implicitly, attend to these very dimensions in our everyday conversations from morning to night. We simply need to restore this attentiveness in an explicit and instrumental way when working with our older clients. We need to pay attention to the subtext of the conversation and ensure that we fully attend and capture the meaning of the interaction.

ATTENDING TO PARALINGUISTIC CUES

To be attentive to the subtext of a conversation with a cognitively impaired older adult, it is important to become sensitized to paralinguistic cues that signal the intent and affect in the conversation. Once again, these are implicit in our everyday perceptions but may be "switched off" in us when language is impaired. These include such things as tone, taste, liveliness, pauses, inflections, breathing, and kinesic signals that indicate meaning and intent such as posture, positioning, eye contact, and touch.

LOOKING FOR AFFECTIVE THEMES

With a correct mind-set, we are in a position to trace the significant affective themes that exist in the inner world of the demented client. As discussed earlier, the lack of logical cognition does not imply the shutdown of emotional life. This is readily apparent in the degree of depression and agitation that frequently exist in the psychological profile of the cognitively impaired elderly. It is important, from a therapeutic point of view, to identify these central themes for the older person and therefore verbally and nonverbally provide therapeutic support for the client. This identification of significant affective themes is an important goal of all psychotherapy and may include what Laborski and Crits-Christoph (1989) referred to as the "central conflictual theme" since many of our significant affective issues are indeed sources of conflict and anxiety.

ATTENDING TO MEANINGFUL RELATIONSHIPS

As noted, the lack of correct identification of family members by the impaired older adult does not necessarily detract from an emotional recognition of these significant relationships. It is quite possible, therefore, to develop an understanding of the key relationships in the older person's life and be able to use that knowledge in an instrumental and therapeutic manner, for example, by making sure that the older person has helpful connections, meetings, even phone calls with important persons in his or her life. If demented patients become confused as to the identity of significant persons in their life and are delusional in their attributions and stories and feelings about those persons, it is frequently (and not unreasonably) assumed that such confusion is simply the effect of neurological damage. It has been suggested, however (Miesen, 1991), that there may be a meaningful pattern to such delusional behavior. Central figures in seemingly delusional material in the older person's awareness may, in fact, provide access for the therapist to key attachment figures in the older person's life. As suggested earlier, general attachment style seems to maintain into late life and even into the inner world of the demented person. The agitation and anxiety frequently found in patients with Alzheimer's disorder, while being an effect of neurological damage, may also be an expression of the sequelae of ambivalent attachment to parental and other significant figures in the person's life. Such a pattern can be tracked by the therapist through sources such as retrospective accounts from family members and the client's nonverbal, subvocal, and paralinguistic clues when discussing these significant relationships.

LOOKING FOR UNFINISHED BUSINESS

The preceding comments suggest a need for the therapist to pay attention to latent unfinished issues in the emotional life of the older person. Apologies never made, love never expressed, anger never resolved, shame never confessed, are all issues that almost essentially are part of the lived experience of human beings and therefore can be expected to figure in the inner lives of older adults even during times of cognitive impairment. The continuity of emotional and affective life make it important for the therapist to attend sensitively to the possibility of such issues, to track their presence in current experience, and to attempt to bring such unfinished issues to conclusion. In many cases, dealing with these issues will take the therapist inevitably into a family therapy mode. It may be that doing family therapy in such contexts cannot be a physically conjoint activity since relatives are not infrequently at great distance. However, it is possible to do therapy with family relationships *within* the individual person or through strategies such as telephone calls and letters to be read to the older person; such strategies are discussed in detail in Duffy (1987). I sensed a very moving example of such unfinished issues in the last days of my own mother as she struggled with a dementing illness. As the eldest daughter in a large family, in her early teens she had been sent to live with a childless family and had been raised by this family through her adolescence and young adulthood. In the less affluent days of large ethnically Irish families, it was not uncommon that a childless, and relatively wealthier family would "adopt" a child from a large family. This had been the situation for my mother. During her earlier life, she had talked about this experience with approval and emphasized the benefits she had gained in terms of resources and educational opportunities. I had, however, often wondered how this had impacted her relationship with her own mother and how she affectively viewed the intensity of that relationship. In her last days, she returned to this theme, albeit with the confused language and themes of the dementing disorder, and I was moved to find that she seemed to be reexamining the intimacy of her own relationship with her mother. It seemed to me that she was trying to resolve a doubt as to whether her mother truly loved her enough to give her away, or did not love her enough to hold on to her. Such moments in the world of a demented person make evident the enormous reality of the remaining personhood and of the poignant and moving themes that exist still in the life of the cognitively confused.

USING TOUCH AS A MEDIUM

The impact of touch in both physical and psychological functioning is by now well accepted. It seems, indeed, that the physical development of the neurological structure of the brain depends on physical stimulation as well as psychological stimulation of the person. Precisely because of this, touch is an intensely personal and provocative part of human relationships. The ambiguity of the meaning of touch and the danger of impropriety have recently led the field of psychotherapy to basically "outlaw" touch as a therapeutic medium. While such vigilance in the meaning and intentionality of touch is highly appropriate in the therapeutic relationship, it is regrettable that such a powerful medium has become less used. Fortunately, in later life, some of the ambiguous (e.g., sexualized) meaning of touch is more resolved (if not absent). It is therefore common in late life to use touch in a familiar, relaxed, and intimate way. Therapists who have worked in nursing homes will be aware that as they move through the facility touch is almost the common language of communication and emotional exchange. It seems as though every greeting is accompanied by touch, by the holding of hands, often continued while conversations progress. In general, institutions are not good for mental health and care must be taken to restore the important dimension of trust into this environment for older adults. Older adults, especially those, who are cognitively impaired and experience the withdrawal of people around them, often become "touch starved" just at that point in their life when touch becomes such a powerful and comfortable medium. This is especially important for communicating with older adults who have dementing disorders. As in our lives in general, much of our feelings and experience, psychologically as well as physically, is present in touch. Touch becomes a powerful vehicle, and as aromatherapy has demonstrated, gentle massage of hands or feet can produce overall therapeutic effects in body and mind. I have personally discovered that an immediate remedy for teeth grinding both in children and in older adults is to gently massage the hands of the person. Within several seconds, the tension responsible for teeth grinding relaxes and the behavior ceases. These are examples of the power of touch in working with all clients but especially among touch and psychologically deprived older adults with dementia.

CONCLUSION

Psychotherapy, including verbal psychotherapy, is not only defensible, but also essential for relieving distress in cognitively impaired clients. Their psychological needs are not less, but frequently greater, than intact clients. The occurrence of comorbid affective symptoms strongly supports this view. And psychotherapy can be directed not only at symptom relief, but also must work sensitively with premorbid and prevailing personality and attachment styles. To disallow verbal psychotherapy for demented clients must signal a restricted and unidimensional view of the therapeutic process that is at odds with the great complexity now understood to be present in every human conversation, including psychotherapy.

REFERENCES

Duffy, M. (1987). The techniques and contexts of multigenerational therapy. *Clinical Gerontologist, 5*, 347–362.

Duffy, M. (1988). Avoiding clinical detachment in working with the elderly in nursing homes. *Clinical Gerontologist, 7*(3/4), 58–60.

Duffy, M. (1997). Individual therapy in long term care settings. In V. Molinari (Ed.), *Professional psychology in long term care.* New York: Hatherleigh.

Feyereisen, P. (1991). Brian pathology, lateralization, and nonverbal behavior. In R.S. Feldman & T. Rime (Eds.), *Fundamentals of nonverbal behavior.* New York: Cambridge University Press.

Grossen, M., & Apolheloz, D. (1996). Communicating about communication in a therapeutic interview. *Journal of Language and Social Psychology, 15*(2), 101–132.

Kendon, A. (1980). Features of the structural analysis of human communicational behavior. In W.V. Von Raffler-Engel (Ed.), *Aspects of nonverbal communication.* Lisse: Swets and Zeitlinger.

Labov, W., & Fanshel, D. (1977). *Therapeutic discourse: Psychotherapeutic: Psychotherapy as conversation.* New York: Academic Press.

Laborsky, L., & Crits-Christoph, P. (1989). A relationship pattern measure: The core conflictual relationship theme. *Psychiatry, 52,* 250–259.

Magai, R. & Cohen, C.I. (1988). Attachment style and emotion regulation in dementia patients and their relation to caregiver burden. *Journal of Gerontology: Psychological Sciences, 538*(3), 147–154.

Miesen, B. (1991). Attachment theory and dementia. In G.M.M. Jones & B.M.L. Miesen (Eds.), *Care-giving in dementia: Research and applications.* London: Routledge/Tavistock.

Papoušek, M. (1995). Origins of reciprocity and mutuality in prelinguistic parent-infant "dialogues." In I. Markova & Wallbott (Eds.), *Mutualities in dialogue.*

Scheflen, A.E. (1980). Systems in human communication. In W.V. Von Raffler-Engel (Ed.), *Aspects of nonverbal communication.* Lisse: Swets and Zeitlinger.

CHAPTER 35

Current Concepts and Techniques in Validation Therapy

Naomi Feil

Validation is not for all older adults. Validation benefits people who are over age 80, disoriented, and whose behavior is age appropriate. The Validation worker looks at three characteristics to determine age-appropriate behavior:

1. Physical characteristics
2. Psychological characteristics
3. Social characteristics.

A 2-year-old child who talks to an imaginary person on the telephone is behaving age appropriately. We do not say that the child is hallucinating. Physically, his logical thinking centers are not fully developed. The child cannot yet classify. He cannot compare real people with another category of people that he has made up. Psychologically, the child develops his imagination and verbal skills. Socially, the child models his parents: He wants to talk to people on the phone.

The same behavior at age 13 would be inappropriate. The 13-year-old's logical thinking centers should be well developed. He should know the difference between the outside and the inside world. His verbal skills and his imagination should be developed. Socially, he should have friends. He should not have to make up people. Behavior that was normal at age 2, becomes abnormal at age 13. Behavior that was logical at age 2, becomes pathological at age 13.

The Validation worker looks at the physical, social, and psychological characteristics of human beings over age 80, what I have called the "old, old or very old." Physically, a 90-year-old will have lost many thousands of brain cells for

The material in this chapter is derived from V/F Validation: The Feil Method. Copyright 1982 and 1992, Naomi Feil.

the past 60 years. He may have suffered little strokes; arteries can harden; not enough blood reaches the brain, and more brain cells die; Alzheimer plagues and neurofibrillary tangles can appear. At age 60 or 70, the brain should not have deteriorated to such an extent. A 60-year-old is different from a 90-year-old—physically, psychologically, and socially.

Psychologically, the 90-year-old prepares for death and wants to tie up loose ends. Often, the 90-year-old restores the past to resolve it. Socially, the 90-year-old struggles to mend broken relationships. With blurry eyesight, he uses his mind's eye to see people from the past to express feelings he has bottled up for a lifetime. Behavior that is appropriate for a 90-year-old is inappropriate for a 60-year-old. The 60-year-old is not yet preparing to die; his brain should not be so deteriorated. Validation was developed with and helps disoriented people over age 80, who are often diagnosed with an Alzheimer-type dementia. Their physical, social, and psychological characteristics are age appropriate.

Validation is a developmental theory and a body of practice with this fundamental belief: In *late life,* the way a human being has lived is of parallel importance to the physical condition of his or her brain. To understand the behavior of very old people who are often diagnosed with an Alzheimer-type dementia, the validating caregiver looks at four factors:

1. The person's physical and mental condition
2. The person's relationship with others
3. The person's ability to express emotions
4. The way the person has faced crises

Empathy with the very old person is essential in Validation practice. To empathize, the validating caregiver acknowledges the intricate relationship between physical deterioration and psychological needs.

IMPORTANCE OF FACING LIFE TASKS

Many psychologists have found that we must face different tasks at different stages in life. At birth, we must learn to trust that we will be nourished. In childhood, we must learn to control our bodies and follow rules. In adolescence, we struggle to find our own identity. In adulthood, we learn to express our emotions, both to ourselves and to those we love. In late middle age, we face physical and social losses, and look for new tasks and new relationships. In old age, our final task is to review life, integrate what we are now with what we were, accept the changes and compromise. We learn not to mourn what we wanted to be and never were. We accept who we are and die with self-respect. Those who have not faced these life tasks from birth to old age, who have never learned to trust others, who have been afraid of facing emotions, who have not learned to express love, anger, fear, and grief, run into serious struggles in old-old age. With increasing physical deterioration to control centers in the brain, emotions that have been suppressed for a lifetime now surface. With weakened brain structures, these old-old can now no longer control strong emotions. Moreover, psychologists have found that bottled up emotions can create physical pain. When these emotions are expressed, they lose their toxicity. The person is relieved. The very old person, who has carried a heavy load of stifled emotions, does not want to die in pain. These old-old often enter a final life struggle: to express strong emotions, to mend broken relationships, to find a meaning and an identity in order to die with self-respect. Validation calls this struggle: *Resolution* vs. *Vegetation*. It is an appropriate struggle at the end of life. When no one listens to the very old person who is struggling to complete their final Resolution task, the person withdraws inward. With little communication from the outside world, the old-old gradually lose speech. Physical damage to eyesight, hearing, mobility, and sensory acuity, speed withdrawal. We see these old-old people stacked in rows, their wheelchairs still, a testament to isolation. Eyes closed, they move towards Vegetation. The Validating caregiver empathizes with the last struggles of the old-old. The Validation body of practice teaches caregivers how to listen with respect.

DEVELOPMENT OF VALIDATION

The Validation theory and method evolved through years of work with Alzheimer-type populations and their families. In 1963, I began working in the Special Service Department , a wing for 30 cognitively impaired residents of the Montefiore Home, a nursing home in Cleveland. All were diagnosed as having some form of dementia, all were over 80 years old. My goals were to renew independent functioning, awareness of present reality, and stimulate existing brain patterns and latent potential. (Feil, 1967; Feil, Shove, & Davenport, 1972). I used the following interventions: behavior modification, psychiatric group work; remotivation; reminiscence; reality orientation; and individual social case work. "I soon found that reality orientation was unrealistic for them. They ignored me and retreated inward, moving even more to their past" (Feil, 1985). When I negatively reinforced their acting out behaviors by isolating them or walking away, the yelling, pounding, hitting, and swearing worsened. They could not reminisce because they had few words. Their attention span was minimal. They could not concentrate on remotivation topics.

In 1967, I began to truly empathize. I no longer expected them to conform to my standards of behavior or to accomplish middle-age tasks. By validating them—acknowledging the truth of their feelings—I discovered that they restored the past to resolve past conflicts. They struggled to justify having lived. They struggled to make peace. As naturally as the adolescent rebels to gain identity, the disoriented old-old clean house before death. They express bottled up feelings at last. When validated, they feel happier and often return to present reality by relating to others. I had to listen to their words, which were few, to the tone of their voices, to their unspoken emotions mirrored in their eyes and movements. I began to tune into them with all my energy and to enter their world. Validation developed, not only by empathizing with the cognitively impaired old-old, but also by reading their social histories and getting to know their families well.

Through the years, I recognized a series of similar patterns. Adult children confided to me that their 90-year-old mothers who complained of men hiding in their beds had often been abused by males. I found out that 90-year-old men who swore and struck male residents often had been severely punished by their fathers. Those who barely survived the Depression, or who had been emotionally robbed by more successful siblings, accused staff of stealing their clothes and money. Very old residents whose mothers had stuffed them with food instead of love, now accused the cook of poisoning their food. Men with a strong work ethic, women whose identity was wrapped around family responsibility, now used familiar body movements to restore work from the past. A 100-year-old woman, lovingly folded a kleenex, then kissed it, whispering, "baby, go to sleep." A former carpenter used his fist as a hammer. These very old "demented" people, with failing speech, now expressed themselves through movements of tongue, teeth, and lips, forming new word-combinations. "Moot ed tet," shouted one woman who wanted to move the table in her room. There was always meaning behind the movements. Case after case, there was always a *reason behind behavior*. When I listened to them closely, acknowledging their anger, fear, or striving for identity, the strong emotions subsided. The old person felt validated. I felt the pleasure of genuine, human communication without words. I shared their relief. I realized that it is not a question of an old person's grip on reality, but it is a matter of unfinished business that has to be resolved or an identity that has to be preserved if the old person is to have peace of mind. Distraction, diversion, re-direction, behavior modification delayed the anger or fear for a moment. But soon, the emotions returned often at double-strength. Listening with empathy helped. The anger, fear, suspicion, moaning, crying lessened. With regular Validation, the acting out behavior often vanished.

DEVELOPMENT OF VALIDATION THEORY

I began searching for theories that would explain the phenomena. Carl Jung (Von Franz & Hillman, 1975) wrote about the . . . "intuitive wisdom inherent in all human beings." The instinctive "knowing" that drives us to preserve ourselves. He wrote about the drive to express buried emotions. He wrote, "the cat ignored becomes the tiger." He wrote about the creative use of objects as symbols. Freud (1938) had originated the idea of "unconscious knowing," and our use of objects as symbols. The term, Freudian symbol is fairly familiar. For example, a knife is a male symbol; a spoon is a female symbol. Our unconscious movements can betray our hidden human drives. The way we move our hands and bodies can reveal hidden human motives. Behaviorist psychologists found that all behavior is purposeful. Facial expressions and voice tones are often more important than speech. Desmond Morris (1985) in his classic book, *Bodywatching, A Field Guide to the Human Species*, illustrated that we can understand human beings by the way they move. Not only gross body movements, but subtle movements of tongue, teeth, and lips are important indicators. Carl Rogers (1942) wrote about the human being's drive to heal. He formulated "client-centered" therapy. He felt that his clients knew, on a deep level of awareness, why they were unhappy. Listening with empathy facilitated their conscious awareness so that they could change neurotic patterns. Abraham Maslow (Koltko-Rivera, 1998) wrote about hierarchies of human needs: We need to express ourselves and be acknowledged, actualize our potential, in order to find meaning in life. All of us have a basic human drive for identity. Erik Erikson (1950, 1963) created a theory of developmental life stages with specific tasks for each stage that need to be faced and accomplished, in order to successfully move onto the next stage. Wilder Penfield (Penfield & Roberts, 1950), the famous neurosurgeon found that we have a mind's eye with which we can see vivid images from the past. In the temporal lobe of the brain, Penfield found different storage areas for sights, sounds, emotions, smells, and tastes. During his neurosurgery, Penfield mapped these areas. Researchers of the brain discovered that early emotionally laden memories stay. What we learn as children is permanently imprinted in the brain's circuits. When recent memory wanes in very old age and controls weaken, early memories often surface. Jean Piaget (1952; Piaget & Inhelder, 1969), the Swiss psychologist, studied infants and young children. He discovered that concrete movements of tongue, teeth, and lips always precede speech. When dictionary words fail in old-old age, early-learned movements such as clucking, rocking, clapping, often return. In quantum physics, empathy is explained as follows: All matter is energy. The human body produces a bioelectric field. All living things generate energy, which is interconnected by mathematical laws. (Davis, 1997). Using all one's energy to feel what the old person feels can bring about a connection. One human being, with a strong desire, can enter into the field of another. This entrance is empathy. Psychologists all agree that empathy is healing. These theories fit the behaviors of the old-old cognitively impaired people with whom I worked. The theories explained the positive results of Validation, and why the other interventions that I had tried for so long did not work.

VALIDATION PRINCIPLES

Out of these theories and years of practice, the following Validation principles evolved:

- We can all see and hear with the mind.
- When sight, hearing, and recent memory fail, the old-old often returns to the past to survive loneliness.
- Humans have many levels of awareness.
- Similar emotions attract. An emotion in present time can trigger a similar emotion from the past.
- The old-old often use objects or people in present time as substitutes (symbols) for people from the past. A hand can become a baby. A caregiver can become a mother-person.

- The old-old, in their wisdom, return to the past to heal themselves.
- Bottled-up feelings hurt.
- Feelings, when validated, are relieved.

THE FOUR PHASES OF RESOLUTION

Resolution, the struggle to wrap up lose ends, happens only if the very old person has been unsuccessful in earlier life tasks and has damage to brain structures that affect recent memory and social controls. The very old who are in Resolution move back and forth in four phases. They tend to remain in one phase most of the time. Which phase the very old person is in depends upon the extent of the physical deterioration and emotional incontinence, which can change within minutes. The validating caregiver recognizes the phase the old person is in at that moment, by carefully assessing the physical characteristics, and then using the appropriate Validation helping techniques. The physical characteristics for each phase of Resolution are found in Table 35.1. There are

Table 35.1   Validation stages.

	Phase One *Malorientation*	*Phase Two* *Time Confusion*	*Phase Three* *Repetitive Motion*	*Phase Four* *Vegetation*
Basic helping cues	Use who, what, where and when type questions Use minimal touch Maintain social distance	Use touch, eye contact, say emotions with emotion, music, and who, what, where type questions	Use touch, eye contact, mirror movements with empathy Use ambiguity, music say emotions with emotions	Use touch, nurturing voice tone, music
Orientation	Keeps time Holds onto present reality Realizes and is threatened by own disorientation	Does not keep track of clock time Forgets facts, names, and places Difficulty with nouns increases	Shuts out most stimuli from outside world Has own sense of time	Does not recognize family, visitors, old friends or staff No sense of time
Body patterns muscles	Tense, tight muscles Usually continent Quick direct movements Purposeful gait	Sits upright but relaxed Aware of incontinence Slow, smooth movements Dancelike gait	Slumped forward Unaware of incontinence Restless, pacing	Placid, minimal body movements, eyes mostly blank or shut, breathing shallow

(continued)

Table 35.1   (Continued)

	Phase One Malorientation	*Phase Two* Time Confusion	*Phase Three* Repetitive Motion	*Phase Four* Vegetation
vocal tone	Harsh, accusatory, and often whining Can sing	Low, rarely harsh Signs and laughs readily	Melodic Slow, steady	
eyes	Focused, good eye contact	Clear, unfocused Downcast, eye contact triggers recognition	Eyes usually closed Repeats early childhood movements and sounds	Self-stimulation is minimal
Emotions	Denies feelings Usually carries a cane, blanket, or sweater	Substitutes memories and feelings from past to present situations	Demonstrates sexual feelings openly	Difficult to assess
Personal care	Can do basic care Seeks personal reminders	Misplaces personal items often Creates own rules of behavior	Few commonly used words Does not listen or talk to others	Rarely responds to voice tone or touch
Communication	Positive response to recognized roles and persons Negative response to those less oriented	Responds to nurturing tone and touch Smiles when greeted	Is not motivated to read or write	None readily apparent
Memory and intellect rules	Can read and write unless blind Sticks to rules and conventions	Can read but no longer writes legibly Makes up own rules	Early memories and universal symbols are most meaningful	Difficult to assess
Humor	Some humor retained	Will not play games Humor not evident	Laughs easily often unprompted	Difficult to assess

Source: Validation: The Feil Method. Used with permission. Copyright 1982 and 1992 Naomi Feil, A.C.S.W.

14 Validation helping techniques. The Validation techniques for each phase are found in Tables 35.2–35.5. However, the Validation techniques are sterile without empathy. The validating caregiver must respect the final struggle to end one's life in peace.

In phase one, Malorientation, the old person is usually oriented to present-day reality and *wants* to be oriented, but has never learned to properly express strong emotions. Bottled up feelings from the past want to surface before death. But, the Maloriented hold tight to their familiar controls. They deny aging. Deep down, they are terrified of increasing memory loss, loss of eyesight, hearing, and social roles. They do not admit their fear. They project onto others. When they misplace a social security check, they accuse the mailman of losing it. They blame. They use people in present time, adult children, nurses, housekeepers as symbols for people from the past. A Maloriented woman whose mother dominated her, displaces her anger on her daughter. A Maloriented nursing home resident whose father neglected him, blames the administrator for neglect. The Maloriented cannot face their emotions honestly. They feel robbed by age. Afraid of losing memory, they accuse others of stealing. They confabulate, make up experiences to cover memory gaps. They felt robbed of happiness when they were young. Similar feelings attract. The fear of losing eyesight can re-ignite a childhood fear of the dark. The Maloriented need a trusting relationship with a nurturing, respectful caregiver who will not argue with them; who understands the final Resolution struggle and who listens with empathy.

Table 35.2   Phase one—malorientation validation techniques.

1. *Center.* Inhale through the nose. Exhale through the mouth. Repeat 8 times. Centering releases frustrations and anger that impede Validation.

2. Avoid emotions by using nonthreatening factual exploring words: "Who," "What," "Where," "When," "How." Avoid confronting the older adult by asking "why." The Maloriented deny their emotions.

3. *Rephrase.* Respond by repeating the older adult's key words, using their rhythms and expressions with *empathy.*

4. *Use polarity.* Help the Maloriented express their feelings without using feeling words. Ask them to tell you the extreme. "What is the worst, (the best, the hardest, etc.)?"

5. *Use their preferred sense.* Build trust by using the sense the older adult uses the most. Listen to their verbs. Do they use visual (see, picture), auditory (listen, hear, loud), or kinesthetic (touch, hurts, feels) verbs? Match their sense.

6. *Help* the person find a solution by imagining a time when the opposite happened. Example: Is there a time when they *don't* poison your food? Maloriented: "When I cook it myself."

7. *Reminisce.* Explore the past to help the older adult recall familiar coping strategies. Words such as, "always," and "never" help trigger early memories of similar situations.
   - The video, *Myrna, the Mal-Oriented*, illustrates techniques.
   - The text, *Validation*, describes the techniques in detail.

Table 35.3   Phase two—time confusion validation techniques.

Use techniques 1–7 for the Maloriented. Add the following:

8. Maintain close, genuine eye contact. Bend or sit and look directly at the person in phase two. Eye contact builds energy and trust.

9. Use a clear, low, nurturing voice-tone. High, weak tones are hard to hear and trigger anxiety. Nurturing, low tones give feelings of safety.

10. *Touch.* People in phase two need touch. Approach from the front to avoid startling. Use fingertips in a light, circular motion. Gentle stroking on the upper cheek can stimulate memories of a mother's touch; fingers on the back of the head can stimulate a father's touch. Where you touch is important.

11. *Ambiguity.* When the person creates their own language, use vague pronouns (he, it, they, someone) to fill for words you don't understand. This keeps communication flowing.

12. *Observe* their emotion and *Match* their emotion. In phase two, people freely express emotions. Feel what the older adult feels.

13. *Say their emotion with emotion.* Your voice and facial expressions match the older adult's emotions. (empathy)

14. *Use music.* Familiar songs learned in childhood and repeated throughout life are permanently imprinted in memory. Older adults who can no longer talk can often sing. A familiar song is often the key to a trusting relationship.

15. *Link* their behavior to their unmet human need. Basic human needs are: To love and be loved; to be useful and active; to express emotions. People in phase two often express these needs by wanting to return home to loved ones or to work. The worker acknowledges the need.

Table 35.4   Phase three—repetitive motion validation techniques.

Use techniques 1, 8–14, and add the following:

16. *Mirror* their movements in space, their finger movements, and their breathing. People in phase three move to early memories. Observe their movements and, with empathy, move the same way. The older adult responds by looking at the Validating Worker. A nonverbal communication flow begins.

Table 35.5   Phase four—vegetation validation techniques.

Use validation techniques 1, 8–14. There may be little or no response. The Validating Caregivers apply the techniques for 30 seconds to 5 minutes. Sometimes eyes flicker, a finger moves, a person smiles.

In phase two, Time Confusion, increasing loss of eyesight, hearing, mobility, recent memory loss make it easy to retreat to the past. The Time Confused no longer struggle to remember clock-time or to recognize people in the present. They give up denying their losses. Now, instead of tracking minutes, they track memories. They retreat to the past, sometimes to resolve it, and often to find comfort by restoring loved ones and work. Vivid images replayed by the mind's eye substitute for damaged sensory equipment. Increasing brain damage brings about loss of social controls. Phase two very old people no longer try to remain oriented. As one 96-year-old woman explained to me, "It's better to be crazy, then it doesn't matter what you do." Human wisdom spills when logical thinking wanes. Another 98-year-old beamed and confessed, "I just had the most wonderful conversation with my mother and my aunt, I didn't have the heart to tell them that they were dead!" They express, without restraint, basic, universal feelings: love, hate, fear of separation, struggle for identity, or loneliness. Validation workers around the world (Fine & Rouse-Bane, 1995; Fritz, 1986; Morton & Bleathman, 1992; Prentczynski, 1991; Sharp & Johns, 1991) have found these emotions expressed by thousands of very old Time-Confused people, in hundreds of nursing homes, day care centers, and communities.

In phase three, Repetitive Motion, there is increasing physical deterioration to the brain and body, but also a retreat inward when no-one has validated them in the earlier phases. When speech centers are damaged and no one communicates, the old-old in phase three nurture themselves by returning to well-remembered prelanguage movements, such as rocking and clucking sounds. The plug on emotions is gone. The very old person freely vents anger, love, sexual feelings, or fear. The desire and the ability to control oneself are gone. The person in phase three is uninhibited, using body parts and objects to express human needs.

In phase four, Vegetation, the elderly person shuts out the world completely. Self-stimulation is minimal, barely enough to survive. Very old people who are chemically or physically restrained in phases two or three, often retreat to Vegetation. Validation workers worldwide have found that Validation can prevent withdrawal to Vegetation. The very old person can keep communicating without words, until he or she dies.

RESULTS OF VALIDATION

Validation was developed with and intended for very old people who are in the final life struggle. Validation leads to significant changes in behavior, wherein the old-old person does not withdraw inwardly, but continues to communicate outwardly. The person does not enter Vegetation. Those that are Validated in phase one, are motivated to stay oriented and function in present time; if Validated in phase two, old-old often keep communicating with dictionary words; when Validated in phase three, the old person does not enter the final phase of Vegetation. Despite continuing deterioration, the old-old maintain communication, either verbally or nonverbally, and die with dignity. Caregivers feel tremendous satisfaction during a Validating Moment, when the old-old person shows relief. Nursing home staff, home health workers, and family caregivers find that their burn-out is reduced. There is less staff turnover with more job satisfaction. Caregivers get pleasure when they communicate with empathy. When validated, the old-old who are struggling in Resolution and who need to communicate with a trusted caregiver, will often begin to use dictionary words, their eyes will light, their walking improves, angry behaviors subside, social controls return, and they find joy in communicating with others. They move to the maximum of their physical capacity. And they die with dignity.

Validation is now used worldwide—11 European countries have Validation teaching centers and 14,000 facilities in North America, Australia, and Europe use Validation.

CASE EXAMPLES

The United States: Emma G. (Mrs. G): Maloriented

Mrs. G: It's about time you showed up. I called your office three times in the last three minutes. You never wear a watch. No wonder you're always late. Another minute would have been too late. Here he comes. Right on time. You can see him if you look at the hole in the curtain. Then he can't see you.

(She shoves the Validation worker (VW) into the correct viewing spot. The worker spots the mailman sorting the mail and placing it in the mail shoot. The mailman, after a furtive glance around, dashes away as fast as he can. This is the fifth time this week that the 91-year-old woman has called the police complaining that the mailman has stolen her social security check and is trying to break into her house to make sexual advances. The police had checked her complaints, found them unfounded, and have called the psychogeriatric hospital to institutionalize Mrs. G For the past six months, the VW has built a bit of trust as she has validated Mrs. G. The fiercely independent old woman absolutely refuses to enter an institution of any kind. She is determined to die in her own home. Her daughter helps her shop and visits daily. Mrs. G survived the Depression. Her husband and son both died in two wars. Her daughter recalls that her mother was never mentally ill, but became bitter, felt cheated by life, and never felt loved. Mrs. G shies away from intimacy and denies her feelings. Whenever the worker tried to explore emotions, Mrs. G found an excuse to leave the room or get rid of the worker. Mrs. G denies her fears and projects them on others. Each time Mrs. G suffers a loss—loss of hearing, loss of recent memory, she blames someone for something. This way she expresses her anger and fear without facing them. She has not achieved integrity: She could not express her disappointments, compromise, and find new ways to fulfill herself. So, now she has entered the final life struggle: Resolution. She sprays others with her emotions in order to express them before she dies.

The VW listens with empathy, genuinely feeling Mrs. G's fears without judging her.

Uses Validation Technique 1: Centering. To Center, the VW focuses on her breath to expel her own frustration and judgments. Mrs. G's claim that the mailman wants sex with her is funny. If the VW chuckles, Mrs. G, though she is almost deaf, will hear the laugh. The worker will lose Mrs. G's trust.

- Focus on a spot about 2 inches below your waist. This is your *Center.*
- Inhale deeply through your nose.
- Fill each organ with your breath. (Exhale through your mouth.)

The VW uses Technique 2: Use nonthreatening factual words to help the person tell you more without exposing their feelings and to build trust.

VW: What do you suppose he is doing?

Mrs. G: As if you didn't know. He stole my check. He put the envelope in his pocket so fast you couldn't see him. Now look at his face. He's planning. Now, see him run! He knows we're watching. He'll be back in a few minutes and sneak behind the bushes.

(Using Validation Technique 3: Rephrasing with empathy. Pick up the rhythms—the tempo of the voice.) Are you saying that he's planning to come back?

Mrs. G: I'm sure of it. He's done it before. And you know what he has in mind.

VW: (Using Validation Technique 4: Polarity. Ask the person to think of the most extreme example.) What is the *worst* thing that he could do to you?

Mrs. G: You're too young to know . . . (raises her eyeballs to heaven. Her hips quiver. Her body shakes.) I don't want to think about it.

VW: (Observing that Mrs. G is expressing her fear of sex physically, since she cannot express her emotions verbally. The Validation principle—"Feelings that are expressed when someone listens, are relieved"—is the basis of these verbal Validation techniques. "When feelings are suppressed, they can become toxic." Mrs. G, in Malorientation, cannot admit her sexual fears, but she can express them without words to the VW worker. After a lifetime of denial, it is too late for Mrs. G to get in touch with her emotions. In old age, when each day brings another crisis, she cannot risk change. She clings to familiar defenses.)

(Using Validation Technique 5: Re-Miniscing. Exploring the past can trigger familiar coping methods which the person can use to survive present day crises.)

Is this new? Did anything like this *ever* happen to you *before?*

Mrs. G: (Her lips firmly set.) Never!

VW: Was your husband a good man?

Mrs. G: I got married too young. I was only 17. I got pregnant and he went to war. I never got to know him. When I got the telegram that he was killed, I threw it away. I tried to forget about him.

VW: Do you think talking about him now, to me, would help?

Mrs. G: I don't know. (She searches the worker's eyes for a moment. Satisfied that the worker is genuinely interested, she cocks her head, peering out the window.) I probably should never have married him. He looked alot like that mailman. Tall, with a brown beard. He walked like him.

VW: (Using Validation Technique 6: Use their preferred sense. Mrs. G uses a lot of visual words. To build trust, the worker also uses seeing words, to speak Mrs. G's language and step into her world with empathy.)

Was he good-looking? What color eyes did he have?

Mrs. G: Brown. A clear liquidy brown. That's what drew me to him. I wanted to jump into his eyes. (She giggles, embarrassed.) That's enough of that silly talk. What's past is past. Over. Finished. (She wipes her hands making a snappy sound, as if to throw the past in the garbage.)

VW: (The Validation worker, recognizing that Mrs. G denies her sexual longing, her fear of being alone, and the losses that aging bring, respects the Maloriented old woman's 30-inch wall. Mrs. G will not let anyone penetrate her defenses. It took 90 years to build the wall, no one can take a brick. She does not want anyone to come close. She does not want touch— she cannot and will not expose her emotions. Feelings come out indirectly. The mailman is a substitute for her husband. She bottled up her anger at him and her sexual feelings for 74 years. Now, before death, in Resolution, the feelings trickle out as she talks about the mailman. The VW listens with empathy. The VW respects this 91-year-old woman who struggles to heal herself as well as she can before she dies.

Using Validation Technique 7: Imagining the opposite. This can spark a memory of a similar solution that worked in the past.

What would your life have been like if you hadn't married so young?

Mrs. G: (Pursing her lips, enjoying the thought, her eyes twinkling.) I would have danced all night. (She giggles again, almost blushing.) I did love to dance. And I was good, too. Everyone said so. You know, I worked at the canteen during the war, dancing with the soldiers. (She wiggles her toes.) I believe these old feet could still do a slow fox trot. What do you think?

VW: You know, there's a senior center not far from your house. They need someone who knows how to dance. Do you think you could help them out once a week?

Mrs. G: Will you take me there? (Her voice trembles.)

VW: (Her voice confident, beaming.) You bet!

[VW's note: The Validation Evaluation of Progress Form showed that Mrs. G accused the mailman only once every three weeks, after six months of Validation. She went, only when the VF worker went with her, to the Senior Center. And she managed to dance with one of the men. Mrs. G is not cured. She has no insight into her unexpressed needs. She will need Validation from an empathic worker until she dies. However, the hope is that, with constant Validation, she can remain in her own home, and that she will not withdraw inward into Time Confusion.]

Berlin, Germany: Margaret S (MS): Time Confused

MS: Will you please, be so kind, I must leave right now. Mamma needs me. She is all alone. You know, she is not well. She's an old lady now. It's not good to leave old people alone.

VW: (Using Validation Technique 8: Direct, prolonged eye contact. In Time Confusion, physical deterioration to eyes, ears, recent memory, and controls increase. Energy level and attention span often decrease. Genuine, close eye contact produces energy, and sparks an intimate relationship. People in present time become loved ones from the past. Logical thinking blurs. Time Confused can no longer place measures of time into separate categories. Minutes, hours, days, months blend. The past becomes the present. Time Confused no longer place people in categories. The VW becomes someone from MS's past.

The VW accepts this 88-year-old woman's memory loss and respects her psychological need to be with her mother. In Resolution, MS struggles with feelings that she has stifled. Her daughter told the VW that MS's mother died during the war of malnutrition. MS never mentioned her mother. MS's daughter believes that her mother has bottled up her guilt. Now, MS struggles to find her mother to express her grief before death. If MS were not Time Confused, she would continue to deny her grief. In old age, MS identifies with her mother. In grieving for her mother, she grieves for herself. She, too, feels old and alone, afraid and abandoned. In Time Confusion, her physical deterioration lets her restore her mother and express her sorrow, so that she can die with some measure of peace.)

MS: (Looks at the VW with deep sorrow.) You understand? You know how she is. I have to go to her.

VW: (Nods, using Validation Techniques 9 and 10: Touch with a nurturing voice-tone.) With increasing damage to control centers, emotions that used to be held in tight check, now spill, uncontrolled. The Time Confused person is still verbal, but responds to nonverbal intimacy.

She is all alone and afraid? Your mother needs you?

(The VW touches MS gently, with the palms of both hands in a light, circular motion on the upper cheek, as she speaks in a low, loving voice. In this way, the VW becomes a mother-person. MS feels safe with the worker. Deep down, in a hidden pocket of awareness, MS knows that her mother died. However, she keeps this knowledge hidden in her subconscious mind. VWs all over the world, have documented hundreds of cases of "demented" very old people who know "the truth," but who deny it in order to mend the past before they die. Therefore, the VW does not lie. The VW never tells MS that she will see her mother later, in order to pacify the old woman. Deep down, the Time Confused know when the worker lies. Then the old person no longer trusts the worker.

Nor does the VW argue, knowing that consciously, the Time Confused woman sees her mother clearly with her mind's eye.)

MS: (Eyes very close to the VW, she begins to cry.) Oh! Yes! She wants to hear my voice. She sings to me.

VW: (Using the Preferred Sense: hearing)

What song do you hear her singing?

(MS has lost cognition. She knows the song but cannot name it. The VW can sing most of the songs of MS's era. Validation Technique 11, Music, is vital when words fail.) Is it, "Guten abend, gute nacht . . . ?" (The VW sings the song. MS's eyes light.)

MS: Sings each word with passion, crying as she sings. (As the VW continues to touch her cheek, they sing together. MS spills her tears. Her grief subsides. She smiles at the worker.)

[VW's note after three months of Validation: Each time MS wants her mother, we validate her. She no longer calls out, nor does she attempt to leave the institution. With Validation every two hours, for three minutes, she feels safe. Her grief is out in the open.

Her speech has improved, as has her gait. She is now the hostess in our Validation group.]

Tempere, Finland: Juhanni R (JR): Repetitive Motion

JR: Mipler befer woffle. Ya!!!

JR, age 92, pounds his right fist hard into the palm of his left fist, over and over, muttering the same sounds, day after day.

VW: (Using Validation Techniques 12, Mirroring, and 13, Observing the Emotion and Matching the Emotion. In Repetitive Motion, controls are gone. The old person has lost awareness of time, place, and person. The kinesthetic nervous system no longer informs the brain of the body's position. Sensory acuity diminishes so that the old person is no longer aware of the outside world. Dictionary words are gone. But early memories remain intact. When recent memory blurs, early, primary emotionally-tinged movements return. The VW now enters the emotional world of the person in phase three of Resolution. Movements of torso, lips, tongue, teeth, jaw, hands and feet substitute for speech to satisfy three basic human needs: Love, identity, and to express emotions.

When no one enters the world of the person in Repetitive Motion, that person withdraws inward. Deprived of outside stimuli, old-old human beings often vegetate. *The VW wants to prevent Vegetation by communicating with that human being.*

After Centering, the VW observes JR and *genuinely* moves with him. The worker picks up his breathing, mirroring his minute body movements: The VW knits his brow, sucks his upper lip with his teeth, scoops his shoulders over his knees, and pounds his fist into his palm, moving with the rhythm of JR. The VW then uses Validation Technique 14: Ambiguity.

You're putting *that one* in the right place? Is it hard work?

VW workers know that there is meaning behind the old person's behavior. Old people in Resolution have a wisdom that does not need logical thinking or clock time or speech. In using an ambiguous pronoun, such as "that one," "it," "someone," "they," the worker establishes communication without knowing the dictionary meaning of the word. VW workers know that the old person is moving for a reason, to satisfy a human need, having lost the words, to express himself.

JR: (Stops pounding and looks at the VW. Eye contact is close, no more than 3 inches from the worker. JR's vision is poor. He squints and grunts.) You betcha! Mipler issa fest woffle.

VW: Does it fit? Is it good wood?

JR was a Master Carpenter. He learned to drive a straight nail at age 5. The VW uses Validation Technique 15: Link the Behavior to the Human Need. In phase three, physical movements mirror psychological needs. JR's facial expression, intense concentration, his shoulders hunched as if he were leaning over a table, are a clue to his human need: to be working, to be busy, to live and die as a carpenter. This old man never learned how to be old, without his work, in a wheelchair in a nursing home. He wants to die with his identity intact—he makes things with his hands. At age 92, he works with wood.

JR: Ya! Fits good. That miffle wood. Better than the woffle.

VW: Is the maple better wood than the other one?

JR: Maple is better. You betcha. Good boy, Anti! (He stops working, slaps the VW's shoulder playfully. Eye contact is close and intimate. The worker has become a coworker from JR's past.)

[VW's notes after six months of Validation, five minutes, four times per day: JR uses many more dictionary words than when we began Validation. It was hard to teach coworkers who do not understand Validation how to Mirror and use Ambiguity. I gave them the Individual Validation Treatment Plan (Table 35.6 on pp. 606–607). They thought it was a game, and that it was not Validation. It is not so easy to teach the principles of Validation. I could not teach my colleagues empathy for JR.]

Validation cannot give life to dead brain cells, but it can wake up sleeping ones. Dormant connections ignite when the old person feels respected!

Vienna, Austria: Helene K (HK): Vegetation

HK lies in her bed in a fetal position. At age 93, her body has almost stopped functioning. Her breathing is slow, movements imperceptible, she makes no sounds. Six months ago, in Repetitive Motion, she constantly screamed for "Hans!" She was finally medicated, then isolated. With no outside stimulation, her body gave up and her voice stilled itself. Now, the VW tries to evoke some response, knowing that HK was isolated too long, and Validation may not work. Timing is important. Validation might have stimulated some communication four months ago.

VW: The VW finds out as much as she can about HK's medical and social history. (History and Baseline Behavior Form is found in Table 35.7 on p. 608.) Sometimes, no history is available, but the worker, knowing Validation Principles, can still use the Validation techniques with empathy.

HK's husband's name was Max. Her two daughters do not communicate with each other. HK ignored her daughters when her husband died. She closed her eyes and began yelling for "Hans!"

Neither daughter recognized that name. HK never expressed emotions to her children, who have stopped visiting her.

Touch. Using the outside of each hand, the VW places her little finger on HK's ear lobes, curving along the side of the neck to the chin. The motion is soft, stroking the side of the neck. This touch often stimulates feelings toward a spouse or lover.

Music. The VW sings, "Du, du, lichts mir ihm herzen," a German love song of HK's generation.

HK: Eyelids flicker. A slight smile twists across her lower lip. A whisper: "Ich liebe dich." Eyes close.

[VW's note: After two weeks of Validation, each day for three minutes, HK's eyes opened more often. I am able to establish direct, close eye contact. She now sings, although weakly, a few notes of the German love song. Once, she whispered, "don't leave me, Hans." My touch, voice tone, and the music stimulate memories of a lover from the past, who left her. She no longer lies lifeless. She now responds to my touch, which has become an anchor. I hope that she will be able to sit up a little, in the next few months.]

THE VALIDATION GROUP

GROUP GOALS

The Validation Group can provide energy that is not possible in an individual communication, heighten attention span (group members interact for 45 minutes to one hour), restore familiar social roles that give identity, provide safe "we" feelings of a close family, help individuals express emotions to each other and problem solve, and enhance social controls when group members limit each other.

After six weeks of weekly Validation Group meetings, workers in ten European countries and in Australia have evaluated and recorded (Table 35.8 on p. 609) Validation Group progress. They have found these results:

1. Speech increases
2. Gait improves
3. Aggressive behavior lessens
4. Less need for sedation
5. Less burn-out for families and staff
6. Group members begin to care about each other
7. Less withdrawal inward

Table 35.6   Individual Validation® Treatment Plan.*

DATE:
V/WORKER:

Resident's Name: _____

Stage: (Maloriented)   (Time Confused)   (Repetitive Motion)   (Combination)

Contact Time: _____   Minutes per Day _____   Minutes per Week _____

SELECT AND APPLY APPROPRIATE VALIDATION TECHNIQUE FROM

COLUMN TWO:

(Write in letter of Validation Technique)

VERBAL VALIDATION:

Topics to Discuss: _____

Unfinished Life Task: _____

Preferred Sense: _____

Validation Technique: _____

NON-VERBAL VALIDATION:

Task-Oriented Movements: (baking, folding, mixing, writing, counting, pounding, serving, napkin stacking, etc.)

(Repetitive Movements to Match and Mirror: Pacing, patting, clucking, swaying, dancing, praying, rhyming, painting, humming, play musical instrument, ball throwing, singing, chanting, poetry, etc.)

Song Titles to Sing: _____

Appropriate Touch: _____
Validation Technique: _____

Sit Resident next to: _____
Encourage them to (sing, talk about, move, touch, etc.)

Equipment Needed: Bean bag, ball, rhythm instrument, food to serve neighbor, paper, pencil, poem, paints, dough, pots to wash, linen to fold, yarn, purse, elastic or parachute, other work materials of music tapes

Source: *Validation: *The Feil Method* ©1988.

Table 35.6   (Continued)

COLUMN TWO

VALIDATION® TECHNIQUES:

I. VERBAL VALIDATION

   A. Observe their Physical Characteristics (eyes, skin tone, muscles, hands, breathing, etc.)

   B. Listen to the words the person uses

   C. Match their preferred sense*

   D. Ask: Who? What? Where? When? How? (avoid Why)

   E. Repeat their key words. Paraphrase. Summarize.

   F. Ask the extreme. (How bad? Worse? Best? etc.)

   G. Reminisce: (How did it used to be before . . .)

   H. Imagine The Opposite: (When are things better? Is there a time when your clothes are NOT STOLEN . . . etc.)

   I. Can we find a creative solution together? What did you do when this happened before? Tap an earlier coping method that worked.

II. NON-VERBAL VALIDATION

   A. Center. Put your own feelings in the closet.

   B. Observe their gut emotion.

   C. Say the emotion out loud with emotion. Match the emotion.

   D. Mirror their movement. Pick up their breathing. Match rhythms.

   E. Link their behavior with the unmet need: love, safety, to be useful, to express gut emotions and to be validated.

   F. Touch: (their cheek with the palm of your hand; the back of the head, the jaw line, the shoulder, the upper arm, etc.)

   G. Maintain genuine eye contact.

   H. Ambiguity. Use a vague pronoun (he, it, someone, that, etc.) when you cannot understand the word-doodles.

   I. Sing familiar songs that match their feelings.

---

* Preferred Sense Words:

Visual: Look, picture, see, notice, watch, clear, bright, etc.

Hearing: Sounds like, loud, scratchy, noisy, clear, still, etc.

Feeling: Feel, hits, strikes, hurts, scary, touches, hard, heavy, etc.

Table 35.7   History and baseline behavior.

Precautions: Diabetic

Sample here and now questions: How long in home or hospital? Like the food? Like roommate? Staff? Do children visit? Hobbies?

Resident: Age, Sex, Race, Birthplace, Employment history.

What work did you do? What did father do? Mother? How many children? Where are parents? Where were you born? What work did spouse do? Children? How old? Who do you miss the most?

Family Background: Socio-economic status. Religious status. Close family relations. (Names)

Loved mother. Father left family often. Misses mother. Misses sister. Loves church. Catholic. Born in Ireland. Family poor. Father laborer.

Love church songs. Prayers.

Health Information: Medical diagnosis.

Length of hospitalization. Medications given. Previous mental or physical illness. Speech. Degree of loss to: Eyes, Ears, Mobility, Sensory acuity, recent memory?

Altzheimer's Late Onset.

Walks well.

Good remote memory. Poor recent memory. Word-doodles. Loss of As-if.

Stage of Disorientation:

Maloriented? Time confused? Repetitive motion? Psychotic behavior? Oriented. Fluctuates between which stages?

Action Pattern:

Customary response to crisis. What precipitated hospitalization?

Typical relationships. Past traumas. Typical response to aging losses. Physical behavior: Muscles, movement in space, eye-contact, response to touch.

What brought you to this home or hospital?

How did you cope with your dear one's death?

In This Home:

Friends? Activities? Movement?

Speech and interaction with others?

Relationship to Staff?

Placement in the institution.

Nighttime behaviors vs. day-time.

Eating behavior.

Prognosis and Treatment Plan:

Overall specific goal for this individual. Baseline behavior. Goal in six months after group intervention.

Recommended Role in Group:

Table 35.8 Therapy evaluation form.

Name	Talks in Group	Makes Eye Contact	Touches	Smiles	Shows Leadership	Participates (Physical)	General Comments on Group Meetings
							Unusual Responses
							Main Recurring Theme
							Plans for Next Week
							Main Conflicts
							Recommendations

KEY: 0 – Never does; 1 – Rarely does; 2 – Occasionally does; 3 – Frequently does; 4 – Always does.

VALIDATION GROUP STRUCTURE

The Validation group develops a rhythm, with a definite structure: a beginning, a middle, and an end. Group cohesion happens after about four meetings, held once each week, for about 45 minutes. Since Time Confused have little recent memory, the group must meet at the same time in the same place. Group members do not remember names, but they remember the face of the worker, familiar voices, songs, and the pleasure in the group meeting. They begin to look forward to the meetings.

The VW enables the group members to assume familiar roles that carry the group forward. The Welcomer greets members; the Song Leader begins the music; the VW engages group members in a topic that relates to unmet human needs. Group members help each other meet their needs for love, safety, usefulness, and to express their feelings. Music, Tough, Mirroring, Saying Emotions with Emotion and Ambiguity are the techniques most used in the Validation group, along with the Verbal Validation techniques.

GROUP COMPOSITION

The selection of group members is crucial to the success of the Validation group (Table 35.9, Selecting Residents for Validation Groups). Maloriented people who deny feelings and cling to present reality do not benefit from a Validation group, where feelings are freely expressed and group members sometimes cannot and will not conform to social rules. The Validation Group Worker must be familiar with individual Validation techniques. The VW must know the phase of Resolution that the person is in most of the time; and must know the history of each individual; their music, their unmet needs, and the unresolved issues that need to be addressed at each meeting. Most important, a Validation group will not succeed without the sanction of the administrator and the director of nursing. The entire staff must know the goals and principles of Validation. The group must meet each week at the same time in the same place. The group

Table 35.9 Selecting residents for Validation Groups.

Questions to Staff and Family. Any YES answers mean Stage 1; 7 or more YES answers indicate a lifetime of Mental Illness. Do NOT include this person in a Validation Group.

1. Has person ever been admitted to a Mental Hospital?
2. Does person blame others for physical losses? (Stage 1)
3. Does person blame others for social losses? (Stage 1)
4. Does person know where he lives? (Stage 1)
5. Does person know where he lived before? The names of his children? The names of staff?
6. Does the resident have a history of retardation?

Table 35.9 (Continued)

7. Does the resident remember an intimate relationship with someone he loved, but blames this person for his losses?

8. Has the person been unable to form an intimate relationship?

9. Does the person hold onto rules rigidly?

10. Is the person wary of expressing feelings?

7 or more YES answers indicate Aphasia; Organic Diseases that do not accompany normal aging losses to vision, hearing, or recent memory. Do NOT include this person in a Validation Group.

1. The person uses correct speech, omitting small connecting words. (and, but, I, they, up, down, etc.)

2. Cries when happy. Laughs when sad. (Aphasia)

3. Swears constantly.

4. Is rigid in body movement. Mechanical. (Without drugs)

5. Dresses well. Is socially correct, but *not* oriented to present time. (Alzheimer's disease)

6. Understands what is said, but cannot express himself. (Aphasia)

7. Has a sense of humor.

8. Can read a newspaper.

9. Can play BINGO, or games with rules.

10. Can sit through a movie without wandering.

11. Does *not* make eye contact or respond to nurturing touch.

12. Does not respond to caring voice-tone.

Questions to ask Residents. Repeated references to the past indicate Stage 2 or 3 Disorientation.

1. Who do you miss most? Your spouse? Your children?

2. What did you do to earn a living?

3. Did you mind leaving your home to move here?

4. What is the worse thing about getting old?

5. How do you overcome sadness?

6. What is the most important thing in life?

7. What happened to you that brought you here?

8. Do you have a lot of pain? (Stage 2 and 3 do not complain of pain as often as more oriented residents)

9. Were you in a hospital? What did the doctors do?

10. Do you like the other people here? If not, why?

11. Do you like the staff? Who don't you like? (Stage 2 or 3 Disoriented will say they live at HOME and do not recognize staff)

members must be up and toileted. Refreshments must be available so that the hostess can assume her social role. If the housekeeping department will not have the same room available, if the nurse will not see that group members are dressed for the meeting, if the dietician will not provide the food, the group will fail. If staff interrupts the meeting, attention span is lost and the meeting ends abruptly. Individual Validation is possible without support from all staff, but the Validation Group cannot survive staff indifference.

The key to successful Validation, both for the individual and in the group, is respect for the very old person who is diagnosed with an Alzheimer's dementia or a related disorder. The validating caregiver accepts the physical deterioration of the old-old and their psychological need to express unresolved emotions, to restore identity and usefulness, and to be loved and safe.

REFERENCES

Babins, L., Dillion, J., & Merovitz, S. (1988). The effects of validation therapy on disoriented elderly. *Activities, Adaptations & Aging, 12,* 73–86.

Davis, C.M. (1996). *Complementary therapies and rehabilitation: Wholistic approaches for prevention and wellness.* Thorofare, NJ: Slack.

Dietsch, J.T., Hewett, L.J., & Jones, S. (1989). Adverse effects of reality orientation. *Journal of American Geriatric Society, 37,* 974–976.

Erikson, E. (1950, 1963). *Childhood and society.* New York: Norton.

Feil, N. (1967). Group therapy in a home for the aged. *Gerontologist, 7,* 192–195.

Feil, N., Shove, L., & Davenport, S. (1972, December). *Pilot study: A new approach for disoriented nursing home residents in a home for the aged.* Paper presented at the meeting of the International Gerontological Society, San Juan, Puerto Rico.

Feil, E. R. (Producer), & Feil, N. (Writer). (1972). *A new approach to group therapy: The Tuesday Group* [Film]. Cleveland: Feil Productions.

Feil, E.R. (Producer), & Feil, N. (Writer). (1974). *Living the second time around* [Film]. Cleveland: Feil Productions.

Feil, E.R. (Producer), & Feil, N. (Writer). (1978). *Looking for yesterday* [Film]. Cleveland: Feil Productions.

Feil, E.R. (Producer), & Feil, N. (Writer). (1980). *The more we get together* [Film]. Cleveland: Feil Productions.

Feil, N. (1985). Resolution: The final life task. *Journal of Humanistic Psychology, 25,* 91–105.

Feil, N. (1989). Validation: An empathetic approach to the care of dementia. *Clinical Gerontologist, 8,* 89–94.

Feil, N. (1991). Validation therapy. In P.K.H. Kim (Ed.), *Serving the elderly* (pp. 89–115). New York: Aldine de Gruyter.

Feil, N. (1992a). Validation therapy with late onset dementia populations. In G. Jones & B.M.L. Miesen (Eds.), *Caregiving in dementia* (pp. 199–218). London: Routledge.

Feil, N. (1992b). *V/F Validation: The Feil method* (Rev. ed.). Cleveland: Feil Productions.

Feil, N. (1993). *The validation breakthrough: Simple techniques for communicating with people with Alzheimer's-type dementia.* Baltimore: Health Professions Press.

Feil, N., & Flynn, J. (1983). Meaning behind movements of the disoriented old-old. *Somatics, 4,* 4–10.

Fine, J.I., & Rouse-Bane, S. (1995). Using validation techniques to improve communication with cognitively impaired older adults. *Journal of Gerontological Nursing, 21*(5), 39–45.

Freud, S. (1938). *The basic writings of Sigmund Freud.* New York: Random House.

Fritz, P. (1986, November). *The language of resolution among the old-old: The effect of Validation therapy on two levels of cognitive confusion.* Paper presented at the meeting of the Speech Communication Association, Chicago.

Jacobi, J. (1971). *Complex/archetype/symbol in the psychology of C.G. Jung.* New Jersey: Princeton-Bollington.

Koltko-Rivera, M.E. (1998). Maslow's "transhumanism." *Journal of Humanistic Psychology, 38*(1), 71–79.

Morris, D. (1985). *Bodywatching: A field guide to the human species.* London: Jonathan Cape.

Morton, I., & Bleathman, C. (1992). Validation therapy: Extracts from 20 groups with dementia sufferers. *Journal of Advanced Nursing, 17,* 658–666.

Penfield, W., & Roberts, L. (1959). *Speech and brain mechanisms.* New Jersey: Princeton University Press.

Piaget, J. (1952). *The origins of intelligence in children.* New York: Norton.

Piaget, J., & Inhelder, B. (1969). *The psychology of the child.* New York: Basic Books.

Prentczynski, J. (1991). *An application of the validation method at the geriatrics care unit of the University Hospital in Reims, France.* Unpublished doctoral dissertation, University of Reims, Department of Medicine, Reims, France.

Rogers, C. (1942). *Counseling and psychotherapy.* Boston: Houghton Mifflin.

Sharp, C., & Johns, A. (1991, November). *Validation therapy: An evaluation of a program at the South Port Community Nursing Home in Melbourne, Australia.* Paper presented at the meeting of the Australian Association of Voluntary Care Associations, Victoria, Australia.

Von Franz, M.L., & Hillman, J. (1975). *Jung's typology.* Zurich: Spring.

Watzlawick, J., & Jackson, D. (1967). *Pragmatics of human communication.* New York: Norton.

CHAPTER 36

Memory Training for Older Adult Medical Patients in a Primary Health Care Setting

MARTHA LI CHIU

Memory problems can affect many aspects of daily life and an individual's sense of self. Over the years, much attention has been paid to memory rehabilitation for patients with serious brain injury and, more recently, to memory interventions for patients with dementia. At the other end of the spectrum, much consideration has also been given to memory training for healthy older adults who are concerned about age-related decline in their memory abilities. However, until now, little has been said about memory training for the many older adults who fall in between these two extremes: those who have not had a brain injury, do not meet the diagnostic criteria for dementia, and yet are not healthy. Instead, people in this category—who have come to be called the "frail elderly"—usually have one or more health problems that are common among older medical patients and can be associated with memory complaints (e.g., cerebrovascular disease; hypertension; diabetes; cardiac, respiratory, renal, or hepatic disease; substance abuse; hearing or vision loss; medication side effects).

In this chapter, after reviewing previous literature on memory training, I describe my current efforts to develop memory interventions for groups of medical outpatients, which include a large proportion of frail elderly. Case vignettes then illustrate the challenges involved in undertaking memory training for older adult medical patients in a primary health care setting.

SELECTED REVIEW OF LITERATURE

The goal of this review is to provide a clinically useful overview of existing psychological memory training interventions. Interventions for brain-injured

614

patients, dementia patients, healthy older adults, and frail elderly are dis-cussed in turn, with an understanding that these heuristic categories over-simplify the varied patients who are seen in actual clinical practice. Overall, this literature reflects a stimulating cross-fertilization of ideas and methods among practitioners of the art of memory training but, as yet, only modest empirical results.

MEMORY REHABILITATION OF BRAIN-INJURED PATIENTS

Organizing Principles
Significant memory impairment can arise from many types of acquired brain damage such as stroke, traumatic brain injury, Korsakoff's syndrome, en-cephalitis, and anoxia. Those who treat patients with such cerebral insults have long debated whether direct restoration of damaged memory function-ing is possible or whether they instead need to focus on helping patients learn to compensate for their impairments. Some have argued that direct re-training of memory provides external stimulation that can facilitate recovery of lost abilities (e.g., Sohlberg & Mateer, 1989a). Many others have concluded that teaching patients compensatory strategies to reduce the severity of their everyday memory problems is a more feasible goal (e.g., Parkin & Leng, 1993; Wilson, 1995).

Guidelines for how to conduct memory rehabilitation with brain-injured patients (e.g., Harrell, Parente, Bellingrath, & Lisicia, 1992; Wilson, 1992) sug-gest that a thorough, multimethod assessment is an essential first step. In ad-dition, ongoing behavioral assessment has been advocated to clarify treatment goals and to evaluate the effectiveness of chosen strategies. The importance of tailoring interventions according to patient characteristics, such as the cause and location of brain damage, level and kind of memory impairment, and type of information to be remembered, has also been noted (e.g., Franzen & Haut, 1991).

Memory training for patients with cerebral trauma has usually been con-ducted in an individualized format. At present, even those who enthusiasti-cally support group training for such patients have suggested that therapists should be prepared to provide supplemental training on an individual basis (Parente & Stapleton, 1993). Yet, clinicians who use both formats have pointed to several advantages to group treatment (e.g., Wilson & Moffat, 1992). These include providing enjoyable socialization experiences for isolated individuals, reducing patients' emotional distress about their memory problems, motivat-ing patients to practice new skills, and making efficient use of therapists' time. Exploratory studies of the effectiveness of memory groups for brain-injured patients have yielded mixed findings. Both the content of training and method for measuring training efficacy seem to be crucial variables. Whereas one study suggested that memory groups may be most helpful for improving par-ticipants' mood and use of external memory aids (Evans & Wilson, 1992), an-other study found possible gains in actual memory functioning, as measured by observational checklists of "everyday memory failures" but not laboratory-based tests (Schmitter-Edgecombe, Fahy, Whelan, & Long, 1995).

Techniques

What specific techniques have been tried to aid brain-injured patients with memory deficits? Direct retraining was an early approach that prevailed for many years in rehabilitation settings. It involved having patients repeatedly practice artificial tasks that were intended to exercise their memory skills. This approach and its underlying assumption—that memory is like a muscle that can be strengthened through repeated exercise—have been criticized as having little empirical support or usefulness (e.g., Glisky & Schacter, 1989).

Another long-standing approach to treating organic memory impairments involved using internal mnemonic strategies (e.g., face-name association procedure, method of loci, PQRST study method, acronyms). Over the years, such techniques have also been criticized for requiring too much effort, overloading the information-processing capability of most brain-injured patients, and failing to generalize easily to everyday life (e.g., Miller, 1992). Wilson (1993) observed that she does not expect amnesic people to apply internal mnemonic strategies on their own. Instead, she emphasized that internal mnemonics are best regarded as tools that relatives and clinicians can employ to teach small amounts of practical information to patients.

External memory aids that have been used in clinical practice include environmental cues (e.g., labels on doors), relatively simple information storage tools (e.g., notepads, memory notebooks, checklists, calendars), and increasingly, an ever-changing variety of electronic products (Harris, 1992). Especially in the past decade, the value of external memory aids for reducing practical memory problems of brain-injured patients has become more recognized. Wilson (1991) reported that 5 to 10 years after patients completed memory training, they used simple external memory aids more than internal memory aids and that those patients who used more external aids tended to live more independently. Some brain-damaged individuals have been shown to improve their everyday memory functioning with new electronic aids, such as an electronic organizer (e.g., Kapur, 1995); but ease of usage and degree of cognitive impairment affect treatment outcome.

Along with heightened interest in external memory aids, an awareness has grown that some form of systematic training is needed to teach memory-impaired people to use them correctly. Thus, rather than simply giving patients a memory notebook with minimal instruction, Sohlberg and Mateer (1989b) developed a three-stage training procedure. It involved acquisition (learning how to use a notebook), application (learning when and where to use notebooks through role play activities), and adaptation (practicing using notebooks in naturalistic settings).

Two specific methods for structuring how clinicians teach new information to amnesic patients have been proposed. In the "method of vanishing cues," patients are usually first provided with steadily increasing cues (i.e.,

L_____, LO____, LOA_ to learn that the word "LOAD" means to transfer a program into a computer) until they respond correctly; and then cues are incrementally withdrawn until, after repeated practice, patients can produce the correct response on their own. The "method of errorless learning" emphasizes keeping patients from guessing and making mistakes while encoding new information, so patients from the start receive all the information they need to succeed (e.g., immediately telling patients what the word "LOAD" means). In a series of studies, Glisky and Schacter (1989) demonstrated that by using the method of vanishing cues even severely amnesic patients could learn basic procedures to use computers in a "hyperspecific" way to perform certain kinds of real-world jobs. However, proponents of errorless learning have argued that the method of vanishing cues is too slow and allows amnesic patients to make too many incorrect responses which, once made, are difficult for them to eliminate (Wilson, Baddeley, Evans, & Shiel, 1994). Their data from controlled group and single case studies suggested that an errorless learning method was superior to an "errorful" method for teaching memory-impaired patients.

Both the methods of vanishing cues and of errorless learning are believed to be enhanced by using a method of expanded retrieval to increase the "robustness and durability of learning" (Wilson et al., 1994, p. 324). Also known as "the spaced retrieval" method, this technique requires patients to rehearse information repeatedly over gradually lengthening time intervals (Moffat, 1992).

Efforts to develop treatments with relevance to everyday memory problems have progressed. Deelman, Berg, and Koning-Haanstra (1994) presented case studies that illustrated their approach to teaching head-injured patients to apply a set of basic rules to reduce personally targeted memory problems (e.g., forgetting people's names, conversations). They observed that both therapists and patients were impressed by "the as yet unquantifiable evidence for post-therapy changes in coping behaviors in everyday life memory problems, for improvement in vocational and social activities, and for a more 'relaxed' attitude towards what might perhaps be a permanently reduced memory capacity" (p. 142). Thus far, in controlled group intervention studies these researchers demonstrated a significant treatment gain at a 4-month, but not a 4-year, follow-up (Milders, Berg, & Deelman, 1995).

MEMORY INTERVENTIONS FOR PATIENTS WITH DEMENTIA

Organizing Principles
Those who treat patients with dementia face the challenge of working with individuals who have an acquired, progressively worsening memory impairment in the context of compromised functioning in at least one other cognitive domain. The pattern of memory deficits differs among various forms of dementia; but most of the existing literature on memory interventions for dementia patients pertains to patients with a diagnosis of Dementia of the Alzheimer's Type (DAT).

Opinions have varied about what memory interventions can accomplish with DAT patients. Some have theorized that cognitive stimulation may improve their memory functioning by influencing hippocampal functions (Sandman, 1993) or by slowing down their rate of cognitive decline (Backman, 1992). Others have proposed that, at best, training can enhance preserved abilities and prolong independent functioning (Camp & McKitrick, 1992). Still others have focused on improving caregivers' interactions with patients (Bourgeois & Mason, 1996).

Efforts to develop memory interventions for dementia patients are still in an early stage. Consequently, general guidelines for how to proceed are few. Backman (1992) suggested that memory training for DAT patients needs to (1) be lengthy, (2) focus on relatively well-preserved cognitive skills, (3) involve the active participation of caregivers, and (4) provide cognitive support at both encoding and retrieval. Camp et al. (1993) recommended approaches that require less cognitive effort, draw on implicit memory, and provide external aids. Camp and Schaller (1989) noted that memory training programs must evoke positive emotional responses from patients to succeed.

Presumably because of the challenges involved in working with such cognitively impaired persons, most reported memory interventions for dementia patients have used an individualized format. Sandman (1993) used small groups for patients and their caregivers, but he did not comment on whether a group format influenced the effectiveness of treatment.

Techniques

A general consensus has emerged that dementia patients have difficulty benefiting from instruction in rather complicated internal mnemonic strategies. For example, Hill, Evankovich, Sheikh, and Yesavage (1987) taught a dementia patient to apply two out of three steps of a face-name association technique. In their investigation of the generalizability of this finding, Backman, Josephsson, Herlitz, Stigsdotter, and Viitanen (1991) found no training gains in 7 out of 8 dementia patients and therefore concluded this mnemonic required cognitive abilities that were too impaired in dementia.

Environmental adaptations and external memory aids have often been used to train patients with dementia. Reality orientation programs have long incorporated aids such as signs and diaries to improve orientation and memory for personal facts (Moffat, 1992). More recent variations on this theme have included using memory wallets (Bourgeois & Mason, 1996) and audio- or videotaped recordings (Arkin, 1992) to help patients remember personal information.

Cognitive stimulation programs that are administered by caregivers have been increasingly advocated. One controlled intervention study of a program of this kind reported that, at a 9-month follow-up, patients in treatment conditions with even minimal caregiver participation showed better memory functioning than wait-list controls (Quayhagen, Quayhagen, Corbeil, Roth, & Rodgers, 1995). Sandman (1993) discovered that, by varying daily routines with enjoyable, new activities, caregivers improved patients' recall of their recent experiences.

How to teach information to DAT patients in a way that does not wear down the treatment provider is a key question. A simplified spaced retrieval method has been shown to be an effective teaching approach for DAT patients (Camp, Foss, O'Hanlon, & Stevens, 1996). Proponents of this technique have hypothesized that it works with DAT patients because it involves relatively spared implicit memory processes and is a form of errorless learning.

New interventions are being developed which are designed to take advantage of research indications that procedural memory skills are also less affected by DAT. In a preliminary study, 3 out of 4 dementia patients showed gains in selected activities of daily living, when they were provided with environmental support and training that was focused on the motor activities involved (Josephsson et al., 1993).

MEMORY IMPROVEMENT PROGRAMS FOR HEALTHY OLDER ADULTS

Organizing Principles

Most studies on memory improvement programs for healthy older adults recruited their community-dwelling volunteer subjects through senior centers or newspaper ads and used screening procedures to exclude people with serious health problems. The usual result was what has been called "a positively selected, nonrepresentative sample of older adults" (Lachman, Weaver, Bandura, Elliott, & Lewkowicz, 1992, p. 294), who often were relatively well-educated and rated themselves in at least fair health, but who were concerned enough about normal age-related memory changes to participate in memory training. Indeed, many of these people probably met the diagnostic criteria for "age-associated memory impairment" (Crook et al., 1986).

Authors of guides to memory improvement for healthy older adults have tended to express high hopes for what is possible to achieve. Some have articulated goals such as helping older people to "gain control" of their memory functioning (Lapp, 1995, p. xvi) or keep their memory "in shape" (West, 1985, p. 27). Others aimed to "anticipate memory problems and . . . prevent them" (Duke, Haley, & Bergquist, 1991, p. 256) or to "restore, in part at least, the memory efficiency" of youth (Caprio-Prevette & Fry, 1996b, p. xvi).

Whereas an individualized format has been the norm for working with brain injury and dementia patients, memory training with healthy older adults has usually been conducted in groups. Evidence suggests that group memory interventions may be more effective for this sector of the population. A meta-analysis of studies on mnemonic training with "normal elderly" concluded that treatment gains tended to be larger when training was conducted in a group format (Verhaeghen, Marcoen, & Goossens, 1992). The importance of taking into account how individual differences in variables such as verbal ability, anxiety, and personality affect response to group treatment has also been investigated (e.g., Gratzinger, Sheikh, Friedman, & Yesavage, 1990).

Interest in designing multimodal interventions is growing. This trend has been in response to greater awareness that memory functioning can be affected by multiple nonmemory factors including a person's mood, level of stress, physical state, use of drugs, social environment, and attitudes toward memory tasks (Herrmann & Palmisano, 1992).

Techniques

While clinical researchers were discovering that patients with brain injury or dementia derived limited benefit from training in internal mnemonic strategies, for many years memory improvement programs involving healthy older adults concentrated on this approach. Verhaeghen et al.'s (1992) meta-analysis indicated that instruction in internal mnemonics appeared to enhance healthy elderly subjects' memory performance, at least on memory tests that allowed them to use their newly learned techniques. Leading contributors to this body of research have shown that the effect of mnemonic training is increased by pretraining in certain skills, such as visual imagery, verbal elaboration, and concentration/relaxation exercises (Yesavage, Lapp, & Sheikh, 1989). Nevertheless, problems in the maintenance and generalization of treatment gains have been observed. In two separate 3-year follow-up studies, researchers found that older adults tended to stop using internal mnemonics after completing training and did not apply them to memory problems they encountered in daily life (Anschutz, Camp, Markley, & Kramer, 1987; Scogin & Bienias, 1988). Stigsdotter Neely and Backman (1993) provided a rare report of maintenance of treatment gains after 3.5 years, but even they cautioned that the treatment effect was seen only on tasks similar to those used in training.

Especially as part of a movement to focus on "everyday memory," awareness has heightened of a need to develop task-specific memory strategies with practical relevance (e.g., West, 1989). Recommendations of memory strategies for healthy older adults have consequently become more eclectic and pragmatic, including external memory aids and classical internal mnemonics, with a primary focus on how they can be applied to everyday memory problems. Indeed, West (1995) advocated a "multiple-strategy, multiple-task approach" (p. 496) to help people see wider applications of strategies that they are learning to use. Clinicians can find in the literature suggestions for reducing common memory problems of older adults, including forgetting names (Lapp, 1995), medications (Leirer, Morrow, Pariante, & Sheikh, 1988), locations of personal belongings (West, 1995), appointments (Scogin & Prohaska, 1993), and activities one intends to do (Duke et al., 1991).

Training in metacognition—teaching individuals to think explicitly about how they remember—has become increasingly recognized as important for memory improvement (e.g., Hertzgog, 1992). Along these lines, Duke et al. (1991) described their "planning to remember" approach as a direct attempt to aid memory functioning by intervening at the level of the executive system that chooses, implements, and monitors the usefulness of memory strategies.

As part of the emphasis on metacognitive memory training, treatments are also being designed to modify older adults' beliefs about their memory, along with their memory functioning. In Lachman et al.'s (1992) controlled intervention study, a program that combined brief cognitive restructuring with memory skills training increased participants' sense of control and perceived ability to improve their memory but did not affect their memory performance. Caprio-Prevette and Fry (1996a, 1996b) developed a longer cognitive restructuring program and showed in a controlled intervention study that their cognitive restructuring group produced greater sustained improvement in memory performance than did a traditional memory strategy training group.

MEMORY TRAINING WITH FRAIL ELDERLY

Scattered in recent literature are indications of growing attention to the memory problems of medically ill older adults. Both Willis (1989) and Park (1992) commented in their reviews of applied cognitive aging research that previous studies focused primarily on healthy subjects. They therefore noted that existing findings may not generalize to frail elderly with chronic illnesses, who indeed may be the most in need of cognitive interventions to help them perform routine activities, such as remembering to take their medications.

Consideration of what kinds of memory training approaches meet the needs of elderly medical patients is just beginning. Park (1992) predicted that, compared with their high-functioning counterparts, frail elderly may benefit more from environmental support and less from internal strategies. Riley (1992) suggested that clinicians who work with frail elderly will need to take into account their limited physical abilities and design interventions with shorter, fewer training sessions and more reliance on homework assignments and self-training.

GROUP MEMORY TRAINING FOR MEDICAL OUTPATIENTS

Memory complaints appear to be among the most common cognitive problems reported by patients and their treatment providers in primary health care settings. In response to this clinical need, I began to develop memory training interventions for medical outpatients, many of whom are older adults who can be considered "frail elderly." Drawing on and integrating ideas from existing literature, my challenge has been to see what does and does not work well with this patient population. Here I focus on describing a group memory training program, but many of the same ideas apply to my work with individuals.

CONCEPTUAL MODEL

In keeping with recent trends in memory training, my approach to working with medically ill older adults is best characterized as task-specific, practical, and multimodal. It is task-specific and practical, because the focus of treatment is on everyday memory problems that patients target as interfering significantly with their daily lives. It is multimodal, because it attempts to take into account various factors that can affect memory functioning; and, in particular, it combines two modules that are designed to improve both memory self-efficacy beliefs and actual memory performance.

The memory group program begins with a cognitive restructuring module that has been primarily influenced by Lachman et al.'s (1992) ideas. Patients are told that the goals of this phase of treatment are to "increase understanding of how our memory works, learn how the way we think about our memory affects our memory functioning, and learn to view our memory as something we can improve." The underlying rationale is that increasing patients' memory self-efficacy beliefs provides a sound foundation for subsequent actual memory training.

Inspired most directly by Duke et al. (1991) but also influenced by others who have advocated a metacognitive approach to memory training, Module 2 focuses on helping patients to "plan to remember." Patients are informed that the goals of this phase are to "decide what strategies we want to use in our daily lives to improve our memory and practice using chosen memory strategies to solve a specific memory problem." In this task-specific form of memory training, patients are encouraged to experiment with an eclectic mixture of techniques until they find the ones that work best for them. The emphasis is on teaching them to think ahead about their everyday memory problems and then develop and practice plans to prevent, or at least reduce, their occurrence. This approach is based on a hypothesis that having patients play a significant role in the generation of solutions to their everyday memory problems will enhance their memory self-efficacy beliefs and they will more likely continue to use their new memory strategies after treatment has ended.

Ways to maintain and generalize treatment gains are built into this program. Because it involves heterogeneous groups of patients who are working on a variety of targeted memory problems, it lends itself to a "multiple-strategy, multiple-task approach" (West, 1995) by showing patients how different memory strategies can apply to the same memory task and how the same memory strategy can apply to different memory tasks. Homework assignments also help patients to identify and practice ways to use memory strategies in their own environments. Booster sessions and follow-up interviews provide patients with further practice and support to work through difficulties in integrating new memory strategies into their daily routines.

DESCRIPTION OF PROCEDURES

Patients begin the memory training program with a multimodal evaluation, which consists of neuropsychological testing, followed by assessment of their metamemory beliefs, mood, and everyday memory functioning. In a pregroup interview, patients then meet individually with group leaders and target a practical memory problem to work on. Since the inception of this program in early 1996, the most frequently chosen problems have been forgetting what people say and forgetting where belongings are put. Examples of other problems that have been addressed include forgetting names, medications, and prospective memory tasks.

The introductory cognitive restructuring module consists of five consecutive 2-hour weekly group sessions. In Session 1, patients are provided with information about multiple factors that can influence memory functioning. They are also introduced to the basic theme of Module 1: the importance of replacing a "shrinking balloon view of memory" (i.e., a view that their memory functioning is inevitably going to worsen and there is nothing they can do to improve it) with a "toolbox view of memory" (i.e., a view that their memory functioning can improve as long as they are willing to exert effort to use appropriate memory strategies). Session 2 presents simplified principles of cognitive restructuring. Patients are taught to notice and challenge automatic negative thoughts that they have about their memory functioning. Session 3 focuses on general principles for memory strategy selection. In Sessions 4 and 5, patients are introduced to a range of external and internal memory strategies and are asked to consider which ones interest them.

The "planning to remember" module starts with an individual consultation session. Based on patients' personal preferences and group leaders' recommendations, plans are made for which memory strategies patients will initially try. Thus far, most have selected simple external memory aids (e.g., writing notes in a daily planner book to remember what people say, keeping belongings in set places to prevent misplacing them, putting up brightly colored signs to remember to take medications); but a few have chosen to use internal mnemonics or electronic cueing devices (e.g., digital voice recorder).

Currently, Module 2 includes five 2-hour weekly group sessions, which are designed to help patients practice and refine their memory strategies until they develop an approach that reduces their targeted memory problems. During group discussions, patients share their progress in applying their chosen memory strategies, with an emphasis on problem-solving of any difficulties that arise. Group leaders also provide detailed suggestions for how to apply certain general memory strategies (e.g., external memory aids, verbal elaboration, organization, and visualization) to patients' specific memory problems.

In-class training exercises are an essential part of Module 2, because they permit patients to go beyond simply talking about their memory strategies to practice using them under the guidance of group leaders. Whenever possible, these exercises attempt to incorporate the principles of errorless learning and expanded retrieval. They frequently involve role plays that simulate real-life situations and are designed to allow patients to practice specific solutions to difficulties they have in implementing their memory strategies. Having repeated opportunity to act out solutions to their memory problems seems to help older medical patients learn more effectively, possibly because this process involves motor encoding in procedural memory. Often such role plays reveal additional needed refinements in memory strategies, which patients then practice during the week in their home environment.

Four weekly optional booster sessions are provided for patients who need more intensive, individualized help and practice. Other patients practice on their own for a month and then return for a "class reunion" follow-up session to discuss group termination issues. Individual meetings are arranged 6 months later to monitor patients' progress in maintaining their treatment gains and to provide added assistance, if necessary.

Group Composition and Size

The memory groups have closed membership and typically consist of two group leaders and approximately six to eight medical outpatients, who are usually referred by their primary care providers. The majority of patients fall into the frail elderly category, because they are over the age of 65, have a variety of medical conditions, and do not have a clear dementia or serious brain injury. Beyond these general, shared characteristics, patients tend to differ widely on important variables, such as their level of intelligence and degree of cognitive impairment.

The ideal may be to form more homogeneous groups with members who are similar in intellectual ability, level of memory impairment, and targeted memory problem. In reality, however, there is clinical pressure to meet, in a timely way, the needs of patients who have expressed an interest in memory training and who cannot wait until enough similar patients are found to start a memory group that is especially suited for them. To work with each patient solely on an individual basis does not seem to be optimal either, because of the many purported benefits from group treatment that have been pointed out in the literature.

Although the issue of whether frail elderly do better in individual or group treatment requires further investigation, I have developed a hybrid approach that is designed to try to reap the benefits of both training formats. I rely on group training to present core shared material. Yet, to tailor the intervention as much as possible to individual patients' needs, I also include strategically timed individual consultations (e.g., pregroup interview to select targeted memory problem, individual consultation at the start of Module 2 to plan initial memory strategy). Moreover, even in the context of group sessions, individuals frequently receive suggestions for applying memory strategies to their particular problems.

Practical Challenges

What are some practical challenges involved in conducting group memory training with frail elderly patients? Special effort is often necessary to keep patients' attention. Helpful techniques include (1) presenting material in lively and interesting ways, using relevant, concrete examples, colorful slides, and entertaining role plays; (2) keeping lectures brief; (3) varying the pace by alternating between small and large group activities; and (4) providing a short break. To facilitate recall of what is presented, written reminders are useful (e.g., recording ideas on a flip chart during class, providing handouts of key points and homework assignments).

Especially when elderly medical patients have 12 years or less of education, as has been true of many in my memory groups, elaborate cognitive restructuring in Module 1 appears to be difficult for them to appreciate. My approach to cognitive restructuring differs therefore from Caprio-Prevette and Fry's (1996a, 1996b) work with high-functioning, well-educated older persons, because it is more abbreviated and does not emphasize having patients identify the specific kinds of cognitive distortions they make. Personalized, real-life examples seem to be more effective than formal lectures for clarifying the difference between negative and positive self-talk. Thus, when patients make self-defeating comments while describing their memory problems, I often reiterate the importance of developing a toolbox view of memory (illustrated by a bright red toolbox that remains in sight at all times as an implicit, external reminder) and help patients to articulate positive coping thoughts that work for them.

In theory, a metacognitive approach to memory training works best when patients with intact executive functions can think ahead on their own about their memory problems and then make plans to prevent them. In practice, many frail elderly patients with weakened executive functions seem to need assistance in planning their memory strategies. Consequently, group leaders often must take a relatively active, guiding role in suggesting ideas and helping to plan specific memory strategies, while respecting patients' preferences.

As a key prerequisite for helping patients to choose effective memory strategies, group leaders need to have derived from preliminary assessment procedures an accurate understanding of each member's memory difficulties. Leaders also should be familiar with the range of memory strategies described in the literature and then must be creative about devising ways to apply these strategies to patients' personal circumstances. Flexibility and patience to keep trying out new solutions is also necessary, because planned memory strategies usually do not work perfectly right away.

An especially challenging aspect of Module 2 is designing meaningful individual practice in a group context. Group leaders must be clear about what they think each patient needs to make progress and then must develop in-class training exercises that permit individuals to work alone or in small groups on their particular points of growth. Keeping patients focused on their targeted memory problems can also be difficult, because some patients are eager to work simultaneously on too many problems. Group leaders must remind patients that they cannot solve everything all at once but that after they succeed in satisfactorily reducing their targeted memory complaint they can work at their own pace to address other problems.

Some elderly patients seem to resist making an effort to try new memory strategies. Fostering a supportive group atmosphere in which members share their experiences and feel encouraged to give one another helpful suggestions is one way to motivate such patients. Other patients are held back by nonmemory factors that interfere with their memory functioning (e.g., marital conflict or hearing loss that affects a patient's progress in remembering what his wife says to him). Finding ways to address these other factors (e.g., referrals for couples therapy or an audiology evaluation) is an important adjunct to successful memory training.

The following case examples illustrate some specific approaches to targeted memory problems and how patients differ in their response to treatment. To preserve confidentiality, identifying details have been altered.

CASE EXAMPLE 1

Mr. A was an 84-year-old male with heart disease and severe vision loss due to macular degeneration, who was especially bothered by difficulty remembering people's names. He had 15 years of education, above-average intellectual skills, and showed on neuropsychological testing no serious cognitive impairments but relative inefficiency in new learning ability. Because he felt unable to remember the names of people he met, Mr. A tended to avoid going out and was therefore becoming increasingly socially isolated.

During memory training, Mr. A was impressed early on with the idea of needing to exert active effort to learn new names. He could not apply a classic face-name association mnemonic, because he could not see clearly enough to notice distinctive features of people's faces. Instead, by monitoring his experience of learning other memory group participants' names, he began to develop his own active encoding strategies. He ended up using a combination of memory strategies whereby he would (1) draw near to people whose names he wanted to remember; (2) notice whatever special characteristics he could, such as a person's general stature, shape, and voice; (3) ask for names to be repeated if he did not catch them initially; (4) keep note cards on which he recorded people's special characteristics, in large print, next to their names; and (5) review his note cards before going to places where he might meet these people. He succeeded in applying these strategies to learn names of memory group participants and a small number of other new acquaintances, but part of the therapeutic challenge involved helping Mr. A to develop more realistic expectations for how many names he could learn at one time.

By participating in the memory group, Mr. A also learned how others coped with their targeted memory problems. Once he felt more confident about his strategies for remembering names, he started to work on the problem of remembering where he puts things. He was especially helped by the simple strategy of always keeping essential belongings (e.g., keys, glasses) in a small box on the kitchen counter, which he called his "memory box."

Flu interfered with Mr. A's participation in later sessions of Module 2 and kept him housebound so much that for a time he had little opportunity to meet new people and practice his strategies for learning names. Yet, at his 6-month follow-up interview, he reported that he still used his name recall strategies whenever he needed them and that therefore remembering people's names was no longer problematic for him. He also was still using his memory box to keep track of essential belongings.

CASE EXAMPLE 2

Ms. B was a 74-year-old female with hypertension, diabetes, and cerebrovascular disease but no clear history of strokes, who was especially troubled by difficulty remembering what people said to her. She had average intellectual skills but only 9 years of education. Due to prior employment in a noisy work environment, she also had significant hearing loss that interfered with the accuracy of her auditory comprehension. Neuropsychological test results indicated selective cognitive deficits, particularly in new learning ability and cognitive flexibility.

During her individual consultation at the start of Module 2, Ms B chose, with the help of a group leader, to try writing down reminders of important things people asked her to do in a pocket-sized daily planner. Progress was initially slow. She had a variety of problems applying her selected memory strategy. She would often forget to keep her daily planner nearby and did not immediately jot things down or regularly review what she wrote. She had difficulty accurately hearing what was said to her and also tended to record overly wordy entries on incorrect dates in her daily planner.

Not until Ms. B repeatedly role-played the correct use of her daily planner did she start to exhibit improvement. She was especially helped by a suggestion that she keep her daily planner open in plain sight whenever she was at home to act as an external reminder to use it. Moreover, during in-class role plays, Ms. B was impressed by how much her hearing loss interfered with her comprehension of what people said to her. She therefore also started to practice asking questions to check whether she had heard and understood correctly. By the last optional booster session, Ms. B demonstrated an ability to remember to telephone a group leader at a certain time on a certain day by writing down this request in her daily planner. Moreover, according to the patient, her family had begun to notice a difference in her behavior and had stopped criticizing her for forgetting what they asked her to do.

At her 6-month follow-up interview, Ms. B reported that she was still using her daily planner to record notes and that her family no longer complained she forgot what they told her. Indeed, she exhibited a maintenance of treatment gains by phoning a group leader, as had been requested several weeks earlier, exactly on time.

CONCLUSION

Memory training with older adult medical patients in a primary health care setting is an evolving enterprise that is so new it is hard at this point to make generalizations about what kind of treatment outcome is usually possible. A program evaluation effort is underway to investigate whether the memory training interventions I am developing yield measurable, lasting, and practical gains in patients' lives. Thus far, there are preliminary encouraging indications that Module 1 is meeting its goal of improving patients' memory self-efficacy beliefs; and most patients who have completed Module 2 have succeeded in reducing the frequency of their targeted memory complaints. Moreover, high ratings on patient satisfaction surveys suggest that, for the most part, patients have felt helped by this group memory training program. However, there are also indications of wide variation in how individuals responded to the treatment; and long-term maintenance and generalization of treatment gains remain to be explored.

Helping memory-impaired patients to practice new strategies to reduce an everyday memory problem may at times seem to be so simple and mundane that clinicians are amazed that activities we take for granted can be so effortful for them. Yet, this overview of memory training approaches is intended to provide the reader with a deeper appreciation for how complex the therapeutic challenge really is. It also suggests that the rewards for clinicians who undertake this challenge lie in the practical, personally meaningful gains patients make in improving the quality of their lives.

REFERENCES

Anschutz, L., Camp, C.J., Markley, R.P., & Kramer, J.J. (1987). Remembering mnemonics: A three-year follow-up on the effects of mnemonics training in elderly adults. *Experimental Aging Research, 13*(3), 141–143.

Arkin, S.M. (1992). Audio-assisted memory training with early Alzheimer's patients: Two single subject experiments. *Clinical Gerontologist, 12*(2), 77–96.

Backman, L. (1992). Memory training and memory improvement in Alzheimer's disease: Rules and exceptions. *Acta Neurologica Scandinavica, 139*(Suppl.), 84–89.

Backman, L., Josephsson, S., Herlitz, A., Stigsdotter, A., & Viitanen, M. (1991). The generalizability of training gains in dementia: Effects of an imagery-based mnemonic on face-name retention duration. *Psychology and Aging, 6*(3), 489–492.

Bourgeois, M.S., & Mason, L.A. (1996). Memory wallet intervention in an adult day-care setting. *Behavioral Interventions, 11*(1), 3–18.

Camp, C.J., Foss, J.W., O'Hanlon, A.M., & Stevens, A.B. (1996). Memory interventions for persons with dementia. *Applied Cognitive Psychology, 10*, 193–210.

Camp, C.J., Foss, J.W., Stevens, A.B., Reichard, C.C., McKitrick, L.A., & O'Hanlon, A.M. (1993). Memory training in normal and demented elderly populations: The E-I-E-I-O model. *Experimental Aging Research, 19*, 277–290.

Camp, C.J., & McKitrick, L.A. (1992). Memory interventions in Alzheimer's-type dementia populations: Methodological and theoretical issues. In R.L. West & J.D. Sinnott (Eds.), *Everyday memory and aging: Current research and methodology* (pp. 155–172). New York: Springer-Verlag.

Camp, C.J., & Schaller, J.R. (1989). Epilogue: Spaced-retrieval memory training in an adult day-care center. *Educational Gerontology, 15*, 641–648.

Caprio-Prevette, M.D., & Fry, P.S. (1996a). Memory enhancement program for community-based older adults: Development and evaluation. *Experimental Aging Research, 22*, 281–303.

Caprio-Prevette, M.D., & Fry, P.S. (1996b). *Memory enhancement program for older adults: A guide for practitioners.* Gaithersburg, MD: Aspen.

Crook, T., Bartus, R.T., Ferris, S.H., Whitehouse, P., Cohen, G.D., & Gershon, S. (1986). Age-associated memory impairment: Proposed diagnostic criteria and measures of clinical change—Report of a National Institute of Mental Health work group. *Developmental Neuropsychology, 2*(4), 261–276.

Deelman, B.G., Berg, I.J., & Koning-Haanstra, M. (1994). Memory strategies for closed-head-injured patients: Do lessons in cognitive psychology help? In R.L. Wood & I. Fussey (Eds.), *Cognitive rehabilitation in perspective* (pp. 117–144). Hove, England: Erlbaum.

Duke, L.W., Haley, W.E., & Bergquist, T.F. (1991). Cognitive-behavioral interventions for age-related memory impairment. In P.A. Wisocki (Ed.), *Handbook of clinical behavior therapy with the elderly client* (pp. 245–272). New York: Plenum Press.

Evans, J.J., & Wilson, B.A. (1992). A memory group for individuals with brain injury. *Clinical Rehabilitation, 6,* 75–81.

Franzen, M.D., & Haut, M.W. (1991). The psychological treatment of memory impairment: A review of empirical studies. *Neuropsychology Review, 2*(1), 29–63.

Glisky, E.L., & Schacter, D.L. (1989). Models and methods of memory rehabilitation. In F. Boller & J. Grafman (Eds.), *Handbook of neuropsychology* (Vol. 3, pp. 233–246). Amsterdam, The Netherlands: Elsevier Science.

Gratzinger, P., Sheikh, J.I., Friedman, L., & Yesavage, J.A. (1990). Cognitive interventions to improve face-name recall: The role of personality trait differences. *Developmental Psychology, 26*(6), 889–893.

Harrell, M., Parente, F., Bellingrath, E.G., & Lisicia, K.A. (1992). *Cognitive rehabilitation of memory: A practical guide.* Gaithersburg, MD: Aspen.

Harris, J.E. (1992). Ways to help memory. In B.A. Wilson & N. Moffat (Eds.), *Clinical management of memory problems* (2nd ed., pp. 59–85). San Diego, CA: Singular.

Herrmann, D.J., & Palmisano, M. (1992). The facilitation of memory performance. In M. Gruneberg & P. Morris (Eds.), *Aspects of memory: Vol. 1. The practical aspects* (2nd ed., pp. 147–167). London: Routledge.

Hertzgog, C. (1992). Improving memory: The possible roles of metamemory. In D.J. Herrmann, H. Weingartner, A. Searleman, & C. McEvoy (Eds.), *Memory improvement: Implications for memory theory* (pp. 61–78). New York: Springer-Verlag.

Hill, R.D., Evankovich, K.D., Sheikh, J.I., & Yesavage, J.A. (1987). Imagery mnemonic training in a patient with primary degenerative dementia. *Psychology and Aging, 2*(2), 204–205.

Josephsson, S., Backman, L., Borell, L., Bernspang, B., Nygard, L., & Ronnberg, L. (1993). Supporting everyday activities in dementia: An intervention study. *International Journal of Geriatric Psychiatry, 8,* 395–400.

Kapur, N. (1995). Memory aids in the rehabilitation of memory disordered patients. In A.D. Baddeley, B.A. Wilson, & F.N. Watts (Eds.), *Handbook of memory disorders* (pp. 533–556). Chichester, England: Wiley.

Lachman, M.E., Weaver, S.L., Bandura, M., Elliott, E., & Lewkowicz, C.J. (1992). Improving memory and control beliefs through cognitive restructuring and self-generated strategies. *Journal of Gerontology: Psychological Sciences, 47*(5), P293–P299.

Lapp, D.C. (1995). *Don't forget! Easy exercises for a better memory.* Reading, MA: Addison-Wesley.

Leirer, V.O., Morrow, D.G., Pariante, G.M., & Sheikh, J.I. (1988). Elders' nonadherence, its assessment, and computer assisted instruction for medication recall training. *Journal of American Geriatric Society, 36*(10), 877–844.

Milders, M.V., Berg, I.J., & Deelman, B.G. (1995). Four-year follow-up of a controlled memory training study in closed head injured patients. *Neuropsychological Rehabilitation, 5*(3), 223–238.

Miller, E. (1992). Psychological approaches to the management of memory impairments. *British Journal of Psychiatry, 160,* 1–6.

Moffat, N. (1992). Strategies of memory therapy. In B.A. Wilson & N. Moffat (Eds.), *Clinical management of memory problems* (2nd ed., pp. 86–119). San Diego, CA: Singular.

Parente, R., & Stapleton, M. (1993). An empowerment model of memory training. *Applied Cognitive Psychology, 7,* 585–602.

Park, D.C. (1992). Applied cognitive aging research. In F.I.M. Craik & T.A. Salthouse (Eds.), *Handbook of cognition and aging* (pp. 449–493). Hillsdale, NJ: Erlbaum.

Parkin, A.J., & Leng, N.R. (1993). *Neuropsychology of the amnesic syndrome.* Hove, England: Erlbaum.

Quayhagen, M.P., Quayhagen, M., Corbeil, R.R., Roth, P.A., & Rodgers, J.A. (1995). A dyadic remediation program for care recipients with dementia. *Nursing Research, 44*(3), 153–159.

Riley, K.P. (1992). Bridging the gap between researchers and clinicians: Methodological perspectives and choices. In R.L. West & J.D. Sinnott (Eds.), *Everyday memory and aging: Current research and methodology* (pp. 182–189). New York: Springer-Verlag.

Sandman, C.A. (1993). Memory rehabilitation in Alzheimer's disease: Preliminary findings. *Clinical Gerontologist, 13*(4), 19–33.

Schmitter-Edgecombe, M., Fahy, J.F., Whelan, J.P., & Long, C.J. (1995). Memory remediation after severe closed head injury: Notebook training versus supportive therapy. *Journal of Consulting and Clinical Psychology, 63*(3), 484–489.

Scogin, F., & Bienias, J.L. (1988). A three year follow-up of older adult participants in a memory-skills training program. *Psychology and Aging, 3*(4), 334–337.

Scogin, F., & Prohaska, M. (1993). *Aiding older adults with memory complaints.* Sarasota, FL: Professional Resource Press.

Sohlberg, M.M., & Mateer, C.A. (1989a). *Introduction to cognitive rehabilitation: Theory and practice.* New York: Guilford Press.

Sohlberg, M.M., & Mateer, C.A. (1989b). Training use of compensatory memory books: A three stage behavioral approach. *Journal of Clinical and Experimental Neuropsychology, 11*(6), 871–891.

Stigsdotter Neely, A., & Backman, L. (1993). Long-term maintenance of gains from memory training in older adults: Two 3 ½-year follow-up studies. *Journal of Gerontology: Psychological Sciences, 48*(5), P233–P237.

Verhaeghen, P., Marcoen, A., & Goossens, L. (1992). Improving memory performance in the aged through mnemonic training: A meta-analytic study. *Psychology and Aging, 7*(2), 242–251.

West, R. (1985). *Memory fitness over 40.* Gainesville, FL: Triad.

West, R. (1989). Planning practical memory training for the aged. In L.W. Poon, D.C. Rubin, & B.A. Wilson (Eds.), *Everyday cognition in adulthood and late life* (pp. 573–597). Cambridge, England: Cambridge University Press.

West, R. (1995). Compensatory strategies for age-associated memory impairment. In A.D. Baddeley, B.A. Wilson, & F.N. Watts (Eds.), *Handbook of memory disorders* (pp. 481–500). Chichester, England: Wiley.

Willis, S.L. (1989). Improvement with cognitive training: Which old dogs learn what tricks? In L.W. Poon, D.C. Rubin, & B.A. Wilson (Eds.), *Everyday cognition in adulthood and late life* (pp. 545–569). Cambridge, England: Cambridge University Press.

Wilson, B.A. (1991). Long-term prognosis of patients with severe memory disorders. *Neuropsychological Rehabilitation, 1*(2), 117–134.

Wilson, B.A. (1992). Memory therapy in practice. In B.A. Wilson & N. Moffat (Eds.), *Clinical management of memory problems* (2nd ed., pp. 120–153). San Diego, CA: Singular.

Wilson, B.A. (1993). Coping with memory impairment. In G.M. Davies & R.H. Logic (Eds.), *Memory in everyday life* (pp. 461–481). Amsterdam, The Netherlands: Elsevier Science.

Wilson, B.A. (1995). Management and remediation of memory problems in brain-injured adults. In A.D. Baddeley, B.A. Wilson, & F.N. Watts (Eds.), *Handbook of memory disorders* (pp. 451–479). Chichester, England: Wiley.

Wilson, B.A., Baddeley, A., Evans, J., & Shiel, A. (1994). Errorless learning in the rehabilitation of memory impaired people. *Neuropsychological Rehabilitation, 4*(3), 307–326.

Wilson, B.A., & Moffat, N. (1992). The development of group memory therapy. In B.A. Wilson & N. Moffat (Eds.), *Clinical management of memory problems* (2nd ed., pp. 243–273). San Diego, CA: Singular.

Yesavage, J.A., Lapp, D., & Sheikh, J.I. (1989). Mnemonics as modified for use by the elderly. In L.W. Poon, D.C. Rubin, & B.A. Wilson (Eds.), *Everyday cognition in adulthood and late life* (pp. 598–611). Cambridge, England: Cambridge University Press.

CHAPTER 37

Management of Alcohol Abuse in Older Adults

LARRY W. DUPREE AND LAWRENCE SCHONFELD

Since the late 1970s, we have been involved in research and treatment of substance abuse among older adults. Beginning with the Gerontology Alcohol Project in 1979 (Dupree, Broskowski, & Schonfeld, 1984), and later in the Substance Abuse Program for the Elderly (or "SAPE"; Schonfeld & Dupree, 1991), older adults with alcohol problems or who misused medications were admitted to demonstration treatment programs at the Louis de la Parte Florida Mental Health Institute of the University of South Florida. These programs consisted of group treatment relying on well-established principles of behavior therapy, including self-management skills and cognitive-behavioral treatment (CBT).

In this chapter, we briefly summarize the evolution of the field using the published literature and then, based on our experience, offer practical methods for assessment and treatment planning. We also refer the reader to more in-depth reviews of the literature on alcohol and aging (e.g., Dupree & Schonfeld, 1998; Schonfeld & Dupree, 1998).

PREVALENCE OF ALCOHOL ABUSE AMONG THE ELDERLY

At the time the GAP program was being developed in 1978, little information about older alcohol abusers was available. Much of the literature involved estimates about the extent of the problem among the general elderly population, as well as reports from several clinical units within veterans hospitals or psychiatry facilities. Early epidemiological surveys suggested that alcohol problems among the general, elderly population ranged from 2% to 10% (Gomberg, 1980). However, those estimates were affected by the age criterion used to define elderly, the method of survey used, and the geographic location of survey respondents. Recent reviews suggest that among the general, community-based population, the estimates for problem drinking and heavy drinking among older people remain about the same as they did about 20 years ago (Adams & Cox, 1997; Beresford, 1995). According to Beresford, at least for heavy drinking among the elderly, there is greater risk for males and the "young-old" (e.g., people in their 50s and 60s), with factors such as ethnicity and marital status having little relationship to heavy drinking.

Among health care settings, the estimates are alarming. We have often cited the astounding report from Congress, which stated that 2.5 million older adults have alcohol problems, and that 21% of hospitalized people age 60 or older have a diagnosis of alcoholism, with related hospital costs as high as $60 billion (HR Report, No. 852, 1992). In their review, Adams and Cox (1997) noted estimates of alcohol problems in primary care settings as being comparable to the general community-based population of elderly (age 60 and older), ranging in some studies from under 4% to about 6%. If focusing only on older men, the percentage increased to about 10%. In emergency rooms, various studies averaged about 14% of elderly having alcohol problems. Among hospital inpatients, the percentage is much higher, ranging from 21% to 60%, with fluctuations dependent on the age-criterion or whether only males are reported (vs. both genders). High estimates have also been obtained in veterans hospitals (Moos, Mertens, & Brennan, 1993).

The conclusions generally drawn are that alcohol problems among older adults are more likely to be identified through less traditional routes than by accessing the same referral sources through which younger substance abusers are entered into treatment. Older individuals are more likely to visit physician offices and require hospitalization. For many, especially older males, alcohol problems are likely to be observed secondarily to other health problems.

TREATMENT ISSUES

Beginning in the 1980s, there was an increased focus on the appropriate form and content of treatment for older drinkers. A major issue was whether separate, age-specific, group treatment programs for older drinkers should be offered. Janik and Dunham (1983) in a nationwide study of treatment programs found that outcomes for younger and older people were similar, and concluded that age-specific programs were unnecessary. In contrast, Kofoed, Tolson, Atkinson, Toth, and Turner (1987) found superior outcomes for older veterans if they attended age-specific treatment, compared with older veterans attending mixed-age treatment.

From the literature, recommendations for treatment have certain common characteristics (Schonfeld & Dupree, 1997). Programs that demonstrated success were likely to employ group treatment in which the staff and clients were "supportive" rather than confrontational; hired and trained staff to work specifically with older people; employed treatment methods for overcoming depression, loneliness, and losses; provided treatment that also enhanced social support; offered treatment at a "pace and content" appropriate for older clientele; and relationships with medical, aging, and other services appropriate for this age group were developed.

The treatment approach developed for the Gerontology Alcohol Project (GAP) attended to these recommendations (Dupree et al., 1984). The GAP employed a three-stage approach: (1) conducting a functional analysis of drinking behavior (each person's drinking behavior and high-risk situations for drinking were identified using a structured interview), (2) teaching clients within a group format to recognize their personal "high-risk situations" for drinking, and (3) teaching clients to use self-management/cognitive-behavioral skills (also in group format) to address their personal high-risk situations or antecedents for use, and relapse prevention. Also, all staff were trained to assess newly admitted clients using a structured interview to identify high-risk situations for drinking, and trained to conduct a series of modules or group treatments delivered in a standardized or consistent fashion thanks to the development of curriculum manuals. A module refers to a group treatment with an accompanying manual consisting of a written curriculum and assessments for rating knowledge and skills gained. Within each module, staff were trained to use a variety of formats to teach the appropriate skills, including lectures, modeling appropriate behaviors, asking clients to rehearse what they would do in certain situations, and asking clients to practice what they learned, either through role playing/rehearsals or through homework assignments. In the next section, we describe the three-stage approach used in the GAP, as well as the Substance Abuse Program for the Elderly (SAPE).

The rationale for the skills training approach of GAP is well grounded in research. Marlatt and Gordon (1985) demonstrated that most relapses are triggered by intrapersonal events such as negative affect (depression, loneliness, anger, frustration) not involving other people, or interpersonal events such as social pressure or conflict with others. Also, the Relapse Prevention (RP) model for intervention offered by Marlatt and Gordon begins with the premise that individuals when faced with a high-risk situation for drinking, most likely experience a slip because they do not have or use adequate, problem-focused coping skills. This results in poor self-efficacy (i.e., decreased confidence about the ability to respond adequately), increases the likelihood of a slip, and potentiates positive expectancies of the effects (or positive consequences) of the first drink. The RP model also suggests that the individual in control of his or her alcohol use is likely to have a repertoire of coping behaviors specific to high-risk situations. Thus, alcohol use has been conceptualized as a general coping mechanism used in situations where other more appropriate coping behaviors are unavailable or unused (Abrams & Niaura, 1987). Moos, Brennan, Fondacaro, and Moos (1990) reported that older problem drinkers, compared with nonproblem drinkers, were more likely to use cognitive and behavioral avoidance responses to manage life stressors; and that problem drinkers who relied more on avoidance (emotional) coping tended to have more drinking problems and reported more depression, physical symptoms, and less self-confidence.

FUNCTIONAL ANALYSIS
OF DRINKING BEHAVIOR

Each client was assessed within the first two weeks using the GAP Drinking Profile (GAP-DP; Dupree & Schonfeld, 1986), a structured interview to identify his or her antecedents and consequences of alcohol use on a "typical day of drinking." The GAP-DP focused on the 30-day period preceding an individual's last drink as well as drinking and treatment history. Most treatment-related questions focus on the *first* drink on a typical day. The information derived from each client's responses was recorded by the interviewer and later used to construct the older abuser's "drinking behavior chain." The drinking behavior chain consists of antecedents such as situations, thoughts, feelings, cues, and urges or self-statements; followed by the behavior, which is the first drink on a typical day of drinking. Staff also identified the individual's consequences of drinking, with special interest in the relatively positive, and immediate or short-term consequences, which typically reinforced drinking.

This approach is also called an A-B-C approach to represent "Antecedents, Behavior, and Consequences"; the behavior is taking a drink of an alcoholic beverage (P.M. Miller, 1976; W.R. Miller & Muñoz, 1976). The A-B-C's can be diagrammed as shown in Figure 37.1. We have also used this schema for intervention with substance and medication abusers. This version of the chain differs from previous versions by showing sequential links occurring over time.

TEACHING OLDER SUBSTANCE
USERS THE A-B-C'S

In the second stage of GAP, clients entered the first group treatment module, also called the "A-B-C's of Drinking." In this module, participants were taught to take the mystery out of their drinking behavior by identifying the components of their personal drinking behavior chain. They learned how drinking (the "B" or behavior within the chain) was preceded by both private

Figure 37.1 The drinking behavior chain.

and observable events, and that the events can be diagrammed as a chain that innervates over time and prompts ultimate drinking behavior. Clients were taught that the antecedent and behavior (A&B) parts of the chain are reinforced and sustained by immediate and positive consequences. Often these reinforcing consequences are expectancies of feeling better, coping better, and so on. They were taught that negative consequences rarely serve as deterrents to drinking.

All clients learned to record their behavior chains using a weekly, self-monitoring log. These logs were used to monitor their personal A-B-C's outside the treatment program and during follow-ups. Each log would be used to describe the circumstances leading up to and following an urge to drink, whether he or she resisted it or actually consumed alcohol and, finally, what happened after that drink.

SELF-MANAGEMENT/COGNITIVE BEHAVIOR THERAPY

Once clients demonstrated that they could successfully identify their drinking behavior chains by acceptable scores on quizzes assessing knowledge in the A-B-C's module, they entered the third stage: a series of modules designed to teach them appropriate skills to prevent relapse. Using self-management approaches and cognitive-behavior therapy, older adults were taught how to cope with common antecedents to drinking and relapse: social pressure to drink, depression, anger/frustration, anxiety/tension, presence of drinking cues, and urges to drink, as well as what to do if he or she experienced a slip or a full relapse.

Self-management involves the use of behavior techniques *by the client* to improve control over his or her own behavior (overt and covert) and over the environment (Kanfer, 1975), whereas cognitive-behavioral therapy (CBT) involves modifications of covert behaviors or private events by the client that only he or she can observe or experience. The goal of CBT with older abusers was to have them acquire the skills necessary to identify and modify self-defeating thoughts and beliefs highly related to unwanted behavior including alcohol misuse or abuse. The benefit of self-management and CBT approaches for older adults is that acquisition of skills necessary to managing antecedents for use, not only helps manage problem drinking, but also enhances both actual and perceived self-control (i.e., the ability to both recognize and manipulate factors involving either excessive drinking or problems in living).

Each session began with a minilecture detailing the rationale, procedures, and objectives for that session. Also, the curriculum used examples pertinent to older rather than younger drinkers; the pace met the needs of older people; cognitively impaired older adults were provided extra, private (booster) sessions with staff as needed to help them master content and continue with the group; and confrontation was not permitted. When slips or relapses occurred and were reported by clients, the unwanted event was reviewed in terms of what skills were not used, and what behaviors or thoughts needed to be enacted to prevent future slips or lapses. To encourage accurate reporting and future use of more appropriate skills, no confrontation or labeling was allowed.

The *social pressure* module emphasized how social pressures to have a drink are common antecedents for drinking and often difficult for problem drinkers because of fears of not being liked if the drink is refused. Older adults are frequently sensitive to shrinking social networks. Also, people drinking and the alcoholic beverage itself are drinking cues. Thus, a common antecedent chain including situations and thoughts (social pressure), feelings (anxiety), and cues often leads to saying "yes" to an offer. We taught the clients how to say "no," while keeping one's friends (if possible). Abilities to refuse a drink were assessed relative to these criteria: Did the person actually say "no?" Have good eye contact with the "pusher?" Did the older adult change the subject to suggest an alternative action to drinking (as well as request that the pusher not do it again)? Each older abuser was taught with vignettes and behavior rehearsal to enact all the noted behaviors to a satisfactory performance level.

In the module dealing with *negative affect* (particularly depression, sadness, and loneliness), sessions began with a minilecture on the influence of thoughts (self-talk) on feelings, that in turn, contribute to alcohol use. Subsequently, clients were taught to recognize the negative and ruminative thoughts that negatively impact how they feel (particularly those feelings known to be antecedents for alcohol use), to use thought-stopping techniques that interrupt and terminate unwanted thoughts and feelings, to make positive and accurate self-statements in correcting negative self-talk, and to perform a quick relaxation technique. Also, problem-solving skills were reviewed. Problem-solving skills were used across all modules each time a client was asked to generate possible solutions to problem situations as well as ways to enact those solutions. Briefly summarized, problem solving includes: (1) recognizing the problem, (2) brainstorming, (3) decision making (rank ordering alternative solutions), and (4) implementation beginning with the higher ranked (likely best) solution until the problem is under control. Potential solutions were addressed in the group until the client was assessed to be behaviorally ready to try them in a natural setting.

The overall process included recognizing one's particular signs of unpleasant feelings or emotions, stopping ruminative thoughts (self-talk), relaxing, making positive and accurate self-statements, and problem solving. The attempt is to break the thoughts → depression (negative affect) → cues → urges (self-statement of "you'll feel better after a drink—have one") chain.

Anger and frustration are feeling states that represent common antecedents (high-risk situations) for alcohol abuse. The drinking chain sequence of events minimally include anger or frustration → urge (e.g., "Have a drink. Forget it"). Older individuals were taught how not to drink for palliative or revenge purposes by acquiring new behaviors that minimized the antecedent conditions (anger/frustration). For many older abusers, anger/frustration can be controlled by learning more assertive behavior. Clients were taught that because of their feelings of anger and frustration, problem drinking would likely continue if they remained passive or aggressive.

Components of assertive behavior, and the resolution of anger and frustration, were facilitated through a memory aid called "DESC." Skill training and rating of client behavior rehearsal centered on four points: *D*escribing the objectionable behavior of the other individual in nonjudgmental language, and asking for the other person's point of view, if not stated; *E*xpressing oneself properly (eye contact, tone of voice, posture, hand gestures, as well as how the objectionable behavior makes the client feel); *S*pecifying a change in the behavior, negotiating or compromising, persisting until the client elicits a change, and saying no to unreasonable demands; and indicating to significant others both the positive *C*onsequences of changing the behavior or the negative ones if not changed.

The result of *anxiety* is tension, worry, nervousness, and so on, which, in turn, often may be an antecedent to drinking (anxiety → urge; e.g., "Have a drink, you'll feel better"). The drinking chain needs to be broken at either the situation-feeling link or the feeling-urge link, and is often done by avoiding anxiety-producing situations and/or by learning anxiety- and tension-reducing skills.

The anxiety/tension self-management sessions also emphasized how thoughts and self-talk could promote unwanted feelings connected to alcohol use. In minilecture, we emphasized *how* one thinks and *what* one thinks have a big influence on how one feels. Using client-prepared lists of anxiety-producing situations, we taught these older adults via behavior rehearsal five steps to managing anxiety and tension: (1) recognize the signs of anxiety in your body (anxiety is manifested differently by many of us), (2) use thought-stopping to terminate ruminative (harmful) thoughts, (3) make a positive and appropriate self-statement (e.g., "I can handle this"), (4) relax, and (5) problem-solve. Clients were trained to criterion across each of the five steps.

The likelihood of drinking increases in the presence of drinking *cues*. Cues are concrete stimuli in a situation such as alcohol itself, certain places (bars, lounges, stadiums, the beach, etc.), hearing others talk about drinking, and seeing others drink. Some cues are not directly related to alcohol. For example, what one does while drinking may later serve as a cue: sitting in a particular chair, fishing, gambling, certain times of the day, special events, or holidays. Thus, older abusers need to recognize the cues relevant to prompting their drinking, as well as skills for controlling those cues.

Clients rehearsed solutions for avoiding or eliminating their particular alcohol cues with the memory aid, "CARD." This mnemonic entails four steps: "C" stands for finding something to do that makes drinking impossible or very difficult (a competing response). "A" stands for an important method of controlling cues: avoid them. Until they gained control over their own drinking, clients were initially encouraged to avoid people who drink and to always avoid people who overdrink. "R" stands for rearrange. Start with the easy cues at home, but one may have to rearrange his or her lifestyle as a whole. "D" is for dispose of it. Get alcoholic beverages out of the house.

Within the module designed to teach older abusers how to manage *urges* to drink, we offered the following information: an *urge* to drink is a strong desire for alcohol, lasts different amounts of time, has a beginning and an end even if one does not drink, can be waited out successfully, is weaker each time it is resisted, is easier to resist the next time, and won't last as long the next time. The urge to drink is more often a self-statement that indicates why one *should* drink and what one *expects* from having a drink. It is not a physical craving. It is a permission (self) statement, or a good reason to drink (e.g., "I can't take many more days at work like this. A drink will help me forget the day"). For drinkers, urges are concluded with some form of this self-statement: "Have a drink."

Older alcohol abusers were instructed that if they had an urge to drink, to use the learned behaviors associated with the "CRASH" memory aid, and to review their personal Consequences Card. A consequence card had the following information: personal consequences of both drinking and not drinking, a brief narrative that reminds one what to do in the presence of an urge to use, and the name and phone number of someone who can help. The CRASH acronym also helped them remember how to respond to an urge to drink. Again, older clients were instructed to remember the *consequences* of drinking and not drinking, to get *rid* of any alcohol or to *remove* themselves from the situation (removing or avoiding any drinking cues), to engage in an incompatible *activity* (one that precludes drinking) and, if reacting to a negative emotional state, to use the *skills* they have learned to manage those feelings. If the urge persisted, they were to call for *help*. Clients were encouraged not to wait until an urge occurred before deciding what to do, to have a plan in the event an urge occurred, and to rehearse that plan while in group sessions.

In the *relapse prevention* module, we discounted the self-fulfilling prophecy of not being able to stop once one has had a drink, or a "slip." We emphasized and reinforced self-control with our clients, and taught them that they can stop. The group leader asked members to describe circumstances leading to previous slips, and to describe what they might do the next time. Clients rehearsed how to handle a slip and were assessed on their plan. Critical points included refraining from negative (condemning) self-statements, generating an initial positive statement ("I can stop"), followed by a person-specific positive self-statement, and to use the self-management skills they acquired. They were encouraged to call for help, and required to memorize (and carry a card in their wallets/purse) with a phone number of a designated person whom they would call.

Slip management skills were evaluated via behavior rehearsal and written assessment. All clients were required to list as many things as possible that they should do in the event of a slip as well as the things they should not do; and recite from memory the names and addresses of people they would turn to for help. The "should do" activities were then rehearsed after review for appropriateness and potential effectiveness.

At discharge, each client was provided with a personalized Do's and Don't's card. Such a card lists the previous steps of what to do in the event of a slip, as well as steps to avoiding situations or feelings most likely to lead that person to slip. The card also emphasizes that the person can stop drinking, and not to make negative self-statements in the event of a slip. Negative self-statements and guilt typically result in continued drinking and unwanted consequences.

In the event of a slip while in the program, clients were asked to present their slips for group discussion and analysis. Using the drinking behavior chain, a staff member would diagram how the slip originated and what might have been done to preclude it. An agreed-on solution was then rehearsed to satisfaction. Thus, slips were used as teaching examples that benefited the client and other group members.

One last comment relates to educating clients regarding calling someone for help at necessary moments. Calling others should not to be construed as a sign of weakness, but as another example of personal control: knowing what to do and doing it.

To illustrate the assessment and treatment process, we present the following case examples from recent admissions to our SAPE program. In this day treatment/outpatient program, clients were assessed at admission, discharge, and follow-up (return appointments at 1, 3, 6, and 12 months postdischarge) using the GAP-DP and follow-up versions of the instrument, the Beck Depression Inventory or "BDI" (Beck, 1972), State-Trait Anxiety Inventory C-2 form (Patterson, O'Sullivan, & Spielberger, 1980), and Geriatric Depression Scale (GDS; Brink, 1982), demographic and medical profiles, and ratings of the client by a spouse or family member using the Profile of Adaptation and Role Skills (PARS; Ellsworth, 1979).

These cases illustrate how we developed a treatment plan using responses from the GAP-DP and corroborated improvement using the other assessments over time. Responses to the GAP-DP allowed staff to identify clients' antecedents to drinking (situations and thoughts preceding drinking, locations for drinking, activities engaged in while drinking, people with whom the client drank, feelings before the first drink, cues and urges to drink), and consequences of drinking (e.g., immediate feelings after drinking begins, the most positive effects or consequences, the most undesirable effects, and longer term, negative consequences over one's life). Much of the focus was on drinking behavior during "a typical day during 30 days prior to the last drink."

CASE EXAMPLE 1

The Widow Who Drank Alone

Typical of many cases we have seen in our programs, Mrs. S lived alone. She was a 65-year-old widow with a mobile home in a rural area. At age 42, she began drinking liquor after work on a daily basis "to ease the discomfort of menopause." She had her first treatment for alcohol problems at age 55 at a community mental health center, and a second treatment following detox at age 57. Around that time, she developed a duodenal ulcer. From age 57 to 60, she worked as a counselor at a local charitable organization.

From age 60 to 64, Mrs. S periodically attended AA meetings and remained abstinent until a close friend died. About the same time, her daughter began a new job, working long hours. Her daughter requested Mrs. S's assistance by asking her to babysit for her two young children. Mrs. S stated that she also wanted to work, but felt pressured by her daughter's request. She reported falling into a deep depression about her losses, that pressure, and her life in general, and began drinking a pint of bourbon each day.

At one point, a neighbor came over to visit while Mrs. S was babysitting and noticed how "sick" she appeared to be. The neighbor took her to a local hospital. At the recommendation of hospital staff, her daughter referred her to our program.

Upon admission to the SAPE, Mrs. S was assessed for mental health and alcohol problems. She scored very high on the STAI-C2 (score = 46), and on the Beck Depression Inventory (score = 18). Mrs. S's daughter rated her mother's emotional well-being and drinking behavior on the PARS scales. Her ratings demonstrated that her mother rated high on anxiety (11), confusion (12), and alienated/depression (12).

Drinking Pattern

In the 30 days preceding her last drink, Mrs. S reported a steady pattern of drinking every day. She reported that her drinking had increased in the previous 3 to 4 months. However, she only reported being intoxicated 5 of the 30 days prior to the last drink. During the 30-day period, Mrs. S reported that she drank up to a fifth of bourbon or vodka on a typical day. Yet, she rated this as being less than the amount she consumed in other, previous 30-day periods.

Drinking Behavior Chain

Mrs. S's drinking behavior chain as derived from the GAP-DP is shown in Table 37.1. As illustrated in this table, Mrs. S usually felt depressed and lonely, or angry at her daughter for wanting her to babysit for the grandchildren. Instead of being active, Mrs. S usually drank at home and alone, hoping that she would feel less lonely or more relaxed. Instead of expressing to her daughter that she did not want to babysit as frequently as she did, she became angry with her daughter without telling her. All immediate consequences of the first drink were positive (e.g., felt relaxed, less lonely, less angry).

While in treatment, Mrs. S attended modules that taught her how to relax without drinking, how to manage depression and loneliness by restructuring her activities, and how to be more assertive in speaking with her daughter about limiting child-sitting duties. She also began job hunting, and began participating in social activities that increased her social support network beyond her family. Her daughter attended several meetings with the staff. She was asked to encourage her mother to get out of the house, and to try to work out a more reasonable child-sitting schedule. Mrs. S successfully completed treatment less than 3 months after admission and was followed up at 1-, 3-, 6-, and 12-month appointments.

During follow-ups, there were occasional slips. At 3 months, she reported drinking on one weekend when she consumed two 16-ounce beers on two consecutive days. On the first day, she reported feeling hot and tired after doing yardwork and drank to cool off. On the second day, she reported feeling lonely and remembered the cold beer in the refrigerator. At the 6-month follow-up she reported consuming another two beers on one day, but remembered her consequences and stopped. Finally, at about 8 months postdischarge, she consumed 4 ounces of bourbon after feeling angry at herself for not being independent, and angry at her daughter. She consumed another 4 ounces of bourbon the next day, then stopped. Although these were noteworthy slips, she did not return to her pretreatment pattern of steady drinking, nor to the pretreatment quantity of consumption (about a fifth per day). More importantly, Mrs. S filled out alcohol self-monitoring logs during the follow-up phase. On several occasions during the follow-ups, she reported feeling the urge to drink,

Table 37.1 Mrs. S's drinking behavior chain.

	Antecedents			→ Behavior	→ Consequences	
Situations/Thoughts	Feelings	Cues	Urges	Drink	Immediate or Short-Term	Long-Term
Home, alone watching TV	Depressed about life; Bored—nothing to do; Restless and tense	Liquor in my cabinet; Beer in refrigerator	"This will help me forget."; "I'll feel less lonely."	Bourbon or vodka; Beer	Less lonely (+); Relaxed (+); Less angry (+); Less depressed (+)	My ulcer will be bothering me (-); Guilty over my past drinking problems (-); My daughter gets angry if she sees me drinking (-)
At my house, babysitting the grandchildren	Angry and pressured about babysitting	Phone call from daughter	"I'm angry at her and want to calm down; to relax."	Bourbon or vodka		
At my daughter's house babysitting	Angry at babysitting	After babysitting grandchildren; Supply of liquor at my daughter's house	"I'd like to take control over my life again. I'm in charge of me."	Bourbon or vodka		

but used the methods learned in group to avoid drinking (e.g., left the house and visited friends, or played bingo, went to the movies, kept busy with housework).

Looking at three major points in time (admission, discharge, and final 12-month follow-up) Mrs. S's self-administered depression scores (Beck Depression Inventory) went from 18 to 6 (no depression) and 4 respectively. Her anxiety scores (STAI C2) dropped from 46 to 31 and 26 respectively. Concomitant ratings by her daughter (PARS scales) indicated large improvement in the areas previously noted (anxiety, depression, confusion).

By the 12-month follow-up, Mrs. S began part-time work at a gift shop, went out regularly with nondrinking friends, and reported maintaining telephone contact with several other friends. On discharge from the 12-month follow-up program, she reported no drinking, no urges to drink, and the relationship with her daughter as improved. Thus, both Mrs. S's and her daughter's ratings indicated that Mrs. S had improved significantly.

CASE EXAMPLE 2

The Man Who Couldn't Say No

Mr. E was a 63-year-old male who had a 40-year history of alcohol abuse, and sought treatment in response to threats of being evicted from the boarding home in which he resided. Mr. E was partially paralyzed (arm and leg), walked with a cane, and had a severe cranial indentation as a result of an auto accident 25 years earlier. Evaluation revealed a Verbal IQ of 103, Performance score of 76, and Full Scale IQ of 90 (placing him in the average range of cognitive functioning). Using the GAP-DP, the following information was obtained.

Drinking Pattern

Mr. E described himself as a "Periodic Drinker" (drinking every so often, but not every day). He reported drinking on 11 of the 30 days, consuming whiskey, vodka, and beer starting about 11 A.M. and ending about 10 P.M., and stopped only when he would get sick. Mr. E reported this 30-day pattern to be similar to his usual drinking pattern. On a typical day, Mr. E started drinking with a half pint of vodka, followed by one and a half quarts of beer. He estimated spending $20 per week on alcoholic beverages. However, he also obtained drinks while in others' homes.

Drinking Behavior Chain

Mr. E's behavior chain is shown in Table 37.2. The information in the table reflects that Mr. E's antecedent conditions included boredom, tension, and anger, as well as a repertoire of drinking related self-statement/urges that sanction use just prior to the first drink on a typical drinking day. In an attempt to diffuse those feelings, he socialized, but with drinkers. They "pushed" him to drink. When alone, he drank to handle the boredom, tension, and anger. Thus, drinking was in response to certain feelings and social pressure (largely from fellow boarding home residents who also drank in response to boredom and repeatedly asked him to either join in or purchase the alcoholic beverages). BDI and GDS scores indicated depression was not a major factor (scores of 2 and 3 respectively). However, he did report a moderate level of anxiety on the State-Trait Anxiety Inventory (a score of 29).

Mr. E's treatment included instruction in the analysis of drinking behavior, training in Drink Refusal (how to manage social pressures to drink), how to manage tension and anxiety, as well as how to be assertive rather than angry or passive. He experienced one slip in

Table 37.2 Mr. E's drinking behavior chain.

	Antecedents			→ Behavior	→	Consequences	
				Drink	*Immediate or Short-Term*	*Long-Term*	
Situations/Thoughts	*Feelings*	*Cues*	*Urges*				
Being bossed by living facility staff	Bored Angry	Hearing people talk about drinking	"I'm tired, need a drink, and no one will know."	Vodka—around 11 A.M. to "help get me started to a high"	Relaxed me (+) Nothing to worry about (+)	Alienated family and others (-)	
Sitting on the porch, doing nothing	Tense	Having folks encourage me to "have a beer"	"I deserve a drink."	Followed by a beer at 4:30 P.M. and at 7–8 P.M.	Have the right outlook on life (+)	Housing threatened (-)	
Thinking about my lost independence		Seeing the places I usually drank in	"I'm 63 years old—I don't need a babysitter!"		Friendly (+)	Medical problems and increased loss of motor control (-)	
Having money available			"I'm restless and bored—a drink would help relax me."		Outgoing (+) Calm (+)	Felt disgusted with myself (-)	
			"Who cares?"		Happy (+)		

the 12-month follow-up and on several other occasions reported urges to drink that he successfully resisted. He became more involved with other residents in nondrinking activities and explored new activities to help occupy at least some of his leisure time. His anxiety dropped to near the lowest possible score (19).

Assessment by the boarding home staff using the PARS rating scale, corroborated his improvement. He was judged to be considerate, cooperative, and interested in what others had to say. They reported rarely seeing him nervous, restless, tense, or having difficulty sleeping. They also reported that he did not drink.

CASE EXAMPLE 3

Man with the Blues

Mr. D was a 69-year-old male who reported several previous admissions to alcohol treatment facilities. At admission to our program, he reported mild depression and alcohol abuse. He showed no signs of psychotic process, nor suicidal ideation. However, he was on probation for larceny with a gun. He lived independently with a woman companion. The following information was obtained from the GAP-DP.

Drinking Pattern

Mr. D reported that prior to admission he was a steady drinker, drinking one or more drinks on 30 out of 30 days, and being intoxicated every day. He also drank about the same time each day, usually drinking beer starting at midnight and ending around dinner time. On a typical day, he drank at least 24 cans of beer. He estimated spending $100 per week on alcoholic beverages.

Drinking Behavior Chain

Mr. D's behavior chain is shown in Table 37.3. Mr. D's drinking was prompted by negative affect (depression, regret, guilt, sadness, and tension), highly salient cues, and desired short-term positive consequences, even though the longer term consequences are very negative. We have repeatedly seen that long-term negative consequences are less influential in stopping drinking in the presence of (actual or remembered) desired short-term consequences of drinking. Mr. D reported that the most desirable thing about drinking was "Euphoria—it lets you forget."

Intervention initially focused on teaching Mr. D how to diagram his personal drinking behavior chain. This gave him some insight into what prompted and supported (reinforced) his drinking behavior. Subsequently, he entered treatment modules specific to his noted antecedents for use/abuse. He successfully completed self-management groups addressing how to manage depression, anger, anxiety/tension, and cues for drinking; and how to prevent relapse.

Beck Depression Inventory scores went from "24" (high level of depression) at admission to zero at discharge and "6" at 6-month follow-up. Parallel depression assessment with the GDS revealed a discharge depression score of 1, with 1-month, 3-month, 6-month, and 12-month follow-up scores of zero, 3, 10, and 6, respectively.

Mr. D modified his lifestyle to reduce the impact of his antecedents and cues for drinking, and remained abstinent throughout his course of treatment despite employment, financial, and interpersonal stressors. Also, he fulfilled all his probation requirements and reestablished relationships with his mother and siblings.

Table 37.3 Mr. D's drinking behavior chain.

	Antecedents			→ Behavior →	Consequences	
Situations/Thoughts	Feelings	Cues	Urges	Drink	Immediate or Short-Term	Long-Term
Alone	Feel down or blue	Refrigerator	"Drinking lets me forget"	Beer over much of the day (midnight to 6–7 P.M.)	"Euphoria—let's you forget" (+)	Alienation of family and friends (-)
Watching TV	Angry	Cooler in the store	"It relaxes me"		Relaxation (+)	Physical health problems (-)
Disappointed in not having accomplished	Guilty	See friends I drink with	"A drink lets me escape from my sadness"		"Escape from reality" (+)	Blackouts (-)
Wants to forget	Anxious	Money in my pocket			Less angry (+)	Arrests (-)
	(all related to "what I have done to my whole life because of alcohol")					Employment problems (-)

646

Mr. D's household companion participated in rating his behavior in the natural setting as part of the follow-up process. Using the PARS, she reported across all follow-up periods that Mr. D was abstinent, almost never had difficulty sleeping, never alluded to life not being worth living, and rarely said people treated him unfairly. Out of a range of 1–4 (almost never to almost always), Mr. D was rated as 2 on items of tension and anxiety. Relative to self-reported feelings of self-esteem and worth, Mr. D showed improvement on a Life Satisfaction Index. Going from a low of 4 to 15 at discharge, to 13, 14, 13, and 12 at 1-, 3-, 6-, and 12-month reporting periods.

CONCLUSION

We have demonstrated the efficacy of a self-management and cognitive-behavioral approach in treating older alcohol abusers, relying on our previous research, as well as the cases presented. We found older adults capable of learning and using these skills to control their drinking. Due to our emphasis on diagramming drinking behavior as the first step in treatment, older adults identified the rationale for the intervention early in the process.

This treatment approach differed from many traditional approaches. The focus of assessment and group discussions is not on the distant past, but rather on recent events (high-risk situations for drinking or recent slips). The content of group discussions is not confrontation, labeling, or dwelling on what went wrong, but instead consists of supportive approaches, teaching the skills necessary to prevent relapse.

In our program, as well as other programs using this approach, older adults also learned to diagram behavior chains related to other problem situations and apply problem-solving skills, as well as coping behaviors they felt were relevant to those situations. Thus, they also experienced a sense of personal control or self-efficacy beyond alcohol-related situations. That is likely to bode them well since they are in a stage of life incorporating frequent change and new coping challenges.

The modular approach benefits staff by providing an assessment instrument (the drinking profile) to identify each client's drinking behavior chain and to develop treatment plans, a prescribed curriculum relevant to the defined drinking behavior chain (including lectures, exercises, role plays, behaviors to be learned and practiced), and assessments to determine whether the information was learned to criterion. Also, when a client's knowledge and performance of skills in the natural setting are judged as satisfactory and capable of managing alcohol use, both clients and staff know when to conclude treatment (and to begin a weaning process from the program). To discharge a client prior to acquisition of antecedent-specific skills is more likely to result in relapse and continued abuse, regardless of how much "insight" the older abuser may have acquired into his or her alcohol abuse.

The program also benefited in that it maintained consistency. Once trained, and by following the written curriculum, staff of various educational levels or even differing treatment philosophies conducted the modules, or substituted for each other as needed, knowing what was covered last and where exactly to pick up. We have found that when staff aren't quite sure what to do in a treatment situation, they resort to prior methods and philosophies. Lastly, our approach is more cost-effective in that it emphasizes a group approach; and third-party payers, as well as quality assurance reviewers, like the structure offered in terms of measures of individual progress, the client's status at any given moment, and progress toward discharge.

The approach outlined in this chapter has value to older alcohol abusers across many areas of their lives, to program staff, and to the parent organization. It meets the treatment criteria suggested by experts in this field and offers a disseminable, skills training approach that attends to the losses, negative affect, and diminished social support networks of older people who turn to alcohol as a coping mechanism.

REFERENCES

Abrams, D.B., & Niaura, R.S. (1987). Social learning theory. In H.T. Blane & K.E. Leonard (Eds.), *Psychological theories of drinking and alcoholism* (pp. 131–180). New York: Guilford Press.

Adams, W.L., & Cox, N.S. (1997). Epidemiology of problem drinking among elderly people. In A. Gurnack (Ed.), *Older adults' misuse of alcohol, medicines, and other drugs* (pp. 1–23). New York: Springer.

Beck, A. (1972). *Depression: Causes and treatment.* Philadelphia: University of Pennsylvania Press.

Beresford, T.P. (1995). Alcoholic elderly: Prevalence, screening, diagnosis, and prognosis. In T. Beresford & E. Gomberg (Eds.), *Alcohol and aging* (pp. 3–41). New York: Oxford University Press.

Brink, T.L. (1982). Screening tests for geriatric depression. *Clinical Gerontologist, 1,* 37–43.

DeHart, S.S., & Hoffman, N.G. (1997). Screening and diagnosis: Alcohol use disorders in older adults. In A.M. Gurnack (Ed.), *Older adults' misuse of alcohol, medicine, and other drugs* (pp. 25–53). New York: Springer.

Dupree, L.W., Broskowski, H., & Schonfeld, L. (1984). The gerontology alcohol project: A behavioral treatment program for elderly alcohol abusers. *Gerontologist, 24,* 510–516.

Dupree, L.W., & Schonfeld, L. (1986). *Assessment and treatment planning for alcohol abusers: A curriculum manual* (FMHI Publication Series, 109). Tampa: University of South Florida.

Dupree, L.W., & Schonfeld, L. (1996). Substance abuse. In M. Hersen & V. Van Hasselt (Eds.), *Psychological treatment of older adults: An introductory text* (pp. 281–297). New York: Plenum Press.

Dupree, L.W., & Schonfeld, L. (1998). *Older alcohol abusers: Recurring treatment issues* (NIAAA Research Monograph) (pp. 339–358). Proceedings of the Alcohol and Aging National Conference, Ipsilanti, MI.

Ellsworth, R.B. (1979). *Personal adjustment and roles skills (PARS) scales.* Roanoke, VA: Institute for Program Evaluation.

Gomberg, E.S. (1980). *Drinking and problem drinking among the elderly.* Ann Arbor: Institute of Gerontology, University of Michigan.

H.R. Report 102-852. (1992). *Alcohol abuse and misuse among the elderly.* Subcommittee on Health and Long-term Care, Select Committee on Aging.

Janik, S.W. & Dunham, R.G. (1983). A nationwide examination of the need for specific treatment programs for the elderly. *Journal of Studies on Alcohol, 44,* 307–317.

Kanfer, F.H. (1975). Self-management methods. In F.H. Kanfer & A.P. Goldstein (Eds.), *Helping people change: A textbook of methods* (pp. 309–355). New York: Pergamon Press.

Kofoed, L., Tolson, R., Atkinson, R.M., Toth, R., & Turner, J. (1987). Treatment compliance of older alcoholics: An elder-specific approach is superior to "mainstreaming." *Journal of Studies on Alcohol, 48,* 47–51.

Marlatt, G.A., & Gordon, J.R. (1985). *Relapse prevention: Maintenance strategies in the treatment of addictive behaviors.* New York: Guilford Press.

Mayfield, D., McLeod, G., & Hall, P. (1974). The CAGE questionnaire: Validation of a new alcoholism screening instrument. *American Journal of Psychiatry, 131,* 1121–1123.

Miller, P.M. (1976). *Behavioral treatment of alcoholism.* New York: Pergamon Press.

Miller, W.R., & Muñoz, R.F. (1976). *How to control your drinking.* Englewood, NJ: Prentice-Hall.

Moos, R.H., Brennan, P.L., Fondacaro, M.R., & Moos, B.S. (1990). Approach and avoidance coping responses among older problem and nonproblem drinkers. *Psychology and Aging, 5,* 31–40.

Moos, R.M., Mertens, J.R., & Brennan, P.L. (1993). Patterns of diagnosis and treatment among late-middle-aged and older substance abuse patients. *Journal of Studies on Alcohol, 54,* 479–487.

Patterson, R.L., O'Sullivan, M.J., & Spielberger, C.D. (1980). Measurement of state and trait anxiety in elderly mental health clients. *Journal of Behavioral Assessment, 2,* 89–97.

Schonfeld, L., & Dupree, L.W. (1991). Antecedents of drinking for early- and late-onset elderly alcohol abusers. *Journal of Studies on Alcohol, 52,* 587–591.

Schonfeld, L., & Dupree, L.W. (1995). Treatment approaches for older problem drinkers. *International Journal of the Addictions, 30,* 1595–1618.

Schonfeld, L., & Dupree, L.W. (1997). Treatment alternatives for older alcohol abusers. In A. Gurnack (Ed.), *Older adults' misuse of alcohol, medicines, and other drugs* (pp. 113–131). New York: Springer.

Schonfeld, L., & Dupree, L.W. (1998). Relapse prevention approaches with the older problem drinker. *Southwest Journal on Aging, 14,* 43–50.

CHAPTER 38

Psychotherapy with the Suicidal Elderly: A Family-Oriented Approach

JOSEPH RICHMAN

The understanding and treatment of the suicidal elderly is based upon life-affirming values and the means for realizing them. Suicide has a great impact upon the living. Virtually everyone has been touched by the suicide of a friend or family member. A suicide hands down a legacy of further suicides from one generation to the next.

In this chapter, the approaches to those in a suicidal despair are presented largely through case histories and illustrations. The basic processes of assessment, treatment, and education are discussed. The first case illustrates the need for flexibility in the beginning therapist and an openness to information and contact with a suicidal person and family. The later examples describe the most frequent situations and challenges, beginning with assessment and crisis intervention, and continuing with treatment procedures. The methods emphasize but are not limited to family therapy.

The foremost influences in my work have been Bowlby's attachment theory (1969, 1973) and its psychoanalytic and sociological underpinnings, especially the role of alienation versus integration. Bowlby is crucial for the understanding of suicidal behavior, especially the feelings of isolation and abandonment in response to loss.

The other influence is Emile Durkheim (1951). His statistical finding of an inverse relationship between suicide rates and social integration is the sociological analogue of Bowlby's findings. Bowlby and Durkheim together summarize the central goals of treatment with the suicidal: the reduction of alienation, despair, and hopelessness, and the restoration of social cohesion, hope, and a sense of belonging.

For a broader view of the research and treatment spectrum, I am indebted to the invaluable annotated bibliography by Osgood and McIntosh (1986). For me, it has been a condensed encyclopedia of research and clinical findings that is still an essential resource for everyone interested in understanding suicide and the treatment of self-destructive people.

A knowledge of demographic, epidemiological, and clinical factors is essential. The highest completed suicide rate occurs in those who are 65 or older. Within this elderly population, there are differences based upon sex, marital status, and racial or ethnic composition. The highest rate is found in White males, with the rate climbing steadily with age. The rate is markedly lower in females where it rises until the mid-50s, and decreases slightly with advanced age. The rates are also lower among nonwhite groups. The suicide rate is higher in those who are single, divorced, or widowed. Marriage protects men more than women, in spite of the stereotype that it is the woman who requires marriage.

Many other factors must also be considered. For a fuller exposition, I recommend Osgood and McIntosh (1986) and McIntosh (1992). The greater the number of danger signs, the greater the suicidal potential. The risk increases if the person is actively suicidal, has a plan, and the means for carrying it out. All these findings are best understood through an integration of clinical, research, and demographic studies. It would be desirable for more research workers to be clinicians and more clinicians to be conducting research.

CASE EXAMPLE

Bernard A., a 59-year-old wheelchair-bound man, had savagely slashed his arms and legs in a suicidal attempt. "I don't want to live this way," he explained. "I have been trapped in this wheelchair for years. I can't walk because I have a spinal tumor, which is benign but inoperable, and I'm in constant pain. I have agonizing arthritis, stomach ulcers, and diabetes, and the diet for one makes the other worse. Would you want to live this way?"

Sympathizing with his plight, and agreeing with his suicidal solution, I arranged for hospitalization, and called in his son from the waiting room. His son presented a different picture. He described a tyrannical father who bullied his children and dominated his wife and the entire family with his illness. On this particular day, there was a huge family argument, which ended abruptly when the patient's wife and three children walked out, leaving him alone in a state of frustration and rage. The patient then made his suicide attempt.

The meeting with the son was a corrective professional experience for me. I learned that for every suicidal situation, the family and interpersonal situation must be explored. Euthanasia and rational suicide were pseudo-solutions and oversimplifications that created barriers to understanding. Fortunately, ignorance can be the beginning of wisdom. That experience with Mr. A. marked the beginning of my explorations into suicide and the family.

THE LIFE-SAVING VALUE OF ASSESSMENT AND RECOGNITION

Therapy begins with assessment, and assessment begins with the recognition that there may be a problem that has to be explored. The following are two similar examples with very dissimilar results.

CASE EXAMPLE

Ernie was a 70-year-old resident of a senior home. He had made a good adjustment until he became obsessed with his bowel functioning. He was labeled "Ernie, the hypochondriac," and subjected to ridicule and laughter, until he jumped to his death. The elderly are often unwilling or unable to state that they are depressed or suicidal. Ernie was presented with a somatic metaphor of being blocked and hopeless. Ernie communicated his suicidal state but nobody heard him.

Sam was an 85-year-old resident of a nursing home, who had made a good adjustment and was involved in many social and intellectual activities, until he became ill. He suffered a heart ailment, which was treated successfully. However, he stated that he had lived his life, that the end was near, and he was ready to die. He took to his bed, and stopped eating.

One doctor on the staff realized that Sam was reacting to a crisis in his life that precipitated a depressive and self-destructive state. The doctor initiated anti-depressant medication. He also called in the relatives and arranged for them to visit more frequently. Within a month, Sam had recovered completely and resumed his satisfying and productive life style. The proper recognition that Sam suffered from a treatable condition saved him from a premature death.

The earlier the recognition of a suicidal risk and the quicker the response, the better the outcome. The elderly are subject to loss, illness, and other factors associated with suicide, but the vast majority *do not* become suicidal. This is a fortunate example of the resilience of the elderly.

CRISIS INTERVENTION

Suicidal acts are largely based upon a current crisis that is built upon unresolved crises in the past. The following is a typical example.

CASE EXAMPLE

Henry B. was a 73-year-old man who had left his wife and family 25 years ago and run away with another woman. Now, he was ill and alone, living in a seedy senior residence, and suffering from Parkinson's disease and a host of other ailments. He made a suicidal attempt on Father's Day, based upon the realization that he was irrevocably alienated from his divorced family.

He became my patient. One of my first acts after establishing contact and the beginnings of a working alliance with him was to call his estranged wife to arrange for a family session. She felt very bitter, but was eager to talk about how he had abandoned her and their children 25 years ago. She could not forgive him, but she said she would help arrange a family meeting although she refused to be present. We held a family session with the patient and his three children, who confronted him directly with his inexcusable behavior 25 years ago. He heard them and that was the beginning of healing. He left his senior residence, which was a long distance from his family, and moved closer to home.

Erwin Stengel (1964) said that the outcome of a suicidal act depends upon its consequences. If it brings people closer, no further suicidal or other self-destructive behavior will take place. If nothing changes, or if the situation becomes worse, the result is further suicidal behavior and completed suicides. Henry B. was an example of people being brought closer. However, the positive outcome would not have occurred without the crisis precipitated by his suicidal attempt, and the intervention of successful crisis intervention and psychotherapy. The call to his ex-wife was an example of the therapeutic value of the telephone. Everyone engaged in crisis intervention should learn about telephone interviewing.

THE FAMILY COMMUNICATION SYSTEM

Secretiveness leads to division and destruction, while openness leads to integration and healing. All symptoms are *communications*, those in the patient and in the family.

CASE EXAMPLE

Miriam D. was an 80-year-old woman who wrote a farewell note, and swallowed a full bottle of sleeping pills while drinking a glass of scotch. She survived only because of a chance phone call from a friend who became concerned when there was no response and notified the police. They arrived to find her comatose. (For further details see Richman,1996b.) After the death of her husband 15 years ago, she had turned to her daughter Jean for solace and support. Unknown to Miriam, her daughter had become a closet alcoholic. Jean died suddenly as the result of a fall while drunk. Her sons and daughters decided to "protect" Miriam by telling her that Jean had died from a brain aneurysm.

The result was almost fatal. When Miriam tried to talk to her grandchildren about their mother, the children reacted with such intense agitation and distress that Rose was taken aback. Secretiveness had became the center of tension and fears of exposure, but Miriam concluded that she was to blame and that the only solution was to put herself out of the way.

She could not admit to others that she was depressed and suicidal. The closest she came was to see her doctor, with the complaint of insomnia. The doctor gave her the sleeping pills, with no investigation into the reasons for her sleeplessness. Miriam naively expected the doctor to recognize how she felt without her having to say so. His failure to do so confirmed her hopelessness, and she used the pills to attempt suicide.

Fortunately, she survived. In the family sessions that followed Miriam was told the true story of her daughter's alcoholism and death. I asked if she would rather not hear such unpleasant details. She replied, "I want to hear this. I want to know the truth." A greater closeness developed with her grandchildren, as well as with her son, from whom she had been estranged. I grew to appreciate her strengths in the year and a half of her therapy.

Attitudes around euthanasia and assisted suicide frequently arise in the treatment of potentially suicidal patients. While Miriam D. was no longer actively suicidal, she continued to feel ambivalent about living. She was particularly concerned about becoming feeble and helpless. During one therapy session with her son Kevin she said, addressing me, "If I ever become unable to care for myself I want you to pull the plug."

I sensed that the message was not for me, and asked Kevin, "How would you feel if Mother became helpless and had no one to care for her but you?"

He replied, "I agree with Mother. I would want someone to pull the plug." I accepted their attitude. However, near the end of the session, I commented to Kevin, "You are very young. Possibly, you will feel different later." (He was 48.)

He agreed. "After all," he said, "I have never had to deal with such a situation. I might feel different."

Mother and son then left. Miriam lagged behind and while her son went for the car, said, "I have such a good feeling." The acceptance and exploration of the expressed wish for assisted suicide removed some of the roadblocks to improved family relationships.

The request for assisted suicide is often based on fears of future illness and disability. At the same time, all suicidal ideation refers to the present situation. Miriam D. was concerned about her current relationship with her son and how much he cared for her. Open discussions of euthanasia can lead to the affirmation of life.

THE SHORT CIRCUITING OF GRIEF AND MOURNING

Edna D. was a 70-year-old woman whose mother had lived with Mr. and Mrs. D. and their daughter from the beginning of their marriage. Edna and her husband worked, while her mother took care of the house. When their daughter was born, her mother took care of the child, in addition to cleaning, cooking, and laundry. Their daughter, grew up, married, and had a child.

Eventually, Edna's mother died, but Edna acted as though her mother were still alive. She talked to her frequently and finally tried to repeat the pattern she had had with her mother by asking her daughter to move in with them. Edna would take care of the baby, clean, do the laundry, and cook. When her daughter refused, Edna become suicidal. Her daughter then became severely depressed and suicidal.

Grief and its vicissitudes was primarily a family matter, at least with suicidal patients (see Richman, 1986, pp. 36–45). Unresolved mourning can usually be traced back to at least three generations in depression and suicide-prone families. The devices used to avoid mourning consist of various measures for keeping the deceased person symbolically alive. Had Edna's daughter been more a part of the grief work together with her parents, the death in the family could have become the beginning of a growth process.

SUICIDE AND THE DESIGNATED FAMILY HEALER

Norman E. was a 16-year-old high school senior who had slashed his wrists, arms, and legs so severely that he almost bled to death. The precipitants included school pressures and peer conflicts, but the family conflicts were prominent. For example, his father had attended a school for gifted children, but transferred to another high school because of conflicts with teachers and other pupils. Years later, he had Norman apply and be accepted at the same school, and then made him transfer to another high school, even though Norman was doing well.

The parents had little communication with each other. His mother had become the financial support of the family since his father had suffered a heart attack. Norman was filled with death anxiety, and felt it was his fault that his father became ill. The son seemed trapped in a symbiotic relationship with his father, while mother became increasingly withdrawn.

A crucial event was the illness and death of Norman's maternal grandmother, who had always disapproved of her daughter's marriage. During grandmother's illness, Norman's mother became increasingly unable to tolerate her husband.

Norman had been sent to the grandmother's funeral far from home, to represent the entire family. Upon his return, he found that his parents had separated and were living apart. He was then pressured by each parent to choose with whom to live. That pressure was the last straw.

In individual therapy, Norman welcomed the opportunity to explore his life and relationships. In family therapy, his mother was preoccupied with the death of her mother, and said that she thought of her day and night. His father started taking better care of himself and began working again, with gratifying success. His mother announced that marital separation was not for her. She returned home, and the family was united once again, this time with a more functional father and a less troubled mother.

The crucial event was the crisis precipitated by the illness and death of the grandmother. That led to another crisis, the breakup of the family, and to a third crisis, Norman's suicidal attempt. Finally, the family received the message to get help.

To understand suicide we must explore at least three generations, especially how the family deals with loss and bereavement. Suicidal events may be inseparable from the relationships between the generations. As with Norman, many suicidal acts can be directly traced to the influence of a grandparent. Fortunately, many suicidal persons have confronted the family heritage and said "enough!" with a beneficial result for present and future generations.

THERAPEUTIC INTUITION AND THE FAMILY CRISIS

I am willing to take a calculated risk with a suicidal patient and try to maintain the person in the community, if hospitalization would disrupt important life roles and activities. But the decision is not an easy one.

CASE EXAMPLE

Frances I., a woman in her mid-70s, was diagnosed as a bipolar disorder, with a history of numerous hospitalizations. She was displaying increasingly pressured speech and bizarre, near-delusional thoughts about her body. As a result, she discontinued her medication. She was in a crisis related to the forthcoming marriage of her son and the rejecting attitude of her prospective daughter-in-law. I was supportive and tried to reduce her anxiety over the wedding and the fear of losing her son.

After the wedding, she said she was feeling much better and denied feeling suicidal. Intuitively, I did not believe her. She did not look at me directly, and her voice had become toneless. Despite her repeated protests, I took her to the psychiatric emergency room to be evaluated for possible admission.

In the interview with the ER resident, she confessed that she was suicidal, and that she had planned to go home and kill herself after the session with me. She was hospitalized.

A DIFFERENT THERAPEUTIC RESPONSES TO A SUICIDAL CRISIS

Maltsberger and Buie (1974) said that suicidal people can accept anger in a therapist; what they cannot accept is rejection and abandonment. Nevertheless, anger is not to be lightly expressed by the therapist, especially if it serves as an outlet for the therapist's problems or feelings.

CASE EXAMPLE

Alice J. was only in her mid-20s when I saw her, but I am including her because of the similarity to Frances I. Both were undergoing a family crisis, but my responses were different.

I saw Alice at the request of her brother, w hom I had evaluated while he was a patient at Jacobi Hospital because of his suicidal behavior. He asked if I could interview his sister who was depressed and suicidal and a patient at another mental hospital. She was a warm and caring woman with two children and a husband who was cooperative and supportive. She wanted to be home. I agreed that she should be with her husband and children and arranged for her to be discharged and continue treatment with me as an outpatient.

The major problem was her identification with a psychotically depressed mother. Her father had not tolerated his wife's depression and was frequently violent. Alice sided with her father. For example, he once stabbed his wife with a pair a scissors, while Alice, then aged 8, looked on approvingly. When Alice married, she did not let her mother come to the wedding.

Soon after the marriage, her mother jumped out a window to her death. In therapy, Alice tearfully said that she feels compelled to repeat her mother's fate, as a form of atonement. Nevertheless, her depression lifted, she functioned well, and her family relationships were good.

One day Alice appeared for her session in an agitated state. Her brother, who had a history of multiple suicide attempts, was hospitalized again. Alice insisted she was now depressed and suicidal and also needed to be hospitalized at the same hospital.

I replied, "You are taking good care of your children and being a good wife to your husband. "You should stay at home and continue doing a good job."

Alice replied, "If you do not hospitalize me, I will stab my two children and jump out the window."

I felt indignant and said angrily, "I think you want to be hospitalized to be with your brother, and that is not a good reason. I will not agree to anything that is not good for you."

Alice left the session, looking very upset, and I proceeded to have an anxiety attack. I waited until she arrived home and called, deciding that I would agree to the hospitalization. However, Alice was cheerful and in good spirits. "I feel fine," she said, "Thank you." I saw her for another year, and there were many problems and ups and downs in her life, but she was never again suicidal.

Events in therapy can occur very rapidly, with no time for considered responses. My response was spontaneous and intuitive, but it was an informed intuition. Her situation was different from her mother's. Alice's husband and his family valued her, wanted her to live, and welcomed her presence.

An understanding of unconscious family processes is a major key to the prevention of suicide. The work of Boszormenyi-Nagy and Spark, (1973) on the "invisible loyalties" behind family ties and the application of the concept of projective identification to family dynamics (Scharff, 1992) lend further support to such a concept.

SUICIDE AS A SYMBOLIC DEATH AND REBIRTH

Andrew K. was a 65-year-old business man with a history of bipolar episodes. During one of these episodes, he decided that suicide was the only way out. He hung himself, but the rope broke. Andrew saw this as a message from God that he was supposed to live. That meant continuing with the treatment that had kept him on an even keel in the past, but that he had periodically discontinued.

Depressed as well as suicidal patients may sink into the depths of despair and unbearable psychic pain. With recovery, there is often a rising out of the abyss to a new world.

One 90-year-old man feared that his daughters wanted to place him in a nursing home. He took an overdose, was hospitalized, and treated successfully. His daughters reassured him that they would not send him to a home. This man left the hospital stating, "I feel that my life is just beginning."

The death-rebirth experience occurs at all ages. Nora, at age 24, had a history of serious suicidal attempts. She said to me in great anger that if she continues in treatment with me she will kill herself. At that point, she entered into a catatonic state.

I thought that hospitalization would be counter-therapeutic. Instead, I called her mother, who came to stay with Nora in her apartment. I saw them both at home for daily therapy sessions. Nora recovered completely in ten days. She wanted to return to her mother's home, but her mother said her daughter had to live her own life.

The experience was a symbolic death, and a rebirth into a more mature and satisfying development and life style. She became notably successful at her career and a subsequent marriage.

THE VALUE OF ONE FAMILY SESSION

One family meeting can sometimes help the patient accept individual therapy. Harry L., was a physically ill, emotionally disturbed 78-year-old man, who was referred by the medical service of the hospital. He resisted psychotherapy, until a family visit was arranged with his three daughters, all of whom lived out of town. They were available for just one meeting. At the end of the family session, the eldest daughter placed her stamp of approval upon the treatment. She said she had misunderstood therapy, thinking it would be the equivalent of a wild and destructive psychoanalysis. That one family meeting marked the beginning of a fruitful working alliance. Mr. L improved physically as well as emotionally, and became an active therapeutic force for others in group therapy.

SUICIDE PACT IDEATION

Just as suicidal ideation precedes an attempted or completed suicide, suicide pact ideation precedes mutual completed or attempted suicides. The frequency of such ideation when one partner is depressed or suicidal is far greater than has been realized.

CASE EXAMPLE

Theodore K. was in individual therapy for the treatment of depression and suicidal impulses. His therapist asked if I would see him and his wife for a family evaluation. Mr. K was 78; his wife, Frances, was 15 years younger. Mr. K reported that they were going to commit suicide together, and Mrs. K nodded in agreement. The precipitant was the departure of their youngest son from the home. "I was left completely alone," explained Mr. K.

"Didn't you have your wife?" I asked.

"We are so much one, that Frances cannot survive without me." Frances nodded in agreement.

"So you would be willing to deprive your three children of both mother and father simultaneously," I commented.

"I never thought of that," Frances said.

Mr. K continued in individual psychotherapy during which his depression and self-destructive impulses were resolved. The implication is that suicidal pact ideation should be explored whenever one member of a couple has exhibited severe depression or suicidal behavior. Such interventions can be life saving, but few people know that the illness, depression, and other precipitants behind suicide pacts can be relieved.

LETHAL MYTH: SUICIDE IS INEVITABLE

A first-year psychiatric resident said, "I hear that you are studying suicide. You might be interested in talking to a case I was just assigned. He is going to commit suicide."

How did this psychiatric resident at the beginning of his training know with such certainty that this new "case" would kill himself? He was told so by an eminent faculty member and the faculty member's wife, who brought in the patient for hospitalization.

I saw Edgar M. (the patient) who was cooperative, friendly, and eager to talk. He was acutely suicidal, but treatable, and basically wanted to live. He became very involved and interested in our discussion of various ways of overcoming his rage and conviction of hopelessness. There seemed little doubt that his anger and family problems could be redirected back into creative activities and social channels. However, that did not happen and the patient killed himself.

His hospitalization could have been a necessary life-saving measure, and the patient agreed that he needed hospitalization. However, beginnings are important. How the patient was introduced by the faculty member became a self-fulfilling prophecy. A hint of the outcome was conveyed by the cold impersonal manner in which the resident spoke about the patient.

Shortly after these events, the faculty member and his wife gave a party for specially chosen friends, who had been invited to say goodbye to the wife since she was committing suicide that evening, with her husband present. The party was videotaped and played on television. The videotape was a pioneering propaganda piece for assisted suicide. Edgar M. was an early sacrifice in the service of the burgeoning assisted-suicide movement.

THE HOSPITAL AS A CENTER FOR TREATMENT SABOTAGE

CASE EXAMPLE

Mary N. was a 78-year-old widow whose daughter, Carol, in her 50s was chronically depressed. Both were in therapy, treated by a social work student. They responded well to treatment, but their therapist left because her hospital training was completed. Carol and her mother were assigned to a new social work trainee. Fortunately, they continued to do well.

However, the hospital policy almost guaranteed that success could not continue. They were assigned a third social work student, but this time they did not connect in a therapeutic manner. Mary's arthritis and other ills escalated. And one day her daughter Carol jumped from the roof of their apartment house, landing in front of her mother while she was cooking supper.

Mary then went to another hospital and became my patient. I was not a trainee, and there was no concern over being abandoned by the therapist, but Carol could no longer join her mother in treatment. Mary was helped to mourn her loss, and she became active at a senior center and her church. She discontinued therapy when she was able to tolerate the smell of red cabbage that she had been cooking when she saw her daughter's body plunge to her death.

The incidence of maladaptive institutional policies extends beyond medicine and psychiatry to all the professions. Such policies should be opposed wherever they are found. When suicide can be traced to the lack of commitment by the hospital or training center, strong countermeasures are necessary. Training institutions can assign the more difficult cases to experienced therapists. Trainees can then receive excellent training as a participant with the senior member. Treatment need not be detrimental to training needs.

Progress in treatment is often preceded by intense therapeutic experiences. Family therapy sessions are often filled with turmoil and intense emotional outbursts, *especially* when the therapy is effective. A barrage of anger, blaming, and other seemingly destructive interactions often appear. The intense affect arouses a corresponding turmoil in the therapist. It is understandable, therefore, that therapists avoid treating the suicidal person and family. Rather than avoidance, it is more desirable that professionals learn how to deal with the stress and other symptoms.

These family meetings may represent the first time that the destructive feelings of the patient and relatives were dealt with constructively and positively. In addition, destructive behavior in the professional clinic, hospital ward, or office has a far different meaning than when it occurs in the home. At some level, the participants know that they are present for a healing purpose. Without that recognition, family meetings can be counterproductive. With that recognition, the open expressions of intense negative affect and attitudes during family therapy may be the beginning of cure. The experience often brings out the family's potential but buried forces of loving, caring, healing, and growth. The main problem is how to handle the arousal of painful and anxiety provoking reactions in the therapist. When successfully accomplished, therapists can help suicidal older adults deal with false cognitive reasoning and emotional despair, revive the intrinsic healing forces that are present, and transform hopelessness into hope.

CONCLUSION

It is especially important to treat older adults because there will not only be many more of them, but they will be youthful and middle aged longer. Some people forecast a higher suicide rate because of the presence of a larger population of older adults in the future and a general increase in the incidence of depression in the present-day young and middle-aged generations. That will presumably make them more vulnerable to suicide when they age. A contrasting view is to exert greater efforts to reach and treat more suicidal people and to apply creative innovations in therapy and society.

The knowledge and experience of older adults form the basis of the successful psychotherapy with suicidal individuals. Suicide is not a rational response to aging, especially now, at the dawning of the age of longevity. It is more rational to recognize and appreciate their assets.

A goal for society is to make the good life available to all. To that end, suicide prevention is everybody's business. Success in such a business requires universal education of the public in the recognition of suicidal risks, dispelling false myths and providing information on how and where to obtain help. Universal education and the cooperation of the media in disseminating information may become one of the most important measures for preventing suicide.

These are among the hopes for the future, to help the suicidal out of despair and into a meaningful and rewarding life, to work toward alleviating the underlying causes, and to be students of the art and science of healing.

REFERENCES

Boszormenyi-Nagy, I., & Spark, G.M. (1973). *Invisible loyalties: Reciprocity in intergenerational family therapy.* New York: Harper & Row.

Bowlby, J. (1969). *Attachment and loss: Vol. I. Attachment.* New York: Basic Books.

Bowlby, J. (1973). *Attachment and loss: Vol. II. Separation.* New York: Basic Books.

Durkheim, E. (1951). *Suicide* (J.A. Spaulding & G. Simpson, Trans.). New York: Free Press.

Goldman, E. (1998). The significance of leadership style. *Educational Leadership, 55*(7), 20–22.

Maltsberger, J.T., & Buie, D.H. (1974). Countertransference hate in the treatment of suicidal patients. *Archives of General Psychiatry, 30,* 625–633.

McIntosh, J.L. (1992). Epidemiology of suicide in the elderly. In A.A. Leenaars, R.W. Maris, J.L. McIntosh, & J. Richman (Eds.), *Suicide and the older adult* (pp. 15–35). New York: Basic Books.

Osgood, N.J., & McIntosh, J.L. (1986). *Suicide and the elderly: An annotated bibliography and review.* Westport, CT: Greenwood Press.

Richman, J. (1986), *Family therapy with suicidal persons.* New York: Springer.

Richman, J. (1993). *Preventing elderly suicide: Overcoming personal despair, professional neglect, and social bias.* New York: Springer.

Richman, J. (1996a). The family and unconscious determinants of suicide in the elderly. In A. Leenaars & D. Lester (Eds.), *Suicide and the unconscious* (pp. 206–216). Northvale, NJ: Jason Aronson.

Richman, J. (1996b) Psychotherapeutic approaches to the depressed and suicidal older person and family. In G.J. Kennedy (Ed.), *Suicide and depression in late life: Critical issues in treatment, research, and public policy* (pp. 103–117). New York: Wiley.

Scharff, J.S. (1992). Projective and introjective identification and the use of the therapist's self. Northvale, NJ: Jason Aronson.

Stengel, E. (1964). *Suicide and attempted suicide.* Baltimore: Penguin.

CHAPTER 39

Ethics of
Treatment in Geropsychology:
Status and Challenges

J. RAY HAYS

This chapter focuses on the ethical demands of mental health practice with elderly persons and their families, with those issues surrounding the decline in ability and capacity of elderly persons, the ethical roles of the practitioners who deal with those elderly persons, their families, and the institutions that provide care for them. The chapter provides a way to examine the development of this relatively new and growing segment of society, a vocabulary for grappling with the ethical dilemmas, and some problems that are distinct with this population. The aim of the chapter is to give the practitioner the tools to cope with the ethical dilemmas presented by elderly persons and their families.

This chapter covers the elements of ethics necessary for the practitioner to deal with the ethical decision making when working with a geriatric population, including the vocabulary of ethics, the conflicts presented in this population, and a method for solving ethical dilemmas when they are identified and confronted. Finally, a proposal is made for a special geriatric ethic, and a suggestion that practitioners working with geriatric clients advocate for an ethic for the elderly that respects their dignity but also affords them the protection they deserve.

NEED FOR THIS TOPIC

The population of the United States is aging through developments in the medical sciences, better nutrition, and healthier lifestyles. As this aging of American society continues, the elderly population is exploring new roles for its members by using more resources and creating new demands on families and professionals (Hays, 1996). Segments within society are created, in part, by the demands placed on society by the members of a group and by what the members of the group can contribute to the larger society. For example, the agrarian culture in Western society, just a little over a hundred years ago, supported a different family structure. An agrarian family requires all hands to accomplish the tasks of farm life. The industrial revolution at the turn of the 1800s moved Western society into an age in which young people were not needed as economic resources for the family. The father worked in a factory, not the fields, and after the development of child labor laws could not take his sons or daughters to the factory until they were old enough to be independent of the family. In this fashion, the industrial revolution created an extended childhood, the adolescent, with the attendant social disruption caused by youths that we are continuing to see.

Just as the adolescent group is partially the product of the industrial revolution, at the other end of the life span a new social class is emerging. With our ability to prolong life through medical innovations, the almost universal medical care for the elderly combined with Social Security for our elderly in the United States, and the socialized care systems that are even more pervasive in Western Europe, we have created a new social phenomenon, namely, the retired elderly, many of whom are fortunate to have leisure and financial resources. As this population grows, older individuals are seeking roles for themselves and forcing society into unexplored frontiers. Professionals who care for this aging population need to explore the changing ethical demands that underlie the treatment that we provide to this population. Why should ethics differ for the geriatric population? Whereas ethical principles remain constant for all populations, the application of and relative weight of those principles may vary with the population served. Just as children receive treatment differently from adults because more weight is given the principle of paternalism and less to the autonomy principle, so also elderly adults may require different treatment than that for younger adults.

In this stage of development, elderly persons may experience decreases in the mental and physical abilities that characterized their youth, a stage in which individuals of mature years can no longer deal with the same level of complexity as in earlier years. I propose a new term, *geriessence,* for use in the discussion of individuals who have reached a stage in their lives in which they no longer have the capacities for independence that characterized them as adults but who have not reached a degree of senescence to meet the criteria for such clinical diagnoses as dementia and are not the subject of clinical concerns over such matters.

TERMS WITHIN ETHICAL ANALYSIS

ETHICAL TERMS

Five general principles underlie discussion of ethics: beneficence, nonmalfeasance, justice, equity, and paternalism. Beneficence, from the Latin, means to do good. The basic tenet of health care is to do good. Nonmalfeasance, again from the Latin, means to avoid doing bad, literally, "no bad do." The term is a principle taken from medicine that is often cited as the first principle of medical care, don't do anything to make the situation worse. Taken together beneficence and nonmalfeasance mean do good and avoid anything harmful and characterize most of the ethical considerations used by patients and physicians to decide a course of medical care.

In this country, justice is often thought to have two aspects, that of procedural justice, or following the rules, and substantive justice, which is much harder to define and has to do with whether the right outcome is reached. The principle of procedural justice is founded on the belief that by following the rules a result will reflect the other ethical principles embodied in the law and by a fundamental belief that everyone should be treated equally. Sometimes, however, following a set of rigid rules leads to a poor outcome, an injustice.

Equity was a form of disputation resolution that developed in reaction to law courts which too rigidly held to procedural rules resulting in outcomes perceived to be unjust. As a result, an alternate court system developed that had differing principles from law courts and enlarged, overruled, or abridged law courts. In this country our legal system has incorporated both the notions of procedural justice and equity into the same court system. However, the principle of examining a legal dispute for its correspondence to the notion of "is the outcome right," which is the essence of equity, remains embedded in our thinking, if not completely in our courts.

The principle of paternalism incorporates the idea that some authority undertakes to supply needs or regulate conduct of those under its control in matters affecting them as individuals. Parents often tell a sick child, "Take this pill. It will make you feel better." That is the essence of paternalism. Historically, the practice of medicine was based largely on paternalism because medicine involved a body of knowledge which was unavailable to the average person. The patient had to rely on the good intentions of the physician to receive the care of that professional. The principle remains to the extent that the patient does not request information from the physician and the physician does not provide it in some form.

LEGAL TERMS

Several legal tools are available to families when dealing with the issues of declining ability of elderly family members. Therapists who deals with such patients and their families should be acquainted with these tools, their potential benefits to the clients and their families, and implications of the use of the tools for the treatment and care of elderly patients:

- *Durable power of attorney for health care.* A durable power of attorney for health care is a legal tool that allows a person to make health care decisions for another individual when the individual who gives the power of attorney becomes incapacitated. A durable power of attorney for health care can be executed at any time and empower a third party to carry out the wishes of the incapacitated person, to act as the surrogate decision maker with full power to choose or refuse care.

- *Advance directive.* An advance directive is a legal tool designed to allow a person to express a desire for the use of extraordinary measures in the event of some untoward outcome, that results in the individual entering a persistent vegetative state. The federal government requires everyone who is admitted to a hospital be given an opportunity to complete an advance directive. The patients do not have to complete the form but must be given the opportunity to consider whether to complete such a form. This raises the consciousness and perhaps the anxiety level of the prospective patient and perhaps their family members about the issues.

These tools empower the elderly person, provide a format and framework for discussion of the issues, and allow families to deal straightforwardly with these issues. On the practitioner's side, those are also benefits.

LAWS, ETHICS, AND MORALS

For the purposes of this chapter, laws are defined as those standards of conduct that are made by some governmental unit (legislative, judicial, executive, or administrative) which are applicable to all persons within the political reach of the governmental unit. Laws generally set a low standard of conduct; that is, laws tell citizens what not to do instead of what to do. Sanctions for violations of laws range from loss of property through loss of liberty to loss of life in some jurisdictions. Ethics are standards of conduct set by any group. Professional codes of conduct are written and set high standards, aspirational goals for the members of the profession. Such codes of conduct are generally written but do not have to be. The maximum sanction for violation of those standards is expulsion from membership: defrocking, excommunication, ejection, dismissal, exile. Morals are those personal standards developed by an individual from genetic endowment, the learning we do from interactions with family, friends, school, church and other sources of experience. In this sense, everyone has a moral standard. The level of the moral standard is either high or low when examined externally against some society standard. The sanction that is experienced when we fail to live up to our personal standards is guilt. When that failure is exposed to public scrutiny, the individual experiences shame.

ETHICAL ANALYSIS

Because three standards are set by laws, ethics, and morals, conflicts may arise when the behavior demanded by one standard is inconsistent with that of another. The process for understanding, reflecting, and choosing a course of conduct when such conflicts arise is ethical analysis. Having the vocabulary to articulate these conflicts assists the practitioner in moving through those situations that demand new levels of consideration from us. Because of the creation of a new class of persons in our society, the retired elderly or *geriessent*, new demands are being placed on us as practitioners to deal responsibly with these conflicts, to help our patients and their families understand the issues, and follow those treatment courses that ultimately seem to serve our patients' best interests.

INFORMED CONSENT

The law on informed consent evolved primarily from medicine but is applicable to mental health practice and to geriatric patients. Obtaining informed consent respects the autonomy of the patient, one of the ethical principles not yet mentioned and which is sometimes thought as being the opposite of the paternalism ethical dimension.

ELEMENTS OF INFORMED CONSENT

The law of informed consent derives largely from surgery rather than from other medical specialties, perhaps because of the dramatic results when surgery goes awry. Medical care is often a matter of placing one's trust in the physician to make appropriate decisions. Medical paternalism was the mode of conduct. Questions such as "What will this treatment do?" were followed by the response, "Trust me. It will make you better." Untoward outcomes were "God's will" or bad luck and not attributed as a failure of care by the physician. As blame for a poor outcome shifted from fate to a lack of skill of the practitioner, from bad luck to medical negligence, so also the reliance on the knowledge of the physician to make the decision to pursue a course of treatment shifted to the right of the patient to make informed decisions about treatment. Physicians became required by courts to discuss the benefits, risks, alternatives to proposed procedures, and the risks of forgoing the proposed procedure. The shift from paternalism to autonomy was among the most important movements in patients' rights of this century. One of the best expressions of the right of self-determination in health care came from a case at the beginning of the century, where Justice Cardozo stated, "Every human being of adult years and sound mind has the right to determine what shall be done with his own body . . . " *Schloendorff v. Society of New York Hospital* (1914, p. 93). Self-determination in medical care has:

> [the] root premise . . . the concept, fundamental in American jurisprudence, that . . . True consent to what happens to one's self is the informed exercise of a choice, and that entails an opportunity to evaluate knowledgeably the options available and the risks attendant on each. The average patient has little or no understanding of the medical arts and ordinarily has only his physician to whom he can look for enlightenment with which to reach an intelligent decision. (*Canterbury v. Spence*, 1972, p. 780)

TRUTH TELLING VERSUS THERAPEUTIC PRIVILEGE

Within the field of mental health this shift from paternalism to autonomy occurred sometimes without thought given to the ability of the patient to make an independent, rational decision. In those situations, the field of psychiatry lagged other areas of medicine simply because of the belief that mental patients could not make reasonable decisions about their care. In Texas, in the case of *Barclay v. Campbell* (1986), a psychiatrist prescribed a neuroleptic medication for a patient who developed tardive dyskinesia. The court ruled that the physician was bound to provide the patient with information that a reasonable person would need to make an informed decision to take medication. Information was to be provided even if the patient was not reasonable and might make a choice different than the physician would make. The physician argued that the patient was not a reasonable person, would make the wrong choice, and that the physician had a duty to provide the treatment without informed consent by a therapeutic privilege. Therapeutic privilege is a term used by physicians to indicate that the physician does not have to inform the patient if the physician does not believe that the patient could use the information reasonably. The Texas court established a standard requiring the physician to inform the patient of all material risks which a reasonable person would want to know of the proposed course of treatment regardless of the patient's ability to use the information:

> Anglo-American law starts with the premise of thorough-going self determination. It follows that each man is considered to be master of his own body, and he may, if he be of sound mind, expressly prohibit the performance of life-saving surgery, or other medical treatment. A doctor might well believe that an operation or form of treatment is desirable or necessary but the law does not permit him to substitute his own judgment for that of the patient by any form of artifice or deception. (*Natanson v. Kline*, 1960, p. 1104)

TREATMENT WITHOUT CONSENT

There are a few well-defined circumstances in which treatment can be provided without the consent of the patient. Circumstances may emerge to demand that intervention occur and consent cannot be obtained. Emergencies may develop when the patient is comatose, as from a motor vehicle accident, or when they represent a threat to themselves, such as a suicide attempt, or when they threaten others, as sometimes happens with elderly demented persons. When such events occur, the force of the state can be brought to bear on the person through involuntary civil commitment proceedings resulting in enforced treatment in an inpatient setting or enforced outpatient care. Some states also provide for forced medication under court order where the patient refuses such medication but the physician believes that such medication may help to resolve, moderate, or control the patient's mental problems or behavior.

There is one other circumstance in which care may be provided without consent and that is where there is a lack of medical feasibility. For example, when a surgeon is operating for a known problem and discovers some other problem after opening the patient, generally the law allows the surgeon to correct the additional problem without first awakening the patient and obtaining consent for the extended procedure since the risk attendant to the expanded surgery is less than the risk of a second general anesthesia. Most surgical informed consent forms now contain the possibility of extension of the surgery for the most commonly seen additional problems found in surgery. Frequently, for example, in abdominal surgery the appendix of the patient is removed as a precautionary matter. Before having that extension of the surgery in the written informed consent form, the surgeon simply removed the appendix and explained it to the patient later. That is an example of medical paternalism due to the lack of medical feasibility. Such circumstances rarely occur in the mental health field.

TREATMENT BY SUBSTITUTED CONSENT

When the patient cannot consent, for whatever reason, and there is no emergency, treatment can be provided by using substituted consent. Courts may appoint a guardian to assist an incapacitated person in matters that affect their lives. Generally, there are two types of guardianships: (1) guardians of the estate, appointed to protect the resources of the ward, and (2) guardians of the person, who have the right to make personal decisions for the person, including consent to medical care. One person may serve as both the guardian for the person and for the estate.

Court-ordered protection for patients may exist in some settings, such as state hospitals, where an independent reviewer may make the medical decisions for patients. Two models of this independent review exist. The first model used for substituted consent was to employ a reviewer in the same facility. In this model of substituted decision making, a physician proposes a course of treatment for a patient. If the patient refuses the proposed treatment, another physician who is employed by the same facility reviews the treatment plan and makes an independent decision of the appropriateness of the proposed treatment. This system is called the "in-house" model and has the inherent risks of possible contamination of the independence of the alternative decision maker and possible collusion between decision makers (You approve my treatment plans, and I'll approve yours). Making the case that such in-house decisions making can be free from the appearance of impropriety is difficult at best. The alternative is to have an outside team or consultant conduct the independent review. This method is called the "outhouse" model and has fewer inherent conflicts than the first model but is more costly.

These models of substituted consent are generally the result of class action suits between some public agency, such as a mental health or mental retardation system, and some patient advocate group that is attempting to gain more civil rights for patients. Generally, such suits were attempts to move from a paternalistic system to one that provided more autonomy for patients. Most of these suits developed during the major push for mental patients' rights in the

1970s. However, the results of such suits and continuing jurisdiction of the courts in these suits may provide appropriate avenues for treatment when patients are not competent but are also not in emergent circumstances.

ECONOMIC FACTORS IN DECISION MAKING

Few of us give thought to the cost of medical care when it is critically needed. However, most of us consider the cost when we pursue elective care. For example, when obtaining orthodontia for our children, parents might do some cost comparisons, balance that against the convenience and reputation of the practitioner, and intangibles such as how we feel about the care that is likely to be provided. This is a kind of cost-benefit analysis that we go through to reach a decision about health care for us or our family members. There is no difference between the decision-making process for an elderly person and a younger adult. The same kind of inquiry, analysis, and balancing occurs in deciding to receive care. However, absent adjudication of incompetence, we do not have the intrusion of the elderly person's children or caregivers into the process of that decision without the elderly person's consent. Generally, the law will favor a cost-benefit analysis approach to medical care when the person who needs the care makes the decision. However, in the case of substituted judgment, the same concern by the surrogate over the cost of treatment is disfavored in the law. The obvious concern is whether the surrogate decision-maker will weigh the concerns in the same way that the elderly person would weigh them. How often have we heard some hysterical parent say, "It doesn't matter what it costs, it's for the children," or, "We'll spend whatever it takes." Such rhetoric, when applied to systems of public health care, does not recognize the limits to the human enterprise of medical care and fails to recognize that there are practitioners who will take advantage of all the resources available regardless of the loss to other sectors of the economy or to the affected families. Despite the reality of the limits of medical care we need to move substituted judgment to the level in which there is truly a substitution of values between the surrogate decider and the incapacitated person. My opinion is that all factors which the elderly person should consider may appropriately, and should, be considered by the surrogate.

FORGOING TREATMENT VERSUS WITHDRAWING TREATMENT

Withdrawing treatment and forgoing treatment are different, but the same type of ethical analysis can be pursued at any decision point in medical care of patients. The risks, benefits, alternatives, and natural history of the disease process if no treatment is undertaken are used to make a decision about pursuing or discontinuing treatment. The same factors are considered when the decision is made to pursue a course of treatment and the discontinuation of a futile course of treatment. What is the likelihood that the treatment will produce the desired outcome? What will be the changes in the quality of life of the patient if a course of treatment is undertaken? How much discomfort will the treatment induce? How much does the care cost? Who will pay? What are the alternatives to the proposed course of treatment? What are the likely outcomes of those alternative treatments? These are the questions that should be raised in an ethical analysis of withdrawing or forgoing treatment.

CURRENT CONUNDRUMS

The following areas are those, that I believe, constitute the most pressing of ethical dilemmas for therapists working with an elderly population. As mentioned, there are no single set or right and wrong outcomes. Each practitioner examining these problems has a moral position that may lead to different courses of action from equally conscientious providers. The key to coping effectively with such problems is in the analysis. Clinical issues unique to older adults include such tasks as forgoing the freedom of driving; making decisions about admission and discharge; pursuing new places to live, such as retirement communities, assisted living homes or nursing homes; executing advanced directives for health care or do not resuscitate orders; and treatment decisions including somatic therapies, such as medication or ECT.

CONFIDENTIALITY

What information to keep private and when to breach the confidential relationship between the therapist and the patient is one of the most problematic and difficult clinical decisions made by therapists. The therapist must respect the elderly person's autonomy, which is embodied in the patient's right to the privacy of medical information but also recognize that adhering to this ethical principle of autonomy may not be in the patient's best interests. The therapist must balance the right to privacy of the patient against the need to provide the best possible care for the patient.

DECISIONS ABOUT CARE

The decision about pursuing care can be subjected to an ethical analysis by considering the various persons who will be impacted by the decision. The major effect of such a decision will be on the elderly person. To the extent that person can make independent decisions, the patient should be provided with information relative to the proposed course of treatment and allowed to decide as an autonomous person, even to the extent of refusal of life-sustaining care (Lo, 1986), such as in *Bartling v. Superior Court* (1984). During healthy periods, he or she should be encouraged to consider what course of treatment he or she would like to have if incapacitated. Using the format of either an advance directive or durable power of attorney for health care, the family or caregivers can pursue these issues of care with the person to obtain an expression of the patient's thoughts. Until the person reaches a stage where decisions are not rational and endanger the person, and a guardianship can be obtained, the family should respect the autonomy of the elderly person. In that sense until there is a decline in rational ability, elderly persons should be treated no differently than younger adults.

Until a guardian is appointed, family and caregivers should respect the autonomy of the elderly person. Psychological tools, such as moral suasion and expressions of care and concern, can be used to move the elderly person toward the decision that seems best for that person and the caregivers. However, as long as the decisions do not endanger the person, they should not be rejected. Decisions to move from a long-term family home that no longer suits the needs of the person, that requires more effort for maintenance and housekeeping than the elderly person can invest, or that is physically challenging, such as a two-story house for a person who is arthritic, are not easily made. Such decisions are not made quickly or without thought to the long-term implications for readjustment of the elderly person and the rest of the family. Moving from an independent living setting into assisted living or nursing home care can be disruptive to the elderly person who may be less psychologically flexible than some younger persons. Regardless of the capacity of the elderly person, respecting his or her autonomy and independence is of major importance in any relative weighting of ethical principles.

DRIVING

There are several areas where the declining ability of the elderly person may impede the ability to act independently. Perhaps the most telling and concrete example is the decision by the elderly person to continue to operate an automobile. As we age, night vision decreases, a well-known physiological process. Visual acuity may deteriorate to the extent that some persons who can drive safely during the day may not be able to do so at night. Many elderly persons note this limitation and voluntarily stop driving after dark. Education may be the key to highlighting such voluntary acts. This procedure respects the elderly person's autonomy and avoids the necessity of the state limiting this freedom. When the person does not voluntarily eliminate night driving what happens? The family or other caregivers may work to educate the person on the safety issues with the aim of achieving the voluntary limitation on driving. Imposition of state action is a last resort when other efforts have failed. The loss of a driver's license can be a devastating blow to the perceived independence of the elderly person and should be treated as a clinical matter. Just as 15-year-olds view with eager anticipation the 16th birthday when they can begin to drive under their own license, at the other end of the life span we cling to the freedom offered by being able to transport ourselves whenever and wherever we choose. Giving up that freedom is a potent, powerful act. When viewed as a voluntary act rather than a coerced action, the achievement is a significant psychological milestone rather than a defeat.

END-OF-LIFE ISSUES

Death is the final task in life. Coping with this reality is the ultimate challenge faced by each of us. Some training for this task, however, comes from the learning that occurs as we cope with the declining ability and eventual loss of our parents or other relatives. The degree to which we learn the lessons of those experiences aids us in that ultimate developmental task. The rules on advance directives and durable powers of attorney for health care, while in the early stages of development, nevertheless are formal, recognized approaches to dealing with the potential problems of terminal illness or incapacitation.

Slow Codes

Problems arise when patients who do not have an advance directive or durable power of attorney for health care become incapacitated and have little, if any, reasonable hope of recovery of function. What happens when such a person arrests in the hospital? Under those circumstances the staff can respond in two ways. The first is prescribed in the procedure manual. When a code is called, staff bring the crash cart as quickly as possible and work to resuscitate the patient. The second way of responding is to "slow code" the patient. Instead of taking the stairs to reach the patient's floor, staff push the elevator call button and wait for the elevator. If your experience in using crowded hospital elevators is similar to mine, you realize this is one way not to get there fast. In the past, some charts were marked to show which patients were to receive such slow codes. Such practice was not condoned legally; it was simply done in some institutions. Regardless of the markings on the patient's chart, staff know whether speed is important and whether all means should be used to resuscitate a patient. Better in my opinion that such procedures be explicit, that policies be established for that determination and openly available to patients and their families prior to admission. Formal ethics case conferences where such decisions are addressed following ethical analysis procedures seem a better approach than leaving the conditions of resuscitation implicit and covert.

How are such decisions reached? What conflicts does this create for the staff who have moral positions that might vary from the ethics embodied by a "slow code?" By dealing with such issues openly, the practitioner can make explicit the institutional ethic that may have been covert. Open discussion of these formerly covert policies can make patients, their families, and staff more comfortable knowing each of the parties is working on the same knowledge base in this delicate area of care. While this common knowledge base may not make the work more comfortable, there is comfort in knowing that each party is equal in participation.

Euthanasia

One area remains largely unformulated in much of the United States but is addressed in most other developed countries: euthanasia. In the dictionary, the term euthanasia is defined as the act of killing or permitting the death of hopelessly sick or injured individuals for reasons of mercy. You will sometimes hear the term "active euthanasia." The terms "killing" or "permitting death" both have the element of intent but differ in the acts which are required of the professional. Thus, adding the term "active" to euthanasia is not redundant but shows an important distinction between "killing" and "permitting" as acts; the first is an act of commission, the second an act of omission.

Many states have considered enacting physician-assisted suicide laws and such legislation has passed or lost by narrow margins. Those narrow margins show the split in the population in attitudes over medical involvement in end-of-life matters. Much newsprint and television time over the past few years has dealt with assisted suicide and the work of Drs. Jack Kervorkian and Georges Reding. These physicians say that they are dedicated not to ending the life of persons but in ending their suffering. The medical procedure they use is called patholysis, from "patho" meaning suffering and "lysis" meaning decomposition or disintegration. The procedure of patholysis is designed to end the suffering of the person. Two elements, in theory, must be present for patholysis to be used: (1) the person must be suffering from some presently incurable disease which causes unendurable suffering, and (2) the person must be capable of making some physical, affirmative act that will initiate the process of patholysis. In one case where patholysis was used, the person was physically incapacitated by amyotrophic lateral sclerosis and could only talk and move his left index finger. No other voluntary physical movement was possible. However, the disease process had left him mentally intact. After much discussion between the person, the family and Dr. Kervorkian, a device was set up to deliver carbon monoxide through a nasal cannula to the person. The tube feeding the cannula was clipped with a plastic device which was attached to a string, in turn attached to the person's finger. The person then pulled the clip from the tube, an affirmative act on his part. This affirmative act was a required element of the patholysis procedure. The physician simply put in place a mechanism in which the person's suffering could end. Each of the several times Dr. Kervorkian has been tried for assisting suicide, he has been acquitted. There can be no better statement of the sentiment of the community in a particular case than that of a jury hearing and weighing all the credible evidence and reaching a decision. Absent legislation in such matters, it is likely that we will continue to have juries decide whether such actions are legitimate use of medical knowledge and the application of science to this final aspect of life.

In the procedures used by Drs. Kervorkian and Reding, one effect of the end of the suffering is the death of the patient. I have watched tapes of patients being attended by Dr. Kervorkian and have no doubt that the persons are fully aware of that effect of the procedure. The patients who have been attended by Dr. Kervorkian have all had clear sensoriums and the disease process has largely left their cognitive abilities intact. Georges Reding, M.D., a retired social psychiatrist, has examined many of the patients attended by Dr. Kervorkian and found them to be capable of making end-of-life decisions. If the person is found not to be competent to make those decisions, then patholysis is not available to those persons. Some of the latest cases in which patholysis has been used are young people who have otherwise non-life-threatening physical problems such as traumatic quadriplegia. We do not need to explore the aspects of these recent cases as they influence the decision to use this procedure for true end-of-life circumstances.

The development of patholysis is, in part, a reaction to medical technological development. McGovern (1996) has stated that modern medical technology which thwarts the normal process of death "forces us to analyze the essentials of good death and to embrace the *ars moriendi* (art of dying) wisdom of earlier centuries" (p. 196). This focus allows us to see what the process of aging and dying offers that is beneficial and contributory to society as well as its negative aspects.

RESOLVING CONFLICTS WITH INSTITUTIONS

When this discussion ensues and policies become explicit that are at odds with the practitioner's beliefs and moral standards, how should we proceed? In many professional ethic codes, there is a provision that requires the practitioner to deal directly with institutional matters that the practitioner believe are illegal, unethical, or that offend the practitioner's moral sense. If the practitioner cannot resolve a legal conflict, the practitioner must resign from the organization. Often, however, no guidance is given when the conflict is over a moral position as opposed to something that may be illegal. Obviously, the line separating what is legal and ethical from what is legal and unethical may not be a bright line. For example, the largest for-profit health care provider in the United States was accused by the federal government of overcharging and overbilling its patients covered by federal insurance programs in an El Paso hospital. The response of the hospital administration was simply, "We do not charge too much; other hospitals charge too little." When is billing of patients illegal? When does care become overtreating, simply to increase revenue? Is aggressive treatment of an individual in an underserved population in a border town simply good medicine, or is it a fraud on the taxpayer? Sometimes there is no clear answer to such questions. Courts will decide when the government prosecutes, however.

PROPOSAL FOR A NEW ETHIC FOR GERIATRIC CARE

Spielman (1986) proposed that for geriatric care we move away from autonomy as the central value in ethics toward realization that as our capacity diminishes we become interdependent, physically and fiscally, and that autonomy may not serve well as the central focus of ethical analysis. She stresses the principles of sociality (recognizing our need for relationships), temporality (recognizing our limitations), and embodiment (respecting the changes of aging) as being more important for geriatric ethics than autonomy. Although these alternative principles noted by Spielman are important, they are also true of each of us, not only the elderly, and should be considered along with all the other ethical considerations required in ethical analysis.

If any shift is required in our thinking in geriatric ethics, we need to move toward education. Education of ourselves, our patients, and their families about the changes which occur with aging, about the need for discussions about change in living circumstances, the nature of care available, and such tools for decision making as advance directives and durable powers of attorney for health care. What needs to be added at this point is not an alteration of autonomy as the central ethical concern in *geriessence* but education as a necessary component of the mix so that it becomes a part of the culture. The proposal is that we consider the central ethic as that of the totality of the circumstances of the patient balancing all the interests of the elderly. Autonomy should not be the central ethic for elderly patients any more than it is for children. This is not to say that the elderly should be treated as children but that as a society we begin to see the declining abilities of the elderly as cause of our concern and appropriate intervention where care is sometimes provided, even when it is unbidden.

The elderly have value to our society through their accumulated experience and can influence the values of our society if allowed. As a society and as individuals we need to respect what these individuals have to offer. Adept practitioners who understand the unique needs of these elderly persons need to make more efforts at public education to elevate the discussion of these issues relating to diminished physical and mental ability and emphasize the abilities enhanced by the aging process—breadth of experience and consequent wisdom.

In the United States, we do not revere the elderly in our society as occurs in some societies. We are not equipped to care for them in our families as in some societies. The elderly become isolated in special communities of retirees, assisted living facilities, and nursing homes. This isolation diminishes the contributions of the elderly to our culture compared with less industrialized nations where the elderly are better integrated with the family. Society needs to define new roles for the elderly just as they need to refine and define their emerging roles. Part of the achievement of this new ethic of aging is to respect the possible contributions of our elderly to our community. The first step in this direction is to respect the ability of the elderly person to make decisions about the future without coercion from family or other caregivers. Absent some reason, the ethical principle of autonomy should be paramount in our practice armamentarium for dealing with elderly persons. Give them the tools to make decisions about their care and then let them decide. Aging is a fact of living. Aging persons as contributing members of the larger society can be the typical experience with that redefinition of roles for the elderly.

CONCLUSION

The revolutions that produced the age of the adolescent and that are producing the age of the geriessent have forced clinical practitioners to confront new ethical demands. Just as the industrial revolution made society more complex through the strides of mechanization, our sciences of the mind have led the revolution in understanding and treating conditions resulting from aging. This chapter provides the clinician with the vocabulary necessary to make decisions about ethical dilemmas that present in a practice with the elderly, the legal bases and rationale for the procedures that are presently used, and a proposal for a new ethic for dealing with our aging population. As legislatures define our ethics by making them laws and as courts resolve some of these thornier issues with which we deal, such as assisted suicide, our field moves forward to more solid foundations for our treatment of elderly persons. As practitioners, we will never be free of ethical conflicts because the problems simply shift as technology advances, forcing us to face frontiers where we have not yet ventured. Personally, and particularly as I age, I hope that you, as a practitioner, look forward as much as I to those challenges.

REFERENCES

Bartling v. Superior Court, 163 Cal. App. 3d 186, 209 Cal. Rptr. 220 (Cal. Civ. App. 1984).

Barclay v. Campbell, 704 S.W. 2d 8 (Tex. 1986).

Canterbury v. Spence, 464 F. 2d 773 (D.C. Cir. 1972).

Hays, J.R. (1996). Legal considerations. In R. L. Dippel & J. T. Hutton (Eds.), *Caring for the Alzheimer's patient* (3rd ed.). Amherst, New York: Prometheus Books.

Lo, B. (1986). The Bartling case: Protecting patients from harm while respecting their wishes. *Journal of the American Geriatric Society, 34,* 44–48.

McGovern, T.F. (1996). Ethical considerations. In R.L. Dippel & J.T. Hutton (Eds.), *Caring for the Alzheimer's patient* (3rd ed.). Amherst, New York: Prometheus Books.

Natanson v. Kline, 350 P. 2d 1003 (Kan. 1960).

Schloendorff v. Society of New York Hospital, 211 N.Y. 125, 105 N.E. 92 (1914).

Spielman, B.J. (1986). Rethinking paradigms in geriatric ethics. *Journal of Religion and Health, 21,* 142–148.

Author Index

Subject Index